Courts of Admiralty and the Common Law

Courts of Admiralty and the Common Law

Origins of the American Experiment in Concurrent Jurisdiction

Steven L. Snell
J.D., LL.M., J.S.D

Carolina Academic Press
Durham, North Carolina

Library of Congress Cataloging-in-Publication Data

Snell, Steven L.
Courts of admiralty and the common law: origins of the American experiment in concurrent jurisdiction / by Steven L. Snell. -- [2nd ed.]
p. cm.
Includes bibliographical references and index.
ISBN 1-59460-173-9 (alk. paper)
1. Admiralty--United States--History. 2. Jurisdiction--United States. 3. Common law. I. Title.

KF1112.S645 2006
343.7309'6--dc22

2006010306

Paperback ISBN 978-1-5310-1068-3

Carolina Academic Press
700 Kent Street
Durham, North Carolina 27701
(919) 489-7486
www.cap-press.com

Printed in the United States of America
2021 Printing

Photo Credits

Front: Pride of Baltimore II, a replica of an 1812-era topsail schooner. Photo courtesy of Pride of Baltimore, Inc. the 501(c)(3) organization that operates Maryland's PRIDE, which relies heavily on private contributions to fulfill its mission. For information call 888-55-PRIDE or visit www.marylandspride.org
Back: H.M.S. Surprise, courtesy of the Maritime Museum of San Diego, 1492 North Harbor Drive, San Diego, CA 92101. Photo by Al Sorkin.

To Betty M. Snell

Contents

The Sources: A Note on Translation, Spelling, and Punctuation

The history of English admiralty jurisdiction is interwoven inextricably with the history of the common law—and with eighteenth-century America's efforts to create a viable judicial system in the early years following independence. While their letters, journals, speeches, and published writings often resonated with the political philosophy of the Enlightenment and the rhetoric of the Revolution, the founders of the new republic were at heart practical men, who revered experience as much as abstract theory in shaping the structure of the new nation. Maritime commerce and adjudication of maritime disputes touched the daily lives of the Framers of the Constitution and the members of the first Congress, and these experiences influenced their thought at least as profoundly as did Montesquieu's theories on the separation of powers. One cannot fully grasp the intricacies of the debate over the judicial branch without some understanding of the history of American admiralty jurisdiction. From the colonial period through the 1780s, America's maritime courts served as the crucible in which solutions for the practical problems of jurisdiction were tested. Thus the surviving records of the admiralty courts, the writings of the merchants and legal-practitioners who litigated in them, and the published works of the jurists who sought to define the scope of their jurisdiction together provide an invaluable resource for those seeking a better understanding of the choices that America's founding generation made in formulating the structure of the federal judiciary. Methodologically, "*Courts of Admiralty and the Common Law*" seeks to shed light on the origins of modern admiralty jurisdiction—as well as on the origins of the federal courts—principally through examining primary sources compiled over a period spanning from antiquity through the eighteenth century.

In addition to the ancient writings—from Cicero to the *Corpus Juris Civilis*—some scholarly legal works of the early modern period originally were written in Latin. In order to facilitate ease in reading and to make the information in this book available to a wide audience, I have translated the Latin sources that I have quoted in the main text. Regrettably, translation at best provides a crude reflection of a text in its original language. Nuances and ambiguities of words and phrases in one language lack perfect analogues in another, forcing the translator to exercise judgment as to which nuances and ambiguities should be stressed in the translation and which may be deemphasized safely (or omitted entirely). A casual glance at how several different (and equally competent) translators render the same Latin passage into English reveals how inevitably subjective the process of translating is. Readers proficient in Latin naturally would prefer to make these judgments for themselves. Out of respect for their preference for reading and interpreting the quoted passages in the original language, I have opted also to reproduce the Latin *verbatim* in the footnotes.

No effort has been made to render the various sources quoted in *"Courts of Admiralty and the Common Law"* into modern English. Archaic spelling, syntax, and punctuation have been preserved throughout. Moreover, as standardized spelling and rules of punctuation are comparatively recent developments in the English language, it is not always possible to distinguish between archaic forms and printers' errors. Some of the quoted material is derived from unpublished sources, such as journals, letters, and lecture-notes, in which the authors employed their own forms of abbreviation and often exercised little care in spelling—with the result that one word may have more than one spelling within the same text. The use of "[*sic*]" to designate departures from standard usage is more of an art than an exact science. I generally have omitted it entirely in medieval and early modern texts, where the reader should not expect modern spelling, reserving its use for inconsistencies in spelling within the same text or for those rare instances in which an archaic form of a word departs so far from its modern equivalent that it requires some clarification. In documents of the eighteenth century and later, in which grammar, spelling, and punctuation have assumed more modern form, I have used "[*sic*]" more liberally to highlight printers' errors and individual authors' personal eccentricities in spelling.

Steven L. Snell
Baltimore, Maryland
June, 2006

Courts of Admiralty and the Common Law

Introduction

"The judicial Power shall extend... to all Cases of admiralty and maritime Jurisdiction..."

Constitution of the United States[1]

Amid heated debates over the structure of the legislative and executive branches, the Framers of the Constitution dispensed with jurisdiction over maritime matters with a single sentence. The allocation was simple and direct; federal courts would hear cases of "admiralty and maritime jurisdiction". Unfortunately, the simplicity of the language chosen did not add to its clarity. The Framers left no record of their reasons for selecting the formulation "admiralty and maritime", and its intended meaning—the scope of jurisdiction conferred—has been long the source of controversy. Moreover, the Framers did not specify which federal courts would hear maritime cases. Unable to reach a consensus, they instead left the structuring of the federal judiciary to the first Congress. The Judiciary Act of 1789, by which Congress established federal district and circuit courts, granted to district courts:

> ...exclusive original cognizance of all civil causes of admiralty and maritime jurisdiction, including all seizures under laws of impost, navigation or trade of the United States, where the seizures are made, on waters which are navigable from the sea by vessels of ten or more tons burthen, within their respective districts as well as upon the high seas...saving to suitors, in all cases, the right of a common law remedy, where the common law is competent to give it...[2]

---

1. U.S. Const., art. III, sec. 2.

2. Judiciary Act of 1789, ch. 20, sec. 9, 1 Stat. 73, 77 (*emphasis added*). Congress subsequently amended the language (28 U.S.C. sec. 1333) to read:

> "The district courts shall have original jurisdiction, exclusive of the courts of the States, of... [a]ny civil case of admiralty or maritime jurisdiction, saving to suitors in all cases all other remedies to which they are otherwise entitled."

Act of June 25, 1948, ch. 646, sec. 1, 62 Stat. 931; Act of May 24, 1949, ch.139, sec. 79,

Rather than pre-empting state courts' power to hear maritime disputes, the first Congress instead opted to grant them concurrent jurisdiction. Nevertheless, even after the passage of more than a century, courts had not identified the precise parameters of this concurrent jurisdiction nor clearly defined the source of substantive law applicable to maritime cases.

On August 15, 1914, the steamship *El Oriente* was moored at Manhattan's Pier 49, where employees of its owner, the Southern Pacific Company, were unloading its cargo. As one of these stevedores attempted to maneuver an electric freight truck laden with lumber backward in the direction of the ship's hatchway, an accident occurred; the stevedore was killed instantly. The widow of the deceased sought relief under New York's Workmen's Compensation Act in a state trial court and prevailed. Subsequently the Appellate Division and Court of Appeals both affirmed the lower court's holding. Dissatisfied with the outcome, the Southern Pacific Company petitioned the United States Supreme Court, contending (among other things) that the trial court's application of the state statute violated Article III, Section 2 of the Constitution, which conferred admiralty jurisdiction on the federal courts. The trial court, attorneys for Southern Pacific maintained, should have applied the "general maritime law" as defined and interpreted by federal trial courts rather than the state statute under which it granted relief. The Supreme Court granted an appeal in 1916, and ultimately Justice McReynolds delivered the court's opinion the following year.[3] Stating that "...in the absence of some controlling statute the general maritime law as accepted by the federal courts constitutes part of our national law applicable to matters within the admiralty and maritime jurisdiction...", McReynolds reversed the lower court's holding.[4] Continuing, he drew inspiration from an admiralty case of the previous century:

> In *The Lottawanna* Mr. Justice Bradley speaking for the court said: "That we have a maritime law of our own, operative throughout the

---

63 Stat. 101. The principal purpose of these amendments was to extend federal jurisdiction to ships' allisions with land-based structures; the amendment to the "Saving-to-Suitors" Clause sparked little congressional debate. *See* S. Rep. No. 1593, H. Rep. No. 1523, 80th Cong., 2d Sess. (1948), *reprinted in* U.S.C.C.A.N. 1898–1905. To date, courts have interpreted the change in language as reflecting Congress' desire to clarify rather than modify the intent of the first Congress. As Justice Black remarked: "We take it that this change in no way narrowed the jurisdiction of the state courts under the original 1789 Act." *Madruga v. Superior Court of California*, 346 U.S. 556, 560 n. 12 (1954).

3. *Southern Pacific Co. v. Jensen*, 244 U.S. 205, 207–214 (McReynolds, J., 1917).

4. *Id.* at 215.

> United States, cannot be doubted. The general system of maritime law which was familiar to the lawyers and statesmen of the country when the Constitution was adopted, was most certainly intended and referred to when it was declared in that instrument that the judicial power of the United States shall extend 'to all cases of admiralty and maritime jurisdiction.'... One thing, however, is unquestionable; the Constitution must have referred to a system of law coextensive with, and operating uniformly in, the whole country. It certainly could not have been intended to place the rules and limits of maritime law under the disposal and regulation of the several States, as that would have defeated the uniformity and consistency at which the Constitution aimed on all subjects of a commercial character affecting the intercourse of the States with each other or with foreign states."[5]

As to the extension of New York's Workmen's Compensation Act to loss of life aboard a vessel engaged in interstate commerce, McReynolds concluded:

> And plainly, we think, no such legislation is valid if it...works material prejudice to the characteristic features of the general maritime law or interferes with the proper harmony and uniformity of that law in its international and interstate relations. This limitation, at the least, is essential to the effective operation of the fundamental purpose for which such law was incorporated into our national laws by the Constitution itself.[6]

Not all of the justices shared McReynolds' assumption that the "general maritime law" was penumbral to the Constitution. It provoked Oliver Wendell Holmes to write what became perhaps his best known aphorism: "The common law is not a brooding omnipresence in the sky but the articulate voice of some sovereign or quasi-sovereign that can be identified..."[7]

McReynolds' opinion in *Jensen* is among the most frequently criticized in the High Court's history. Over the ensuing decades, the Court has beaten a slow retreat from its expansive stance on federal jurisdiction and its aggressive

---

5. *Id.* at 215. For the context from which McReynolds selected the quote, *see The Lottawanna*, 88 U.S. 558 (Bradley, J., 1875, upholding a state-created home-port lien for "ship's necessaries").

6. *Id.* at 216.

7. *Id.* at 222 (Holmes, J., dissenting).

approach to pre-emption of state substantive law in maritime actions.[8] Nonetheless, few commentators have noted the irony of *Jensen*. One might expect such an opinion from a Supreme Court dominated by New Deal appointees, or later from the Court over which Chief Justice Warren presided. For very different reasons, one also might expect such an opinion a century earlier from the Federalist admiralty scholar Richard Peters or the scholarly, cosmopolitan, Republican-turned-Federalist Joseph Story. James Clark McReynolds, however, stands as the Court's most staunch defender of states' rights in the twentieth century, and yet he drafted an opinion so far-reaching in its implications for federal power that it would have made John Marshall and Joseph Story blush. A Southerner whose family retained Confederate sympathies long after the Civil War had ended,[9] McReynolds often championed the cause of the states against what he perceived as the federal government's overreaching.[10] Nonetheless, it was McReynolds who set federal admiralty jurisdiction's high-water mark. The irony of *Jensen* bears closer examination.

---

8. *See e.g., Just v. Chambers*, 312 U.S. 383 (1941); *Standard Dredging Corp. v. Murphy*, 319 U.S. 306 (1943); *Davis v. Department of Labor and Industries*, 317 U. S. 349 (1942); *Hess v. United States*, 361 U.S. 314 (1960).

9. One biographer observes that McReynolds' father refused to take an oath of allegiance to the Union after the war and that he even gave instructions that he was to be buried such that his grave was aligned with that of Jefferson Davis. *See* James E. Bond, I Dissent: The Legacy of Chief Justice James Clark McReynolds (Fairfax, Virginia: George Mason University Press, 1992) at 7 (hereinafter Bond).

10. Bond remarks: "One can... discern an implicit outline of [McReynolds'] 'American system' in his opinions. It is basically Jeffersonian. The national government was supreme within the powers granted to it, but those powers were limited and were to be construed narrowly. State governments retained substantial authority to legislate, but their powers, too, were limited. Individual citizens retained rights that no government, state or national, however responsive to transient majorities, could abridge." *Id.* at 125. In his own words, McReynolds' views on federalism are best represented by his dissenting remarks in *Steward Machine Co. v. Davis*, in which he wrote that:

> "... 'the preservation of the States, and the maintenance of their governments, are as much within the design and care of the Constitution as the preservation of the Union and the maintenance of the National government. The Constitution, in all its provisions looks to an indestructible Union, composed of indestructible States.' [*quoting Texas v. White*, 74 U.S. 700, 725 (Chase, C. J., 1869)]. The doctrine thus announced and often repeated, I had supposed was firmly established. Apparently the States remained really free to exercise governmental powers, not delegated or prohibited, without interference by the Federal Government through threats of punitive measures or offers of seductive favors."

301 U.S. 548, 599 (1937). For discussion, *see* Bond at 128–129; *see also* general discussion of McReynolds' views on states' rights and federalism at 95–98, 104–107, 136.

McReynolds' tenure on the bench is arguably the most controversial in the history of the Supreme Court. He dissented more times than any federal judge in history.[11] His treatment of his fellow justices was often condescending and abusive; his hatred of Roosevelt and the New Deal is well documented. Indeed, McReynolds' behavior was the principal impetus behind Roosevelt's attempt to "pack" the Court in 1937.[12] Some modern criticism has sought to reconcile McReynolds' usual support of states' rights with his apparently anomalous decisions in *Jensen* and its progeny by contending that the justice always favored the application of the law least favorable to impecunious plaintiffs. The accusation is unfair.[13] His rudeness and personal prejudices made McReynolds an easy target in his own life-time, and no less so for modern critics. Nevertheless, his colleagues (who knew him best) were reluctant to ascribe base motives to him. Brandeis, a frequent recipient of McReynolds' barbs and snubs, found him "one of the most interesting men on the Court",[14] and Holmes conceded that he was a "useful and quite suggestive man" with "special knowledge and experience", whose "doubts and difficulties are always worth considering".[15] Neither personal biases nor intellectual failings provide an adequate explanation for his opinion in *Jensen*. A better explanation lies instead in the nexus between McReynolds' thought-processes and the nature of admiralty jurisdiction itself.

If his contemporaries' observations were accurate, McReynolds held tenaciously to a strong preference for order. All papers on his desk were neatly

---

11. Bond, *supra* note 9, at 108–109.

12. *Id.* at 53–56, 83–85, 99–103.

13. McReynolds' lack of tact and controversial opinions notwithstanding, those who knew him well attested to the high value he placed upon honesty, and much of the criticism he received in his years on the Supreme Court stemmed from his inflexible personality and his tendency to view all legal questions as moral questions. Bond, *supra* note 9, at 7–8, 15. Moreover, he owed his appointment to the Court largely to progressive Democrats' misunderstanding of his motives for zealous "trust-busting" while serving as Attorney General. Wilson ascribed his zeal to "progressive" views. In fact, the ultra-conservative McReynolds leaned more to *laissez-faire* policies than to social reform for the benefit of the underprivileged. His rigorous enforcement of the antitrust laws stemmed instead from righteous indignation at the unscrupulous behavior of monopolists rather than from dissatisfaction with the free-enterprise system *per se*. For McReynolds, honesty and morality were paramount in business transactions just as they were in one's private life. *Id.* at 31–32, 39, 49–51.

14. Bond, *supra* note 9, at 123.

15. Letter from Oliver Wendell Holmes, Jr., to Harold J. Laski (Oct. 9, 1923), *published in* The Holmes-Laski Letters: The Correspondence of Mr. Justice Holmes and Harold J. Laski, 1916–1935 (2 vols., Mark DeWolf Howe ed., Cambridge, Massachusetts: Harvard University Press, 1953), Vol. I, at 552 (hereinafter Holmes-Laski Letters).

stored in their proper pigeon-holes. His intellectual work-habits mirrored the physical; Brandeis observed his strict adherence to jurisdictional forms.[16] His terse writing style, coupled with his propensity for omitting detailed discussion of case law, reflected not a lack of legal acumen,[17] but rather a desire to avoid *obiter dicta* and an overriding belief that the *ratio decidendi* of a well-reasoned opinion was virtually self-evident. Matters were either black or white, and engaging in a detailed exegesis on the nuances of the various shades of grey merely served to clutter the issue.[18] Judges were to resolve cases not so much by creative insight and intellectual inspiration as by clarity of perception and diligence in attention to detail.[19] His penchant for order had served

---

16. *See* Bond, *supra* note 9, at 4–5, 133.

17. Holmes felt that the reasoning behind McReynolds' opinions was often more profound than the manner that he chose for expressing it. As he once wrote to Laski: "McR[eynolds] doesn't do himself justice in his opinions. He is often acute in suggestion and has worked on useful legislation." Letter from Oliver Wendell Holmes, Jr. to Harold J. Laski (March 26, 1922), *published* in Holmes-Laski Letters, *supra* note 15, Vol. I, at 413.

18. As one biographer has summarized McReynolds' processes of legal reasoning and writing:

> "McReynolds' opinions ran short because...he cited little supporting authority and did not discuss the authority he did cite.... In some opinions he declined to cite case authority at all. He rarely cited secondary authority other than standard treatises, and he seldom quoted from the cited works or entered into any discussion of them.... Unwilling to concede that a proposition might be doubtful, McReynolds also generally declined to discuss contrary authority.... Sometimes, McReynolds would dismiss contrary authority on *ipse dixit* alone. When the Justice did feel compelled to discuss contrary authority, he engaged in the most limited factual discussion possible. His 'blind' citation of supporting authority and his cursory treatment of contrary authority probably reflected both his confident assumption that the correct result was self-evident and his desire to avoid any obiter, which he abhorred."

Bond, *supra* note 9, at 58–60.

19. Bond reprints the following comment that McReynolds made later in life regarding reliance on self-discipline and hard work:

> "My early training was to do well the task at hand—not to quit until accomplished, and that early training, I think, has been of great value to me. A will to work is a powerful aid to success in any line. Genius is very rare indeed."

Id. at 2–3. Unfortunately, though a "will to work" may produce quantity, quality is very much a product of genius. Legal reasoning is not the creation of an assembly line, and as Oliver Wendell Holmes once observed, when judges differ in their opinions, it is not because one of them is not doing his sums correctly. *See* "The Path of the Law", *in* Oliver Wendell Holmes, Jr., Collected Legal Papers (New York: P. Smith, 1952) at 167, 180. Irrespective of whether McReynolds lacked the genius of a Holmes or a Brandeis, a belief that a case has only one pre-ordained "correct" outcome awaiting judicial discovery is psy-

him well in law school, particularly in the eyes of his mentor, John Minor. Minor's *Institutes*[20] (in fact his lectures in published form) gave the future justice his first exposure to maritime jurisdiction. Voluminous and methodical, the *Institutes* were a product of their age. Christopher Langdell and his fellow "legal scientists" still held sway in the mainstream of legal academia—long before Walter Wheeler Cook, Jerome Frank and those "legal realists" who followed launched their attack on legal positivism. The legal scientists approached law as a biologist approaches biology. Law was systematic; law could be reduced to logical principles. For Minor organizing his *Institutes*, this meant extrapolating clear substantive rules from a myriad of cases and reducing them to well-indexed, well-ordered outline-form. For those seeking order, however, case law can be a source of endless frustration. While the scientists sought to reduce precedent to general rules of law, every practicing litigator faced daily the awkward fact that some cases always run afoul of the expected pattern. This fact formed the basis of the legal realists' scholarship of the 1930s and 1940s, but is seldom addressed legal scientists' writings of a generation earlier.

In reading Minor's treatise, one is struck first by the clarity and systematic order of the material, and second by the dearth of discussion of case law. Minor acknowledges his debt to Matthew Hale and William Blackstone in the structure and organization of his work.[21] He fails to emphasize, however, the influence of Hale and Blackstone on the substance of his work as well, particularly as it relates to admiralty jurisdiction. He gives a summary of English admiralty jurisdiction largely in accord with the two great English scholars. The High Court of Admiralty held sway over matters arising at sea; the common law governed matters arising on land. Between the two—the high and low water-marks set by the ebb and flow of the tide—lay concurrent jurisdiction.[22] Turning to American practice, however, Minor reproduces the Eng-

---

chologically limiting. One holding such a belief is more likely to lapse into formalism in deciding cases, and may have difficulty envisioning the full panoply of solutions that a more open, creative mind could conceive. In short, one with McReynolds' work-habits would be susceptible to intellectual tunnel-vision.

20. John B. Minor, Institutes of Common and Statute Law (4 vols., 1st ed. 1875; 4th ed., Richmond: Anderson Brothers, 1891) (hereinafter Minor). John B. Minor spent his career on the faculty of the University of Virginia School of Law, where he taught both McReynolds and Woodrow Wilson. *See* Bond, *supra* note 8, at 15, 37.

21. *See* Minor, *supra* note 20, Preface To The First Edition, Vol. I, at vii.

22. Minor outlines the rules for admiralty jurisdiction in England in a manner consistent both with that of Matthew Hale's intellectual predecessor, the seventeenth-century Chief Judge of Common Pleas and King's Bench, Sir Edward Coke, and that of the eigh-

lish rules of the eighteenth century almost *verbatim*. Absent from the treatise is detailed discussion of the Judiciary Act of 1789 and its impact on the maritime jurisdiction of the state and federal courts.[23] A century had elapsed between Congress' creation of concurrent admiralty jurisdiction and the drafting of Minor's treatise. In that time, courts had struggled with a variety of issues—whether federal judges were permitted to fashion new rules of maritime law in the absence of acts of Congress; whether state courts were obligated to follow federal judge-made rules of substantive maritime law; whether federal courts must apply state statutes in preference to substantive rules created by federal judges. Moreover, there was the nineteenth century's great struggle to define "admiralty and maritime" itself, through which the Supreme Court ultimately extended federal jurisdiction to inland waters. All of this experience, the growing pains of America's experiment with federalism, the treatise omits. It paints instead a picture of harmony and order that belies the con-

---

teenth-century legal scholar Sir William Blackstone:

> "The High Seas, beginning at Low-water Mark. These are subject to the jurisdiction of the *Admiralty* courts, and not to that of the Courts of common law. Between high and low water, where the sea ebbs and flows, the common law and the Admiralty have *divisum imperium*, an alternate jurisdiction; one upon the water when it is full sea, the other upon the land when it is at ebb."

Id., Vol. I, at 55. In this view, jurisdiction is defined solely by geography, and the geographical overlap in jurisidction is limited to the ebb and flow of the tides. Moreover, as the sea is either at ebb or full tide, it is never possible for both the admiralty and the common law to have concurrent jurisdiction over the same case.

23. With regard to state and federal maritime jurisdiction under Article III of the Constitution and the Judiciary Act of 1789, Minor observes:

> "The main or high seas are for some purposes part of the realm of the United States, and over them the Federal courts of admiralty exercise, in respect of vessels and citizens of the United States, a jurisdiction both civil and criminal. The main sea begins at *low-water* mark; but between the high-water mark and the low-water mark, where the sea ebbs and flows, the common law, whether administered in the Federal or in the State courts, and the admiralty, have *divisum imperium*, an alternate jurisdiction; one upon the water, when it is full sea; the other upon the land, when it is at ebb."

Id., Vol. I, at 57–58. It would appear that in Minor's view, the Constitution and Judiciary Act did nothing to change the allocation of jurisdiction that prevailed in England before the American Revolution. Admittedly, Minor acknowledges elsewhere that geography is controlling only in tort (an accurate statement in 1875), while subject-matter determines jurisdiction in contract. *Id.*, Vol. III, at 1028. This implies that one would have the option of bringing action for breach of a maritime contract either in admiralty or at common law, but Minor fails to discuss the possibility. Throughout the remainder of the treatise, Minor neglects to examine the ramifications of concurrent jurisdiction in the context of admiralty.

flict (or even chaos) that one would expect when two separate sets of courts interpret the same body of substantive law.

McReynolds abhorred chaos and disorder. To be sure, he was not the first to press for uniformity in interpretation of substantive maritime law. Many expressed the same desire in the 1780s. One might speculate that McReynolds' opinion in *Jensen* was influenced in part by current events. Scarcely a month earlier, President Wilson had asked Congress for a declaration of war. Under the circumstances, the need for uniformity of maritime law would be especially deeply felt as the nation's navy and merchant fleet prepared to enter the European conflict.[24] Nevertheless, McReynolds continued to draft admiralty opinions grounded in the same *ratio decidendi* even after the armistice,[25] much to the chagrin of Holmes.[26] Justice Stone was equally critical, claiming that

---

24. In his *Address to a Joint Session of Congress* (April 2, 1917), Wilson asked Congress for a declaration of war, stating that the Imperial German Government had adopted a "new policy" which:

> "...has swept every restriction aside. Vessels of every kind, whatever their flag, their character, their cargo, their destination, their errand, have been ruthlessly sent to the bottom without warning and without thought of help or mercy for those on board, the vessels of friendly neutrals along with those of belligerents. Even hospital ships and ships carrying relief to the sorely bereaved and stricken people of Belgium...have been sunk with the same reckless lack of compassion or of principle."

reprinted in The Papers of Woodrow Wilson (69 vols., Arthur S. Link ed., Princeton: Princeton University Press, 1983), Vol. 41, at 519–520.

25. Of all of *Jensen's* progeny, the most notable is *Chelentis v. Luckenbach S.S. Co.*, 247 U.S. 372 (1918), holding that it was unconstitutional for a state court to apply a state statute providing a remedy for an injury occurring at sea, thereby limiting an injured party's remedies to those recognized by the general maritime law as interpreted by the federal courts. Among the progeny of *Jensen* for which McReynolds drafted opinions after the war were *Knickerbocker Ice Co. v. Stewart,* 253 U.S. 149 (1920) (holding that Congress could not constitutionally authorize courts to apply states' workmen's compensation statutes for injuries occurring at sea, since to do so would threaten the uniformity of the general maritime law); *Washington v. W.C. Dawson and Co.*, 264 U.S. 219 (1924) (extending the holding in *Knickerbocker* to include acts of Congress that would have permitted application of state workmen's compensation statutes to injuries sustained by longshoremen); *Robins Dry Dock and Repair Co. v. Dahl,* 266 U.S. 449 (1925) (rejecting the application of a state law requiring that an employer provide a safe workplace in the case of a shipyard worker injured while repairing a vessel docked in a New York port.) Despite his general objections to the application of state statutes in maritime cases, McReynolds did hold in *Western Fuel Co. v. Garcia,* 257 U.S. 233 (1921) that application of a state wrongful-death statute to the death of a stevedore was sufficiently "local" in nature that it would not offend the uniformity of the general maritime law.

26. Reflecting over the decade in which McReynolds drafted the opinions in *Jensen* and its progeny, Holmes wrote:

"Justice McReynolds has set admiralty law back a century..."[27] Despite occasional protests, McReynolds was not alone on the Court in his quest for uniformity. The majority of his brethren endorsed his opinions.[28] On reflection, this is not surprising. McReynolds had provided a bright-line solution—albeit one that in application often resembled the bed of Procrustes more than the judgment of Solomon. Minds far less driven by the need for order and

---

> "McReynolds is the boss in Admiralty because he has carried through a series of decisions that I don't believe in at all—although I don't [believe] he had any special knowledge before his victories in that field."

Letter of Oliver Wendell Holmes, Jr. to Harold J. Laski (Feb. 22, 1929), *published in* HOLMES-LASKI LETTERS, *supra* note 15, Vol. II, at 1133, 1135. Despite his reputation, Holmes' own record in admiralty matters has been the target for much criticism. He never fully accepted the legal fiction of "personification of vessels"—the cornerstone of the American action *in rem*—once writing with a touch of sarcasm that:

> "A ship is the most living of inanimate things.... It is only by supposing the ship to have been treated as if endowed with personality, that the arbitrary seeming peculiarities of the maritime law can be made intelligible, and on that supposition they at once become consistent and logical."

OLIVER WENDELL HOLMES, JR., THE COMMON LAW (1st ed. 1881; 59th printing, Boston: Little, Brown & Co., 1923) at 26–27. His difficulty with personification of vessels influenced his decision in *The Western Maid*, 257 U.S. 419 (1922), in which he held that a sovereign nation's acquisition of a vessel extinguished all existing maritime liens, grounding his decision in the doctrine of sovereign immunity. The suit, as critics were quick to point out, was against the personified vessel *in rem*, not against the sovereign government. Judge Charles Merrill Hough, the noted admiralty scholar, critiqued the anomalous result in print shortly thereafter. *See* Charles M. Hough, *Admiralty Jurisdiction—of Late Years*, 37 Harv. L. Rev. 529 (1924); for discussion of the Holmes/Hough debate, *see* G. EDWARD WHITE, JUSTICE OLIVER WENDELL HOLMES: LAW AND THE INNER SELF (New York: Oxford University Press, 1993) at 374–376. Holmes fared little better in his approach to admiralty and federalism. If McReynolds' approach sacrificed the states' interests to produce greater uniformity in substantive law, Holmes' approach did the opposite. His "gap theory", under which judges would apply state statutes in preference to creating new "common law" rules in admiralty, provided a mechanism for selecting applicable rules. Nonetheless, this mechanism threatened the uniformity of the maritime law and simultaneously ignored both federal and state interests. Ultimately, the Supreme Court rejected "gap theory" as unwieldy. For discussion, *see e.g.* David. P. Currie, *Federalism and the Admiralty: The Devil's Own Mess*, 1960 Sup. Ct. Rev. 158, 167–173 (hereinafter Currie, *Devil's Own Mess*).

27. *Quoted in* BOND, *supra* note 9, at 69.

28. Despite his curmudgeonly reputation, of the total of 503 opinions that McReynolds drafted during his tenure on the Supreme Court, his brethren endorsed 401 of them unanimously. Moreover, even Holmes conceded that many of their fellow justices looked to the former antitrust lawyer for guidance in admiralty matters. *See* discussion, *supra* note 26.

simplicity have felt the same frustration with concurrent admiralty jurisdiction,[29] and some have responded to the same siren's song that Holmes and Stone believed had lured the High Court to founder on the shoals in *Jensen*. Even after more than eighty years of scathing criticism, *Jensen*'s promise of bright-line rules for choice of substantive law has retained its luster for some modern critics.[30]

The precise parameters of the states' jurisdiction over admiralty and maritime cases remain a source of controversy today. To date, the Supreme Court has not offered a solution either as simple or as comprehensive as that envisioned by McReynolds in 1917. One should not judge the Court harshly; by its very nature concurrent jurisdiction is prone to a certain level of friction and discord. In other contexts, we accept this friction as an unfortunate byproduct of other values that we seek to preserve. One reasonably might ask why the Framers of the Constitution did not create lower federal courts with exclusive admiralty and maritime jurisdiction, or why the members of the first Congress opted to save common-law remedies in admiralty cases. These men clearly understood the potential for friction inherent in concurrent jurisdiction in other contexts. Were there potential benefits of concurrent jurisdiction that they expected on balance to outweigh the obvious disadvantages? To answer this question, it is necessary to examine "admiralty and maritime jurisdiction" and the activities that it governed as the Framers and the first Congress understood them.

Maritime Commerce and the Eighteenth-Century American Economy

In the winter of 1776, the colonies had been at war for nearly a year. The Continental Congress' declaration of independence was still several months

29. As Professor Currie once remarked of the Supreme Court's *ad hoc* retreat from *Jensen* and its progeny:

> "When the Supreme Court takes a more active view of its responsibilities in developing a rational common law of the sea, and when it pays more attention to relevant state and federal interests and to consistency between decisions, it may escape the tangle and seaweed which has long obstructed the development of this branch of the law..."

Currie, *Devil's Own Mess*, *supra* note 26, at 221.

30. *See e.g.* David J. Bederman, *Uniformity, Delegation, and the Dormant Admiralty Clause*, 28 J. Mar. L. & Com. 325 (1997).

away, and the hope for achieving recognition as an independent nation was precarious at best. Even if the colonies were to secure their independence, grave doubts remained as to whether the fledgling nation could survive alone in a world dominated by military alliances of the Old World's powers. At the height of the crisis, Thomas Paine offered his fellow Americans a word of encouragement. It was in Continental Europe's best interest, he maintained, for America to be free:

> Our plan is commerce, and that, well attended to, will secure us the peace and friendship of all Europe; because, it is the interest of all Europe to have America a *free port.* Her trade will always be a protection...[31]

Commerce would win America its independence, and commerce would preserve it. Paine knew his audience well. "Commerce" in the eighteenth century was *maritime* commerce. To his readers, New England shipowners and Southern planters alike, free trade meant freedom from the British Navigation Acts—a principal impetus behind the independence-movement. It is a fortunate revolution that finds its means and its ends in such harmony. Paine's comment was not merely clever rhetoric or the product of wishful thinking. In the 1770s, America's greatest asset was its overseas trade, and in particular the ships that facilitated it.

From their founding, the colonies were dependent on the sea. Ships brought settlers to the New World, and ships formed the life-line that permitted their settlements to survive in their early years. The sea provided the means by which the British mercantilist system operated—the conduit through which raw materials and cash-crops entered England for resale throughout Europe and through which English manufactured goods were sold to the colonists at a significant profit to English merchants. Obviously in the early days, the business of trade and shipping was centered in London, but in time the colonists themselves became significant participants in maritime commerce at all levels. From the beginning of the eighteenth century until the eve of the Revolution, the population of the thirteen colonies grew nearly tenfold to more than two million.[32] Modern writers often have characterized the American colonies as "agrarian". Admittedly, a substantial portion of the pop-

---

31. Thomas Paine, *Common Sense* (1st ed. Feb. 14, 1776), *reprinted in* THOMAS PAINE, COLLECTED WRITINGS (Eric Foner ed., New York: Library of America, 1995) at 5, 24.

32. *See* UNITED STATES DEPARTMENT OF COMMERCE: BUREAU OF THE CENSUS, HISTORICAL STATISTICS OF THE UNITED STATES: COLONIAL TIMES TO 1957 (Washington, D.C.: United States Government Printing Office, 1960) at 756.

ulation was engaged in agriculture, but the colonies' towns and cities—particularly their port-towns—were growing rapidly in size and economic importance throughout the century.[33] Estimates place the percentage of Americans in the colonies' largest cities engaged in maritime commerce at between one fifth and one quarter of the population; another one in twenty was employed in the building or fitting of ships.[34] In scarcely three generations, the principal locus for colonial maritime commerce had moved from London to the shores of the New World. Moreover, the colonists were the authors of their own prosperity; the amount of direct investment of overseas capital in colonial shipping and mercantile enterprises was negligible.[35] Development of shipping facilitated the development of ancillary industries. In addition to those providing goods and services to merchants and shipowners (*e.g.* stevedores, warfingers, sail-makers, ships' chandlers, and repair yards), the colonists also had begun to insure their own vessels and cargoes against loss.[36]

---

33. One set of estimates places the population of America's principal ports in 1775 at approximately 175,000, or roughly eight percent of the colonies' total. *See* Jacob M. Price, *Economic Function and the Growth of American Port Towns in the Eighteenth Century*, 8 Perspectives in American History 121 (1974) (Appendix A, Appendix B at 175–177) (hereinafter Price, *Port Towns*). The largest of these—Philadelphia, Boston, New York, Charleston, Newport, and Baltimore—accounted for roughly 110,000 of the total. No estimates are available for the population of towns of under 3,000 inhabitants, although a substantial number of such towns existed in 1775 along the coast, and many of their inhabitants derived their livelihood directly or indirectly from the sea.

34. *See Id.*, Appendix C at 181–183. (The estimates are for the cities of Philadelphia and Boston.) *See also* Marcus Rediker, Between the Devil and the Deep Blue Sea: Merchant Seamen, Pirates, and the Anglo-American Maritime World, 1700–1750 (Cambridge: Cambridge University Press, 1987) at 61–62 (corroborating Price's figures indicating that twenty-five percent of the population of the major colonial ports derived their livelihood from maritime commerce) (hereinafter Rediker).

35. James F. Shepherd & Gary M. Walton, Shipping, Maritime Trade and the Economic Development of Colonial North America (Cambridge: Cambridge University Press, 1972) at 43, 152 (hereinafter Shepherd & Walton, Shipping, Maritime Trade); *see also* John J. McCusker, "Sources of Investment Capital in the Colonial Philadelphia Shipping Industry", *in* Essays in the Economic History of the Atlantic World (John J. McCusker ed., London: Rutledge, 1997) at 245–246, 252–253 (hereinafter McCusker, "Investment Capital").

36. The rise of American brokers helped to reduce transactions-costs, which, in the words of one recent commentary, "represented a considerable savings for colonial merchants". *See* John J. McCusker & Russell R. Menard, The Economy of British America: 1607–1789 (Chapel Hill: The University of North Carolina Press, 1991) at 347–348 (hereinafter McCusker & Menard). The rise of domestic insurance brokerage, coupled with improvements in actuarial practices and reduction of risks (principally piracy), al-

The world of the eighteenth-century American entrepreneur was far different from that of his twenty-first century counterpart. Today buyers and sellers of goods are rarely directly involved in the business of carriage. Even their contacts with carriers are often by proxy; an assortment of middlemen—brokers and freight-forwarders—usually handle the details of contracts of affreightment for them. Such was not the case in the eighteenth century. "Vertical integration" was the norm. It was common for American merchants, particularly those in New England, to own the vessels that carried their goods to foreign markets.[37] Indeed, the most common route to becoming a successful merchant was to begin one's career as a ship's master.[38] As master, one was obliged to learn not only skills of navigation, but also the business of running a ship, from interpreting sailors' contracts of employment, or "ship's articles",

---

lowed insurance coverage to improve from a range of 70% to 90% per loss to between 98% and 99% in most cases without a commensurate increase in the premium. The resulting savings significantly reduced costs for shipowners and merchants. *See* GARY M. WALTON & JAMES S. SHEPHERD, THE ECONOMIC RISE OF EARLY AMERICA (Cambridge: Cambridge University Press, 1979) at 121 (hereinafter WALTON & SHEPHERD, ECONOMIC RISE). Nevertheless, American marine insurance was still in its infancy. One commentator provides the following description of how marine insurance operated in America in the 1770s:

> "Marine insurance in eighteenth-century America was still an individual rather than a corporate enterprise. Ports with substantial commerce usually had one or more insurance offices that wrote policies, posted them, and settled balances between the insurers and the insured for a fee. The actual capital was put up by individuals or partnerships, who signed their names at the bottom of the policies—hence the term underwriter—for the posted rate. No money changed hands at this point. The contract simply stipulated that the insured would pay the insurers the stated premium on their subscriptions whether or not the vessel came to grief. If the vessel did not complete its intended voyage, the amount of the premium was deducted from the amount for which the underwriters were liable. Balances between the insured and the underwriters customarily remained unsettled for some time, especially in cases of distant losses, where proof was required before underwriters would honor the policies. If no one subscribed at the rate initially posted, those seeking insurance had to offer more favorable terms or do without."

RICHARD BUEL, JR., IN IRONS: BRITAIN'S NAVAL SUPREMACY AND THE AMERICAN REVOLUTIONARY ECONOMY (New Haven: Yale University Press, 1998) at 97–98 (hereinafter BUEL).

37. See SHEPHERD & WALTON, SHIPPING, MARITIME TRADE, *supra* note 35, at 51–52. *See also* SAMUEL ELIOT MORISON, THE MARITIME HISTORY OF MASSACHUSETTS, 1783–1860 (1st ed. 1921, *reprinted* Boston: Northeastern University Press, 1979) at 24–25, 290 (hereinafter MORISON).

38. *See* Stuart Bruchey, *Success and Failure Factors: American Merchants in Foreign Trade in the Eighteenth and Early Nineteenth Centuries*, 33 Bus. Hist. Rev. 272, 281 (1958).

to contracting for repairs to the vessel by means of "bottomry bonds".[39] It was the master, not the owners, who would appear in court on behalf of a vessel should litigation arise. In colonies lacking a formal institution for promoting knowledge of admiralty law among members of the bar, ships' masters often had a greater practical knowledge of the substantive maritime law than did most practicing attorneys. The most successful of these ships' masters eventually purchased their own ships, hired others to sail them, and commenced new careers as "men of commerce". When one spoke of "commerce" in the 1770s, one meant foreign trade.[40] Apart from small-scale retailers, all merchants' activities were inextricably tied to the sea. Arcane as "admiralty law" may appear to businessmen of today, it was an integral part of the working life of every successful merchant of the eighteenth century. The same applied to the colonial bar. Just as some legal specialties today have the reputation of being "sophisticated", so also in the late colonial period, the best-educated attorneys gravitated to commercial law, of which a significant part was maritime law.[41] It was these classes, the successful merchants and the elite members of the colonial bar who represented them, who were to become the leading figures of the Revolution—as well as those responsible for shaping the form of the new government after independence was achieved.

As the century progressed, American merchant-shipowners became more productive. Innovations in technology played at most a minor role in this increased productivity.[42] Sail-driven ships changed little throughout the century,[43] and the still relatively small size of markets served by American ports

39. For discussion of a master's duties in construing contracts of employment and negotiating bottomry bonds, under which he pledged the hull as security for services rendered to the ship, *see infra* Chapter II, notes 104, 145 and text accompanying.

40. *See* Currie, *Devil's Own Mess*, *supra* note 26, at 163; Jonathan M. Gutoff, *Original Understandings and the Private Law Origins of the Federal Admiralty Jurisdiction: A Reply to Professor Casto*, 30 J. Mar. L. & Com. 361, 391 (1999) (hereinafter Gutoff).

41. For discussion of the practice of those colonial attorneys who handled maritime cases, *see infra* Chapter II, notes 225–229 and text accompanying.

42. *See* McCusker & Menard, *supra* note 36, at 270; Shepherd & Walton, Shipping, Maritime Trade, *supra* note 35, at 6–7, 9.

43. Ironically, the British tax laws actually retarded the development of improved hull designs. Ships' tonnage was measured according to a fixed ratio, which calculated depth at one half of the beam. Thus to obtain a better tax rate, naval architects were obliged to design ships with short keels and "kettle-shaped" bottoms. This maximized the available cargo-space per measured ton, but produced vessels that were slow and clumsy. In the early republic, the Americans preserved this technique for measuring registered tonnage, abandoning it finally in the mid-nineteenth century. For the formula used in calculating tonnage and its implications for tax rates and ship design, *see* John G. B. Hutchins, The American Maritime Industries

often prevented the use of larger ships, which cost less to operate per ton than smaller vessels.[44] Some factors contributing to improvements in productivity were beyond the control of the colonists, such as a reduction in levels of piracy.[45] Others were the result of their own initiative. These included significant reductions in time spent in port and reductions in insurance rates (the latter in part a product of improved actuarial methods).[46] In all, the productivity of American merchant shipping increased at a rate approaching one percent *per annum* for the century preceding the Revolution.[47] Despite the Nav-

---

AND MARITIME POLICY, 1789–1914 (Cambridge, Massachusetts: Harvard University Press, 1941) at 216–218 (hereinafter HUTCHINS); *see also* MORISON, *supra* note 37, at 14 n. 1.

44. Ships of larger size required fewer men per ton to sail them and generally had more cargo space in relation to their external dimensions. Nevertheless, a very large ship filled with one type of cargo might easily flood the market, thus reducing profits per unit and conceivably leaving the owners with a surplus that could not be sold without incurring the expense shipping it to another port. For discussion, *see e.g.* Gary M. Walton, *A Measure of Productivity Change in American Colonial Shipping*, 21 Econ. Hist. Rev., 268 (2d ser., 1968) (hereinafter Walton, *Measure of Productivity*). In addition, there is some evidence that in the era before steam-power, shipowners preferred several smaller ships to a few larger vessels as a method of risk-spreading. *See* MORISON, *supra* note 37, at 97.

45. So long as pirates were a serious threat, shipowners responded by carrying additional guns and additional crew to man them in case of attack. Eighteenth-century artillery was both expensive and heavy, thus adding to the owners' fixed costs while simultaneously decreasing the ships' carrying capacity. Moreover, additional crew added to variable costs—no insignificant sum for colonial owners—as a scarcity of labor compelled them to pay higher wages than their European competitors. For discussion *see* Christopher J. French, *Productivity in the Atlantic Shipping Industry: A Quantitative Study*, 17 Journal of Interdisciplinary History, 613, 615–616, 620, 626–631 (1987). For statistics on the wages of colonial sailors, *see* REDIKER, *supra* note 34, at 52, 104–105, 136–137, 303–306.

46. The technology of the era limited the number of voyages a ship could make between ports in a calendar year. By reducing time spent in port, ships were able to make an extra voyage, significantly increasing annual revenue. Time and techniques required for lading had not changed, but business practices had. One significant component in saving time in the process of lading was the innovative practice of stationing importers' agents in colonial ports. Others were the product of the colonists' own initiative. One should not underestimate the cumulative effects of small measures taken for reducing costs. By early in the following century, American ocean-carriers dominated world markets, largely through improvements in efficiency of business practices—not superior technology or cheaper inputs. For discussion of improvements in productivity of colonial shipping, *see* Gary M. Walton, *Sources of Productivity Change in American Colonial Shipping*, and 20 Econ. Hist. Rev. 67, 77 (2d ser., 1967); SHEPHERD & WALTON, SHIPPING, MARITIME TRADE, *supra* note 35, at 6–9, 73–85, 90, 157–159; Walton, *Measure of Productivity*, *supra* note 44, at 268; French, *supra* note 45, at 615–631.

47. Shepherd and Walton estimate the increase in productivity conservatively at .8% per year from 1675 through 1775, yielding a total increase of 200% on the London-to-

igation Acts, American merchants took control of an increasingly large portion of the British carrying trades as the century progressed. By the 1770s, colonists owned one-third of all British tonnage.[48] American prosperity was aided further by British merchants' liberal use of short-term credit, which provided a much-needed additional source of capital. For those merchants who used it wisely, short-term credit formed the foundation of colonial fortunes.[49]

The sea provided another source of income for the colonists. British and colonial merchants alike needed ships, and America, unlike much of Europe, had a large supply of timber. While the costs of colonial labor were comparatively high, raw materials were inexpensive.[50] The savings in costs of materials offset the additional cost of labor sufficiently to shift a large portion of British shipbuilding to American ports; current scholarship reveals that as much of one third of total British registered tonnage was built in the thirteen colonies.[51] In the early days, the shipbuilding industry was heavily concentrated in New England, but over time colonies further south also began building ships.[52] By 1771, Massachusetts built only about one out of every three American vessels,[53] by which time ships ranked fifth among all colonial exports, accounting for an estimated 140,000 pounds sterling per year.[54] Ship-

---

New York route between 1699 and 1775; McCusker and Menard concur. *See* Shepherd & Walton, Shipping, Maritime Trade, *supra* note 35, at 64, 68, 71, Appendix 3 at 188–203; *see also* McCusker & Menard, *supra* note 36, at 266. Walton's earlier article places the figure somewhat higher, at a 1.35% uncompounded annual increase in productivity throughout the eighteenth century. Walton, *Measure of Productivity*, *supra* note 44, at 268, 276.

48. McCusker, "Investment Capital", *supra* note 35, at 246.

49. *See* Walton & Shepherd, Economic Rise, *supra* note 36, at 105–106.

50. *See* Hutchins, *supra* note 43, at 130–137, 144–149.

51. Working from a combination of eighteenth-century sources (including *Lloyd's Register* and Lord Sheffield's revised report of 1784) and twentieth-century historians' estimates, economic historian Jacob Price arrives at a figure of more than 30% as the percentage of British ships that were built in America. *See* Jacob. M. Price, *A Note on the Value of Colonial Exports of Shipping*, 37 J. Econ. Hist. 704, 715 (1976) (hereinafter Price, *Note*).

52. Price, *Port Towns*, *supra* note 33, Appendix F at 185 (providing statistics for the tonnage built in each of the thirteen colonies).

53. *Id.* at 146.

54. Economic historian Jacob Price makes the following estimates of the value of shipbuilding to the colonial American economy:

> "Thus, instead of the range of £ 46,000–105,000 suggested by Walton and Shepherd for the value of colonial shipping sales, we now have an estimate of £ 120–180,000, with a figure in the vicinity of £ 140,000 appealing most strongly to the present writer. The £ 140,000 estimate is distinctly on the conservative side. It makes no allowance for the value for North American smaller vessels (sloops

building was not the only colonial occupation that owed its existence to the sea. Each port had its share of warfingers, boatmen, stevedores, warfbuilders, underwriters, ships' chandlers, and those who supplied provisions and naval stores to merchant and naval vessels.[55] In many instances, maritime pursuits were not merely an integral part of the local economy; they were the only reason for a town's existence.

For agrarian colonies lacking in domestic manufacturing,[56] trade was clearly critical to their economic well-being. Even in the early years, trade served as a catalyst for improving the allocation of resources and the expansion of colonial agriculture.[57] Estimates have placed commodity exports at more than

---

> and schooners) sold in the West Indies unless they visited British or Irish ports and were inspected for Lloyd's. Nor does it make any allowance for colonial-built vessels sold in Spain or Portugal or sold in London to non-British owners who employed them in trade that fell outside the network of Lloyd's inspectors.... In short... I would say that ca. 1763–1775 shipbuilding in the Thirteen Colonies totaled about 40,000 measured tons and was worth about £ 300,000 sterling, of which at least 18,600 tons worth £ 140,000 were sold abroad. Given these estimates, American colonial shipbuilding, a neglected industry, does appear to have made a significant contribution to late colonial export earnings."

See Price, *Note*, *supra* note 51, at 722. *Cf.* Shepherd & Walton, *supra* note 35, at 96, for the statistics that Price critiques.

55. *See* Price, *Port Towns*, *supra* note 33, Appendix C at 177–185.

56. Shepherd & Walton, Shipping, Maritime Trade, *supra* note 35, at 23–24, estimates that only ten percent of Americans were engaged in manufacturing on the eve of the Revolution.

57. As Shepherd & Walton explain:

> "[I]t is important to keep in mind the importance of overseas trade and the market economy as a source of colonial income, as opposed to self-sufficient or subsistence economic activities. While overseas trade and market activity may not have comprised the major portion of all colonial economic activity, the importance of the market was that of improving resource allocation.... We argue that while subsistence agriculture provided an important base to colonial incomes and was a substantial share of average per capita income, changes in incomes and improvements in welfare came largely through overseas trade and other market activities. Not only did improvements in productivity occur primarily through market activities, but the pattern of settlement and production was determined by market forces. This pattern changed slowly and unevenly, spreading from the waterways and distribution centers along the Atlantic seaboard into the interior. The geographical location of the population near available water transport resulted primarily from the wide differences in the costs of transportation by water and by land. Few settlers were completely independent of the market, and most colonists were engaged, at least part-time, in production for markets. Furthermore, the costs of transportation in the colonies were particularly important for

twelve percent of total colonial output.[58] Trade with overseas ports was matched by a burgeoning intercolonial coastal trade, reaching forty percent of the total for foreign trade in the middle colonies and sixty percent in New England.[59] Despite the importance of trade with Britain and foreign nations, much has been made of the colonies' trade deficit. Admittedly, a sizable proportion of Britain's total exports went to the American colonies,[60] and roughly three-fourths of all goods imported by the colonies came from Britain.[61] As one would expect in a mercantilist system, more than half of all colonial exports went to Britain and Ireland.[62] Equally predictable are the regional statistics. The Southern colonies, with their cash-crops of tobacco, rice, and in-

---

> such items as tobacco, rice, indigo, fish, wheat, lumber, and others, which were typically high bulk items in relation to their value. In fact, there were few goods that could bear the costs of overland shipment of any great distance, and, as a result, resources responded to market forces and production and exchange centered near cheap water transport."

Id. at 25–26.

58. *See e.g.* James F. Shepherd & Samuel H. Williamson, *The Coastal Trade of the British North American Colonies, 1768–1772*, J. Econ, Hist. 783, 801 (1972) (hereinafter Shepherd & Williamson) (placing the estimated percentage of total output attributable to commodity exports as between 11.5% and 13.5%). McCusker and Menard make the following observations:

> "Assuming total incomes per capita to have been between £ 11.00 and £ 12.50, exports contributed from 11 to 13 percent of the whole. If we include the value of ships sold abroad (£ 140,000) and an estimate of invisible earnings (£ 820,000), per capita income from foreign trade rises to £ 1.75 and exports contributed 14 to 16 percent of total income. If we further add the value of commodity exports in the coastal trades (£ 715,000), the per capita figure reaches £ 2.10, 17 to 19 percent of the total. This seems a substantial share of colonial income. It would be slightly higher were a reliable estimate of invisible earnings in the coastal trade available, substantially higher if attention was confined to market transactions and production for home use excluded."

McCusker & Menard, *supra* note 36, at 85–86. *See also* Shepherd & Walton, Shipping, Maritime Trade, *supra* note 35, at 44.

59. Shepherd & Williamson, *supra* note 58, at 801; *see also* the corroborating figures of Shepherd and Walton, *supra* note 58.

60. One set of figures estimates that 25% of total British exports went to the North American colonies. *See* Walton & Shepherd, Economic Rise, *supra* note 36, at 167.

61. Shepherd and Walton place the value of British goods imported by the thirteen colonies at four million pounds sterling in 1772. Their figures for imports from southern Europe and the West Indies are 84,000 pounds and 964,000 pounds (C.I.F. values) respectively for the same year. Shepherd & Walton, *supra* note 35, at 104, 113.

62. For the years 1768–1772, Shepherd and Walton estimate the total average value of American exports to Britain and Ireland at 1.9 million pounds sterling (F.O.B. prices), while

digo, were the principal exporters.[63] Modern research has debunked the once-held notion that Southern planters' mounting debts to London's merchants precipitated the Revolution.[64] There were in fact deficits in the colonists' trade with Britain in the 1770s, although these were not as great as one might suppose upon a cursory examination of the balance of payments in the sale of commodities. The South, stereotypes notwithstanding, actually experienced surpluses in the first half of the decade,[65] while New England and the Mid-Atlantic colonies instead bore the brunt of the deficits.[66] From the earliest days of the preceding century, the people of Massachusetts recognized their vulnerability to trade deficits with the mother country. They lacked a cash-crop, and their few manufactured goods could not compete favorably at home with English goods despite the additional costs of transporting the latter across the Atlantic. Initially, the colonists adopted policies aimed at limiting their consumption of English products, but soon thereafter, they discovered that rev-

---

exports to southern Europe, Africa, and the West Indies totaled roughly 1.6 million pounds (also F.O.B. prices). *Id.* at 94–95.

63. Shepherd and Walton give figures of £ 766, 000, £ 312,000, £ 117,000 as the average annual colonial exports of tobacco, rice, and indigo respectively for the years 1768–1772. Together with bread and flour (£ 412,000) and dried fish (£ 287,000), these commodities constituted roughly half of all colonial exports. The South produced virtually all of the tobacco, rice, and indigo exported, and contributed a significant portion of the exported bread and flour as well. Among the five leading exports (excluding ships), the northern colonies dominated only the trade in dried fish. *Id.* at 92–98. The authors calculate the average *per capita* exports for 1770 in pounds sterling by region at £ .85 for New England, £ 1.0 for the Mid-Atlantic Colonies, £ 1.8 for the Upper South, and £ 1.55 for the Lower South. *Id.* at 101. It is thus clear that the export-trade of the colonies was skewed in favor of the South.

64. For figures and analysis debunking this notion, *see* Walton & Shepherd, Economic Rise, *supra* note 36, at 105–106. The deteriorating relations between the thirteen colonies and the mother country in the 1770s cannot be explained solely in terms of the colonists' pursuit economic self-interest. Admittedly, there is evidence that the British Navigation Acts produced a drag on the colonial economy amounting to roughly 1% to 3% of the colonial gross "national" product. *Id.* at 173–174. Nevertheless, such burdens fell disproportionately on New England. The movement for independence received as much support in Virginia as in the north, despite regional trade surpluses on the eve of the Revolution. *Id.* at 106.

65. If one considers commodities alone (exclusive of shipbuilding and services), one finds that the South experienced surpluses in its trade with Great Britain and Ireland in 1768 and 1769, while it experienced small deficits in the first three years of the next decade. If one includes their trade with the West Indies, Africa, and southern Europe, however, they managed surpluses in their total foreign trade in the years 1770 and 1772 as well. *See* Shepherd & Walton, Shipping, Maritime Trade, *supra* note 35, at 115.

66. *Id.* at 114–116.

enue from shipping could offset in part the deficit in commodities' trade.[67] Investments in shipping born of local necessity soon restructured the economy of all the colonies. Economies of scale dictated that one port become the *entrepôt* for the colonies, and Boston's initial investment bore fruit.[68] Despite significant deficits in trade in commodities, New England earned sizable sums in the carrying trades.[69] While the statistics for the Southern and Mid-Atlantic colonies are not so striking, they also profited by carrying goods by sea to domestic and foreign markets.[70] The results were dramatic. In spite of average annual deficits of 1.3 million pounds sterling in colonial trade in commodities with the world as a whole, and an annual average deficit of £ 1.8 million

---

67. McCusker & Menard, *supra* note 36, at 96. As the authors explain, the people of New England:

> "...learned that the shipping business itself could generate considerable credits, and merchants soon accepted both the risks and the benefits of the 'carrying trade'. The New Englanders became the Dutch of England's empire. The earnings from these endeavors joined with a successful subsistence agriculture and a growing domestic market to create a flourishing economy, though one less prosperous than the plantation economies to the south."

Id. at 92.

68. As Price concludes:

> "[P]art of the concentration at Boston must be seen as arising from the very complexity of the trade.... [T]he complexity of the trade required a 'comprehensive entrepôt', and not simply a 'shipping point' for fish. Sloops going southward in the coastal trade carried not just fish but other New England produce (including some crude manufactures) plus manufactures from Britain and salt from either Iberia or the West Indies. Sloops in the West Indies trade carried fish, horses, flour, and provisions (including some bought from the more southerly colonies) and manufactures and wine from Europe. To England went not only the furs and forest products (particularly turpentine) of New England but sugar from the West Indies and tobacco from the Chesapeake. With trade of this complexity, there were advantages in concentration in a single mart town, or general entrepôt, where one man's surplus could fill another's vessel, and external economies of linkages could be realized."

Price, *Port Towns*, *supra* note 33, at 142–143.

69. Estimated earnings for New England's overseas shipping industry in the years from 1768 through 1772 range from £ 296,000 to £ 354,000 per year, with an average of £ 327,000. New England's carrier-trade with Britain yielded earnings £ 55,000 to £ 66,000 annually for the same period, with an average of £ 61,000. *See* Shepherd & Walton, *supra* note 35, at 128.

70. *Id.* Estimates of earnings in overseas shipping for the years 1768 through 1772 for the Mid-Atlantic colonies ranged from £ 165,000 to £ 188,000, with an average of £ 177,000. For the Southern colonies during the same period, the figures range from £ 89,000 to £ 110,000, with an average of £ 97,000.

in trade with the mother country,[71] some modern scholars estimate that earnings from the service sector narrowed the annual deficit to between £ 50,000 and £ 100,000.[72] Others contend that when a more accurate accounting is made of so called "invisible earnings" from the service sector, we will discover that the colonies in fact experienced a surplus.[73] Virtually all of these service-sector earnings accrued in the carrying trades.[74] When one examines all of the figures, the conclusion is inescapable. The carrying trades and the related mar-

---

71. *Id.* at 115. The figures are for the years 1768 through 1772. The year 1769, a good year for the Americans' trade balance, is offset by 1771, their worst before the Revolution. The average of the figures for the three remaining (and more typical) years thus remains at roughly the same as that for the five years as a whole. As one might infer, the trade deficit with Britain is greater than the total trade deficit because the colonies earned surpluses in their trade with the rest of the world.

72. *See* Shepherd & Williamson, *supra* note 58, at 803. The authors have included surpluses earned in shipbuilding together with traditional "invisibles" (*i.e.* carrying trades, marine insurance, interest, and other services) in arriving at this estimate. The figures given by Shepherd and Walton in their book of 1972 are somewhat less favorable to the colonists, but they do reaffirm the conclusion that earnings from "invisibles" such as the carrying trades, marine insurance, and shipbuilding did much to alleviate the colonists' deficits in commodities-trading:

> "For the period 1768–72, at least, the resulting estimates strongly suggest that earnings from invisibles were very important as a source of sterling to the colonies. For the North American colonies, the average annual deficit remaining on the balance of commodity trade for this five-year period was £ 1,331,000. Estimates of their annual average shipping earnings for this period were £ 610,000 and estimates of other invisible earnings were £ 222,000. Thus, an estimated 62 per cent of the deficit from commodity trade was paid by these invisible earnings."

Shepherd & Walton, Shipping, Maritime Trade, *supra* note 35, at 116. It should be noted that the authors' totals are based on their assumption that earnings from sale of ships abroad was in the range of £ 46,000 to £ 105,000 per year. *Id.* at 96. If Jacob Price is correct, shipbuilding for sale abroad yielded the colonists between £ 120,000 and £ 180,000, with a figure of £ 140,000 as the preferred estimate. This would increase the figure for total invisible earnings by an amount of somewhere between £ 15,000 and £ 134,000 *per annum*—representing a significant increase in the authors' estimate of a 62% offset against the deficit in commodity-trade. *See supra* note 54; *see also* Price, *Note*, *supra* note 51, at 722.

73. *See* McCusker & Menard, *supra* note 36, at 72. The authors applaud the efforts of Shepherd and Walton, the most accurate and comprehensive at the time of their publication, but note several deficiencies in their analysis. First, they fail to take smuggling into account; if smuggling were widespread, it would further tip the balance of trade in the Americans' favor. Second, they agree with Price (*see supra* notes 54, 72) in concluding that some of the estimates of invisibles given by Shepherd and Walton may be low. *Id.* at n. 2.

74. Shepherd & Walton, Shipping, Maritime Trade, *supra* note 35, at 117. For the value of other invisibles, *see Id.* at 134.

itime industries that supported them were more than important to the colonies; they were the linchpin that held the colonial economy together.

The Impact of Independence on American Maritime Trade

The colonies' declaration of independence had a profound effect upon the American economy. Much of this effect was a product of the Revolution itself; war inevitably interrupts the usual course of business. Nonetheless, some of the changes were not the direct result of armed conflict. The former colonies found themselves outside of the ambit of the British Navigation Acts, but this new-found freedom came at a price. American merchants lost many of the trading privileges they had enjoyed as part of the British Empire. Initially, the economy struggled. The British blockade and closure of British ports to colonial vessels wreaked havoc on the American carrying trades until the French entered the war, occupying the attention of the Royal Navy, disrupting the blockade, and leaving the Americans free to pursue trade wherever opportunities presented themselves.[75] As the war drew to a close, merchants—unencumbered by the Navigation Acts but unassisted by Britain's protective

75. The state of American trade during the Revolution, a topic deserving of book-length treatment, received perhaps its best one-paragraph summary in McCusker & Menard, *supra* note 36, at 361, outlining a four-stage sequence of development first suggested by economic historian Curtis Putnam Nettles:

> "During the first stage, lasting from the nonimportation agreement of late 1774 to April 1776, prohibitions on trade by the British government and by Congress and the closing of old markets effectively curtailed foreign commerce and led to acute shortages of imported goods. In late 1774 and early 1775, Congress tried to stop all trade by employing the weapons of boycott and embargo, but once the fighting started, it sanctioned a limited exchange with foreign nations. The second stage began in April 1776, when Congress removed all restrictions on foreign trade; it lasted until mid-1778. This stage was marked by a flourishing commerce with France and with the foreign West Indies but also by a fairly successful British naval blockade of the principal northern ports, which limited volume and kept risks and costs high. Wartime trade peaked in the third period, from mid-1778 to early 1782, as increasing demands on the Royal Navy limited its ability to maintain a tight blockade and as the French, the Spanish, and the Dutch entered the war. During 1782, however, the last of [the] four periods, this flourishing trade with Europe and the islands declined sharply as the British concentrated an increasing share of their naval operations on attacks against American merchant shipping."

umbrella—scrambled to re-establish their old trade patterns while pursuing new avenues for commerce. To a great extent, they were successful; by the end of the decade, they were exporting at levels that equaled or even exceeded those of the pre-war period.[76] Despite a shortage of capital, even shipbuilding had begun to recover by 1783; financially-burdened merchants ordered new vessels, recognizing that the investment was essential to ensure their ability to compete in post-war international markets.[77]

Opinion was divided on the state of the American economy. Benjamin Franklin wrote to an acquaintance in 1786:

> America never was in higher prosperity, her produce abundant and bearing a good price, her working people all employed and well paid, and all property in lands and houses of more than treble the value it bore before the war; and, our commerce being no longer the monopoly of British merchants, we are furnished with all the foreign commodities we need, at much more reasonable rates than heretofore. So that we have no doubt of being able to discharge more speedily the debt incurred by the war, than at first was apprehended.[78]

For a more detailed analysis of trade and the American economy during the Revolution, *see generally* Buel, *supra* note 36.

76. McCusker & Menard, *supra* note 36, at 370–371. For a statistical analysis, *see e.g.* James F. Shepherd & Gary M. Walton, *Economic Change after the American Revolution: Pre- and Post-War Comparisons of Maritime Shipping and Trade*, 13 Explorations in Economic History 397 (1976) (hereinafter Shepherd & Walton, *Economic Change*). The authors conclude:

> "Overall, there was an increase in the real value of exports of about 37% from 1768–1772 to 1790–1792, assuming that the customs data upon which these comparisons have been based are reasonably accurate."

Id. at 412.

77. Shipbuilding had continued throughout the Revolution, though most of the vessels constructed sacrificed cargo-space for speed. "Blockade-runners" and privateers (typically sharp-built schooners) are not economical vessels in peace-time. Financial hardships notwithstanding, many merchants recognized the necessity of procuring larger ships for peace-time trade, thereby giving a much-needed boost to a shipbuilding industry that by some estimates had been second only to tobacco producers in overseas sales-revenues before the war. *See* Buel, *supra* note 36, at 240–244.

78. Letter from Benjamin Franklin to M. Le Veillard (March 6, 1786), *quoted in* Merrill Jensen, The New Nation: A Short History of the United States During the Confederation, *1781–1789* (New York: Alfred A. Knopf, 1950) at 249 (hereinafter Jensen). Franklin's correspondence with others in this period reflected the same optimism. For discussion, *see* Charles A. Beard, An Economic Interpretation of the Constitution of the United States (1st ed., 1913; *reprinted* New York: The Free Press, 1986) at 47. Franklin's remarks proved prophetic; the United States did in fact retire its war-debt

Others were less optimistic. Predictably, the most dire prognoses came from the Northern ports. Scarcely a year after Franklin penned his remarks, William Cushing of Massachusetts lamented that:

> ...Commerce is in a wretched Situation unregulated, unprotected, unproductive of Revenue—that All the world are become our Carriers, except only that we ourselves—are in a manner excluded;—Shipbuilding & navigation in a great measure cease;—while hundreds of Our Carpenters—& hundreds of our honest Seamen on the coast with men of numerous other trades & businesses dependent on these now lie still for want of employ; in short, the intrest [*sic*] of all classes of men through the community is essentially affected—from the Ocean to the wilderness.[79]

In tying the fate of the whole economy to the success of maritime commerce, Cushing was not alone. In 1787, the *Essex Journal* observed: "...this town depends principally on Ship-building for its subsistence", adding that the decline in trade "is the cause of an almost universal stagnation of business among all classes of men".[80] An editorial in the *Boston Gazette* contended that "half of our sailors are out of business", "our traders [are] involved in debt", and "our merchants have been sinking money ever since the peace".[81] John Jay expounded upon the same theme, writing:

---

by 1800, largely through foreign trade in commodities facilitated by the comparative advantage of the nation's carrying trades. *See* Buel, *supra* note 36, at 254.

79. Draft of a Speech (Feb. 4, 1788), *published from manuscript in* The Documentary History of the Ratification of the Constitution (18 vols., John P. Kaminski & Gaspare J. Saladino eds., Madison: State Historical Society of Wisconsin, 1976–2000) Vol. VI, at 1439 (hereinafter Ratification). The date of the speech, and indeed much of the material in print decrying the state of the carrying trades and the economy in general, is from the period immediately following the publication of the Convention's final draft of the Constitution. Lobbying for support for the new form of government, the federalists often exaggerated the nation's economic difficulties, offering the Constitution as a panacea for the economy's ills. Allowing for differences in politics and perceptions, the private nature and slightly earlier date for Franklin's letter (*supra* note 78) argue for greater objectivity and accuracy. For a quantitative analysis of the economy during this period, *see generally* Shepherd & Walton, *Economic Change*, *supra* note 76; Rhoda M. Dorsey, *The Pattern of Baltimore Commerce During the Confederation Period*, 62 Maryland Historical Magazine 119 (1967) (hereinafter Dorsey).

80. The anonymous author signed his name "A". *Essex Journal* (Oct. 10, 1787), *reprinted in* Ratification, *supra* note 79, Vol. IV, at 65, 66.

81. Editorial by an anonymous Federalist lobbying for ratification of the Constitution, published in the *Boston Gazette* (Oct. 15, 1787), *reprinted in* Ratification, *supra* note 79, Vol. IV, at 80.

> Our shipyards have almost ceased to disturb the repose of the neighborhood by the noise of the axe and hammer; and while foreign flags fly triumphantly above our highest houses, the American Stars seldom do more than shed a few feeble rays about the humble masts of river sloops and coasting schooners. The greater part of our hardy seamen, are plowing the ocean in foreign pay; and not a few of our ingenious shipwrights are now building vessels on alien shores.[82]

Admittedly, there were problems. American merchants, eager to profit from the re-opening of trade with Great Britain, had obtained British goods on credit and had miscalculated American demand, leading to glutted markets for some commodities and financial ruin for those who had erred in their estimates.[83] In addition, the lack of a centralized trade policy worried many. By 1785, many states had begun to enact tariff acts less as a means for collecting revenue than as a precaution against the recession—and for the protection of local manufacturing interests.[84] Concerns over the lack of a national trade policy precipitated the convening of the Annapolis Convention in 1786.[85] As one

---

82. John Jay, *An Address to the People of the State of New York, on the Subject of the Constitution* (1787), *reprinted in* PAMPHLETS ON THE CONSTITUTION OF THE UNITED STATES, PUBLISHED DURING ITS DISCUSSION BY THE PEOPLE, 1787–1788 (Paul Leicester Ford ed., Brooklyn, New York, 1888) at 67, 73 (hereinafter Ford, PAMPHLETS).

83. JENSEN, *supra* note 78, at 185–191. The author summarizes the events that began in May of 1783, as foreign goods flooded American ports:

> "These goods came to markets adequately if not oversupplied. Credit and easy terms were offered American merchants to induce them to buy. They bought, and they bought too much.... The boom that started as a buying spree by war-prosperous Americans in the seaport towns continued as a credit-supported balloon and too few, indeed, realized that such beauteous moments in history have but one inevitable end. The collapse did not come suddenly in one great panic. Actually, from the end of the war on, it was plain that matters were getting worse in the seaport towns. By the spring of 1784 the glutted market, the scarcity of specie, and the overextension of credit all combined to produce a serious commercial depression, although imports continued to arrive during the spring of 1784."

Id. at 185, 187.

84. *See* William Appleton Williams, *The Age of Mercantilism: An Interpretation of the American Political Economy*, 1763–1828, 15 William & Mary Quarterly 419, 423 (3d ser., 1958) (hereinafter Williams).

85. For discussion of the Annapolis Convention, *see e.g.* STANLEY ELKINS & ERIC MCKITRICK, THE AGE OF FEDERALISM: THE EARLY AMERICAN REPUBLIC, 1788–1800 (New York: Oxford University Press, 1993) at 43, 102 (hereinafter ELKINS & MCKITRICK).

might expect, the self-styled "federalists" saw in the economic woes of 1783–1784 a symptom of America's vulnerability under the Articles of Confederation, and used the recession and its aftermath to full rhetorical effect in their call for a stronger national government. Federalist rhetoric notwithstanding, the recession was short-lived, and the economy was showing marked signs of improvement by the time the Constitutional Convention convened in the spring of 1787. The nation owed much of this financial recovery to trade, and in particular to the carrying trades.[86]

American merchants experienced a precipitous fall in their exports to Britain and a slow but steady decline in their trade with the West Indies, but they compensated with expansion of their trade with France, Holland, the Mediterranean, and East Asia.[87] A principal factor contributing to America's economic recovery was the growth of its interstate trade, and in particular the coastal fleet that carried it.[88] Nevertheless, as exaggerated as some of the fed-

---

86. The state of the American economy in the 1780s has been the source of nearly as much controversy among modern scholars as among the original disputants. Relying largely upon materials available in the eighteenth century and upon Timothy Pitkin's landmark study of 1816 (revised 1835) Jensen maintains that the post-war period saw little difference the level of American imports of British goods, while the level of American exports to Britain initially fell sharply but subsequently experienced steady annual growth from 1784 through 1792. *See* JENSEN, *supra* note 78, at 195–197. The unfavorable trade balance with Britain was offset by gains in trade with the rest of the world. Relying again largely upon Pitkin's figures, Jensen observes: "Wherever statistics have come down to us they show the same trend: rapid increase of shipping after the war." *Id.* at 214. Jensen admits that Pitkin's figures may not be entirely accurate (*Id.* at 197 n. 4) but finds empirical evidence for federalists' claims of impending economic catastrophe wholly lacking. He concludes: "There is nothing in the knowable facts to support the ancient myth of idle ships, stagnant commerce, and bankrupt merchants in the new nation." *Id.* at 218; discussion at 245–246. *See also* TIMOTHY PITKIN, A STATISTICAL VIEW OF THE COMMERCE OF THE UNITED STATES (1st ed., 1816; *reprinted* New York: Augustus M. Kelley, 1967) at 30.

87. JENSEN, *supra* note 78, at 198–214.

88. Rhoda Dorsey's case-study of Baltimore under the Articles of Confederation is illustrative. Ties to Philadelphia and the Mid-Atlantic region added diversity to Baltimore's import/export business and carrying trades that Boston lacked. Thus it weathered the difficulties of the mid-1780s more easily than the ports of New England. Despite mixed success in foreign trade with France and Southern Europe, the city's commerce grew "due to the rapid rise in entries from American ports". While Baltimore expanded its trade with other American ports in the 1780s—the "single factor most responsible" for its increase in prosperity—it also acted as a catalyst for economic growth in other American cities. Dorsey, *supra* note 79, at 125–132. As she observes:

> "The rise of Baltimore shipping engaged in the American trade of the port is indicative of the expanding interests and capabilities of the city. Significantly enough, however, it was paralleled by the rise of New England bottoms engaged

eralists' forecasts of financial catastrophe had been, the structure of the Articles of Confederation left much to be desired. Even if economic conditions were relatively good under the circumstances, the form of government was not well suited to a nation heavily dependent upon trade. The Articles failed to vest in Congress the authority to levy taxes, instead requiring that national revenue be raised through the states at Congress' request. Not all states were willing to pay their fair share, and the national government often found itself under-funded.[89] In addition to the practical deficiencies in such a system, forcing Congress to go hat-in-hand to the state legislatures was bad for the nation's public image, creating the impression that the nation was weak and incapable of defending itself.[90] The decentralized nature of the Confederation likewise failed to inspire confidence in the new nation's ability to conduct commerce. Lord Sheffield, architect of Britain's post-war economic policy toward the United States, wrote in 1783:

> in trade with Baltimore. By 1787, 124 of the entries in domestic trade to Baltimore were locally owned and 92 were New England bottoms."

Id. at 133.

89. The Articles of Confederation provided that:

> "Article VIII. All charges of war, and all other expenses that shall be incurred for the common defense or general welfare, and allowed by the united states in congress assembled, shall be defrayed out of a common treasury, which shall be supplied by the several states, in proportion to the value of all land within each state, granted to or surveyed for any Person, as such land and the buildings and improvements thereon shall be estimated according to such mode as the united states in congress assembled, shall from time to time direct and appoint. The taxes for paying that proportion shall be laid and levied by the authority and direction of the legislatures of the several states within the time agreed upon by the united states in congress assembled."

Reprinted in RATIFICATION, *supra* note 79, Vol. I, at 86, 89. For discussion of Congress' difficulties in raising revenue, *see e.g.* MAX FARRAND, THE FRAMING OF THE CONSTITUTION OF THE UNITED STATES (New Haven: Yale University Press, 1913) at 1–12.

90. In addition to the usual assortment of free-lance freebooters, merchant ships of the eighteenth century were forced to contend with corsairs harbored by the Barbary States. Despite the power of the Royal Navy, even Britain had concluded that it was cheaper to control such state-sponsored predation through payment of tribute rather than *via* naval action. In America in the 1780s, opinion was divided as to the proper course of action. Adams suggested the British approach—offering bribes in exchange for "passes" permitting American merchantmen to sail unmolested along the North African coast. Jefferson disagreed, preferring instead to strengthen the American navy. John Jay opted for a less expensive measure, namely commissioning privateers, but Congress was reluctant to act. Enterprising American merchant-captains found a more expedient solution; they procured forged British passes and papers and flew the Union Jack while sailing the Mediterranean. For discussion, *see* JENSEN, *supra* note 78, at 211–213.

> "It will not be an easy matter to bring the American States to act as a nation; they are not to be feared as such by us. It must be a long time before they can engage, or will concur, in any material expense.... In short, every circumstance proves, that it will be extreme folly to enter into any engagements, *by which we may not wish to be bound hereafter.* It is impossible to name any material advantage the American States will, or can give us in return, more than what we of course shall have. No treaty can be made with the American States that can be binding on the whole of them. The act of Confederation does not enable Congress to form more than general treaties: at the moment of the highest authority of Congress, the power in question was with-held by the several States. No treaty that could be made, would suit the different interests. *When treaties are necessary, they must be made with the States separately. Each State has reserved every power relative to imports, exports, prohibitions, duties &c. to itself. But no treaty at present is necessary.*"[91]

The vulnerabilities Sheffield observed were obvious to the Americans themselves.[92] Without a better mechanism for raising national revenue, providing for defense of American merchant vessels on the high seas, and negotiating treaties for the regulation of international trade, the United States' reliance on maritime commerce as the catalyst for economic growth was precarious at best. All were agreed that modifications in the national government's structure were needed. Nevertheless, the nation remained divided on how best to reform it.

---

91. Sheffield's *Observations on the Commerce of the United States* was first published as a brief report in 1783. The following year, the author released a second edition of the controversial work, this time supporting his arguments with statistics gleaned chiefly from British customs records. For the quoted passage, *see* John [Holroyd], Lord Sheffield, Observations on the Commerce of the American States: A New Edition, Much Enlarged, With an Appendix, (2d ed., London: J. Derbett, 1784; *facsimile reprint* New York: Augustus M. Kelley Publishers, 1970) at 198–200 *(emphasis in the original)* (hereinafter Sheffield (rev. ed., 1784)).

92. It is worth noting that Sheffield's *Observations* were read on both sides of the Atlantic. In 1783—before Sheffield could revise and reissue his report—Philadelphia printer Robert Bell marketed his own reprint of Sheffield's first edition. The title page of this first American edition, which for reasons lost to posterity was bound together with a reprint of John Adams' old (and utterly unrelated) *Essay on the Canon and Feudal Law*, indicates that the volume was offered for sale at a price of half a dollar. The printer also reproduced the title and text but neglected to identify Sheffield as the author. *See* [John Holroyd, Lord Sheffield] Observations on the Commerce of the American States with Europe and the West Indies, Including the Several Articles of Import and Export. Also, An Essay on the Canon and Feudal Law, By John Adams Esquire (1st ed., Philadelphia: Robert Bell, 1783; *facsimile reprint* New York: Research Reprints Inc., 1970).

Maritime Commerce and American Foreign Policy

Americans were well-acquainted with Sheffield's *Observations* and the policies they spawned, but not all were convinced that the United States was inevitably at the mercy of its more powerful trading partner. John Adams wrote to Jefferson in August of 1785:

> The words "Ship and Sailor", still turn the Heads of this People. They grudge to every other People, a single ship and a single seaman. The Consequence of this Envy, in the End, will be the loss of all their own. They seem at present to dread American Ships and Seamen more than any other. Their Jealousy of our Navigation is so strong, that it is odds if it does not stimulate them to hazard their own Revenue.[93]

At the core of Adams' indictment of the British position is skepticism regarding the viability of the British mercantile system. In the words of Adam Smith, the system was grounded in "the encouragement of exportation, and the discouragement of importation."[94] In theory, it rested upon the notion that a nation's wealth, and by extension its national security, were to be measured by its reserves of precious metals. Out of these it would be able to pay the expenses of war should the need arise. Lacking indigenous supplies of gold and silver, Britain could obtain them only through export-trade, and care had to be taken to ensure that more specie flowed into the country in payment for exports than was exported in payment for foreign goods. The colonies were to supply Britain with raw materials and to purchase manufactured goods from the mother country. To implement this policy, beginning in the seventeenth century Parliament had enacted a series of Navigation Acts. From Adam

---

93. Letter from John Adams to Thomas Jefferson (Aug. 4, 1785), *published in* THE ADAMS-JEFFERSON LETTERS: THE COMPLETE CORRESPONDENCE BETWEEN THOMAS JEFFERSON AND ABIGAIL AND JOHN ADAMS (2 vols., Lester J. Cappon ed., Chapel Hill: The University of North Carolina Press, 1959), Vol. I, at 48, 49. Writing more than a decade later, Thomas Paine makes virtually the same observation of British mercantilism as does Adams, namely that a multilateral agreement for trade on "Most-Favored-Nation" terms, coupled with an exclusion of Britain, would turn Britain's Navigation Acts from the basis of national prosperity into the mechanism of the nation's economic ruin. *See* THOMAS PAINE, COMPACT MARITIME (Washington D. C.: Samuel Harrison Smith, 1801) at 11–12.

94. ADAM SMITH, AN INQUIRY INTO THE NATURE AND CAUSES OF THE WEALTH OF NATIONS (1st ed., 1776; Edwin Cannan ed., New York: Modern Library, 1937), Bk. IV, Ch. VIII, at 607 (hereinafter SMITH, WEALTH OF NATIONS).

Smith onwards, economists—with good reason—have condemned mercantilism as inefficient.[95] For Britain's policy-planners, however, efficiency was subordinate to national defense, and they were willing to forego financial gain in favor of a stronger military position among their fellow European nations.[96] In the colonial period, American merchants had coped with Britain's restrictive trade policies as best they could.[97] With independence came freedom from

---

95. The goal of mercantilism was to make one's own nation more wealthy than its trading partners, even at the cost of efficiency and a reduction in Gross National Product. Only through such a strategy, proponents argued, could a nation be safe from military aggression. *See* LAWRENCE A. HARPER, THE ENGLISH NAVIGATION LAWS: A SEVENTEENTH-CENTURY EXPERIMENT IN SOCIAL ENGINEERING (1st ed., 1939; *reprinted* New York: Octagon Books, 1973) at 10, 18, 42, 343, 347, 362–372 (hereinafter HARPER); *see also* discussion, *infra* Chapter II, notes 45–53 and text accompanying. Even if one concedes that a nation may be better off settling for less wealth in absolute terms than to risk having less than its neighbors, Britain's treatment of its own colonies is as puzzling to modern eyes as it was to the colonists themselves. The Navigation Acts prevented the colonists from selling their products in Britain, thus reducing the income (in specie) with which they could have purchased British manufactures. Smith recognized the problem. The first to identify that which modern economists call "deadweight losses", he was also the first to associate them with British mercantilism's relations with its own colonies. *See* SMITH, WEALTH OF NATIONS, *supra* note 94, Bk. III, Ch. VII, at 595–596.

96. A major component of British mercantilism was its preferential treatment of English bottoms. For discussion, *see infra* Chapter II, notes 54–60 and text accompanying. On first glance, this would appear to be merely an extension of mercantilism's principle of maintaining a trade surplus into the carrying trades. For Sheffield, however, there was something more. An undercurrent running through his *Observations* is a belief that a strong merchant fleet is essential to national security. Both ships and sailors would be invaluable additions to the Royal Navy in time of war. He remarks that: "[o]ur great national object is to raise as many sailors and as much shipping as possible", and he emphasizes that the merchant fleet is the "nursery of our seamen". SHEFFIELD (rev. ed., 1784), *supra* note 91, at 93 n., 168, 200. Sheffield returns repeatedly to his principal theme—the necessity of protecting both the carrying trades and the shipbuilding industry. *Id.* at 86, 135–138, 187, 206–208, 217, 237 (protection of the carrying trades); at 86, 252–253 (shipbuilding). To do so, Britain must at all costs retain the Navigation Acts, which form "the basis of [her] great power at sea", through which she has secured "the trade of the world". *Id.* at 214–217.

97. Benjamin Franklin gave perhaps the most succinct summary:

> "Britain, acting on the selfish and perhaps mistaken Principle of receiving nothing from abroad that could be produced at home, would take no Articles of our Produce that interfered with any of her own; and what did not interfere, she loaded with heavy Duties. We had no Mines of Gold or Silver. We were therefore oblig'd to run the whole World over, in search of something that would be receiv'd in England. We sent our Provisions and Lumber to the West Indies, where Exchange was made for Sugars, Cotton, &c. to remit. We brought Mollasses [*sic*] from thence, distill'd it into Rum, with which we traded in Africa, and remitted

the enforcement of the Navigation Acts as domestic law, only to be replaced by application of those same Acts under their new status as foreign trading partner.

As a theory, mercantilism retained vitality among the educated classes on both sides of the Atlantic even after the Revolution. For the men of the Framers' generation, this was the economic theory with which they had grown up and had grown accustomed, and old habits die slowly. Against this tradition were set the innovations of Adam Smith, with their faith in the "invisible hand" and the interplay between supply and demand. In theory, Smith and his followers favored *laissez-faire* policies domestically and free trade in international commerce, while mercantilists supported state-sponsored regulation designed to increase one's own supply of hard currency at the expense of one's neighbors. In practice, however, most late eighteenth-century politicians drew support for their positions from each theory, producing hybrid policies grounded in both. Modern historians may find justification for some of these hybrid policies, just as modern scholars of antitrust law justify measures which, though admittedly economically inefficient, nonetheless serve political goals.[98] Other hybrids appear merely inconsistent, products of either rhetorical obfuscation or slipshod analysis. Even Sheffield, the quintessential British mercantilist,[99] periodically abandoned his theoretical roots in favor of

---

> the Gold Dust to England. We employ'd ourselves in the Fisheries, and sent the Fish we caught, together with Quantities of Wheat Flour, and Rice, to Spain and Portugal, from whence the Amount was remitted to England in Cash or Bills of Exchange. Great Quantities of our Rice, too, went to Holland, Hamburg &c., and the Value of that was also sent to Britain. Add to this, that contenting ourselves with Paper, all the hard Money we could possibly pick up among the Foreign West India Islands, was continually sent off to Britain, not a Ship going thither from America without some Chests of those precious Metals."

"The Retort Courteous", *reprinted in* BENJAMIN FRANKLIN, WRITINGS (J.A. Leo Lemay ed., New York: The Library of America, 1987) at 1122, 1123–1124.

98. *See e.g.* HARPER, *supra* note 95, at 18, 42, 235–238, 253, 343, 347, 362–372; *see also* discussion, *infra* Chapter II, at 50–53.

99. Most of Sheffield's treatise is grounded in traditional mercantilist theory. Confronted with the argument that permitting British subjects to buy American ships would both lower the costs of transportation for British merchant/shipowners and give Americans sterling with which to purchase more British goods, he objects vigorously, citing the impact of shipbuilding upon other British industries (sail-makers, rope-makers, etc.). He also cites the importance of shipbuilding to national defense, distinguishing the relatively harmless relaxation of the Navigation Acts in the market for woolens from relaxation in the market for ships, the cornerstone of the Royal Navy. SHEFFIELD (rev. ed., 1784), *supra* note 91, at 245, 252–253. Similarly, he rejects a weaker version of the same policy—namely permitting British subjects to purchase American-built ships so long as they are willing to

Smith's brand of economics—at times with real insight.[100] In America, the debate over the regulation of maritime commerce reflected the larger debate over regulation of the economy in general. As the decade progressed toward the drafting and subsequent ratification of the Constitution, participants in both public and private discussions drew alternately from mercantilist and Smithian economics.[101] The choice of one's theory was not necessarily dictated

---

pay an additional tax. *Id.* at 258. Just as he opposes allowing British subjects to purchase American ships, *a fortiori* he opposes allowing foreign-flagged vessels to enter British ports on terms equal to British bottoms, contending that a relaxation of the Navigation Acts would encourage America's southern states to build ships—to the detriment of British naval supremacy. *Id.* at 249. For the same reasons, he favors the establishment of a monopoly in fisheries, ignoring the "deadweight loss" in the British domestic market for fish in order that the Americans do not build more ships for their fishing fleet. *Id.* at 126. In addition, in true mercantilist manner, he makes a distinction between the establishment of duty-free ports in Britain itself and similar ports in the colonies, the latter of which he views as a threat to the British monopoly. *Id.* at 255.

100. Sheffield is not always a doctrinaire mercantilist. In a passage worthy of Adam Smith, Sheffield acknowledges the concept of "comparative advantage", observing as regards the market for pine-tar: "The best reason for encouraging a trade with the American States for these articles, is, that our merchants would procure them in barter for the manufactures of our own country." *Id.* at 71–72. Elsewhere, his departures from traditional mercantilist thinking are more startling. He questions the wisdom of Britain maintaining overseas colonies, contending that the nation's costs in protecting the West Indies exceed the revenues they produce. *Id.* at 152, 166. Canada, he argues, should be given greater political autonomy if Britain wishes to use its timber, ships, and raw materials as replacements for those lost through the American Revolution. *Id.* at 175–183. Finally, he commits the ultimate heresy for any mercantilist; he calls into question the wisdom of a system that encourages emigration of its own people to overseas colonies:

> "Nothing can be more impolitic, at least in a commercial nation, than a fondness for foreign dominions, and a propensity to encourage distant colonization, rather than to promote domestic industry and population at home. The internal trade of Great Britain is much greater than its external commerce. The best customers of the manufacturers of Britain, are the people of Britain. Every emigrant consequently, from being the best customer, becomes the worst; and from being a soldier or a sailor, who may be brought forward on the day of danger, ceases to be of service to the State in any shape."

Id. at 239–240. It is a rare mercantilist who would question the wisdom of a nation maintaining an overseas empire.

101. Contrary to oversimplified stereotypes, the debate over the virtues of mercantilist/protectionist policies versus free trade did not split cleanly along party-lines—with federalists supporting the former and antifederalists supporting the latter. The appeal of mercantilism spanned the length of the political spectrum; at one time or another Timothy Pickering, John Adams, Alexander Hamilton, James Madison, and even Thomas Jefferson advocated mercantilist policies. *See* Williams, *supra* note 84, at 427. Jefferson, gen-

by one's politics. While federalists David Ramsay of South Carolina[102] and Thomas Russell of Massachusetts[103] defended the Constitution on mercantilist grounds, fellow federalist James Iredell championed the same cause with inspiration from *The Wealth of Nations.*[104]

---

erally a free-trade advocate, was joined at various times by Elbridge Gerry, Richard Henry Lee, George Wythe, and even the federalist Adams. *See* CATHY D. MATSON & PETER S. ONUF, A UNION OF INTERESTS: POLITICAL AND ECONOMIC THOUGHT IN REVOLUTIONARY AMERICA (Lawrence: University of Kansas Press, 1990) at 34 (hereinafter MATSON & ONUF); Williams, *supra* note 84, at 424–426, 432 (Madison's mercantilist policies discussed); Merrill D. Peterson, *Thomas Jefferson and Commercial Policy*, 22 William & Mary Quarterly 584, 589, 598, 603 (3d ser., 1965) (outlining Jefferson's occasional departures from supporting free-trade policies and endorsement of mercantilist policies) (hereinafter Peterson).

102. Addressing his fellow South Carolinians, Ramsay defended legislative protection for New England's shipowners in terms virtually identical to Sheffield's defense of the Navigation Acts (*supra* note 99):

> "The eastern states, by the revolution, have been deprived of a market for their fish, of their carrying trade, their ship-building, and almost of every thing but their liberties. As the war has turned out so much in our favour, and so much against them, ought we to grudge them the carrying of our produce, especially when it is considered, that by encouraging their shipping, we increase the means of our own defense?"

David Ramsay ["Civis"], "An Address to the Freemen of South Carolina on the Federal Constitution", *reprinted in* Ford, PAMPHLETS, *supra* note 82, at 371, 377.

103. Boston merchant and banker Thomas Russell defended ratification of the Constitution on traditional mercantilist grounds; as the records of the state's ratifying convention relate:

> "[I]t had always been the policy of trading nations, to secure to themselves the advantages of their carrying trade.... [Russell] then went into an accurate and interesting statement of the quantities of produce, which were exported from the several States—and shewed the ability of the States, to furnish among themselves, shipping fully sufficient for the transportation of this produce: which, he observed, if confined by the general government to American vessels, while the restriction would not increase the rates of freightage, to the southern States, as the northern and middle States *could* produce a surplusage of shipping, and a spirit of competition, would call forth the resources; would greatly increase our navigation—furnish us with a great nursery of seamen—give employment not only to the mechanicks, in constructing the vessels, and the trades dependent thereon, but to the husbandman, in cutting down trees, for timber, and transporting them to the places of building..."

Debates in the Massachusetts Convention (Feb. 1, 1788), *published in* RATIFICATION, *supra* note 79, Vol. VI, at 1403–1404. *Cf.* Sheffield's comments, *supra* note 99.

104. While not explicitly crediting Smith, the federalist Iredell gives one of the debates' better examples of modern economic theory used in support of ratification:

> "[Antifederalists] fear, that a [simple 50%] majority of the States may establish

When the Framers and the delegates to the various states' ratifying conventions debated public policy, first and foremost they debated the Constitution's impact on the economy—and specifically its impact on maritime trade. The debate was not carried on in a vacuum; Britain's Navigation Acts always lurked in the background. The challenge for federalists and antifederalists alike was to determine how best to promote growth in the nation's economy—and how to respond to Sheffield's mercantilist policies. Some sought to respond in kind, erecting barriers to entry in American markets and insulating domestic industries from British competition. Others sought solutions in the theories of Adam Smith and the doctrine of free trade, convinced that the market's "invisible hand" would smite the British lion if given the opportunity. For both groups, maritime commerce was the fulcrum upon which their plans for government

---

> regulations of commerce which will give great advantage to the carrying trade of America, and be a means of encouraging New England vessels rather than Old England. Be it so. No regulations can give such advantage to New England vessels, which will not be enjoyed by all other American vessels, and many States can build as well as New England, though not at present perhaps in equal proportion."

Continuing, he adds a footnote to explain the point further:

> "Some might apprehend, that in this case as New England would at first have the greatest share of the carrying trade, the vessels of that country might demand an unreasonable freight. But no attempt could be more injurious to them as it would immediately set the Southern States to building, which they could easily do, and thus a temporary loss would be compensated with a lasting advantage to us; the very reverse would be the case with them. Besides, that from that country alone there would probably be competition enough for freight to keep it on reasonable terms."

James Iredell, "Observations on George Mason's Objections to the Federal Constitution", *reprinted in* Ford, PAMPHLETS, *supra* note 82, at 333, 357–358. Thus Iredell identifies classical economics' prerequisite for monopolization—barriers to entry—while adding his own insight, namely that the self-correcting market will encourage new entrants, thereby increasing the number of American bottoms and driving the price of domestic freights downward. In addition, it would drive freights down on the international market as well—to the advantage of American consumers—and would provide America with more ships and sailors, which would be available for national defence should the occasion arise. Despite the decidedly modern tone of Iredell's analysis, it is given in the context of mercantilist protective measures designed to prevent British ships from competing effectively in the American market. He adds further: "And what could conduce more to the preservation of the Union than allowing to every kind of industry in America a peculiar preference!... Is it not the aim of every wise country to be as much the carriers of their own produce as they can be?" *Id.* at 358. Iredell's remarks thus serve as an excellent example of how mercantilism and market-based economic theories could coexist in hybrid form in the mind of one eighteenth-century policy-planner.

turned. Federalist Tench Coxe, a supporter of legislation protecting domestic manufacturing, nevertheless recognized also the importance of exporting agricultural surpluses. Improvements in internal navigation and regulations favorable to the grain-trade would reduce costs, thus enhancing the position of American exports in world markets.[105] Fellow federalist Timothy Pickering defended northern shipping and mercantile interests, supporting plans aimed at ensuring that goods entering and leaving American ports did so in American bottoms.[106] Of all the federalists, Hamilton's economic policies were the most complex and the most frequently misunderstood.[107]

Attacked by his critics as an Anglophile, a latent monarchist, and an apologist for northern commercial interests, Hamilton nonetheless differed greatly in his views from Pickering and other northern federalists.[108] Hamilton had made a detailed study of *The Wealth of Nations* and made use of Smith's ideas in his own writings, but he also supported measures designed to protect American manufacturing in ways that bore strong resemblance to Sheffield's mercantilism. Of pivotal importance to Hamilton's plan for the national economy was a significant but manageable national debt; this debt would serve two purposes. First, it would provide a source of capital and thus serve as a catalyst in the growth of the economy;[109] second, it would give the social classes to

---

105. *See* Matson & Onuf, *supra* note 101, at 70, 150–151.

106. *See* Williams, *supra* note 84, at 431.

107. A detailed analysis of Hamilton's economic philosophy is a topic worthy of an entire monograph and is obviously beyond the scope of the present work. For brief discussions in the secondary literature, *see e.g.* Williams, *supra* note 84, at 428–431; Elkins & McKitrick, *supra* note 85, at 259–261, 279–282; Industrial and Commercial Correspondence of Alexander Hamilton, Anticipating His Report on Manufactures (Arthur Harrison Cole & Edwin F. Gay eds., Chicago: A. W. Shaw Co., 1928), Introduction at xv–xxviii (hereinafter Hamilton, Industrial and Commercial Correspondence).

108. *See* Hamilton, Industrial and Commercial Correspondence, *supra* note 107, Editor's Notes for the Report on Manufactures, at 233, 241.

109. Hamilton's *Report on Manufactures* (1791) is the culmination of a decade of thought on the structure of the American economy. In it, he makes the following observation on the importance of a national debt:

> "But though a funded debt is not, in the first instance, an absolute increase of capital, or an augmentation of real wealth; yet, by serving as a new power in the operations of industry, it has, within certain bounds, a tendency to increase the real wealth of a community, in like manner, as money, borrowed by a thrifty farmer, to be laid out in the improvement of his farm, may, in the end, add to his stock of real riches."

Report on Manufactures, in *Id.*, at 278. For public reaction to the *Report*—both pro and con—*see e.g.* Matson & Onuf, *supra* note 101, at 166–168.

which the central government is indebted a stake in preserving the government.[110] Moreover, in the long run, he believed that future growth of the American economy depended upon manufacturing.[111] Manufacturing would facilitate diversification, freeing the economy of dependence on a handful of cash-crops and insulating the nation against dire consequences should the price of these crops fall on world markets.[112] Hamilton, like Smith, believed in the virtues of free trade, but felt that the American economy was not sufficiently mature to profit by it. As a result, he eschewed Smith's simple model based on "comparative advantage", contending instead that the nation needed to protect its infant manufacturing industries from foreign competition until such time as they were strong enough to compete in world markets without preferential treatment at home.[113] Nevertheless, Hamilton's long-range plans for the United States as a manufacturing nation never blinded him to the contingencies of the moment. He accepted a trade deficit with Britain for the foreseeable future,[114] and he understood well that the new government would have to win the support of merchants and shipowners as well as manufacturers in

---

110. As Elkins and McKitrick contend:

> "He did not want holdings in the public debt widely dispersed. He wanted the resources which they represented concentrated as much as possible in the hands of a particular class of men, because he wanted those resources maximally available for productive economic uses."

ELKINS & MCKITRICK, *supra* note 85, at 117. While the authors make their remark in relation to national debt in the form of old Continental dollars, the same principle should hold for future debt as well. This "particular class of men", viewing the federal government as a highly useful source of capital, would tend to work toward its preservation.

111. *See* JOHN C. MILLER, THE FEDERALIST ERA: 1789–1801 (New York: Harper & Brothers, 1960) at 64–65 (hereinafter MILLER).

112. *See Report on Manufactures, in* HAMILTON, INDUSTRIAL AND COMMERCIAL CORRESPONDENCE, *supra* note 107, at 282–283; *see also* ELKINS & MCKITRICK, *supra* note 85, at 259–261.

113. For the specific content of Hamilton's proposals, see *Report on Manufactures, in* HAMILTON, INDUSTRIAL AND COMMERCIAL CORRESPONDENCE, *supra* note 107, at 289–300. Miller summarizes them in a nutshell:

> "The aid Hamilton recommended in his Report on Manufactures was calculated to stir the blood of even the most lethargic and self-satisfied businessman: protective tariffs; bounties for the establishment of new industries; premiums for improvements in quality; awards for the encouragement of inventions, particularly of labor-saving machinery; and exemption from duty of essential raw materials imported from abroad."

MILLER, *supra* note 111, at 65.

114. *See* ELKINS & MCKITRICK, *supra* note 85, at 124, arguing that Hamilton rejected the plan endorsed by Jefferson and Madison calling for "reciprocity" in trade with Britain,

order to survive.[115] He also understood the importance of the government's investment in infrastructure—and particularly in aids to navigation.[116]

Jefferson's economic policies were nearly as complex as Hamilton's, and perhaps more crucial in setting the tone for debate on the structure of the new nation. While Hamilton's incorporation of Smith's new economics and his emphasis on manufacturing placed him somewhat out of the mainstream of his mercantilist Northern colleagues, Jefferson's policies more closely reflected the interests of the Southern planter-class from which he had come. Sufficiently pragmatic to reject the economic isolationism that one might expect from a thinker wedded to the notion of a republic of yeomen-farmers,[117] Jefferson believed in the importance of trade—even more than Pickering and merchant-shipowners of the Northeast. Jefferson had been the principal architect of America's trade policy in 1784.[118] Believing that Europe's traditional system of balance of military power spelled disaster for the young nation, Jefferson sought a way of circumventing it while at the same time providing for the nation's security. He found his solution in a marriage between Adam Smith's free trade and Emmerich de Vattel's concepts of treaty-formation. Vattel had maintained that nations could create binding law through express

---

fearing that the British would pull out of American markets in retaliation, thereby depriving the United States of much-needed tax revenues from British imports.

115. MATSON & ONUF, *supra* note 101, at 164. When he courted the support of shipowners and merchants, it was not mere political expediency. He recognized that foreign trade spurs growth in other sectors of the economy. *Id.* at 149.

116. In his *Report on Manufactures*, Hamilton defends spending tax-money for improvements in navigation, contending that: "Good roads, canals, and navigable rivers, by diminishing the expense of carriage, put the remote parts of the country more nearly upon a level with those in the neighborhood of the town. They are, upon that account, the greatest of all improvements..." HAMILTON, INDUSTRIAL AND COMMERCIAL CORRESPONDENCE, *supra* note 107, at 298.

117. As he wrote in 1785:

> "Were I to indulge my own theory, I should wish them [the Americans] to practice neither commerce nor navigation, but to stand with respect to Europe precisely on the footing of China. We should thus avoid wars, and all our citizens would be husbandmen.... But this is theory only, and a theory which the servants of America are not at liberty to follow."

Letter of Thomas Jefferson to G. K. van Hogendorp (Oct. 13, 1785), *quoted in* Peterson, *supra* note 101, at 589. For discussion of Jefferson's reasons for rejecting economic isolation, *see also* MATSON & ONUF, *supra* note 101, at 69–70.

118. *Id.* at 609. Jefferson had formulated his plan after Sheffield's *Observations* had overcome opposition led by the Earl of Shelburne, a disciple of Adam Smith who had tried unsuccessfully to move Britain toward free trade. *See* ELKINS & MCKITRICK, *supra* note 85, at 69, 130. Had Shelburne succeeded, it is likely that Jefferson's plan would have fared better.

agreement. The law of nations, grounded in the law of nature, recognized such agreements as positive law, giving rise to rights that the community of nations must recognize.[119] The intended effect of Jefferson's use of commercial treaties was two-fold. Politically, reliance on treaties, and the law of nations that gave them force, would reinforce America's independence. Economically, the ties of trade that the treaties established would give European trading partners access to goods at a cheaper price than would be possible otherwise. Thus Europe's respect for the law of nations and economic self-interest would perform the function of America's national defense. Commercial treaties were more in line with the ideological underpinnings of a republic than were military alliances, and, unlike standing armies, such treaties did not drain the public coffers.[120] While Jefferson found that his plan did not work so well in practice as in theory,[121] he continued to support trade as a catalyst for economic growth and a guarantee of national security into the 1790s.[122]

The conclusion is inescapable. For Northern merchants and shipowners and Southern planters, for mercantilists and free-traders alike, international

---

119. *See* Peter Onuf & Nicholas Onuf, Federal Union, Modern World: The Law of Nations in an Age of Revolutions, 1776–1814 (Madison, Wisconsin: Madison House, 1993) at 108, 111 (hereinafter Onuf & Onuf). For discussion of Vattel's theory of the law of nations and its relation to the law of nature, *see infra* Chapter IV, notes 164–174.

120. Onuf & Onuf, *supra* note 119, at 103–113; Elkins & McKitrick, *supra* note 85, at 70.

121. Jefferson found in the 1780s that European nations were less interested in his plan for a low-tariff regional trade zone than he had expected. *See* Peterson, *supra* note 101, at 593–594. Gradually, he began moving away from free trade in the 1790s, after the ratification of the Constitution. Williams, *supra* note 84, at 433. The trend began with his policy of "reciprocity", designed to coerce Britain into accepting more favorable terms of trade. *See* Elkins & McKitrick, *supra* note 85, at 380–381. It ended, quite disastrously, with the Embargo, which so damaged the efficacy of his second term in office. *See* Onuf & Onuf, *supra* note 119, at 182–184.

122. As Secretary of State, Jefferson published his *Report on the Privileges and Restrictions on the Commerce of the United States in Foreign Countries* on December 16, 1793. The *Report*, though virtually an anachronism when finally released, represented the culmination of Jefferson's work on the use of commercial treaties to preserve America's national security. For text, *see* Thomas Jefferson, Writings, (Merrill D. Peterson ed., New York: Library of America, 1984) at 435–448. The *Report* recites the nation's difficulties with promoting low-tariff trade, but concludes with a note of optimism:

> "Still, it must be repeated that friendly arrangements are preferable with all those who will come into them; and that we should carry into such arrangements all the liberality and spirit of accommodation which the nature of the case will admit."

Id. at 448.

commerce and the carrying trades were the key to a healthy economy—and indeed to the nation's survival. To be sure, these groups differed among themselves as to *how* maritime trade should be regulated. Pickering and his colleagues sought protection for Northeastern commercial interests and ocean-carriers. Hamilton, the pragmatist, sought long-term prosperity in manufacturing, but was aware that his plan required the support of the wealthy mercantile class until the economy became more mature and diversified. Jefferson, the theoretical innovator, saw in American maritime commerce a means of extricating the fledgling country from the entanglements of European alliances while simultaneously providing much-needed markets and higher prices for Southern agricultural products. It is not, as some commentators have argued, that Americans of the Framers' generation did not believe in state-sponsored intervention in the economy or specifically in protecting and promoting maritime industry.[123] America had a long-standing tradition of governmental intervention as a means for promoting economic growth.[124] The first Congress continued this tradition by enacting statutes regulating the collection of duties on tonnage, the registration of vessels, the rights of seamen, and the maintenance of lighthouses and other aids to navigation.[125] Americans' concern for maritime commerce was no less apparent earlier during the process of ratification. Commercial interests were instrumental in ensuring the adoption of the Constitution. There is perhaps no better testimony to coastal New England's reaction to ratification than a letter posted on the day Massachusetts' convention concluded its work and announced its final vote. That very day, the author optimistically observed, a

---

123. *See e.g.* William R. Casto, *The Origins of Federal Admiralty Jurisdiction in an Age of Privateers, Pirates, and Smugglers*, 37 Am. J. Legal Hist., 117, 138 (1993), contending:

> "Many modern scholars have noted...that the Founding Generation was...interested in promoting and protecting the maritime industry. There is, however, virtually no basis—other than anachronistic assumptions—for concluding that this modern concern figured significantly into the original consensus on the need for national admiralty courts. The only specific evidence that has been advanced to support the Founding Generation's concern for the protection and support of the maritime industry are brief remarks by James Madison and Edmund Randolph at the Virginia Ratification Convention."

124. For descriptions of early efforts in promoting economic growth through governmental intervention and regulation, *see* McCusker & Menard, *supra* note 36, at 331–342 (in the colonial period); Williams, *supra* note 84, at 421 (during the Revolution and under the Articles of Confederation).

125. For a list of statutes and discussion, *see infra* Chapter IV, notes 17–20, 120 and text accompanying.

long-idle Boston shipyard received an order for three large merchant-ships.[126]

When the men of the founding generation debated the Constitution—its drafting, its interpretation, and its implementation—they did so invariably with an eye to economic as well as political concerns. When they debated the economy, invariably they looked to maritime commerce. Common sense dictates that their concern would extend also to maritime law and maritime jurisdiction. Clear—and *uniform*—rules can reduce the costs of doing business and encourage growth in any sector of the economy. On first reflection, it would seem reasonable to expect the first Congress to vest jurisdiction over all maritime matters exclusively in the federal courts, thereby ensuring uniform interpretations of the substantive law. Nevertheless, the first Congress opted to grant concurrent jurisdiction to the state courts in matters in which the common law offered remedies. The decision was counterintuitive; in other contexts eighteenth-century Americans were keenly aware of the potential for friction inherent in concurrent jurisdiction. In other contexts, they understood that *concurrent* jurisdiction would threaten uniformity in the substantive rules. Why, one reasonably might ask, would the first Congress jeopardize much-valued uniformity by allowing two sets of courts to interpret the same body of substantive law? The answer lies in their view of the substantive rules themselves. In their experience, the substantive maritime law was unchanging. In contrast with the common law, an ever-evolving amalgam of rules refined incrementally through the ages, they believed the maritime law to have devolved intact to succeeding generations from remote antiquity. It mattered little which courts enforced the maritime law, as all courts—federal, state, or foreign—applied its unchanging rules alike. To understand why the men of the founding generation believed this body of law to be unchanging, we must examine both its history and the life-experiences of eighteenth-century Americans.

126. Letter from Jeremy Belknap to Ebenezer Howard (Feb. 10, 1788), *published in* RATIFICATION, *supra* note 79, Vol. VII, at 1625.

Chapter I

"Although I am a professor of the common law, yet I am so much a lover of truth and of learning, and of my native country, that I do heartily persuade that the professors of that law, called Civilians (because the civil law is their ruler), be not discountenanced nor discouraged: else whensoever we shall have ought to do with any foreign Prince or state, we shall be at a miserable loss, for want of learned men in that profession."

Sir Francis Bacon[1]

In *DeLovio v. Boit*, the seminal case establishing the parameters of federal admiralty jurisdiction, Joseph Story wrote:

> The language of the constitution will therefore warrant the most liberal interpretation; and it may not be unfit to hold, that it had reference to that maritime jurisdiction, which commercial convenience, public policy, and national rights, have contributed to establish, with slight local differences, over all Europe; that jurisdiction, which, under the name of consular courts, first established itself upon the shores of the Mediterranean, and, from the general equity and simplicity of its proceedings, soon commended itself to all the maritime states; that jurisdiction, in short, which, collecting the wisdom of the civil law, and combining it with the customs and usages of the sea, produced the venerable Consolato del Mare, and still continues in its decisions to regulate the commerce, the intercourse, and the warfare of mankind.... Of this great system of maritime law it may truly be said, "*Non erit alia lex Romae, alia Athenis, alia nunc, alia posthac; sed omnes gentes, et omni tempore, una lex, et sempiterna et immortalis, continebit.*"[2]

1. 1616 draft letter to George Villiers, Duke of Buckingham, *reproduced in* Daniel Coquillette, Francis Bacon (Stanford: Stanford University Press, 1992) at 10.

2. *DeLovio v. Boit* (Case No. 3, 776), 7 F. Cas. 418, 443 (C.C, D. Mass., 1815). The quote in Latin, which translates as "There will not be one law for Rome, and another for

Thus Story paints a picture of clarity. The history of maritime jurisdiction and substantive law have descended to the modern world through a careful process in which evolving maritime customs are grafted onto the body of the civil law, thereby forming a coherent system of maritime law, the origins of which may be traced to antiquity through an unbroken chain of tradition. Much the same sentiments were echoed a generation later by Erastus Benedict, the author of the treatise that, after seven editions, remains the standard reference work in the field today. With regard to the origins and sources of English maritime law, he remarked blandly: "The Black Book of the Admiralty, is an ancient book or register of admiralty laws, decisions, ordinances, and proceedings and acts of the King, the Admiral, and the Court of Admiralty of England, from the earliest periods.... It has been always considered, by all writers on maritime law, as a book of great authority, containing the ancient rules or statutes of the English Admiralty."[3] Unfortunately, the *Black Book of the Admiralty*, the purported repository of the history of English maritime law and practice, was known more by reputation and passing references in the works of seventeenth-century legal commentators than by first-hand knowledge. Indeed, at the date of publication of the first edition of Benedict's treatise, the original *Black Book* had been lost for more than four decades, and there was no reliable copy of the full text.[4] To approach the history of English admiralty jurisdiction, one must grapple with the most turbulent eras in England's past. The Admiralty Court survived through the most significant upheavals of English history,—the War of the Roses, the Reformation, the Civil War, the Glorious Revolution, the Act of Union, and finally the revolt of England's American colonies. It witnessed the demise of the feudal system, the beginnings of the enclosure movement, and the onset of the Industrial Revolution. It reached its zenith

---

Athens, nor one body of law now and another in the future, but instead among all people and for all times, the same imperishable and eternal law shall apply", is taken from Cicero, *De Re Publica*, Bk. 3, Sec. xxii, and is today best remembered by legal scholars for its use by Lord Mansfield in *Luke v. Lyde*, 97 Eng. Rep. 614, 617 (K.B. 1759). It is worth noting that Story himself used the quote again three decades later in *Swift v. Tyson*, 41 U. S. 1, 19 (1842).

3. Erastus C. Benedict, The American Admiralty: Its Jurisdiction and Practice, With Practical Forms and Directions (1st ed., New York: Banks, Gould & Co., 1850) sec. 53 at 31 (hereinafter Benedict (1st ed.)).

4. The Black Book of the Admiralty (*Rerum Britannicarum Medii Aevi Scriptores* (Rolls Series)): No. 55 *Monumenta Juridica*, (Sir Travers Twiss ed., London: Her Majesty's Stationery Office, 1871; Kraus reprints, 1965), Vol. I (hereinafter Twiss, Vol. I).

in Henry VIII's efforts to transform England into a first-rate economic power, while its powers ebbed to their lowest point just as the British Empire achieved its greatest political and economic influence. Yet despite its participation in significant events throughout five hundred years of British history, the origins of the Admiralty Court and the law that it applied remain largely shrouded in mystery.

One reason for our limited understanding of the early history of the Court is the paucity of court records. It was not until the late eighteenth century that Judge William Scott (later Lord Stowell) first commissioned the publication of formal reports of the Court's judgments.[5] The Court did keep its own records, but owing to the limited value of precedent these records are frequently less complete than those kept by the common-law courts.[6] Moreover, our knowledge of the substantive maritime law is somewhat hampered by the

---

5. Henry Bourguignon, Sir William Scott, Lord Stowell: Judge of the High Court of the Admiralty, 1798–1828 (Cambridge: Cambridge University Press, 1987) at 61. For discussion, *see* L. Kinvin Wroth, *The Massachusetts Vice Admiralty Court and the Federal Admiralty Jurisdiction*, 6 Am. J. Legal Hist. 251, 265 (1962); *see also* David R. Owen & Michael C. Tolley, Courts of Admiralty in Colonial America: The Maryland Experience, 1634–1776 (Durham: Carolina Academic Press, 1995) at 11 (noting that it was Stowell who introduced into admiralty the practice of relying upon precedent) (hereinafter Owen & Tolley).

6. William Holdsworth, A History of English Law (London: Methuen & Co., 1924), Vol. V, at 127–128, 137 (hereinafter Holdsworth). These records were kept in Latin from 1524 through 1731—with a brief hiatus during the Interregnum, during which they were kept in English—and in English again from 1731 onwards. *Id.* at 137. The condition in which the Court's records were filed has remained a source of frustration for legal scholars to the present day. As one editor of the only collection of sixteenth-century admiralty examinations to date extracted and published from these files once remarked: "To find documents relating to any particular case it is necessary to make a complete search through the files or volumes for the relevant period. Nor is there any ordered arrangement, it being quite common to find the sentence (or judgment) of a particular case in an earlier file, or in an earlier part of the same file, than the libel of the plaintiff or the allegation of the defendant. Indeed there is no guarantee that all the material documents relating to any one case will be found at all." High Court of Admiralty Examinations (Ms. Volume 53) 1637–1638 (Publications of the Anglo-American Records Foundation, Vol. II, Dorothy O. Shilton, Richard Holworthy, & Eric G. M. Fletcher eds., London: Butler & Tanner, 1932) Introduction (Fletcher) at xvii–xviii. For a general discussion of the practice of keeping records in the English courts prior to the sixteenth century, *see* S. E. Thorne, *Courts of Record and Sir Edward Coke*, 2 Toronto L. J. 24 (1937). During the late eighteenth century, some of the Doctors of Civil Law who practiced before the Admiralty Court began depositing the notebooks containing synopses of the cases that they had heard with the Registrar of the Court. Among these are those of eighteenth-century practitioners Sir Edward Simpson and Sir Edward Burrell. *See* Owen & Tolley, *supra* note 5, at 11.

lack of published legal treatises on maritime law.[7] More readily available sources on the early history of admiralty jurisdiction are the various statutes regulating the jurisdiction of the Court and a fairly large assortment of patents granted to the Lord High Admiral as well as to judges, and even to royal governors of England's overseas colonies.[8] Nevertheless, in the absence of evidence of how the grants of power conferred by these patents were construed in practice, these form at best an incomplete—and potentially misleading—impression of the scope of admiralty jurisdiction in the seventeenth and eighteenth centuries. A second impediment to our understanding of the Court's early history is the common law's principle of *stare decisis*. Judges recognize the importance of grounding their decisions in precedent, even in cases of first

---

7. Alain Wijffels, "*Ius Gentium* in the Practice of the Court of Admiralty around 1600", *in* The Roman Law Tradition (A.D.E. Lewis & D.J. Ibbertson eds., Cambridge: Cambridge University Press, 1994) at 121. (According to Wijffels, this deficiency also plagued practitioners at the time, particularly in the area of prize law.) As one commentator has observed: "[A] Scottish civilian, W. Welwod [also spelled "Welvod" or "Welwood"], published a rough collection of these laws in *Sea Law of Scotland*. [In 1607], Welwod's *Sea Law* constituted the entire printed resources of the English law merchant beyond scattered references in the common law treatises—and Welwod's book was not English." *See* Daniel R. Coquillette, The Civilian Writers of Doctors' Commons: Three Centuries of Juristic Innovation in Comparative, Commercial and International Law (Berlin: Duncker & Humblot, 1988) at 128 n. 176 (hereinafter Coquillette, Civilian Writers). *See also Id.* at 128 for lack of published treatises on civil and maritime law in England. The volume to which Professor Coquillette refers is now available in facsimile: William Welvod [also spelled "Welwod" Welwood" or "Welvvod"], The Sea-Law of Scotland (facsimile of Robert Welgrave ed., 1590: *reprinted as* No. 565, The English Experience—Its Record in Early Printed Books Published in Facsimile (New York: De Capo Press, 1972)) (hereinafter Welvod, The Sea-Law of Scotland).

8. Reginald Marsden, one of the few scholars to be remembered today for his extensive contributions both to maritime legal history and to the practicing bar, noted that he was able to identify 3,500 documents relating to admiralty jurisdiction. *See* R. G. Marsden, "The High Court of Admiralty in Relation to National History, Commerce, and the Colonisation of America—A.D. 1550–1650", *in* Transactions of the Royal Historical Society, Vol. 16 (New Series: London, 1902) at 69, 70 (hereinafter Marsden, "High Court"). He also notes that the instance and prize records were separated in 1625, facilitating the beginning of the distinction between the Court's prize and instance jurisdictions. *Id.* at 79. Unfortunately, availability of documents does not guarantee their clarity. As Marsden observed: "In the Latin documents are many words not found in Du Cange [presumably Charles du Fresne du Cange, *Glossarium ad Scriptores Mediae et Infimae Latinitatis* (1678)]". *Id.* at 86. An excellent published source for documents is Documents Relating to the Law and Custom of the Sea (2 vols., R.G. Marsden ed., London: The Navy Record Society, 1915–1916), though the editor has selected a disproportionate amount of material related to privateering and piracy.

impression. Unfortunately for nineteenth-century judges, lack of published admiralty opinions often forced them to fabricate history to fill gaps in what was known from court records of the Court's early jurisdiction and of the law that it applied. In some cases, this gap-filling took the form of deductive reasoning, inferring the content of the missing information by reference to known facts. In others, judges looked to treatises to establish the parameters of jurisdiction and the content of substantive rules when published precedent was lacking. English admiralty treatises were of two varieties. Those of the first variety, which sought to define the scope of the Court's jurisdiction, were products of the seventeenth century, a period in which the Court was embroiled in the struggle between the English civilians and the common lawyers over maritime and commercial business as well as in the larger struggle between the Crown and Parliament for political control of the nation. Obviously, the authors of these works were aware that their value lay in their rhetorical impact, not their historical accuracy. That is not to say that these political polemics were devoid of intrinsic logic or that they would necessarily make poor models on which to base a legal system. One should, however, be wary in accepting as historical fact anything contained in these works that cannot be corroborated by earlier sources. The authors of the second variety of English admiralty treatise—which addressed substantive law as well as jurisdiction—sought to reconcile conflicting rules and create a coherent foundation upon which future case law would rest. Of these, the most conspicuous example is Arthur Browne, the American-born and Irish-educated civil-law scholar whose "*Compendious View of the Civil Law, and of the Law of Admiralty*" first appeared in print in 1797.[9] While their goal may have been socially useful, their attempts to tie up all loose ends convey a somewhat inaccurate impression of an extensive body of maritime law unchanged since antiquity.

The purpose of this chapter is first to identify the sources of the substantive law that came to be applied in maritime cases in the eighteenth century and, secondly, to examine the struggle between the civilians and the common-law bar over maritime jurisdiction. Through this we can gain some understanding not only of the actual history of the Court of Admiralty and of the law it applied, but also of how maritime law and jurisdiction would have been perceived by members of the American colonial bar in the late eighteenth century.

9. Arthur Browne, A Compendious View of the Civil Law, and of the Law of Admiralty, Being the Substance of a Course of Lectures Read in the University of Dublin (2 vols., 3d ed. [1st American ed.], New York: Halstead & Voorhies, 1840) (hereinafter Browne). For a detailed history of the life and career of the author, *see generally* Joseph C. Sweeney, *The Admiralty Law of Arthur Browne*, 26 J. Mar. L. & Com. 59 (1995).

The Continuity of Substantive Maritime Law

Maritime law is as old as maritime commerce. The earliest extant codification of maritime law is found in the Code of Hammurabi of the eighteenth century B.C.[10] Broadly construed, the subject-matter that "maritime law" regulates may be grouped into four general subcategories. First are relationships among persons. These include agency (as between shipowner and ship's master), labor agreements (between shipowner and crew), partnership agreements, joint venture agreements, and the lender/borrower relationship of ship mortgages.[11] In addition, there are the contractual relationships between carriers and either cargo owners or passengers, as well as those between shipowners and those who provide supplies or services to their vessels. The second subcategory includes what may be termed obligations toward persons and property, including the duties of the shipowner, master, and crew for preventing harm both to the ship's own passengers or cargo and also to the hulls, cargoes, and passengers of other vessels.[12] Thirdly, maritime law provides rules

---

10. Stanley S. Jados, The Consulate of the Sea and Related Documents (University of Alabama Press, 1975), Introduction at xii (hereinafter Jados, Consulate of the Sea).

11. Of necessity, this generalization involves a certain level of oversimplification. Over time, maritime industry has spawned a whole assortment of "middle-men", such as charterers and freight forwarders, among whom the contractual relations are governed by the substantive maritime law of many—though not necessarily all—modern nations. Moreover, in legal systems in which ships are "personified"—thus enabling them by legal fiction to enter into contracts to which their owners may not be parties—the question of agency becomes more complicated, as a court must ascertain whether the ship's master was acting as agent for the ship itself. (For a general discussion of personification of vessels, *see Tucker v. Alexandroff*, 183 U.S. 124, 138 (1902).) Different legal systems are divided on the question of whether an employment contract between a shipowner and a ship's master is cognizable in admiralty, with the traditional English position being that it is not (*see* Browne, *supra* note 9, Vol. II, at 94, critiquing the policy behind the traditional rule). In the ancient and medieval world, the usual contractual arrangement for carriage of cargo was what today would be called a "voyage charter", although various other business arrangements, including joint ventures and partnership agreements, occasionally were encountered. (For discussion, *see e.g.* Walter Ashburner, The Rhodian Sea Laws: Edited from the Manuscripts (Oxford: Clarendon Press, 1909), Introduction at ccxlii (hereinafter Rhodian Sea Laws)). The relationship between ship-mortgager and mortgagee long has been a subject of maritime litigation, as extant records reveal that the Athenian orator Demosthenes wrote speeches for at least three such cases (*see Id.* at cxii).

12. The general distinction between the first and second subcategories would be expressed in common-law terms as the difference between claims *ex contractu* and *ex delicto*, a distinction lacking a precise analogue in the civil law. It is worth noting that some claims

for apportionment of losses for acts of nature, often referred to as "perils of the sea." These rules include both those for exoneration of ship, shipowner, master, and crew for damage to cargo as well as those of "general average", the rules of which seek an equitable distribution amongst various cargo owners for losses sustained through perils of the sea.[13] Finally, there is salvage. Salvage is *sui generis*, bearing little resemblance to any other concept in Western law. Rules of salvage—which throughout European history have varied from one nation and era to another—may be grounded in one of three concepts. First, the property right in a wrecked vessel may escheat to the state. Secondly, a wrecked vessel may become *res nullius*, title to which is subject to being claimed by whomever first locates it and obtains possession of it. Thirdly, while title to the wrecked vessel may remain with the owner, the law may require that the owner pay a reward to anyone who saves the damaged property and restores it to him.[14]

The earliest set of laws recognized as binding among the various states engaged in trade in the Mediterranean was that of the island of Rhodes. About this Rhodian Law, the seventeenth-century English jurist John Selden wrote:

> Of all the ancient Lords of the Sea the *Rhodians* are the most renowned; chiefly in this respect, becaus [*sic*] the Sea-Laws which were used and in full force and virtue in both the Empires, were borrowed from them, and put into the *Digests* by *Justinian*.[15]

---

in a modern American court would straddle the first two categories. A shipowner, for example, has a duty to provide a seaworthy vessel, breach of which would constitute a tort. Nevertheless, claims for damage to cargo also may sound in contract as breach of the terms of carriage in a charterparty or bill of lading.

13. The theory underlying contribution and general average is that if one merchant's cargo is thrown overboard to prevent the ship from foundering, his loss in effect has saved the ship and—in some cases—the cargo of other merchants whose property would have been lost but for the sacrifice their fellow businessman's goods. In compensation, it is equitable that those who benefited from the sacrifice should partially compensate for the loss. While this basic concept is common to all definitions of general average, subtle variations on the rule developed in various ports in Europe from antiquity through the middle ages. Examination of these variations is the most reliable means of ascertaining the origins of and relationships among particular codes of maritime law that evolved in Europe in the medieval period (*see* Twiss, *supra* note 4, Vol. III, at xxxiii.)

14. For an overview of how English law addressed issues of salvage at various times, *see* Browne, *supra* note 9, Vol. II, at 47–53.

15. John Selden, Of the dominion, or Ownership, of the Sea: Written First in Latin, and Entitled, *Mare Clausum seu De Domino Maris* (Marchamont Nedham trans., London: William Du-Gard, 1652) Bk. I, Ch. x, Sec. v, at 59 *(emphasis in the original)*. (Selden's Latin original was completed in 1635, but as his translator Nedham notes

Beginning from the same premises, the seventeenth-century English civilian Sir Richard Zouch concluded that over time the Rhodian Law had become part of the law of nations, which, he contended, was to be construed according to the civil law.[16] Hence, Zouch maintained, the civil law governs all maritime contracts.[17] The conclusions of Selden and Zouch—as well as the assumptions on which they rest—bear closer examination.

Book 14 of the *Digest of Justinian* contains much of the substantive maritime law of the late Roman Empire.[18] The degree to which it replicates the

---

in his "Epistle Dedicatorie", it was "lockt up in a Language unknown to the greatest part of that Nation whom it most concern's [*sic*]". Departing from my usual practice of citing to sources in their original language wherever possible, I have opted to cite Selden's work in the form in which it was best known both to his own contemporaries and to readers today, even if Nedham's English is perhaps less elegant than Selden's Latin.)

16. Richard Zouch[e], The Jurisdiction of the Admiralty Asserted, Against Sir Edward Coke's *Articuli Admiralitatis*, In XXII Chapter of His Jurisdiction of the Courts (London: Francis Tyton & Thomas Dring, 1663) at 6–9, 66–67 (hereinafter Zouch).

17. *Id.* at 56.

18. Dig. 14.1–14.2, *in Corpus Iuris Civilis* (Latin edition, C. M. Galisset ed., Paris: Janet & Cotelle, 1830). While the first two subsections of Book 14 are devoted primarily to maritime law, other books of the *Digest* also contain scattered references to rules applicable to maritime activities. For example, Book 4.9 addresses liability of ship's personnel for loss of property entrusted to them, while Book 4.9.7 (Ulpianus, *Ad Edictum* 18) establishes liability of the master for actions of the crew. Other maritime provisions are those of *Digest* 19.2, which include passengers' action against a shipowner for losses resulting from the latter's failure to retain a pilot (19.2.13.2, Ulpianus *Ad Edictum* 32), shipowner's liability for loss resulting from transfer of cargo to a vessel not named in the contract of affreightment (19.2.13.1, Ulpianus *Ad Edictum* 32), and the divisibility of bulk cargo in calculating damages for loss at sea (19.2.2.31, Alfinus). In content, the provisions range from the very general and predictable, such as *Digest* 44.7.5.6, which establishes liability of a shipowner for acts committed on his vessel by third parties, to rules that apply to very fact-specific situations, such as *Digest* 9.2.27.24 (Ulpianus *Ad Edictum* 18), which provides penalties for scuttling a merchant vessel, and *Digest* 9.2.29.2–4 (Ulpianus *Ad Edictum* 18), which addresses collision of vessels. The level of specificity often approaches the absurd proportions of some law-school hypotheticals, such as *Digest* 19.2.17.7 (Ulpianus *Ad Edictum* 18), which notes that a child born while a ship is in transit does not have to pay for his passage. Occasionally, rules that appear to be related in subject-matter are found in different books. For present purposes, the most relevant examples are found in Book 41. According to *Digest* 41.1.9.8 (Gaius *Institutes* 2), jettison does not relieve an owner of title to his cargo, and such cargo cannot be salvaged by third parties until the owner has abandoned it (Dig. 41.7.7). Similarly, a wrecked vessel remains the property of the shipowner and cannot be salvaged until he abandons it (Dig. 41.1.58). Salvage of a vessel or cargo that has not been abandoned would result in a four-fold penalty (Dig. 41.1.44, Ulpianus *Ad Edictum* 19).

earlier laws of the island of Rhodes is open to question, as no text of its Hellenistic-era laws and customs were preserved for posterity.[19] Book 14.1 regulates the obligations and liability of the shipowner. It defines "*exercitor*" ("shipowner") and "*magister*" ("master" or "captain") and outlines the principles of agency that govern the relationship between them, under which the *exercitor* is liable for all agreements made and expenses incurred by the *magister*, so long as they were within the authority granted to him by the *exercitor*. These include contracts for carriage of cargo, for repair of the ship, and for seamen's wages.[20] It notes that while an *exercitor* is liable for the *delicti* of members of the crew, he or she is not likewise liable for their contracts.[21] It also briefly addresses the ownership of vessels by partnership, and the liability of the partners to third parties.[22] In addition, Book 14 contains rules on jettison and contribution for loss of cargo at sea, which the text denominates "*De Lege Rodia De Jactu*", or The Rhodian Law of Jettison. The text begins as follows:

> The Rhodian Law admonishes that, if a jettison of cargo is made for the purpose of lightening the vessel, that which was given up for the benefit of all should be restored through the contributions of all. If,

---

19. Some traditions trace the ancient Rhodian Laws back a half of a millennium earlier, to 900 B.C. *See e.g.* BENEDICT (1st ed.), *supra* note 3, sec. 179 at 98. *See also* JAMES ALLAN PARK, A SYSTEM OF MARINE INSURANCES: WITH THREE CHAPTERS ON BOTTOMRY, ON INSURANCES ON LIVES, AND ON INSURANCES AGAINST FIRE (1st ed., London: T. Whieldon, 1787; *reprinted* Philadelphia, Joseph Crukshank, 1789), Introduction at v, contending that the Rhodians had established "... a system of marine jurisprudence, to which even the *Romans* themselves paid the greatest deference and respect, and which they adopted as the guide of their conduct in naval affairs. These excellent laws not only served as a rule of conduct to the ancient maritime states; but as will appear from attentive comparison of them, have been the basis of all modern regulations respecting navigation and commerce. The time at which these laws were compiled is not precisely ascertained: but we may reasonably suppose, it was about the period when the *Rhodians* first obtained the sovereignty of the sea, which was about 916 years before the era of Christianity."

20. DIG. 14.1.1.7 states in relevant part:

> *Non autem ex omni causa praetor dat in exercitorem actionem, sed eius rei nomine, cuius ibi in praepositus fuerit, id est, [si] in eam rem praepositus sit, utputa, si [ad] onus vehendum locatum sit, aut aliquas res emerit utiles naviganti, vel si quid reficiendae navis causa contractum vel impensum est, vel si quid nautae, operarum nomine, petent.*

21. DIG. 14.1.1. It is worth noting that the status of "*exercitor*" is not limited to men; the *Digest* emphasizes people of either gender, including slaves, may function in the capacity of ship-manager, so long as they are adults.

22. DIG. 14.1.2–14.1.4 (Ulpianus *Ad Edictum* 29).

> with the ship in peril, goods are jettisoned, the owners of the lost goods, if they were subject to a contract of carriage, are able to proceed under the contract against the master of the vessel. He in turn is able to proceed in contract against the owners whose goods were thereby preserved, in order that the losses be divided proportionately.[23]

The remainder of the text construes the meaning of this general rule through a series of specific examples, in one of which the author notes that the owner of the ship, whose property is saved from foundering through jettison, also must contribute.[24] Taken as a whole, the legal principles elucidated by the examples are as follows. First, a claim for contribution lies only where there has been a loss of property: *i.e.* the cargo or the ship and/or its tackle. Second, the loss must have been caused by an intentional act, the purpose of which was to save the vessel and the remaining property aboard. Third, contribution lies only if the sacrifice of property succeeded preserving the ship and/or its cargo.[25] Provided all three conditions were met, the party whose property was jettisoned for the common good was entitled to compensation for the loss. Thus Book 14.2 is the oldest surviving text describing rules that today are known as "general average".

The material contained in the *Digest* is not the only text of "Rhodian Sea Laws" that is extant today. There is a collection of sea-law manuscripts in Greek (the earliest of which dates from the tenth century A.D.), of which some have appended to them "*telos nomou Rhodionos*" or similar titles.[26] The content of

---

23. Dig. 14.2.1–2 (*my translation*). The passage reads as follows in the original Latin: *Lege Rodia cavetur, ut, si levandae navis gratia iactus mercium factus est, omnium contributione sarciatur, quod pro omnibus datum est.... Si laborante nave, iactus factus est, amissarum mercium domini, si merces vehendas locaverant, ex locato cum magistro navis agere debent; is deinde cum reliquis, quorum merces salvae sunt, ex conducto, ut detrimentum pro portione communicetur, agere potest.*

24. Dig. 14.2.2 (Paulus *Edict.* 34).

25. *Id.* For discussion, *see also* Ashburner, Rhodian Sea-Laws, *supra* note 11, Introduction at cclvi. It is worth noting that the act of lightening the ship need not preserve it until it arrives safely in port. *Digest* 14.2.4.1 notes that if cargo is jettisoned—thereby saving the ship—and the ship is subsequently lost before arriving at its destination, any cargo recovered from the wreck would be required to contribute to the owners of the jettisoned cargo, apparently on the rationale that had the ship sunk earlier in the voyage, the cargo that was salvaged would not have recovered. For discussion, *see* Ashburner, Rhodian Sea-Laws, *supra* note 11, Introduction at ccliii.

26. Ashburner, Rhodian Sea-Laws, *supra* note 11, Introduction at lxvii.

the manuscripts is likely much older, with linguistic analysis placing the origin somewhere between the seventh and ninth centuries A.D.[27] Nevertheless, such a date would make the laws a product of late antiquity rather than of the Hellenistic period, thereby post-dating rather than pre-dating the *Digest*.[28] Walter Ashburner, who edited the Rhodian Sea-Law manuscripts in the early portion of the twentieth century, concluded that the laws were of Byzantine origin and had been collected and arranged for insertion into the now fragmentary Book LIII of the *Basilica*, the code of the Byzantine Empire.[29] Assuming this to be

---

27. *Id.* at lxvi. In examining these manuscripts, Ashburner notes that the various texts of the Sea-Laws remain virtually unchanged through the centuries. *Id.* at xlviii. While there are a few changes—some to be ascribed to clerical error and others that resulted in abridged articles—there were no substantive innovations. *Id.* at xlix. From this, he forms two conclusions. First: "The law-book is still of practical importance.... The Sea-law must, even down to the fifteenth century, have represented the maritime law for some parts of the Mediterranean." *Id.* at xlix. His second conclusion is that: "the circumstances with which [the Sea-law] dealt did not materially change from the time of its original composition until near the time when it ceased to be copied.... There seems to have been very little alteration, except for the worse, in the navigation and commerce of the Mediterranean between the eighth and thirteenth centuries. It is with the thirteenth century that the commercial renascence begins, which made the literary and artistic renascence possible." *Id.* at l. Further on in the Introduction, Ashburner makes a similar observation in defending his decision to "illustrate a code of law by materials dating the oldest of them three hundred years after it was compiled"; he notes: "The date at which a statute received its present shape is not necessarily the date of the law which it contains; and the form of a commercial document may easily be centuries older than the document itself. So long as the conditions which make the law remain unaltered, the law itself remains unaltered. Between the ninth and thirteenth centuries, there was probably less change in the conditions of commerce and navigation than there has been in the last twenty-five years [from 1884–1909]." *Id.* at cxv.

28. The manuscripts of the Rhodian Sea-Laws are divided into three parts, the first of which is an "*auctoritas*" or imperial prologue, which purports to "give a sanction to the Sea-laws from declarations of various Roman emperors". This *auctoritas* appears in various manuscripts in two forms, one apparently an abridgement of the other, but no surviving manuscript that incorporates the *auctoritas*—in either the long or short form—can be dated earlier than the twelfth century. Ashburner concludes that the *auctoritas* is a creation of a later date, intended to lend the authority of antiquity to the text. For discussion, *see* ASHBURNER, RHODIAN SEA-LAWS, *supra* note 11, Introduction at lxxi–lxxiv.

29. Selecting one palimpsest as the best overall text of the Sea-Laws, Ashburner posits that there were in fact two editions of the Sea-Laws: one drafted to stand as an independent document and another, which he dubs the "vulgate", that was drafted for incorporation into the *Basilica*. *Id.* at xlvii; liii; xcviii. He gives his qualified assent to the proposition that the *Basilica* paraphrased material contained in the *Corpus Juris Civilis*—of which the *Digest* is a part—without adding to it. *Id.* at civ. Nevertheless, he maintains that the Rhodian laws, which were not originally part of the *Corpus Juris Civilis*, were inserted as

accurate,[30] the Rhodian Sea-Laws would be of little use in establishing the continuity of substantive maritime law from ancient Rhodes through the later phases of the Roman Empire, but it might prove useful in establishing a link between the civil law of Rome and the maritime law of the middle ages.

A common thread running through all medieval collections of sea-laws is the principle of general average. Nevertheless, while all extant medieval European codes include the concept of contribution for losses incurred at sea, not all of these legal systems formulated the concept in exactly the same way. Subtle variations in the rules for general average serve as *indicia* of the origin of a particular set of sea-laws, providing insight into its relation to other bodies of maritime law. Thus the best evidence that one set of laws is descended from another—or that both share a common precursor—is similarity in treatment of losses caused by perils of the sea.[31] The *Digest*, as noted above,

---

an Appendix to Book 53 of the *Basilica*. *Id.* at cix–cx. Ultimately maintaining that the Sea-Laws post-dated the *Corpus Juris* and pre-dated the *Basilica*, Ashburner summarizes his conclusions:

> "The Sea-law was put together from material of very different epochs and characters. Some of it was possibly from treatises in the nature of a 'Complete Merchant', guides to a gentleman engaging in business (c. 11). Other parts may have come from enactments of Byzantine Caesars; but the mass of it must be derived from local customs. Some provisions which originally had nothing to do with maritime affairs have been doctored in order to bring them within the purview of the Sea-law. There are traces of a South Italian origin for some of the chapters. Part III of the Sea-law, as we have it, was evidently composed to be a part of Book LIII of the Basilica. Part III and Book LIII fit in together and form a complete body of maritime law, while each separately is imperfect. I therefore infer that a second edition of the Sea-law was made either by, or under the direction of, the men who compiled the Basilica. Perhaps at this time Part II [of the Sea-law] was severed from Part III. Our texts represent in substance the second edition—what I call the vulgate—but there are traces of the earlier one or even of the texts out of which the earlier one was composed." *Id.* at cxiii.

Ashburner concedes that his theory would lead one to ask why, if the Sea-Law pre-dated the *Basilica*, are there no extant texts in pre-vulgate form independent of the *Basilica*? He responds that monasteries would have had an incentive to copy the "imperially authorized version" rather than an earlier edition. Thus the earlier editions have not survived in later copies as have the versions drafted for insertion into the *Basilica*. *Id.* at cxiii–cxiv.

30. Ashburner's contention that the Rhodian Sea-Laws are no older than the seventh century has not gone unchallenged. Working from Greek texts in the Vatican's collections, the Italian scholar G.L. Perugi has argued for earlier origins. *See* Owen & Tolley, *supra* note 5, Introduction at ix n. 2, *citing* G. L. Perugi, *Lex Rhodiorum Nautica* (Greek critical text, Rome: Ambrosian Library, 1929).

31. Twiss, *supra* note 4, Vol. III, at xxxiii, states: "...the provisions on the subject of contribution in cases of jetison...may be regarded as a crucial test of the diversity of ori-

provided for contribution only where the loss of property resulted from a deliberate act, the purpose of which was to sacrifice that property with the intention of saving the ship and/or its remaining cargo.[32] The matter is not so simple under the Rhodian Sea-Laws. Some articles replicate the rules contained in the *Digest*.[33] Others, however, expand the circumstances under which contribution would be available.[34] As Ashburner explains:

> Intermingled with these chapters [*i.e.* Chapters 9 and 38, which reproduce the Roman rule for contribution] are others which lay down an entirely different rule. Many accidents happen to a ship or its cargo, whether on the sea or in harbour. The ship may be wrecked, run into, burnt, or attacked by pirates. The cargo may be lost, wetted, or plundered. Now the Sea-law lays down in many places that, where there is a loss of this nature for which no one is to blame, ship and cargo, so far as saved, are to contribute to ship and cargo, so far as lost. There is no question here of a sacrifice for the common safety. It is only necessary that a loss shall occur in the course of the maritime adventure for which neither the owner of the property lost nor any other partaker in the maritime adventure can be held responsible. The result of the principle is that, by entering into the maritime adventure, you insure to a certain extent the ship on which you sail and the goods of your co-adventurers, while on the other hand you are insured to the same extent by the owners of the ship and the other goods on board.[35]

---

gin of any two systems of maritime law..." For Twiss, writing as a legal historian in the late nineteenth century, this conclusion was easy to draw. Nearly a century earlier, it was not so easy for Arthur Browne. Unlike Twiss, whose purpose was descriptive, Browne sought to provide a sound foundation upon which evolving maritime practice would build. To do so, it was necessary to emphasize the continuity of the law and its intrinsic logic. *See supra* note 9 and text accompanying. Commenting on the rules of general average, Browne remarked: "The laws on average and contribution [of Roman law] do not materially differ from those of modern days, and have served as models for them." BROWNE, *supra* note 9, Vol. II, at 36.

32. *See supra* note 24 and text accompanying.

33. Chapters 9 and 38 of the Sea-Laws reflect the rules of contribution outlined in *Digest* 14.2, with a few innovations. The prerequisites for contribution remain unchanged—*i.e.* there must be a deliberate sacrifice of property, which has the effect of saving other property. Unlike the Roman law, however, each of these chapters provides a formula for measuring the value of lost property. For discussion, *see* ASHBURNER, RHODIAN SEA LAWS, *supra* note 11, Introduction at cclviii–cclix.

34. *Id.*

35. *Id.* at cclvii–cclviii.

This approach to general average, under which contribution is available for all losses incurred through perils of the sea, constitutes a marked departure from the law of the *Digest*, indicating influences from sources beyond the civil law, or at the very least showing that local innovation had modified significantly the law that Byzantium had inherited from Rome. Thus rather than being the first link in the chain that connects the ancient civil law to the maritime law of the Renaissance, the Rhodian Sea-Laws are instead the first reflection of a process that would come to dominate maritime law in the middle ages—the trend toward absorption of the local customs of merchants and mariners into positive law. Future maritime law would continue to be influenced by the codified Roman law, but it would not be copied from it.

The seeds for the gradual evolution of customs of the sea into codes of maritime law were sown as the Roman Empire in the West was supplanted by various invaders from northern Europe. To maintain the economies and social stability of occupied portions of the former Empire, the conquerors adopted a policy of applying not their own laws, but rather the laws of the conquered territories. In short, each person was to be judged according to the law of his own people. For merchants and mariners, this policy opened the door for local custom becoming part of the positive law.[36] In many fields of purely domestic law, this approach would lead to highly diverse substantive rules. Such was not the case, however, for the evolving *lex maritima*. For merchants and mariners, more than any other social classes, geographical mobility was part of daily life. Moreover, merchants and mariners often spent more time interacting with those of their own professions in foreign ports than with their own countrymen. Their needs, habits, and expectations cut across national boundaries, producing a certain measure of uniformity of custom in ports and marketplaces throughout Europe. Moreover, each country that wished to encourage foreign trade recognized the advantages to be gained from promulgating rules and reg-

---

36. Thomas Lambert Mears, "The History of the Admiralty Jurisdiction", *in* SELECT ESSAYS IN ANGLO-AMERICAN LEGAL HISTORY, Vol. II, 312, 323 (Boston: Little, Brown & Co., 1908). *See also* TWISS, *supra* note 4, Vol. III, at lxxxi, noting: "[A]t the time when the enterprises of the Italian Republics in the South and the Hanse Confederation in the North were indirectly co-operating to bring about a great commercial revolution in Europe, merchants and mariners were left at liberty to set laws for themselves, and the usages of one locality were readily adopted by another, as soon as the superior convenience and equity of them were recognized. This result was greatly facilitated by a wise provision of the Visigothic Code, which was received in Spain and in the South of France, under which merchants from beyond the sea were allowed to have their disputes settled by their own judges according to their own laws."

ulations that matched the existing customs of the international community of merchants and mariners. In the language of modern economics, uniform rules reduce transactions-costs.[37] That is not to say that social and economic forces created a universal body of substantive law from the Adriatic ports to the towns of the Baltic. Local variations remained, but differences were generally subtle, matters of degree rather than differences in kind. Nevertheless, as with the *Digest* and the Rhodian Sea-Laws, these subtle differences provide vital clues regarding which sets of local customs became models for similar rules adopted in other ports.[38]

By the ninth century, as the written Roman law had begun to fade from memory, many port cities in Europe elected men experienced in maritime and commercial affairs to sit alongside of their municipal judges and provide the court from memory with the applicable substantive rules of maritime law. This system proved adequate so long as the number of maritime cases on the docket remained fairly small. As commerce expanded and maritime cases became more common, however, many saw the advantages of a written set of sea-laws. Moreover, the process was aided by the fact that the clergy, whose responsibility it was to record municipal ordinances before the introduction of the printing press, had gained through the Crusades a greater familiarity with nautical customs.[39] By the eleventh century, written law had begun to replace oral tradition in adjudication of commercial and nautical matters.[40] Over

---

37. Twiss, *supra* note 4, Vol. III, at lxxxi.

38. *See e.g. Id.* at lxvi, in which Twiss rejects the contention that the Table of Amalfi is the source of the Consulate of the Sea (or "*Consolato del Mare*") on the grounds that the rules of general average are too dissimilar to warrant the conclusion that the two codes are related. (For use of rules of contribution to establish origins of maritime codes, *see supra* note 30 and text accompanying.)

39. Twiss, *supra* note 4, Vol. II, at xl–xli.

40. Twiss, *supra* note 4, Vol. IV, at xciv. Written law also brought with it changes in the structure of the courts, as Twiss explains: "The eleventh century seems to have been a period when grave difficulties were experienced in many cities in keeping up the knowledge of their good customs by oral tradition, and when it was found necessary to appease the controversies, which arose amongst the citizens themselves on the subject of their customs, by reducing them into writing. A want seems to have been felt about the same time of a municipal magistracy of a more energetic character than that of the *prud'hommes* [*i.e.* elected experts on nautical practice who sat along side of the judges], whose interpretation of written laws would have weight with their fellow citizens, and the magisterial office of Consul...found a welcome reception in the great commercial cities..." *Id.* Elsewhere, Twiss contends that in addition to issues of convenience, changes in socio-economic power structure played a significant part in the movement to reduce oral customs to writing. He maintains: "The twelfth century, however, was the commencement of a new era in Europe...."

the next few centuries, collections of sea-laws were compiled in European ports in all parts of the Continent. Among those best known to posterity are the Table of Amalfi, the Ordinances of Trani, the Assizes of Jerusalem,[41] the Laws of Wisby, the Consulate of the Sea, and the Rolls of Oleron. All are known today only through later copies, a circumstance that has led to much academic controversy regarding their respective ages. The Laws of Wisby have received occasional attention in modern English and American case law and legal scholarship.[42] They were mentioned in the works of William Welwood, the sixteenth-century Scottish scholar whose works on maritime law were the first of that *genre* to be published in England.[43] Nevertheless, references to the Baltic code are few in English case law, and they generally factor into discus-

---

The knowledge of the principles of the Feudal Law had hitherto been the privilege of the few, and the uncertainty of a law, which rested solely on unwritten custom, had become intolerable to the populations, who found themselves subject to the arbitrary decisions of judges administering a law, the principles of which were only known to the judges themselves." *Id.*, Vol. IV, at xx.

41. Twiss provides texts of these three sets of maritime law in Volume IV. For the Table of Amalfi, *see* Twiss, *supra* note 4, Vol. IV, at 3*ff.*; for the Ordinances and Customs of the Sea Published by the Consuls of the City of Trani, *see Id.* at 523*ff.*; for the Assises of the Latin Kingdom of Jerusalem, *Id.* at 499*ff.* For the origins and relationships among these various compilations, *see generally Id.*, Introduction.

42. *See e.g.* Grant Gilmore & Charles L. Black, Jr., The Law of Admiralty (2d ed., New York: Foundation Press, 1975) at 6–7. For nineteenth-century references, *see* Henry M. Flanders, A Treatise on Maritime Law (Boston: Little, Brown & Co., 1852), Ch. 1, sec. 24-31 at 18–27; Benedict (1st ed.), *supra* note 3, sec. 183 at 99.

43. William Welvvod [Welwood], An Abridgement of All Sea-Lawes, Gathered Forth of All Writings and Monuments Which Are to Be Found among Any People or Nation, upon the Coasts of the Great Ocean and Mediterranean Sea (facsimile of Humphrey Lownes ed., 1613: *reprinted as* No. 565, The English Experience—Its Record in Early Printed Books Published in Facsimile: New York: De Capo Press, 1972), Title 22 (identifying the code as a Dutch translation of the laws of Oleron intended for use in trade with the Baltic ports) (hereinafter Welvvod, Abridgement). Welwood is in error in concluding that the Laws of Wisby were Dutch in origin and only later adopted in the Baltic ports, and his error was replicated two generations later by Zouch, who cited him as authority. *See* Zouch, *supra* note 16, at 6. Twiss observes that that in addition to incorrectly identifying the code's provenance, Welwood also cites a provision that appears in none of the extant texts of the Wisby Laws. He concludes that the Wisby Sea Laws were not well known in England either in the seventeenth century or earlier. *See* Twiss, *supra* note 4, Vol. IV, at lix. As for their importance and legal effect in the northern ports wherein they were promulgated, Twiss remarks that the Laws are "simply a compilation of maritime customs or judgments reduced into writing, which have not been confirmed by any superior authority, but have obtained the sanction of general use and observance from the intrinsic equity and convenience of their provisions." *Id.* at lxxxii. He observes further the

sion in the scholarly literature only in conjunction with other compilations—in particular the Rolls of Oleron and the Consulate of the Sea—when an author wishes to reinforce the antiquity and uniformity of a rule.

Of all the medieval sea-laws, the Consulate of the Sea (or *Consolato del Mare*) is the most controversial. Citations to it are more frequent than to the Laws of Wisby, and in many of those citations, it stands as the sole authority. In American jurisprudence, Chancellor Kent identified it as the most important source of European commercial law that has survived from the middle ages.[44] To Americans, it is perhaps best remembered, however, for its use by Joseph Story in *DeLovio v. Boit*.[45] On the other side of the Atlantic, Lord Mansfield cited it as authority in *Luke v. Lyde*, correctly identifying its Spanish origins.[46] Nevertheless, the reputation of the Consulate of the Sea has always been better known to the common-law world than has the text itself. Indeed, it had not been available in English until Sir Travers Twiss' translation was published in 1874 as part of the collection of documents that he appended to his edition of the *Black Book of the Admiralty*.[47] An Italian version of 1549—translated from the original Catalan—was the mechanism by which the Consulate of the Sea had become known throughout Europe, lead-

---

Wisby Town Law's Preamble provides for use of such customs in adjudication where no written law is found within the Town Law itself. *Id.* at lxxxiii.

44. James Kent, Commentaries on American Law (1st ed., New York: O. Halstead, 1826–1830), Vol. III, at 10.

45. *See supra* note 2 and text accompanying. Ironically, this best known citation to the text in American jurisprudence contains an error in translation. Justice Story, working from an Italian translation of a text that was originally written in Catalan, replicated in English a mistake first made by the Italian translator. For discussion, *see* Twiss, *supra* note 4, Vol. III, at lxxiv–lxxv. Reliance on translations was not unique to Story. Arthur Browne makes several references to the Consulate of the Sea—*see* Browne, *supra* note 9, Vol. II, at 163, 170, 185—all of which rely on an Italian translation. Both examples serve to illustrate the limited knowledge of the origins of the Consulate, even among scholars of the caliber of Story and Browne, as well as the scarcity of reliable texts of early maritime law prior to Pardessus completing his critical edition of collected sea-laws in 1845.

46. For discussion of Mansfield's use of the Consulate of the Sea, *see* Twiss, *supra* note 4, Vol. III, at xxvi. Among other prominent citations to the Consulate in English case law were those by Lord Stowell in *The Aquila*, 1 C. Rob. 37, 43 (1798) and in *The Ceylon*, 1 Dods. 105, 116 (1811).

47. Twiss, *supra* note 4, Vol. III, at lxxiii. A contemporary English edition of the Consulate of the Sea—based on Francis Celelles' text (*see infra* note 49)—is now available in Jados, Consulate of the Sea, *supra* note 10. Jados' edition of the Consulate—which lacks a Catalan text to accompany the translation—also contains an introduction explaining the cultural *milieu* in which the Consulate was created.

ing to the once popular misconception that Italy was the source of the rules themselves.[48] The form in which these rules became known was a comparatively late compilation—dating from 1494—of materials considerably older.[49] Even these, however, cannot be traced through extant documents to a date earlier than 1283, thus eliminating them as a possible source for the Rolls of Oleron, which form the foundation of English substantive maritime law.[50] It is not, however, to documents of the thirteenth century but rather to the somewhat questionable text of 1494 that subsequent commentators and case law have made reference. Walter Ashburner, the editor of the Rhodian Sea-Laws, repeatedly exhibited a dismissive contempt for this text of the Consulate, at one point remarking:

> It must be admitted that there is [in the Consulate] an ancient nucleus of custom; but the greater part of the work consists of ingenious suggestions by learned men, which were probably never practiced by any mariner or enforced by any court. No maritime code of the middle ages has such an air of unreality about it. Until it has been separated into its constituent parts, it must be used with great caution.[51]

To the extent that the Consulate of the Sea was used in England at all—with "great caution" or otherwise—it was used by judges and commentators of the seventeenth century or later to bolster arguments grounded in indigenous English custom and case law. To find the source of the medieval maritime law that became foundation for the rules that prevailed in eighteenth-century England, we must look elsewhere.

---

48. Twiss, *supra* note 4, Vol. III, at xxxi–xxxiii. For evidence that Catalan is the original language of the Consulate, *see Id.* at xxxiii–xxxiv; Jados, Consulate of the Sea, *supra* note 10, Introduction at xii–xiii.

49. The *Editio Princeps* of 1494, once housed in the National Library of Paris, was the basis of the edition published in the first decade of the sixteenth century by Francis Celelles to remedy the lack of an accurate text of the Consulate. Twiss, *supra* note 4, Vol. III, at xxvii–xxviii; xli–xlii. Celelles' text became the source of the 1549 Italian edition and all other foreign-language editions. *Id.* at xli–xliv.

50. Twiss, *supra* note 4, Vol. II, at lxvi. Twiss outlines the reasons for rejecting earlier dates for the sources of the Consulate (*Id.* at lix), and rejects as later propaganda the "Acceptations" that preface Celelles' edition and claim endorsement from Pope Gergory VII, who had been widely respected as a jurist. *See Id.*, Vol. III, at lviii. Twiss' views represent the modern "orthodox" answer regarding the origins of the Consulate of the Sea that have prevailed for the last century. Nevertheless, the subject was once hotly debated, and Twiss' views—resting as they do on circumstantial evidence—may be superseded if additional documentary evidence ever comes to light.

51. Ashburner, Rhodian Sea Laws, *supra* note 11, at cxx–cxxi.

The island of Oleron, situated in the Atlantic off the coast of France, was a dependency of the duchy of Aquitaine in the twelfth century. Surviving records show it to have been a frequent destination of foreign shipping in the twelfth and thirteenth centuries, and by the fourteenth century, its law had become sufficiently well known that the Mayor's Court had become a popular forum in which foreign mariners and merchants adjudicated their claims.[52] It is from Oleron that the first body of substantive maritime law entered the English legal system, though the precise mechanism by which it did so remains open to question. One of the more colorful accounts is provided by John Selden, who claimed that the "Judgments of the Sea" had been promulgated in Oleron by Richard the Lionhearted upon his return from the Crusades, and from there had been taken by Richard back to England. This explanation, as fanciful as it may sound, was adopted subsequently by no less eminent a scholar than William Prynne, the seventeenth-century commentator best remembered today for his insightful—if vitriolic—response to Sir Edward Coke's *Fourth Institute*.[53] His contemporary, Matthew Hale, rejected the assertion unceremoni-

---

52. Twiss, *supra* note 4, Vol. II, at lv. Twiss notes that—second only to the Ordinances and Customs of the Sea of the Consuls of Trani—the sea-laws of Oleron are the oldest extant body of European maritime law. *Id.*, Vol. II, at xliii; xlvii. With regard to the sources of the substantive law of Oleron, Twiss observes:

> "We know not how it happened that Eleanor of Guienne or Richard I. of England was able to collect together a body of maritime judgments, which proved to be so faithful and so complete a mirror of the customs observed in the trade between the ports of the Atlantic seaboard of France and those of the rest of Europe, that they have been accepted as law for centuries in the ports of the North Sea and of the Baltic equally as of the Mediterranean Sea, unless it was that the Maritime Court of Oleron was in advance of other courts in keeping a careful record of the decisions of its judges, and so possessed a body of judge-made law, which would have been sought for in vain in the neighboring courts of Bordeaux and of Rochelle."

Id., Vol. IV, at cxxix.

53. Twiss, *supra* note 4, Vol. I, at lviii; Vol. II, at xlvii–xlviii; li. Selden drew support for his contention that Richard promulgated the Laws of Oleron and sent them back to England through his reading of a passage in the Roll "12 Edward III", generally known as the "*Fasciculus Superioritate Maris*". For further discussion, *see* Reginald G. Marsden, Select Pleas in the Court of Admiralty: A. D. 1390–1404 and 1527–1545, Vol. II (London: Publications of the Selden Society, Vol. 6, 1892), Introduction at xxx (hereinafter, Marsden, Select Pleas II). *See also* William Prynne, Brief Animadversions on, Amendments of, and Additional Explanatory Records to the Fourth Part of the Institutes of the Lawes of England, Concerning the Jurisdiction of the Courts, Compiled by the Late Famous Lawyer, Sir Edward Cooke, Knight (London: Thomas Ratcliffe & Thomas Daniel, 1669) at 109 (hereinafter Prynne, Brief Animadversions).

ously with a single sentence: "But yet it seems to me very doubtfull whether Richard I made these Lawes, or whether they were made sooner than the year 1266, which was about 50 Hen. III."[54] To understand the divergent views, context is important. When Selden recorded the anecdote about Richard in *Mare Clausum*, he was attempting to refute Grotius' contention that no nation had the power to promulgate legislation for the high seas. If Richard—as King of England—had issued laws while in Aquitaine that were applicable throughout the Atlantic coast, it would show—*contra* Grotius—that there was precedent for an English monarch extending his nation's sovereignty over the ocean.[55] The argument admittedly is highly attenuated, and it is likely that it would have been met with skepticism from objective scholars even in Selden's own day. *Mare Clausum* was, however, political propaganda in the guise of legal history, and Prynne, no more likely than Hale to be impressed by its sophistry, nevertheless appears to have been willing to applaud its assertions so long as they comported with his own politics.[56]

Seventeenth-century politics aside, modern commentators remain divided on how the maritime law of Oleron came to be adopted for use in England. Subsequent to the publication of *Mare Clausum*, historians established that Selden's story is inconsistent with what is known about Richard's whereabouts after his return from the Holy Land.[57] A variation of Selden's account, however, retains some support. In this version, first suggested by Cleirac, the seventeenth-century French scholar whose text of the Sea-Laws of Oleron was recognized as authoritative by England's High Court of Admiralty from the judgeship of Sir Leoline Jenkins through 1709, Eleanor of Aquitaine instigated the project of compiling the customs of the sea prevailing in French ports into a maritime code, naming it after her favorite island, Oleron. Unfortunately, Cleirac offered no evidence to support his conjecture. Twiss, examining the time-frame and personalities involved, found concrete evidence lacking, but

---

54. Matthew Hale, "*A Disquisition Touching the Jurisdiction of the Common Law and Courts of Admiralty in Relation to Things Done Upon or Beyond the Sea, and Touching Maritime and Merchants' Contracts*", *published in* M. J. Prichard & D. E. C. Yale, Hale and Fleetwood on Admiralty Jurisdiction (London: Publications of the Selden Society, Vol. 108, 1993) at 61 (hereinafter Hale and Fleetwood).

55. Twiss, *supra* note 4, Vol. II, at xlvii–xlviii.

56. Unlike those of Selden and Prynne, Hale' treatise, which was completed sometime between publication of Prynne's work (which Hale mentions) in 1669 and his retirement from the Chief Justiceship if King's Bench in 1676, was never intended for publication; hence Hale had no motive to resort to political rhetoric. *See* Hale and Fleetwood, *supra* note 54, Introduction at xvii–xviii.

57. Twiss, *supra* note 4, Vol. II, at li.

conceded that Cleirac's account should not be dismissed lightly.[58] Other commentators have been more skeptical. In the introduction to their critical edition of Hale's heretofore unpublished manuscript on the Courts of Admiralty, M. J. Prichard and D. E. C. Yale argue for a gradual absorption, concluding their examination of the subject with the contention that: "The judgments of Oleron entered English maritime law apparently in consequence of trade with Aquitaine and Bordeaux, not as the result of any political decision or legislative act by English kings who were dukes of Aquitaine."[59]

As the precise means by which the maritime law of Oleron was adopted in England remains open to question, so also does the date of its reception.[60] A

58. *Id.*, Vol. II, at xlviii–li.

59. Hale and Fleetwood, *supra* note 54, Introduction at xxxiv.

60. Nomenclature poses a further problem in attempting to ascertain when maritime law from Oleron first made its way into English legal proceedings. A cursory examination of the tables of contents in Volumes I and II of Twiss' edition of the *Black Book* and related documents would reveal that there are a plethora of manuscripts of sea-laws with titles related to the island of Oleron. Readers are encouraged to examine Sir Travers' Introductions to each of the four volumes in order to gain a better understanding of the complex history of the Oleron manuscripts. A short summary may be helpful. The oldest of the texts are those commonly referred to as the "Judgments of the Sea". These should not be confused with the Custumary of the Commune of Oleron, a medieval work of a somewhat later date, about which Twiss writes:

> "The most interesting chapters... are those which are concerned with maritime matters, which, when put in controversy, were adjudged in the Mayor's Court, to which foreigners had free access. There are as many as sixteen or seventeen chapters on matters connected with shipping, some of which indeed had reference to questions which might arise in harbour, or within territorial waters, but others were of a more general character, such as questions respecting partnerships in vessels, the duty of masters, the rules of contribution in cases of jetison, and of compensation in certain cases of collision, which might have well found a place amongst the 'Judgments of the Sea', if they had not been of more modern origin."

Twiss, *supra* note 4, Vol. II, at lxxvii.

A greater source of potential confusion is posed by the various texts of the "Judgments of the Sea" themselves, commonly referred to as the "Rolls of Oleron". The text published by Cleirac in the seventeenth century, which Twiss calls the "Roll of the Judgments of Oleron", is a somewhat longer work of a later date. *Id.*, Vol. II, at lxxviii–lxxxii, Vol. I, at lxiv (noting that Cleirac's text was roughly double the length, containing 47 rather than the 24 articles found in the oldest manuscripts of the "Judgments of the Sea"). Nevertheless, Cleirac's text, while derived from less ancient sources, was treated as an authoritative text of the oldest of the sea-laws associated with the island of Oleron, and was cited as authoritative by the High Court of Admiralty from the Restoration through 1709. *Id.*, Vol. IV, at lvi–lvii.

Bristol inquest of 1351 confirms that they were in use by the reign of Edward III,[61] roughly a decade after the establishment of England's first Admiralty Court.[62] Other evidence indicates that they were in use somewhat earlier—in the reign of Edward II (1307–1327)—having received the approbation of the Magistrates of the Corporation of the City of London for use in the City Courts, which at that time adjudicated maritime and commercial disputes.[63] The existence of two manuscripts of "The Charter of Oleron of the Judgments of the Sea" in the Archives of the City of London, dating to 1314 and 1321–28 respectively, would serve to confirm that the sea-laws of Oleron were in use in the early portion of the fourteenth century.[64] With regard to the century between the reign of Richard the Lionhearted (1189–1199) and Edward II, however, evidence is more tenuous.[65]

While England's adoption of the Sea-laws of Oleron predated the establishment of the Court of Admiralty, it was to the records of that tribunal that subsequent generations of practitioners—both of the civil and the common law—looked to ascertain the substantive rules of English maritime law. About these records, John Exton, the seventeenth-century civil-law scholar and judge of the High Court of Admiralty, wrote:

---

61. For discussion, *see* Timothy J. Runyan, *The Rolls of Oleron and the Admiralty Court in Fourteenth Century England.*, 19 Am. J. Leg. Hist. 95, 98–99 (1975) (hereinafter Runyan).

62. *See* Prynne, Brief Animadversions, *supra* note 53, at 119. For discussion by modern commentators, see Mears, *supra* note 36, at 319; *see also* Twiss, *supra* note 4, Vol. I, at lxi.

63. Twiss, *supra* note 4, Vol. I, at lxi.

64. *Id.*, Vol. I, at lviii–lx. The manuscripts are the "*Liber Memorandorum*" (1314), deposited in the Record Room of the Guildhall, and the "*Liber Horn*" (transcribed between 1321 and 1328), named for Andrew Horn, a prominent legal scholar of the day. Twiss identifies two other English manuscripts of the "Judgments of the Sea". The first, a copy of the *Liber Memorandorum*, is in the Bodleian Library; the other, preserved in the library of Corpus Christi College, Cambridge, appears to be from the reign of Edward II (1307–1327).

65. While the *Black Book of the Admiralty* incorporates both the "Judgments of the Sea" and various ordinances of kings from Henry I (1100–1135) through Edward I (1272–1307), *Id.*, Vol. I, at lvi–lvii, the handwriting in the text itself indicates that it was transcribed no earlier than the reign of Henry IV (1399–1413), *Id.*, Vol. III, at x, leaving open the possibility that the ordinances pre-dated the introduction of the sea-laws of Oleron into England. While Prynne was obviously correct in noting that an ordinance of King John (recorded as Article 25 in the *Black Book*) appears to amend a rule contained in the "Judgments of the Sea", it does not necessarily follow that the "Judgments of the Sea" were already in force in their entirety at the time King John issued his ordinance. For discussion, *see Id.*, Vol. I, at lxi.

> There are likewise ancient Statutes of the Admiralty to be observed, both upon the Ports and Havens, the high Seas, and beyond the Seas, which are comprised in an old authentick Book, called *The black Book of the Admiralty*, which Statutes are ingrossed upon Vellam in the said Book, and written in an ancient hand, in the ancient French Language, which plainly shew the Admirals Jurisdiction to be upon the Ports and Havens, as well as upon the high Seas.[66]

Among the statutes incorporated into the *Black Book of the Admiralty* were the Sea-laws of Oleron. Though long a touchstone of substantive sea-law, the *Black Book*'s utility to the High Court declined as many of the matters over which the Court had exercised jurisdiction were transferred to the common-law courts, and by the third decade of the nineteenth century the *Book* itself had disappeared from the Court's archives. Nevertheless, the *Black Book* contained the core of what had become English maritime law, and in the interest of legal history, the Master of Rolls included the *Black Book* among those medieval legal texts selected for publication in his proposal to the Treasury in 1857. The editor selected for the project was Her Majesty's Advocate General, Sir Travers Twiss. Lacking both the book itself and a reliable copy of the full text, Twiss was forced to reconstruct its contents from an assortment of manuscripts of various documents that the original book had contained, resulting in a published edition of the *Black Book* in 1871.[67] Shortly thereafter, the original was discovered in a trunk containing the private papers of a deceased registrar of the Court, and examination of its contents confirmed that Sir Travers' reconstruction was highly accurate.[68] This episode in the history of the *Black Book* highlights two often overlooked points. First, Twiss' ability to reconstruct the *Black Book* from various other manuscripts illustrates the fact

66. John Exton, The Maritime Dicaeology, Or Sea-Jurisdiction of England (London: Richard Hodgkinson, 1664), Bk. 2, Ch. xi, at 115 (hereinafter Exton). Exton's statement that the *Black Book* was written wholly in Old French is somewhat misleading, as the section Twiss labels the "*Ordo Judiciorum*" was composed in Latin (*see text in* Twiss, *supra* note 4, Vol. I, at 178–220), and the following section, "*De Officio Admiralitatis*", while originally drafted in Law French, appears in the *Black Book* in a Latin translation by Thomas Rowghton, Registrar for the Court during the reign of Henry VI (*Id.*, Vol. I, at 221–245). For discussion of Rowghton's Latin translation, *see Id.*, Vol. I, at 221; Introduction at lxxiii. For discussion of whether French or Latin was the original language of "Section C" of the *Black Book*, which precedes the "*Ordo Judiciorum*" in the text and contains the Sea-laws of Oleron, *see Id.*, Vol. I, at liii–liv.

67. *See generally* Twiss, *supra* note 4, Vol. I, Introduction.

68. Twiss, *supra* note 4, Vol. III, Introduction at vii–xiii.

that the book post-dated the law that it contained; in short, it was a compilation of older texts of various origins rather than a comprehensive medieval maritime code. Second, when case law and treatises from the eighteenth and nineteenth centuries make reference to the substantive law of the *Black Book*, the authors are citing a work known in their times only through synopses in secondary sources.

With the discovery of the original *Black Book*, it was possible to form certain conclusions regarding its age. Analysis of handwriting reveals that the oldest portions date from the reign of Henry VI (1422–1461), though some of the material that it contains pre-dates the reign of Edward III (*i.e.* 1327). The book consists of ten parts, the first seven of which relate directly to admiralty matters. The first two parts (generally referred to as A and B), consist of ordinances of the King and Council relating to the Lord Admiral. The fifth and sixth parts respectively are the *Ordo Judiciorum*, a procedural treatise, and Thomas Rowghton's *De Officio Admiralitatis*, followed by a set of documents relating to the tenure of John Holland, Duke of Exeter, as Admiral. Between these sets of documents are Parts C and D, which contain the bulk substantive maritime law in the book. Part C consists of thirty-nine "indigenous" English rules relating to the Admiralty, followed by the twenty-four articles derived from the Laws of Oleron, which are followed in turn by ten additional substantive maritime-law articles of English derivation together with an eleventh article, purporting to date from the reign of King John, which requires merchant ships to lower their sails when hailed by English naval vessels. Twiss estimated the original date of compilation of this material as somewhere between 1360 and 1369. Part D contains the eighteen articles of the Inquisition of Queenborow, which was held in 1375, followed by a set of fifty-two articles from the reign of Henry V (1413–1422) and ten more derived from the reign of Henry VI (1422–1461).[69]

Some of the law in Part C resembles rules that are still in force today. Among the Laws of Oleron, modern practitioners would recognize the seaman's right to maintenance and cure, the master's power to incur expenses for the benefit of the ship, the master's duties in loading cargo, and the rule for calculating damages when ships collide. While the rules may have changed over time, the medieval laws, like their modern counterparts, also addressed issues of wreck and jettison, including valuation for general average. One provision established liability for a merchant for failing to load his cargo within the prescribed time, thus laying the groundwork for the modern concept of

69. Twiss, *supra* note 4, Vol. I, at xxviii–xli.

"demurrage". Several provisions addressed seamen's labor contracts, providing insight into the development of modern law regulating "ship's articles". Not all of the Laws of Oleron and the ten English rules, however, left a lasting impression on modern practice. Those which have disappeared range from the trivial—such as the seaman's right to a wine ration (predictably, of French derivation)—to the startling—as with the indigenous English rule that provided for the decapitation of a negligent pilot.[70] The bulk of the eighteen articles of the Inquisition of Queenborow pertain to seamen's rights and obligations under their labor contracts. The supplemental sixty-two articles that follow address a variety of issues, including criminal law (murder and mayhem) and wreck (rights to flotsam, jetsam, and deodands). Of particular interest are Articles 51 and 52 (from the reign of Henry V), which call for an inquiry when a suit regarding maritime matters is filed in a common-law court rather than in a court of admiralty.[71]

---

70. For additional discussion, *see* Mears, *supra* note 36, at 326–328. The Laws of Oleron, together with the eleven English additions to them in the *Black Book*, are found in Twiss, *supra* note 4, Vol. I, at 89–132. The master's power to incur expenses for the benefit of the ship is found in Article 1; Article 7 establishes the forerunner to the modern seaman's right to maintenance and cure. The master's duties in the handling of cargo are outlined in Article 10, while Article 15 establishes the rule for splitting damages in case of collision. The Laws of Oleron provide additional guidance in apportioning damages when ships at anchor run afoul of each other in Article 16. Articles 8 and 9 of the Laws of Oleron govern jettison, while Article 32 of the English rules addresses valuation for general average. Articles 3 and 4 address respectively the effect of wreck upon the rights of seamen to their wages and upon the rights of the parties to a contract of carriage. Article 22 provides that a merchant whose failure to load his cargo within the agreed period of time must pay damages to the shipowner. The first of the English rules, Article 25, relieves both parties to a contract of carriage of their obligations if rendered impossible by "acts of princes". Article 29 establishes the sailor's right to his ration of wine. The provision for the death penalty for a negligent pilot—Article 34—is an extension of the civil liability of the pilot for the negligent wrecking of a ship as outlined in preceding article. Of particular interest is Article 31, which provides that a master may discharge cargo and demand freight after 21 days. This provision supplied the rule applied at the Birstol inquest—discussed *supra* note 61 and text accompanying—and was described as one of the Laws of Oleron. As no text of the Laws of Oleron outside of England contains this provision, it indicates that the laws of the French island had been in use in England long enough for the distinction between them and the indigenous laws to have become blurred. For discussion, *see Id.*, Vol. III, at xi–xii.

71. The Inquisition of Queenborow, together with the rules added under the reigns of Henries V and VI, are reproduced in The Rolls Series edition of the *Black Book:* Twiss, *supra* note 5, Vol. I, at 133–177. Articles 29 and 30 address murder and mayhem respectively. Wreck is addressed in Articles 41, 42, and 74.

While the *Black Book* itself eventually disappeared from sight, the influence of its contents—in particular the Laws of Oleron—would remain the cornerstone of substantive maritime law in England for the next four centuries. As late as the close of the seventeenth century, Sir Leoline Jenkins, Judge of the High Court of Admiralty following the Restoration, made reference to the law of the *Black Book*, admonishing in his charge at Admiralty Sessions: "These are your Bounds, Gentlemen, the Particulars you are to enquire of, deduce from these three Heads; The Laws of the Realm, the Laws of Oleron, and the Laws of the Admiralty."[72] Nevertheless, the law did not remain static. Changes began as early as the thirteenth century, when Edward I altered Oleron's rule of contribution (inherited from the *Digest*), whereby shipowners were required to contribute *pro rata* according the value of their ships and personal effects aboard, amending it to require shipowners' contributions only for any of their own merchandise aboard which they intended to sell upon reaching port.[73] Over time, English maritime law added new concepts to the

72. Sir Leoline Jenkins, "A Charge Given at a Session of Admiralty within the Cinque Ports, Sept. 2, 1668", *reprinted in* WILLIAM WYNNE, THE LIFE OF SIR LEOLINE JENKINS, JUDGE OF THE HIGH COURT OF ADMIRALTY, AND PREROGATIVE COURT OF CANTERBURY &C. AMBASSADOR AND PLENIPOTENTIARY FOR THE GENERAL PEACE AT COLOGN AND NIMEGUEN, AND SECRETARY OF STATE TO CHARLES II. (2 vols., London: Joseph Downing, 1724), Vol. I, at lxxxv–lxxxvi (hereinafter WYNNE). Further on in the charge, Sir Leoline elaborated:

> "The *Laws of Oleron*, are the ancient universally received Customs of the *Western* Part of the World; which *Rich.* I. of immortal Memory, being upon his Return from the Holy War, thought fit to review and reform; and then to give them the Stamp of his Royal Authority. These Laws all the Sea-faring Nations of this *Western* Part the World, soon after received and entertained from the *English*, by way of Deference to the Soveraignty of our Kings in the *British* Ocean, and to the Judgment of our Countrymen in Sea-Affairs."

Id. at lxxxvii (*emphasis in the original*).

73. Matthew Hale reproduces this Ordinance of Edward I *verbatim* in Latin in his "*Disquisition*": *see* HALE AND FLEETWOOD, *supra* note 54, at 63–64. For discussion, *see* TWISS, *supra* note 4, Vol. I, at lxx; Vol. II, at xxxii–xxxiv. This new rule, laid down in 1285, is included in the *Coutumier* (or Custumary) of Oleron (*see supra* note 59) in Chapter LXXXVIII, which Twiss reproduces in Vol. II, at 254–402. It is worth noting that despite the importance of rules of general average to modern scholars in ascertaining whether sets of maritime law are derived from common sources, actual cases of general average are comparatively rare. In editing his edition of the pleas of the medieval Admiralty Court, Reginald Marsden was able to identify only one case involving general average before 1545. *See* REGINALD G. MARSDEN, SELECT PLEAS IN THE COURT OF ADMIRALTY: A.D. 1390–1404 AND A.D. 1527–1545, VOL. I (Publications of the Selden Society, Vol. 6, 1892), at lxxii (hereinafter MARSDEN, SELECT PLEAS I).

core of the Oleron text. Some, as Jenkins indicated, were statutory creations. One Tudor-period law provided rules for adjudicating issues related to charterparties, seaworthiness of vessels, marine insurance, foreign contracts, and bills of exchange.[74] Other new concepts were a product of judicial recognition of changing practices in the maritime world, such as the Admiralty Court's recognition of the validity of "contracts of consortship", the "bill obligatory", and the claims of materialmen.[75] The first case of spoil was tried at admiralty

74. 32 Hen. VIII., c. 14. For discussion of the statute's treatment of seaworthiness, charterparties, foreign contracts, bills of exchange, and marine insurance, *see* Mears, *supra* note 36, at 352–353. The experiment of having marine insurance claims tried at admiralty was short-lived; in 1601 another statute granted jurisdiction over marine insurance claims to a separate tribunal. (*See* HALE AND FLEETWOOD, *supra* note 54, Introduction at lxxxi.) When this also proved unsatisfactory, it fell to the common-law courts to develop the substantive law of marine insurance, much of which can be traced to Lord Mansfield. (*See*, MARSDEN, SELECT PLEAS II, *supra* note 53, at lxxx.)

75. "Contracts of consortship"—private arrangements for organization of convoys to provide mutual protection from pirates and privateers—arose during the middle ages and persisted down to the seventeenth century. *See* Marsden, "High Court", *supra* note 8, at 82–83. Surviving examples of "contracts of consortship" are rare, particularly in print. Marsden has reproduced a variation of this form of contract from manuscript in DOCUMENTS RELATING TO THE LAW AND CUSTOM OF THE SEA (2 vols., R.G. Marsden ed., London: The Navy Record Society, 1915–1916), Vol. I, at 272–273. This "Consortship Agreement entered into by Lord Thomas Howard and John Watts", dating from 1591, is unusual in that it is an agreement of mutual support and defense among privateers rather than among merchant vessels traveling in convoy. Marsden also provides an example of the more familiar type ("Articles of Consortship for the Wine Fleet"), dating from 1576. *Id.* at 205–209. The "bill obligatory" (or "*billa obligatoria*")—the forerunner of the "bottomry bond" common in nineteenth-century practice—provided for the advance of funds for the purchase of ship's necessaries (or even cargo), with an interest in the ship itself serving as security for the loan. In this form of contract, which became popular in the first half of the sixteenth century, "the money [was] usually expressed to be payable in a stated number of days after the ship's arrival at her port of discharge." MARSDEN, SELECT PLEAS I, *supra* note 73, at lxxii. The history of materialmen's claims in English admiralty law is complex. Sir Leoline Jenkins observed that when a ship was sold at judicial auction, the Admiralty Court traditionally had paid materialmen if funds remained after all other claims were satisfied—treating materialmen's claims in effect as low-priority liens—although this practice had come under attack in the seventeenth century by the common lawyers, who contended that such decisions of the Court were *ultra vires*. (*See* Leoline Jenkins, "Letter to King in Council", *in* WYNNE, *supra* note 72, Vol. II, at 746–747. *See also* Mears, *supra* note 36, at 362–363.) BROWNE, *supra* note 9, Vol. II, at 134, traces materialmen's claims to the Laws of Oleron (Article 1). The issue that provoked later controversy was not whether materialmen had valid claims, but rather whether they could enforce those claims *in rem* in a court of admiralty rather than *in personam* in the courts of common law.

in 1357, marking the beginning of what was to become one of the Admiralty Court's most lucrative sources of business for centuries to come.[76] The Admiralty Court continued to develop law in the field of criminal law, as well as contract law relating to partnership, affreightment, and even shipbuilding, before losing its jurisdiction over these matters to the common law in the seventeenth century.[77] While the rules governing seamen's labor contracts had been set out in some detail in the *Black Book*, nevertheless the law continued to evolve in this area too.[78] Sir Leoline Jenkins became the first judge to appoint experts for fact-finding in a collision case, and the Court initiated a change in the substantive maritime law by laying down the rule that losses

---

76. Lionel H. Liang, *Historic Origins of Admiralty Jurisdiction in England*, 45 Mich. L. Rev. 163, 167 (1946) (hereinafter Liang).

77. Despite the general expansion of admiralty jurisdiction under Henry VIII, the Admiralty Court lost jurisdiction over criminal matters in 1537. Mears, *supra* note 36, at 352. Admiralty's jurisdiction over contracts of affreightment ended with *Jurato v. Gregory*, 1 Ventris 32 (1669). (For discussion, *see* Hale and Fleetwood, *supra* note 54, Introduction at lxxxvii.) In *Freeman contra Lydyard* (File of Prohibitions No. 20, 1602), a writ of consultation permitted the Admiralty to proceed in adjudicating a dispute over a shipbuilding contract. (For discussion, *see* Marsden, Select Pleas II, *supra* note 53, at lvi.) Today, such contracts do not sound in admiralty in either British or American law. Despite Jenkins' best efforts to preserve jurisdiction over partnership disputes for the Admiralty in his speech before the House of Lords in 1670, the jurisdiction was lost to the common law. *See* Sir Leoline Jenkins, *"Argument, in Behalf of a Bill to Ascertain the Jurisdiction of the Admiralty, in the House of Lords"*, *reprinted in* Wynne, *supra* note 72, Vol. I, at lxxvi, lxxxviii.

78. As one commentator has noted: "Mariners were hired in one of three ways. They were paid a set wage for the journey, allowed to freight their own cargo in space allotted to them (*mareage*) or granted a share of the profits of the freight by the master. Only the first of these methods of payment is known to Roman law." Runyan, *supra* note 61, at 99 (*citing* Articles 18 and 20 of the Laws of Oleron). *See* also Dorothy Burwash, English Merchant Shipping, 1460–1540 (Toronto: University of Toronto Press, 1947) at 42–43. While the Laws of Oleron and the Inquisition of Queenborow dealt with seamen's wages in great detail, the rights of seamen occasionally were altered by statute. Moreover, as occurrences came before the courts that were unforeseen by the compilers of the medieval maritime laws, they were at times obliged to create new rules. (*See generally* Browne, *supra* note 9, Vol. II, at 155–188.) The Admiralty Court's chief innovation in the area of seamen's wages was procedural rather than substantive, as the procedure under which the Court operated—derived from the civil law—permitted joinder of all mariners in a single action for their wages. Joinder of wage-claims, not possible under the common law, reduced the transactions-costs for individual sailors, for whom an individual suit for wages at common law would have been prohibitively costly. For discussion, *see e.g.* Jenkins, *"Argument"*, *in* Wynne, *supra* note 72, Vol. I, at lxxxii; *see also* Zouch, *supra* note 16, at 147.

were to be divided equally where both vessels were at fault in a collision.[79] The High Court of Admiralty also has been credited with innovation in the law of salvage, being the first court to award to salvors a "moiety", or award of half the monetary value of property saved at sea.[80] From the middle ages onwards, the Court began to assert rights to the "droits of the Admiralty", which—depending on factual context—could include "royal fish", flotsam, jetsam, deodands, or even wrecked vessels.[81] In addition, over the next few centuries, the

---

79. In 1673, Jenkins first employed nautical experts in fact-finding in a case of collision. MARSDEN, SELECT PLEAS II, *supra* note 53, at lxxix–lxxxv. With regard to collision, Article 15 of the Laws of Oleron provided for apportionment of damages equally between vessels if a moving vessel were to strike a vessel at anchor (technically an "allision" in modern parlance). Marsden observes that with the exception of *Handcocke v. Payne*, an arbitral decision of 1539, there is no surviving evidence of equal apportionment of damages in a case of collision in the sixteenth century. MARSDEN, SELECT PLEAS I, *supra* note 73, at lxxii; text of decision reproduced at 90. Elsewhere, he remarks that:

> "During the sixteenth century collision cases are very rare. In the seventeenth century they abound. There is no sentence of any judge prior to Sir Julius Caesar for division of loss; full damages were always given, or none. The judges who succeeded Caesar, for a collision caused by the defendant's fault, sometimes gave full damages, sometimes half, sometimes less than half. Sometimes they gave half damages where there was no fault in either ship, and sometimes where the cause of collision was left in uncertainty. Not until 1789 was the loss divided where both ships were in fault; and not until 1824 was it decided that the loss must, in such case, be divided equally."

MARSDEN, SELECT PLEAS II, *supra* note 53, at lxxxiii.

80. Arguably the granting of a "moiety" to salvors may be traced to the Assizes of Jerusalem. TWISS, *supra* note 4, Vol. IV, at 517. (For discussion, *see* Mears, *supra* note 36, at 332 n. 1.) BROWNE, *supra* note 9, Vol. II, at 53, credits Thomas Rowghton (translator into Latin of the "*De Officio Admiralitatis*" in the *Black Book of the Admiralty*—*see supra* note 65) with the rule, noting that the award of a moiety is an English creation not employed on the Continent. Marsden mentions a case of 1333 in which salvors were granted a moiety of the cargo of fish salvaged from a French vessel (*see* MARSDEN, SELECT PLEAS I, *supra* note 73, at xxvi). Nevertheless, Marsden contends, ambiguities regarding title to wrecks (*i.e.* whether the wrecked ship remained the property of the owners or droits of the Admiralty) placed a salvor's right to sue for a moiety on precarious ground until 1633, when a decision by Judge Henry Marten confirmed the salvors' right to an award. (For discussion, *see* MARSDEN, SELECT PLEAS II, *supra* note 53, at xxxvi–xxxvii.)

81. As Mears explains:

> "The droits or perquisites formerly attaching to the office of Lord High Admiral, as enumerated in their later patents, consisted of flotsam, jetsam, ligan, treasure, deodands, derelicts found within the admiral's jurisdiction, all goods picked up at sea, all fines, forfeitures, ransoms, recognizances and pecuniary punishments, all sturgeons, whales, porpoises, dolphins, and gramupses, and all such large fishes, all ships and goods of the enemy coming into any creek, road, or

Admiralty Court grappled with the problem of conflicting claims to wrecks and their contents, as the shipowners, salvors, the Lord Admiral, and even the Crown asserted rights to hulls, tackle, and cargoes of wrecked vessels.[82]

> port by stress of weather, mistake, or ignorance of the war, all ships seized at sea, salvage, together with a share of prizes."

Mears, *supra* note 36, at 318–319. (With regard to the technical vocabulary, "jetsam" refers to portions of a ship or its cargo that wash ashore, while "flotsam" refers to those portions that remain afloat. "Ligan" (sometimes spelled "lagan" or "lagon") are items to which bouys are attached before they are thrown overboard, so that the owners can retrieve them later. "Deodands" are either items that cause the death of a person at sea, or the personal effects found on the body of the deceased. "Derelicts" are vessels intentionally cast adrift, to which the owners have relinquished all claim of title.) Marsden, noting the broad—and potentially overreaching—powers granted by the Admiral's patent, makes the rather startling observation that: "an important—perhaps the chief—purpose of the Admiral's Court was the collection of perquisites and forfeitures." MARSDEN, SELECT PLEAS II, *supra* note 53, at xxiii; xviii. Jenkins provides a list of the perquisites of the Admiral that were removed and vested in the Crown in the reign of Charles II. Sir Leoline Jenkins, "Another Charge at a Sessions of Admiralty, Held at the Old Bailey", *reprinted in* WYNNE, *supra* note 72, Vol. I, at xc, xcviii.

82. The substantive law of wreck in English legal history is deserving of monograph-length treatment. For present purposes, a brief summary should suffice. Roman law was very protective of rights to property experiencing casualty at sea. Even where cargo was jettisoned intentionally, its owners retained title, and anyone who appropriated jettisoned property—whether found on land or retrieved from the sea—was criminally liable for theft. (*See* DIG. 41.1.9.8.) Where the ship itself suffered calamity, the law was similarly protective of the owners' rights:

> "If at any time it should happen that a ship is driven to wreck upon the shore, or if it should allide with any other part of the land, it would continue to belong to its owners. My [the emperor's] imperial treasury would not interfere [with the property right]. For in what sense would the imperial treasury justly have an interest in a third party's misfortune, such that profit should be sought from such a lamentable occurrence."

CODE J. 41.5.1 (Imp. Constantinus A.) (*my translation*). The owners' interest in their property was preserved for one year after its recovery (CODE J. 41.5.2). By contrast, in early medieval English law, portions of a wreck or its cargo adrift on the high seas were *res nullius*, subject to being claimed by whomever first found and retrieved them. On the other hand, portions of a wreck that washed ashore would escheat to the Crown, excepting (as Bracton noted) ship's timbers of minimal value. (*See* MARSDEN, SELECT PLEAS II, *supra* note 53, at xxxix.) With the enactment of 3 Edward I, ch. 4 in 1276, if any person or animal escaped the wreck alive, the original owners would have one year and a day to claim their property, after which time it would escheat to the local lord upon whose property it washed ashore. Thus a "wreck", properly understood, was either a vessel and its cargo that remained unclaimed for the statutory period or one from which there had been no survivors, while a "derelict" was a vessel that had been abandoned intentionally. (For discussion, including the legal significance of whether the damaged vessel washed ashore or re-

While the maritime law continued to evolve from the fourteenth through eighteenth centuries, knowledge of its rules most often was confined to those legal practitioners who specialized in the field. Owing to the lack of published reports, particularly for the Court of Admiralty, acquiring this knowledge proved difficult. The unpublished records of the Court of Admiralty often would contain only the result of a case, minus the *ratio decidendi*. Thus, frequently the only detailed written accounts of the outcome of litigation were the notations in the private notebooks of the practitioners themselves.[83] Predictably, it was the mercantile classes, those with the most at stake in being able to assess accurately their rights and potential liabilities under the law, who most desired some means of gaining access to understanding substantive maritime law. The obvious response to this demand was the publishing of practical manuals, which would give merchants the information that they needed in order to conform their conduct to the rules recognized and enforced by the courts. Unfortunately, the authors of these treatises were hampered by the same lack of information that precipitated the need for such treatises in the first place. Nevertheless, beginning at the end of the sixteenth century, a handful of works on substantive maritime law began to appear in print in England.

The first[84] of these works was that of William Welwood. Welwood (sometimes spelled "Welwod"), a professor of mathematics and civil law at St. An-

---

mained at sea, *see* BROWNE, *supra* note 9, Vol. II, at 47–49. For one of the better brief treatments of the history of the law of wreck in England, *see* Mears, *supra* note 36, n. 1 at 331–335. For a synopsis of the history of the law together with a practical assessment of the state of the law of wreck at the end of the seventeenth century, *see* CHARLES MOLLOY, *DE JURE MARITIMO ET NAVALI*: OR A TREATISE ON AFFAIRS MARITIME AND OF COMMERCE (3d ed., London: John Bellinger, 1682) at 337–345 (hereinafter MOLLOY, (3d ed., Bellinger)).) The rule that had declared a vessel to be a wreck if no "person, dog, or cat" survived continued to be applied through the eighteenth century. It was finally overturned by Lord Mansfield in *Hamilton v. Davis*, 5 Burr 2732 (1771). (It should be noted that when portions of wrecked vessels were recovered from the shore rather than from the high seas, jurisdiction lay with the common-law courts.)

83. *See* discussion, *supra* notes 5 and 6 and text accompanying.

84. One might contend that the William Fleetwood's "*Certen Notes Declaring Admirall Jurisdiction*", *circa* 1568 (*reprinted in* HALE AND FLEETWOOD, *supra* note 54, at 121–254) is the first treatise on substantive maritime law of this period, as the title includes the assertion that the work contains "*a Declaration When the Civill Lawe or the Common Lawe of the Realme Is to Be Used in any Admiral Court for the Triall of such Matters as Be There to Be Heard or Determined*". Fleetwood, a member of Middle Temple, sergeant-at-law, and longtime member of Parliament, relied—in his own words—upon both the civil and common law, as well as statutes and even the Bible in drafting his treatise, which is remarkable chiefly for being one of the few defenses of the civil-law jurisdiction of the Admiralty Court ever

drews, had published in 1590 a brief outline of maritime law entitled "*The Sea Law of Scotland*".[85] After James succeeded Elizabeth to the English throne in 1603, Welwood sought to win recognition from the Scottish-born sovereign through publication of a revised and expanded version of his earlier work, which first appeared in print in 1613 under the name "*An Abridgement of All Sea-Laws*".[86] The substance of the work, however, was aimed at a broad audience in which the author included "sea-faring persons in every order, whether Commanders, Iudges, Skippers, Mariners, Merchants, Passengers, Fishers, Ferryers, Watermen, &c."[87] This relatively short work (77 pages in length) drew upon a patchwork of sources, including the medieval codes of Oleron and the Baltic ports, as well as the Roman law. Welwood described the relationship between the ancient Roman law—the basis of the civil law of his day—and the medieval maritime codes and statutes as follows:

> Notwithstanding all these many, divers, and late Statutes and Ordinances made and set forth these sixeteene hundreth years, by the nations, people & Princes above written, in the decision of causes, and iudging of Sea-faring controversies; that fragment of the *Rhodian* law, extant and Latinized by [mid-sixteenth century scholar] *Simon Shardius*, intituled by him, *Leges navales Rhodioru* [*sic*] & *selecta Leges Rhodiorum*, with the interpretations and commentations, devised thereupon by the olde Romane *Iurisconsults* insert in the *Pandects*; together with the constitutions made by the Romane Emperours, contayned in the *Cod.* and *Novells* at large: as it were by common consent of Nations, obtaines the prerogative throughout all *Europe*; as in *Great Britaine*, *Germany*, *France*, *Italie*, and *Spaine*. Such is the force and authority of the Civill Romane Lawe amongst all Nations Christian.[88]

Thus Welwood creates the impression that the medieval maritime customs and enactments were outgrowths of the civil law of Rome, re-enforcing the im-

---

written by a practitioner of the common law. Nevertheless, the alphabetically-arranged treatise addresses substantive matters—such as charterparties, deodands, "jetzon", "flotzon" and wreck—as incidental or ancillary to the principal purpose of outlining the parameters of the Admiralty Court's jurisdiction.

85. WELVOD, THE SEA-LAW OF SCOTLAND, *supra* note 7. The title was somewhat misleading, as the pamphlet-sized volume of civil law contained no Scottish innovations. *See* COQUILLETTE, CIVILIAN WRITERS, *supra* note 7, at 128 n. 76. For Welwood's biographical details, *see* HOLDSWORTH, *supra* note 6, Vol. V, at 10–11.

86. WELVVOD, ABRIDGEMENT, *supra* note 43, at 6–7.

87. *Id.* at 4.

88. *Id.* at 4–5.

pression—or perhaps more accurately the illusion—of international uniformity resting upon unbroken ties to a body of law from antiquity, the force of which remained binding on all of Renaissance Europe. While one would expect a Scot to display a greater affinity for the civil law than his English counterparts, his insistence upon the continuity of maritime law from antiquity to the early modern age appears strained. The most striking feature of Welwood's statement, however, is its ambiguity. Did the "Civill Romane Lawe" retain its authority and force because subsequent customs and statutes were grounded in it, or because the "common consent of Nations"—the *ius gentium*—had been recognized by and incorporated into the civil law of Rome and was thus (at least in a civilian's eyes) as much a part of the civil law as were the Roman laws themselves? This question, while seldom addressed, is lurking behind much of the struggle between the civilians and the common lawyers for control of maritime jurisdiction throughout the seventeenth century.[89]

If Welwood had cast his net broadly to encompass a wide range of prospective readers, the same cannot be said of Gerard Malynes. Malynes, who was born in 1586 in Belgium of English parents, spent his life grappling with issues of international trade and currency rather than with concepts of law. He served the English Crown in the capacity of a trade commissioner in the Low Countries and later as a commissioner of mint affairs.[90] Proficient in nine languages, including Latin, he often acted as a translator for the king and an assortment of visiting dignitaries. Moreover, Malynes spent fifty years of his life involved in currency exchange, insurance, and international trade.[91] Thus when his *Consuetudo, vel Lex Mercatoria* was published in 1622, it is not surprising that it was directed at his fellow merchants. Indeed, unlike Welwood's

89. Characterizing the *lex maritima* as the part of the *ius gentium*, however, posed a practical problem for the English civilians who were seeking to protect admiralty jurisdiction from encroachment by the common law, as it was equally possible for the common lawyers to argue that if such customs were binding on all nations, they were by definition incorporated into the Common Law of England, and as such should be enforced in the common-law courts. *See* Coquillette, Civilian Writers, *supra* note 7, at 135.

90. *Id.* at 133.

91. Gerard Malynes, *Consuetudo, Vel Lex Mercatoria*. Or the Ancient Law-Merchant (London: Adam Islip, 1622), which has long been out of print, recently was made available to modern readers in a critical edition by Katie F. Hamilton (Phoenix: Metheglin Press, 1995) with the words "The Merchant's Almanac of 1622" appended to Malynes' original title. Hamilton preserved Malynes' original spelling, but there are changes in the pagination. As this edition is more readily available than facsimiles of the first edition, all references in this work will be to Hamilton's text. For the biographical information on Malynes, *see* Hamilton's Foreword at i-3–i-4.

treatises, *Consuetudo* was not really work on maritime law, but rather a practical merchant's manual that addressed maritime matters in conjunction with other mercantile concerns. Of the three books that make up the *Consuetudo*, only Book I contains chapters devoted to maritime law. As one would expect, Malynes, the experienced merchant, opted to focus on topics largely ignored by legal scholars, such as marine insurance, while devoting significantly less attention to the issues of collision, seamen's wages, and droits of the Admiralty that had preoccupied the compilers of the medieval codes.[92] Also missing from the *Consuetudo* are the endless series of hypotheticals that one encounters in the *Digest* and in much of the medieval materials. To a great extent, omission of these hypotheticals reflects Malynes' ambivalent feelings toward scholars of the civil law, about whom he remarks:

> [D]ivers... doctors and learned of the civile Law, have made many long discourses and volumes of bookes of the questionable matters falling out amongst Merchants, for and concerning merchandise, which are yearely observations or booke cases and precedents; by the reading whereof, Merchants are like rather to metamorphose their profession and become lawyers, than truely to attaine to the particuler knowledge of the said Customes or Law-merchant: For they have armed questions and disputations full of quillets and distinctions over-curious and precise, and many of them to small purpose...[93]

Nevertheless, Malynes cites civilians when it serves his purpose, even for those matters, such as charterparties and marine insurance, in which his practical experience was at its most extensive.[94]

---

92. The relevant Chapters of Book I are 21–35, the bulk of which (24–28) address "assurances" (*i.e.* marine insurance). Of the remaining Chapters, 21 and 22 address charterparties, bills of lading, and the master's duties to the merchant, while Chapter 32 addresses partnership in voyages. Chapter 31 discusses bottomry, while Chapters 33 and 34 contain general information on shipping and navigation (including an abridgement of the Hanse Sea-laws in Chapter 33). Chapter 29 deals with shipwreck. The remaining two chapters address what today would be referred to as public international law of the sea. *See* MALYNES, *CONSUETUDO* (Hamilton ed.), *supra* note 91, at 98–137.

93. *Id.* at 7.

94. Malynes opted for the convention of referring to material gleaned from the works of civil-law scholars as the work of "civilians" rather than identifying the authors by name "to avoid ambiguity and uncertaintie in the Contents of the Booke". *Id.* at 9. For his use of civilian writings in the context of insurance, *see* Chapter 28, *Id.* at 115; for civilian support in his discussion of charterparties, *see* Chapter 21, *Id.* at 100. In addition to works of civilians, Malynes draws heavily from the Laws of Oleron and the sea-laws of the Baltic ports.

As to the source of the law merchant itself, Malynes contends that it is grounded in reason and the law of nature:

> Reason requireth a Law not too cruell in her Frownes, nor too partiall in her Favors. Neither of these defects are incedent to the Law-Merchant, because the same doth properly consist of the Custome of Merchants in the course of Trafficke, and is approoved by all Nations.... I have intitled the Booke, according to the ancient name of *Lex Mercatoria*, and not *Ius Mercatorum*; because it is a Customary Law approved by the authoritie of all Kingdomes and Commonweales, and not a Law established by the Soveraigntie of any Prince, either in the first foundation or by continuance of time.[95]

Nevertheless, despite this definition, Malynes is careful to distinguish the law merchant from the *ius gentium*, which he admits often has been described in the same terms. Both, he concedes, derive their binding force by a tacit acknowledgement of custom among nations. *Ius gentium*, however, may be a product of a transitory consensus among sovereigns, while the *lex mercatoria*, formed over time through a trial-and-error refinement of customs, is more reflective of true "reason" and "nature".[96]

The same demand that prompted Malynes to write the *Consuetudo* also served as the impetus behind the publication of two other prominent treatises on the *lex mercatoria* in the mid-seventeenth century. John Marius, as had Malynes before him, directed his *Advice Cocerning Bills of Exchange* toward a readership of merchants.[97] This work on a narrow trade-law subject remained influential for generations, and was even praised by Kent nearly two centuries after its publication for the thoroughness of its treatment of its subject.[98] The second treatise, Charles Molloy's *De Jure Maritimo et Navali*, however, was unique in that its author aimed the book principally at a new readership—the common lawyers—who through changes in the allocation of maritime ju-

95. *Id.* at 3 (*inconsistencies in spelling reproduced from the original text*).

96. *Id.* at 6. Extending this notion of the self-correcting benefits of rules that develop over time, Malynes echoes the writings of Coke and Hale (perhaps unintentionally) when he remarks that: "Customes are the best interpreters of Lawes, either for suppressing of vice, or establishing of Vertue". *Id.* at 7.

97. JOHN MARIUS, ADVICE CONCERNING BILLS OF EXCHANGE (1st ed. 1651; 2nd ed., London: W.H. for Nicholas Bourne, 1655) (hereinafter MARIUS). For discussion of how the common law and the civil law respectively treated the topic of bills of exchange, *see* COQUILLETTE, CIVILIAN WRITERS, *supra* note 7, at 215–254.

98. KENT, COMMENTARIES, *supra* note 44, Vol. III, at 126.

risdiction were taking an increasingly active part in litigation of matters that scarcely three generations earlier had been the exclusive province of the civilians of the Court of Admiralty.[99] Despite the title, the bulk of substantive maritime law in *De Jure Maritimo* is contained in Book II's sixteen chapters, which cover such topics as charterparties, contribution, marine insurance, bottomry, barratry, and wreck.[100] As one would expect, many of Molloy's citations are to common-law authorities, from Bracton to Coke and Selden. First published in 1676, the popular treatise underwent revisions for eleven editions, the last of which was published in 1793.[101] Its popularity, however, was no guarantee against criticism. *De Jure Maritimo*—for the most part a distillation of the works of earlier authors—lacked both originality and an underlying theoretical framework. In places, it also lacked detail; Kent compared Molloy's treatment of bills of exchange unfavorably with that of his contemporary Marius, characterizing it as superficial, a view shared by some modern commentators.[102] Nonetheless, designed as a comprehensive summary of commercial

---

99. For discussion, *see* Coquillette, Civilian Writers, *supra* note 7, at 140–146.

100. Molloy's treatise is subdivided into three "Books". Charterparties, freight, and demurrage are addressed in Chapter 4 (Molloy, (3d ed., Bellinger), *supra* note 82, at 227–236), while contribution and "assurance" are addressed in Chapters 6 and 7 respectively (*Id.* at 246–264). Chapter 11 deals with bottomry (*Id.* at 288–298). "Barratry", a master's theft or usurpation of a vessel for his own purposes, is covered in Chapter 3 (*Id.* at 218–226). Wreck is the topic of Chapter 5 (*Id.* at 237–245). The first two chapters cover the rights and obligations of shipowners and masters (*Id.* at 201–217). Chapter 10, for which Molloy received much criticism from scholars of later periods, addresses bills of exchange (*Id.* at 272–287). For discussion, *see infra* note 101 and text accompanying.

101. Despite the Latin title, the bulk of the text of the first edition was in English, and it was sufficiently popular to prompt the publishing of a second edition the following year in 1677. None of the eleven editions were mere reprintings of preceding editions; each contained new material reflecting evolution of the substantive law. All references contained herein (unless noted otherwise) are to the third edition of 1682. Unfortunately for future generations of legal scholars, two London printers, John Bellinger and Thomas Passenger, each produced third editions of *De Jure Maritimo* in 1682. Predictably, the pagination was not identical. I have opted to use the text of Bellinger, the publisher of the first two editions, largely because it is more frequently found in libraries' rare book rooms and microform collections. Thus to avoid confusion, references will be to Molloy, (3d ed., Bellinger).

102. *See* Kent, Commentaries, *supra* note 44, Vol. III, at 126 (contrasting Molloy's treatment of bills of exchange with that of Marius). Professor Coquillette shares much of Kent's opinion on Molloy's lack of thoroughness as a legal scholar, but he concedes that his book is "clear, well-indexed, and readable". *See* Coquillette, Civilian Writers, *supra* note 7, at 140–148. For an interesting discussion on how the common law and the civil law differed in substantive treatment of bills of exchange, *see Id.* at 217–254.

and maritime law written for practitioners of the common law, it was unique in its time, and its influence was felt at the bar and bench alike. Even Lord Mansfield cited it, and did so in no less conspicuous a place than in the seminal maritime and commercial case *Luke v. Lyde*.[103] While Mansfield's use of Molloy's work lent an air of legitimacy to it, in doing so he also had ushered in a new era. The flexible business practices of the *lex mercatoria* and *lex maritima*, praised by Malynes because they had been refined through the ages by practical use, had become rigid, rendered static and immutable by the common law's doctrine of *stare decisis*.[104]

By the time of Arthur Browne, who began his study of the civil law while Mansfield occupied the bench, the High Court of Admiralty retained jurisdiction over seamen's wages and express hypothecation, as well as torts committed at sea; for all other matters, jurisdiction was vested in the courts of common law.[105] Nevertheless, it was not differences in the substantive maritime law

---

103. *Luke v Lyde*, 97 Eng. Rep. 614, 617 (K. B. 1789) (*citing* the 5th ed. of *De Jure Maritimo*, *paraphrasing* Malynes' *Consuetudo*). For discussion of the accuracy of Burrows' published report of Mansfield's opinion in this case, which involved apportioning of freight costs after the loss of a vessel, *see* James Oldham, The Mansfield Manuscripts and the Growth of English Law in the Eighteenth Century (2 vols., Chapel Hill: University of North Carolina Press) Vol. I, at 168–169. Mansfield also cited Molloy in *Pillans v. Van Mierop*, 97 Eng. Rep. 1035, 1041 (K. B. 1765) (removing the requirement of consideration from commercial contracts).

104. Coquillette contends that to some degree, the civilians were in agreement with Malynes in the need for mercantile rules flexible enough to change with evolving commercial practices. Coquillette, Civilian Writers, *supra* note 7, at 153, 157. With regard to the situation that prevailed after Mansfield incorporated the customs and usages of merchants into the common law, however, Coquillette observes:

> "Coke's views, as expanded by Molloy and Blackstone, contained the seeds of future common law rigidity. If a custom was substantive and demanded by the requirements of a universal reason, its contents, once determined, were determined forever, particularly within a common law precedent system. As [Professor John] Baker has observed, 'Lord Mansfield's law was binding on his successors; and so, to the extent that it embodied mere current usage, it froze the practice of Georgian merchants as the permanent law of England.' Change in the customs and the needs of merchants could not easily change the law merchant once it was so defined and incorporated.... This was...precisely the reason why Ridley [the seventeenth-century English civilian] refused to consider the law merchant part of the 'law of nations', but insisted that it was a special law for merchants instead."

Id. at 132.

105. "Express hypothecations" are those in which a master, needing repairs or supplies for his ship while in a foreign port, signs agreements pledging an interest in the ship itself in exchange for the needed goods or services. Browne characterizes the extent of admiralty

applied by the Admiralty Court that distinguished it from the common-law courts. Indeed, in the time of John Exton, who served as judge of the High Court of the Admiralty after the Restoration, there were few differences in the *lex maritima* as interpreted by the Admiralty and common law respectively; the significant difference instead lay in the procedures employed.[106]

The foregoing examination of the history of substantive maritime law in England leads to two conclusions. First, contrary to the view propounded by seventeenth-century civilians who defended the jurisdiction of the High Court of Admiralty against perceived common-law encroachments, the *lex maritima* of the middle ages was not the nation's inheritance from Imperial Rome, recorded in the *Corpus Juris Civilis* and passed down for a millennium through successive generations to the Plantagenet kings of England. Much of the law of the *Corpus Juris*—the Civil Law of Rome—had been abrogated (or at least greatly modified) by the customs later recorded in the medieval maritime codes. In short, there is nothing about maritime law—either intrinsically or historically—which makes it a part of the civil law. To the extent that the civil law could lay claim to it at all, it would be (as Welwood suggested) under the concept of *ius gentium*, and it is a precarious theory that would seek to make customary *lex maritima* a part of the civil law merely because the civil law acknowledged circumstances under which its customs were binding.[107] Nevertheless, the civil law *is* relevant to maritime law in England because the court that once adjudicated most maritime matters—the High Court of Admiralty—utilized procedures borrowed from the civil law. Secondly, at the close of the eighteenth-century, a legal practitioner wishing to educate himself on some specific point of maritime law would have experienced great difficulty.

---

jurisdiction at the outset of the nineteenth century as follows:

> "The result of our enquiries... as to the extent of the jurisdiction in the instance court of admiralty, which is at present seemingly allowed by the law courts, is, that it is confined in matters of contract to suits for seamen's wages, or those on hypothecations; in matters of tort to actions for assault, collision, and spoil; and in quasi contracts to actions by part owners for security, and actions of salvage; but if a party institute a suit in that court on a charter-party, for freight..., in a cause of [general] average and contribution, or to decide the property of a ship, and be not prohibited [by writ from a common-law court], I do not see how the court could refuse to entertain it..."

BROWNE, *supra* note 9, Vol. II, at 121–122. Elsewhere, Browne is highly critical of rules of jurisdiction based upon locality rather than subject-matter, observing that it would be absurd for a court of admiralty to entertain an action for breach of a promise of marriage simply because it had been made at sea. *Id.* at 94.

106. COQUILLETTE, CIVILIAN WRITERS, *supra* note 7, at 186.

107. *See supra* note 88 and text accompanying.

England lacked a substantive maritime code, and records of maritime decisions—both those of the Admiralty Court and those of the common law—were not published. Moreover, as precedent was of limited importance to the civil-law adjudicature of the Admiralty Court, its records, even if made available, lacked the detailed descriptions of *ratio decidendi* associated with modern published opinions. These obstacles would have posed little concern for an experienced practitioner in London, who would have relied upon his own memory and notebooks, as well as the advice of his colleagues, to arrive upon the applicable rule of law. For the less experienced colonial practitioner, there were only the treatises, which (as we have seen) drew almost indiscriminately upon an assortment of sources—merchants' customs, the Roman law, medieval codes of England and of foreign ports, English statutes, civil-law commentators, Coke, Selden, classical authors, and even the Bible—leaving the inexperienced advocate with at best a muddled impression of the substantive law and its origins. The resulting confusion was compounded by the fact that colonial practitioners were well aware of the struggle between the High Court of Admiralty and the common-law courts for jurisdiction over maritime matters, which manifested itself in America with uncertainty regarding the proper channels for appealing in England the maritime decisions of the plantations' courts.[108]

The Struggle for Jurisdiction

"So far there is unimpeachable evidence", Sir Travers Twiss observed, "that before the Admiral's jurisdiction was established in England, and the decision of questions of contract and tort on the high seas was assigned to the Admiral's Court, there were courts in England whose province it was to administer a common Law Marine to foreign equally as to British merchants and mariners."[109] Indeed, there is no record of the office of Admiral before 1293, and prior to the reign of Edward III, maritime matters were tried by the common-law courts, chancery, or in some cases the King's Council.[110] Commercial matters involving small sums often found their way into the "piepowder

108. *See e.g.* Owen & Tolley, *supra* note 5, at 190–200; *see also* Helen Crump, Colonial Admiralty Jurisdiction in the Seventeenth Century (London: Longmans, Green & Co., 1931) at 161–163.

109. Twiss, *supra* note 4, Vol. II, at xxxvii.

110. Marsden, Select Pleas I, *supra* note 73, Introduction at xv.

courts", or courts of the fairs, the summary procedures of which saved litigants both time and expense.[111] In addition, there were the courts of the Cinque Ports, which continued to try maritime causes centuries after the creation of the Admiralty Court, deriving their claim to jurisdiction from the general terms of their charters and the antiquity of the practice.[112] Insight into the procedure employed by local port courts has been preserved in the Domesday of Ipswich, the contents of which date from the reign of King John.[113] The earliest reference to judicial powers vested in the Admiral dates to 1337, when commissioners were appointed to try cases involving sailors of the fleet. The evidence indicates that these commissioners convinced Edward III of the need for a full-fledged permanent admiralty court three years later, in the wake of

---

111. In 1303, the king gave sanction to these tribunals—already active since the previous century—thereby providing a guarantee that foreign merchants would have access to inexpensive and speedy procedures for resolution of their disputes. As with the common-law courts, the piepowder courts kept rolls, some of which survive today. The most common type of maritime claim litigated here was breach of a contract of carriage. As England in the thirteenth and fourteenth centuries was principally an exporter of raw materials, it was not then the commercial center that it later became. As a result, foreign merchants often selected other *fora* for resolving their disputes, and thus the English piepowder courts—unlike their Continental counterparts—played at best a minor role in the development of English commercial law. For discussion *see* HOLDSWORTH, *supra* note 6, Vol. V, at 106–114.

112. The "Cinque Ports"—Dover, Sandwich, Romney, Hastings, and Hythe—derived their name and privileges from William the Conqueror. While these same privileges subsequently were extended to Winchelsea and Rye, the name "Cinque" was retained. For discussion, *see* Liang, *supra* note 76, at 176. It was fairly common for the charters of other coastal towns to retain a more limited jurisdiction over wrecks, and as late as the nineteenth century, the towns of Dunwich and Southwold attempted simultaneously to assert jurisdiction over the same salvaged barrel of whisky. *See* MARSDEN, SELECT PLEAS II, *supra* note 53, at xxii.

113. Ipswich, or "Gippeswich", which traces its origins to the Saxon period, received its charter from King John in the second year of his reign. TWISS, *supra* note 4, Vol. II, at x–xi; xvii. The Domesday itself dates from this period, although the surviving manuscripts, from which Sir Travers derives his text, are of the fourteenth century. *Id.* at lxxxiii–lxxiv; 16–209 (text of Domesday). The Ipswich text was not particularly unique in its own time; other maritime towns maintained similar records. Unfortunately, it is one of the few of its kind to have survived, for, as Twiss notes: "The Domesdays of the English maritime boroughs are so far valuable as they disclose to us the existence of borough courts in England at a very early period administering a customary Law of the Sea to passing mariners, and the Domesday of Ipswich helps to carry back our knowledge of this practice to a period almost contemporaneous with the reign of Richard I." *Id.* at xxxvii. Twiss observes further that the Court of Ipswich (unlike the High Court of Admiralty of the Tudor period) utilized a jury in adjudicating maritime matters. *Id.* at lxx.

the Battle of Sluys.[114] Within twenty years, the new Court of Admiralty had been granted instance jurisdiction, *i.e.* the power to adjudicate disputes of a maritime nature between private parties.[115] The Inquisition of Queenborow established the procedures that were to be used in the court.[116]

It must be emphasized that this new court—unlike the common-law courts—was a creation of royal prerogative.[117] This prerogative was not with-

---

114. Marsden, Select Pleas I, *supra* note 73, at xli, xxxvi. There is some debate regarding whether the admiral exercised judicial powers—or organized a court under his auspices—somewhat earlier. Zouch identifies an ordinance of Edward I, which provided:

> *"That every Contract made between Merchant and Merchant, or betwixt Merchant and Mariner beyond the Sea, or within the flood-mark, shall be tried before the Admiral, and no wayes elsewhere."*

(emphasis in the original). Zouch, *supra* note 16, at 108. Liang, *supra* note 76, at 164, observes that: "It would serve no useful purpose to attempt here, were it possible, to fix with certainty the date of the establishment of the admiralty court." Nevertheless, despite the controversy, it appears safe to assume that the court was created in the first half of the fourteenth century.

115. In 1354, 27 Ed. III, Stat. 2, c. 13 removed the requirement that foreign merchants sue at common law for recovery of goods taken by pirates and subsequently offered for sale on English soil, and by 1357, the Admiral was adjudicating cases of spoil. For discussion, *see* Liang, *supra* note 76, at 166. The Admiral's patents of 1360 and 1361 granted a more general instance jurisdiction to the Admiral and his court. Marsden, Select Pleas I, *supra* note 73, at xlii.

116. Marsden, Select Pleas I, *supra* note 73 at xlvii. The text of the Inquisition of Queenborow, the fourth section of the *Black Book of the Admiralty*, is reproduced in Twiss, *supra* note 4, Vol. I, at 133–177. For a brief description of the method of commencing an action in the Court of Admiralty, *see* Marsden, Select Pleas I, *supra* note 73, at lxxi–lxxii.

117. Liang, *supra* note 76, at 167. As a prerogative court, its powers were defined in the royal patents issued to the admirals. From the earliest period, these patents had provided for the appointment of "deputies" (*i.e.* vice-admirals) and "lieutenants" to enable the admirals to carry out their duties. *See* The Black Book of the Admiralty, Part A, *in* Twiss, *supra* note 4, Vol. I, at 3. "Lieutenants" later were held to be judges. See Wynne, *supra* note 72, Vol. II, at 706. Twiss, *supra* note 4, Vol. I, at 409, reproduces the patent issued to Sir Thomas Beaufort as Admiral. As initially there were several admirals, there were as many admiralty courts. Over time, as the powers of the office of Admiral became consolidated into one person, so also the various admiralty courts became unified under the name "High Court of Admiralty". This, however, did not end the practice of holding admiralty sessions in ports outside of London. Courts of Vice-Admiralty, subordinate to the High Court, were instituted in English ports—and later in the colonies—to adjudicate maritime matters. Despite receiving appointment from the admiral rather than directly from the Crown, by the reign of Elizabeth it was established that the Judge of the High Court could continue to adjudicate cases even in the event of the death of the admiral. *See* Mears, *supra* note 36, at 354; Marsden, Select Pleas II, *supra* note 53, at xii. For general discussion of the power of the admiral to appoint judges, *see* Liang, *supra* note 76, at 169; Mears, *supra* note 36, at 336–338; Marsden, Select Pleas I, *supra* note 73, at lix–lx.

out bounds; the parameters of the court's jurisdiction periodically were expanded and contracted by statute. Nevertheless, its grounding in royal authority gave it the opportunity to develop along its own course, independent of the traditions of the common law. From the beginning, the court's most striking feature was its adoption of the civil law.[118] To be sure, the civil law had several procedural advantages over the common law of the time. The civil law's rules for joinder of parties greatly simplified litigation, particularly in cases of seamen's wages.[119] This was crucial for ordinary sailors, as the costs of litigating in the common-law courts often would have exceeded their recoveries, or if not, at the very least the length of the proceedings would have forced many either to forego their wages for the voyage in dispute or to lose the opportunity of employment on the next ship to sail.[120] In addition to joinder of parties, the civil law also permitted wage-claims and claims for freight arising out of the same voyage to be tried together.[121] Added to these specific advantages, the civil law held several more general procedural advantages over the common law, which were readily recognized by merchants. One notable difference was that the rules of evidence provided for the substitution of depositions in place of live testimony, a feature that could prove especially beneficial by permitting witnesses to return to useful occupations at sea rather than

---

118. *Id.* at 169.

119. For joinder in suits for seamen's wages *see e.g.* Zouch, *supra* note 16, at 147. The civil law's rules of joinder were helpful in other forms of disputes, such as those between joint holders of merchandise (*see Id.* at 143–144) and part-owners of a vessel in an action of account (*see* George F. Steckley, *Merchants and the Admiralty Court During the English Revolution*, 22 Am. J. Legal Hist. 137, 171 (1978) (hereinafter Steckley)). Steckley also notes that: "Private merchants who together wrote maritime insurance could join to sue the policyholder for the premium." *Id.* at 171.

120. Jenkins emphasized this point in his speech before the House of Lords:

> "And the Mariners had better lose the Wages of a whole Voyage, than not to go off [on] the next [ship] that offers itself. They and their Families would be starved by staying at Home till the Term, and then the Wages recovered would scarce quit the Costs, when every one is forced to bring his Action singly (as he must) at Common Law."

Jenkins, *"Argument,"* *in* Wynne, *supra* note 72, Vol. I, at lxxxii. Jenkins' statement contains another important advantage that admiralty had over the common law. While not an intrinsic part of the civil law, English admiralty courts—unlike courts of common law—did not limit their adjudication to terms meeting at fixed times in the year. Indeed, after the creation of vice admiralty courts by royal patent in 1536, merchants and mariners across the realm had immediate access to maritime courts, which sat daily from "tide to tide". *See* Liang, *supra* note 76, at 177–178.

121. *Id.* at 80. *See also* Browne, Vol. II, *supra* note 9, at 86.

remaining idle in port awaiting a common-law trial.[122] As for the other principal advantages, Holdsworth explains:

> The reasons why the Admiralty was assuming this jurisdiction are obvious. In the first place, the connection between cases which arise in connection with merchant shipping and those which arise out of foreign trade must always be close. In the second place, the common law rules as to venue prevented the common law courts from assuming jurisdiction over such cases. In the third place, the civil law procedure of the Admiralty, because it was based on the technical ideas of the civil law, was far more intelligible to the foreign merchant than the procedure of the common law courts.... [Nevertheless,] even in this medieval period there were signs that the court of Admiralty would not be permitted to get a monopoly of this kind of business without a struggle.[123]

Ultimately, the focal point for critics of the Admiralty Court was the fact that it could operate without a jury.[124] By dispensing with the jury, the court was

---

122. *See* Zouch, *supra* note 16, at 129. For discussion, *see also* Steckley, *supra* note 119, at 172; Coquillette, Civilian Writers, *supra* note 7, at 178. Although sworn statements were entered into evidence, the Admiralty Court also permitted live testimony. For the rules applicable to live testimony, *see* Browne, *supra* note 9, Vol. II, at 420–425.

123. Holdsworth, *supra* note 6, Vol. V, at 128. Under "the common law's rules of venue", a common law court could not assert jurisdiction over a contract signed on foreign soil or a tort committed outside of the geographical limits of a county of England. For discussion, *see* Marsden, Select Pleas II, *supra* note 53, at xliii.

124. Through the course of the long and bitter struggle between the civilians and the common lawyers, it was axiomatic that admiralty courts operated without juries. For the common lawyers, trials sans juries were reviled as destructive of liberty, while the civilians emphasized the advantages in efficiency, especially given the role of the English jury in the medieval and Renaissance periods. (For discussion of the role of early juries, *see e.g.* Coquillette, Civilian Writers, *supra* note 7, at 108). Contemporary impressions of Admiralty's stance on use of juries is perhaps best expressed by Fortescue, who maintained that juries were omitted because: "...in these cases there be no neighbors found, by whose oathes, Iuries of twelue men may bee made, as in contractes, and other cases, arising within the Realme of England is accustomed to bee done." John Fortescue, *De Laudibus Legum Angliae* (London: Companie of Stationers, 1616) at 74. Nevertheless, juries were employed on occasion in Admiralty. Although the "Common Courts" convened daily under the vice-admiralty patents (*see supra* note 120) sat without juries, the "Courts of Enquiry", which convened twice per year under those same patents to address matters inimical to the "peace and safety of the Commonwealth", utilized juries of twelve to fifteen men. Liang, *supra* note 76, at 177–178. During his tenure as Judge of the High Court of Admiralty in the late Tudor period (*circa* 1591), Sir Julius Caesar "rode circuit" to various ports in remote corners of the Realm. His instructions for juries at these Admiralty Sessions are still

able to streamline its procedure, but efficiency came at a price.[125] A legacy of Saxon times reinforced in Article 39 of *Magna Carta*, the jury was the cornerstone of common-law procedure.[126] Admittedly, the lack of a jury was generally not troubling to foreign merchants accustomed to Continental commercial courts. Nevertheless, in time it became a convenient target for the common-law faction, a symbol which simultaneously showed that the Admiralty Court was a potential threat to civil liberties and, perhaps more importantly, "non-English". This notion, nascent in the fourteenth century, was to become a centerpiece of the Parliamentarians' attack on royal prerogative at the outset of the Civil War, and still later a much-recited "grievance" among American pamphleteers as strained relations with the mother country reached the breaking point in the 1770s.[127]

---

extant. *See* MARSDEN, SELECT PLEAS II, *supra* note 53, at xvii, xxxii n. 3; *see also supra* note 72 and text accompanying for Sir Leoline Jenkins' instructions at Admiralty Sessions.

125. It has often been argued that the procedures of the civil law were less cumbersome and time-consuming than those of the common law. While it is certainly true that a court that holds daily sessions is more expeditious than one that holds sessions only twice per year, Admiralty's daily sessions were not an intrinsic part of the civil law. With regard to the length of time required to try an admiralty case, Holdsworth observes:

> "[Admiralty's] procedure, though it was the lengthy procedure of the civil law, and not the summary procedure used by the Star Chamber, the Chancery and the Court of Requests, or by the commercial courts of the Continent, was at least as well, if not better, adapted to the trial of commercial cases than the equally lengthy procedure of the common law."

HOLDSWORTH, *supra* note 6, Vol. V, at 138–139. Nevertheless, the Admiralty Court was able to reduce time and costs in simple cases through use of an expedited procedure. *See* BROWNE, *supra* note 9, Vol. II, at 428.

126. There is no end to the panegyrics composed in honor of the English common-law jury. Blackstone's terse description of the esteem in which the institution was held—at least in common-law rhetoric—serves as a prototypical example:

> "...whether or no their juries consisted precisely of twelve men, or were bound to a strict unanimity; yet the general constitution of this admirable criterion of truth, and most important guardian both of public and private liberty, we owe to our Saxon ancestors."

WILLIAM BLACKSTONE, COMMENTARIES ON THE LAWS OF ENGLAND (4 vols., 1st ed., Oxford: Clarendon Press, 1765–1769; *reproduced in facsimile with commentary,* Chicago: University of Chicago Press, 1979), Vol. IV, at 407 (hereinafter BLACKSTONE).

127. Liang, *supra* note 76, at 169–170 (observing that a petition was presented to Parliament in 1371 seeking redress from trials sans juries). For the controversy regarding the lack of a jury in colonial vice-admiralty proceedings, *see e.g.* CARL UBBELOHDE, THE VICE ADMIRALTY COURTS AND THE AMERICAN REVOLUTION (Chapel Hill: University of North Carolina Press, 1960) at 77.

Initially, the Admiralty Court flourished. After its founding, common-law courts could continue to try maritime cases, but only by special commission.[128] By the mid-1360s, the common-law courts had acknowledged that the Admiralty was a "*court of record*", the decision of which was to be regarded as *res judicata*.[129] The Admiralty Court even had gone so far as to interfere with proceedings before common-law courts.[130] This was soon to change. Amid mounting pressures from the borough courts and the courts of common law, the Admiralty was further shaken by a series of irregularities in the court of the Admiral of the West, John Holland, Earl of Huntingdon.[131] The response was swift. In 1389, Parliament enacted a statute limiting the Admirals' jurisdiction:

> ITEM, Forasmuch as a great and common Clamour and Complaint hath been oftentimes made before this Time, and yet is, for that the Admirals and their Deputies hold their Sessions within divers Places of this Realm as well within Franchise as without, accroaching to them greater Authority than belongeth to their Office, in Prejudice of

---

128. Marsden, Select Pleas II, *supra* note 53, at xliii. In addition, in 1361 the Council determined that "felonies, trespasses and injuries" occurring at sea should be tried at admiralty rather than at common law. While this policy enhanced the scope of admiralty's jurisdiction by granting express recognition of admiralty's power to adjudicate these claims, it did not do so at the expense of the common law, which in the fourteenth century lacked jurisdiction over matters occurring outside of the counties of England. *See* Mears, *supra* note 36, at 329.

129. Marsden, Select Pleas I, *supra* note 73, at xlv, notes that:

> "In 1364 a writ of *supersedeas* issued to the justices commanding them to stay proceedings in a case of nuisance which was pending before them against Lionel de Bradenham upon an indictment for driving piles into the bed of certain creeks or waters near Colchester. The *supersedeas* issued upon the ground that the matter had been dealt with in the court of the admiral, and the record of the proceedings before the admiral is referred to in the writ. It appears, therefore, that at this date his court was recognized by the courts at Westminster as a court of record."

In 1369, a case involving a charterparty came to the same result, when the defendants' vessel was discharged from arrest following the production of a certificate showing that the defendants had prevailed in proceedings before the Admiralty Court. *Id.* at xlvi. These cases reconfirm the status of an admiral's tribunal as a court of record as laid out in an ordinance that Twiss contends dates from the reign of Richard I. Twiss, *supra* note 4, Vol. I, at xlvii.

130. Marsden, Select Pleas I, *supra* note 73, at xliv–xlv (citing a case of wreck of 1365).

131. *Id.*at l–li; Liang, *supra* note 76, at 170. Among other complaints against Holland were the removal of causes from the Court of the West to Southwark, on the south side of the Thames in London. Mears, *supra* note 36, at 330 n. 1.

> our Lord the King, and the common Law of the Realm, and in diminishing of divers Franchises, and in Destruction and impoverishing of the common People: It is accorded and assented, That the Admirals and their Deputies shall not meddle from henceforth of any Thing done within the Realm, but only of a Thing done upon the Sea, as it hath been used in the Time of the noble Prince King Edward, Grandfather of our Lord the King that now is.[132]

In response to the "great and grievous Complaint of all the Commons...that the Admirals and their Deputies do incroach to them divers Jurisdictions", this general admonition to the Admirals was followed two years later by a second statute providing more specific restrictions on the matters over which their courts had cognizance:

> ...It is declared, ordained, and established, That of all Manner of Contracts, Pleas, and Quarrels, and all other Things rising within the Bodies of the Counties, as well by Land as by Water, and also of Wreck of the Sea, the Admiral's Court shall have no Manner of Cognizance, Power, nor Jurisdiction; but all such Manner of Contracts, Pleas, and Quarrels, and all other Things rising within the Bodies of Counties, as well by Land as by Water, as afore, and also Wreck of the Sea, shall be tried, determined, discussed, and remedied by the Laws of the Land, and not before nor by the Admiral, nor his Lieutenant in any wise. Nevertheless, of the Death of a Man, and of a Maihem done in great Ships, being and hovering in the main Stream of great Rivers, only beneath the Bridges of the same Rivers nigh to the Sea, and in none other Places of the same Rivers, the Admiral shall have Cognizance; and also to arrest Ships in the great Flotes for the great Voyages of the King and of the Realm; saving always to the King all Manner of Forfeitures and Profits thereof coming; And he shall have also Jurisdiction upon the said Flotes, during the said Voyages only: saving always to the Lords, Cities, and Boroughs their Liberties and Franchises.[133]

Parliament reinforced these two statutes in 1400 with an enactment providing for punative damages against a party filing an action in Admiralty Court

132. 13 Ric. II, Stat. 1, c. 5. (1389), Statutes of the Realm: Printed by the Command of His Majesty King George the Third (*reprinted* Buffalo: William S. Hein, 1993) Vol. III, at 62 (hereinafter Statutes of the Realm).

133. 15 Ric. II, c. 3 (1391), *in* Statutes of the Realm, *supra* note 132, Vol. III, at 78–79.

in contravention of 13 Ric. II, c. 5.[134] It is perhaps not surprising that the Admiralty retained jurisdiction over matters occurring on the high seas, as they lay beyond the "bodies of counties", the traditional limits of the common law's reach. It is also not surprising that Parliament sought to curtail the Admiralty's overreaching; even such staunch defenders of the Admiralty as Zouch and Jenkins later would concede that the admiralty courts of the fourteenth century had exceeded their powers and encroached on those of the common law.[135] What *is* surprising is the manner in which Parliament chose to define the admiralty jurisdiction. Rather than enumerating the matters over which the Admiralty would retain jurisdiction, Parliament grounded jurisdiction on the principle of geography. It mattered not that charterparties related to a maritime activity; charterparties—and all other maritime contracts signed on English soil—became the province of the common law.[136] Moreover—and most importantly—the common law's jurisdiction was exclusive.

---

134. In addition to requiring the party to pay punative damages to his opponent, he was also to pay damages to the Crown:

> "...the King...hath ordained and stablished, that as touching a Pain to be set upon the Admiral, or his Lieutenant, that the Statute and the Common Law be holden against them; and that he feeleth himself grieved against the Form of the said Statute [13 Ric. II, Stat. 1, c. 5], shall have his Action by Writ grounded upon the Case against him that doth so pursue in the Admiral's Court, and recover his double Damages against the Pursuant; and the same Pursuant shall incur the Pain of Ten Pounds to the King for the Pursuit so made, if he be attainted."

2 Hen. IV, c. 11, *in* STATUTES OF THE REALM, *supra* note 132, Vol. III, at 124.

135. *See* ZOUCH, *supra* note 16, at 41. Jenkins contends that:

> "...They complain that the Admirals came into the Franchises of Lords; but the Lords of Franchises had nothing to do with trying of *maritime Contracts* [*italics in original*] by the maritime Law; the Invasion therefore made upon them, was in meddling with the Land Affairs properly depending before them, which the Admirals had no Right to do..."

Jenkins, "*Argument*", *in* WYNNE, *supra* note 72, Vol. I, at lxxviii.

136. While English civilians and modern scholars alike have been critical of a system of jurisdiction that denies that a contract is maritime because it was signed on *terra firma*, we are perhaps tempted to forget that a contract signed at sea would by the same logic be within the jurisdiction of the admiralty. The classic example is the following *reductio ad absurdum* by Browne:

> "...[I]f, on an East India voyage, one passenger should agree that his daughter should be married to the son of another passenger, and thereupon marriage articles or settlements were drawn, no man pretends that any question arising upon their construction would be triable in the admiralty..."

BROWNE, *supra* note 9, Vol. II, at 94–95.

Throughout the next century, the Admiralty Court languished in comparative obscurity, deprived of jurisdiction over most traditional maritime causes. In 1470, Parliament further eroded the powers of the Court by allowing concurrent jurisdiction to Chancery to hear cases of spoil.[137] The political unrest of the fifteenth century provided few opportunities for any English institution to develop or flourish. As the country was torn apart in the struggles between the Houses of Lancaster and York, it was inevitable that the Admiralty would not escape unscathed. Despite its reduced powers, there is evidence that a significant portion of those cases over which the Court retained power remained unheard.[138] To this point, the conflict between the admirals' courts and the courts of common law had been largely personal, with the various emoluments of the jurisdiction—wrecks, jetsam, royal fish, and most importantly the fees collected for litigating maritime causes—at the center of the controversy.[139] With the advent of the Tudor period, the pecuniary motives of individual judges and advocates on both sides were overshadowed by the conflicts resulting from a shift in economic policies. The England that Henry VII found upon ascending to the throne had been plagued for two generations by internal strife. When his son, Henry VIII, succeeded him, scarcely a quarter of a century had elapsed since the reign of Richard III, and England's economy remained a relative backwater by the standards of other western European nations. Expansion of international trade—particularly the export of manufactured goods

---

137. Marsden, Select Pleas I, *supra* note 73, at lv.

138. There is some question as to whether the dearth of fifteenth-century records is a product of poor record-keeping or an actual decrease in business before the court during this period of unrest. As one commentator observes:

> "It was not to be expected that the admiralty court would immediately find its place in the juridical system. Institutions are the products of slow growth which must be shaped to time and circumstances. There was a place for an admiralty court in England, but its effective functioning needed particular conditioning. The Fifteenth Century could scarcely be called a propitious time for such development. It was a century of conflict and unrest. Besides the preoccupation with the French Wars, there was the constant dissension at home between the Houses of York and Lancaster, which weakened administrative control. It will be readily seen that in admiralty, as doubtless in other jurisdictions, there was necessarily no decrease in the volume of business which should come before the court. It may only be inferred that, because of the laxity of control, many causes never came to be heard. Contemporary documents furnish little information as to the business of the admiral's court during this period. "

Liang, *supra* note 76, at 171–172.

139. Marsden, Select Pleas II, *supra* note 53, at xxiii. *See also supra* notes 81 and 135 and text accompanying.

rather than raw materials—would have served the dual purpose of correcting England's trade imbalance and creating an environment conducive to the development of the financial institutions that later were to become the backbone of the British economy from the Industrial Revolution to the present day. As Henry sought to close the economic gap with his principal European rivals, he did so through a reassertion of royal prerogative.[140] Thus the Admiralty Court became the linchpin in Henry's plan for two reasons. First, as a prerogative court, it was subject to greater royal control than were the courts of common law. Secondly, the Court already operated under the procedural rules of the civil law, making its procedures more familiar to Continental merchants than were those of the courts of Westminster. By shifting to the Admiralty Court the greater share of commercial causes (particularly those involving contracts of affreightment and bills of exchange), it was hoped that England would become a more attractive market for European business interests.[141] With such purposes in mind, a statute enacted in 1540 sought to implement Henry's reforms through expansion of the admiralty jurisdiction.[142]

Despite the new legislation, there remained the problem of the statutes of Richard II, which established geographical limitations upon the Admiralty Court. These statutes had not been repealed by the subsequent legislation. Henry attempted to circumvent the geographical limitations through the language of the royal patents granting to the Admiral the authority to set up courts and try cases under the *lex maritima*. These, drafted in Latin, generally contained the phrase "*statutis in contrarium non obstantibus*", thereby carving out an exception to the restrictive terms of the fourteenth-century acts.[143] Predictably, this move produced a substantial degree of uncertainty regarding where the admiralty jurisdiction ended and that of the common law began, much as had occurred with the creation of the admiralty courts in the fourteenth century. By this time, however, the stakes were higher, and the ensuing years saw the beginnings of a conflict that was to reach its climax in the judgeship of Sir Edward Coke some fifty years later. In 1566, early in the reign

140. Steckley, *supra* note 119, at 141–142.

141. For a critique of the civil law's handling of substantive law governing bills of exchange, *see* Coquillette, Civilian Writers, *supra* note 7, at 215–254.

142. 32 Hen. VIII, c. 14, *in* Statutes of the Realm, *supra* note 132.

143. Mears, *supra* note 36, at 351–352. The phrase, which translates as "with statutes to the contrary notwithstanding", generally is referred to in the shortened, singular form; hence the scholarly literature dubs these "*non obstante* clauses". Marsden, Select Pleas I, *supra* note 73, at lviii, reproduces in the original Latin excerpts—including the "*non obstante* clause"—from the patent issued in 1525 to Henry, Duke of Richmond.

of Elizabeth, common-law opposition blocked an attempt to vest the Court of Admiralty with the full commercial jurisdiction of its counterparts on the Continent.[144] This coincided with the common law's relaxation of its rules of venue, under which courts of common law were able to circumvent the geographic limitations on their jurisdiction through use of legal fictions, thus permitting them to assert cognizance over foreign contracts, a class of cases over which admiralty had possessed unchallenged power in the reign of Henry VIII.[145] In response to a series of complaints beginning in 1570, the Queen sent a letter to the Mayor of London warning the city's courts not to interfere with the Admiralty's adjudication of matters relating to foreign contracts.[146] By 1575, Admiralty received a special commission for exclusive jurisdiction to hear cases of affreightment, bills of exchange, express hypothecation, marine insurance, and ships' necessaries.[147] The same year produced negotiations between the judges of the common law and the Admiralty Court regarding the limits of the jurisdiction of each, which the civilians maintained resulted in the common-law judges agreeing not to meddle in maritime matters.[148] The last extension of the admiralty jurisdiction in the Tudor period occurred in 1586, though ma-

---

144. Holdsworth, *supra* note 6, Vol. V, at 153.

145. *Id.* at 140–141.

146. Mears, *supra* note 36, at 353.

147. *Id. See also* Marsden, Select Pleas II, *supra* note 53, at xii–xiii.

148. Prynne reprints the text of the agreement, which contains the following terms:

> "That the Judge of the Admiralty, according to such ancient order as hath been taken 2 Ed. 1 by the king and his Council, and according to the Letters Patents of the Lord Admiral for the time being, and allowed of by other kings of this land ever since, and by Custome, time out of memory of man, may have and enjoy the cognition of all Contracts, and other things arising as well beyond, as upon the Sea, without any Let, or Prohibition. That the said Judge, may have and enjoy the knowledge and breach of Charter-parties, made between Masters of Ships, and Merchants, for voyages to be made to the parts beyond the Seas, and to be performed upon, and beyond the Sea, according as it hath been accustumed, time out of mind, and according to the good meaning of the Statute of 32 H[en.] 8 c. 14. though the same Charter-parties happen to be made within the Roialme [*sic*]."

Prynne, Brief Animadversions, *supra* note 53, at 98–99. There is, however, some debate as to whether this agreement was ever concluded. While the text itself is extant, there is no surviving manuscript containing the signatures of the judges of King's Bench. Zouch, who also reprints the text (*see* Zouch, *supra* note 16, at 120–122), relates the following:

> "...Sir Edward Cook answers, that the supposed agreement, had not been delivered unto them, but having heard the same read before his Majesty (out of a Paper not subscribed with the hand of any Judge) they answer, that for so much thereof as differs from their present Answers, it was against the Laws and Statutes

terialmen's right to file their claims in admiralty remained a source of tension and controversy throughout the remainder of Elizabeth's reign.[149]

The heightened importance that the Tudor monarchs placed upon the Court of Admiralty was not the only reason that its jurisdiction came into conflict with the common law at the close of the sixteenth century. Coincident with the expansion of the Admiralty Court's powers were changes in the common law itself, facilitating a three-pronged attack on the powers of the prerogative court. First there was the development of the action of *assumpsit* as a mechanism by which the common law could assert jurisdiction over a variety of commercial matters. The second was a change in the rules of venue, whereby courts of common law were able to assert cognizance over matters occurring beyond the geographical boundaries of England's counties. Finally, there was the writ of prohibition.

Among the matters litigated in admiralty, *assumpsit* proved most valuable to plaintiffs in matters relating to bills of exchange. As one modern commentator has observed:

> [I]t was part and parcel of the general development of *assumpsit* to enable the enforcement of all parol undertakings. And, since there were no set formulae in *assumpsit*, it was possible to adapt its forms to charge the various parties to bills of exchange.[150]

> of the Realm, and therefore the Judges of the Kings Bench never assented thereunto, as it is pretended, neither doth the phrase thereof agree with the Terms of the Laws of the Realm."

Id. at 118. Zouch contradicts Coke's account, but the truth of the matter is still open to question. *Id.* at 119. For a modern assessment of the alleged compromise of 1575, *see* MARSDEN, SELECT PLEAS II, *supra* note 53, at xiv.

149. For discussion, *see* Mears, *supra* note 36, at 354.

150. *See* "The Law Merchant and the Common Law before 1700" *in* J. H. BAKER, THE LEGAL PROFESSION AND THE COMMON LAW: HISTORICAL ESSAYS (London: Hambledon Press, 1986) at 356. Of course, new forms of action would have been of little use to the plaintiff in the absence of a body of commercial law with which to resolve the case. Baker gives the following explanation of how the courts of common law dealt with the *lex mercatoria* in actions of *assumpsit*:

> "The plaintiff in *assumpsit* could omit all mention of custom, and at trial ask the judge and jury to notice a mercantile custom as warranting the implication of an undertaking in the circumstances. Or he could declare on a specific 'custom of the realm' used by merchants, which probably had the same effect, since the allegation of such a custom, though helping to focus attention on a form of words, was surplusage. Or he could rely on an immemorial local custom, which had to be proved as fact. None of these alternatives treats the law merchant as a body of law akin to foreign law. This may be why, so far as we can tell from the reports, no reliance was placed in this period on learned treatises of the law merchant or

This new form of action, which was first used in the reign of Henry VIII to assert money-claims, also proved useful in a broad range of commercial transactions, including partnership agreements and contracts of insurance.[151] Of perhaps greater impact in the battle over maritime jurisdiction was the change in the common law's rules for venue. This took the form of the adoption of what came to be known as the "Cheapside fiction". The courts of common law, as noted previously, had no power to adjudicate contracts concluded at sea or on foreign soil. Nevertheless, as the place of contracting was treated as a formal requirement in pleading rather than as a fact at issue in the case, courts of the sixteenth century began to circumvent the geographical limitations through use of legal fictions. As Prynne later was to explain:

> ...[S]ome Common Lawyers and Courts, to enlarge their Jurisdiction beyond its antient [*sic*] limits, and diminish the Admirals, have by a *new strange poetical fiction*...surmised, that Contracts, Bargains, Obligations, Charter-parties made, and things done by Merchants and Marriners in any Foreign Country, Port, Creek, Haven, City beyond the Sea, or any Shore thereof...was made or done at such a place of that name in the Parish of *Bow* in *Cheapside*, within the City of *London*...and so by this new-coyned untraversable fiction, which must be admitted for truth, though never so false and impossible, transporting whole Kingdoms, Countries, Cities, Rivers, Ports, Creeks, Shores in foreign parts, into *Cheapside* in *London*...(which no Miracle nor Omnipotency it self can do...) they pretend and resolve that the Contract, Bargain, and thing done beyond the Sea, is now become triable only at the Common Law, not in the Admiralty, by the Law of *Merchants, Oleron*, or the *Civil Law*...[152]

> of mercantile practice or of the laws of nature, and why no calls were made on the Civil lawyers for their evidence or assistance. Mercantile customs were either local facts or they were the common law of England. In so far as judges took notice of such customs as common law, they were not taking over for their own use a pre-existing body of jurisprudence."

Id. at 367.

151. *See Id.* at 354–356. While *assumpsit* gained prominence under the reign of Henry VIII, Maitland has traced its origins earlier—to the fifteenth century—although he observes that the full potential of the flexible and adaptable writ had not yet been exploited by plaintiffs. *See* F. W. Maitland, Equity, Also the Forms of Action at Common Law: Two Courses of Lectures (1st ed. 1909; *reprinted* Littleton, Colorado: Fred B. Rothman & Co., 1999) at 28–29.

152. Prynne, Brief Animadversions, *supra* note 53, at 95 *(emphasis in the original)*.

The result—as the common lawyer Prynne correctly observes—was to permit a court of common law to adjudicate a dispute over a contract of affreightment signed in Marseilles, so long as the aggrieved party added boiler-plate language indicating that the French port was located in the London ward of Cheapside or elsewhere on English soil. The practice was similarly condemned by the civilians,[153] though it was to find an unlikely defender in Matthew Hale.[154]

Of all causes of friction between the common law and the Court of Admiralty, none played so great a role as did the writ of prohibition. Unlike the action of *assumpsit*, which gave plaintiffs access to the courts at Westminster for a narrow range of commercial matters, leaving the strictly "marine" causes of action—such as express hypothecation, salvage, general average, and seamen's wages—to the Admiralty Court, the writ of prohibition touched virtually every variety of claim known to the law of the sea. Similarly, unlike the "Cheapside fiction", which merely provided an alternate forum in which aggrieved parties could file their claims, the writ of prohibition permitted the courts of common law to invade the inner workings of the Court of Admiralty, disrupt its process of adjudication, and overturn its decisions. Throughout the seventeenth century, the writ became the subject of numerous speeches, letters, and books, with defenders and detractors expending hundreds of pages extolling its utility and denouncing its disruptive effects. In all

---

153. Zouch, *supra* note 16, at 130–131 also offers a condemnation of the practice. The "Cheapside fiction" drew its most vehement criticism from authors of the mid-seventeenth-century, for whom its clear absurdity and wanton overreaching made it the perfect target for arousing animosity against the common lawyers. Nevertheless, there is evidence to show that the legal fiction was regarded as a hackneyed and somewhat disreputable device even in the reign of Elizabeth. *See* Steckley, *supra* note 119, at 145.

154. In his posthumously published treatise on admiralty jurisdiction, Hale defends the practice of using legal fictions to establish jurisdiction over matters involving "Bonds, Specialties or Covenants" likening them to "Contracts and other transitory actions":

> "...[F]or as well as a Jury of Cornwall may take Notice of a Deed made at New-castle, which is a transitory thing, so they may take Notice of a transitory thing done in France or Spain or any Place of the World;...[which] is in truth a fiction, but such a fiction as is only to accommodate a Proces and a [*venire facias*] for a Jury, and goes not at all to the Substance of the matter.... And though fictions be a shew of something that is not, yet there is scarce any well Ordered Law, nay, not the Civil Law, but hath its fictions."

Hale and Fleetwood, *supra* note 54, at 23–24. In fairness to Hale, it should be noted that his position had been that the common law should have jurisdiction over foreign contracts concurrent with that of the Admiralty. As such, the courts at Westminster would have provided plaintiffs with alternate *fora*, rather than divesting Admiralty of its power to adjudicate such matters. *See Id.* at 4–11.

this literature, John Godolphin, judge of the High Court of Admiralty during the Interregnum, provides perhaps the most succinct definition:

> A *Prohibition* in the sense most adequate to the purpose in hand, is a Writ forbidding to hold Plea in a Matter or Cause supposed to be without the Jurisdiction and Cognizance of that Court where the Suit depends.[155]

In essence, the writ of prohibition permitted a court of common law to stay the proceedings in the Court of Admiralty if it found that the latter court's cognizance over a matter was *ultra vires*.[156] With a substantial overlap in the jurisdiction claimed by the common law and the Admiralty, "*ultra vires*" was

---

155. John Godolphin, *Synegoros Thalassios*: A View of the Admiral Jurisdiction Wherein the Most Material Points Concerning That Jurisdiction Are Fairly and Submissively Discussed (1st ed. 1661; *reprinted* London: George Dawes, 1685) at 72 (hereinafter Godolphin).

156. The procedure for granting prohibitions developed over time. The form in which it would have been known to eighteenth-century practitioners—both in England and the American colonies—is set out in detail by Blackstone:

> "The party aggrieved in the court below [in this case, the admiralty court] applies to the superior court [*i.e.* the court of common law], setting forth in a suggestion upon record the nature and cause of his complaint, in being drawn *ad aliud examen*, by a jurisdiction or manner of process disallowed by the laws of the kingdom: upon which, if the matter alleged appears to the court to be sufficient, the writ of prohibition immediately issues; commanding the judge not to hold, and the party not to prosecute, the plea. But sometimes the point may be too nice and doubtful to be decided merely upon a motion: and then, for the more solemn determination of the question, the party applying for the prohibition is directed by the court to *declare* in prohibition; that is, to prosecute an action, by filing a declaration, against the other, upon a supposition, or fiction, that he has proceeded in the suit below, notwithstanding the writ of prohibition. And if, upon demurrer and argument, the court shall finally be of opinion, that the matter suggested is a good and sufficient ground of prohibition in point of law, then judgment with nominal damages shall be given for the party complaining, and the defendant, and also the inferior court, shall be prohibited from proceeding any farther. On the other hand, if the superior court shall think it no competent ground for restraining the inferior jurisdiction, then judgment shall be given against him who applied for the prohibition in the court above, and a writ of *consultation* shall be awarded; so called, because, upon deliberation and consultation had, the judges find the prohibition to be ill founded, and therefore by this writ they return the cause to it's [*sic*] original jurisdiction, to be there determined, in the inferior court. And, even in ordinary cases, the writ of prohibition is not absolutely final and conclusive. For, though the ground be a proper one in point of *law*, for granting the prohibition, yet, if the *fact* that gave rise to

a matter of considerable controversy, and a clash between the two sets of courts was inevitable.[157] The conflict was further exacerbated by the fact that use of the writ was not restricted to cases in progress; it was also available to overturn final decrees in Admiralty.[158] The theoretical justification given by the courts of common law was that the Court of Admiralty was not a *court of record*, and as such a decision in Admiralty could not be regarded as *res judicata*.[159] In practice, as one would surmise, this theory provided a dissatisfied party with the opportunity to obtain a "second chance" by launching a collateral attack on the Admiralty Court's decision.

The Admiralty had a similar weapon of its own, known as the "contempt procedure", under which a proctor whose client had been sued at common law for breach of a contract signed on foreign soil could produce before an admiralty judge a copy of the complaint. In turn, the admiralty judge would then issue a summons to the common-law plaintiff to appear and give evidence to show that his actions were not in violation of the Admiralty's jurisdiction. If he was unable to do so and refused to withdraw his complaint, the judge was empowered to imprison him for contempt of court until he withdrew the common-law action.[160] Nevertheless, this "contempt procedure" did

> it be afterwards falsified, the cause shall be remanded to the prior jurisdiction."

3 Blackstone, *supra* note 126, Ch. 7 at 113–114.

157. As the passage from Blackstone, *supra* note 156, implies, a court's first step in reviewing an application for a prohibition was to examine the complaint—or "libel"—filed with the admiralty court for defects "on its face" that would divest the maritime tribunal of jurisdiction. An experienced civilian would have been careful to contend that the cause of action arose "*super altum mare*" ("on the high seas") rather than *in causa maritima* or *infra jurisdictionem maritimam* in order to minimize the chance that a prohibition would be issued. Neverthelss, where the common law conceded that locality was not dispositive—as in wage-cases—the usual formula of "*super altum mare*" could be omitted without risk of triggering a prohibition. *See* Hale and Fleetwood, *supra* note 54, Introduction at liii., lvi.

158. Hale and Fleetwood, *supra* note 54, at liv.

159. As Prichard and Yale observe:

> "[T]he common law courts had the last word through prohibition, fortified by their claim to have the last word in statutory interpretation.... There can be no doubt that in the area of actual litigation the weapon of prohibition gave the courts of common law the upper hand over jurisdictional claims, for the writ was more than an injunction. It prohibited the Court itself. The civilians were in no position to deny the writ itself: they could only complain of its abuse."

Id. at lviii.

160. *See* Steckley, *supra* note 119, at 146–147. For his description of the "contempt procedure" Steckley credits an 1829 edition of Francis Clerke's *Praxis*. Clerke's work, written in Latin in the latter years of Elizabeth's reign, was first published posthumously in the year

---

1667. While undoubtedly of early origins, the "contempt procedure" receives no mention in the first published edition, Francis Clerke, *Praxis Curiae Admiralitatis Angliae* (London: William Crooke, 1667), nor in the subsequent edition published by Crooke in 1679, both of which contain 63 Titles. The "contempt procedure" is addressed, however, in the edition of Clerke's *Praxis* published in 1743 by Sir Edward Simpson. In compiling his edition, Simpson had used two manuscripts in the collection of Trinity Hall, Cambridge. *See* [Francis Clerke], *Praxis Supremae Curiae Admiralitatis... Cui Adjiciuntur Articuli Magistri Rowghton* (Edward Simpson ed., London: C. Bathurst, 1743) *Praefatio ad Lectorem* (*not paginated*). These manuscripts—transcribed by Sir Robert Wyseman and Dr. Thomas Eden respectively—contain 68 Titles and date from the mid-seventeenth century. In the ensuing seventy years between Clerke's initial drafting of his *Praxis* and the first published edition, various civilians had made copies for their personal use, and predictably these copies varied in some details. Nevertheless, scribal errors may not account for the omission of references to the "contempt procedure" in all early published editions of the *Praxis*. One commentator maintains that Clerke continued to make revisions of his own manuscript over a period of years. Thus the Wyseman/Eden texts—containing additional information—are copies of Clerke's revised manuscript, completed later in life. *See* J. Duncan M. Derrett, *The Works of Francis Clerke, Proctor (A Chapter in English Romano-Canonical Law)*, 40 *Studia et Documenta Historiae et Iuris* 52, 64–65 (1974). Simpson's Latin edition, not widely distributed in the eighteenth century, received its first rendering into English in 1809 by American legal scholar John Elihu Hall. The last two Titles address the contempt procedure:

> "The Proctor for the party injured is accustomed in those cases, to allege before the Judge of the Court of Admiralty, that a certain person, under colour of a maritime contract made and concluded without the kingdom, pretending that his client was indebted to him in a certain sum of money, had caused him to be arrested in a secular Court: and to inform the Judge in a summary manner of the truth of this allegation, he exhibits a copy of the complaint, or, as it is called, the declaration, filed in the secular Court. And he prays the Judge to decree that the said plaintiff be attached, until he shall appear in the Court of Admiralty, to answer articles in a case of contempt, which it is usual for the Judge to grant upon an inspection of the declaration."

John E. Hall, The Practice and Jurisdiction of the Court of Admiralty; In Three Parts (Baltimore: George Dobbin & Murphy, 1809), Bk. II, Tit. 67 at 115–116. Title 68 provides further that:

> "And if he [*i.e.* the plaintiff] confess the fact, he is to be admonished forthwith to withdraw the aforesaid action. If he do this without delay, it is usual for the Judge not to consider him in contempt. But if he pertinaciously adhere to it and refuse to withdraw the action, although it is confessedly a cause of maritime jurisdiction, he is to be pronounced in contempt, and is to be committed to prison, and there detained until he withdraw the aforesaid action."

Id., Bk. II, Tit. 68 at 116. If Derrett is correct in concluding that Clerke continued to revise his work over a period of several years, one would expect his later editions added only those arcane, odd pieces of information that escaped his mind in the first draft. Had the contempt procedure been utilized frequently, Clerke undoubtedly would have mentioned it in the earlier drafts on which the published editions by Crooke were based.

not place the Court of Admiralty on an equal footing with the courts of Westminster in the battle over jurisdiction. The courts of common law were firmly established as courts of record; their decrees were binding. In the sixteenth and seventeenth centuries, however, the Admiralty Court's status as a court of record was open to question. It is clear that it had been so recognized in its earliest days.[161] Following the retrenchment in the reign of Richard II, the Court's status and powers were less clearly defined, and by the Tudor period the issue of whether the Court was a court of record had become the focal point of the conflict between the common lawyers and the civilians for two reasons. First, with the final decree of a court of record, a matter became *res judicata*, and as such was no longer vulnerable to a writ of prohibition. Second, only a court of record was empowered to accept a "recognizance". In its normal course of business, the Admiralty Court routinely accepted "stipulations", or sums held by the court as assurance that the plaintiff's (or more properly "libellant's") claim would be satisfied in the event that he should prevail on the merits.[162] If the Admiralty Court had not been a court of record and if these stipulations could have been construed as recognizances, the foundation of the Court's procedure would have been *ultra vires* and violative of the common law. The common lawyers' penchant for equating stipulations with recognizances showed a lack of full understanding of the role that stipulations played in the civil law; stipulations and recognizances were not identical. One modern commentary notes the crucial distinction: "The nature of the Admiralty stipulation was clearly not in form close to that of a common law recognizance. The recognizance acknowledged a debt due to the King; the stipulatory undertaking was a promise to the other party."[163] Nevertheless, the

---

161. *See supra* note 129 and text accompanying.

162. "Stipulations" are required at various stages of litigation under the civil law. The most notable is described in Title 11 of Francis Clerke's *Praxis*, a late sixteenth-century Latin treatise on the curial law of the English admiralty, published posthumously in 1667. Clerke observes that the *reus* ("respondent" or defendant) should provide securities to the court in an amount sufficient to satisfy the claim in the event he should held liable, as well as an amount sufficient to cover the court costs as determined by the judge. CLERKE, *PRAXIS* (1667 ed.), *supra* note 160, Title 11 "*De Introductione fidejussorum per Reum & stipulatione ab iis captanda*" at 8–9. The procedure is roughly equivalent to the modern practice of posting of a bond to secure the release of an arrested ship, for which it is likely to have served as a model.

163. While not the only distinction between civil-law stipulations and common-law recognizances, this observation by Yale and Prichard gets closest to the heart of the matter. HALE AND FLEETWOOD, *supra* note 54, Introduction at lxi. Arthur Browne offers the following distinction:

"In this stipulation the sureties, and the party by his sureties, expressly submit

power of interpretation remained with the courts of common law, and as the sixteenth century drew to a close, a clash of wills was imminent.

Edward Coke is a study in contrasts, and arguably the most controversial figure in English legal history. Born in Norfolk just outside the town of Norwich in 1552, he studied Latin at an early age, entered Trinity College, Cambridge in 1567, was admitted to Inner Temple in 1572, and was called to the bar in 1578. Having practiced law and served in Parliament, he received appointment as Attorney General in 1594. By 1606, he had been elevated to Chief Justice of Common Pleas, a position that he would retain until, much against his will, political rivals maneuvered in 1613 to have him "promoted" to the Chief Justiceship of King's Bench and membership in the Privy Council, positions of greater prestige (if fewer material rewards) than his previous appointment.[164] Ironically, despite this long and prosperous career, it was in old age—and in the disgrace of removal from office—that Coke achieved historical immortality.[165] Certainly his contemporaries, Lord Burghley and his

---

> to the jurisdiction of the court, and consent, in case of default in the performance of the conditions, that the admiralty process shall issue against them. This stipulation, though in the nature of a recognizance, differs from the security usually so termed; it subjects the persons and goods of the stipulators, but it doth not enable the admiralty to issue process against their lands. It must also be observed, that the bail are not liable beyond the extent of this fidejussory caution, and that the security doth not affect them in a court of appeal, where the impugnant must get fresh fidejussors."

BROWNE, *supra* note 9, Vol. II, at 409–410.

164. For Coke's biographical details, *see generally* CATHERINE DRINKER BOWEN, THE LION AND THE THRONE: THE LIFE AND TIMES OF SIR EDWARD COKE (1st ed., Boston: Little, Brown & Co., 1956). Considering his status in the history of English law, biographical studies of Coke are in short supply. Apart from Bowen's National Book Award winning book—which was written for a general audience rather than for scholars—material on Coke generally has been directed at specific times in his life or toward specific topics. Historian Stephen D. White has examined Coke's latter years and his role in Parliament on the eve of the English Civil War. *See* STEPHEN D. WHITE, SIR EDWARD COKE AND "THE GRIEVANCES OF THE COMMONWEALTH", 1621–1628 (Chapel Hill: University of North Carolina Press, 1979) (hereinafter WHITE, SIR EDWARD COKE). Professor White addresses Coke's early life in his Introduction at 3–23, with much of the information being drawn from Bowen's earlier work. Holdsworth provides a monograph-length look at Coke's work as a judge and legal scholar in his multi-volume history. *See* HOLDSWORTH, *supra* note 6, Vol. V, at 423–493.

165. Coke was dismissed from office as Chief Justice of King's Bench in November of 1616. He had been rebuked once before by James I five years earlier—while serving on the bench of Common Pleas—for improper use of the writ of prohibition. The charges against him, drafted by Bacon, again included abuse of the writ of prohibition and meddling in mat-

son, Robert Cecil, wielded more power and influence in their time than did Coke, and yet their names today are little more than historical footnotes to all but students and scholars of the Elizabethan Age. In his exile from public life, Coke was to compile his *Reports* and write his *Institutes*, the two works that more than any others were to influence English legal education from their publication through the end of the eighteenth century. Moreover, that influence was to cross the Atlantic. Under the guidance of Jeremiah Gridley, the young John Adams was to study Coke's *Institutes* together with the *Institutes of Justinian*.[166] Thomas Jefferson hailed Coke as the harbinger of eighteenth-century Whiggism, and expressed deep regret that his works had of late given way to those of the conservatives Blackstone and Mansfield.[167] A generation later, even after Blackstone's *Commentaries* had come to dominate the training of aspiring lawyers, Coke remained relevant. As a young man, Joseph Story—who mastered the comparatively straightforward *Commentaries* easily—was to struggle with the complexities of Coke's *First Institute*, or "*Coke on Littleton*" as it had come to be known.[168] Unlike his contemporary Francis

---

ters properly pending before the Admiralty Court. Coke, with time on his hands, used the opportunity to make some revisions to his *Reports*, of which eleven of the total of thirteen already had been published. Although he was subsequently reinstated in his place on the Privy Council, his clashes with the Crown did not end there. Several years later, after the dissolution of the Parliament in which Coke had sponsored a bill to give the courts of common law control over Chancery, he found himself confined in the Tower while his papers were searched for evidence of treason. Eventually cleared of the charges, he was prevented from serving in the Parliament of 1626 when James appointed him sheriff—a position that disqualified him from taking a seat in Parliament. Once again, Coke used his exile from the public life of London to write, this time completing his *Fourth Institute*. *See* Bowen, *supra* note 164, at 324–325; 374–388. *See also* Holdsworth, *supra* note 6, Vol. V, at 439–449.

166. *See* Daniel R. Coquillette, "Justinian in Braintree: John Adams, Civilian Learning and Legal Elitism, 1758–1775", *in* Law in Colonial Massachusetts (D. R. Coquillette ed., Charlottesville: University of Virginia, 1984) at 369–370. *See also* Bowen, *supra* note 164, at 513.

167. Bowen, *supra* note 164, at 153. However much Jefferson was fond of citing Coke for rhetorical effect, in his private correspondence he was not always so complimentary. *See e.g.* his letter to John Page of Christmas, 1762: "I am sure, to get through old Coke this winter.... Well, Page, I do wish the Devil had old Coke, for I am sure I never was so tired of an old dull scoundrel in my life..." *reprinted in* Thomas Jefferson, Writings (Merrill D. Peterson ed., New York: Library of America, 1984) at 735. With regard to Coke's influence on subsequent generations—particularly eighteenth-century Whigs—*see* J. G. A. Pocock, The Ancient Constitution and the Feudal Law (1st ed., Cambridge: Cambridge University Press, 1957) at 45–46 (hereinafter Pocock).

168. *See* R. Kent Newmyer, Supreme Court Justice Joseph Story: Statesman of the Old Republic (Chapel Hill: University of North Carolina Press, 1985) at 39–41.

Bacon, Coke eschewed reductionist theories, and in general lacked a developed political ideology.[169] Complex as it was, Coke's work became known to posterity largely for its aphorisms. "*Aliquis non debet esse judex in propria causa*"—"No one should act as judge in his own case"; "*Lex est tutissima cassis*"—"The law is the safest shield".[170] Yet among these none resounded so loudly as "*The common law hath admeasured the King's prerogative*".[171]

As Elizabeth's Attorney General, Coke had defended royal prerogative, yet his career on the bench and in Parliament was marked by opposition to it under the reign of her successor. To a great extent, this was a reflection of differences in the two monarchs rather than changes in Coke's own politics and thought.[172] Where Elizabeth had been politically astute, understanding how to preserve the delicate balances among the various constituencies of the Realm, James asserted prerogative not as a convenient tool to accomplish particular ends, but rather as something between the cornerstone of a political ideology and the sacred tenet of a religion. Indeed, so seriously did James take the prerogative by which the kings of England established admiralty courts that he once adjudicated an admiralty case himself.[173] To Coke, this was intolerable. The tension was compounded by James' frequent lack of tact. Coke, not a paragon of tactfulness himself, saw in the common law a means by which the excesses and indiscretions of the King could be kept in check. "*Lex est tutissima cassis.*" In *Calvin's Case*, he had observed:

> ...[O]ur daies [*sic*] upon the earth are but as a shadow, in respect of the old and ancient dayes and times past, wherein the Laws have been by the wisdom of the most excellent men, in many successions of ages, by long and continual experience (the trial of right and truth) fined and refined, which no one man (being of so short a time) albeit he had in his head the wisdom of all the men in the world, in any one age could

---

169. Holdsworth, *supra* note 6, Vol. V, at 434; Bowen, *supra* note 164, at 508.

170. *See* Bowen, *supra* note 164, at 278–280, 315–316. The first quote is from *Bonham's Case. See* [Edward Coke], The Reports of Sir Edvvard Coke, K[night], Late Lord Chief Justice of England...Faithfully Rendered into English (1st English ed., London: W. Lee, M. Walbanck, D. Pakeman, & G. Bedell, 1658), Part VII at 113b, 118a (hereinafter Coke, Reports). "*Lex est tutissima cassis*" is the motto that Coke had inscribed on the rings he gave to attendees at the banquet he hosted upon being created Serjeant-of-Law in 1606. More properly translated "law is the safest *helmet*", Coke later incorporated this motto into his *Second Institute. See* Edward Coke, The Institutes of the Laws of England (London: E. and R. Brooke, 1797), Part II at 56 (hereinafter Coke, Institutes).

171. *Quoted in* Bowen, *supra* note 164, at 291.

172. *Id.* at 293–294.

173. *See* Matthew P. Harrington, *The Legacy of the Colonial Vice-Admiralty Courts*, (Part I) 26 J. Mar. L. & Com. 581, 588 (1995).

> never have effected or attained unto. And therefore it is *optima regula, qua nulla est verior aut firmior in jure, Neminem oportet esse sapientiorem legibus,* no man ought to take upon him to be wiser than the laws.[174]

Coke's defense of the common law—which bears a remarkable resemblance to Malynes' defense of the *lex mercatoria*[175]—addresses only the *wisdom* of placing the common law above the will of the King. To affirm its *legitimacy*, Coke was obliged to ground the theory in the English Constitution. To do so, he had recourse to English history. The Common Law, he contended, had reigned supreme in England since "time out of mind"; the King obtained his authority under its auspices—not *vice versa*. While even today one might argue that some common-law rules in fact ante-date human memory, it was clear that the Norman Conquest did not. It would have been all too easy for proponents of royal prerogative to point to 1066 A.D. as marking the end of the ancient law of England and the beginning of an era in which all legitimate power and law flowed from the Crown. Through some imaginative historiography, Coke was able to work around this obstacle, ironically with some help from William the Conqueror himself. The Norman policy of allowing local customs to govern the Saxon population had become, in the hands of English chroniclers, William's ratification of the "laws of King Edward the Confessor", of which an apocryphal version (drafted in the twelfth century to remedy the lack of an original text) was later incorporated by reference into the King's coronation oath, where it was to remain until 1688.[176] While characterizing the Conquest as confirmation of existing law enabled Coke to assert the common law's independence from—and precedence over—royal prerogative, it produced a conundrum. If the common law had existed from time immemorial, pre-

---

174. Coke, Reports, *supra* note 170, *Calvin's Case,* Part VII at 1, 3b.

175. *See* discussion, *supra* note 96 and text accompanying. It is ironic that these defenders of the common law and the law merchant respectively chose such similar terms in which to voice their arguments. Nonetheless, "evolution of rules through the ages" can be both emotionally appealing and logically compelling. As one modern commentator has observed:

> "Institutions which have survived this process for a long time must be presumed to have solved innumerably more problems than the men of the present age can imagine.... The wisdom which they embody has accumulated to such a degree that no reflecting individual can in his lifetime come to the end of it, no matter how he calls philosophy and theoretical reason to his aid."

Pocock, *supra* note 167, at 36.

176. For discussion, *see Id.* at 42–46.

dating royal prerogative and therefore "admeasuring" it, how should one account for the fact that the law was in a constant state of evolution and flux? Coke failed to provide an adequate answer. When Hobbes later attacked Coke on this very point, Matthew Hale took up the challenge of defending him, observing that it was not the *content* of the law that had survived intact since Saxon times, but rather the common law's *process* of defining law incrementally through case law that gave it its claim to precedence. Hale's response—which appears consistent with Coke's own writings—provides him with an escape from the paradox, but Coke himself had not made the point explicitly.[177] Ultimately, this failure, coupled with his somewhat questionable approach to historiography, was to leave Coke vulnerable to attack intellectually, not only in his own time, but also by a succeeding generation of civilian scholars.

Although prohibitions had prompted complaints to the Crown as early as the 1570s, they had been comparatively rare in the sixteenth century.[178] With Coke's elevation to the bench in 1606, the situation changed. In 1611, Daniel Dun, Judge of the Admiralty Court, filed a formal eight-part complaint with the Council, to which Coke replied.[179] Years later, Coke was to publish his reply to Dun in his *Fourth Institute*.[180] Of his eight responses, Coke's replies

---

177. For Hale's critique of Hobbes, *see* "Sir Matthew Hale's Criticisms on Hobbes' Dialogue of the Common Laws", *reprinted in* HOLDSWORTH, *supra* note 6, Vol. V, Appendix at 499–513. For discussion, *see also* POCOCK, *supra* note 167, at 163–177.

178. *See* HALE AND FLEETWOOD, *supra* note 54, Introduction at xlix (noting that J. H. Baker has compiled a full list of cases of the early sixteenth century in which prohibitions were issued; these are published in the Publications of the Selden Society, Vol. 94 (1978) at 73 n. 4).

179. The first four claims related to prohibitions issued in cases of: 1) contracts concluded at sea, 2) transmarine contracts, 3) stipulations taken, and 4) charterparties. The fifth related to Common Pleas ignoring "*non obstante*" clauses in admirals' patents; the sixth related to Coke's contention that matters arising on rivers beneath the first bridges were not within admiralty jurisdiction. The seventh claim was that Common Pleas had violated the Agreement of 1575; the final claim encompassed in general terms any abuses left out of the first seven. HALE AND FLEETWOOD, *supra* note 54, Introduction at xcvi–xcviii. Dun's cause for alarm was not so much the volume of cases for which prohibitions had been granted—the records list only fewer than fifty in James' reign through 1611—but rather the precarious position in which Coke's interpretation of jurisdiction had placed Dun's own court. *Id.* at xcviii. *See also* Steckley, *supra* note 119, at 143 (noting that only forty-five prohibitions were issued in the first eight years of James' reign, while the Admiralty Court averaged roughly four hundred cases per year).

180. COKE, INSTITUTES, *supra* note 170, Part IV, Ch. XXII at 134–136.

to Dun's third and fifth claims—which were directed at the status of the Admiralty Court itself—were the most damaging. As to the fifth—regarding Common Pleas' disregard for the "*non obstante*" clauses in the admirals' patents—Coke responded in effect that the jurisdiction of the common law cannot be diminished by royal prerogative, rendering the king's patents nugatory—and *ultra vires*. With respect to the third claim—relating to Admiralty's use of stipulations—Coke wrote:

> The court of the admiralty proceeding by the civill law is no court of record, and therefore cannot take any such recognisance as a court of record may do. And for taking recognisances against the lawes of the realme, we finde that prohibitions have been granted, as by law they ought. And if an erroneous sentence be given in that court, no writ of error, but an appeale before certain delegates do lye, as it appeareth by the statute of 8 Eliz. *reginae*, cap. 5. which proveth that it is no court of record.[181]

Though Coke was forced to defend his use of prohibitions before the Privy Council in 1611, the clash between the common-law courts and the civilians remained unresolved, and would resurface again intermittently throughout the next several decades.[182] It should be noted that prohibitions were not a problem for Admiralty alone; all prerogative courts suffered similarly. The ecclesiastical courts often bore the brunt of the common law's attack upon royal prerogative,[183] and Coke himself, as a member of Parliament, sought to expand the powers of the courts of common law at the expense of the Courts of Chancery, Wards, and Exchequer.[184] John Godolphin, the civilian who was to support Parliament in the Civil War, attributed the zeal with which Coke and his common-law brethren pursued jurisdiction over admiralty matters to greed, a view shared

---

181. *Id.*, Ch. XXII at 135. With regard to Coke' remark about appeals, beginning in the reign of Henry VIII, appeals in Admiralty were heard by "*judices delegati*", or "delegates", who were doctors of the civil law appointed by the king. Hale and Fleetwood, *supra* note 54, Introduction at lxxix. Having received Coke's response to their eight complaints, Dun and his colleague Henry Marten wrote a refutation, "A replye to my L[ord] Co[ke] his answare to the greevances of the Admiralty exhibited to his Majestie by the [Lord] Admirall and his officers" (Adm. Reg. MS. (Extracts), f. 51; HCA 30/4), which Prichard and Yale reprint in an appendix to Hale and Fleetwood at 300–312.

182. Bowen, *supra* note 164, at 323–325; Hale and Fleetwood, *supra* note 54, at xcix.

183. Holdsworth, *supra* note 6, Vol. V, at 429.

184. White, Sir Edward Coke, *supra* note 164, at 58–65.

by Prynne, himself a common lawyer.[185] Admittedly, Coke was personally driven by a desire to acquire wealth, and his overbearing personality and tendency to resort to vituperative attacks when challenged have led critics—seventeenth-century and modern alike—to attribute base motives to him. His treatment of criminal defendants and implacable distrust of Catholics are distasteful to modern sensibilities.[186] As one biographer observed: "His manner was abrupt at times to rudeness; his faults bordered rather on brutality than subservience."[187] It was his behavior toward those in power as much as his politics that resulted both in his removal from office and his later imprisonment in the Tower.[188] Nevertheless, it was not greed that induced Coke to introduce into Parliament a bill for preventing defendants from removing cases to the central courts in London in an effort to raise plaintiffs' costs. Despite protests from the civilians to the contrary, Coke believed strongly in reducing costs to litigants—and keeping less pecunious litigants on a par with their more affluent opponents—through vesting jurisdiction in local rather than London courts.[189] Moreover, it was not concern for his own worldly prosperity that induced him, at the request of Commons, to stand before the House of Lords and present the Petition of Right, challenging the authority of James' son, Charles I, to order arbitrary imprisonment and to levy taxes without consent of Parliament.[190] In the end, it was not

---

185. GODOLPHIN, *supra* note 155, Introduction (*not paginated*): He remarks:

> "...[H]e is more then [*sic:* "than"] of an audacious spirit, that dares invade the Laws Prerogative.... As Reason is the soul of the Law, so Jurisdicitons may be styled the faculties of that soul, being reduced to act or excercise as they are accomodated to this or that object; Consequently therefore to confound Jurisdictions, is to obliquitate the Rule of all Humane actions, specially if any thing less than *Bonum Publicum*, under a vizior be the Authour of that confusion. *Mine* and *Thine* divide the world betwixt them; in Private transactions they are unhappy Monosyllables, but in Publick affairs, they may be of most dangerous Consequence..."

For discussion of Prynne's characterization of the common law's encroachment on the Admiralty as the product of motive "for gain, not for the public good", as well as a survey of modern scholars' propensity to attribute the common-law faction's attack on the Admiralty Court's jurisdiction to jealousy and greed, *see* DAVID W. ROBERTSON, ADMIRALTY AND FEDERALISM (Mineola, New York: Foundation Press, 1970) at 32–34 n. 25.

186. HOLDSWORTH, *supra* note 6, Vol. V, at 426–427; for specific examples in Coke's life, *see generally* BOWEN, *supra* note 164.

187. BOWEN, *supra* note 164, at 79.

188. *See e.g. Id.* at 370–390; 452–457; HOLDSWORTH, *supra* note 6, vol. V, at 440–441.

189. For discussion of Coke's support of legislation to prevent removal of cases to central courts—as well as general information about his support of legislation to curb abuses in the court-system—*see* WHITE, SIR EDWARD COKE, *supra* note 164, at 50–66, 76–77.

190. *See* HOLDSWORTH, *supra* note 6, Vol. V, at 456; BOWEN, *supra* note 164, at 493–504; WHITE, *supra* note 164, at 261–274.

avarice, jealousy, or personal enmity that provided Coke with the principal impetus toward asserting that the prerogative courts were not courts of record.[191] To admit otherwise would have been for Coke to threaten the independence of Parliament and to elevate the will of the king above the supremacy of the common law, that repository of justice which (in Coke's imaginative historiography

---

191. Yale and Prichard observe that prize cases, the Admiralty Court's most lucrative source of business, were never the targets of prohibitions during this period, thus providing compelling evidence that greed was not the principal motive for the attack on admiralty jurisdiction by Coke and the common lawyers. HALE AND FLEETWOOD, *supra* note 54, Introduction at xlviii. One commentator has argued that Coke's definition of "court of record" was directed at establishing that Parliament was such a court. The accepted definition of "court of record" is one in which the "testimony to all that had been done before it is conclusive [and]...[may not] be impeached by witnesses who had been present at the trial." The account of proceedings was recorded in Latin upon a parchment roll. Thorne, *supra* note 6, at 31. Coke amended this definition, identifying a "court of record" as one with the power to fine and imprison. Historically, his definition is suspect. The power "to fine" is derived from the expression "*finem facere*" ("to make an end") in medieval case law, by which a person secured release from prison through a payment. It is likely that Coke, fully fluent in Latin, would have been aware that construing "*finem facere*" in the sixteenth-century sense of a "fine" was anachronistic. *Id.* at 38–40. Thorne finds similar problems with Coke's history of the power to imprison. *Id.* at 42–44, 47. Rejecting the often-cited position that Coke's definition was directed principally at thwarting the powers of admiralty, chancery, and the ecclesiastical courts, he instead contends that Coke used it to defend the claim of Parliament (which kept no roll) to judicial preeminence:

> "During the period the power to fine and imprison was habitually exercised by the council, star chamber, chancery, admiralty, and high commission, and it is difficult to believe that even Coke cherished the thought that they might be deprived of these powers because their proceedings were not properly kept in accordance with common-law custom. Whether or not this thought lay behind his formulation, and we believe that it played at most a minor part, it is clear that in this field his remarks had little or no effect. Elsewhere, however, they bore magnificent fruit, for it was with more than a casual eye toward parliament that they were framed. Coke had determined that parliament should again become the judicial body that it had been in the fourteenth century, the highest court in the land, which would mean a court above the council-made courts as well as at the apex of the common law. It was the last step in the war he had been waging for the supremacy of the common-law courts over the courts of equity.... That the lords, and the commons as well, should be courts of record was imperative, but neither kept a formal Latin record enrolled on parchment.... If, however, the power to fine and imprison, legally and rightfully exercised, characterized the court using these powers as one of record, the problem would be satisfactorily solved."

Id. at 48.

if not in historical fact) had defined rights and obligations in the Realm since time immemorial.

By 1628, Coke had served in his last Parliament. Coke—that "masterful, masterless man", as Frederic Maitland later was to characterize him[192]—retreated into study and scholarship for the remaining six years of his life. The struggle over maritime jurisdiction, however, did not die with him. On the contrary, as tensions between Parliament and the Crown escalated, the struggle moved into its most crucial phase. In 1632, the judges of the common law and of the Admiralty arrived at a compromise—reminiscent of their similar attempt in 1575—but this time the agreement was adopted by Privy Council and ratified by the king. In essence, the compromise protected the Admiralty Court against prohibitions in matters concerning foreign contracts, contracts concluded at sea, and claims (such as those of materialmen) in which the vessel itself, rather than its owners, was named as a party. Similar treatment was to be accorded to suits for mariners' wages or breach of contracts of carriage, even if signed within the Realm, so long both parties conceded that the contract itself was valid. The common-law courts also were enjoined against issuing prohibitions in cases of contracts concluded or injuries sustained on English rivers beneath the first bridges.[193] Unfortunately—as had happened so frequently before—this compromise failed to produce the desired result, prompting the merchants of London to attempt a novel approach. In 1641, contending that "The Common law doth not provide in all causes concerning Maritime affairs, and is not so well understood as the Civil Law beyond the seas", the Masters of Trinity House joined two other groups of merchants in petitioning the House of Lords to settle the dispute by vesting jurisdiction over maritime and commercial matters in the Court of Admiralty.[194] When Parliament failed to act, in 1646 another group of merchants approached Commons, requesting:

> ...that some speedy Remedy may be provided for the Hearing of Suits for Marriners Wages and Freight together in an Admiralty way and in Foreign Contracts, wherein the Petitioners, Factors and others, are

---

192. Frederic William Maitland, English Law and the Renaissance (1st ed. 1901; *reprinted* Littleton, Colorado: Fred B. Rothman & Co., 1985) at 29.

193. Exton reproduces the text of the 1632 agreement, signed before Council in February of 1633, as an appendix in his *Dicaeologie*. *See* Exton, *supra* note 66, at 262–263. For discussion, *see* Liang, *supra* note 76, at 181–182; Mears, *supra* note 36, at 357–358.

194. For discussion of the history of events in Parliament leading up to the passage of the Ordinance of 1648, *see* Steckley, *supra* note 119, at 148–158.

> enforced to make notarial Contracts according to Civil Law and Customs of those Countries.[195]

Over the next two years, the various factions in both houses of Parliament debated the fate of the merchants' petition, with support generally being stronger in Lords and opposition concentrated in Commons. Eventually, however, Parliament reached consensus; the product was the Ordinance of 1648, which granted to the Court of Admiralty jurisdiction over charterparties, bills of lading, and freight, but forbade it to entertain suits involving bills of exchange. Although the Ordinance addressed many of the merchants' requests, it was not intended as a permanent solution; it was to expire after three years if not renewed by Parliament. The act was reinforced the following year by an ancillary statute, forbidding the courts of common law from issuing prohibitions to the Admiralty Court in matters properly before it. Ultimately, Parliament was to renew these statutes four times, thereby keeping them in force throughout the Interregnum. In spite of this legislation, problems persisted. In the waning years of the Protectorate, merchants again sought relief from Parliament, but the attempt failed when a bill to reinforce admiralty jurisdiction over foreign contracts was voted down despite Cromwell's support. The final effort to resolve the matter during the Interregnum ended in 1659, when Commons debated—but declined to pass—a bill designed to make foreign civil-law contracts enforceable in the Admiralty Court.[196]

Parliament's eleven-year effort to settle jurisdiction over maritime matters reveals two important points. First, merchants, who for obvious reasons were desirous of settling the question, generally preferred to have their disputes resolved in a civil-law forum. Admittedly, had Parliament ended the uncertainty by selecting either forum as sole adjudicator, it would have saved the mercantile community significant time and expense by guaranteeing that a decision rendered in one court would not have been open to collateral attack in the other. Nonetheless, Trinity House and other merchant-groups expressed more than a preference for a bright-line jurisdictional rule; they expressed a preference for the substantive and curial law of their trading partners on the Continent. Secondly, despite Parliament's efforts, the courts of common law continued to interfere with proceedings before the Admiralty Court. This was

195. *Quoted in Id.* at 155. It should be noted that, with the establishment of the Commonwealth, Parliament abolished the office of Lord High Admiral (*see* Mears, *supra* note 36, at 358), although the Admiralty Court continued to operate, with the pro-Parliament civilian John Godolphin as judge.

196. Steckley, *supra* note 119, at 159–166.

due in large part to the relative political clout of the two warring factions. The civilians lacked the power to protect themselves from encroachment by the common law. With the overthrow of the monarchy, they also lost political influence—the ear of the king—which might have offset the common lawyers' advantages in numbers and financial resources. The result was a protracted battle in which the civilians were able to gain concessions on paper, only to lose them in the actual practice of litigation. Initially, this produced an ambiguity in England's maritime jurisdiction. As time went on, however, that which had been mere ambiguity began to crystallize into the underpinnings of a new theory of jurisdiction. The grey area of uncertainty—where both the common law and admiralty claimed power—became in the scholarly literature of the next decade a system of concurrent jurisdiction.

Concurrent Jurisdiction

Despite legislative gains during the Commonwealth, the English civilians were no closer to achieving freedom from prohibitions than in Coke's tenure on the bench of Common Pleas. When a plan to secure Charles II's support for granting the Admiralty Court exclusive jurisdiction over maritime contracts failed, the civilians were forced to take stock of their position and reevaluate their priorities.[197] The civilian practitioners—or advocates—were never numerous; the rigorous course of study kept their numbers small. Eight additional years were required at Oxford or Cambridge for those who already had completed the requirements for Master of Arts. The doctors of civil law had organized themselves in 1430, and their "College", as it came to be known, was officially founded in 1511, the second year of Henry VIII's reign. By 1557, they had relocated to Mountjoy House (near St. Paul's Cathedral), which they were to occupy until the Great Fire of 1666 claimed the building. New construction began shortly thereafter on the same site, and the civilians were to remain at their new quarters from 1671 through 1858, when the surviving members voted to dissolve the College and distribute its assets among themselves. From the granting of their Royal Charter in 1768, the formal title became "The College of Doctors of Law, Exercent in the Ecclesiastical and Admiralty Courts", but in popular parlance—from the days of Mountjoy House through the dissolution of the College—their chambers were known as "Doc-

197. *Id.* at 166.

tors' Commons".[198] Charles Dickens, who as a young man had been a reporter at Doctors Commons,[199] later was to offer a characterization of it as:

> ...a little out-of-the-way place, where they...play all kinds of tricks with obsolete old monsters of acts of Parliament, which three-fourths of the world know nothing about, and the other fourth supposes to have been dug up, in a fossil state, in the days of the Edwards. It's a place that has an ancient monopoly in suits about people's wills and people's marriages, and disputes among ships and boats.[200]

The image may be an apt description of the civilians' abode in its waning years, but in the late seventeenth century, the civilians still had one great battle ahead of them before succumbing to the superior political, financial, and numerical strength of practitioners of common law.

At the time of the Restoration, the civilians retained two advantages. The civil law was still favored by merchants. In addition, as Francis Bacon once had observed, amongst the states of Europe, the "law of nations" was part of the civil law, and a civil-law education was indispensable for English as well as Continental diplomats.[201] Indeed, Sir Leoline Jenkins' career as an ambassador was at least as noteworthy as his career on the Admiralty bench.[202] Nevertheless, it had become clear that the civilians could not hope to re-establish and protect their monopoly over maritime contracts. Instead, they sought the more modest goal of protecting their courts from the writ of prohibition. Moreover, as professional academics rather than politicians, the method that they selected for their counterattack was the written word. The struggle for English admiralty jurisdiction had passed into the phase known to history as the "Battle of the Books". Admittedly, "battle" is somewhat misleading. This contest lacked the parry-and-thrust polemics of the American Revolution's pamphleteering wars; instead the civilians generally aimed their barbs at their

---

198. *See* F. L. WISWALL, JR., THE DEVELOPMENT OF ADMIRALTY JURISDICTION AND PRACTICE SINCE 1800 (Cambridge: Cambridge University Press, 1970) at 75–81; COQUILLETTE, CIVILIAN WRITERS, *supra* note 7, at 22–25.

199. *See* WILLIAM S. HOLDSWORTH, CHARLES DICKENS AS LEGAL HISTORIAN (New Haven: Yale University Press, 1928) at 9. It is worth noting that prior to working at Doctors' Commons, Dickens had been in the office of a common lawyer by the name of "Charles Molloy"; Holdsworth declines to mention whether he also practiced maritime law or whether he was a descendent of the author of *De Jure Maritimo et Navali*. *Id.*

200. CHARLES DICKENS, DAVID COPPERFIELD (1st ed. 1850; *reprinted*, Nina Burgis ed., Oxford: Clarendon Press, 1981), Ch. XXIII at 292.

201. *See* quote, *supra* note 1.

202. *See generally* WYNNE, *supra* note 72.

favorite foil and bogeyman, the deceased Sir Edward Coke. It is not that the common lawyers did not reflect on maritime jurisdiction. Matthew Hale, Chief Justice of King's Bench, wrote an insightful treatise, but the work was not intended for mass consumption and was not published in his lifetime. William Prynne, the Puritan common lawyer, wrote a treatise on the subject which *was* published, but the chief target of his often splenetic pen was not the civilians, but Coke.

Prynne's writings provide some insight into how the common-law bar of the late 1600s viewed maritime jurisdiction. Prynne applauds Coke's contention that maritime and commercial contracts entered into within the boundaries of an English county—"*infra corpus comitatus*"—are within the exclusive jurisdiction of the courts of common law. Nonetheless, he parts company with Coke on the issue of foreign contracts, jurisdiction over which he concedes to the Admiralty Court. For Prynne, as for Coke before him, locality rather than subject-matter is dispositive in ascertaining which court has power to adjudicate. Moreover, for Prynne, the lines on a map also provide a bright-line jurisdictional rule. Where the common law has jurisdiction, the Admiralty does not, and *vice versa*.[203]

The first among the civilians to champion the cause of the Admiralty Court after the Restoration was Sir Richard Zouch. Zouch had been appointed judge of the Court in 1641, had lost his office during the Interregnum, and had regained it in 1661, only months before his death. Always politically cautious, he had avoided confrontations with the common-law faction in his lifetime, but his *Jurisdiction of the Admiralty of England Asserted*, published posthumously in 1663, shed its author's usual timidity in favor of a direct assault on Chapter XXII of Coke's *Fourth Institute*.[204] It took the form of nine "assertions" that contradicted Coke, citing sources ranging from the *Black Book of the Admiralty* to Selden.[205] Zouch is unique in his rejection of geography as the litmus test for jurisdiction. The crux of his argument against territorial jurisdiction comes in Assertion Five. Turning one of Coke's own canons of statutory construction against him, Zouch maintains that the purpose of the statutes of Richard II was to prevent the admiral's court from interfering with

203. *See* Prynne, Brief Animadversions, *supra* note 53, at 75–78; Hale and Fleetwood, *supra* note 54, Introduction at cx–cxii.

204. Coquillette, Civilian Writers, *supra* note 7, at 174–176.

205. The nine assertions are set out in the first two (*not paginated*) pages following the author's note "To the Reader" in the first edition of Zouch, *supra* note 16, and are reproduced by Prichard and Yale in Hale and Fleetwood, *supra* note 54, Introduction at cxiii–cxiv.

contracts to be performed on land. In the end, *situs* is important, but the place of performance—not the place of making—determines which court shall have cognizance.[206]

While Zouch defended the Admiralty Court's power to hear all maritime-contract cases, events of the last several decades had convinced him that exclusive jurisdiction was no longer a possibility. Emphasizing the unique advantages of the *lex maritima*, he argued instead more narrowly for freedom from common-law interference:

> It is not hereby intended that the Courts of Common Law cannot or do not take notice of the Law-Merchant, in Merchants cases, but that other things likewise considered, it might be thought reasonable, if they so desire, to allow them the choice of that Court, where the Law-Merchant is more respected, than to confine them to other Courts, where another Law is more predominant.[207]

Zouch's suggestion—concurrent jurisdiction—was not altogether novel; it had been employed previously in a few specific contexts.[208] Nonetheless, the proposed scope was novel, and if adopted it would have preserved the mainstay of the civilians' practice. Moreover, Zouch implies that—if left to their

---

206. *See* Zouch, *supra* note 16, at 57–63. Zouch measures the language of the Preamble of 15 Rich. II, c. 3 against Coke's Latin maxim (*Id.* at 59) requiring that specific statutes take precedence over more general ones and (with some help from Ulpian—*Id.* at 63) concludes that the statute, read in context, would concede to the Admiralty Court cognizance over contracts to be performed at sea. Zouch's creativity in shifting jurisdictional analysis away from locality to a "maritime-activity standard" should not be underestimated. It was not until the later half of the twentieth century that the "maritime-activity test" fully displaced locality in American law. *See Executive Jet Aviation Inc. v. City of Cleveland*, 409 U. S. 249 (1972) (abolishing the "locality test" for establishing federal admiralty jurisdiction in maritime tort actions). As for Zouch using Coke's canons of construction against him, he repeats the technique in Assertion Six, where—beginning with a Preamble of a statute of Edward II—he concludes that the admiralty jurisdiction extends to ports and rivers. *Id.* at 83; for discussion, *see* Joanne Mathiasen, *Some Problems of Admiralty Jurisdiction in the 17th Century*, 2 Am. J. Legal Hist. 215, 226–227 (1958) (hereinafter Mathiasen).

207. Zouch, *supra* note 16, at 144–145. Zouch further develops his notion of concurrent jurisdiction in Assertion Six, in which he observes that the Admiralty and the courts of common law have *divisum imperium* (shared jurisdiction) in areas falling between the high and low tide-marks. In other localities, either the common-law courts or the Admiralty Court may exercise jurisdiction, depending upon the subject-matter of the suit; Zouch terms this form of overlapping jurisdiction "*conjunctum imperium*". *Id.* at 101–102. (For discussion of "*divisum imperium*", *see supra* Introduction, note 22.)

208. For example, the Court of Requests for a time had concurrent jurisdiction over matters of salvage, spoil, reprisal, and prize. Holdsworth, *supra* note 6, Vol. V, at 139.

own preferences—the merchants and mariners would have entrusted the lion's share of the maritime business to Doctors' Commons rather than the Inns of Court. In this latter point, modern critics concur. As events throughout the Interregnum reveal, merchants preferred the Admiralty Court, and its decline resulted more from litigants' fear of prohibition than from the common law's ability to attract litigants through innovation in its procedural or substantive law.[209]

John Godolphin stands as a reminder against oversimplified analyses of history. A civilian *and* a Puritan, Godolphin backed Parliament in the Civil War. Under the Commonwealth, he replaced Zouch as judge of the Admiralty Court, and relinquished the bench at the Restoration. Nevertheless, his views on jurisdiction transcended politics, and his *Synegoros Thalassios* (published in 1661) generally has more in common with his fellow civilian, the royalist Zouch, than with the parliamentarian Coke.[210] He clearly shared with Zouch a belief that subject-matter, not geography, should determine jurisdiction:

> A Marine Contract may be made, and a Nautical Debt contracted as well by Land as by Sea, for security whereof Obligation may be afterwards made at or beyond the Sea, and be within the Cognizance of the Jurisdiction of the Admiralty; which would not signifie much in this or any Nation, if it could not administer Justice in any Cases save only such as have their Birth, Life and Death, their foundation, negotiation, and consummation precisely *Super altum mare*; specially where a surmise or suggestion may be material *quoad examen*, though the Case oft-times happens to prove otherwise, *quoad merita*.[211]

Like the merchant-petitioners of the Interregnum, Godolphin condemned the lack of certainty in jurisdiction at least as much as its distribution between the common law and the Admiralty:

209. *See e.g.* Steckley, *supra* note 119, at 174; HALE AND FLEETWOOD, *supra* note 54, Introduction at cxxvii–cxxviii. *But see* COQUILLETTE, CIVILIAN WRITERS *supra* note 7, at 215–254 (contending that the common law prevailed over the rival civil law in part because it adapted to the demands of merchants).

210. *See* COQUILLETTE, CIVILIAN WRITERS, *supra* note 7, at 186–187. As to the political leanings of Godolphin's writings, it should be noted that *Synegoros Thalassios* was published in 1661; one commentator has argued that Godolphin intentionally downplayed his parliamentarian sympathies and embraced royalist views on prerogative in order to appease the Crown and salvage his career. *See* Mathiasen, *supra* note 206, at 232–234.

211. GODOLPHIN, *supra* note 155, at 101. Godolphin nonetheless uses geography as *indicia* of whether matters are "maritime". For discussion, *see* Mathiasen, *supra* note 206, at 231–232.

> Though Merchants and Mariners *qua tales* be not such able Lawyers as to know *how* their Maritime Cases should be determined according to the exact Rule of Law, yet they are such able Supports to any Nation or Kingdom, that they are not to be left *sub incerto, where* or in what tribunal to find that Rule under such quality of Juridical Competency, as not to run hazards by Land as well as by Sea…[212]

While not embracing concurrent jurisdiction as explicitly as Zouch, Godolphin did express his belief that the common-law and admiralty jurisdictions should be able to coexist without conflict.[213]

The third civilian to publish a work on maritime jurisdiction in the early 1660s was John Exton. A graduate of Trinity Hall, Cambridge and successor to Zouch on the bench, Exton held judicial office during both the Interregnum and the Restoration. Published in 1664, the year after Zouch's *Jurisdiction of the Admiralty Asserted* and three years after Godolphin's *Synegoros Thalassios*, Exton's *Maritime Dicaeologie* also grounded jurisdiction in subject-matter rather than geography.[214] Moreover, like Godolphin, Exton sought to avoid conflicts between Admiralty and the common law through the distinction between maritime and land-based activities:

> In all which I have endeavoured neither to eclipse the honour, power, or least right of the Municipall Laws of this Kingdome, nor in any sort to detract from the renown of the Reverend and Learned Professors thereof, but hope I have manifested that the upholding of both Jurisdictions, and the restraining of each of them to its proper limits and confines, will be more advantageous to this Kingdome and the Inhabitants thereof, then [*sic*] the suffering either of them to swallow up or devour the other.[215]

---

212. *Id.*, sixth page of Introduction (*not paginated*) (*emphasis in the original*).

213. *See e.g. Id.* at 127–128; for discussion *see* Mathiasen, *supra* note 206, at 235

214. *See e.g.* Exton, *supra* note 66, at 43 (maintaining that maritime jurisdiction depends on whether a case relates to maritime activity or commerce), and at 252–253 (contending that a charterparty ought to fall within the cognizance of the Admiralty, although singed on land, because it is "made of and concerning a ship"). In general, the *Third Book*, devoted to jurisdiction over maritime contracts, addresses the preference for subject-matter over *situs* in allocating jurisdiction. *Id.* at 180–261.

215. *Id.*, third through fourth page of *Epistle Dedicatory (not paginated)*. For Exton's scheme for allocating jurisdiction, *see Id.*, Bk. II, Ch. I at 41–44. With regard to why each set of courts is best confined to its own subject-matter, Exton observes that the law applied by each would have gaps if applied to matters more properly within the jurisdiction of the other:

Ultimately, as a practical solution, Exton advocated a return to the compromise of 1632,[216] which would have secured for the Admiralty Court the scope of jurisdiction contained in the Ordinance of 1648, together with cognizance over bills of exchange.[217]

By the end of the decade, both Zouch and Exton were dead, and Godolphin had only eight more years to live. None would see the final stages of the struggle for jurisdiction nor the civilians' ultimate defeat. In their last efforts to preserve a significant role for the ancient Court, the civilians turned for leadership to Exton's successor on the bench, Sir Leoline Jenkins. Jenkins, a Welshman educated at Jesus College, Oxford, had sided with the royalists in the Civil War. In 1664, the forty-one year old civilian joined Doctors' Commons, and within a year received appointment as assistant to Exton, succeeding him upon his death three years later.[218] As with Mansfield, Jenkins authored no books or treatises; his writing is known to posterity through the posthumous publication of his opinions, letters, and speeches. Among these one speech stands out; in 1670, he appeared before the House of Lords to speak on behalf of a bill designed to resolve the conflict between the common law and the Admiralty regarding maritime jurisdiction. Having been defeated in a similar attempt seven years earlier, the civilians had regrouped, and they had pinned their hopes upon Jenkins' ability to sway Parliament.[219] His speech was not lengthy, amounting to no more than ten pages in fine print, but its concise defense of the admiralty jurisdiction exceeded both in organization and rhetorical effect the rambling and often tedious works of Godolphin and Exton.

The speech begins cautiously, with Jenkins stating: "I am to expect no Aids from the Civil Law, but am to make out what I shall offer to your Lordships,

---

> "If the power and privileges of either of these Jurisdictions should be decayed, or but impaired, though the other should be left never so entire, yet could not the effects of Justice in the one supply the defects in the other: For the Laws of the Land are no more fit to regulate the Affairs of the Sea, nor the Laws of the Sea any more apt to rule the business of the Land, then [*sic*] a horse is fit for a sea Voyage, or a ship for a land Journey."

Id. at 136.

216. *See supra* note 193 and text accompanying.

217. Exton, *supra* note 66, at 262–263. For discussion *see* Coquillette, Civilian Writers, *supra* note 7, at 184.

218. Coquillette, Civilian Writers, *supra* note 7, at 189–190.

219. *Id.* at 191–192. Ironically the most complete collection of Jenkins' work is the two-volume set published in 1724 and edited by William Wynne, a common lawyer, not a civilian.

by the peculiar Law and Practice of this Kingdom".[220] He anticipates a common-law rebuttal, and cites both Coke and Selden in an effort to meet the opposition on its own terms and to counter the lurking suspicion that the civilians are promoters of "foreign law". In a two-pronged attack, Jenkins argues both law and policy. On the side of policy, he maintains first that competing claims to jurisdiction produce inefficiency. To encourage the growth of trade, the nation must assure merchants that favorable decisions in the Court of Admiralty are secure from collateral attack in the courts of common law. Moreover, for some classes of cases, including suits for seamen's wages, Admiralty procedures are less costly and time-consuming for litigants than their common-law counterparts. Finally, the Admiralty Court can grant relief in many commercial cases—such as foreign contracts—over which the common law concededly lacks jurisdiction.[221] On the side of law, Jenkins remarks:

> All Merchants Abroad make their Contracts according to the marine or civil Law, the Differences therefore upon those Contracts, should not be judged by a Law that hath nothing in it, either provisional or decisive in such Cases.[222]

Having explained how the existing jurisdictional arrangement was detrimental to commerce, he turns his attention to his proposed solution. First, jurisdiction should be based on subject-matter, not locality:

> I hope, My Lords, I may take Leave to measure maritime Causes, by the same Rules and Reasons that we do other distinct Classes and Species of Causes; the *meer Locality* does not make a Cause maritime, but the Analogy that this Species has with others: For it was observed yesterday, that the sealing of a Bond or Lease *super altum mare*, would not make it cognisable in the Admiralty; I submit it to your Lordships then, whether the sealing of a *Charter-Party* to go from *London* to *Lisbon*, can make the Cause a Land Cause; since the main Scope of the Charter-Party is to be performed on the Sea, and nothing of the Undertaker's Business is to be performed upon the Land; and therefore by a Parity of Reason, that Case ought to be cognisable in the Admiralty, and not at Common Law.[223]

---

220. Sir Leoline Jenkins, "*Argument, in Behalf of a Bill to Ascertain the Jurisdiction of the Admiralty, in the House of Lords*" (1670), *reprinted in* WYNNE, *supra* note 72, Vol. I, at lxxvi.

221. *Id.*, Vol. I, at lxxxi–lxxxii.

222. *Id.*, Vol. I, at lxxxii.

223. *Id.*, Vol. I, at lxxvii (*emphasis in the original*).

Secondly, it is not necessary to eliminate all overlapping jurisdiction in order to create a workable system:

> But whether this of *encouraging so many young students*, of *satisfying Foreign Traders*, of giving *Dispatch to Mariners*, and to material Men the Security which they like best, shall be esteemed *real Conveniencies* or not; yet I hope, My Lords, to conclude with something that will give all Parties content, and must be understood to be a *Conveniency*; it is, that we of the Admiralty are content, that Suitors may have *their Option* of the Court they would sue in: If Mariners will go for their Wages, Owners for their Freight, Merchants for their Damages, Material Men for their Money, to the Common Law, we shall not in the least regret it: But if they choose rather to come to the Admiralty, (as they certainly will not, unless they find the Dispatch quicker, the Proceedings less chargeable, and the Methods of Judgment and Execution more suitable to their Business) we desire leave to receive them, and to do them Justice, without the Danger of a penal Statute, and without the Interruption of Prohibitions when once we are possessed of the Cause. And this is all we desire.[224]

This, in the end, was Jenkins' solution: let the parties choose their forum. Concurrent jurisdiction would have salvaged the civilians' practice and preserved merchants' access to the expedited procedures of the civil law. Nonetheless, Jenkins' speech failed. Its conciliatory tone reveals much. When one negotiates from a position of power, graciousness and magnanimity may be appropriate, but olive branches are unnecessary. The civilians tried one final time in 1685, again without success. By the end of that year, Jenkins was dead, and the civilians' efforts to preserve their ancient jurisdiction had died with him.[225]

John Marius, the author of the much-cited book on bills of exchange, had admonished his readers: "The right dealing Merchant doth not care how little he hath to do in the Common Law, or things of that nature."[226] Despite deficiencies in their rules of procedure, the courts of common law had secured for themselves cognizance over maritime causes. Hale, writing in the late

224. *Id.*, Vol. I, at lxxxv (*emphasis in the original*).

225. For a discussion of this bill, drafted in 1685 by Thomas Bedford, *see* Hale and Fleetwood, *supra* note 54, Introduction at cxxiv–cxxv n. 2; *see also* Coquillette, Civilian Writers, *supra* note 7, at 197.

226. Marius, *supra* note 97, (2d ed., 1655), "To the Reader" (*not paginated*).

1660s, treats the question of jurisdiction as already settled. Nonetheless, Hale's views do not entirely mirror those of Coke. With regard to substantive law, Hale concedes that the civil law has a role to play in filling gaps in England's domestic maritime law.[227] As for jurisdiction, Hale accepts the broad reach of the common-law courts and the restricted role for Admiralty envisioned by Coke, but he arrives at his conclusions in a different way. Missing is any discussion of exclusive jurisdiction grounded in geography. Jurisdiction over foreign contracts and transitory actions arising *super altum mare* is concurrent.[228] Analytically, Hale is thus closer to Zouch and Jenkins than to Coke and Prynne, though for him the scope of overlapping jurisdiction is considerably smaller. More significantly, by the close of the seventeenth century, "concurrent" has become an established part of the vocabulary of discourse on English jurisdiction.

Zouch had warned of the social dangers inherent when power is not allocated evenly between two sets of courts, observing: "[with] one Jurisdiction being the greater, a more potent may soon swallow up the other, not onley to the prejudice of the subjects for whose good the diversity of Courts were erected, but also the wrong of the Prince from whom those Jurisdictions are derived."[229] The admonition fairly sums up the experience of the Admiralty Court in the 1600s. By the eighteenth century, however, the atmosphere had begun to change. Through years of adjudication, the courts of common law were beginning to develop expertise and precedent in maritime matters in which the civilians and Prynne had lamented they were lacking. Moreover, the political climate had changed. In the early seventeenth century, much of the conflict between the courts of common law and the Court of Admiralty had been a reflection of the larger struggle between Parliament and the Crown. Gone was the conflict between royal prerogative and the ancient rights of Englishmen, and with it much of the friction of Catholic versus Protestant, Puritan versus Anglican, and English nationalism versus Continental cosmopolitanism that had characterized the 1600s. Riding the theory of mercantilism, Great Britain—as the nation had become with the Act of Union in 1707—faced new challenges and conflicts with the growth on an overseas empire. By the mid-1700s, the courts of common law were less concerned with using prohibitions to make a political point; the common-law bench recognized that parties often sought refuge in the courts of common law for strategic advan-

227. Hale, "*Disquisition*", Hale and Fleetwood, *supra* note 54, at 58.

228. *Id.* at 44–48, 107.

229. Zouch, *supra* note 16, at 131.

tage rather than to escape the abusive overreaching of a royal tribunal. Thus Judge Holt routinely had dispensed with the requirement of "*super altum mare*" in a narrow range of cases (such as those for seamen's wages),[230] and Mansfield later was to end the practice of collateral attacks on final decrees in Admiralty, noting that a party waived the right to apply for a prohibition if it were not asserted in a timely manner.[231]

Arthur Browne, who had commenced his study of admiralty jurisdiction in the 1770s, summarized the state of admiralty jurisdiction two centuries after the reign of the Tudors. While the rigid geographical rules had been relaxed to a degree, subject-matter was yet to replace locality as the basis for maritime jurisdiction.[232] Nevertheless, this relaxation had produced a sphere in which arguably both courts of admiralty and courts of common law had cognizance; as Browne observes:

> ... the extent of jurisdiction in the instance court of admiralty, which is at present seemingly allowed by the law courts, is, that it is confined in matters of contract to suits for seamen's wages, or those on hypothecations; in matters of tort to actions for assault, collision, and

---

230. *See* Hale and Fleetwood, *supra* note 54, Introduction at lvi.

231. In *Buggin v. Bennett,* 4 Burr. 2035, 2037 (K.B., 1767) *(emphasis in the original),* Mansfield held that:

> "If it appears on the *face of the proceedings* 'that the Court below have *no jurisdiction,'* a prohibition may be issued at any time, either before or *after sentence*: because all is a *nullity*; it is *coram non Judice*. But where it does *not* appear upon the face of the proceedings, if the defendant below will *lie by*, and suffer that court to go on under *apparent* jurisdiction, (as upon a contract made at sea,) it would be unreasonable that this party who when defendant below has thus lain by, and *concealed* from the Court below, a *collateral* matter, should come hither *after sentence* against him there, and suggest that *collateral* matter as a cause of prohibition, and obtain a prohibition upon it, *after all this acquiescence* in the jurisdiction of the court below."

232. Browne observes:

> "Thus we see, when we leave the plain principle of the subject matter determining the jurisdiction, there is no rest for the sole of the foot; and surely it seems but consistent, that as a contract, though made upon the sea, if not relative to maritime affairs, is triable only in the courts of common law; so a contract made upon the land, if relative solely to maritime affairs, ought to be cognizable in the admiralty: for as Sir L[eoline] Jenkins observes, how can the execution of a charter-party upon land to go from London to Lisbon make a cause a land cause, since the main scope of the charter-party is to be performed on the sea, and nothing of the *undertaker's* business is to be performed upon the land?"

Browne, *supra* note 9, Vol. II, at 90 *(emphasis in the original).*

> spoil; and in quasi contracts to actions by part owners for security, and actions of salvage; but if a party institute a suit in that court on a charter-party, for freight, in a cause of average and contribution, or to decide the property of a ship, and be not prohibited, I do not see how the court could refuse to entertain it; and I have some reason to think that this my opinion is supported by very high authority.[233]

Thus if Browne is correct, *in the absence of a prohibition*, the scope of admiralty jurisdiction at the close of the eighteenth century was as broad as that envisioned by Jenkins in his speech before Parliament more than a century earlier. Courts of admiralty possessed concurrent jurisdiction over most maritime matters. Admittedly the phrase "in the absence of a prohibition" is of crucial importance; for a party filing a breach-of-charterparty case in an admiralty court, the threat of prohibition would have hung over the proceedings like the sword of Damocles. Nevertheless, Mansfield's decision in *Buggin v. Bennett* had eliminated the risk of incurring high costs in litigating a case to final outcome before one court, only to repeat the entire process before another tribunal later. Moreover, it should be noted that much of the strategic advantage of launching a collateral attack in a second court disappears when that second tribunal lacks bias or animosity toward the court in which the case was first filed, and it is more difficult to raise an opponent's costs by filing in another court when his attorney is admitted to practice in both venues. In Scotland, where the civil law applied to marine and "terrine" matters alike, advocates were able to appear before both the civil and the maritime courts, and there was less tendency for parties to ask one court to enjoin proceedings of another.[234] A similar set of incentives applied in the American colonies. Lacking a "Doctors' Commons" of their own, the colonists were obliged to admit their common-law attorneys to practice in their vice admiralty courts, thereby deterring the rise of professional rivalries in competition for fees. This facilitated the development of a system of concurrent jurisdiction between the courts of vice admiralty and the courts of common law, which functioned relatively smoothly until the admiralty courts once again became caught up in a larger political struggle, this time between the colonial merchants and the Crown.

---

233. *Id.*, Vol. II, at 121–122.

234. *See* Hale and Fleetwood, *supra* note 54, at xlviii. *See also* *Acta Curiae Admirallatus Scotiae: 1557–1661* (Publications of the Stair Society, Vol. 2, Thomas Callander Wade ed., Edinburgh: Robert MacLehose & Co., 1937), Introduction at xxvi. It should be noted that the High Court of Admiralty of Scotland was a court of record. *Id.* at xxvi–xxvii.

CHAPTER II

> *"To what is urged of new powers granted to the Courts of Admiralty, or the extension of authority conferred on the judges, it may be answered in a few words, that [the American colonists] have themselves made such regulations necessary; that they are established for the prevention of greater evils..."*
>
> Samuel Johnson[1]

In the hundred years since Sir Edward Coke's retirement from Parliament, much had changed. England had survived civil war and witnessed the abolition and reinstitution of the monarchy. The Glorious Revolution had placed William and Mary upon the English throne. Sir Matthew Hale, whose tenure as Chief Justice had been second in influence only to that of Coke himself, had been dead for fifty years, while Mansfield's ascent to the bench was still three decades away. With the Act of Union in 1707, England and Scotland had been joined, becoming the nation of Great Britain. Ironically, the nation had emerged from the turmoil of the seventeenth century stronger rather than weaker. No longer was Britain an economic backwater. Economic growth, the elusive goal of Henry VIII, had transformed it into a modern nation with power rivaling any on the Continent, despite a century lacking the political stability that Henry had thought indispensable for his country's survival. One catalyst of this transformation had been trade. By the third decade of the eighteenth century, these changes had become manifest in the physical appearance of London itself; in the wake of the Great Fire, centuries of medieval clutter gave way to wider streets and spacious structures better suited to the city's new role as a mercantile and financial center. Fresh from a tour of the English countryside, Daniel Defoe paused to give his impres-

1. Samuel Johnson, Taxation no Tyranny: An Answer to the Resolutions and Address of the American Congress (London: T. Cadell, 1775) at 63 (hereinafter Johnson, Taxation.)

sions of the capital, a city of more than a million inhabitants and a "center of...commerce and wealth":[2]

> There is one great work yet behind, which, however, seems necessary to a full description of the city of London, and that is the shipping and the Pool; but in what manner can any writer go about it, to bring it into any reasonable compass? The thing is a kind of infinite, and the parts to be separated from one another in such a description, are so many, that it is hard to know where to begin.... That part of the river of Thames which is properly the harbour, and where the ships usually deliver or unload their cargoes, is called the Pool, and begins at the turning of the river out of Lime-house Reach, and extends to the Custom-house-Keys: In this compass I have had the curiosity to count the ships as well as I could, *en passant*, and have found above two thousand sail of all sorts, not reckoning barges, lighters or pleasure boats, and yatchs; but vessels that really go to sea.[3]

With these two thousand ships, Defoe observed "the business of export and import...is so prodigiously increased" that "[t]he revenue, or income, brought in by these warfs, inclusive of the warehouses belonging to them, and the lighters they employ, is said to amount to a prodigious sum; and, as I am told, seldom so little as forty thousand pounds per annum."[4] Adjacent to these moorings stood the newly renovated and enlarged architectural centerpiece, the Customs House.[5]

In the reign of Henry VIII, only somewhere between 3,000 and 5,000 Englishmen had made their living at sea; two centuries later that number had increased to 60,000.[6] By the early portion of the eighteenth century, a full

---

2. Daniel Defoe, A Tour Through England and Wales, Divided into Circuits or Journies (1st ed., 3 vols., 1724–1726; *reprinted,* Peter Davies ed., London: J. M. Dent & Sons, 1927), Vol. I, at 322, 335.

3. *Id.* at 347–348.

4. *Id.* at 342.

5. *Id.*

6. *See* Marcus Rediker, Between the Devil and the Deep Blue Sea: Merchant Seamen, Pirates, and the Anglo-American Maritime World, 1700–1750 (Cambridge: Cambridge University Press, 1987) at 290 (hereinafter Rediker). Rediker's estimates for the number of English sailors in the mid-sixteenth century are very conservative. While the ensuing thirty years—those of Hawkins, Drake, and the defeat of the Spanish Armada—were certainly a period of great growth, historian Lawrence Harper has estimated that England had more than 15,000 seamen scarcely one generation after the Rediker's first benchmark year, indicating a rate of growth of between 300% and 500% in three decades. *See* Lawrence A. Harper, The English Navigation Laws: A Seventeenth-Century Experiment in Social Engineering (1st ed. 1939; *reprinted* New York: Octagon Books,

twenty-five percent of Londoners were dependent upon maritime commerce for their livelihood.[7] In the thirty years preceding the Glorious Revolution, the tonnage carried by English ships increased at the rate of between two and three percent *per annum*. Spurred by policies that encouraged the growth of the merchant fleet, English tonnage itself grew from 68,000 at the time of the Spanish Armada to 162,000 at the Restoration, burgeoning to 581,000 on the eve of the American Revolution.[8] Moreover, in the century following the Civil War, the percentage of that tonnage engaged in foreign commerce doubled to more than fifty percent, with the greatest gains occurring in the first fifty years.[9] The traditional trade routes to northern Europe experienced increased activity, while those with southern Europe, dominated by the export of dried fish from the Grand Banks, expanded into Portuguese and Spanish ports. Trade with the East Indies was protected by a government-granted monopoly and concentrated in the import of luxury goods—such as silk, porcelain, and tea.[10] Nevertheless, it was through trade with its colonies in the New World that the nation would experience its greatest economic growth.[11]

1973) at 322 (hereinafter HARPER). Nevertheless, even using Harper's numbers, it is clear that the number of sailors in England increased at a significant rate over a span of less than two centuries.

7. REDIKER, *supra* note 6, at 21. Growth of the English maritime industry was not limited to London. Rediker notes that: "By 1740 London had lost a considerable share of its trading eminence to the western ports of Bristol, Liverpool, and Glasgow. Whereas in 1702 London had handled 43 percent of all English trade, that figure by 1751 had shrunk to 28 percent; outport tonnage increased to 72 percent of the total." *Id.* at 41–42.

8. *See* HARPER, *supra* note 6, at 339. While the author observes: "The task of determining the tonnage of English shipping resembles that of solving a cross-word puzzle" (*Id.* at 322), his statistics bear close resemblance to those of Rediker and McCusker (*infra* note 11). He describes the formulae by which he arrives at his figures in Chapter XXII at 327.

9. REDIKER, *supra* note 6, at 301–302. Rediker observes: "Although commercial statistics of the early modern period are notoriously fragmentary and difficult to interpret, the overall patterns in the growth of English trade are fairly clear.... The proportion of English tonnage engaged in foreign trade increased from 26.1 percent in 1660 to 45.9 percent on 1702, and further to 52.3 percent in 1773." HARPER, *supra* note 6, at 339 estimates the percentages somewhat higher, contending that 304,000 of 581,000 tons were engaged in foreign trade in 1773.

10. REDIKER, *supra* note 6, at 36–40.

11. There is some debate regarding the level of impact that England's colonial trade had on the development of its economy. In the period between 1752 and 1754, 33% of its imports came from its American colonies, while exports and re-exports of goods from England to the colonies represented 20% and 18% respectively of all goods leaving the country. *See* JOHN J. MCCUSKER & RUSSELL R. MENARD, THE ECONOMY OF BRITISH AMERICA: 1607–1789 (Chapel Hill: University of North Carolina Press, 1985) at 40 (hereinafter Mc-

From humble beginnings in Jamestown in 1607, the colonies' population grew twenty-four fold between the years 1650 and 1770.[12] Not surprisingly, much of the colonies' economic activity was tied in some manner to the sea; as in England, nearly one quarter of the working male population of Boston, Philadelphia, and New York derived its livelihood from maritime activities. Where Defoe had witnessed two thousand vessels moored in London's Pool, within less than a generation his colonial counterparts could count 1,500 ships that called New England's ports their home.[13] Predictably, maritime litigation in the colonies began almost as soon as maritime commerce itself. The pinnace "*Dove*", dispatched in 1634 by Leonard Calvert and his brother Cecil, Lord Baltmore, to carry the first settlers to Maryland, was sued by her own master for unpaid wages.[14] In 1625, it was a matter arising in Virginia that tested the High Court's power to adjudicate breaches of foreign con-

---

Cusker & Menard); *see also* Harper, *supra* note 6, at 271, stating that 36.5% of imports arriving at the port of London were from the American colonies. Nevertheless, these statistics may not convey the whole picture. English ledgers of the day failed to take account of various services as well as goods, thus omitting crucial information on the value of the carrying trades. McCusker & Menard at 75–76. Moreover, as one commentator has argued, in addition to the direct effects of the colonial trade on the economy, certain secondary effects must be considered. The colonial trade offered opportunities for utilizing domestic resources—including manpower—which in the absence of the trade would have been underemployed. Secondly, colonial demand placed additional pressure on scarce resources, thereby providing further incentives for technological innovation. Finally, economies of scale in the colonial trades required larger firms, which in turn spurred growth and improved efficiency in the insurance industry and facilitated the development of innovation in credit arrangements. *See* Jacob Price, *Colonial Trade and British Economic Development*, 14 *Lex et Scientia* 101, 122–123 (1978).

12. McCusker & Menard, *supra* note 11, at 53–54. Basing their estimates on assumptions of .3% (conservative) and .6% (somewhat more liberal) annual rate of economic growth from 1650–1774, the authors calculate the gross "national" product of the colonies to have reached somewhere between $327 million and $278 million respectively by 1720 (measured in 1980 dollars).

13. Rediker, *supra* note 6, at 61–65.

14. *See* David. R. Owen & Michael C. Tolley, Courts of Admiralty in Colonial America: The Maryland Experience 1634–1776 (Durham: Carolina Academic Press, 1995) at 23–24 (hereinafter Owen & Tolley). While the case involving the "*Dove*" has not been published, an abstract is available in Peter Wilson Coldham, English Adventurers and Emigrants, 1609–1660: Abstracts of Examinations in the High Court of Admiralty with Reference to Colonial America (Baltimore: Geneological Publishing Co., 1985), *Orchard v. Lord Baltimore* (H.C.A., 1636) at 64–65 (hereinafter Coldham, Abstracts: 1609–1660). For further discussion of the proceedings before the High Court of Admiralty, *see* Helen Crump, Colonial Admiralty Jurisdiction in the Seventeenth Century (New York: Longmans, Green & Co., 1931) at 75–76 (hereinafter Crump).

tracts.[15] Even the *Mayflower* did not escape unscathed; the Pilgrims' ship became the subject of a whaling dispute in 1626.[16] As one would expect, governmental infrastructure in the colonies was sadly lacking in these early years, and all three of these matters were litigated in London. Nonetheless, it soon became apparent that trying all maritime cases in England would be impractical and costly. Local tribunals were needed, first for handling a steady stream of instance cases, and soon thereafter to adjudicate prize cases also. Moreover—and most importantly—England needed *fora* for enforcement of the legal cornerstone of its mercantilist policies, the Navigation Acts.

Practicality was essential. Neither the colonists nor those in power in England had vested interests in structuring colonial admiralty courts in conformity with political ideology. The colonists cared little whether juries were a Saxon legacy to modern Englishmen or whether the common law existed from time immemorial and held precedence over royal prerogative. They were, however, concerned with having their private disputes decided expeditiously. The matter stood much the same in England. The struggle over admiralty jurisdiction, an outgrowth (and often a microcosm) of the conflict between the Crown and Parliament, had run its course before there arose a need for defining and demarking maritime jurisdiction in the colonies. Resolution of colonial instance cases and the occasional prize case were important to those in power in England, but only in order to keep the wheels of commerce well lubricated,[17] not to make a symbolic point to political rivals by holding up one tribunal as superior to another. Even with the Navigation Acts, where the government's interest was stronger than in private disputes, it was the revenue itself—rather than the mechanisms of enforcement—with which the government was most concerned. As one commentator later was to remark: "the mother country was more interested in enforcing the laws than in establishing nice lines of demarcation between jurisdictions as a matter of form."[18] As a result, colonial maritime jurisdiction came to be dispersed among many

---

15. For discussion of King's Bench's denial of a prohibition in *Tucker v. Cappes*, 2 Rolle 492 (1625), *see* M. J. PRICHARD & D.E.C. YALE, HALE AND FLEETWOOD ON ADMIRALTY JURISDICTION (London: Publications of the Selden Society Vol. 108, 1992), Introduction at lxxxvi.

16. R. G. Marsden, "The High Court of Admiralty in Relation to National History, Commerce, and the Colonisation of America—A.D. 1550–1650", *in* TRANSACTIONS OF THE ROYAL HISTORICAL SOCIETY, Vol. 16, (New Series: London, 1902) at 69, 89.

17. *See* REDIKER, *supra* note 6, at 119 (noting that swift and inexpensive resolution of disputes over seamen's wages was important to the English economy and hence also of great concern to the nation's policy-makers.)

18. HARPER, *supra* note 6, at 189.

courts—some common-law and others operating under the aegis of the High Court of Admiralty—with a substantial area in which both common-law and civil-law courts held concurrent jurisdiction. In England, the rivalry between the common lawyers and the civilians intensified the conflict, but such was not the case in America. There was no "Doctors' Commons" in the colonies. Only one doctor of civil law immigrated to America to serve as a judge, and there is no record of an English civil-law practitioner crossing the Atlantic.[19] As a result, colonial vice admiralty courts—civil-law tribunals—were forced to admit common-law attorneys to practice. To do so, the vice admiralty courts were obliged to make some concessions in the fine points of curial law, creating hybrid procedural rules that sought to preserve the efficiency of the civil-law system while simultaneously permitting colonial attorneys to conduct trials in much the same way they did in the provincial courts.[20] Thus colonial lawyers proceeded *in rem* and consolidated seamen's claims for wages into a single suits for whole crews, but filed "pleas" and "demurrers", not "libels" or "answers". Parties were more often "plaintiffs" and "defendants" than "libellants", "claimants", "impugnants" or "respondents".[21] Moreover, overlapping jurisdiction produced hybrid procedures in the common-law courts as well. On occasion these provincial courts even entertained suits *in rem*.[22]

To better accommodate the needs of their litigants, the colonial courts also frequently dispensed with the geographical limitations of the statutes of Richard II.[23] For certain classes—shipowners, ship-builders, chandlers, seamen, and particularly merchants—occasional litigation was part of the costs of their respective occupations. Unlike modern forum-shopping, in which parties compare substantive rules in selecting a court, colonial litigants were more concerned with comparing rules of procedure. That court was best which adjudicated most quickly and inexpensively. Moreover, those whose business operations necessarily involved occasional trips to court, such as mer-

---

19. The only English doctor of civil law to immigrate to America was William Spry, who became judge of the ill-fated and short-lived Vice Admiralty Court established in Halifax in 1764 for the enforcement of the trade acts. For discussion, *see* Owen & Tolley, *supra* note 14, at 39–40, 175.

20. *See e.g.* Matthew P. Harrington, *The Legacy of the Colonial Vice-Admiralty Courts* (Part II), 27 J. Mar. L. & Com. 323, 324–325 (1996) (hereinafter Harrington (Part II)).

21. *See e.g.* Charles Merrill Hough, Reports of Cases in the Vice Admiralty of the Province of New York and in the Court of Admiralty of the State of New York: 1715–1788 (New Haven: Yale University Press, 1925), Introduction at xiii (hereinafter Hough, Vice Admiralty of New York).

22. *See e.g.* Owen & Tolley, *supra* note 14, at 182–187.

23. 13 Rich. II, c. 5 (1389); 15 Rich. II, c. 3 (1391).

chants, preferred having their disputes resolved in familiar surroundings with familiar procedures. It mattered not to a merchant that one charterparty was signed in the colony and another was signed overseas. As both are the same type of contract, should not the same court construe their respective terms? From a businessman's standpoint, the jurisdictional restrictions of the statutes of Richard II made little sense. Subject matter—not locality—should determine jurisdiction. Not all colonies responded to these social pressures in the same way. Some recognized the medieval limits, while others, relying upon broad grants of jurisdiction in the colonial vice-admiralty patents, permitted their maritime courts to hear causes arising *infra corpus comitatus*.[24] Most, however, recognized a substantial sphere of activities in which both admiralty courts and common-law courts had cognizance, and left the selection of the appropriate forum to the convenience of the parties.

Left to their own devices, the colonial courts found a means of adjudicating private maritime disputes in a manner satisfactory to all classes that had regular recourse to the judicial system. Admittedly, the writ of prohibition appears occasionally in the colonial records, but does so as the merchants' weapon in revenue cases, not instance cases. This chapter seeks to explore how colonial courts' development of hybrid rules of procedure and flexible jurisdictional rules shaped merchants' and shipowners' expectations of how a system of maritime courts should function. In addition, it examines how the evolving scheme of overlapping jurisdiction influenced the Framers' understanding of how American courts traditionally had handled maritime cases, and provides a point of reference for examining the jurisdictional scheme that the First Congress incorporated into the Judiciary Act of 1789.[25]

The Early History of Maritime Litigation in the American Colonies

Maritime disputes arose in America before the founding of permanent colonies. As early as the sixteenth century, various entrepreneurs had acquired from the Crown patents granting fishing rights in the North Atlantic off Newfoundland. To enforce their monopoly-rights and settle disputes among them-

---

24. There is no evidence that the statutes of Richard II were in force in either Virginia or Maryland (Owen & Tolley, *supra* note 14, at 28 n. 13, 138), although Rhode Island recognized the English limitations on jurisdiction. *See* Frederick Bernays Wiener, *Notes on the Rhode Island Admiralty*, 46 Harv. L. Rev. 44, 62 (1933) (hereinafter Wiener).

25. 1 Stat. 77 (1789).

selves, the patentees sought to establish a vice admiralty court in 1615.[26] When settlements were established, some rudimentary means of preserving law and order was required, but creation of a specialized tribunal for maritime disputes was not initially a priority. As historian Helen Crump has observed:

> The first work of a new settlement is concerned with the need of food and shelter; for niceties of law there is no time. In a young community justice is of necessity often rude and ready, though the experience of the settlers soon led to the development of a simplified system based on English law. But admiralty courts are highly specialised and are concerned only with maritime affairs, so that as long as a colony had little trade there was no need for an admiralty court. From the point of view of the settler the ordinary court, usually the council, was all that was necessary, and if the admiralty courts had been left to develop naturally in the colonies, they would only have appeared as the growth of trade warranted.[27]

As one would expect, records from this phase of colonial history are incomplete. Nevertheless, surviving documents offer a glimpse into how various colonies first chose to handle maritime disputes. In Maryland in 1639, the Lord Proprietor[28] had submitted to the colony's Assembly a draft of a bill to establish a maritime court that would "enjoy use and exercise all or any the said or the like powers privileges authorities and Jurisdictions within this Province as the high Court of Admiralty in England enjoys or may enjoy use and exercise within the Realm of England".[29] When the bill failed to pass, the colony vested admiralty jurisdiction in the Provincial Court, which heard its first maritime case in 1643 and continued to entertain all instance actions until the founding of first vice admiralty court in 1694. Even into the eighteenth century, the Provincial Court would retain concurrent jurisdiction over instance cases, sitting in admiralty with or without a jury at the parties' request.[30]

---

26. It is worth noting that this court utilized juries. *See* Crump, *supra* note 14, at 25–29.

27. *Id.* at 24.

28. Maryland was a proprietary colony from its founding in 1634 through 1689. From 1689 through 1715, it was under royal government, passing back into proprietary rule at the end of that period. Joseph H. Smith, "The Foundations of Law in Maryland" *in* Law and Authority in Colonial America (George Athan Billias ed., Barre, Massachusetts: Barre Publishers, 1965) at 92.

29. Owen & Tolley, *supra* note 14, at 53. The authors reproduce the text of the bill from manuscript in Appendix H at 387–388.

30. *Id.* at 79–83. In the early period, the Provincial Court consisted of the governor and council sitting in a judicial capacity. With regard to the use of juries, the authors note

Other colonies had similar experiences. The charter of Massachusetts provided for admiralty jurisdiction, but the colony did not see fit to create a special tribunal to try maritime cases. These cases were heard instead by the colony's common-law courts, and a jury—though not required—was permissible if one of the parties desired it.[31] In 1660, Virginia vested power in the governor and Council to hear maritime cases, granting them broad jurisdiction exceeding that of the High Court of Admiralty.[32] In its early years, Connecticut empowered its courts of common law to decide maritime cases under the "laws of Oleron", a practice that continued even after independence and the ratification of the Articles of Confederation.[33] Lacking a vice admiralty court of its own until the mid-1700s, Rhode Island was obliged to confer cognizance

---

that the parties opted for a jury in only eleven of the forty maritime cases for which records survive, and of those in only nine of the thirty filed after 1694, when litigants had the option in filing in the Vice Admiralty Court instead. The statistics indicate that among differences in procedures employed by the two courts, the availability of a jury was seldom dispositive in parties' selection of a forum.

31. *Id.* at 37–39; 47–49. In his study of the Massachusetts Vice Admiralty Court, L. Kinvin Wroth makes the following observation regarding the colony's formative period: "In the earliest years of the Massachusetts Bay Colony, a few maritime cases, suggesting a relatively simple commerce, came up in the ordinary courts. More complicated matters were referred for arbitration to a committee with power to examine witnesses under oath." L. Kinvin Wroth, *The Massachusetts Vice Admiralty and the Federal Admiralty Jurisdiction*, 6 Am. J. Legal Hist. 250, 253 (Part I), 347 (Part II) (1962) (hereinafter Wroth). Portions of this article subsequently were reprinted in LAW AND AUTHORITY IN COLONIAL AMERICA, *supra* note 28, at 32–73.

32. As governor-and-Council was not a "vice admiralty court" in the usual meaning of the term, the Assembly's disregard for the limitations of the Statutes of Richard II is not as surprising it might first appear. The act provided that the governor and Council would:

> "...have full power and authority of a Court of Admiralty to cognoss [*sic*], determine, and administer justice in all things pertaining to sea-faring, that shall appertaine, happen, or fall out within the jurisdiction of this collonie, either between mariner and merchant, or mariner and master, as likewise all complaints, contracts, offences, pleas, exchanges, assecurations [*sic*], debts, counts, charter-parties, covenants, and all other writings concerning lading and unlading of shipps, freights, hyres, and all other business among sea affairs done on the water and when within the limits of the jurisdiction of Virginia, or the laws and cognizance thereof, with the cognition of writs, the causes and actions of reprisals, of letters of marque, to take stipulations, cognitions and instructions."

Published in OWEN & TOLLEY, *supra* note 14, at 28.

33. CHARLES ANDREWS, "The Vice-Admiralty Courts" *in* THE COLONIAL PERIOD OF AMERICAN HISTORY, Vol. IV (New Haven: Yale University Press, 1938), at 232 (hereinafter ANDREWS); HENRY J. BOURGUIGNON, THE FIRST FEDERAL COURT: THE FEDERAL APPELLATE PRIZE COURT OF THE AMERICAN REVOLUTION, 1775–1787 (Philadelphia: The Amer-

over instance cases upon its common-law courts.[34] When the Dutch ceded possession of New Amsterdam to the English, they left behind a body of substantive law and a fully functioning system of courts to administer it. From 1664 through 1685 the English introduced both the common law and new courts to administer it, among which the Court of Assizes had jurisdiction over criminal matters and private disputes involving large sums.[35] Nevertheless, the Mayor's Court, a vestige of the old Dutch regime, handled most of the maritime business in New York. Generally, this court acted under a special commission from the governor to sit as a court of admiralty, but there is evidence that it occasionally heard cases involving seamen's wages or maritime contracts of its own initiative.[36] In Pennsylvania, the colony's charter had given the proprietor authority to establish courts with power to hear cases arising "by land and by sea". These charter-rights notwithstanding, in the decade between the colony's founding and England's decision to create vice admiralty courts for America, William Penn refrained from erecting a maritime court, preferring instead to allow the courts of general jurisdiction to decide maritime disputes.[37]

If dissatisfied with local colonial courts, litigants could opt for English courts instead. When merchants were on opposite sides of the Atlantic, this option had its advantages, particularly in breach-of-contract cases where the colonial party had an agent in London. Records show that the High Court of Admiralty continued to hear such cases even after Parliament authorized the Crown to create vice admiralty courts in America.[38] For those doing business

---

ican Philosophical Society, 1977) at 195 (hereinafter BOURGUIGNON, FIRST FEDERAL COURT).

34. For discussion, *see* RECORDS OF THE VICE-ADMIRALTY COURT OF RHODE ISLAND, 1715–1752 (Dorothy S. Towle ed., Introductions by Charles Andrews and Dorothy S. Towle, Washington D. C.: American Historical Association, 1936), Introduction (Towle) at 81–100 (hereinafter Towle, RECORDS).

35. *See* Herbert Alan Johnson, "The Advent of Common Law in Colonial New York" *in* LAW AND AUTHORITY IN COLONIAL AMERICA, *supra* note 28, at 74–87.

36. *Id.* at 82–83.

37. Matthew P. Harrington, *The Legacy of the Colonial Vice-Admiralty Courts* (Part I), 26 J. Mar. L. & Com. 581, 595–600 (1995) (hereinafter Harrington (Part I)). When an act of Parliament gave the Crown the power to establish a vice admiralty court in the colony in 1696, Penn appeared before the Board of Trade in person, protesting that to do so would violate his proprietory rights. Moreover, to reinforce his argument, he threatened to create a maritime tribunal of his own, though ultimately he abandoned the scheme.

38. *See e.g.* CRUMP, *supra* note 14, at 76. To date, the decisions of the High Court of Admiralty in the seventeenth and eighteenth centuries have not been published. For those wishing to examine the records without traveling to England, genealogist Peter Coldham

further north, there were the courts of Scotland. In 1681, the Scottish Parliament had vested in the nation's Admiralty Court cognizance over "all maritim and sea-faring causes, forreigne and domestick, whether civil or criminal, whatsoever within this realme, and over all persons as they are concerned in the same."[39] Records survive for ten cases filed before the creation of courts of vice admiralty in the colonies, and for eight more between that time and the

has assembled in two volumes abstracts of all of the High Court's cases related to America for the period 1609–1733. For the years 1609–1660, he has identified 185 cases. *See* COLDHAM, ABSTRACTS: 1609–1660, *supra* note 14. He has identified 183 more for the period 1661–1733. See PETER WILSON COLDHAM, ENGLISH ADVENTURERS AND EMIGRANTS: 1661–1733: ABSTRACTS OF EXAMINATIONS IN THE HIGH COURT OF ADMIRALTY WITH REFERENCE TO COLONIAL AMERICA (Baltimore: Geneological Publishing Co., 1985). Coldham's recently published supplement to the two-volume set includes materials dating back to 1625 that were omitted in the earlier edition, as well as materials for the years from 1733–1777. About the latter, Coldham remarks:

> "The principal reason why the series has not hitherto been continued up to the beginning of the Revolutionary War is that, by an act of apparent bureaucratic vandalism, the HCA Examination Books in Instance cases after 1745 were early in the last century ordered for destruction together with other unique HCA records. An attempt has therefore had to be made to compensate for the loss of these papers by consulting alternative and subsidiary records to be found scattered amongst HCA and Treasury sources. In this way a conspectus of the work of this court in cases affecting the American colonies has now been effected up to the year 1777."

PETER WILSON COLDHAM, MORE ENGLISH ADVENTURERS AND EMIGRANTS, 1625–1777: ABSTRACTS OF EXAMINATIONS IN THE HIGH COURT OF ADMIRALTY WITH REFERENCE TO COLONIAL AMERICA (Baltimore: Geneological Publishing Co., 2002), Introduction at v. This supplement identifies an additional 239 cases related to the 13 colonies.

39. The text of the Act is reproduced in the Introduction *(not paginated)* of DAVID DOBSON, AMERICAN DATA FROM THE RECORDS OF THE HIGH COURT OF ADMIRALTY OF SCOTLAND, 1675–1800 (Baltimore: Clearfield Co., 2000) (hereinafter DOBSON). Dobson's book provides summaries of cases in the unpublished court records of the High Court, which are housed in the West Register House, Charlotte Square, Edinburgh. For an account of the jurisdiction of the Scottish Admiralty court in the late seventeenth century, *see* JAMES [DALRYMPLE], VISCOUNT OF STAIR, THE INSTITUTIONS OF THE LAWS OF SCOTLAND, DEDUCED FROM ITS ORIGINALS, AND COLLATED WITH THE CIVIL, CANON, AND FEUDAL LAWS, AND WITH THE CUSTOMS OF NEIGHBOURING NATIONS (2d ed.1693; David M. Walker ed., University Presses of Edinburgh and Yale, 1981), Bk. II, Tit. 2, Sec. 2 at 314 (over prize); Bk. IV, Tit. 1, Sec. 58 at 797 (over prize and maritime causes); Bk. IV, Tit. 37, Sec. 4 at 943 (scope of Court's jurisdiction). If the subject-matter of the cases that Dobson summarizes are representative (*see infra* note 40), the Court routinely exercised in practice a wider jurisdiction than Stair attributes to it. *See also* *ACTA CURIAE ADMIRALLATUS SCOTIAE*: 1557–1661 (Publications of the Stair Society, Vol. 2, Thomas Callander Wade ed., Edinburgh: Robert MacLehose & Co., 1937), Introduction at xvii–xviii (noting that the Admi-

Act of Union in 1707.[40] Contrary to expectations, with the merger of England and Scotland, the flow of American cases into the Scottish court actually increased. Between 1707 and 1776, the court heard nearly two hundred cases related to colonial navigation and commerce.[41] For most litigants, however, the courts of England and Scotland were not a practical alternative. Geography *per se* posed no serious inconvenience so long as parties had a choice of litigating either in the colonies or in the mother country, but it was not the locality, but rather the civil-law procedures that induced those for whom the costs were not prohibitive to file their claims in the High Court of Admiralty. Even with their hybrid procedures, flexible rules of evidence, and ability to jettison the jury if the parties so desired, the colonial common-law courts could not compete with the Admiralty Court in experience with substantive maritime law. Colonial merchants and shipowners desired a specialized tribunal to supplement—not replace— the existing courts, but their influence alone was not sufficient to induce England to create one at their behest. Thus the colonies were to remain without vice admiralty courts until England itself found a use for them.

Vice Admiralty Courts and the Navigation Acts

The term "vice admiral" dates from 1536, though the office itself has its origins earlier in the reign of Henry VIII. Created to carry out many of the du-

---

ralty Court's jurisdiction "covered seafaring questions, and a wide interpretation was given to that definition" and citing examples).

40. Dobson, *supra* note 39, at 1–10. Of the ten cases adjudicated before 1696, five are commercial and two involve wages. Of the remaining three, there is one claim for freight, one prize case, and a materialman's claim for payment for victualling a ship. The facts alleged in several of these cases attest to the breadth of the maritime jurisdiction exercised in Scotland. Neither claim for wages was made by a "seaman" in the traditional sense. One was filed by a cartographer and the other by an agent whose job it was to sail to America and report to investors on the condition of their plantation. Similarly, one of the commercial cases involved the breach of a contract to establish a settlement, a "maritime" matter only in that a ship was required for transportation.

41. *Id.* at 11–85. Dobson identifies 181 cases with connections to the American colonies litigated by the Scottish court, of which suits relating to contracts of carriage (charterparties and bills of lading) were the most numerous, with a substantial percentage of the rest being divided among commercial contracts and seamen's wages. In addition, there were a few cases relating to partnership disputes, maritime torts, materialmen's claims, bottomry, prize, and salvage.

ties of the Lord High Admiral, these officers were responsible for protecting the coasts from piracy and for ensuring that the Crown received its share of wrecks, flotsam, jetsam, and royal fish. Moreover, each vice admiral was required to establish a court and to appoint a deputy learned in civil law to serve as its judge. These courts were authorized to adjudicate maritime disputes between private parties and were required to hold sessions at convenient times. In time, all maritime counties in England had their own vice admiralty courts.[42] The judges and registrars were compensated out of the fines and fees collected by the courts.[43] In the Tudor and Stuart periods, the vice admiralty extended no further than the coasts of England and Ireland, but as trade with England's New World possessions grew, pressures mounted for the creation of vice-admiralty jurisdictions for the plantations as well. Though each colony needed a vice admiralty court for somewhat different reasons, one common thread underlay the decision to expand the scope of vice-admiralty jurisdiction into America. As historian Helen Crump observed:

> In the New World the vice-admiralty courts originated in the circumstances of the various colonies, in trade at Boston or Jamestown, in wreck at Bermuda, in prize and piracy in the West Indies, but the courts developed under the aegis of the Imperial government for the purpose of enforcing an imperial trade policy…[44]

In Restoration England, trade policy was mercantilism. Admittedly, since the advent of modern economic thought—from Adam Smith to Alfred Marshall to John Maynard Keynes—mercantilism has had a bad reputation. We are conditioned to respond to "mercantilism" much as modern chemists and physicists respond to "alchemy". It is important, however, to see seventeenth and eighteenth century mercantilism in the context of the times that produced it. More was at stake than "economic efficiency". National security was of paramount importance. It was widely believed that the key to security was the ac-

---

42. *See* Crump, *supra* note 14, at 13–14. All business of the court was to be conducted in the presence of a registrar (or "register" as the office later was called in the colonies) who kept the court's records.

43. In the early period, the judges received a share of flotsam, jetsam, and wreck, thus even inducing some judges of the High Court of Admiralty to "ride circuit" in order to augment their fees. After 1636, however, all perquisites of the Admiralty were handed over to the Crown, while the judge, registrar, and marshal were to be paid out of the "amerciaments and profitts" of the court, with the judge receiving half and the other two officers dividing the balance between them equally. *Id.* at 16–19.

44. *Id.* at 183.

quisition of bullion, without which the nation could not wage war.[45] A domestic economic policy based on efficiency looks only to the size of one's own slice of the pie, irrespective of the size of the slices obtained by one's trading partners. When one's trading partners are also potential enemies in war, however, relative wealth becomes relevant, and it may be better to settle for less in absolute terms than to risk having less than one's competitors.[46] For England, the motives for adopting mercantilist policies were especially strong, as the country lacked natural sources of gold and silver. Moreover, as an island nation, England lacked other resources, including timber, which rendered it vulnerable if war were ever to cut off supplies when they were most needed. Lack of inexpensive indigenous timber was particularly troubling, because without it English shipbuilders could not hope to compete with foreign builders, and thus would not be available to supply the Royal Navy in time of crisis.[47] Self-sufficiency, England's policy-planners thought, would solve the problem. Jamestown had failed to produce the much desired bullion, but the Atlantic seaboard was covered with timber. Soon Virginia had found a cash-crop in tobacco, a ubiquitous weed with the potential to erase England's trade deficit. When the common economic wisdom of the day converged with a new-found supply of natural resources, the seductive allure of mercantilism was irresistible. The nation had found a way to convert theory into practice. As Adam Smith later was to remark: "one of the principal effects of those discoveries has been to raise the mercantile system to a degree of splendour which it could never otherwise have attained to."[48]

---

45. As Harper explains:

> "The danger of war explains much that might otherwise be difficult to understand in English mercantilism. It clears up the apparent paradox of the adoption, by a country in which agricultural interests predominated, of legislative programs which redounded principally to the merchants' advantage. The explanation lies in the correlation supposed to exist between national security, bullion, and foreign trade. War was managed by the 'power of money', and it was believed that no nation could be 'accounted safe, or mistress of its liberties' without an adequate supply. Since England had no gold or silver of her own, she could acquire the bullion upon which the monetary system rested only by exporting more merchandise than she imported. Hence the landed gentry could be persuaded to pass legislation intended to promote a favorable balance of trade."

HARPER, *supra* note 6, at 9–10.

46. *Id.* at 375–376.

47. *Id.* at 10.

48. ADAM SMITH, AN INQUIRY INTO THE NATURE AND CAUSES OF THE WEALTH OF NATIONS (1st ed., 1776; Edwin Cannan ed., New York: Modern Library, 1937), Bk. IV, Ch. VII at 591 (hereinafter SMITH, WEALTH OF NATIONS).

The "encouragement of exportation, and the discouragement of importation," Smith wrote, "are the two great engines by which the mercantile system proposes to enrich every country."[49] Historian Lawrence Harper summarized England's trade policy in a nutshell, remarking: "The main concern of Parliament was to reserve the plantation trade for English shipping, to give England a monopoly of certain colonial products, and to help her in retaining the colonial market."[50] Monopolies, as Smith was quick to point out, are not efficient.[51] By restricting the markets into which the colonists could export their goods, England forced America to absorb much of the economic cost of mercantilism. These policies no doubt raised prices of some commodities for English consumers as well. Nevertheless, the policies bolstered English shipbuilding and the carrier-trades, both essential to national security, for which the Crown and Parliament were willing to overlook a certain modicum of inefficiency.[52] As Harper later was to observe:

> In so far as seventeenth-century theorists attempted any reconciliation of individual interest and public welfare, it rested on the assumption that there was an ideal balance which, if attained, would secure national prosperity as well as individual advancement.... Followers of Adam Smith must not misunderstand the nature of the assumption. It did not rely upon any doctrine that the "invisible hand" of Providence would supply the necessary guidance, if only man would not interpose his puny efforts. Mercantilists probably believed as devoutly in the wisdom and omnipotence of the Diety as did Smith, but they placed less reliance upon the assumption, "the Lord will provide" than upon the proverb, "God helps those who help themselves".[53]

Theoretical purists working in Smith's tradition today may condemn the practice, but few, if any, nations ever have practiced *laissez-faire* trade policy. Regulation is inevitable; at stake is merely the matter of degree. To judge whether

---

49. *Id.*, Bk. IV, Ch. VIII at 607.

50. Harper, *supra* note 6, at 242.

51. Smith, the first writer to examine what economists now call "deadweight losses", explains:

> "In the trade to America, [England] endeavours to engross as much as possible the whole market of its own colonies, by fairly excluding all other nations from any direct trade to them.... Monopolies of [this kind] always attract to the particular trade in which they are established, a greater proportion of the stock [*i.e.* "capital"] of the society than what would go to that trade of its own accord."

Smith, Wealth of Nations, *supra* note 48, Bk. IV, Ch. VII at 595–596.

52. Harper, *supra* note 6, at 343, 347, 362–372.

53. *Id.* at 18.

a particular policy was successful, one would have to place a price on national security and then attempt to assess whether the measures adopted achieved their goals at the lowest possible cost.

The forerunner of England's seventeenth-century Navigation Acts was enacted during the Commonwealth in 1651. Eschewing the complexities of earlier efforts at trade regulation, Parliament concentrated upon imports. The plan was fairly simple: goods entering England should do so directly from the nation of origin and should be carried either in that nation's ships or in English-flagged vessels. Admittedly, there were some exceptions, as where the port from which a particularly commodity was first shipped was not in the nation of origin.[54] Nevertheless, the general thrust of the statute was to cut off "middle-men" and prevent transshipment of goods destined for English markets.[55] Following the Restoration, Charles II refused to recognize legislation promulgated by the Commonwealth, and Parliament was obliged to re-enact the trade statute in 1660, but not before making some significant changes. The Act of 1651 was fairly straightforward, stating a general rule and providing exceptions. By contrast, its successor assumed the legality of importing in foreign vessels, but provided an extensive list of enumerated goods that could enter English ports only if carried in ships of the country of origin or in English bottoms.[56] Colonial exports remained largely unaffected; the Act banned

54. For a detailed summary and analysis of the Act of 1651, including the exceptions to the rule requiring the carriage of imported goods by English vessels, *see* JOHN REEVES, THE LAW OF SHIPPING AND NAVIGATION (1st ed. 1792; 2d ed., London: W. Clarke & Sons, 1807), Part II at 35–41 (hereinafter REEVES).

55. HARPER, *supra* note 6, at 38, 48–49. Parsing the provisions of all of the Navigation Acts is beyond the scope of the present study. Even Harper, whose own work on the Acts exceeds five hundred pages, provides the caveat: "A complete statement of the law of navigation throughout its history would require a book many times the size of this." *Id.* at 387. He provides a useful summary of the seventeenth-century Acts in an Appendix at 387–414. For additional information on the Acts, as well as the customs system that enforced them, *see* ELIZABETH EVELYNOLA HOON, THE ORGANIZATION OF THE ENGLISH CUSTOMS SERVICE 1696–1786 (1st ed., 1938; *reprinted* New York: Greenwood Press Publishers, 1968) (hereinafter HOON).

56. For discussion, *see* HARPER, *supra* note 6, at 51–53. Harper provides the following list of enumerated goods:

> "The specified goods constitute a somewhat impressive list, including as they did, all Russian goods, as well as masts, timber, boards, foreign salt, pitch, tar, rosin, hemp or flax, raisins, figs, prunes, olive oils, corn or grain, sugar, potashes, wines, vinegar, and spirits called aqua vitae, or brandy-wine, together with currants and Turkish goods. But calculated from the London import figures for 1663 and 1669, they composed only slightly more than 50 percent of Europe's trade with England in weight and less than 50 percent in value."

exportation of only seven commodities.[57] It was however the next of the Navigation Acts, the Staple Act of 1663, that had the greatest impact on American colonial trade. With some exceptions, it provided that all European goods bound for America first pass through England. In addition, it required that all such goods be transported by English-built vessels.[58] A decade later, the Staple Act was supplemented by another statute, which established duties for intercolonial coastal trade and overhauled the mechanisms for enforcement.[59] Finally, in 1696 Parliament extended the Staple Act's provision on "English-built ships", requiring that all trade with the American colonies—import, export, and intercolonial coastal—be restricted to vessels built in England or its overseas possessions. In addition, to facilitate enforcement, the Act also provided for the establishment of vice admiralty courts in the colonies.[60]

It is not surprising that England would erect courts of vice admiralty in the colonies; they were sorely needed to adjudicate instance and prize cases. Enforcement of the Navigation Acts, however, marked a significant change in the traditional role of the Admiralty.[61] In England, breaches of trade acts were

---

Id. at 53. The resulting legislation provided less protection than its predecessor of 1651, but when supplemented two years later by the Act of Frauds of 1662 (14 Car. II., c. 11), which provided for the loss of both goods and the vessel of anyone importing a number of products for which the Dutch were the world's principal middle-men, English merchants finally received the protection that they had sought, while the English government succeeded in foreclosing rival Holland from a significant share of the European market. It is worth noting that while the Trade Act of 1660 permitted ships flagged by the nation of origin of their cargoes to trade with English ports, it excluded all but English-owned ships from trading with the American colonies. For purpose of the Act, an "English ship" was English-owned, and sailed by an English master and a crew of whom at least three-fourths were also English, yet it need not have been English-built. Moreover, the Act classed as "English" ships owned by colonists and navigated by a colonial master and a crew of whom three-fourths were colonists. Similarly, vessels constructed in any of England's overseas possessions were classified as "English-built." For discussion, *see* Harper, *supra* note 6, at 388–390; *see also* Reeves, *supra* note 54, Part II at 232–261.

57. The seven goods enumerated in the Navigation Act of 1660, 12 Car. II, c. 18, xviii, were cotton wool, dyewoods, fustic, ginger, indigo, sugar, and most importantly tobacco. Over the next seven decades, an assortment of statutes added to this list, banning the export of commodities ranging from rice and molasses in 3 & 4 Anne, c. 3, xiv (1705) to coffee, skins, and potash in 4 Geo. III., c. 15, xxvii (1764).

58. For discussion of the Staple Act, 15 Car. II., c. 7 (1663), *see* Harper, *supra* note 6, at 60–61.

59. *See* 25 Car. II, c. 7 (1673). For discussion, *see* Harper, *supra* note 6, at 60, 397.

60. *See* 7 & 8 Gul. III., c. 22 (1696); Harper, *supra* note 6, at 60–62, 360, 390.

61. Vesting jurisdiction over violation of navigation acts in an admiralty court was a departure from seventeenth-century practice but not entirely novel. In the previous cen-

tried in the Court of Exchequer, operating under a hybrid procedure that employed both the civil law and that mainstay of common-law adjudication, the jury.[62] Although the High Court of Admiralty was not empowered to hear trade-act cases, Parliament provided that a violation of the trade acts could be tried "in any of His Majesties Courts of Record att Westminster, or in any Court in His Majesties Plantations, where such Offence shall bee committed",[63] thereby granting a potentially broader jurisdiction to vice admiralty courts than that enjoyed by the High Court itself.[64] This radical departure from traditional practice did not go unnoticed, and in time the colonists would come to resent their lack of input in the decision-making process. Nonetheless, as one commentator has observed: "it would seem that Parliament, which had restricted Admiralty in the first place, was free to abrogate these restrictions".[65] Having thus overcome legal objections to the vesting of jurisdiction, a practical problem remained; the Act of 1696 assumed the existence of colonial courts in which trade-act cases could be tried. Section II of the Act implies that the cases could be filed in the colonies' common-law courts, but such a move would have stripped the Crown of much of its control over the process of enforcement. Edward Randolph, Surveyor General for the American colonies and the prime instigator behind the Act, had urged its passage out of a conviction that the colonial authorities were too lax in their enforcement of the Navigation Acts.[66] He had suggested instead that jurisdiction be entrusted

---

tury, 5 Eliz., c. 5, xx (1562–63) had granted jurisdiction both to the Lord High Admiral and to justices of the peace to try offences.

62. For discussion, *see* Harper, *supra* note 6, at 111–112.

63. 7 & 8 Gul. III., c. 22, i (1696), *in* Statutes of the Realm: Printed by the Command of his Magesty King George the Third (*reprinted* Buffalo: William S. Hein, 1993).

64. The Navigation Acts addressed trade regulation in a piecemeal fashion, and Parliament had not been particularly careful to repeal or amend provisions in earlier legislation that were at odds with later enactments, with the result that the various acts contained inconsistent and conflicting language. The Act of 1696, which had been intended in part to clarify ambiguities in the allocation of jurisdiction, instead compounded the problem. It was clear that the courts of Westminster—including Exchequer—had jurisdiction. It was also clear that the High Court of Admiralty—which was not regarded as a court of record at this time—was not empowered to hear trade-act cases. Section II of the Act of 1696 appears to grant jurisdiction both to colonial courts of common law and to colonial vice admiralty courts (which ironically received their powers from the High Court of Admiralty, for which adjudication of trade-act cases was *ultra vires.*) Section VII of the same Act, however, gave jurisdiction to colonial vice admiralty courts, but appears to withhold it *sub silentio* from the colonial common-law courts. For discussion, *see* Owen & Tolley, *supra* note 14, at 104–107; *see also* Harper, *supra* note 6, at 186–187.

65. Wroth, *supra* note 31, at 355.

66. Towle, Records, *supra* note 34, Introduction (Andrews) at 12–14. Owen & Tolley, *supra* note 6, at 110–111. Despite Randolph's vehemence, it was not he, but mem-

to colonial courts of exchequer, patterned after the Court of Exchequer in England. His suggestion was rejected. Such courts were established in Barbados, the Leeward Islands, and Bermuda, but among the American colonies only in New York was a court of exchequer founded. In the remainder of the colonies, the provincial courts were competent to adjudicate most matters handled by the English Exchequer; in addition, as the Court's procedures were as alien to the common-law bar as were those of the High Court of Admiralty, there was no practical reason to prefer courts of exchequer to courts of vice admiralty.[67] Moreover, apart from hearing trade-act cases, the colonies had little use for courts of exchequer. On the other hand, the colonies already had need of vice admiralty courts. While prize and instance cases alone provided insufficient impetus for creating the courts, their expedited procedures would provide merchants and mariners with a welcome addition to the colonies' judicial system.[68] As violation of the Navigation Acts necessarily involved ships, admiralty's well-defined procedures for arrest of vessels made vice admiralty courts attractive *fora*.[69] Finally, vice admiralty courts had one decided advantage over courts of exchequer; they operated without juries.[70]

---

bers of the House of Lords who first suggested that vice admiralty courts hear trade-act cases. Randolph's statements to the Board of Trade reflect the views of many of his English contemporaries, who characterized American colonial juries as biased in favor of smugglers. Having conducted a survey of surviving case law, Harper, *supra* note 6, at 195, disagrees, observing: "Investigation has disclosed information regarding 46 jury trials which took place in various colonies, and the records show that 25 trials, or 54.4 percent, resulted in convictions. The proportion of convictions becomes 69.6 percent, if the Randolph seizures in New England are omitted because of the peculiar circumstances surrounding them."

67. Harper, *supra* note 6, at 183–184. Both the Court of Exchequer and the High Court of Admiralty could proceed *in rem*, utilizing procedures derived from the civil law; however, the Court of Exchequer, unlike the Court of Admiralty, employed a jury. For details of the procedure employed by the Court of Exchequer in adjudicating trade-act cases, *see* Hoon, *supra* note 54, at 277–280.

68. Harper, *supra* note 6, at 184–185. Crump, *supra* note 14, at 125–126, 183, discusses the need for admiralty courts in Bermuda to hear cases of wreck and in Jamaica to hear prize cases.

69. In her Introduction, Dorothy Towle provides a detailed account of the vice-admiralty procedure for arrest of vessels as part of her overview of trial procedures in the Vice Admiralty Court of Rhode Island. Towle, Records, *supra* note 34, at 91–95.

70. Crump, *supra* note 14, at 2, maintains that colonial vice admiralty courts were required by law to use juries when adjudicating trade-act cases, but in practice this was ignored. Her conclusions appear to be based upon English attorney Roger Mompesson's advice to William Penn regarding construction of the language of Section 10 of the 1696 Act, which provided that "there shall not bee any jury but of such only as are Natives of Eng-

There had been vice admiralty courts in the colonies before the passage of the Act of 1696. In the early years, the Admiralty had conferred vice-admiralty powers upon colonial governors.[71] By 1662, the new governor of Jamaica had received instructions to set up a vice admiralty court, principally to try prize and piracy cases, the latter of which were beyond the jurisdiction of the High Court of Admiralty.[72] Though American colonial governors had the power to create vice admiralty courts, that power was not exercised until 1679, when New York governor Edmund Andros established a maritime court, borrowing personnel from the Mayor's Court, the colony's traditional forum for maritime litigation.[73] Immediately following the Glorious Revolution, the Lords of the Admiralty authorized the High Court to issue new patents to colonial governors, conferring upon them the title of "vice admiral" and enabling them to create vice admiralty courts, but withholding the usual power

---

land, or Ireland or are borne in His Majesties Plantations". Mompesson contended that the statute required that juries be empaneled in trade-act cases. While this interpretation suited the interests of Mompesson's client, under a more objective reading, Section 10 stated rules for the composition of juries in common-law courts, which had concurrent jurisdiction over trade-act cases. The practical effect of the provision was to exclude from jury-duty Scots and Scottish immigrants in the American colonies, who were subjects of the Crown but—prior to the Act of Union—were deemed citizens of a foreign jurisdiction. Thus the purpose was not to require civil-law tribunals to utilize juries, but rather to provide guidelines for jury-selection among those courts in which juries were already required. For discussion, *see* Winfred Trexler Root, The Relations of Pennsylvania with the British Government, 1696–1765 (New York: D. Appleton & Co. for University of Pennsylvania Press, 1912) at 97–98 (hereinafter Root).

71. From the Restoration through 1673, the Admiral's seal was kept at the Lord Admiral's registry rather than at the High Court, and it was the registry that issued vice-admiralty patents to colonial governors. *See* Crump, *supra* note 14, at 150–151.

72. Owen & Tolley, *supra* note 14, at 29; Crump, *supra* note 14, at 105–107. Despite approval for creation of a court, the Jamaican vice admiralty court was technically not properly constituted. As Crump observes: "There was an admiralty court working between 1657 and 1660, but it was not legally established by the admiralty commissioners, nor could [Governor] Doyley get any answer from them about the legal position of the court". *Id.* at 101. Nonetheless it was this court, established on questionable authority and exercising "a wider jurisdiction than any English vice admiralty court", that most influenced the scope of jurisdiction later exercised by vice-admiralty courts on the American mainland. *Id.* at 116.

73. *Id.* at 29–30. Whether this court ever convened is a matter of speculation. Owen and Tolley contend that it did not, citing a letter of 1705 from Lord Cornbury, then governor of New York, to the Board of Trade, indicating that no "regular Court of Admiralty" had been established in the colony before 1696. *Id.* at 30. Judge Hough located no vice admiralty records for New York pre-dating 1715, although he admits that the extant records are not complete. Hough, Vice Admiralty of New York, *supra* note 21, Introduction at xi.

to appoint the judge, marshal, and "register", thereby permitting England to retain greater control over the courts.[74] In 1694, Governor Nicholson established a court of vice admiralty in Maryland, becoming the first to create a fully-functioning maritime court in mainland America founded upon a patent issued by the High Court.[75]

Pursuant to the Act of 1696, the King instructed the High Court of Admiralty to grant commissions to colonial governors to create vice admiralty courts and to appoint a judge, marshal, and registrar for each of them. Anticipating opposition in the proprietary colonies, the scheme called for the creation of ten districts, in which each chartered colony was joined with a royal colony. As a result, Massachusetts Bay (having received a new charter in 1691) was joined with New Hampshire and Rhode Island, while Connecticut, New York, and East New Jersey formed a second district. Pennsylvania, the Lower Counties, and West New Jersey were grouped together, and Virginia was joined with North Carolina and the Bahamas. Maryland and South Carolina each received its own court. The remaining four districts were Jamaica, Barbados, Bermuda, and the Leeward Islands.[76] As had been expected, trouble began almost immediately in various colonies,[77] particularly in Pennsylvania,

---

74. *See e.g.* Warrant for Commission of Governor Lionel Copley [of Maryland] as Vice Admiral, October 21, 1691 (LC: Adm. 2: Vol. 1045 Part I, at 110), *published in* Owen & Tolley, *supra* note 14, Appendix D at 369. "Register" became the standard American spelling for the English "registrar". The commissions to other colonial governors contained similar language prohibiting them from appointing the judge, marshal, and register of their respective courts. *Id.* at 31. Instead that power was reserved for the admiralty commissioners. After 1696, governors were granted the power to appoint officers to vice admiralty courts in the event of an incumbent's death. *See* Crump, *supra* note 14, at 154.

75. Owen & Tolley, *supra* note 14, at 31, 285. Francis Nicholson (himself a vice admiral) succeeded Copley as governor upon the latter's death in 1693; on the day that he took the oath, his first official act was to initiate the process by which the first permanent vice admiralty court was established. Despite the restrictions in the patents issued by the High Court, Nicholson appointed all officers of the new court; moreover the first matter it heard was a prize case, for which the patents had granted no express power to adjudicate. For a summary of the case and the founding of the court, *see Id.* at 283–285.

76. *Id.* at 33. The seats of the courts for the four "merged" districts were Massachusetts (established 1699), New York (1696), Pennsylvania (1698), and Virginia (1698). The courts of Maryland and South Carolina were established in 1694 and 1697 respectively. *See also* Towle, Records, *supra* note 34, Introduction (Andrews) at 14, (noting that: "No vice admiralty court was established in Georgia until quite late in the colonial period.")

77. Opposition was strongest in the chartered colonies. As historian Winfred Root observes:

> "In Rhode Island, the governor rendered the commission of the new judge ineffectual by refusing to administer to him the oath of office. The governor of Con-

where the proprietor, William Penn, protested that the new court violated the colony's rights under its charter. The charter gave Penn the authority to create courts and appoint judges to hear "what Causes soever", and he resented what he perceived as the Crown's intrusion into the colony's affairs and its abridgement of his proprietary rights.[78] Thus began a struggle between the

---

> necticut refused to recognize the commission, holding it to be an infringement of the charter. The judge in South Carolina complained of great discouragement offered him by the government. The governor and council in the Bahamas openly denounced the commission, and the judge in fear of his life was forced to flee."

ROOT, *supra* note 70, at 97.

78. The charter provided:

> "And wee doe likewise give and grant unto the Said William Penn and his heires and to his and their Deputies and Lieutenants such power and authoritie to appoint and establish any Judges and Justices Magistrates and Officers whatsoever for what Causes soever...and to doe all and every other thing and things which unto the compleate Establishment of Justice unto Courts and Tribunalls formes of Judicature and manner of Proceedings doe belong altho in these presents expresse mencion bee not made thereof..."

Charter of the Province of Pennsylvania, THE STATUTES AT LARGE OF PENNSYLVANIA IN THE TIME OF WILLIAM PENN: COMPILED UNDER THE AUTHORITY OF THE ACT OF MAY 19, 1887 (1st ed.1896; *reprinted with supplement by* Gail McKnight Beckman, New York: Vantage Press, 1976), Vol. I, at 111, 113. It should be noted that the powers granted by Pennsylvania's charter were not as broad as those of colonies founded earlier. Having learned from a half-century's experience, Privy Council carefully circumscribed Penn's charter-rights to ensure that the colony respect England's trade policy. Conformity with the trade acts became an express term of the charter, and the Crown retained the right to station customs officers in any port that Penn designated as an *entrepôt* for foreign or colonial goods. The proprietor was required to name an agent in London who would be legally responsible for the colony's compliance with the Navigation Acts. Furthermore, Pennsylvania's legislation was made subject to review by Privy Council. As for the language employed in the grant of authority to establish courts, it is virtually identical to that contained in the governors' commissions in the royal colonies, such as New York, in which it was written that:

> "And we do by these presents, give and grant unto you all power and authority, with the advice and consent of our said council, to erect, constitute and establish such and so many courts of judicature and public justice, within our said province and the territories under your government, as you and they shall think fit and necessary for the hearing and determining of all causes, as well criminal as civil.... And we do hereby authorize and empower you to constitute and appoint judges and justices of the peace and other necessary officers and ministers in our said province.... And we do hereby give and grant unto you...full power and authority to erect one or more Court or Courts Admiral within our said province and territories for hearing and determining of all marine and other causes and matters, proper therein to be heard..."

Crown and the chartered colonies that would carry over into the next century. Years later, Samuel Johnson would offer the most succinct summary of the Crown's position:

> To their Charters the Colonies owe, like other corporations, their political existence. The solemnities of legislation, the administration of justice, the security of property, are all bestowed upon them by the royal grant. Without their Charter there would be no power among them, by which any law could be made, or duties enjoined, any debt recovered, or criminal punished.
>
> A Charter is a grant of certain powers or privileges given to a part of the community for the advantage of the whole, and is therefore liable by its nature to change or revocation. Every act of Government aims at publick good. A Charter, which experience has shewn to be detrimental to the nation, is to be repealed; because general prosperity must always be preferred to particular interest.[79]

While the Crown did not abrogate the charter altogether, it did choose to ignore the language that gave the proprietor the right to establish courts and select officers to staff them. Penn responded by requesting an audience with the Board of Trade, and in 1696 he received the opportunity to appear before the Board in person to challenge the establishment of a vice admiralty court in his colony.[80]

Both legally and politically, Penn was on shaky ground. The scope of the 1696 Act was clear; it had declared null and void any colonial legislation in conflict with the Navigation Acts, leaving no room for the colony to create courts or promulgate its own procedures for enforcing the trade acts.[81] The issue would turn upon whether as a matter of law the Act was to be read as reneging portions of Penn's authority as granted in the charter. Having heard Penn's arguments, the Board declined to issue a decision, opting instead to refer the matter to Privy Council. His direct appeal to the Crown failed, paving

---

English translation of the Commission to Lord Cornbury, *published in* ERASTUS BENEDICT, THE AMERICAN ADMIRALTY: ITS JURISDICTION AND PRACTICE (5th ed., Albany, New York: Banks & Co., 1925) Sec. 657 at 789–790 (hereinafter BENEDICT (5th ed.)). Thus it was not the language of the charters and commissions *per se* that produced the clash between the colonial officials and the Crown in the chartered colonies, but rather that charters fostered in colonial leaders a more independent stance in their relationships with the Crown.

79. JOHNSON, TAXATION, *supra* note 1, at 26–27.

80. Harrington (Part I), *supra* note 37, at 595–596.

81. 7 & 8 Gul. III, c. 22 (1696); for discussion, *see* Harrington (Part I), *supra* note 37, at 593.

the way for the High Court of Admiralty to establish a vice admiralty court and appoint a judge.[82] In defeat, however, Penn had raised an issue that was to plague American judges long after independence. In its zeal to implement its trade policies, Parliament had granted to the new court powers of enforcement not enjoyed by the High Court itself. Moreover, these powers were not carefully circumscribed by the geographical limitations that applied to all English admiralty jurisdiction; the new court was to have cognizance over all violations of the trade acts irrespective of whether they were alleged to have occurred on the high seas, in port, or even on navigable rivers. In England, this would have proven difficult to reconcile in law, but in practice it would have been of little importance, as English rivers above their mouths generally are not navigable. In America, however, Penn contended, differences in topography made this extension of jurisdiction objectionable in practice as well as in principle. As he explained:

> Our settlements are upon the freshes of navigable rivers and creeks, where the river may be from two to three miles over, to a stone's cast over, and 100 miles from the ocean, and the Court of Admiralty by virtue of the seventh and eighth of the king [*i.e.* the Act of 1696], pretends not only to try cases that relate to the King's revenue as to unlawful trade or piracy, but whatever is done in the rivers or creeks other ways, as debts for victuals, beer, sails or anything relating to the building of small craft; so that they have swallowed up a great part of the Government here, because our commerce, by reason of the nature of our settlements, is so much upon the river and small creeks of it; and determining these causes without a jury, gives our people the greatest discontent, looking upon themselves as less free here than at home, instead of greater privileges, which were promised.[83]

Penn's protests notwithstanding, by establishing vice admiralty courts in the colonies, the Crown had not only created *fora* in which violations of the trade acts could be punished, but also venues where merchants could sue for damage to cargo, shipowners for freight, sailors for their wages—and where materialmen could file their claims *in rem* for the purchase-price of barrels of salt-pork or beer. Furthermore, such claims were not to be limited by geography; subject-matter was to govern jurisdiction. Eventually, Penn's worst fears were alleviated; his colony's government and courts were not "swallowed up".

82. Harrington (Part I), *supra* note 37, at 596–597.
83. *Reprinted in* Root, *supra* note 70, at 97.

Jurisdiction over both trade-act cases and instance cases was held to be concurrent, and parties were allowed their choice of forum.[84] Sir Leoline Jenkins dream, moribund for a generation in England, was to come to fruition in America.

The Provincial Vice Admiralty Courts

Despite initial controversy, by 1700, all seven provincial vice admiralty courts had opened their doors for business. Unfortunately, many of their records have been lost. As admiralty records, unlike those of the English common-law courts, were not irrefutable evidence of the proceedings that they memorialized, less care was taken for their preservation. Moreover, they were kept on paper rather than parchment, making them more susceptible to decay.[85] Some documents were victims of fire in the colonial period; others were lost in the turmoil of the Revolution.[86] Lack of published reports proved frustrating even to eighteenth-century commentators. John Reeves, the author of the leading eighteenth-century work on English maritime and trade law, lamented the dearth of published decisions in trade-act cases, beginning his treatise with a laconic apology: "One great source…of illustration, and that which principally commands the attention of the professors of the law, is extremely deficient in this branch of jurisprudence."[87] Nevertheless, enough

---

84. Harrington (Part I), *supra* note 37, at 593.

85. *See* Crump, *supra* note 14, at Preface (*not paginated*), 131–132. For the history of the common-law courts' practice and significance of the common-law courts keeping records on parchment, *see generally* S. E. Thorne, *Courts of Record and Sir Edward Coke*, 2 Toronto L. J. 24, (1937).

86. In Maryland, for example, the provincial vice admiralty court sat from 1694–1775; however, extant records cover only the period from 1754–1775. There is some evidence that the earliest records were lost in court-house fires in 1699 and 1704, while the whereabouts of the later records are still a mystery. Owen & Tolley, *supra* note 14, at 134 n. 157, 389–391. Many of the early records of Virginia's vice admiralty court were lost when fire destroyed the Capitol in Williamsburg in 1747. *See* Proceedings in the Court of Vice-Admiralty of Virginia, 1698–1775 (George Reese ed., Richmond: Virginia State Library, 1983) Introduction at ix (hereinafter Reese, Vice-Admiralty of Virginia). Of the four regional vice admiralty courts created in 1767 to supplement those established pursuant to the 1694 Act, all records except those of the Boston court were lost by the end of the Revolution. *See* Carl Ubbelohde, The Vice Admiralty Courts and the American Revolution (Chapel Hill: University of North Carolina Press, 1960) at 158.

87. Reeves, *supra* note 54, at 4.

remains to sketch a rough estimate of the relative volume of the various types of cases that came before them.[88]

Given the history of the creation of vice admiralty courts in the American colonies, it would be natural to assume that trade-act cases dominated their dockets. For both the Crown and Parliament, enforcement of the Navigation Acts and collection of revenue were of paramount importance, and it is not surprising that they overhauled the colonial legal system in order to combat illicit trade. Nonetheless, there remains the question of whether the problem was as serious as eighteenth-century observers believed. Despite the panicked warnings of Randolph and others, modern research has shown that the government overestimated smuggling's impact on the British economy.[89] In the colonies in particular, the evidence indicates that smuggling did not constitute a major portion of total trade.[90] Moreover, of the many who operated in

---

88. *See e.g.* Rediker, *supra* note 6, at 315, noting that research has identified documents relating to 2,200 cases tried in various admiralty courts.

89. One barometer of the overall level of smuggling is the level of illicit traffic in the tea-trade. It was common practice to smuggle tea together with heavier commodities, such as brandy, which would serve as ballast. As a result, tea constituted about 25% of total seizures of contraband in the latter half of the eighteenth century, while tea and spirits together accounted for roughly half. In 1745/46 and 1783, committees in Parliament released reports estimating the level of smuggling in the tea-trade. The latter report, based in part upon evidence submitted by the East India Company, is likely to have overestimated the level of illicit trade intentionally, as the Company was lobbying for more stringent enforcement of the Navigation Acts. (William Pitt's estimates—made at the same time—placed the level at roughly 40% of those of the East India Company.) Having accounted for changes in consumers' preferences and elasticities of demand, one commentator has identified the following general trends. From the founding of the colonial vice admiralty courts through the 1740s, the level of smuggling rose significantly; following the lowering of the tax on tea in 1745, the level of illicit trade dropped precipitously. During the 1770s, the level of trade in contraband items once again increased; however, even at its height in this period, it accounted for less than 20% of total British imports. For discussion, *see* W. A. Cole, *Trends in Eighteenth-Century Smuggling*, 10 Econ. Hist. Rev. (New Series: Issue 3), 395–410 (1958); for discussion of author's methodology, *see* W. A. Cole, *The Arithmetic of Eighteenth-Century Smuggling*, 28 Econ. Hist. Rev. (New Series: Issue 1) 44–49 (1975).

90. With regard to exports from the colonies, Harper concludes that "illicit trade constituted only a small fraction of the legitimate commerce". Harper, *supra* note 6, at 263. Illegal imports are somewhat more difficult to measure. Only 6% of all commodities that entered the colonies legally between 1770 and 1772 were regulated goods from Europe. *Id.* at 266–267. For smuggled goods to have had a significant impact on the overall colonial economy, their value would have to have been several times as great as that of comparable goods which entered legally. Although concrete figures for smuggling are lacking, it is well established that after the early days of the colonies, an unfavorable balance of trade with the mother country produced a net indebtedness. In short, the colonists' legitimate trade

the illicit markets, comparatively few were apprehended. Responsibility for enforcement of the trade acts was not centralized, but rather shared among various governmental entities,[91] resulting in a lack of efficiency.[92] The Customs officers faced numerous obstacles and disincentives in their work,[93] and in the colonies in particular the unpopularity of their offices provoked frequent harassment.[94] As a result, it has been estimated that the revenue col-

---

was based on credit. Thus the colonies' trade deficit with Britain provides circumstantial evidence that the colonists were not financially able to engage in illicit trade on the large scale that the British government and modern commentators alike have ascribed to them. For discussion, *see Id.* at 267–271

91. The Treasury, Commissioners, and Customs bore primary responsibility for enforcement, while the Crown, Privy Council, the Lords of Trade, and the Navy also had a hand upholding the trade laws. HARPER, *supra* note 6, at 134, 140–147, 178.

92. *Id.* With regard to the efficacy of the process of enforcement, Elizabeth Hoon observes:

> "Despite the best of these efforts, effective procedure against illicit trade was not assured, for there were many discouragements to officers: they were often intimidated by the power and organizations of the smugglers; there was sometimes uncertainty of customs backing in a seizure, and danger of counter-suits by the runners; charges of prosecution were costly; the process of the law was slow; prejudiced juries and justices frequently failed to convict; sales of goods often enough brought little, owing to low appraisements, large lots, combinations in bidding, and delays in payments of shares of seizures."

HOON, *supra* note 55, at 286.

93. *Id.* at 275. If the officer was willing to incur the costs of prosecution personally, he could recover as much as a moiety (*i.e.* one half) of the proceeds of the condemnation if he were to prevail. Expenses at trial, however, were high, and the officer faced the possibility of a counter-suit (*see supra* note 92). Furthermore, there was no guarantee that he would prevail. If he opted for prosecution at the expense of the Crown, he could reduce his out-of-pocket expenses and protect himself against counter-suit, but the Crown would claim a larger percentage of the proceeds. One of these disincentives was removed in 1736; the Crown assumed responsibility for legal defense in counter-suits so long as the customs officer had followed the prescribed rules in making the seizure. *Id.* at 286.

94. One pamphleteer offered graphically detailed advice to his fellow colonists on how to deal with an offending customs officer:

> "First strip a Person naked, then heat the Tar untill it is thin, & pour it upon the naket [*sic*] Flesh, or rub it over it with a Tar Brush, *quantum sufficit*,—after which, sprinkle decently upon the Tar, whilst it is yet warm, as many Feathers as will stick to it—then hold a lighted Candle to the Feathers & try to set it all on Fire: if it will burn so much the better: but as the Experiment is often made in cold Weather; it will not then succeed—take also an Halter, & put it round the Person's Neck, & then cart him the Rounds."

Peter Oliver, "Origin and Progress of the Rebellion in America, to 1776", British Museum, Egerton Mss. 2671, *published in* UBBELOHDE, *supra* note 86, at 117.

lected in the colonies amounted to no more than 25% of the cost of enforcement.[95] In the end, the provincial vice admiralty courts, created to enforce the trade laws, tried comparatively few trade-act cases.[96]

Of all varieties of cases adjudicated by the provincial vice admiralty courts, claims for seamen's wages were by far the most numerous.[97] The conditions

---

95. *Id.* at 43.

96. Charles Andrews offers the following summary of the surviving records of trade-act litigation in the vice admiralty courts:

> "Smuggling and illicit trading...have ever had an attraction for the reader of colonial history, who is always liable to exaggerate their extent, because of the want of any very precise information about them.... Certainly activities of this kind do not bulk large in the vice-admiralty proceedings. Even in Massachusetts, probably the chief offender among the colonies, the great majority of cases concerns wages, desertions, assault upon the high seas, and other matters that fall within the class of strictly marine causes. The number of trials for illegal trading, recorded in the proceedings of the vice-admiralty courts (as far as we have of them) of Rhode Island, Pennsylvania, Maryland, South Carolina, and Antigua, is very small, amounting to less than five per cent of the whole. The percentage is rather higher in North Carolina, but on the other hand in New York the number is negligible.... No one of the vice-admiralty court records discloses attempts at illicit trade on any extended scale; for even the cases that are entered are comparatively petty or, relatively speaking, unimportant."

ANDREWS, *supra* note 33, at 240–241. The figures from Massachusetts lend support to Andrews' assertion. Of the extant 726 cases decided between 1718 and 1772 for which subject matter can be identified, instance cases outnumbered trade-act cases 453 to 262, with prize cases accounting for the balance. *See* Wroth (Part II), *supra* note 31, at 367. Of the 60 extant case-records from North Carolina, only 23 involved the Navigation Acts. *See* OWEN & TOLLEY, *supra* note 14, at 37. Andrews' contentions regarding Maryland are not entirely accurate. The records for the colony are fragmentary, but as the surviving sample is sufficiently large and the missing records sufficiently random, it is possible to form some conclusions regarding the place of Navigation-Act cases in Maryland's vice admiralty court. Of 62 instance cases, only fourteen were filed in the vice admiralty court, with the colony's various common-law tribunals adjudicating the remainder. On the other hand, of the 48 Navigation-Act cases for which records survive, only 21 were heard by the vice admiralty court. The statistics in part reflect the fact that trade-act cases were tried in common-law courts before 1694 for lack of another venue. Nonetheless, fourteen instance cases were filed in the vice admiralty court after 1694, as compared with 21 trade-act cases. These instance cases, together with five prize cases and one matter related to a procedural issue, constituted nearly half (49%) of cases filed in admiralty for which records are extant. *Id.* at 103. Though Andrews may have overstated his point, the records tend to support the conclusion that the provincial vice admiralty courts were not principally venues for trying violations of the Navigation Acts.

97. The records for the colony of Massachusetts are among the most extensive that have survived. Of the 815 cases filed between 1718 and 1772 for which records are extant, 318

that sailors endured in the colonial merchant fleet were almost unimaginable by modern standards. Of life at sea in the 1700s, Samuel Johnson once quipped:

> No man will be a sailor who has contrivance enough to get himself into a jail; for being in a ship is being in a jail, with the chance of being drowned.... A man in a jail has more room, better food, and commonly better company.[98]

That which provided Johnson with occasion for light-hearted sarcasm was for many the road to a dangerous and (all too frequently) short life. The average

---

involved claims for wages. Wroth (II), *supra* note 31, at 367. In North Carolina, the eleven suits for wages were the most numerous category among 37 instance cases. OWEN & TOLLEY, *supra* note 14, at 37. Records from Virginia are sparse, and the sampling may be too small to form an accurate conclusion. Contrary to Charles Andrews' contention that all of Virginia's records were lost (*see* Towle, RECORDS, *supra* note 34, at 80), George Reese managed to locate scattered records for the years 1688–1700, 1758, and 1770–1775 in collections of private papers. Among the nine cases for which at least partial records exist, two were claims for seamen's wages. *See* Reese, VICE-ADMIRALTY OF VIRGINIA, *supra* note 86, at ix, 8–11, 80, 91–93, 115. In Maryland, where seamen often filed their claims in the Provincial Court, Owen and Tolley have identified four cases (out of a total of fourteen surviving instance suits) in which mariners sought to recover wages in the colony's vice admiralty court. OWEN & TOLLEY, *supra* note 14, at 103; Appendix at 309, 317, 320, 324. New York appears to be the exception to the rule that suits for wages dominated the dockets in colonial vice admiralty courts; most such cases were heard by the courts of common law. *See* ANDREWS, *supra* note 33, at 251.

98. JAMES BOSWELL, LIFE OF JOHNSON, (6 vols., George Birkbeck Hill ed., revised ed. by L. F. Powell, Oxford: Clarendon Press, 1934) Vol. I. (1709–1765), at 348. Lest one judge Johnson harshly for his apparent flippancy at the plight of sailors, it should be noted that the sailors themselves often resorted to similar sarcasm in describing their own lives. Stan Hugill, the last surviving professional shantyman, published the following words to a popular shanty, dating from the days of the Atlantic packet ships of the early nineteenth century and generally sung as the men took their last turn at the pumps as the ship approached port:

> "The work wuz hard an' the voyage wuz long,
> The sea wuz high an' the gales wuz strong...
> The grub wuz bad an' the wages low,
> But now once more ashore we'll go...
> We'd be better off in a nice clean gaol,
> With all night in an' plenty o' ale,
> An' it's time for us to leave her!"

SHANTIES FROM THE SEVEN SEAS: SHIPBOARD WORK-SONGS AND SONGS USED AS WORK SONGS FROM THE GREAT DAYS OF SAIL, COLLECTED BY STAN HUGILL (Stan Hugill ed., Mystic, Connecticut: Mystic Seaport Museum, revised ed. 1994) at 218.

"able seaman" in the merchant service was in his late twenties; fewer than thirteen percent of them were over forty. Only two-thirds were sufficiently literate to sign their own names.[99] In the first half of the eighteenth century, the average monthly pay for foremastmen was between one and two pounds sterling per month in peace-time, rising by around fifty percent in time of war.[100] Occupying the lowest rung of the social ladder, "Jack Tar" lacked bargaining power and found himself at the mercy of those with whom he dealt. As one contemporary observer once told an eighteenth-century grub-street writer: "merchants are a pack of sharpers, masters of ships a parcel of arrant knaves, a vessel but a doubtful confidant, and the sea a mere lottery".[101] Sailors moved "from port to port in search of a few shillings more a month, beer that did not stink, biscuit that did not move by itself, a safer ship, or a less brutal master."[102]

A master's authority over his ship was absolute, and his relations with his crew were not always congenial. As historian Charles Andrews remarked:

> Captains and masters were truculent men, much given to swearing and blasphemy, to beating, bruising, and maltreating their sailors, threatening to cut off their ears, to whip 'em raw, or to blow out their brains. They pinched them in provisions, knocked them about with impunity, and met their complaints with abuses and insults, often to the terror of the men's lives.[103]

Futhermore, and often unfortunately for merchant seamen, the master would determine unilaterally whether a sailor had breached the terms of his employment contract, the "portage bill",[104] thus forfeiting his wages for the voy-

---

99. Rediker, *supra* note 6, Appendix A: "Age Distribution Among Deep-Sea Sailors, 1700-1750" at 299–300; Appendix D: "Literacy in the Merchant Shipping Industry, 1700–1750" at 307.

100. *Id.* at 123; Appendix C: "Wages in the Merchant Shipping Industry" at 304–305.

101. Edward ["Ned"] Ward, The London Spy: The Vanities and Vices of the Town Exposed to view (1st ed. 1698–1703; Arthur Lawrence Hayward ed., London: Cassell & Co., 1927) at 270.

102. Rediker, *supra* note 6, at 291.

103. Towle, Records, *supra* note 34, Introduction (Andrews) at 26.

104. In the seventeenth and eighteenth centuries, seamen's labor contracts ("ship's articles" in nineteenth-century parlance) were known as "portage bills" or "portledge bills". *Id.* at 25. *See also* Several Orders Made in the General Court at Boston in New England, October 14, 1668, Maritime Affaires, Sec. 5 at 10–11:

> "...Masters...shall make clear agreements with their Marriners, and Officers, for their wages, and those agreements enter into a Book...a copy whereof the Master as a *portlige bill* shall leave with the owners..."

(*emphasis added*), *reproduced in* Records of the United States of America: A Micro-

age. Admittedly, the monetary value of individual cases generally was not large. Taken collectively, however, maritime labor was indispensable for the preservation of British trade policy, and if Britain wanted its merchant ships to sail, it had to guarantee a sufficient level of fair treatment for British sailors to induce them to remain at sea.[105] Fair laws, however, would have been useless in the absence of procedures that would give the generally impecunious sailors cost-effective access to redress.[106] By 1705, the debate over whether the High Court of Admiralty had jurisdiction over wage-disputes had ended;[107] Parliament had granted the Court explicit cognizance over these claims, elim-

---

FILM COMPILATION, Mass. B.2 Reel I, 1661–1742 (William Sumner Jenkins ed., Washington, D. C.: Library of Congress Photoduplication Service, 1949).

105. For discussion, *see e.g.* REDIKER, *supra* note 6, at 119, observing:

> "The proliferation of vice-admiralty courts throughout the British Empire in the seventeenth century was part of the overall expansion and rationalization of commerce. One of the main functions of these courts was to handle seafaring wage disputes. By 1700 admiralty law had clearly established criteria to guarantee seamen's pay.... Vice-admiralty judges recognized the indispensability of maritime labor to the orderly movement of commodities and the accumulation of capital, and they did not hesitate to condemn and sell merchantmen at public auction. Since the colony, the court, and the judge benefited by such sales, numerous ships and cargoes were sold to satisfy wage contracts."

106. *See e.g.* the observation of Sir Leoline Jenkins: "And the Mariners had better lose the Wages of a whole Voyage, than not to go off on the next that offers itself" *in "Argument, in Behalf of a Bill to Ascertain the Jurisdiction of the Admiralty, in the House of Lords"* (1670), *published in* WILLIAM WYNNE, THE LIFE OF SIR LEOLINE JENKINS, JUDGE OF THE HIGH COURT OF ADMIRALTY, AND PREROGATIVE COURT OF CANTERBURY &C. AMBASSADOR AND PLENIPOTENTIARY FOR THE GENERAL PEACE AT COLOGN AND NIMEGUEN, AND SECRETARY OF STATE TO CHARLES II (2 vols., London: Joseph Downing, 1724), Vol. I, at lxxix, lxxxii.

107. This debate was more often manifest in the political polemics of the seventeenth century's "Battle of the Books" than in actual case law. Years later, Arthur Browne was to summarize the common lawyers' position as expounded by Holt, remarking: "And, in truth, Lord Chief Justice Holt had no better answer to make...but this, that it was an indulgence to the poor sailor, and that in his case *communis error facit jus*..." ARTHUR BROWNE, A COMPENDIOUS VIEW OF THE CIVIL LAW, AND OF THE LAW OF ADMIRALTY, BEING THE SUBSTANCE OF A COURSE OF LECTURES READ IN THE UNIVERSITY OF DUBLIN (2 vols., 3d ed. [1st American ed.], Halstead & Voorhies, 1840), Vol. II, at 86–87 (hereinafter BROWNE). In essence, the common law refrained from exercising its power to pre-empt the Admiralty Court out of pity for the plight of mariners. Nevertheless, however rare, common-law courts occasionally did issue prohibitions in wage-cases. A manuscript in the Admiralty Register records a case in which a common-law judge issued a prohibition in an action for seamen's wages, reasoning that the employment contracts had been made in London "in the parish of the St. Mary Bow within the Body of the County of the City". *Swanton v. Dove* (1604), *published in* HALE AND FLEETWOOD, *supra* note 15, at 282–283.

inating the threat of prohibition.[108] Adopting the practice of the High Court, the colonial vice admiralty courts permitted an entire crew to join their claims against the vessel, with a considerable savings in expense.[109] In addition, the admissability of depositions avoided numerous delays and permitted witnesses to return to sea.[110]

The outcome of suits for wages was not a foregone conclusion. Courts recognized several affirmative defenses for refusal to pay. Mutiny, theft of cargo, refusal to work in a storm, desertion, and "neglect of duty" all constituted grounds for forfeit of wages.[111] Proof of desertion alone would not guarantee exoneration from liability. Seamen were entitled to their pay even after deserting provided they could show that the ship had altered its course without authority or that provisions had been insufficient.[112] They were also entitled to desert if they had been subjected to cruel and inhuman treatment.[113] As captains were entitled by law to use force to put down mutinies, determining whether treatment was "cruel and inhuman" often required that judges make close calls on when such force was either unwarranted or excessive.[114] *The*

108. 4 & 5 Anne, c. 3 (1705). For discussion, *see* Hale and Fleetwood, *supra* note 15, Introduction at lxxi. Despite the ban on prohibitions for wage-claims, Frederick Wiener has identified one case in Rhode Island in which a prohibition was sought. *See* Wiener, *supra* note 24, at 44, 53. Wiener publishes the case, *Shilcock v. Bannister*, 2 R. I. Adm. Pap. 34 (1743), in an Appendix to his article at 85–86.

109. *See e.g.* Owen & Tolley, *supra* note 14, at 142 (noting the advantages in proceeding *in rem* and joinder of claims). For discussion of the civil-law procedure, which permits joinder of claims for seamen's wages, *see* Browne, *supra* note 106, at 155.

110. *See* Owen & Tolley, *supra* note 14, at 17–18, 189–190; *see also* Harrington (Part II), *supra* note 20, at 350.

111. Towle, Records, *supra* note 34, Introduction (Andrews) at 25–26. "Neglect of duty" included, among other things, drunkenness and laziness, for which sailors' wages were reduced rather than entirely forfeited.

112. *Id.* at 26. While the defense of desertion existed in the colonial period, it was not common. In his survey of New York case law, Hough identifies *Bush v. McRuth* and *Nosworthy v. The Glaudina*, two unpublished cases adjudicated after independence (1786) as the first two times that the defense appears in the records of New York. Hough, Vice Admiralty of New York, *supra* note 21, at 254.

113. Towle, Records, *supra* note 34, at 26.

114. Judges generally showed greater tolerance for a captain's violence where he was able to establish that he had responded to a credible threat that sailors would take over the ship. For example, in New York, the vice admiralty court held a master liable for striking seamen who were not performing their duties to his satisfaction, but exonerated Captain White of the *Doddington* for discharging a pistol at a crew member during an attempt to seize the ship. *See Gordon v. Blake* (1755); *McFarlin v. White* (1750), *published from manuscript in* Hough, Vice Admiralty of New York, *supra* note 21, at 84, 25–27. It should

Hannah, heard by the Vice Admiralty Court of Maryland in 1763, illustrates both the substantive law that applied to desertion and the procedural advantages of allowing an entire crew to consolidate their claims into one action. Pooling their resources, the seamen were able to retain two attorneys, who framed the issue as follows:

> That by the marine and civil law and every other law violent and inhuman treatment is a legal discharge of whatever covenants of time of service mariners or other set of men may have entered into and executed and by the said marine and civil law mariners are entitled to their wages for their work and service done to the time of departure from their ship for such legal cause any agreement covenants or articles to the contrary notwithstanding.[115]

Despite language in the ship's articles by which the sailors had agreed to forfeit their entire wages in the event of desertion,[116] the judge found that that the master's treatment had been inhumane, and awarded the libellants damages. Apart from establishing in America the rule by which sailors could allege cruelty as a defense to a claim of desertion,[117] the case is most memorable for the identities of the libellants' attorneys. William Paca was to become a signer of the Declaration of Independence, governor of the newly independent state of

---

be noted that White had paid McFarlin his wages before the suit commenced. Thus the allegation of mutiny was an affirmative defense to a claim for assault and clearly not fabricated as an excuse for withholding wages.

115. Brief of the libellants in *Edwards v. The Hannah* (1763), *reproduced from manuscript in* Owen & Tolley, *supra* note 14, at 324. It should be noted that in the absence of published reports, the selections from cases and case-summaries of the decisions of the Vice Admiralty Court of Maryland in this collection are the only published source for the Court's decisions. For a bibliography of the extant archival material examined by Owen and Tolley, *see Id.* at 389–392.

116. Unfortunately, shipowners often sought to deprive sailors by private agreement of wages to which they otherwise would have been entitled by operation of law. A more common form was a clause in ship's articles that barred mariners from collecting wages earned on out-bound voyages in the event that the ship was lost while returning home. Applying principles of equity, courts generally refused to enforce such clauses. *See* Henry J. Bourguignon, Sir William Scott, Lord Stowell: Judge of the High Court of Admiralty, 1798–1828 (Cambridge: Cambridge University Press, 1987) at 68–69 (hereinafter Bourguignon, Stowell).

117. Judge Ashur Ware, the noted scholar of maritime and civil law, later adopted into federal law the principle that Judge Steuart enunciated in *The Snow Hannah*; *see Sherwood v. McIntosh* (Cas. No. 12,778), 21 F. 1924 (D. Maine, 1826, holding that seamen who desert their ship on account of inhumane treatment remain entitled to their wages.)

Maryland, judge of the national prize court established by the Continental Congress, and finally the first judge of the Federal District Court in Maryland. His colleague was also signer of the Declaration of Independence, future Supreme Court Justice Samuel Chase.[118] In the absence of the procedural rule that permitted joinder of seamen's wage-claims, it is unlikely that impecunious seamen would have been able to afford legal representation, and access to the services of the highest caliber of legal talent of the day would have been out of the question. It also appears to have helped that courts were generally sympathetic to the claims of seamen.[119] Thus even in these early vice-admiralty cases there appear reflections of later English[120] and American[121] case law, in which courts acknowledged sailors' relative lack of bargaining power.

---

118. For discussion, *see* Owen & Tolley, *supra* note 15, at 226, 324–325.

119. Scholarly opinion is divided on the degree to which colonial vice-admiralty judges sympathized with seamen in wage-cases. Charles Andrews makes the following observation:

> "...[I]nsufficient attention has been paid to [vice admiralty courts'] great usefulness as the guardian of the rights of the seamen.... In none of the leading ports, particularly on the continent...could commerce have been carried on without the aid of these courts and in none of them did there exist agencies which pursued their humanitarian work with more regard for justice and fair dealing than did the justices of the vice-admiralty.... As far as the records bear witness... I have yet to find an instance of manifest partisanship or injustice on the part of a colonial judge of vice-admiralty..."

Andrews, *supra* note 33, at 251–252. On the other hand, examining much of the same evidence, Marcus Rediker concludes:

> "The historian...does not always have the advantage of knowing how judges weighed the evidence they heard. Such knowledge, even when available, does not, of course, always reflect the truth of the case. Judges rendered numerous verdicts that supported the interests of merchants and captains even when the evidence and the law stood firmly on the side of the common tar."

Rediker, *supra* note 6, at 315. He declines, however, to give statistics or concrete examples to support his contention. Owen and Tolley perhaps should be given the last word in the matter, citing the "special solicitude of the admiralty" for seamen while observing that of the twelve suits for seamen's wages adjudicated in Maryland for which records survive (four by the vice admiralty court and eight by the courts of common law), the seamen prevailed in all twelve. *See* Owen & Tolley, *supra* note 14, at 3, 145.

120. Judge Scott (later Lord Stowell) of the High Court of Admiralty once wrote: "The common mariner is easy and careless, illiterate and unthinking; he has no such resources, in his own intelligence and experience in habits of business...", setting the tone for interpretation of ship's articles in nineteenth-century case law. *See The Julianna*, 2 Dod. 504, 509 (H.C.A., 1822). During his tenure on the bench, Scott ruled in favor of seamen in 32 of the 43 cases in suits for wages among cases for which reports were published. *See* Bourguignon, Stowell, *supra* note 116, at 78.

121. In the early years of American jurisprudence, Joseph Story would remark:

Other substantive rules relating to seamen also begin to appear in the colonial period. When a ship was arrested, condemned, and sold at judicial auction and the resulting fund was insufficient to cover all claims, the wage-claims of seamen were paid before those of other claimants.[122] A court of admiralty may seize a vessel, even when it is in possession of a common-law court, in order to adjudicate a claim for seamen's wages filed *in rem* against the vessel itself.[123] The colonial records reveal no case in which a seaman recovered in tort for injury caused by the unseaworthiness of his ship,[124] but there is evidence of the evolution of the modern doctrine entitling sailors to "maintenance and cure".[125] As in England, colonial vice admiralty courts followed the general practice of denying masters' claims for wages when filed

---

> "Every court should watch with jealousy an encroachment upon the rights of seamen, because they are unprotected and need counsel; because they are thoughtless and require indulgence; because they are credulous and complying.... They are emphatically the wards of the admiralty.... They are considered as placed under the dominion and influence of men, who have naturally acquired a mastery over them; and as they have little of the foresight and caution belonging to persons trained in other pursuits in life, the most rigid scrutiny is instituted into the terms of every contract, in which they engage."

Harden v. Gordon (Case No. 6047), 11 F. Cas., 480, 485 (C.C., D. Maine, 1823).

122. *See e.g. Mills v. Ship "Anne" of Newcastle*, (Provincial Court of Maryland sitting in Admiralty, 1692), *published in full from manuscript in* Owen & Tolley, *supra* note 14, Appendix B ("Record of the Ship Anne of Newcastle") at 339–352; for additional discussion, *see Id.* at 226.

123. *Johnson v. Ship "Ann"* (Vice Admiralty Court of New York, 1764), *published from manuscript in* Hough, Vice Admiralty of New York, *supra* note 21, at 214–215. There is some question of whether this procedural advantage was available in all jurisdictions. In his study of instance cases in Massachusetts, Wroth, *supra* note 31, at 353–354, contends that sailors filed the majority of wage-claims *in personam* against the ships' owners.

124. Owen & Tolley, *supra* note 14, at 227; Wroth, *supra* note 31, at 350.

125. Bourguignon, Stowell, *supra* note 116, at 73–74; Owen & Tolley, *supra* note 14, at 226–227. The law was still in its formative stages, however, and courts were not yet in agreement regarding the extent of a seaman's right to maintenance and cure. In *Trapier v. Banister* (Vice Admiralty Court of Rhode Island, 1743) *reproduced from manuscript in* Towle, Records, *supra* note 34, at 500–502, the court deducted the cost of medical expenses rendered to the libellant in Jamaica from the amount that the respondent owed him. It should be noted, however, that evidence at trial indicated that the seaman, Trapier, had not been taken ashore to receive treatment, and furthermore that he subsequently returned to his duties for the duration of the voyage. Traditionally, "maintenance and cure" was owed to a sailor who was treated for his injuries or illness on shore; often the sailor was left behind when the ship left port. For origins of the doctrine, *see* The Black Book of the Admiralty (Rerum *Britannicarum Medii Aevi Scriptores* (Rolls Series)): No. 55 *Monumenta Juridica* (Sir Travers Twiss ed., London: Her Majesty's Stationery Office, 1871,

in rem, reasoning that the master's contract bound the owners, not the ship, and thus was cognizable only in the courts of common law.[126] Despite their reputation as legally uncomplicated, seamen's claims for wages occasionally raised novel issues, forcing the vice admiralty courts to exercise creativity in making new law. The Vice Admiralty Court of New York, for example, held that a seaman who had signed articles to sail with one master could demand payment and release from his contract if the owners were to replace the master with another.[127] In another case, the Court held that sailors who aided in sailing a retaken prize ship were to be paid wages out of the salvage award.[128]

Kraus reprints, 1965) Vol. I, "Laws of Oleron" (Part C), Art. 7, at 94–97. The last edition of Charles Molloy's *De Jure Maritimo et Navali* edited during its author's lifetime, gives the following rule for seamen's maintenance and cure:

> "[I]f any of the *Mariners* be in any ways wounded, or do become ill in the service of the Ship, he is to be provided for at the charges of the Ship; and if he be so ill as not fit to travel, he is to be left ashore, and care to be taken that he hath all accommodations of humanity administered to him: and if the Ship is ready for a departure, she is not to stay for him; if he recover, he is to have his full wages, deducting the Masters charges which he laid out for him."

Charles Molloy, *De Iure Maritimo et Navali*: Or A Treatise of Affairs Maritime and of Commerce (3d. ed., London: John Bellinger, 1682), Bk. II, Ch. III, Sec. V. at 221 (hereinafter Molloy (3d. ed. Bellinger)).

126. Towle, Records, *supra* note 34, Introduction (Andrews) at 25. Nonetheless, the practice of denying masters relief in claims for wages was not followed universally. In Massachusetts, the vice admiralty court adopted a pragmatic approach. When the master's contract specified hire for wages, a claim for nonpayment sounded concurrently in admiralty and common law. When the master's compensation (in whole or in part) involved receipt of a share in the vessel herself, the master was limited to filing his claim *in personam* against the owners. Wroth, *supra* note 31, at 353.

127. *See Flood v. Snow "Hector"* (Vice Admiralty Court of New York, 1750), *reproduced from manuscript in* Hough, Vice Admiralty of New York, *supra* note 21, at 71–73.

128. The facts in *Covertry v. Snow "Doddington"* (Vice Admiralty Court of New York, 1748) are complicated, and unfortunately the record is not as complete as a modern scholar would like. The *"Doddington"* was captured as a prize by the French, but later abandoned by them. Her English captain and his crew then retook possession of the vessel and sailed it to Scotland, where the captain loaded a cargo of salt—at his own expense—and proceeded back to New York. The captain then claimed a salvage award for restoring the vessel to the owners. As the seamen's original contract had ended with the capture of the *Doddington*, they also sought relief from the court. Cases in which third parties claimed salvage for retaking a prize-ship are not unprecedented in the eighteenth century, but it is highly unusual for the retaking to be accomplished by the same captain and crew who originally lost the vessel. The judge's decision reflected the creativity and imagination due under such unusual circumstances. The captain was granted a salvage award for restoring the *Dod-*

In addition to providing *fora* in which seamen could sue for their wages, on occasion, the vice admiralty courts rendered humanitarian aid to vessels that arrived in port damaged and short of provisions.[129] They did so as part of their administrative functions, which formed a significant portion of the courts' work. Among these functions were the issuing of letters of marque and the ordering of surveys to ascertain the condition of vessels.[130] There is even one recorded instance of a court—acting on instructions of the Lords of Admiralty—conducting an investigation to determine whether a privateering raid aimed against French possessions had violated Dutch neutrality.[131] The courts' administrative duties regarding surveys often paralleled their adjudicative powers over wrecks and salvage. Cases of wreck were rare in vice admiralty courts of colonial times,[132] but not entirely un-

---

dington to her owners, and he was not required to pay freight to the owners for the cargo of salt that he brought back from Scotland. The crew, whose contracts had terminated with the capture of the ship by the French, also were paid a salvage award—in the amount that they would have earned under their employment contracts—out of the proceeds of the sale of the vessel at judicial auction. The decision is reproduced from manuscript *in* HOUGH, VICE ADMIRALTY OF NEW YORK, *supra* note 21, at 32–35.

129. *See* ANDREWS, *supra* note 33, at 252–253; Towle, RECORDS, *supra* note 34, Introduction (Andrews) at 61–62.

130. With regard to the courts' role in ordering surveys, Andrews explains:

> "Should a ship run ashore or ground upon a reef, the services of the court were immediately called into play and a survey resulted. On receipt of an application or petition from the captain, the judge issued a warrant, sometimes on his own initiative, sometimes on an instruction from the governor or council, authorizing a committee to examine the boat, determine its position and the nature of its injuries, and report either to himself or to the council the extent of the damage. If the hull was too far gone to be worth saving, he might order it to be sold where it was for what it would bring. The owner, as well as the captain, might apply to the court for a survey, in order to obtain attested evidence upon which to base a claim for insurance money, or else he might ask the court to determine the exact cost of refloating and refitting in order that the necessary data might be at hand in making up an audit. In such cases the court acted somewhat in the capacity of a receiver, issuing orders, providing for surveys and examinations, approving estimates and costs, paying bills, and determining fees."

ANDREWS, *supra* note 33, at 254. Although vice admiralty courts' role in ordering surveys is often ignored in the scholarly literature, Andrews has identified thirteen such cases among the fragmentary records in South Carolina alone. *Id.* at 253 n. 1. Wroth, *supra* note 31, at 367, has identified seventeen in Massachusetts.

131. For discussion of Judge Strengthfield's investigation in 1746, *see* Wiener, *supra* note 24, at 52–53.

132. CRUMP, *supra* note 14, at 17. Wroth, *supra* note 31, at 367, observes that of 936 extant cases from Massachusetts, there were only twelve cases involving salvage.

known.[133] Traditionally, courts have awarded up to a moiety (fifty percent) of the salved property, with the value the award varying according to the difficulty and danger faced by the salvors. Nonetheless, courts generally had made a distinction between the recovery of a wrecked vessel (for which a salvor would receive an award, with the residual value reserved for the owners) and an abandoned or "derelict" vessel (which as *res nullius* could be claimed by the salvor.)[134] It is not clear that American vice admiralty courts always recognized this distinction, as on several occasions courts granted salvage awards to individuals who had rescued abandoned vessels.[135] Another

---

133. *See e.g. Brigantine "William and Thomas"* (Vice Admiralty Court of Maryland, 1745), *reproduced from manuscript in* Owen & Tolley, *supra* note 14, at 316–317; *Brigantine "Swan"* (Vice Admiralty Court of Maryland, 1753: survey and distribution of the proceeds of a salvage sale) summarized *in Id.* at 319–320. On occasion, cases of wreck and salvage were addressed by the colonial courts of common law as well. *See Schooner "Tasker"* (Maryland Provincial Court, 1750); *Ship "Greyhound"* (Maryland Governor and Council, 1750), *Id.* at 318–319. Fact-patterns in such cases occasionally were novel. Crump, *supra* note 14, at 40, notes the case of the *"Mary Rose"*, salvaged where she sank in Boston Harbor. A gun retrieved from the wreck—in which had been hidden coins worth thirty pounds sterling—accidentally discharged, showering the onlooking crowd with money. When the crowd refused to return the coins, the contract-salvor was forced to initiate proceedings against the onlookers for recovery of his property.

134. Attorneys for William Penn once made the distinction between a ship lost through negligence or perils of the sea and one intentionally abandoned by its owners, contending that the ship *"St. Louis"* (Vice Amiralty Court of Pennsylvania, 1699), had become *res nullius* through abandonment. For discussion, *see* Root, *supra* note 70, at 101–102; Harrington (Part I), *supra* note 37, at 558–559. At one time in English history, an abandoned vessel, or "derelict", that washed ashore would escheat to the Crown as a "droit of the admiralty", while one that was salved at sea could be claimed by the salvor. Reginald G. Marsden, Select Pleas in the Court of Admiralty: A.D. 1547–1602, Vol. II (London: Publications of the Selden Society, Vol. 11, 1897), Introduction at xxxix (hereinafter Marsden, Select Pleas II). For statutory changes to this rule, *see* Molloy (3d ed., Bellinger), *supra* note 125, at 337–345. For discussion of the complex history of the substantive English law of wreck and salvage, *see* Thomas Lambert Mears, "The History of the Admiralty Jurisdiction", *in* Select Essays in Anglo-American Legal History, Vol. II (Boston: Little, Brown, & Co., 1908), n. 1 at 331–335. *See also* discussion, Chapter I, notes 81–82 and text accompanying.

135. It is not always clear whether the results in these cases turned upon a different rule of substantive law or on an interpretation of facts—through which the courts concluded that the alleged "derelicts" had in fact not been abandoned willfully. For example, *see Carlton v. Goods of Ship "Friends Good Will"* (Vice Admiralty Court of New York, 1730), *published from manuscript in* Hough, Vice Admiralty of New York, *supra* note 21, at 10–11. Later, during the Articles-of-Confederation period, the state admiralty court was very specific in concluding that the salvor of an intentionally abandoned vessel was entitled to no more than a salvage award rather than outright possession. *See March v. Goods of Brigantine "Port Roseway"* (New York State Court of Admiralty, 1785), *reproduced from manu-*

feature common to the eighteenth century was the granting of salvage awards to anyone who recaptured an English or colonial vessel, with the original owner receiving the residual value when it was sold at judicial auction.[136] As in modern practice, the colonial records reveal that salvage awards were granted both to those who salved property under contract with the vessels' owners[137] and to those whose services had not been solicited.[138]

Sir Leoline Jenkins had lamented the fate of English materialmen, whose access to the High Court of Admiralty often had been barred by writs of prohibition.[139] Claims for "ship's necessaries" were rare in vice admiralty courts,[140] but appear occasionally in the extant records.[141] In some jurisdictions, common-law courts issued prohibitions in these cases.[142] In others judges found a practical solution; the court would assume jurisdiction so long as both parties desired the rules of procedure and evidence employed in the vice admi-

---

script in Id. at 244–248. More typical of the traditional rule is *Burchall v. Snow "Jolly Bachelor" and Goods*, (Vice Admiralty Court of Rhode Island, 1743), *reproduced from manuscript in* Towle, RECORDS, *supra* note 34, at 226–235, in which the court awarded salvage after finding that sailors remained alive on a disabled and drifting vessel.

136. *See e.g. Troy v. Snow "Halifax Packet"* (Vice Admiralty Court of New York, 1761), *reproduced from manuscript in* HOUGH, VICE ADMIRALTY OF NEW YORK, *supra* note 21, at 188–190; *Williams v. Sloop "Prosperous Polly" and Lading* (Vice Admiralty Court of New York, 1762), *reproduced in Id.* at 199–201; *Bill v. Snow "Confirmation" and Lading and Snow "Speedwell" and Lading* (Vice Admiralty Court of New York, 1749), *reproduced in Id.* at 41–46; *Troupe v. Brig "Ave Maria"* (Vice Admiralty Court of New York, 1748), *reproduced in Id.* at 46–48. Courts also allowed salvage when a crew recaptured a vessel that had turned pirate. Towle, RECORDS, *supra* note 34, Introduction (Andrews) at 31.

137. *Flowers v. Ship "Alexander"* (Vice Admiralty Court of Rhode Island, 1742) *reproduced from manuscript in* Towle, RECORDS, *supra* note 34, at 161–166.

138. *Burger v. Brigantine "Mary"* (Vice Admiralty Court of New York, 1770), *reproduced from manuscript in* HOUGH, VICE ADMIRALTY OF NEW YORK, *supra* note 21, at 233–234.

139. Jenkins, "*Argument*", *in* WYNNE, *supra* note 106, at lxxxiv.

140. Towle, RECORDS, *supra* note 34, Introduction (Andrews) at 31. Wroth, *supra* note 31, at 367, has found records for only thirteen claims by materialmen in the extant records of Massachusetts.

141. *See e.g. The Schooner "Liberty"* (Vice Admiralty Court of Maryland, 1770), *in* OWEN & TOLLEY, *supra* note 14, at 334–335. The case consolidated chandlers' claims for necessaries with a shipwright's claim for breach of a contract to build a vessel. Since the mid-nineteenth century, American law has held the latter claim to be outside federal admiralty jurisdiction. *See People's Ferry Co. v. Beers*, 61 U. S. 393 (1857).

142. *See e.g.* Wiener, *supra* note 24, at 53; *see also Potter v. Owners of the "Greyhound"* (Vice Admiralty Court of Rhode Island, 1747, holding that a court of vice admiralty does not have cognizance over a claim for necessaries), *reproduced from manuscript in* Towle, RECORDS, *supra* note 34, at 413–417.

ralty courts.[143] The colonial courts of common law asserted exclusive jurisdiction over these cases in some colonies, and concurrent jurisdiction in others, with the result that many materialmen's claims were litigated in the provincial courts. Nevertheless, common-law courts did not always employ juries in these cases.[144] Materialmen's claims appeared more frequently in vice admiralty courts when they were secured by bottomry bonds. This form of contract, which pledged the hull of the vessel in exchange for repairs or necessaries, constituted an express hypothecation[145] of the type generally held to be within the jurisdiction of the High Court of Admiralty and thus immune to prohibition. While not numerous, records of several cases of this type have survived.[146] Although the bond might specify only a part-interest in the ves-

---

143. Towle, Records, *supra* note 34, Introduction (Andrews) at 31.

144. *See e.g. The "Recovery"* (Provincial Court of Maryland, 1644); *The Ship "John and Benjamin"* (Provincial Court of Maryland, 1736), *in* Owen & Tolley, *supra* note 14, at 241, 312–313.

145. In his adaptation of the work of the eighteenth-century French scholar Balthazard Emerigon (1716–1785) for the American market, John Hall gives the following definition of "express hypothecation":

> "I adopt the definition which M. Pothier gives of this contract. 'The contract of maritime loan', he says, 'is an agreement by which one, who is the lender, lends to another, who is the borrower, a certain sum of money, upon the condition that if the thing upon which the loan has been made, should be lost, by any peril of the sea, or *vis major*, the lender shall not be repaid, unless what remains shall be equal to the sum borrowed; and that if the thing arrive in safely, or in case that it shall not have been injured, but its own defect or the fault of the master and mariners, the borrower shall be bound to return the sum borrowed, together with a certain sum agreed upon as the price of the hazard incurred.'"

John E. Hall, An Essay on Maritime Loans, From the French of M. Balthazard Marie Emerigon: With Notes (Baltimore: George Dobbin & Murphy, 1809) at 24. In France, governed by the civil law, the admiralty courts' cognizance over such agreements was unproblematic. In England and its colonies, however, jurisdiction over this form of contract—instrumental in the development of the modern maritime lien—remained with the courts of admiralty because it was first developed as a means of raising funds in foreign ports. The common law lacked jurisdiction over foreign contracts. As one modern commentary explains:

> "The master of a vessel caught in a foreign port without funds to pay for repairs or supplies could pledge the vessel for a bottomry loan payable only if the vessel completed her voyage (thus giving rise to exorbitant interest rates). This was an express hypothecation of the vessel, well known in the civil law as an '*hypothèque*'."

Owen & Tolley, *supra* note 14, at 12.

146. *Sloop "Polly and Fanny"* (Vice Admiralty Court of Virginia, 1770), *reproduced from manuscript in* Reese, Vice-Admiralty of Virginia, *supra* note 86, at 83–84; *Ship "John-*

sel, the materialman nonetheless could sue to have her sold at auction to satisfy the claim, with the proceeds divided between him and her owners.[147] Conflicts over ownership of vessels were not restricted to bottomry-bond cases. Given the value of ships and the great risks involved in maritime ventures, quite frequently investors sought to limit their potential losses by purchasing shares in several vessels rather than owning one outright. As a result, disputes among partners were fairly common, usually arising when one set of owners wished to send their ship on a voyage while another group did not.[148] In general, disputes over possession of a vessel were tried in admiralty, and disputes regarding ownership were tried at common law.[149] In some colonies, the common-law courts issued prohibitions when vice admiralty courts entertained these actions.[150] It is likely that the majority of these matters were tried at common law;[151] nonetheless, a number of partnership disputes and "petitory" suits were heard in the provincial admiralty courts.[152]

Collisions were rare in the eighteenth century, and when they occurred, the damage was often minimal.[153] They occurred most frequently in crowded harbors and channels, but the parties disposed of most of these matters without

---

ston" (Vice Admiralty Court of Maryland, 1763) *in* Owen & Tolley, *supra* note 14, at 326–327.

147. *Howard v. Moiety of "The Charming Sally"* (Vice Admiralty Court of New York, 1759), *reproduced from manuscript in* Hough, Vice Admiralty of New York, *supra* note 21, at 164–165.

148. Towle, Records, *supra* note 34, Introduction (Andrews) at 30.

149. Owen & Tolley, *supra* note 14, at 149.

150. Wiener, *supra* note 24, at 53.

151. Towle, Records, *supra* note 34, Introduction (Andrews) at 30. Examples of cases filed in common-law courts include *The Sloop "Fanny and Molly"* (Provincial Court of Maryland, 1744), *in* Owen & Tolley, *supra* note 14, at 314–315; *Frigate "Expedition"* (Provincial Court of Maryland, 1664), *in Id.* at 256–258; *Bayley v. Staplefort [The Barque "Providence"]* (Provincial Court of Maryland, 1665, *affirmed by* Governor and Council, 1674), *in Id.* at 261–262.

152. "Petitory actions" involve title to vessels. Owen & Tolley, *supra* note 14, at 149. Wroth, *supra* note 31, at 367, identifies 26 cases involving "part ownership and possession" which were filed in the Vice Admiralty Court of Massachusetts between 1718 and 1747. Examples of disputes between partners from other jurisdictions include *Averill v. Blackstock* (Vice Admiralty Court of Rhode Island, 1750), *reproduced from manuscript in* Towle, Records, *supra* note 34, at 528–529; *Belknap v. Schooner "Elizabeth"* (Vice Admiralty Court of Rhode Island, 1752), *reproduced in Id.* at 554–557.

153. Owen & Tolley, *supra* note 14, at 2. The authors note that there is no record of a collision being litigated in Maryland. *Id.* at 139. Wroth, *supra* note 31, at 367, identifies only five cases in Massachusetts, the colony in which maritime litigation was most common and for which the extant records are most complete.

recourse to litigation.[154] Generally, collisions between sail-driven craft merely cause damage to rigging, but occasionally—when the disparity in size is great enough—one vessel may sink another.[155] A few such cases survive, but the records are too scant to form any conclusions concerning how the colonial courts interpreted the rule requiring the splitting of damages in collision-cases.[156] Also rare in the colonial period are cases of general average; this oldest of maritime claims—origins of which can be traced to antiquity—is almost wholly absent from the colonial records.[157] There are, however, colonial

---

154. Towle, RECORDS, *supra* note 34, Introduction (Andrews) at 31; ANDREWS, *supra* note 33, at 232–233.

155. In 1703, a ship was libelled in Massachusetts for striking and sinking a sloop, resulting in the loss of the smaller vessel and her cargo. For discussion, *see* Towle, *supra* note 34, at 31. The few surviving records from the Vice Admiralty Court of Virginia include one collision-case. The ship *"Peter"* under full sail struck the disabled sloop *"Patty"*, resulting in the loss of the *"Patty"* and her cargo. Unfortunately, the record is fragmentary, and the surviving portion does not indicate the outcome or the rule of substantive law that the court applied. *Welch v. The Ship "Peter"* (Randolph, J., Vice Admiralty Court of Virginia, 1772), *reproduced from manuscript in* Reese, VICE-ADMIRALTY OF VIRGINIA, *supra* note 86, at 95–96.

156. One modern commentary explains:

> "The admiralty has always had its own rule which was and is markedly different from the common law rule that the plaintiff's negligence bars all recovery. For 800 years the admiralty divided the loss equally, that is to say, the party with the lesser damage paid to the other one-half of the difference between their losses. This originated with the *Rolls of Oleron* and was again promulgated in the *Marine Ordinance of Louis XIV (1681)*."

OWEN & TOLLEY, *supra* note 14, at 14. While Article 15 of the Laws of Oleron (*see* BLACK BOOK, *supra* note 125, Vol. I, "Rolls of Oleron" at 108–109) did provide for the splitting of damages in cases of allision (*i.e.* where a moving vessel strikes another moored or at anchor), before 1539 there is no record of a case in which a court apportioned losses in a collision-case where both ships were at fault. *See* MARSDEN, SELECT PLEAS IN THE COURT OF ADMIRALTY: A. D. 1390–1404 AND A. D. 1527–1545, VOL. I (London: Publications of the Selden Society, Vol. 6, 1892), Introduction at lxxii, *text of decision reproduced from manuscript* at 90. Throughout the next century, the High Court of Admiralty applied various rules for assessing damages in collision-cases. MARSDEN, SELECT PLEAS II, *supra* note 134, Introduction at lxxxiii–lxxv. For further discussion, *see supra* Chapter I, n. 79 and text accompanying.

157. Wroth, *supra* note 31, at 367, has located records for only six cases of general average in the records for Massachusetts. There are no surviving records for general-average cases in Maryland, Virginia, Rhode Island, or New York. The lack of general-average cases in the eighteenth-century colonial records is not altogether surprising; they were equally uncommon in England in that era. As Henry Bourguignon explains in his biography of Sir William Scott, who ascended to the bench of the High Court at the end of that century:

> "Scott had no occasion to discuss the doctrine of general average, though he cer-

cases that preserve a tradition from the middle ages—the "droits of the Admiralty."[158] While there are vestiges of the medieval rule, whereby wrecks on shore are perquisites of the admiralty,[159] this category of cases generally is limited to the Admiralty's claim on drift whales. The archaic rule was fairly straightforward; whales that washed ashore were the property of the Admiralty.[160] Nonetheless, in the whaling ports of New England, dead whales were a mainstay of the local economy, and occasionally disputes arose as to whether drift whales had died natural deaths (making them droits of the Admiralty) or from wounds inflicted by a whaler's harpoon[161] (thereby triggering an in-

---

> tainly was familiar with it. Probably by Scott's day, average adjusters calculated these cases which were then settled without court involvement."

BOURGUIGNON, STOWELL, *supra* note 116, at 114.

158. Sir Leoline Jenkins gives the following list of the "droits", or perquisites, of the admiralty at the close of the seventeenth century, noting that these had reverted to the Crown with Charles II's ascension to the throne:

> "Lastly, There are several *Rights* and *Emoluments* belonging to the ancient Office of *High Admiral* of *England*, that are at this Time, by Surrender of his Royal Highness, returned to, and vested in the Crown; and it has always been the Course of this Court to give them in Charge. You [members of the jury] are to enquire therefore of those that have seiz'd and taken to themselves Wrecks at Sea, having neither Grant nor Prescription whereby they may lawfully do it. Of those that have posses'd themselves of *Flotsons, Jetsons, Lagons, Derelicts, Deodands, Treasure-Trouve,* the Lord High Admiral's *Tenths* in Men of War, *Royal Fishes,* such as Whales, Sturgeons, Porpoises, Shares in the Casualties, and *ejectamenta maris*, the Goods of Pirates, the Goods of Enemies in the late wars, the Goods of Traitors, Felons, Out-laws, *Felones de se,* when lying within the Jurisdiction of the Admiralty; or of any other Rights or Perquisites belonging to that Office."

"A Charge given at an Admiralty Sessions held at the Old-Baily, by Sir L. Jenkins. Taken by a good Hand." *in* WYNNE, *supra* note 106, Vol. I, at xc, xcviii–xcix (*emphasis in the original*).

159. *See e.g. Charleton v. Divers Goods Saved Out of the Ship "Friends Good Will"* (Vice Admiralty Court of New York, 1729), *reproduced from manuscript in* HOUGH, VICE ADMIRALTY OF NEW YORK, *supra* note 21, at 10–11, in which the court—having awarded salvage and deducted fees for the officers of the court from the proceeds of the sale—declared the balance be paid to the "Receiver for the Rights and Perquisites of the Admiralty." For discussion of the medieval rules relating to the droits of the admiralty, *see* Chapter I, notes 81–82 and text accompanying.

160. *See* Towle, RECORDS, *supra* note 34, Introduction (Andrews) at 33.

161. *See* ANDREWS, *supra* note 33, at 233–234. In 1706, Governor Dudley of Massachusetts wrote to the Board of Trade regarding the colonists' disregard for the Admiralty's claim on drift whales. As it was at times difficult to ascertain whether a whale had died a natural death or from injuries sustained through freeing itself from a whaler's harpoon, the colonists always assumed the latter, thereby granting title to local whalers rather than to the Admiralty. *Id.* at 234 n. 1. These cases were surprisingly common; Wroth, *supra* note

digenous set of American rules for determining title to the carcass).[162] Occasionally, colonial vice admiralty courts heard disputes between whalemen, among which the most famous pitted James Otis against John Adams, noteworthy not only for the identity of the attorneys but also for Adams' use of Roman law in ar-

31, at 367, identifies twenty-four such matters adjudicated by the Vice Admiralty Court of Massachusetts between 1718 and 1772, with the highest concentration (twenty) being heard between 1718 and 1726.

162. *Id.* at 234. Generally, whalers preferred to settle disputes among themselves through their own form of arbitration. The rules were often detailed, and by the end of the eighteenth century whalers fishing the same waters had begun to commit these rules to writing, in effect creating by contract substantive law that sovereign nations had not seen fit to promulgate. A drift whale could be distinguished from a whale killed by whalers by one of two methods. If the whale had been killed but not yet hoisted out of the water, it was marked with a pennant (known as a "waif"). If it had escaped and subsequently died of its wounds, the owner's mark on the harpoon itself would identify the rightful claimant. *See* Granville Allen Mawer, Ahab's Trade: The Saga of South Sea Whaling (New York: St. Martin's Press, 1999) at 97–103. Lamenting the lack of positive law to govern the matter, Herman Melville gave history's most famous synopsis of whalers' customs for assigning title to a whale:

> "[Whalers] have provided a system which for terse comprehensiveness surpasses Justinian's Pandects and the By-laws of the Chinese Society for the Suppression of Meddling with Other Peoples' Business. Yes; these laws might be engraven on a Queen Anne's farthing, or the barb of a harpoon, and worn round the neck, so small are they. I. A Fast-Fish belongs to the party fast to it. II. A Loose-Fish is fair game for anybody who can soonest catch it. But what plays the mischief with this masterly code is the admirable brevity of it, which necessitates a vast volume of commentaries to expound it. First: What is a Fast-Fish? Alive or dead a fish is technically fast, when it is connected with an occupied ship or boat, by any medium at all controllable by the occupant or occupants.... Likewise, a fish is technically fast when it bears a waif.... These are scientific commentaries; but the commentaries of the whalemen themselves sometimes consist in hard words and harder knocks—the Coke-upon-Littleton of the fist. True, among the more upright and honorable whalemen allowances are made for peculiar cases, where it would be an outrageous moral injustice for one party to claim possession of a whale previously chased or killed by another party. But others are by no means so scrupulous."

Herman Melville, Moby Dick, or, The Whale (1st ed. 1851; critical ed.: Harrison Hayford, Hershel Parker, & G. Thomas Tanselle eds., Evanston: Northwestern University Press, 2001) Ch. 89, at 395–396. Despite Melville's assessment of the "terse comprehensiveness" of the custom, the text of an agreement amongst whalers that Mawer cites (at 97–98) is quite detailed, providing rules for a large variety of possible fact-patterns. As to whether informal custom or contractual obligation generally prevailed over "the Coke-upon-Littleton of the fist", Melville would have been in a better position to judge than most modern commentators.

guing the case.[163] Unfortunately, the outcome of the case is unknown, but it serves to show that eighteenth-century colonial attorneys and judges would not reject offhandedly the notion that the substantive maritime law of Rome continued to apply to private actions, either through incorporation into English law or as part of the binding customs that constituted the law of nations.[164]

By act of Parliament, the High Court of Admiralty lost jurisdiction over criminal matters in 1537, though the Court retained jurisdiction *in rem* over pirates' ships and goods.[165] The act, however, did not apply to the colonies,

---

163. The case was *Doane v. Gage* (Vice Admiralty Court of Massachusetts, 1769). The records of this case, which ultimately was withdrawn from the court and decided through arbitration with the mutual consent of the parties, are published in LEGAL PAPERS OF JOHN ADAMS (L. Kinvin Wroth & Hiller B. Zobel eds., Cambridge, Massachusetts: Belknap Press, 1965), Vol. II, Case No. 43, at 68–97 (hereinafter LEGAL PAPERS OF JOHN ADAMS). The crew of Adams' client, Captain Doane, had harpooned a whale that later was captured by a whale-boat from Gage's ship. As Daniel Coquillette explains:

> "So the key issue was simply whether Doane's boat was attached to the whale when Gage struck it, or whether the whale was a "loose" whale. No less than seventy-four witnesses, thirty-four for Doane and forty for Gage, would testify. John Adams represented Captain Doane and Robert Treat Paine and James Otis represented Captain Gage. Never was a dead whale given such posthumous dignity. He was fought over by seventy-four eyewitnesses, two signers of the Declaration of Independence—one a future President of the United States—and the great James Otis!"

Daniel R. Coquillette, "Justinian in Braintree: John Adams, Civilian Learning and Legal Elitism, 1758–1775", *in* LAW IN COLONIAL MASSACHUSETTS (Daniel Coquillette ed., University of Virginia Press, 1984) at 359, 383–386 (hereinafter Coquillette, "Justinian"). In an effort to counter the rule laid out in *Justinian's Institutes*, 2.1.12, under which an animal that escapes capture becomes once again *res nullius*, Adams cited *Digest* 41.1.5, which maintains that he who first wounds an animal retains title to it so long as he continues his pursuit, even if another overtakes it before he does. *Id.* at 385–386; LEGAL PAPERS OF JOHN ADAMS at 73–75. (For texts cited by Adams, *see* *CORPUS JURIS CIVILIS* (Latin ed., C. M. Galisset ed.: Paris: Janet & Cotelle, 1830), J. INST. 2.1.12 at 135; DIG. 41.1.5 at 1330.)

164. Coquillette, "Justinian", *supra* note 163, at 385–386. For discussion of the relationship between Roman substantive maritime law and English law of the early modern period, *see* Chapter I, notes 107–108 and text accompanying.

165. *See* 28 Hen. VIII, c. 15 (1536); for discussion *see* Thomas Lambert Mears, "The History of the Admiralty Jurisdiction", *in* SELECT ESSAYS IN ANGLO-AMERICAN LEGAL HISTORY (Boston: Little, Brown & Co., 1908), Vol. II, at 312, 351–352. Despite the loss of criminal jurisdiction, the High Court of Admiralty retained some jurisdiction over piracy, as Mears explains:

> "In the case of piracy...the criminal aspect was disregarded, the proceedings being for restitution, and no preliminary conviction was required, as was the case where the Lord High Admiral proceeded *pro interesse suo*, upon his royal grant

and the vice-admiralty commissions contained broad grants of criminal jurisdiction.[166] In 1700, Parliament enacted the Piracy Act, which provided that colonial trials for piracy be tried under civil-law rules in special sessions of Oyer and Terminer.[167] The Piracy Act of 1717 amended these provisions, substituting common-law for civil-law procedures, thus guaranteeing defendants the right to a jury.[168] Despite these acts, criminal proceedings in colonial vice admiralty courts were rare. Although there are a few extant records of prosecutions for assault,[169] there are no surviving records of felonies being tried in these courts.[170] The vice admiralty courts, however, did on occasion try another variety of criminal case. By an act of 1722, Parliament had sought to

---

> of *bona piratarum*."

Id. at 320–321.

166. *See* Owen & Tolley, *supra* note 14, at 221. For an example of the grant of criminal jurisdiction to colonial vice admirals, *see* the Commission of Governor Lionel Copley as Vice Admiral (1691), extending to him the power:

> "... [T]o take cognizance of, and proceed in, all... causes, suits, crimes, offences, excesses, injuries, complaints, misdemeanors, or suspected misdemeanors... within the maritime jurisdiction of our Vice-Admiralty of our province and territory of aforesaid Maryland, by sea or water, on the banks or shores of the same howsoever done, committed, perpetrated, or happening."

Reproduced as Appendix D *in Id.* at 369, 370–371.

167. 11 & 12 Will. III, c. 7 (1700)

168. 4 Geo. I, c. 11 (1717).

169. *See* Owen & Tolley, *supra* note 14, at 34 (noting that there are records for cases of assault in Rhode Island and New York). Dorothy Towle has located two case of criminal assault prosecuted in the Vice Admiralty Court of Rhode Island: *Selman v. Gardner* (1727/28) and *Spencer v. Gardner* (1727/28), the former resulting in acquittal and the latter in a fine. Towle, Records, *supra* note 34, at 123–125. Hough, Vice Admiralty of New York, *supra* note 21, has identified several civil actions for assault in his published records of the Vice Admiralty Court of New York: *Thomas v. Bryson* (1759) at 179, *Gillaspie v. Hynes; Linster v. Hynes* (1762) at 210–214, *Gordon v. Blake* (1755) at 84, *White v. Hall* (1754) at 80–81, but only one case of criminal assault: *The King v. White* (1754) at 81.

170. Owen & Tolley, *supra* note 14, at 34. Wroth, *supra* note 31, at 357, identifies one criminal case of piracy tried in admiralty in Massachusetts; however, the court that heard *Rex v. Snow "Elizabeth"* (1726) was a special court of admiralty convened solely for this case rather than the Vice Admiralty Court of Massachusetts. Similarly in 1712 in South Carolina, a court convened by special commission—with the colony's vice admiralty judge presiding—tried and convicted the pirate Stede Bonnet; the pirates Quelch and Kidd were tried in similar manner. Properly speaking, however, these were not vice-admiralty trials. Owen & Tolley, *supra* note 14, at 165, 167. Nonetheless, as with the High Court of Admiralty, the vice admiralty courts of the colonies retained civil jurisdiction *in rem* over pirates' ships and goods (*see supra* note 165), and Wroth, *supra* note 31, at 367, observes that the Court of Massachusetts heard a total of three piracy cases. *Id.* at 367.

protect standing timber for use as masts and spars for the Royal Navy, and the vice admiralty courts were given jurisdiction over alleged violations of the act, which forbade the cutting of trees of more than two feet in diameter measured three feet from the ground. A royal official, the "Surveyor of His Majesty's Woods", had the responsibility of identifying all trees of such size and marking them with a symbol—the "King's broad arrow"—as a warning to colonial loggers. The Surveyor's staff being small and incapable of protecting the trees, it was relatively easy for colonists to ignore the law and to poach timber marked for naval use. Nonetheless, the Surveyor on occasion did identify the perpetrators, bringing action against them personally and against the timber *in rem*, in order to reclaim the logs for the Navy.[171]

Another class of cases heard by the vice admiralty courts was prize. In an era when nations found it cost-effective to augment the strength of their navies through issuing letters of marque, seizures were common, and England had opted to handle the process of distributing awards through judicial rather than administrative proceedings.[172] Thus all captured vessels were formally con-

---

171. ANDREWS, *supra* note 33, at 247. In the parallel proceedings of *Wentworth v. Dean* and *Rex v. Three White Pine Trees* (Vice Admiralty Court of New York, 1769), John Wentworth, the King's Surveyor, brought an action against three men for illegally cutting timber marked with the "broad arrow" and another against the trees *in rem*. The defendants were incarcerated (one for four months and the other two for three), after failing to pay a substantial fine for destruction of the Crown's property. *Reproduced from manuscript in* HOUGH, VICE ADMIRALTY OF NEW YORK, *supra* note 21, at 228–233.

172. Prior to the reign of Elizabeth I, prize cases generally were heard by the "Commissioners for causes of depredation". *See* JOHN E. HALL, THE PRACTICE AND JURISDICTION OF THE COURT OF ADMIRALTY (Baltimore: Philip H. Nicklin & Co., 1811) at 82 (hereinafter HALL, JURISDICTION AND PRACTICE). In the wake of the defeat of the Spanish Armada, Privy Council issued an order that sought to streamline the process of condemning prizes by vesting exclusive jurisdiction in the High Court of the Admiralty:

> "It ys further ordered that all shipps, goods, and merchandizes, taken by vertue of eany commission of reprisall aforesaid shalbe kepte savely, and noe part of that sould, spoyled, wasted, nor diminished, till judgement hath first passed in the high courte of the Admiralty that the said goodes are a lawful prize; otherwise the said commission to all purposes to be voide, as well to the taker as to all other who shall buy or intermeddle with the said goodes or eany part thereof."

"Order of Council that all captures should be brought in for adjudication in the Admiralty Court"—Admiralty Court, Exemplifications 29, No. 113 (1589), *published in* DOCUMENTS RELATING TO LAW AND CUSTOM OF THE SEA (R. G. Marsden, ed., London: Navy Record Society, 1915–1916), Vol. I, at 252. (hereinafter Marsden, DOCUMENTS). In 1602, the Queen issued a proclamation that reinforced the power of the High Court of Admiralty to hear prize cases. HALL, JURISDICTION AND PRACTICE, at 82–83. One eighteenth-century author implies that the change in procedure may reflect changes in international custom

demned in the courts of admiralty.[173] The patents of the judges of the High Court of Admiralty did not specifically mention prize, but by the reign of Elizabeth I, the judges had assumed the jurisdiction.[174] In 1625, the High Court began to separate its records in prize cases from those in instance cases, and soon thereafter differences in the two jurisdictions began to evolve.[175] As Lord Mansfield later was to write:

> The Court of Admiralty is called the Instance Court; the other the Prize Court. The manner of proceeding is totally different. The whole system of litigation and jurisprudence in the Prize Court, is peculiar

---

and practice, which came to require full-fledged adjudication by a court in place of summary administrative proceedings:

> "By the Maritime Law of Nations, universally and immemorially received, there is an established method of determination, whether the capture be, or not be, lawful prize. Before the ship or goods can be disposed of by the Captor, there must be a regular judicial proceeding, wherein both parties may be heard, and condemnation thereupon as prize, in a Court of Admiralty, judging by the Law of Nations and Treaties."

Anthony Stokes, A View of the Constitution of the British Colonies, in North-America and the West Indies, at the Time the Civil War Broke out on the Continent of America (London: B. White, 1783), Ch. XIII, "Of the Court of Vice Admiralty" at 270, 275 *(citations omitted)* (hereinafter Stokes).

173. Although the courts of common law never seriously challenged the power of the High Court of Admiralty to try prize cases, they did dispute the authority of the Court to try cases relating to goods despoiled at sea that were later brought ashore on English soil. Matthew Hale had been of the opinion that the courts of common law had concurrent jurisdiction in such cases. Hale and Fleetwood, *supra* note 15, Introduction at xci.

174. Owen & Tolley, *supra* note 14, at 155. Eventually, Parliament reinforced centuries of tacit acknowledgement and the proclamation of Elizabeth I (*supra* note 172), and formally vested jurisdiction over prize in the High Court of Admiralty. As Henry Bourguignon explains:

> "Although there was authority for the admiralty court to assert inherent jurisdiction over prize cases, at least after 1702 it became the practice for the Lord High Admiral or the Lords High Commissioners of the Admiralty at the outbreak of each war to issue special commissions to the High Court authorizing the judge to hear cases of prize. The Prize Act of 1708 gave parliamentary recognition to the admiralty court's prize jurisdiction and gave to the captors (whether a naval vessel or privateer) a statutory right to the whole of the prize, thereby surrendering any right of the king to a share. Parliament throughout the eighteenth century re-enacted the Prize Act in essentially the same form at the start of each war."

Bourguignon, First Federal Court, *supra* note 33, at 14.

175. Marsden, "High Court", *supra* note 16, at 79.

> to itself: it is no more like the Court of Admiralty, than it is to any court in Westminster-Hall.[176]

Among the differences were the procedures for admitting evidence and for handling appeals. When sitting in either prize or instance, the Court eschewed oral testimony. It received witnesses' testimony on the instance side in the form of affidavits and depositions; when acting as a prize court, evidence was in the form of standing interrogatories.[177] The High Court of Delegates heard appeals in instance cases; in prize cases they went to the Lords Commissioners of Prize Appeals.[178] The most striking contrast between the Court's prize and

---

176. *Lindo v. Rodney*, 2 Douglas' Reports 613, 614; 99 Eng. Rep. 385, 386 (K. B., 1781). As Bourguignon notes:

> "The procedures for prize adjudication became well defined by the late seventeenth century.... The Council in 1665 outlined procedures for a trial in the prize court. Without departing from this basic outline, Parliament, by the various prize acts of the eighteenth century, more fully spelled out the details of prize adjudication."

Bourguignon, First Federal Court, *supra* note 33, at 17. The procedures that the Council promulgated in 1665—directed at expediting the adjudication of prize cases during the Dutch Wars—were as follows:

> "8. That upon notice given to the Court of Admiralty of the seizing and bringing into any port of any prize, the court shall send forth a proces to be hanged up on the Exchange, or other most publique place, whereby all that pretend to have anie right to claime may come and enter theire claimes in court in such cases where such claime is allowed; and if noe person shall come in to claime within fourteene daies after the publication of the said proces then the court shall forthwith proceed towards adjudication; and in case anie one shall come in to claime, if the goods shalbee perishable, the court shall forthwith order an appraisement and sale, and though they shall not appeare to bee perishable, yet if the claimer shall have a commission into foreigne parts for the proofe of his property, then the court shall alsoe order an appraisment and sale as aforesaid. 9. That the Court of Admiralty shall sit twice a weeke, or oftener as occasion shall require, to give dispatch to the affaire of prize shipps and goods."

"Rules for the Admiralty court in the adjudication of prizes" (1665) Lansd. MSS. 194, f. 18b, *published in* Marsden, Documents, *supra* note 172, Vol. II, at 53, 56. (These rules were also reproduced in Wynne, *supra* note 106, Vol. I, at xii.)

177. Owen & Tolley, *supra* note 14, at 155. A set of these "standing interrogatories"—boiler-plate questions to be answered under oath by the vessel's master in prize proceedings—are reproduced in Stokes, *supra* note 172 at 334–340. For a comparison to the interrogatories drafted by the parties themselves for use in instance cases, see those employed by Adams and Otis in *Doane v. Gage*, Legal Papers of John Adams, *supra* note 163, Vol. II, Case No. 43, at 93–97.

178. *Id.* at 155; Bourguignon, First Federal Court, *supra* note 33, at 11.

instance jurisdiction was in the applicability of the jurisdictional statutes of Richard II. In instance matters, the Court's jurisdiction was limited to matters arising beyond the boundaries of English counties; no such limitation applied to prize cases. Even if goods had been removed from a vessel and taken ashore on English soil, the Court retained jurisdiction. Subject-matter—not locality—governed jurisdiction in prize cases.[179]

As with the High Court of Admiralty, neither the commissions of colonial governors nor those of the vice-admiralty judges specified jurisdiction over prize cases.[180] Despite the lack of an express jurisdictional grant, the colonial courts heard prize cases, reasoning that they fell under the general rubric of "maritime causes".[181] Recognizing the impracticality of requiring that all prizes be taken to England for trial, the government remained silent, allowing the practice of trying prize cases in vice admiralty courts to flourish.[182] Any ques-

---

179. Owen & Tolley, *supra* note 14, at 155. For the text of 13 Rich. II, c. 13 (1389) and 15 Rich. II, c.3 (1391) and discussion, *see* Chapter I, notes 132–136 and text accompanying.

180. Owen & Tolley, *supra* note 14, at 156. Extant commissions—issued by the High Court of Admiralty in Latin—today are available in their original language only in manuscript. There are, however, several published sources for these documents with their texts translated into English. For an example of a judge's commission issued before Parliament passed the American Act, *see* "The Commission of Nicholas Greenbury as judge of the court of Vice Admiralty, August 27, 1696", *published as* Appendix E *in Id.* at 377–380. For examples of the scope of maritime jurisdiction granted in colonial governors' commissions, *see e.g.* "The Warrant for the Commission of Governor Lionel Copley as Vice Admiral, October 21, 1691", *published as* Appendix D *in Id.* at 369–376; "Commission of Lord Cornbury, governor of New York" (precise date unknown), *published in translation in* Benedict (5th ed.), *supra* note 78, Sec. 657, at 789–790. While it is now somewhat difficult to find, Stokes, *supra* note 177, reproduces examples of commissions in the original Latin in Chapter IV at 166–176.

181. Owen & Tolley, *supra* note 14, at 156. For examples of prize cases heard by colonial vice admiralty courts before they formally received prize jurisdiction, *see Pink "John"* (Maryland Court of Vice Admiralty, 1694); *Ship "St. Paul"* (Maryland Court of Vice Admiralty, 1703, 1704), *Id.* at 283–285; 298–299.

182. Revenue, not concern for the legality of prize proceedings, provided the impetus for resolving the ambiguities of colonial prize jurisdiction. As Charles Andrews observes:

> "It would appear, therefore, as if, before the passage of the [American Act, *infra* note 183], prize jurisdiction in the colonies was exercised without any special authorization from England. In all probability neither [Prince George of Denmark, Consort to Queen Anne and Lord High Admiral of England] nor the authorities in England knew much about the general situation and cared less about the place of trial and the methods employed than they did about the prize money, the fines, and the forfeitures. Where the cases were tried was of less importance than was the securing of the financial rights of queen and Admiralty. The latter were

tion as to whether the courts could hear prize cases was laid to rest in 1707, when Parliament enacted the "American Act", which provided for adjudication of prize cases in the colonial vice admiralty courts.[183] While never as numerous as instance cases, cases of prize constituted roughly 33% of all matters heard by the colonies' admiralty courts from 1703–1763,[184] their numbers augmented by the frequent wars in which Britain was involved in the eighteenth century.[185] In general, prize cases were of two types. First, there were actions initiated by privateers, who captured ships under letters of marque; in addition, there were actions brought by the Royal Navy against vessels for trading with the enemy.[186] In order for a court to condemn a vessel as a prize, it

---

> troubled because of reports that the governors were interfering in the disposal of prizes and were conniving at the misuse or embezzlement of monies obtained from their sale."

Towle, Reports, *supra* note 34, Introduction (Andrews) at 37. To remedy this loss of revenue, the authorities in England sought to tighten control over the way in which prize cases were handled in the colonies. As a first step, the moribund Prize Office was re-instituted in 1669 under warrant from the Treasury, which together with the Admiralty, appointed "receivers", whose duty it was to "take into custody all ships and goods seized as prize and brought into colonial ports." To further ensure the integrity of the process, the colonial vice admiralty courts were given express jurisdiction over prize eight years later. *Id.* at 38–41.

183. "An Act for the Encouragement of Trade to America", 6 Anne, c. 37 (1707). In addition to vesting jurisdiction over prize cases in the vice admiralty courts, the Act also authorized the High Court of Admiralty to grant colonial governors the power to issue letters of marque, and, more importantly, abolished the custom of claiming a portion of the prize for the Crown, thus providing privateers with an additional incentive by allowing them to keep the whole value of the prizes they captured. Despite the explicit grant of jurisdiction, there is evidence of colonial courts of common law issuing prohibitions in prize cases. *See* Bourguignon, First Federal Court, *supra* note 33, at 26.

184. Towle, Records, *supra* note 34, Introduction (Andrews) at 41; Harrington (Part II), *supra* note 20, at 330. This percentage represents an average, and the ratio of prize cases to other cases varied greatly from one colony to another. In Maryland, prize cases accounted for only five of forty-one vice-admiralty cases for which we have records. In New York, prize cases totaled 56% of all matters heard, and in Rhode Island, 41% of those matters for which we have records involved prize. Owen & Tolley, *supra* note 14, at 103, 152–153. On the other hand, in Massachusetts, where the vice admiralty court handled the largest volume of business in the colonies, Wroth, *supra* note 31, at 367, identifies only eleven prize cases.

185. Prior to the Seven Years' (or "French and Indian") War (1756–1763), Britain fought the War of the Spanish Succession (1702–1713) and the War of the Austrian Succession (1740–1748). Rediker, *supra* note 6, at 32.

186. Owen & Tolley, *supra* note 14, at 156. It should be noted that a privateer acting without a valid letter of marque would forfeit his prize, the proceeds of which would escheat to the Crown. *See dicta in The Snow "Le Bon Rencontre" and Lading* (Court of Vice

was necessary to prove that its owners were of a belligerent rather than neutral nation—a fact not so easily determined in an age in which fraud was rampant and ships often carried several sets of papers.[187] On occasion, courts found that while the ship herself belonged to citizens of a neutral country, the cargo was owned by enemies. In such a case, the court would release the vessel but order that the cargo be sold.[188] Apart from issues of ownership, the courts' most challenging determinations of fact concerned whether nearby vessels had played a significant role in a capture,[189] and, if so, to what degree they

---

Admiralty of New York, 1759), *published from manuscript in* HOUGH, VICE ADMIRALTY OF NEW YORK, *supra* note 21, at 100–111. (Unfortunately, the records containing the final disposition of this case, rendered in 1764, have been lost; *see* note at 111.)

187. Towle, RECORDS, *supra* note 34, Introduction (Andrews) at 41. For examples of cases in which ships "coloured" their papers to evade capture, *see Roome v. Ship "Vryheyd" (or "La Liberté") and Lading* (Court of Vice Admiralty of New York, 1758); *Lush v. Ship "Dagerloed" and Lading* (Court of Vice Admiralty of New York, 1758), *published from manuscript in* HOUGH, VICE ADMIRALTY OF NEW YORK, *supra* note 21, at 138–140, 140–142. (In each case, the offending vessel carried Dutch papers while engaging in trade with France.)

188. Towle, RECORDS, *supra* note 34, Introduction (Andrews) at 41. A surviving example of a case in which cargo was held to be a lawful prize—while the ship itself was released—is *Roome v. Ship "St. Fernando"* (Court of Vice Admiralty of New York, 1758), *published from manuscript in* HOUGH, VICE ADMIRALTY OF NEW YORK, *supra* note 21, at 131–137. *"The St. Fernando"*, unlike *"The Dageroed"* (*supra* note 187), carried no passport from the King of France authorizing it to trade in French ports. Despite some inconsistencies in the various documents found aboard—the Dutch papers, the charterparty, and bills of lading—the court found insufficient evidence to condemn the vessel herself as a prize. Nonetheless, finding evidence that the cargo "must...have been in trust for...French subjects", the court declared it a lawful prize.

189. Although proximity to a vessel taken as a prize was a prerequisite to sharing in the proceeds, it was not alone sufficient. The Vice Admiralty Court of New York offered this explanation of the general rule:

> "...[I]f 2 vessells having Letters of Marque meet at sea, and one of them take a prize before the other can Come up, Nevertheless the Last Vessell being Ready and Prepared for Battle has a Right to the Moiety of the Prize. That I take to be Just and agreeable to Reason. Because it is supposed that the Inducement to the Enemy to submitt sooner than otherways she would have done, was the other's being in sight and using all her Endeavours to Come up, to the assistance of the ship Engaged, and therefore Ought to be entituled to the Moiety,—Tho the Vessell Engaged with the enemy should be a vessell of much superior Force. But had they both been Engaged, In that Case I Conceive they would have shared in proportion to the Bigness of the Vessell, Number of Men and Largeness of the Guns."

Rosewell v. Pink "Annunciation" and Lading (1746), *published from manuscript in* HOUGH, VICE ADMIRALTY OF NEW YORK, *supra* note 21, at 27–28. In this matter, however, the court found that the privateering sloop *"Hector"*, though nearby, did not come to the assistance of

were to share in the proceeds of the sale. In assigning shares in a prize, judges exercised broad discretion.[190] Although the substantive prize-law was fairly straightforward, resolution of these cases was not always easy. To the extent that the surviving records reveal the courts engaging in fine points of legal reasoning, the most frequently addressed legal issues concern presumptions. Nevertheless, since the decisions tend to be fact-specific and the records fragmentary, it would be difficult to extrapolate detailed rules governing presumptions from the surviving materials.[191]

The final class of cases heard in the colonial vice admiralty courts were those for breach of maritime contracts. With the exception of express hypothecation,[192] contracts made at sea, and arguably those made on foreign soil, maritime contracts were deemed outside of the jurisdiction of the High Court of Admiralty.[193] As the various colonies adopted different positions on

---

the ship *"Triton"*, and thus did not share in the award. The court used similar reasoning to deny a moiety to the sloop *"Phoenix"*, noting that in addition making an effort to reach the prize-vessel in time to join in the engagement, it must be shown that the approach of the second privateer induced the prize-vessel to surrender. *See Ship "Le Heureuse"* (1748), *published from manuscript in* HOUGH, VICE ADMIRALTY OF NEW YORK, *supra* note 21, at 38–40.

190. Towle, RECORDS, *supra* note 34, Introduction (Andrews) at 41.

191. Among the extant cases, the New York Vice Admiralty Court's opinion in *Rutgers v. Ship "Isaac Gally"* (1758) comes closest to generating general rules for presumptions in prize cases:

> "...(first) [the ship] sailed from amsterdam to a french port, traded there with the enemy, and came last from the Dominions of the french King; & since by the french Laws of Trade no foreigner can maintain a Traffic with their colonies, it must be supposed that the true proprietors of the ship & lading in Question are frenchmen. (2d) The Lading being of the produce & manufacture of the dominions of France it follows, that it once was french property and the claimant is therefore driven to take off the presumption that it is so still, by full and concluding proof of a Transfer to neutrals. (3dly) The consignation of the outward bound cargo to...two frenchmen, who tis said purchased this Lading with the produce of the other, is another very suspicious circumstance. (4thly) There is proof that the proprietors of part of the Lading are concealed...(5thly) The concealment of papers at sea upon sight of our men or war and privateers, affords a strong presumption of the enemy's Interest; since no reason can be assigned for a neutral subject concealing papers not Evinsive of french property..."

Published from manuscript in HOUGH, VICE ADMIRALTY OF NEW YORK, *supra* note 21, at 159–160.

192. Wroth, *supra* at 31, at 351. For discussion of express hypothecation and bottomry bonds, *see supra* notes 145–146 and text accompanying.

193. *See* BROWNE, *supra* note 107, Vol. II, at 120–121; Jenkins, *"Argument"*, *in* WYNNE, *supra* note 106, Vol. I, at lxxix. For discussion, *see* Chapter I, notes 203–233 and text accompanying.

the degree to which the jurisdictional statutes of Richard II limited colonial courts, the number and variety of maritime-contract cases litigated in the vice admiralty courts varied from one colony to another. In general these cases were not so numerous as seamen's-wage cases, but nevertheless constituted a significant portion of cases tried. In Massachusetts, where the scope of admiralty jurisdiction was construed broadly, the variety was greatest.[194] In one case in 1733, the court held that a contract to build a vessel was within its cognizance—indicating a broad scope of jurisdiction indeed—as even today shipbuilding contracts do not sound in admiralty.[195] The court also entertained pilotage-claims, an action on a charterparty, a cargo-claim, and claims for breach of contracts to carry passengers.[196] One of these latter cases is particularly interesting, in that the court held that the vessel was bound to the passengers through an "hypothecation" created by a voyage charter to carry immigrants to Philadelphia, thereby presaging the later development of the modern maritime lien.[197] In Maryland, where actions on maritime contracts

---

194. Wroth, *supra* note 31, at 367, identifies seventeen matters involving contracts to transport passengers, charterparties, and payment of freight, in addition to a shipbuilding contract.

195. *Alfrey v. The Snow "The Charming Molly"* (Vice Admiralty Court of Massachusetts, 1730), *discussed in Id.* at 354.

196. *Id.* at 351, 354.

197. *Palatines v. Lobb ("The Loving Unity")* (Court of Vice Admiralty of Massachusetts, 1732) involved the breach of a contract to carry passengers from Rotterdam to Philadelphia. The master of "*The Loving Unity*" failed to distribute provisions to the passengers, resulting in the deaths of more than one hundred of them. Finding the existence of a hypothecation on the basis of a transportation-contract was novel for the eighteenth century. As a practical matter, it allowed the court simultaneously to assert jurisdiction (and avoid prohibition) and to provide a fund for payment of claims in the event that the plaintiffs prevailed on the merits. As Wroth explains:

> "The contract of transportation had bound the vessel to performance, and the court based its jurisdiction upon that 'hypothecation'. The existence of something very like a maritime lien was recognized here, not only as a basis for jurisdiction, but as an incident of the remedy. The court's decree ordered the master to pay various damages and provided that in the event of default, the vessel should be sold and payment made out of the proceeds. The case is also an example of the assumption of jurisdiction solely on the basis of the maritime subject matter of the contract, without reference to the location in which it had been drafted. Since the performance bond here involved was not technically an hypothecation, the court was clearly entering an area where prohibition would have been possible."

Wroth, *supra* note 31, at 351–352. Though Wroth's observation regarding vulnerability to a writ of prohibition is ostensibly correct, it is unlikely that a provincial court would have

were more often tried in the Provincial Court,[198] the extant records nonetheless contain two suits for breach of contract, one involving a charterparty[199] and the other an agreement to build a vessel and equip her with necessaries[200]—indicating that the vice admiralty court and the courts of common law held concurrent jurisdiction over maritime contracts. In Rhode Island, there is some evidence that parties sought prohibitions in contract-cases,[201] and one case from New York indicates that at least some contracts were beyond the jurisdiction of that court.[202] Nonetheless, the general pattern that emerges when one examines the records of all colonies collectively shows

---

issued one, as the common law's jurisdiction over a contract signed on foreign soil was dubious at best. Admiralty's jurisdiction over a bottomry bond is not contingent on its place of making. By stretching the definition of "hypothecation"—applying the same rule to a transportation-contract that it applied to bottomry bonds—the court expanded the scope of admiralty jurisdiction over contracts. The court's approach no doubt appealed to the plaintiffs, for whom the provincial courts could offer no relief. Moreover, extending "hypothecation" to the contract made the ship herself liable. In light of the extent of the losses suffered, the master's personal liability would have provided little assistance to those who lost family members—particularly those who were their families' principal wage-earners.

198. Owen & Tolley, *supra* note 14, at 143, note that of the fourteen colonial cases involving charterparties, all but one were adjudicated in the Provincial Court.

199. *Ship "Dolphin"* (Vice Admiralty Court of Maryland, 1718), *in* Owen & Tolley, *supra* note 14, at 305–308. It should be noted that the losing party launched a collateral attack on the Vice Admiralty Court's jurisdiction in the Provincial Court. It was to no avail. As the authors observe: "The outcome was not surprising considering that Samuel Young was judge in both courts", a circumstance that helps to explain why prohibitions were never a source of controversy in Maryland.

200. *Sewell v. Schooner "The Liberty"* (Vice Admiralty Court of Maryland, 1770), *in Id.* at 334–335.

201. *See Potter v. Owners of "The Greyhound"* (Vice Admiralty Court of Rhode Island, 1747) (contract to provide necessaries for a vessel), *published from manuscript in* Towle, Records, *supra* note 34, at 413–417.

202. *Castriot v. Nicoll and Waddell* (Vice Admiralty Court of New York, 1759), *published from manuscript in* Hough, Vice Admiralty of New York, *supra* note 21, at 167–168. The terse, one-paragraph opinion lacks a detailed statement of facts and a well-phrased *ratio decidendi.* It appears that the libellant alleged that he made a contract to share prize-money with the respondents prior to going to sea; the court dismissed for lack of jurisdiction. It is not clear whether the court regarded this contract as beyond its cognizance because it was made on land or (as is more likely) because it did not fall within any recognized class of maritime contracts. In America in the nineteenth century, when admiralty came to be distinguished from common law by the combination of the *in rem* action and the maritime lien, this contract would not have sounded in admiralty.

that the courts of common law and the courts of vice admiralty shared jurisdiction over most contracts that today would be called "maritime", though litigants' preferences for one venue over another varied greatly from one colony to the next.[203]

Factors Influencing Choice of Forum

Parties considered a variety of factors in selecting one venue over another. First, there was geographical convenience. In the days before mechanized transportation and modern hotels, the amount of time spent and inconvenience incurred in traveling to a court was a significant concern to any prospective litigant, particularly where the sums of money at stake were not large—as was the case with many claims for seamen's wages. In addition, there were personal factors—such as the character of individual judges, their reputations, and the their relationships to members of the community. With the exception of New York, Boston, and Philadelphia, no eighteenth-century American city had a population of more than 15,000,[204] and even in those cities, the merchant and shipowning classes and the bench and bar often formed a rather small community, the members of which knew each other.[205] Moreover, in such close-knit communities, the opportunity for conflict of interest was great, encouraging litigants to take care not to file their cases in a forum in which the judge—a close friend or family member—would have been obliged to recuse himself. Leaving aside these considerations—both of which relate to the personal lives of individual parties—there are three other sets of criteria that influenced litigants' choice of forum. First, there was the substantive law. While this factor may have greatest influence upon choice of forum today, it played an insignificant role in the decision-making process in the American colonies. Secondly, there was the curial law—the rules of procedure and evidence employed by each court. Not only were the rules themselves different, but the time required to litigate a matter from beginning to end differed also,

203. Owen & Tolley, *supra* note 14, at 152.

204. In 1770, Philadelphia was the largest metropolitan area in the colonies, with a population of 30,000, while New York and Boston had 25,000 and 16,000 inhabitants respectively. The population of Charleston was 12,000; that of Newport, Rhode Island was 11,000. Baltimore and Norfolk, the two largest cities in the Chesapeake Bay region, had roughly 6,000 inhabitants each. There were no more than 3,700 people living in Annapolis, and the population of Williamsburg has been estimated at 2,000. *See* McCusker & Menard, *supra* note 11, at 131.

205. For discussion, *see* Ubbelohde, *supra* note 86, at 9.

thus making the vice admiralty courts preferable to courts of common law in those matters for which swift adjudication was desirable. Finally, where knowledge of particular maritime and commercial practices were crucial to proper adjudication, it is reasonable to assume that parties would have preferred the forum with the most experience in such matters.

A prerequisite for appointment to the bench of the High Court of Admiralty was a doctorate in civil law from either Oxford or Cambridge.[206] In the provincial vice admiralty courts, there was no such requirement.[207] Most vice admiralty judges were born in the colonies. Although they received their commissions from the High Court of Admiralty, it was the colonial governors who in practice controlled the process of appointment. As a result, many appointees were political supporters of the governors who appointed them.[208] Moreover, vice admiralty judges were not required to be members of the bar. Of the fifteen men who served as judge of Maryland's court, only four were attorneys,[209] and from 1694 through 1776, only three registrars (or "registers"

---

206. F. L. Wiswall, Jr., The Development of Admiralty Jurisdiction and Practice since 1800 (Cambridge: Cambridge University Press, 1970) at 75–81; Coquillette, The Civilian Writers of Doctors' Commons: Three Centuries of Juristic Innovation in Comparative, Commercial, and International Law (Berlin: Dunker & Humblot, 1988) at 22–25. *See also* discussion, Chapter I, note 198 and text accompanying.

207. Owen & Tolley, *supra* note 14, at 175.

208. *Id.* at 6–9. Historians disagree about the degree of influence that colonial governors had in the process of appointment. Andrews contends that:

> "The difficulty [regarding appointments] was never wholly settled in colonial times, for while the governors seem to have had at least a traditional right to name the officers of the court and certainly did so in some instances, in actual practice the appointments were usually made at Whitehall by Admiralty warrant. Men who solicited or bought the officers [*sic:* "offices"] turned to the Admiralty for its approval and conformation, until it was generally understood in the colonies that patronage had best be sought across the water."

Towle, Records, *supra* note 34, Introduction (Andrews) at 19. In response, Ubbelohde maintains: "Even in colonies where judges requested permanent commissions from the Admiralty, the governors' appointments were accepted and the commissions were issued automatically", Ubbelohde, *supra* note 86, at 8, offering support for his position by noting: "the fact that the governors controlled the appointments is evidenced by the correspondence of the Lords Commissioners of the Admiralty. See, as examples, the following and their endorsements: Edward Cornwallis to Admiralty, Dec. 2, 1750; James Glenn to Admiralty, Sept. 23, 1752; Peregrine Hopson to Admiralty, Apr. 14, 1753; all in PRO, Admir. 1, 3818." *Id.* at 8 n. 8.

209. Owen & Tolley, *supra* note 14, at 178–179. The only Maryland judge for whom a full set of decisions has survived is George Steuart, who was appointed to the bench in 1754. Steuart, a physician with no formal training in law, rendered decisions in eleven mat-

in colonial parlance) were members of the bar.[210] Virginia's experience parallels that of Maryland; its judges often lacked formal legal training, although most had extensive practical experience.[211] In Rhode Island, the level of legal qualifications ran the full gamut from an experienced judge with a degree from Oxford, to one whose "principal qualification was probably wholly pragmatic: he owned a number of privateers".[212] Nonetheless, the lack of formal training does not appear to have affected the quality of service that the courts provided, and an examination of the extant records reveals that the decisions which these judges rendered generally were consistent with the interpretations of the substantive maritime law propounded by the High Court of Admiralty in the same era.[213]

There were, however, two respects in which the vice admiralty judges aroused controversy. Operating without a jury, the judges were both interpreters of law and triers of fact. In the former capacity, the surviving decisions reveal a higher level of competence and sophistication than one might expect given their limited formal training. In the latter role, they occasionally received criticism from their contemporaries. In some colonies, it was common for judges to hold several offices simultaneously, potentially compromising their

---

ters, all of which are consistent with generally accepted rules of English maritime law of the mid-eighteenth century.

210. *Id.* at 180–181. The register was a position of great importance, with duties ranging from those of a clerk of the court to those of a magistrate or assistant judge. For one register, Benjamin Nicholson, the position served as a stepping-stone to appointment as judge of Maryland's prize court during the Revolution. The three attorneys who held the position were William Gladden (1694–1708), Benjamin Nicholson (1760–1763), and Reverdy Ghiselin (1763–1775).

211. Those who served as officers of the vice admiralty court of Virginia often had long political resumés prior to being appointed to the court. Offices that various appointees held included attorney general, surveyor general, treasurer of the colony, commander of militia, clerk of the General Court, member of the House of Burgesses, and member of His Majesty's Council in Virginia, which served as both the upper house of the legislature and the highest common-law tribunal (*i.e.* the General Court) in the colony. *See* Reese, Vice-Admiralty of Virginia, *supra* note 86, at 6–7.

212. *See* Wiener, *supra* note 24, at 67–68. Oxford graduate Robert Lightfoot, who occupied the bench from 1753–1758, had served previously as a judge of vice admiralty in the southern colonies. While lack of formal legal training was not unusual for judges in the colonies, the appointment of privateer John Gidley, who served from 1743–1744 (during the war with Spain), must have aroused amusement even in that era. Nonetheless, this variety of pragmatism was not unprecedented in the history of colonial appointments; Harper, *supra* note 6, at 103–104, notes that an applicant for a position as a customs officer listed as his principal qualification his extensive experience as a smuggler.

213. For discussion, *see e.g.* Owen & Tolley, *supra* note 14, at 179.

objectivity.[214] The reason was often practical, as neither the Crown nor the High Court of Admiralty had provided vice-admiralty judges with a fixed salary. Instead, judges were paid out of the fees collected by the court, creating an incentive in certain cases—such as prize or salvage—for the judge to render the verdict that would most profit the officers of the court.[215]

Anthony Stokes—barrister of Inner Temple, loyalist, and former Chief Justice of Georgia—published an account of the practice in the colonial courts of vice admiralty in his *View of the Constitution of the British Colonies* in 1783. The principal purpose of the chapter on admiralty[216] is to provide in print various forms for use by practitioners, with the author's commentary interspersed throughout. In it, he is quite critical of the quality of training of both bench and bar in the colonies before the Revolution, remarking at one point that: "There are very few Admiralty forms to be met with in print; and those used in the Colonies are too loose and inaccurate to deserve notice."[217] His overall impression of the attorneys and judges of the colonial courts is equally disparaging:

---

214. Maryland poses the best example. It was not uncommon for one man to hold multiple judgeships, even during the "royal" and "second proprietary" periods (*i.e.* after 1689). *See e.g.* Judge Young's dual role as judge of both the Provincial Court and the Court of Vice Admiralty in adjudicating *The Ship "Dolphin"* (1718), discussed *supra* note 199 and text accompanying; *see also* Owen & Tolley, *supra* note 14, at 178–179.

215. Thomas Corbett, compiler of the "Secretary of the Admiralty's Precedent Book" (*circa* 1730) on file at the Library of the Admiralty, observed that the vice-admiralty judges: "having no Salaries, consult nothing but their Fees, and prostitute the dignity of the courts for the sake of gain". The solution, he said, was to establish a fund for paying salaries out of the money that the Crown acquired from the "droits of the admiralty". Unfortunately, this could not be done—he contended—until the Crown reasserted its rights to its perquisites, which of late had been co-opted by the colonial governors. *Quoted from manuscript in* Crump, *supra* note 14, at 159. For discussion of the droits of the admiralty and how colonial courts dealt with them, *see supra* notes 158–161 and text accompanying.

216. Stokes, *supra* note 172, Ch. XIII, "Of the Court of Vice-Admiralty" at 270–371.

217. *Id.* at 275. Lest one conclude that Stokes is merely venting his anger at the judges and attorneys of the thirteen rebellious colonies, his opinion expressed elsewhere of papers filed with the vice admiralty court of the "loyal" colony of Antigua is no higher. Stokes remarks:

> "The Copies of the Depositions, and of some other of the Vice-Admiralty Precedents which I got at Antigua, were so loose and incorrect, that I found it necessary to alter them in different places to make sense of them; and several ungrammatical and other inaccurate expressions which were in the manuscript yet remain, from my overlooking them in the proof-sheets.... However, with all their imperfections, those Antigua Precedents may have their use, as there are no other Vice-Admiralty forms in print."

Id. at 356–357.

> Of all the Barristers who practiced in the Colonies, and afterwards returned to England, few have attempted to practice at the bars here; for the following reasons: The Judges in the Colonies being, in general, unacquainted with the Law, order and decorum are not properly attended to, and little improvement can be got under such masters.
>
> Most matters that arise in the Colonies are founded in litigation, and not in intricacy; and, as the gentleman [*sic*] of the bar in general go out there at an early period in life, before they are arrived at any considerable share of knowledge, they have it not in their power to gain much experience in the Colonies, and most of the Judges not being bred to the profession of the law, the Advocate, who has the greatest fluency, may sometimes be considered as the ablest lawyer.[218]

As a barrister who both returned to England and resumed a legal career, Stoke's account is suspect. Even assuming it to be somewhat accurate as regards the majority of colonial judges and practitioners, it should be remembered that the majority of colonial lawyers did not practice before the courts of vice admiralty. Even the most mundane maritime litigation had the potential to pose one or more issues that required some familiarity with foreign law or the law of nations.[219] John Adams had found use for his command of Latin—acquired through years of reading Cicero—as he sifted through civil-law commentators and the *Corpus Juris Civilis* for legal guidance in determining the fate of a dead whale,[220] and in his earliest education, he found the time amidst his readings of Coke and statutory law to examine the Laws of

218. *Id.*, Ch. XII, "Of the Counsel and Attornies in the Colonies", at 269–270.

219. As Stokes admits, for any colonial practitioner handling prize cases, the most useful texts were "Grotius of War and Peace, Bynkershoeck's [*sic*] Questiones Jurispublici [and] Vattel's Law of Nations." *Id.* at 277–278. Jeremiah Gridley, advising the young John Adams on a course of reading for admission to the bar, did not restrict the use of treatises on the law of nations to prize cases, observing: "Indeed a Lawyer through his whole Life ought to have some Book on Ethicks or the Law of Nations always on his Table." Diary and Autobiography of John Adams (L. H. Butterfield, Leonard C. Faber, & Wendell D. Garrett eds., Cambridge, Massachusetts: Belknap Press, 1961), Vol. III, *Autobiography*, at 272 (hereinafter Diary and Autobiography of John Adams).

220. For text of papers filed with the court in *Doane v. Gage* (Court of Vice Admiralty of Massachusetts, 1769), *see* Legal Papers of John Adams, *supra* note 163, Vol. II, Case No. 43, at 68–97. For discussion of the case, *see supra* notes 163–164 and text accompanying.

Oleron and the *"Lex Mercatoriae"*.[221] Adams was not alone among his colonial colleagues in his belief that the practice of law entailed serious study of legal history, legal theory, and comparative law.[222] Adams, Jeremiah Gridley, Robert Auchmuty (later a vice admiralty judge), and others established a pri-

---

221. *See* LEGAL PAPERS OF JOHN ADAMS, *supra* note 163, Vol. I, "Adams' Student Notes" (1758), at 2–3. Twenty years later, Adams waxed sentimental about the Island of Oleron as he gazed it in the distance, interrupting an anecdote about a ship-board swindler and his flea repellant long enough to remark: "We have been becalmed all day in Sight of Oleron... I feel a Curiosity to visit this Island of Oleron so famous in Antiquity for her Sea Laws, at least I take this to be the Place." DIARY AND AUTOBIOGRAPHY OF JOHN ADAMS, *supra* note 219, Vol. II, *Diary* 1771–1781 (March 29, 1778), at 290–291.

222. In his *Autobiography*, the young Adams, already immersed in the study of "Bracton, Britton, Fleta and Glanville", offers the following description of how the "elite" of the colony's bar sought to improve the quality of education required for admission to the courts:

> "Looking about me in the County, I found the practice of Law was grasped into the hands of of Deputy Sheriffs, Pettyfoggers and even Constables, who filled all the Writts upon Bonds, promissory notes and Accounts, received the Fees establised for Lawyers and stirred up many unnecessary Suits. I mentioned these Things to some of the Gentlemen in Boston, who disapproved and even resented them very highly. I asked them whether some measures might not be agreed upon at the Bar and sanctioned by the Court, which might remedy the Evil? They thought it not only practicable but highly expedient and proposed Meetings of the Bar to deliberate upon it. A Meeting was called and a great Number of regulations proposed not only for confining the practice of Law to those who were educated to it and sworn to fidelity in it, but to introduce more regularity, Urbanity, Candour [*sic*] and Politeness as well as honor, Equity and Humanity, among the regular Professors. Many of these Meetings were the most delightfull Entertainments, I ever enjoyed. The Spirit that reigned was that of Solid Sense, Generosity, Honor and Integrity: and the Consequences were most happy, for the Courts and the Bar instead of Scenes of Wrangling, Chicanery, Quibbling and ill manners, were soon converted to order, Decency, Truth and Candor."

Id., Vol. III, *Autobiography*, at 274. While one might be tempted to view these meetings cynically as an attempt to limit the number of practitioners in an effort to capture a greater share of the fees, there is evidence that many participants sincerely wished to improve the quality of standards for admission to the bar. Adams' account of the proceedings of his law-club (*infra* note 223 and text accompanying) reflects serious legal discussions, not political strategies for restricting admission to the bar to members of society's elite. Daniel Coquillette offers the following observation:

> "Of course it could also be argued that Adams' professional elitism and his emphasis on intellectualism were not-so-subtle devices to promote a narrow professional monopoly. They probably were. But...learning was the one and only way that the then humble, but able, Adamses, Gridleys, and Danas could compete with the great families of patronage and wealth.... If this was a restrictive

vate "law club", which engaged in discussions of Coke, English feudal law, the *Corpus Juris Civilis*, and even Cicero's oration for Milo—all for the purpose of enhancing the quality of law-practice in Massachusetts.[223] While Stokes saw the colonies' separation from England as a liability, depriving attorneys of much-needed technical proficiency and inhibiting their intellectual growth, Gridley saw only greater opportunity—a legal environment demanding of the colonial practitioner a wider panoply of talents and challenging him in ways unknown to his English counterparts:

> A Lawyer in this Country must study common Law and civil Law, and natural Law, and Admiralty Law, and must do the duty of a Counsellor, a Lawyer, an Attorney, a sollicitor, and even of a scrivener, so that the Difficulties of the Profession are much greater here than in England.[224]

In the eighteenth century, as today, some legal specialties took on the reputation of "sophisticated", and with the colonies' economic well-being dependent upon maritime commerce—particularly the carrying trades—it was only natural that the vice admiralty courts attracted men of the highest level of legal talent. In New York over a fifty-year period (1739–1789), twenty-five attorneys handled eighty percent of the business of the vice admiralty court.[225] Though these men did specialize in maritime litigation, they did not restrict their practices to it. As Judge Hough observes:

---

practice, its restriction emphasized talent and training, not wealth and privilege." Coquillette, "Justinian", *supra* note 163, at 399–400.

223. The association, created for "the study of Law and oratory", was called "Sodalitas", and it met once per week for two years, ending with the death of Gridley in 1767. The Diary and Autobiography of John Adams, *supra* note 221, Vol. I, *Diary* (January 24, 1765), at 251–258; Vol. III, *Autobiography*, at 385–386. For discussion, *see* Coquillette, "Justinian", *supra* note 163, at 376–382.

224. Diary and Autobiography of John Adams, *supra* note 221, Vol. I, *Diary 1755–1770*, at 55. Adams notes both that Gridley had corresponded with Dr. Dickins, Regius Professor of Law at Cambridge, regarding the study of civil law and that he had advised Judge Lightfoot of the Rhode Island Court of Vice Admiralty on sources of maritime law. It speaks well of Gridley's reputation as a maritime lawyer and scholar that Robert Lightfoot—an Oxford graduate with prior experience as a vice admiralty judge in the southern colonies—would seek his advice. For biographical information on Lightfoot, *see* Wiener, *supra* note 24, at 68. *Id.*

225. Hough, Vice Admiralty of New York, *supra* note 21, at xxiv. The author gives brief biographies of various practitioners who appeared before the vice admiralty court at xxiv–xxvii.

> ...it was the earliest specialized bar in America, not because the practitioners did nothing else; on the contrary, Admiralty was in most cases the least of their activities, but the men who got and kept business at that bar were the best the Colony produced.[226]

It was much the same in the other colonies.[227] In Maryland, of the 429 lawyers who were admitted to practice between 1666 and 1775, extant records can confirm that only eighteen filed maritime actions in either the Vice Admiralty Court or the Provincial Court. Moreover, as in New York, for each of these men, maritime law constituted only a portion of his practice.[228] Despite the small number of Maryland's attorneys who handled maritime cases, most had very distinguished careers. Five had been admitted to one of the Inns of Court, a credential highly unusual among colonial practitioners. Ten served as Attorney General of the colony; two would become governor. Seven later would serve as judges, among whom were William Paca and future Supreme Court Justice Samuel Chase.[229]

Irrespective of their innate talents, colonial attorneys lacked a Doctors' Commons or Inns of Court of their own. Unlike their English counterparts, they did not devote a decade of their lives to academic study of the fine points of maritime law under the tutelage of experienced scholars (as did the civilians), nor did they enter chambers at one of the Inns to learn from experienced barristers, who had begun to handle the bulk of English instance cases

---

226. *Id.* at xxiv.

227. Wiener, *supra* note 31, at 70, notes: "...the men who practiced in the Rhode Island admiralty were, like their brethren in New York, leaders of the bar." He supplies brief biographies both for members of the colony's vice-admiralty bar and for its judges (both those who served as deputy-judges under the auspices of the Massachusetts Vice Admiralty Court and those who received their commissions directly from the High Court of Admiralty). *Id.* at 66–71.

228. Owen & Tolley, *supra* note 14, at 174–175.

229. *Id.* at 176–178. Thomas Notley and William Paca each held the office of governor. The former also had served as Chief Justice of the Provincial Court; the latter had an illustrious career, serving first on the bench of the Continental Congress' Prize Court and later as judge of the Federal District Court in Maryland. Paca remained involved in politics throughout the period of the Articles of Confederation, and became an ardent spokesman for the right of the people to exercise control over their representatives in the debates held in the Maryland House of Delegates on the eve of the Constitutional Convention. For discussion of his role in the debates (and that of his one-time law-partner Samuel Chase—*supra* notes 115–118 and text accompanying), *see* Gordon S. Wood, The Creation of the American Republic: 1776–1787 (Chapel Hill: University of North Carolina Press, 1969) at 291–293, 369–372.

as the seventeenth century progressed. Thus colonial practitioners' ability to replicate the maritime practice of English courts was dependent in part upon their access to published sources of substantive and procedural law. In the absence of published admiralty reports, they lacked first-hand knowledge of the law that the High Court of Admiralty applied. By the late eighteenth century, this included the substantive rules of express hypothecation and bottomry, seamen's rights and obligations, salvage, general average, maritime torts (*e.g.* collision), droits of the admiralty, and prize. Although the courts of common law had assumed jurisdiction over some maritime matters—such as charter-parties and marine insurance—reports of common-law decisions were neither as complete nor as widely available as today. This is reflected in the practice—adopted by English and colonial practitioners alike—of keeping "common-place books".[230] Therefore, as a practical matter, colonial lawyers learned what they knew of English maritime practice through secondary sources.

It is difficult to know to what extent works on substantive maritime law were available in the colonies. John Adams, who owned one of the largest law libraries in America, expressed familiarity with the "Laws of Oleron", though nowhere in his *Diary* or *Autobiography* does he mention which of the many editions he had read.[231] Throughout much of the colonial period, Connecticut's law required that its courts of common law apply the "laws of Alleroone" to disputes over maritime contracts.[232] During the Revolution, Virginia enacted a statute drafted by Thomas Jefferson that provided for the establishment of a court of admiralty, which was to apply the Laws of Oleron, the Rhodian Law, and Roman law—to the extent that these had been incorporated into the law of England.[233] There is not, however, any indication of whether the legislators of either Connecticut or Virginia had copies of these texts ready at hand or instead used these terms as a form of shorthand to refer to the rules

230. In an era when published reports and digests were comparatively rare, common-place books—consisting of personal notes on precedents assembled by the attorneys themselves—were indispensable tools for litigators. Even the scholarly Jeremiah Gridley, who owned one of the largest legal libraries in the colonies, kept a common-place book. Diary and Autobiography of John Adams, *supra* note 221, Vol. I, *Diary*, at 55. The editors of the Legal Papers of John Adams, *supra* note 163, Vol. I, No. 2 at 3, have reproduced Adams' own common-place book, which he began compiling in 1759.

231. *See* Legal Papers of John Adams, *supra* note 163, Vol. I (1758), at 2–3; *see also* *supra* note 221 and text accompanying.

232. *See* Towle, Records, *supra* note 34, Introduction (Andrews) at 28–29; Andrews, *supra* note 33, at 232–233.

233. For discussion, *see* Ubbelohde, *supra* note 86, at 196–197.

of maritime custom and practice then currently in use in most European ports.[234] Legislators in both Maryland[235] and Massachusetts introduced bills for regulating maritime conduct, and the latter succeeding is passing a maritime statute in 1668. While Massachusetts' statute governing "Maritime Affaires" is quite detailed, reflecting extensive knowledge of traditional rules applying to contracts of affreightment, seamen's rights and duties, and general average, it does not incorporate by reference earlier maritime codes.[236] Among

---

234. To date, the most complete quantitative study of law books in the colonies is HERBERT ALAN JOHNSON, IMPORTED EIGHTEENTH-CENTURY LAW TREATISES IN AMERICAN LIBRARIES, 1700–1799 (Knoxville: University of Tennessee Press, 1978) (hereinafter JOHNSON, LAW TREATISES). Professor Johnson compiled a list of all books contained in the law libraries of twenty-one colonial attorneys, including John Adams, Thomas Jefferson, John Jay, Francis Dana, and St. George Tucker, the editor of the well-known American edition of Blackstone's *Commentaries*. From the publication of the first edition in 1647, Cleirac's collection of sea-laws was the most widely available source for the Laws of Oleron. Though his edition reproduced a later version of the Laws—almost twice the length of that contained in the *Black Book of the Admiralty* (*see supra* Chapter I, note 60 and text accompanying)—Sir Leoline Jenkins nevertheless adopted it for use as the official text of the High Court of Admiralty. Until 1705, this remained the only edition in print available in England, though John Godolphin had reproduced a copy of this version as an appendix to *Synegoros Thalassios* in 1661. In 1705, Alexander Justice published *A General Treatise of the Dominions and Laws of the Sea*, with a second edition (greatly revised) appearing in print in 1709, with the author's name omitted. Both of these editions included texts of the Laws of Oleron translated into in English, with that of 1709 taking as its source the second edition (*circa* 1671) of Cleirac's work. Sir Travers Twiss remarks that: "It is a scarce book, but it is to be met with occasionally in public sales." *See* THE BLACK BOOK OF THE ADMIRALTY (*RERUM BRITANNICARUM MEDII AEVI SCRIPTORES* (ROLLS SERIES)): No. 55 *MONUMENTA JURIDICA* (Sir Travers Twiss ed., London: Her Majesty's Stationery Office, 1871, Kraus reprints, 1965) Vol. IV, at liv–lvii. Nonetheless, Professor Johnson notes that copies of Justice's book were found in the libraries of Judge Theophilus Parsons of Massachusetts (1705 ed.), John Jay (1709 ed.), Thomas Jefferson (reprint of 1709 ed.), and John Mercer of Virginia (edition unknown), JOHNSON, LAW TREATISES, at 34, thus establishing both that a text of the Laws of Oleron was available in the colonies and that the available text was of a later version of the Laws.

235. The "Act for Erecting a Court of Admiralty" (March 19, 1639) had provided that the court's judgments should conform to:

> "...the Laws of this Province or (in default thereof) to the Judgments which usually are or ought to be given in the same or the like causes by the custom or Law Merchant of England or in the Admiralty Court of England as near as the said Admiralty Judge or Judges Commiss. or Commissrs. Shall be able to determine."

reproduced from manuscript in OWEN & TOLLEY, *supra* note 14, Appendix H at 387–388. The Assembly declined to enact the bill into law.

236. Several Laws and Orders, Made at the General Court of Boston in New England, October 14, 1668, Maritime Affaires, at 9–14 (*reproduced in* RECORDS OF THE STATES OF

all books on substantive maritime law, references to only one—Molloy's *De Jure Maritimo et Navali*[237]—appear in the extant records.[238] Studies to date have yet to uncover a copy of Gerard Malynes' treatise in colonial law libraries, although the work was sufficiently well-known for it to have been incorporated by reference into a bill rejected by Massachusetts' lawmakers in 1650.[239] Also missing from the law libraries of the colonies were the works of Welwood, Fleetwood, Zouch, Exton, and, somewhat surprisingly, John Marius.[240] Hale's

---

THE UNITED STATES OF AMERICA: A MICROFILM COMPILATION, Mass. B.2 Reel I 1661–1742, William Summer Jenkins ed., Washington, D. C.: Library of Congress Photoduplication Service, 1949). An earlier maritime statute, introduced in 1650 and incorporating the *lex mercatoria* as outlined by Gerard Malynes, had failed to pass in 1650. *See* CRUMP, *supra* note 34, at 53. Despite the lack of a specific reference to Malynes in the text of the 1668 statute (*see* Wroth, *supra* note 31, at 254 n. 14), on close reading of Malynes' treatment of collision, wages, and general average, Wroth maintains that the statute of 1668 is also derived from his *Consuetudo, vel Lex Mercatoria*. For discussion of Malynes' work, *see* Chapter I, notes 90–96 and text accompanying.

237. Johnson located copies of various editions of Molloy's treatise in twelve of the twenty-one colonial law libraries that he examined, noting that Jefferson owned the seventh edition of 1722, while Adams owned the eighth edition of 1744. John Jay and St. George Tucker each owned a copy of the two-volume ninth edition—the last published before the Revolutionary War. JOHNSON, LAW TREATISES, *supra* note 234, at 40–41. For discussion of *De Jure Maritimo et Navali*, *see* Chapter I, *supra* notes 99–104 and text accompanying.

238. *See* OWEN & TOLLEY, *supra* note 14, at 175, 224 (noting that Molloy's treatise was owned by several Maryland practitioners whose libraries have been catalogued and that it was cited for authority in the colony's Provincial Court.); *see also* BOURGUIGNON, FIRST FEDERAL COURT, *supra* note 33, at 180–181 (noting that colonial courts cited Molloy in prize cases). Nevertheless, while Molloy's book undoubtedly was owned in the colonies, opinion is divided regarding how often the book was used in practice. Joseph Smith, writing more than two decades before Owen and Tolley, had not yet found any evidence of courts relying Molloy; he remarks: "At least one book on the subject, Molloy's *De Jure Maritimo et Navali*, was owned by some lawyers in the Province [of Maryland]. That this body of law was resorted to by any city or admiralty court seems doubtful." *See* Smith, "Foundations of Law in Maryland", *supra* note 28, at 102.

239. *See* CRUMP, *supra* note 34, at 53; *see also* discussion, *supra* note 236 and text accompanying.

240. JOHNSON, LAW TREATISES, *supra* note 234, did not uncover a copy of Marius' popular treatise on bills of exchange in the twenty-one colonial libraries that he examined. While this is not definitive proof that the work was unknown in the colonies, it is worth noting that Johnson also makes no mention of Marius in his monograph on the law merchant in colonial New York, a substantial portion of which is devoted to bills of exchange. *See* HERBERT ALAN JOHNSON, THE LAW MERCHANT AND NEGOTIABLE INSTRUMENTS IN COLONIAL NEW YORK, 1664–1730 (Chicago: Loyola University Press, 1963). Nonetheless, as Marius' *Advice Concerning Bills of Exchange* (1651) remained suf-

work on maritime jurisdiction remained unpublished until the twentieth century, although other works by Hale were available.[241] Similarly, there is no record of *Synegoros Thalassios*, but other titles by Godolphin appear in colonial records.[242] Nonetheless, other works on maritime law and the law merchant were read in the colonies,[243] including *Justinian's Institutes* and *Digest*.[244] Among the most common books that addressed the law of the sea were treatises on the law of nations, including the works of Selden, Grotius, Pufendorf,

---

ficiently influential to warrant comment by James Kent in his *Commentaries* in the early nineteenth century, one would infer that it was a lack of availability of the text rather than obsolescence that accounts for the absence of references to it in the colonial records. (For discussion of Marius' work and Kent's critique, *see* Chapter I, *supra* notes 97–98 and text accompanying.)

241. The works by Hale found amongst those in colonial law libraries include *De Successionibus apud Anglos*, *The History and Analysis of the Common Law of England*, and *Historia Placitorum Coronae*. *See* JOHNSON, LAW TREATISES, *supra* note 234, at 27–28.

242. While Johnson did not find the well-known *Synegoros Thalassios* in the library records that he examined, seven of the twenty-one practitioners owned the comparatively obscure *The Orphan's Legacy: or, A Testimentary Abridgement*. *Id.* at 25–26. For discussion of Godolphin's *Synegoros Thalassios*, *see* Chapter I, *supra* notes 210–213 and text accompanying.

243. JOHNSON, *supra* note 234, at 5, 32, notes that several law libraries contained the second and third editions (1761 and 1783) of Wyndham Beawes' *Lex Mercatoria Rediviva: or the Merchant's Directory* and also the first and second editions (1718 and 1729) of Giles Jacob's *Lex Mercatoria: or the Merchant's Companion*.

244. It is clear from the extant proceedings of *Doane v. Gage* (*see supra* note 220 and text accompanying) that Adams had access to both the *Institutes* and the *Digest* in the original Latin. Moreover, Adams makes numerous other references to reading Roman law in the original language. (*See e.g.* DIARY AND AUTOBIOGRAPHY OF JOHN ADAMS, *supra* note 219, Vol. I, *Diary*, at 251–258, noting that the Sodalitas Club read and discussed the *Corpus Juris Civilis*). On the other hand, Johnson's survey of the contents of private law libraries identifies only two copies of the *Institutes*—and both were translated into English. *See* JOHNSON, LAW TREATISES, *supra* note 234, at 18. The answer to the apparent discrepancy may be that Johnson's sampling was not sufficiently large to be representative. On the other hand, Adams himself may provide a clue to the whereabouts of books mentioned in cases and private correspondence which do not appear in Johnson's list. In his first meeting with Gridley, he mentions that he borrowed a copy of *Justinian's Institutes* (in the original Latin) with Vinnius' notes from the Harvard College Library. DIARY AND AUTOBIOGRAPHY OF JOHN ADAMS, *supra* note 219, Vol. III, *Autobiography*, at 271. A cursory comparison of sources cited in modern law review articles with their authors' own personal libraries would reveal that most scholars borrow more books than they own. Moreover, Gridley's act of loaning books to the young Adams reflects a social custom more prevalent in the eighteenth century (when books were scarce) than today. In short, one would expect that an eighteenth-century book's circulation greatly exceeded its sales.

and Vattel.[245] The first edition of Sir James Park's *A System of the Law of Marine Insurances* was not available until 1787, although records indicate that the work appeared in America shortly after its publication in England.[246] John Reeves' *Law of Shipping and Navigation* and Arthur Browne's *A Compendious View of the Civil Law and of the Law of Admiralty* would not appear in print until shortly after the colonies achieved independence,[247] but Blackstone's *Commentaries*, first published in 1769, became instantly popular.[248] Coke's *Institutes*—particularly the *First Institute*, or "*Coke-on-Littleton*"—remained a mainstay of legal education and a working tool for practicing lawyers throughout the colonial period.[249]

---

245. Hugo Grotius' *De Jure Belli et Pacis*, and works by Baron Samuel von Pufendorf, Emmerich de Vattel, and John Selden appear in the records both in their respective original languages and in translation. For holdings in colonial law libraries, *see* JOHNSON, LAW TREATISES, *supra* note 234, at 27 (Grotius: in Latin and English), 46 (Pufendorf: in Latin, French, and English), and 54 (Vattel: translated into English), 50 (Selden: complete works in Latin).

246. JAMES ALLAN PARK, A SYSTEM OF THE LAW OF MARINE INSURANCES (1st ed., London: T. Whieldon, 1787; *reprinted* Philadelphia: Joseph Crukshank, 1789). For holdings, *see* JOHNSON, LAW TREATISES, *supra* note 234, at 43.

247. The first edition of Browne's treatise was published in Dublin in 1797–1799, followed shortly thereafter by an edition in London in 1802–1803. *See* Joseph C. Sweeney, *The Admiralty Law of Arthur Browne*, 26 J. Mar. L. & Com. 59 (1995). The first edition of Reeves' work (see *supra* note 54) was published by E. & R. Brooke and J. Sewell in London in 1792. (In the same year, another printing of the work was produced in Dublin by T. Burnside for E. Lynch and P. Wogan.) Reeves' earlier and more popular work—*History of the English Law from the Time of the Saxons to the End of the Reign of Philip and Mary* (London, 1787)—is listed among the holdings of colonial libraries. JOHNSON, LAW TREATISES, *supra* note 234, at 47–48.

248. WILLIAM BLACKSTONE, COMMENTARIES ON THE LAWS OF ENGLAND (4 vols., 1st ed., Oxford: Clarendon Press, 1765–1769; *reproduced in facsimile with commentary,* Chicago: University of Chicago Press, 1979). Blackstone made the study of law considerably easier than it had been before 1768. As Adams remarks:

> "At this Time October 1758 the Study of the Law was a dreary Ramble, in comparison of what is at this day. The Name of Blackstone had not been heard, whose Commentaries together with Sullivans Lectures and [John] Reeves's History of the Law [*see supra* note 246], have smoothed the path of the Student, while the long Career of Lord Mansfield, his many investigations and Decisions, the great Number [of] modern Reporters in his time and a great Number of Writers on particular Branches of the Science have greatly facilitated the Acquisition of it."

DIARY AND AUTOBIOGRAPHY OF JOHN ADAMS, *supra* note 219, Vol. III, *Autobiography*, at 273–274. Nearly half of the libraries that Johnson examined contained copies of Blackstone's *Commentaries*. JOHNSON, LAW TREATISES, *supra* note 234, at 6–7.

249. *See e.g.* DIARY AND AUTOBIOGRAPHY OF JOHN ADAMS, *supra* note 219, Vol. I, *Diary*, at 174 (Adams reads Coke on advice of Gridley), 255 (Sodalitas Club agrees to read

Lack of formal institutions (such as the Inns of Court and Doctors' Commons) for legal instruction—coupled with the colonies' practice of admitting all lawyers to practice in both the courts of common law and the courts of admiralty—prevented the polarization of the colonies' practitioners into two rival factions, as had occurred in England with the civilians and the common lawyers. Moreover, lacking access to published admiralty reports and to many of the leading maritime treatises of the day forced colonial attorneys to fall back of the those resources that were ready at hand. However "provincial" the colonial bar may have been at its inception in the seventeenth century, the businessmen—merchants and shipowners—who formed the clientele of the America's maritime lawyers were men of the world, intimately acquainted with the customs and practices of eighteenth-century marine commerce, and their experience, more than formal education, no doubt provided colonial practitioners with their greatest legal resource. As regards the printed material—sources of law in the more traditional sense—the colonists made good use of the few available books on the *lex maritima*, but it appears that they made little (if any) distinction between civil-law sources, such as the *Corpus Juris Civilis*, and common-law sources, such as Molloy.[250] Thus, for the colonial bar at the close of the eighteenth century, the difference between adjudication in an admiralty court and adjudication in a court of common law was not one of substantive law, but rather of procedure.

Commenting on the dearth of published materials on admiralty procedure in the colonies, the common-law judge Anthony Stokes remarks:

> The only book that I have met with, which treats of the practice of the High Court of Admiralty in England, is Clerke's *Praxis Admiralitatis*; and this is the book used by the practitioners in the Colonies.... [T]here are few Admiralty forms to be met with in print...[251]

Coke's *First Institute*). For holdings of Coke's works in colonial libraries, *see* JOHNSON, LAW TREATISES, *supra* note 234, at 13–14.

250. Molloy himself contributed to the blurring of the distinction between substantive civil law and substantive common law with regard to maritime matters. *De Jure Maritimo* routinely cites Roman law alongside of English statutes and Coke, creating the impression that both bodies of substantive law have been melded together into a seamless and coherent system of rights, duties, and obligations. For examples, *see* MOLLOY (3rd ed., Bellinger), *supra* note 125, Bk. II, Ch. II "Masters of Ships, their Actions considered in reference to cases both private and public" at 208–217: (*vis major*—defined according to the civil law—relieves a master of liability for damage to cargo) Sec. II at 209; (rules governing deviation of course derived from the *Digest*) Sec. XII at 212.

251. STOKES, *supra* note 172, Ch. XIII, "Of the Court of Vice-Admiralty", at 271.

It is clear that copies of Clerke's book crossed the Atlantic, although the precise number is questionable. Even more questionable is the degree to which either lawyers or courts relied upon it.[252] At least one modern commentator has argued that the procedure of the colonial vice admiralty courts more closely resembled Clerke's account from the late 1500s than the actual procedures employed by the High Court of Admiralty during the eighteenth century.[253] Samuel Betts, federal judge for the Southern District of New York and a noted authority on admiralty law in the early years of federal practice, maintained that the vice-admiralty procedures had been derived directly from the civil law of Continental Europe rather than from the High Court.[254] Implic-

---

252. JOHNSON, LAW TREATISES, *supra* note 234, at 13, found copies in only two of the twenty-one libraries the records of which he examined—those of Theophilus Parsons and Thomas Jefferson. The edition in each collection is that of T. Browne and J. Senex, printed in London in 1722. Today, this edition is quite rare, although Jefferson's copy still exists—preserved as part of the collection that its owner sold to establish the Library of Congress. I had the opportunity to examine this book in the Library's special collections. It is worth noting that it contains the original Latin text and an English translation by an anonymous translator on facing pages, indicating that the work was more likely to have been intended for reading by those with a passing interest in comparative law rather than as a working tool for civilians whose practice before the High Court of Admiralty required fluency in Latin. The High Court continued to keep its records in Latin until 1731, nine years after Browne and Senex published this edition of Clerke's work. *See* WILLIAM HOLDSWORTH, A HISTORY OF ENGLISH LAW (London: Methuen & Co., 1924), Vol. V, at 137. Jefferson, proficient in Latin, in all probability would not have selected a version containing a translation if a "civilians'" edition had been available. The work was already an antique from the previous century at the time of its publication by William Crooke in 1667. For discussion, *see* Chapter I, *supra* note 160 and text accompanying. The reasonable inference to be drawn from all the circumstantial evidence is that while colonial practitioners with personal copies may have consulted *Praxis Curiae Admiralitatis Angliae* occasionally, neither colonial attorneys nor judges relied upon Clerke as heavily as Stokes would have his readers believe.

253. Wroth, *supra* note 31, at 266. Wroth's assertion rests in part on the changing nature of the *in rem* action in the eighteenth century. With regard to Clerke's approach to the action *in rem*, Wroth remarks:

> "This process resembles foreign attachment more than it does the modern *in rem* action. There is no lien against a specific thing, and the action is in terms of a personal obligation, rather than an obligation incurred by certain goods or a certain vessel."

Id. at 265. As a result, the procedures came to resemble the *in rem* procedure of Roman law more than the procedure described by Clerke.

254. Samuel Betts, a contemporary of Joseph Story, makes the following observation in 1838:

> "The archives of the admiralty in this district [*i.e.* New York] for more than seventy years up to the Revolution, exhibit a striking similitude between its meth-

itly, these characterizations both rest in part on the changing nature of the action *in rem* in the eighteenth century.

Originally a mechanism for compelling one's party-opponent to appear before the court *in personam* by attaching his property, the action *in rem* began to evolve into an action directly against the vessel and/or goods themselves. According to Clerke, an *actor* (*i.e.* "libellant" in modern admiralty practice or "plaintiff" in common-law terms) is to proceed against the vessel, its tackle, and/or goods aboard in the event that the owner cannot be found within the country. The ship and/or its cargo are to be arrested under a warrant executed by a marshal, who is to take possession of the *res* for the court pending the outcome of the proceedings.[255] In the event that the owner fails to appear *in*

> ods of procedure and those of the civil law. Some formalities of the English Admiralty common to the canon courts, were employed in the colonial admiralty courts also for a considerable period and passed down to the United States tribunals, but they have been gradually diminishing, until all processes not necessary to the direct and effective action of the court have, in a great measure disappeared from the practice. It was manifestly the general acceptation of the profession in this country at the adoption of the Federal Constitution, that the admiralty courts here were conducting their proceedings in conformity to the principles and rules of the civil law, and that the course of the English admiralty was not an authority or guide in that matter, and such was clearly the understanding of the first congress."

Samuel R. Betts, A Summary of Practice in Instance, Revenue and Prize Causes, in the Admiralty Courts of the United States, for the Southern District of New-York; and also on Appeal to the Supreme Court (New York: Halstead & Voorhies, 1838), Introduction at x. As to the means by which he arrives at his conclusion, he remarks:

> "The decisions of the English court of admiralty [and] of the colonial court of this district and its usages...have been carefully examined, so far as these materials were accessible to the author."

Id. at xi. As to what extent the materials were accessible to the author is open to speculation. Charles Hough, himself a federal judge in New York and a noted scholar of admiralty law, came to a different opinion in examining the records of the vice admiralty court of New York a century later, and one can only wonder if materials available to Betts had been lost in Hough's time.

255. Clerke outlines the procedure for the arrest of vessels and cargo in Title 24:

> *"Omnia in praecedentibus titulis sunt intelligenda, quando Persona Rei sit arrestata in causa Civili. Nunc tractabitur de arrestandis Bonis Rei. Si igatur latitat, vel forsan abfuerit extra regnum, quo minus possit arrestari, tunc si habureit aliqua bona, merces, vel navem, vel navis aliquam partem, seu cymbam super mare, vel infra fluxum & refluxum maris, tunc impetrandum est Warrantum ad hos effectus, Ad arrestandum talia bona, vel talem navem, &c. ad N. id est, ad reum debitorem spectantia, in quorumcumque manibus existentia, & ad citandum apud bona hujusmodi N. debitorem in specie, ac omnes alios in genere, jus & interesse in bonis hu-*

personam, he is declared contumacious, and ultimately the *res* may be sold in satisfaction of the *actor*'s claims.[256] If, however, the owner appears in person and provides security, the action shifts from one against the vessel and/or cargo to one against the owner *in personam*.[257] While Clerke's procedure works

---

> *jusmodi habentes, aut habere pratendentes [sic: i.e. "praetendentes"], ad comparendum tali dei, N. Mercatori in quadam causa civili & maritima, de justitia responsuros."*

FRANCISCO [FRANCIS] CLERKE, *PRAXIS CURIAE ADMIRALITATIS ANGLIAE* (London: William Crooke, 1667) Tit. 24, at 21 (hereinafter, CLERKE, *PRAXIS*). The Title reads as follows in English:

> "Everything in the preceding Titles is to be understood as applying to cases in which the person of the Defendant has been arrested in a civil cause. Now it is necessary to address the manner in which the Defendant's goods are to be arrested [*i.e.* "attached"]. Thus if he is in hiding or has fled out of the country—so that it is not possible to arrest him personally—and yet he has goods, merchandise, or a ship, or any part of a ship, or boat, either upon the high seas, or within the ebb and flow of the tide, a Warrant is to be obtained to these effects: For the arrest of any such goods, or such ship, etc., belonging to the Defendant/Debtor—in the hands of whomsoever they may be—citing the Defendant/Debtor specially together with his arrested goods. All others who have or purport to have any sort of right or interest in the goods are to be present on the specified day to answer the Plaintiff/Merchant in a civil and maritime cause."

(*my translation*). The marshal or other officer of the court then arrests the goods or vessel, at the same time giving notice to all parties with a purported interest in the arrested property to appear on the specified day to defend their claims against the Plaintiff. *Id.* Title 25 at 22.

256. *See Id.*, Titles 31–32, at 27–29; *see also* BROWNE, *supra* note 107, Vol. II, at 396–405.

257. Clerke describes the process by which the goods are released and the "*actor*" or plaintiff then proceeds directly against the "*reus*" or defendant in Title 33, which states:

> *"Saepe contingit, quod sicut in personali actione persona alicujus sit arrestata propter debitum, cum nullam debetur; ita aliquando bona tua arrestantur pro debito supposito. In isto igatur casu quamprimum notitiam habueris bona tua arrestata esse, ne eadem per defaultas, modo praemisso, contra te recuperentur, & in poenam tuae contumaciae adversarius tuus ex primo decreto mitteretur in possessionem eorundem, expedit ut compareas; & si introduxeris fidejussores de respondendo actioni institutae ad omnes effectus in titlo (11) de Introductione fidejussorum per reum, tunc relaxandum est arrestatum praedictum & bona tibi tradenda sunt. Et actor tenetur fidejubere, libellare, ac debitum petitum probare, & in causa procedere in omnibus, ut in actione instituta contra personam debitoris..."*

Title 33 reads as follows in English:

> "Just as it often happens that a person is arrested in a personal action for a debt that he does not owe, thus also your goods may be arrested for a supposed debt. Therefore, in such a case, whenever you receive notice that your goods have been arrested (or "attached"), it is advisable that you should make an appearance,

well enough in theory for the time in which it was written (*i.e.* the 1590s),[258] the second phase—the *in personam* component—became increasingly vulnerable to the writ of prohibition early in the next century. The development of the modern action *in rem* against the vessel-as-person—recognizable to modern American practitioners—can be traced to Admiralty's efforts to shield itself from the writ of prohibition. This was accomplished by borrowing from the civil law of Europe, thus transforming the *in rem* procedure of Clerke's English civil law into the full-fledged *in rem* procedure derived from the law of Rome.[259] Ultimately, this process facilitated the development of the cor-

---

> lest—in the manner described previously—your goods be recovered from you through default and awarded to your adversary, in penalty for your contumacy. If you provide securities in response to the commenced action—fulfilling all requirements contained in Title 11 "Regarding the Introduction of Securities on behalf of the Defendant"—then the arrest is to be terminated and your goods returned to you. And the Plaintiff is required to provide security, to initiate the libel, and to prove the existence of the debt, just as [though initially he had commenced] the action against the Defendant himself..."

Id. at 29–30 (*my translation*).

258. As Clerke's treatise is unique in its subject-matter, it has been cited as authoritative by eighteenth-century and modern scholars alike. In the absence of Clerke, the sum total of our knowledge of procedure before the High Court of Admiralty would be limited to that which could be gleaned through inference from Admiralty records preserved in manuscript. Thus one is tempted to place great weight on Clerke, who has left us our only detailed and systematized treatment of the subject. Nonetheless, in places the text has more of the appearance of an academic work than of a practical guide-book. To supplement his description of practice before the Admiralty Court, he openly borrows from his knowledge of the ecclesiastical courts, apparently to fill gaps in his own experience. (*See* Clerke, *Praxis*, *supra* note 255, Titles 46, 49, at 39, 41.) Even Arthur Browne, who relies heavily on Clerke as a source, acknowledges Clerke's tendency to fall back on his knowledge of the ecclesiastical courts to explain the practice in the Admiralty Court. *See* Browne, *supra* note 107, Vol. II, at 413, 418. Even as Clerke was writing his treatise in the 1590s, the battle over prohibitions was already in full-swing, as is reflected in Judge Julius Caesar's letter to King's Bench in 1592. *See* Hale and Fleetwood, *supra* note 15, Introduction at xcv. *See also* discussion, Chapter I, *supra* notes 144–149 and text accompanying. In light of these events, one should approach with a modicum of caution the notion that Clerke's *Praxis* reflected accurately practice before the Admiralty Court in his own day.

259. While the procedure of the High Court of Admiralty was undoubtedly "civil-law" in character, it did not represent a complete incorporation of the entire body of ancient Roman-law procedure. The Roman *actio in rem* permitted the *actor* (or "plaintiff") to assert a right in the thing itself; the right was not contingent upon—or affected by—the rights of other parties. (For contrast, consider, for example, how the common law treats "purchasers in good faith" with regard to property obtained by fraud.) The *actio in personam*, on the other hand, alleged some particular individual's liability to the *actor*, aris-

nerstone of contemporary admiralty law, the maritime lien. Nonetheless, in the colonial period, this transformation was not yet complete, and in colonial courts the distinction between *in rem* and *in personam* was often indistinct.[260]

---

ing out of the relationship between them. As legal historian William Buckland once observed:

> "The *iudex* in an *actio in rem* is directed to condemn the defendant if the *res* proves to be the plaintiff's. In an *actio in personam* the direction is to condemn if it appears that the defendant is lawfully bound to pay."

W. W. Buckland & Arnold D. McNair, Roman Law and Common Law: A Comparison in Outline (Cambridge: Cambridge University Press, 1936) at 67. In Title 33 of Clerke's *Praxis* (*supra* note 257), the right is clearly against owner of the *res* (*i.e.* "*bona*") personally, and the *res* may stand in the place of the owner only if he were to refuse to appear personally.

In the eighteenth century, the High Court of Admiralty retained jurisdiction over express hypothecation (the pledging of the vessel's bottom: *see supra* note 145), adjudicating such matters in a manner consistent with Buckland's description of the civil-law *actio in rem* as practiced by Roman jurists. As these contracts generally were made in foreign ports, the common law had conceded jurisdiction over them to the Admiralty. The novelty in the colonial vice admiralty courts' practice lies in how they imputed liability to the *res* in the absence of an express agreement binding the *res* itself rather than its owners. The case of *Palatines v. Lobb*, *supra* note 197, provides an excellent example. The Vice Admiralty Court of Massachusetts held that the ship "*Loving Unity*" herself was liable for the death of passengers—even in the absence of an express agreement to bind the hull, and despite a contract that ostensibly made the carriers personably liable for damage occurring through breach of the voyage-charter. The court's reasoning in "*The Loving Unity*" is thus more consistent with the ancient Roman model described by Buckland than with Title 33 in Clerke's *Praxis*. It is not clear that colonial vice admiralty courts always structured their thinking in accordance with that of the court of Massachusetts in "*The Loving Unity*"; from the records, it likely that a procedure more akin to Clerke's governed many claims for seamen's wages.

As for Judge Betts contention (*supra* note 254) that the civil law of Continental Europe (*i.e.* the Roman formulation of the *in rem* action) was employed in the colonial vice admiralty courts, it should be read with some caution. Betts clearly recognized that a transformation was in progress in the colonial period—a transformation that would be completed by Betts, Joseph Sory, and others of their generation in the early years of American independence. In a system grounded in *stare decisis*, the judiciary—even while innovating—often feels obliged to assert that innovation already has taken place in an earlier time. The modern *in rem* action—and the modern maritime lien that arose with it—were evolving but not yet fully developed in the colonial period. The federal judiciary, Judge Betts' contemporaries, were to complete the development in the early nineteenth century, and true to form in a *stare-decisis* system, they were to credit their predecessors with it.

260. For discussion, *see e.g.* Wroth, *supra* note 31, at 266–267. With regard to the changing nature of the action *in rem*, Wroth remarks:

> "The practice in Massachusetts bears greater resemblance to that set out by Clerke than it does to anything that went on in the High Court in the eighteenth century. As far as can be determined in the absence of file papers, the Massachusetts

It is clear that the Americans introduced some innovations into the practice of the High Court of Admiralty. Most notable among these was a streamlining of the procedure, designed to make adjudication less time-consuming. Despite its procedural advantages over the common law, litigation before the High Court of Admiralty was often protracted. As one modern commentator has explained:

> The traditional procedure of the High Court, as it had developed from the relatively simple action outlined by Clerke, was well known for its complexity and its ponderous slowness. In the *in rem* action, the libellant first had to enter four appearances on successive court days at which no claimants appeared. In an *in personam* action, complicated security arrangements and a lengthy series of appearances were necessary before the libel was produced in court. Similar proceedings were necessary before the answer was filed. [Moreover], there was further delay before award of the proceeds. While this cumbersome process was greatly simplified and speeded up for seamen's

---

> court drew no formal line between *in rem* and *in personam* actions. In the majority of cases the process seems to be *in personam* in the first instance. In many actions entitled *in rem*, recovery is decreed against the owner personally, with no indication that he had filed any formal stipulation."

Id. at 266. If one overlooks the fact that Wroth is writing of Massachusetts rather than New York, on first glance, Wroth's conclusions appear to be at odds with those of Betts (*supra* note 254). On closer examination, however, this is not necessarily so. Both contend that the procedures of the colonial courts differed from those of the High Court of Admiralty. Traditionally, the High Court would have exercised greater precision than the colonial courts in distinguishing an action *in rem* from one *in personam*. Wroth chooses to emphasize the vice admiralty courts' inconsistency—which allowed recovery in like cases either against the goods themselves or against their owners—while Betts opts to concentrate on the colonial courts' expansion of the action *in rem* beyond express hypothecation into implied hypothecation. Both processes tended to expand the scope of matters for which the *in rem* action was available. Continuing, Wroth addresses Betts' theme:

> "The action *in rem* seems to have been relied upon primarily in cases in which no respondent to an *in personam* suit could be found within the jurisdiction, but the action was also extended to include a practice of the traditional maritime law, for which Clerke does not expressly provide. It was recognized that there were certain obligations for which a vessel was liable even when her master appeared personally. In this primitive form of maritime lien, satisfaction could be had either *in rem* or *in personam* regardless of the original form of the action, and no formalities regarding the distribution of proceeds were observed. The Massachusetts court thus applied a flexible combination of the colony's own longstanding maritime tradition and Clerke's *in personam* process."

Id. at 266–267.

> wage actions and in certain other cases, in most instances the ordained procedure was followed. Contemporary examples suggest that time was distinctly not of its essence.[261]

Though simplified procedures were available, Arthur Browne admits that generally they were reserved for cases of little monetary value.[262] Seamen no doubt appreciated the expedited procedures, but this provided little consolation to merchants and shipowners, whose cases were generally of considerably greater value. The colonial vice admiralty courts attempted to remedy this by making the procedures in cases of greater value less complicated and time-consuming than those of the High Court.[263] Moreover, reflecting the common-law experience of American attorneys, the terms of art that the vice admiralty courts employed were often those of the common law rather than of the English Admiralty Court.[264] While testimony was generally in the form of depositions and interrogatories, colonial admiralty courts on rare occasions heard oral testimony.[265] Lacking fear of the writ of prohibition, the colonists availed themselves of the procedure for maritime attachment, moribund in England since Coke occupied the bench of Common Pleas.[266] The one area in which

---

261. Wroth, *supra* note 31, at 267.

262. Browne, *supra* note 107, Vol. II, at 428. He explains:

> "Indeed, in causes heard *summarissime*, as are sometimes suits for seamen's wages, they are, sometimes after publication, ordered at once to be heard summarily next court day. And indeed in some of their suits, when trifling, there is no publication, witnesses being only examined *viva voce* at the hearing; and it is said in a note on Title 19 of Clerke's Practice, even that their petition need not be in writing, though it uniformly is so."

263. Wroth, *supra* note 31, at 267–268. Wroth credits the colonists' reliance on Clerke's *Praxis* for the simplification, though he admits that his conclusion is speculative. Even if Clerke did influence the way in which vice admiralty courts opted to handle instance cases, it is clear that this theory does not supply a complete answer. The vice admiralty courts' inconsistent treatment of actions *in rem* and *in personam*—evidence of a nascent maritime lien emerging in the colonies—clearly was not derived from Title 33 of the *Praxis* (*see supra* note 257). It is more likely that written sources, such as the *Praxis*, were intermingled with the practical experience of the colonial bar's greatest resource—their own clients—together with the dictates of common sense, to create the hybrid form of procedure that characterized the colonial courts in the late 1700s.

264. Wiener, *supra* note 24, at 48; Hough, Vice Admiralty of New York, *supra* note 21, Introduction at xiii; Wroth, *supra* note 31, at 267–268.

265. Reese, Vice-Admiralty of Virginia, *supra* note 86, at 81; *see also* discussion of the expedited procedure outlined by Browne, *supra* note 262.

266. "Maritime attachment" is in essence the procedure described by Clerke in Title 33 (*supra* note 257). In most colonies, prohibition was not a serious threat in instance cases, thus allowing the vice admiralty courts to release arrested property and assume jurisdic-

the colonial courts were not able to innovate was in the handling of appeals. As John Exton once had observed, there "was no regular channel of appeal from a colonial [admiralty] court."[267] The following century brought little clarification. Immediately after the founding of the vice admiralty courts, appeal was to Privy Council, though within a decade the High Court of Admiralty had become the appropriate tribunal. The matter was complicated by the vice admiralty courts' jurisdiction over trade-act cases. As the High Court was denied jurisdiction over these cases in the first instance, the opinion persisted that Privy Council should be the appropriate appellate court, and by 1748, Privy Council and the High Court had concurrent jurisdiction over vice-admiralty appeals. Moreover, there was the High Court of Delegates, which heard appeals in cases litigated in the first instance by the High Court. After 1766, the High Court ceased to hear appeals from the colonies, leaving Privy Council and the Delegates with appellate jurisdiction in colonial instance cases.[268] Ambiguity as to the proper channel for appeals contributed a third disincentive to the geographical inconvenience and the increased expense[269] of pursuing an appeal on the other side of the Atlantic. As a result, few colonial cases were appealed to England.[270] Thus ironically, it was not the threat of the writ of prohibition, the lack of civil-law training among members of the judiciary and bar, the indispensability of the jury, nor the intrinsic advantages of the common-law courts and the law they applied that provided the colonists with the impetus to forsake the courts of vice admiralty in favor of the courts of common law. The vice admiralty courts met these challenges with hybrid procedures, practical knowledge of maritime commerce, and common sense. The greatest obstacle to the courts' domination of the con-

---

tion over a defendant *in personam* after receiving from him sufficient security. When entertaining classes of instance matters that were outside of the jurisdiction of the High Court of Admiralty—such as charterparties—the vice admiralty courts varied in their approach, at times opting for attachment followed by *in personam* jurisdiction and in others for *in rem* jurisdiction. (*See supra* note 260.) For discussion of how this procedure was used in the colonial courts, *see* Harrington (Part II), *supra* note 20, at 350–351; Owen & Tolley, *supra* note 14, at 17, 187–188. *See also* Browne, *supra* note 107, Vol. II, at 434–435, describing maritime attachment in England. Maritime attachment has been preserved as a part of modern Admiralty practice, with the modern rules being outlined in Fed. R. Civ. P., Supplemental Admiralty Rule B.

267. *Quoted in* Harper, *supra* note 6, at 201.

268. Towle, Records, *supra* note 34, Introduction (Andrews) at 20–24.

269. Crump, *supra* note 14, at 163–164.

270. *See e.g.* Hough, Vice Admiralty of New York, *supra* note 21, at xiv, xvii, identifying only one case decided by the vice admiralty court that was appealed to the High Court of Admiralty.

current jurisdiction that they shared with the courts of common law was the only one that was beyond their power to influence or control—the litigants' preference for swift and inexpensive appeals close to home.

Vice Admiralty Jurisdiction on the Eve of the Revolution: A Final Appraisal

In England there persisted a perception that the provincial vice admiralty courts—created to enforce the trade acts—had become biased in favor of colonial merchants.[271] While it is true that these courts were staffed largely by men born in the colonies, surviving statistics of their ratios of prosecutions to convictions do not demonstrate excessive leniency.[272] Nonetheless, enforcement of the trade acts was costing Britain four times as much as the country collected under them,[273] and there was a natural tendency for policy-makers both to find a convenient scapegoat and to seek a quick solution. It came in 1764 in the form of a new court, established in Halifax with Dr. William Spry, civilian of Doctors' Commons, as its judge. As originally envisioned, this court would provide an alternative to the provincial admiralty courts for the trial of trade-act violations. Judge Spry was to receive a salary of eight hundred pounds sterling *per annum*, to be paid out of the Crown's share of the forfeitures, with the balance to be paid out of the proceeds of sale of old naval stores in the event that the forfeitures were insufficient. The court was to have original jurisdiction over both instance and navigation-act cases. Chief among the new court's responsibilities, however, was that of hearing appeals from the provincial vice admiralty courts in cases of alleged violations of the acts of trade, particularly the recently enacted Stamp Act. Halifax, selected as being more geographically convenient and politically favorable for the British authorities, was not so for those who were intended to use the court. For two years the court sat virtually idle, finally being deprived of its appellate jurisdiction with the repeal of the Stamp Act. Shortly thereafter, Spry departed Halifax, leaving a surrogate in charge of the court.

---

271. *See e.g.* Ubbelohde, *supra* note 86, at 52–53.

272. *See e.g.* Owen & Tolley, *supra* note 14, at 117. Records survive for 21 cases involving alleged breaches of the acts of trade adjudicated by the Vice Admiralty Court of Maryland. Of these, the defendant prevailed in only one, with the outcome unknown in three more.

273. Ubbelohde, *supra* note 86, at 46.

Britain's first experiment in consolidating colonial vice admiralty jurisdiction had failed.[274]

Within a year of the creation of Dr. Spry's court, a proposal was circulating in the Treasury that called for the replacement of the new court with four regional courts, but the plan was rejected and lay forgotten for two years. In 1767, however—in the wake of the colonists' protests and the repeal of the Stamp Act—Parliament enacted the Townshend Acts, and in them incorporated Treasury's plan for regional vice admiralty courts. These courts would be placed in Charleston, Philadelphia, Boston, and Halifax, serving respectively the regions of the South, the Mid-Atlantic Colonies, New England, and the present-day maritime provinces of Canada. The plan jettisoned the requirement that the judges have doctorates in civil law, and the judges were permitted to appoint surrogates to sit for them.[275] In addition to jurisdiction over the acts of trade, the new courts were given jurisdiction over instance cases.[276] As for the provincial courts of vice admiralty, the new courts were established to supplement them, not replace them, and it was assumed that they would soon wither away through lack of business.[277] Nonetheless, on the assumption that the provincial courts would continue to operate at least for a short time, the regional courts were given the power to entertain appeals from them.[278]

---

274. *Id.* at 3–4, 48–56, 72–106.

275. *Id.* at 128–133.

276. *Id.* at 156, 159. As planned, the new courts in fact did adjudicate a variety of instance matters, including cases involving seamen's wages, charterparties, damage to cargo, surveys, and an assortment of commercial contracts, although as tensions between the colonists and Britain escalated, a greater proportion of these cases found their way into other provincial courts.

277. *Id.* at 152–155. To the extent that this occurred, it did so only in the four ports that received the new regional courts. Halifax had never possessed a "provincial" vice admiralty court, and the new court replaced Dr. Spry's court. In Charleston, the new regional vice admiralty court and its provincial counterpart coexisted side-by-side, with each hearing cases while the other was not in session. In Massachusetts, Robert Auchmuty, judge of the provincial vice admiralty court and one-time member of the law club "Sodalitas" (*see supra* note 223), was appointed judge of the new regional court and promptly merged the two tribunals, although he was obliged to appoint a judge to serve in his place in the provincial vice admiralty court of New Hampshire, where he had held joint appointment. Only in Pennsylvania did the provincial vice admiralty court wither away, unable to compete with the new regional vice admiralty court in Philadelphia, and even here it continued to exist in form long after it ceased to hear cases.

278. *Id.* at 156–158. Of the four regional courts, records survive for only one—Auchmuty's court in Boston—and those end with the year 1772, thus giving us at best an incomplete view of practice before these courts. Among the surviving records, there is evidence of the court in Boston hearing only two appeals from the provincial vice admiralty courts, and both of these cases involved alleged breaches of the acts of trade.

Established as they were to enforce the acts of trade, the regional courts of vice admiralty became a focal point for colonists' criticisms from their inception in 1768. The court at Philadelphia was the subject of a protracted pamphlet-war between lawyer John Rush and the court's judge, Robert Ingersoll—each writing under a pseudonym—with the former contending that the court deprived the colonists of all Englishmen's right to trial by jury.[279] Of course, the vice admiralty courts had been trying instance cases without juries for generations without serious complaints, but in the volatile political climate of 1774, rhetorical impact mattered more than historical fact, and one would not expect complete objectivity from Rush under the circumstances. In autumn of that same year, the newly convened Continental Congress issued a Declaration of Rights and Grievances, which condemned the acts of Parliament that had "extend[ed] the powers of the admiralty courts beyond their ancient limits, [and] deprive[d] the American subject of trial by jury..."[280] The theme was echoed in Philadelphia two years later, when the Continental Congress severed the colonies' ties to Britain, asserting that George III had "combined with others to subject us to a jurisdiction foreign to our constitution, and unacknowledged by our laws, giving his Assent to their Acts of pretended Legislation: ...For cutting off our Trade with all parts of the world: For imposing Taxes on us without our Consent: For depriving us, in many cases, of the benefits of Trial by Jury..."[281]

Despite exaggerations in the heat of political battle, the vice admiralty courts—both the regional courts and the provincial courts—had become controversial. In the years immediately preceding the Revolution, the number of instance cases on the dockets of the vice admiralty courts declined.[282] As the colonies moved closer to armed conflict with Britain, it was only natural that many colonists with private disputes would cease to avail themselves

---

279. *Id.* at 183–189.

280. Journals of the Continental Congress (34 vols., Worthington Chauncey Ford ed., Washington D. C.: 1904–1937), Vol. I, at 71.

281. The Declaration of Independence, para. 15, 18–20 (U.S. 1776).

282. Ubbelohde, *supra* note 86, at 159–160. Wroth, *supra* note 31, at 367, notes that instance cases constituted slightly more than eighty percent of all matters heard by the Vice Admiralty Court of Massachusetts between 1718 and 1747. No records are available for the next nineteen years. For the period from 1765 through 1772, the last year for which records are extant, 112 of 171 cases involved alleged violations of the acts of trade, while only eight can be identified as instance cases. For the remaining fifty cases, insufficient information remains to ascertain the issues involved. Even assuming that all were instance cases (statistically an unlikely assumption), it is nevertheless clear that much private maritime litigation shifted to other *fora* during the era of the Stamp Act and the Townshend Acts.

of a forum that—no matter how practical and convenient—was increasingly associated in the public imagination with British oppression. This should not, however, obscure the fact that from their founding at the close of the seventeenth century through the 1760s, the provincial vice admiralty courts had provided the colonists with a means of recovering their wages, vindicating their rights, and enforcing their contracts. Perhaps more importantly, these courts had provided the litigants with a choice. A potential plaintiff was able to weigh the alternatives, determining whether the opportunity to cross-examine witnesses in open court and availability of a jury mattered more than the speed of summary civil-law procedures or the ability to consolidate several related actions into one. Even for the same person, the choice may have varied from one dispute to another. The courts of admiralty had jurisdiction over foreign contracts, and when one's party-opponent resided abroad, even the most stalwart advocate of jury-trials and testimony *viva voce* would have appreciated the opportunity of attaching a party-opponent's property and collecting depositions before witnesses sailed away on their next voyage. For cases involving larger sums or requiring special expertise—such as ships' surveys—a more distant forum nevertheless would have been worth the additional time spent in traveling and living away from home. The hallmark of colonial maritime jurisdiction was its flexibility. Through seventy years of experimentation, the colonists had learned the advantages of both the civil and the common law, and these experiences formed a valuable legacy for the generation that met in Philadelphia in the summer of 1787 to draft the Constitution.

Chapter III

"The most bigotted idolizers of state authority have not thus far shewn a disposition to deny the national judiciary the cognizance of maritime causes. These so generally depend on the laws of nations, and so commonly affect the rights of foreigners, that they fall within the considerations which are relative to the public peace."

Alexander Hamilton[1]

In the early hours of the morning of November 2, 1843, roughly ninety-five miles upstream from New Orleans, the steamboat *DeSoto* struck the steamer *Luda*, sending her to the bottom of the Mississippi. The matter reached the Supreme Court four years later, where the justices debated whether federal admiralty jurisdiction reached a collision between vessels on the inland waters of the United States.[2] In construing the limits of Article III's grant of admiralty jurisdiction, the justices sought guidance from those scraps of paper still extant from the Constitutional Convention, comprising all that remained of the legislative history of Article III.[3] It was not the first time that

1. The Federalist (Jacob E. Cooke ed., Middleton, Connecticut: Wesleyean University Press, 1961) No. 80, at 538 (hereinafter The Federalist).

2. *Waring v. Clarke*, 46 U.S. 441 (1846).

3. The deliberations of the Convention had been held in secret, and with the Convention's closing, the secretary was instructed to deliver the journal and other papers generated by the delegates to George Washington, the Convention's President—which he did after destroying an assortment of loose papers that he deemed unimportant. Washington in turn entrusted the papers to the Department of State nine years later, where they were to remain until a joint resolution of Congress in 1818 ordered that they be published. President Monroe assigned the task of overseeing the papers' publication to Secretary of State John Quincy Adams, who succeeded in completing the task the following year, when a Boston printer released the roughly 500-page "*Journal, Acts, and Proceedings of the Convention*". This volume formed the principal source for Justice Wayne in tracing the history of the Admiralty Clause in *Waring v. Clarke*. For the history of the publication of the *Journal*, *see* The Records of the Federal Convention of 1787 (3 vols., Max Farrand ed.,

the High Court had sought to ascertain how far the Framers had intended federal maritime jurisdiction to extend,[4] nor would it be the last. Their deliberations completed, Justice Wayne delivered the opinion of the Court. Of the Framers' intent, he remarked:

> It is remarkable, too, that the words, "all cases of admiralty and maritime jurisdiction", as they are now in the constitution, were in the first plan of government submitted to the convention, and that in all subsequent proceedings and reports they were never changed.[5]

Justice Wayne's inquiry did not begin and end with the debates at the Convention; he understood that the delegates of 1787 did not work in a vacuum. The debates were as much a reflection of practical experiences of the participants as of ideology. As Delaware's John Dickinson had observed: "Experience must be our only guide. Reason may mislead us."[6] Accordingly, for Wayne the key to the meaning of Article III's language lay beyond the proceedings themselves. For twelve pages, the majority opinion painstakingly traces the history of admiralty jurisdiction from the statutes of Richard II and Henry IV through the states' handling of maritime matters during the Revolution. Along the way, Wayne cites John Holt, Matthew Hale, and Arthur Browne, critiques Sir Edward Coke and Anthony Stokes, and examines how maritime jurisdiction was exercised in America from the colonial vice admiralty courts to the states' maritime courts of the 1780s.[7] Limited by available sources, in places the opinion is not historically accurate.[8] It is the Court's approach to the issue, however,

---

New Haven: Yale University Press, 1966), Vol. I, at xii–xvii (hereinafter FARRAND, RECORDS).

4. The Supreme Court first addressed the scope of federal admiralty jurisdiction in *Glass v. The Sloop Betsey*, 3 U.S. 6 (1794).

5. *Waring v. Clarke*, 46 U.S. at 457.

6. *See* MAX FARRAND, THE FRAMING OF THE CONSTITUTION (New Haven: Yale University Press, 1913) at 204 (hereinafter FARRAND, FRAMING).

7. *Waring v. Clarke*, 46 U.S. at 452–463.

8. Justice Wayne is silent as to which plan of government incorporated the words "all cases of admiralty and maritime jurisdiction". Four plans were introduced, and among them none contained the language eventually employed in Article III. In 1847, however, the only published source of for the Convention's proceedings was the *Journal* prepared by John Quincy Adams in 1819. This contained a version of the plan submitted by Charles Pinckney, "Article 9" of which provided that the cognizance of the federal judiciary would extend "to all cases of Admiralty & maritime jurisdiction". The authenticity of this draft was questioned by both Madison and Rufus King, and later scholarship confirmed that the draft that Pinckney had sent to J. Q. Adams was not the original that Pinckney had introduced at the outset of the Convention. Nonetheless, this was the source available to Wayne,

and not its conclusions, that may seem out of place to modern eyes. It is rare for a modern opinion to examine cases more than a few decades old. Medieval case law and seventeenth-century treatises are fodder for antiquarians and legal historians; they do not ordinarily provide rules of decision and establish parameters of jurisdiction for the modern world. Nonetheless, *Waring v. Clarke* is neither wholly anomalous nor a product of a quaint nineteenth-century approach to legal reasoning. It reflects instead a process that remains a part of maritime adjudication today. In part, this is due to a question posed but never adequately answered in the 1780s. To what extent are American maritime jurisdiction and substantive law a domestic creation rather than a ratification—or incorporation—of a jurisdictional regime and a body of law that pre-date the Constitution?

As the delegates assembled in Philadelphia in the summer of 1787, it soon became clear that their task would extend beyond a mere overhauling of the Articles of Confederation. Fundamental weaknesses in the system—most notably the Continental Congress' inability to collect revenue and enforce its resolutions—required a more comprehensive solution. The national government needed a new structure. Less certain, however, was the form this new government would take. Implicit in the debates that followed was a belief in checks and balances and in separation of powers, grounded both in ideology and in a deep-rooted suspicion of concentrations of power born of colonial experience.[9] Montesquieu had written that the three principle functions of government—the legislative, the executive, and the judicial—must be distributed amongst different branches of government,[10] though he also ac-

---

and he incorporates its historical inaccuracies into his analysis. For discussion, *see* FARRAND, RECORDS, *supra* note 3, Vol. III, Appendix D at 595–604. *See also* J. Franklin Jameson, "Studies in the History of the Federal Convention", *in* AMERICAN HISTORICAL ASSOCIATION, ANNUAL REPORT (H.R. Doc. No. 461) (2 vols. Washington, D.C., 1903), Vol. I, at 111, 112–115 (hereinafter Jameson); Harrington Putnam, *How the Federal Courts Were Given Admiralty Jurisdiction*, 10 Corn. L.Q. 460, 465–468 (1925) (hereinafter Putnam). For further discussion, see *infra* notes 112–118, 141–150 and text accompanying.

9. For the notion that separation of powers formed a base-line of agreement among federalists and antifederalists alike, *see e.g.* THE ANTIFEDERALISTS (Cecelia M. Kenyon ed., Boston: Northeastern University Press, 1966, *reprinted* 1985), Introduction at lxxxi (hereinafter Kenyon).

10. [CHARLES LOUIS] DE SECONDAT, BARON DE [LE BRÈDE ET DE] MONTESQUIEU, THE SPIRIT OF LAWS, TRANSLATED FROM THE FRENCH, WITH CORRECTIONS AND ADDITIONS COMMUNICATED BY THE AUTHOR (1st English ed., Thomas Nugent trans., London: J. Nourse & P. Vaillant, 1750), Bk. XI, Ch. VI, at 215–218, 225–226 (hereinafter MONTESQUIEU). Published a mere two years after the French original by a translator who had exchanged correspondence with the author, this edition underwent several printings and

knowledged that "the three powers may be very well distributed in regard to the liberty of the constitution, tho' not so well in respect to the liberty of the subject."[11] As to how to ascertain when balance among branches of government also promoted optimum liberty for the citizen, Montesquieu was silent, admonishing his readers:

> I should be glad to inquire into the distribution of the three powers, in all the moderate governments we are acquainted with, and to calculate thereby the degrees of liberty which each may enjoy. But we must not always exhault a subject so far, as to leave no work at all for the reader. My business is not to make people read, but to make them think.[12]

The delegates *did* think, and as influential as Montesquieu was for them, it is unlikely that his advise, even if he had chosen to publish it, would have closed the rift that emerged as the delegates began to polarize into opposing camps over the issue of how much power to vest in the national government. This rift was not restricted to a difference of opinion regarding the distribution of power between the national government and those of the states; it also reached the fundamental question of how the proposed constitution would protect the liberties of individual citizens against encroachments by the national government. For both of these issues, the debate over the structure of the federal courts and the extent of their jurisdiction became crucial.

The battle over the Constitution was hard-fought, and the debates intensified rather than mollified the antagonisms and differing visions of the various participants. Their work, begun in May, concluded less than four months later in mid-September. As the proceedings drew to a close, the aging Benjamin Franklin expressed his views of the process:

> I doubt, too, whether any other Convention we can obtain, may be able to make a better constitution; for, when you assemble a number of men, to have advantage of their joint wisdom, you inevitably assemble with those men all their prejudices, their passions, their errors of opinion, their local interests, and their selfish views. From such an assembly can a *perfect* production be expected? It therefore

---

would have been more readily accessible in Britain and the American colonies alike than was the French edition. For the high regard in which Montesquieu was held in late eighteenth-century thought, *see e.g.* Kenyon, *supra* note 9, Introduction at lxxvii, lxxx.

11. Montesquieu, *supra* note 10, Bk. XI, Ch. XVIII, at 253.

12. *Id.*, Bk. XI, Ch. XX, at 259.

> astonishes me, Sir, to find this system approaching so near to perfection as it does...[13]

Agreement on a final text came at a price. Article III provided that: "The judicial Power shall extend...to all Cases of admiralty and maritime Jurisdiction..."[14] The final draft, however, relegated to Congress the decision-making on the structure of the federal judiciary and left to the federal courts the task of defining the parameters of "admiralty and maritime".

The purpose of this chapter is to take up the inquiry begun by Justice Wayne—namely how did the language "all cases of admiralty and maritime jurisdiction" become a part of Article III and how did the Framers construe the phrase? In other words, why did the Framers opt to grant the power to hear maritime cases to the federal courts rather than to those of the states, and, secondly, what was their understanding of the scope of that jurisdiction? This latter question gives rise to another. To what extent did the delegates believe that the law of nations limited their power to define the scope of admiralty jurisdiction?

The Maritime Jurisdiction of the States

Since the opening shots of the war were fired on Lexington Green in April of 1775, the British navy had stifled much of colonial commerce, in some cases seizing and condemning colonial vessels without formal trials. Deprived of their usual sources of revenue, some New England shipowners opted to make the best of a bad situation and began fitting out their idle merchant ships as privateers, intending to recoup their losses by seizing British merchant ships. Concerned that anarchy might result if this practice were not regulated, Washington wrote to the Continental Congress.[15] On November 25, 1775, Congress responded with a Resolution regulating captures from the enemy. It forbade masters of colonial ships from taking prizes in the absence of a com-

---

13. Benjamin Franklin, Speech in the Convention at the Conclusion of Its Deliberations (Sept. 17, 1787), *in* BENJAMIN FRANKLIN, WRITINGS (J.A. Leo Lemay ed., New York: Library of America, 1987) at 1139, 1140.

14. U.S. CONST. art. III, sec. 2.

15. JOURNALS OF THE CONTINENTAL CONGRESS: 1774–1789 (34 vols., Worthington Chauncey Ford ed., Washington, D.C.: U.S. Government Printing Office, 1904), Vol. III, at 371–373 (hereinafter CONTINENTAL CONGRESS). For discussion, *see e.g.* HENRY J. BOURGUIGNON, THE FIRST FEDERAL COURT: THE FEDERAL APPELLATE PRIZE COURT OF THE REVOLUTION 1775–1787 (Philadelphia: The American Philosophical Society, 1977) at 44–48 (hereinafter BOURGUIGNON, FIRST FEDERAL COURT).

mission from either Congress or one of the colonies. In addition, it made provision for the first American admiralty courts to be erected independent of British authority:

> 4. That it be and is hereby recommended to the several legislatures in the United Colonies, as soon as possible, to erect courts of Justice, or give jurisdiction to the courts now in being for the purpose of determining concerning the captures to be made as aforesaid, and to provide that all trials in such case be had by a jury under such qualifications, as to the respective legislatures shall seem expedient.[16]

The Resolution also provided that in all such cases, "an appeal shall be allowed to Congress".[17] Massachusetts, a hotbed of privateering activity since the outbreak of hostilities, had not waited for congressional approval; the assembly had divided the colony into three districts and established a court in each with the authority to try prize cases.[18] Other colonies soon followed. Rhode Island responded quickly, creating a "Maritime Court" in January of 1776.[19] That same month, Virginia granted a panel of three judges the power to decide prize cases; nine months later it created a full-fledged admiralty court under an act drafted by Thomas Jefferson.[20] Between April and July of 1776, South

---

16. Continental Congress, *supra* note 15, Vol. III, at 373–374.

17. *Id.* at 374.

18. The act was passed on November 1, 1775, and Washington enclosed a copy in his letter to Congress. For discussion, *see* Bourguignon, First Federal Court, *supra* note 15, at 44; *see also* Franklyn C. Setaro, *The Formative Era of American Admiralty Law*, 5 N.Y.L. Forum 9, 30 (1959) (hereinafter Setaro).

19. Rhode Island was to alter the structure of its court several times before it was replaced by the federal court system in 1789; as one commentator explains: "In Rhode Island a Maritime Court was established in January, 1776. The act was amended in October, 1776. On the 9th of May, 1780, it was replaced by a Court of Admiralty, and the right of appeal to Congress was curtailed." J. C. Bancroft Davis, "Appendix to the Decisions of the Supreme Court of the United States: From September 24, 1789, to the End of October Term, 1888", in 131 U.S. ii, xxi (1889) (hereinafter Davis, Appendix); *see also* Setaro, *supra* note 18, at 30; Putnam, *supra* note 8, at 462.

20. Jefferson's draft is significant both for its choice of substantive law and for its extension of state admiralty jurisdiction to private maritime causes:

> "The court shall have cognizance of all causes heretofore of admiralty jurisdiction in this country, and shall be governed in their proceedings and decisions by the regulations of the Continental Congress, Acts of Annual Assembly, English statutes prior to the fourth year of the reign of King James the First, and the laws of Oleron, the Rhodians and Imperial laws, so far as the same have been heretofore observed in the English courts of admiralty, save only in the instances hereinafter provided for."

Carolina, Connecticut, Maryland, New Hampshire, and North Carolina also founded maritime courts; that autumn, Georgia and New Jersey did the same.[21] Despite its ports being occupied by the British, New York established an admiralty court on July 31, 1776, appointing Robert Morris as judge.[22] Within two years, there were maritime courts in all thirteen of the colonies.[23]

Cited in Putnam, *supra* note 8, at 461–462. The act underwent revision in 1779. *Id.* at 462; *see* discussion *infra* note 25. The degree to which Jefferson and his colleagues in the Virginia legislature understood the medieval maritime codes that were incorporated by reference into the statute is open to debate. In her catalogue of the books which Jefferson sold to the Library of Congress, Millicent Sowerby notes that Jefferson owned two works on the Rhodian Laws, that of Claude Emmanuel Joseph Pierre, Marquis de Pastornet on the influence of the Rhodian laws in the ancient world, and an English work entitled *A Treatise on the Maritime Laws of Rhodes* by Alexander Crowcher Schomberg. These works, however, were first published in 1784 and 1786 respectively—a decade too late to have been of assistance in framing the language of the Virginia statute. *See* Catalogue of the Library of Thomas Jefferson (5 vols., E. Millicent Sowerby ed., Washington D.C.: The Library of Congress, 1953), Vol. II, at 369–370. His copy of an obscure work listed in the inventory as *Scriptores de Jure Maritimo, sc. Stymmanus, Kuricke, Loccenius, et Heineccius* was published in 1740, though the records reveal that Jefferson did not acquire his copy until 1789. (Ironically, this book and a copy of William Wynne's *Life of Sir Leoline Jenkins* were both lost when Jefferson loaned them to President James Madison in 1815, indicating that Jefferson was not alone among America's political leaders in his use of arcane civil-law texts in the early days of the republic.) *Id.* at 368–369. Nonetheless, Jefferson did own a copy of Estienne Cleirac's *Us, et Coustumes de la Mer* (a later edition published in 1661), the standard reference work on ancient and medieval maritime codes used by the High Court of Admiralty in the time of Sir Leoline Jenkins. Unfortunately, Sowerby was unable to determine whether Jefferson purchased his copy before or after drafting the statute. *Id.* at 368. Also in the inventory was a 1686 edition of Malynes' *Consuetudo*, with appendices containing the Laws of Oleron and Wisby and Zouche's *Admiralty of England Asserted. Id.* at 357. As with Cleirac, however, the date of purchase is unknown. Other titles of interest in Jefferson's collection were Molloy's *De Jure Maritimo* (8th ed., acquired in 1787), Marius' *Advice Concerning Bills of Exchange* (1790 repirnt of 2d ed.), two editions of Clerke's *Praxis Curiae Admiralitatis Angliae* (2d Latin ed. of 1679; English/Latin ed. of 1722: dates of acquisition unknown), Browne's *Compendious View of the Civil & Admiralty Law* (1802), and Coke's *Fourth Institute. Id.* at 361–364. The general trend reflected in Jefferson's purchases indicates that he began collecting books on the civil law, the law merchant, and maritime law seriously in the 1780s and continued to do so through his second term as president. This tells us little regarding his knowledge of maritime law at the time of the Revolution, but does provide us with a microcosm of America's fascination with civil-law maritime texts in the early federal period.

21. *Id.* at 463 n. 9. *See also* Davis, Appendix, *supra* note 19, at xx–xxii; Setaro, *supra* note 18, at 30–32.

22. Putnam, *supra* note 8, at 462.

23. *Id.* at 463.

Washington had requested the creation of admiralty courts for reasons narrowly focused on the waging of war. When the colonies broke with Britain, however, private parties also lost access to convenient *fora* for filing maritime claims. Though in several colonies business gradually shifted away from the vice admiralty courts to the locally-controlled colonial common-law courts in the few years preceding 1775, the vice admiralty courts nonetheless had remained available for private actions when claimants believed their unique expertise was required. The Revolution deprived private parties of these specialized tribunals. As was the case a century earlier, when the private sector's desire for maritime courts alone was insufficient to spur their creation, so too in 1776 the impetus for establishing the courts would have to come from elsewhere. In the 1690s, merchants and shipowners took full advantage of vice admiralty courts erected for hearing trade-act cases; the merchants and shipowners of the 1770s—desiring courts of their own—soon found their own use for the states' new prize courts. Most of the new state courts of admiralty welcomed private actions.

Virginia clearly welcomed private suits in its newly constituted admiralty court. Moreover, the act creating it—authored by Jefferson—also named the "laws of Oleron, the Rhodians, and the Imperial laws, so far as the same have been heretofore observed in the English courts of admiralty" as providing the rules of decision.[24] Whether by design or by oversight, however, the plain language of the statute applied the restrictive statutes of Richard II to the scope of the court's jurisdiction. This impediment was removed three years later when the legislature enacted amendments drafted by George Wythe.[25] Connecticut declined to create a separate maritime court, but granted to its common-

---

24. For the text of the 1776 statute, *see supra* note 20. For discussion, *see also* Davis, Appendix, *supra* note 19, at xxii; *see also* Jonathan Gutoff, *Original Understandings and the Private Law Origins of the Federal Admiralty Jurisdiction*, 30 J. Mar. L. & Com. 361, 379–380 (1999) (hereinafter Gutoff).

25. There is some controversy regarding whether Jefferson's draft was intended to limit the court's jurisdiction to contracts signed at sea or abroad. Despite being widely read, Jefferson would have been more familiar with the jurisdiction actually exercised by the colonial vice admiralty courts than with medieval English statutory law. Unfortunately, the surviving case law from Virginia does not reveal conclusively whether the colony recognized the limitations of the statutes of Richard II. The surviving instance cases include claims for seamen's wages, collision, and bottomry, all cognizable in admiralty even under the narrowly-construed admiralty jurisdiction described by Hale and Prynne. *See* PROCEEDINGS IN THE COURT OF VICE-ADMIRALTY OF VIRGINIA: 1698–1775 (George Reese ed., Richmond: Virginia State Library, 1983) at 8–11, 91–93 (seamen's wages), 95–96 (collision), 83–84 (bottomry). In 1779, George Wythe drafted amendments to the act of 1776 that deleted

law courts the power to sit in admiralty to hear prize cases, adjudicating under the laws of the state, the law of nations, and the civil law.[26] These same courts, when adjudicating instance cases, were technically courts of common law, but since the colonial period, they had been instructed to apply the Laws of Oleron to private maritime actions.[27] Unlike Virginia, New Jersey was quite specific in limiting the jurisdiction of its maritime court, providing that "the Court of Admiralty shall be liable to the Prohibition of the Supreme Court of Judicature, in like Manner and with like Effect as the Prohibition of the Court of King's Bench in *England* in like Case."[28] Nevertheless, this limitation would have been superfluous had the assembly not intended the court to hear instance suits.[29] Of the

---

the language "English statutes prior to the fourth year of the reign of king James the first". Again, it is unclear as to whether this was intended to extend the jurisdiction of the court or merely to clarify ambiguous language; Wythe's draft is silent as to whether the court was intended to have cognizance over maritime contracts signed on Virginia's soil. For discussion, *see* BOURGUIGNON, FIRST FEDERAL COURT, *supra* note 15, at 69–71. The decree in an unpublished case from 1778 ultimately may shed some light on whether Virginia's State Court of Admiralty applied the English jurisdictional restrictions. The matter resulted in an award of one-fourth the value of the sloop "*Adventure*" and her cargo to the libellants. Unfortunately, the decree fails to mention the subject-matter of the libel. Should additional information come to light, it may provide a definitive answer to the question of whether Virginia adopted the statutes of Richard II. *See Richard Barron, James Barron, et al., v. The Sloop "Adventure" and Cargo,* (Virginia State Court of Admiralty, decided Jan. 18, 1778) (unpublished opinion, The Tucker-Coleman Collection, 40 T79 Box 70, on file with the Special Collections of Swem Library, College of William & Mary). For the text of the statutes of Richard II and discussion, *see* Chapter I, notes 132–136 and text accompanying.

26. *See* Davis, Appendix, *supra* note 19, at xxi; *see also* BOURGUIGNON, FIRST FEDERAL COURT, *supra* note 15, at 63–64.

27. *Id.* at 64; *see also* CHARLES M. ANDREWS, THE COLONIAL PERIOD OF AMERICAN HISTORY (New Haven: Yale University Press, 1932), VOL. IV: ENGLAND'S COMMERCIAL AND COLONIAL POLICY, at 232–233.

28. New Jersey Session Laws, 6th Assembly, 1st Sitting, Dec. 18, 1781, *quoted in* BOURGUIGNON, FIRST FEDERAL COURT, *supra* note 15, at 68 (*emphasis in the original*).

29. New Jersey made instance jurisdiction explicit in legislation passed in 1781, which amended the earlier act regulating the admiralty court; the 1781 statute provided:

> "...that the Judge of the Admiralty hold a Court of Admiralty and therein have cognizance in...all controversies, suits and pleas of Maritime Jurisdiction, and thereupon the said Judge shall pass sentence and decree according to the maritime law and the law of nations, and the ordinances of the Honorable, the Congress of the United States of America and the laws of the State.

Quoted in Setaro, *supra* note 18, at 31. Thus the statute also incorporated two existing bodies of substantive law—the customary maritime law and the law of nations—as a supplement to the enactments of the legislature and Congress.

court of admiralty in Delaware little is known, though provision was made for it under the state's constitution.[30]

Of the states in the South, the experience of North Carolina is best documented. The statute passed in November of 1777 granted the new prize court jurisdiction over instance matters as well, drawing the lines of jurisdiction over "all Matters and Transactions that are in their Nature maritime" broadly even by today's standards.[31] While in most states, the newly created prize courts were also vested with instance jurisdiction, in South Carolina the process was reversed; the court created to hear "maritime causes" soon was granted the power to judge prize cases as well.[32] The court in Georgia was established strictly as a prize court, though as a practical matter, it was ineffective, since the state's ports were under British occupation for much of the war.[33] This was not the case with Maryland, where the Chesapeake ports remained open during Revolution. Three weeks before the ratification of the Maryland State Constitution in 1776, the state adopted a resolution establishing a court of admiralty.[34]

---

30. Davis, Appendix, *supra* note 19, at xxi; Setaro, *supra* note 18, at 30.

31. In addition to "Suits for Freight, Mariners Wages, Breach of Charter Parties" and salvage, the statute granted cognizance over "Suits for building, repairing...or the necessary Victualing for a Ship". Claims of materialmen were circumscribed by the "home-port doctrine" by the nineteenth century, while shipbuilding contracts are still beyond the jurisdiction of modern admiralty courts in both the United States and Britain. The statute is also noteworthy for its distinction between claims *in rem* against the vessel and those *in personam* against the owners, though in form it more closely resembles foreign attachment than an *in rem* action for enforcing a modern maritime lien. For text of the statute and discussion, *see* Bourguignon, First Federal Court, *supra* note 15, at 73–74.

32. *Id.* at 71–72. In adjudicating prize cases, Bourguignon notes that the admiralty court of South Carolina "ignored the resolves of Congress specifying the proportion of recaptured vessels to be awarded to the recaptors in lieu of salvage." *Id.* at 71. Lack of uniform standards would plague Congress throughout the war and ultimately become as issue at the Constitutional Convention in 1787.

33. *Id.* at 74.

34. *See* Emory H. Niles, The Revolutionary Court of Admiralty of the State of Maryland 1776–1789. Address Before the Lawyers' Round Table, Maryland Club, Baltimore (Dec. 8, 1941) (transcript available through the Maryland Historical Society Library) at 3–5 (hereinafter Niles). Judge Niles reproduces the text of the resolution, which provides:

> "...that a court of admiralty be established for the trial of such captures and seizures, with full power to take cognizance of all libels on account of such captures and seizures; and to proceed to a final determination and decree thereon.... This court to be held at such place as the judge shall think convenient for the trial of such captures and seizures as are or shall be made aforesaid."

Id. at 4–5. While the resolution provides detailed provisions for the court's structure and emphasizes geographic flexibility in handling prize cases—the purpose for which it was first established—it is silent as to the substantive law to be applied. *Id.* at 5.

While the court was to utilize "the process and form of proceeding... usual in the courts of admiralty", it also made provision for impaneling a jury if either party requested one.[35] In addition, though clearly structured as a prize court, the Maryland court soon began to entertain instance actions as well.[36] Initially from 1776 through 1781, the majority of matters heard by the court involved prize, though after 1783—as the number of matters on the docket doubled—private maritime claims dominated the business before the court.[37]

In July of 1776, New Hampshire passed a statute providing for the creation of a "Court Maritime" for trial of prize cases, patterning it on that of Massachusetts; this court was to employ a jury in all cases.[38] Unfortunately, it shared a common characteristic with its counterpart in Massachusetts: neither statute permitted an appeal to a national tribunal.[39] Massachusetts, the first colony

---

35. *Id.* at 5.

36. *See* David R. Owen & Michael C. Tolley, Courts of Admiralty in Colonial America: The Maryland Experience, 1634–1776 (Durham, North Carolina: Carolina Academic Press, 1995) at 220 (hereinafter Owen & Tolley). The source of the court's power to hear instance cases remains unclear; as Judge Niles explains:

> "[I]ts power to determine civil cases may have been later granted by statute or simply assumed by the Court for from 1783 onward, the Court exercised definite civil jurisdiction in cases of seamen's wages, assault, bottomry and other matters."

Niles, *supra* note 34, at 6–7. In either case, it is clear that pressure from the private sector transformed a tribunal conceived for hearing prize cases into a forum for resolving private disputes.

37. Judge Niles observes that from 1776 through 1781—during the Revolution—twenty-nine cases were decided, the majority of which were cases of prize. There are *lacunae* in the records from 1782 and 1783. For the period 1784 through 1787, the number of cases on the court's docket increases to fifty. In addition, "the whole character of litigation changes.... Out of the fifty, thirty-four were for seamen's wages, and ten for assault on seamen. Of the remaining six, one was for supplies furnished a vessel; one was for work and labor upon a vessel; one for unlawful discharge, and one for the removal of a Master for incompetence. Two were for forfeiture for breach of the custom and navigation laws." Niles, *supra* note 34, at 12–14.

38. The text of the New Hampshire statute is set out *verbatim* in *Penhallow v. Doane's Administrators*, 3 U.S. (3 Dall.) 54, 56–60 (1795). For discussion, *see* Bourguignon, First Federal Court, *supra* note 15, at 64–65.

39. The statutes of both states actually did provide for an appeal to Congress, but only when the ship that captured the prize was outfitted at the expense of the national government. It should be remembered that the Massachusetts statute on which New Hampshire patterned its own act was enacted in 1775, before Congress passed its resolution vesting appellate power in the national government. *See supra* notes 15–18 and text accompanying. New Hampshire, by contrast, enacted its statute on July 3, 1776, when the resolution of Congress was already in force. It is unclear as to whether this was an oversight in draft-

to enact a substantive maritime code[40] and the first state to create a maritime court, established its court before the Continental Congress had adopted its resolution of November, 1775, allowing for appeals in prize cases to be heard by the national legislature. Under pressure from Congress, in 1778 it amended its legislation to provide for appeals to Congress in cases where the property rights of citizens of foreign nations "in amity with this [state] and the United States of America" were asserted.[41] This court utilized juries in its proceedings and heard private disputes as well as cases of capture.[42]

Pennsylvania stands as an excellent example of how states periodically restructured their admiralty courts to alleviate problems unforeseen at the time the courts were established. Enacting its first statue in 1776, Pennsylvania provided for trials by jury and avoided the problem that plagued Massachusetts and New Hampshire by providing for appellate review of prize cases by Congress. Two years later, the state extended the jurisdiction of the court to encompass private maritime disputes, to be determined according to the laws of Pennsylvania and the general maritime law. At the same time, however, it limited appeals to issues of law; facts found by juries could not be reviewed on appeal. Embarrassed by its clash with Congress over the case of the sloop *Active*, in 1780 the state jettisoned its limitations on the scope of appeal, allowing Congress to review facts as well as law. In addition, it eliminated the jury entirely, opting instead for civil-law procedure modified by the use of testimony *viva voce* in place of interrogatories.[43]

British troops occupying the port of New York rendered its court ineffective until their withdrawal. By 1784, however, the court was open for busi-

---

ing or a deliberate effort to ignore Congress. Ultimately in 1779, under pressure from Congress, New Hampshire amended its law to permit an appeal to Congress in all prize cases. For discussion, *see* BOURGUIGNON, FIRST FEDERAL COURT, *supra* note 15, at 64.

40. For the text of the statute, *see* Several Laws and Orders, Made at the General Court in Boston in New England, October 4, 1668, Maritime Affairs, at 9–14 (*reprinted in* RECORDS OF THE STATES OF THE UNITED STATES OF AMERICA: A MICROFILM COMPILATION, Mass. B.2 Reel I 1661–1742, William Sumner Jenkins ed., Washington, D.C.: Library of Congress Photoduplication Service, 1949); for discussion, *see* L. Kinvin Wroth, *The Massachusetts Vice Admiralty Court and the Federal Admiralty Jurisdiction* (Part I), 6 Am. J. Legal Hist. 251, 254–255 (1962); *see also* Chapter II, note 236 and text accompanying.

41. For the text of statute and discussion, *see* BOURGUIGNON, FIRST FEDERAL COURT, *supra* note 15, at 64–65.

42. *See* Gutoff, *supra* note 24, at 379–380.

43. *See* BOURGUIGNON, FIRST FEDERAL COURT, *supra* note 15, at 66–67. The author gives a detailed account of the conflict between the state of Pennsylvania and the Continental Congress in the matter of the *Sloop Active* in Chapter III. *Id.* at 101–134.

ness, and surviving records indicate that its dockets were dominated by instance cases, including express hypothecation, salvage, claims for seamen's wages, and the claims of materialmen.[44] Alexander Hamilton, a practitioner before this court, appeared as counsel in only one trial for prize, but he represented clients in two matters involving bottomry as well as in two salvage cases.[45] Nonetheless, one faction of the common-law bar succeeded in 1787 in lobbying the legislature to pass an act limiting the jurisdiction of the court of admiralty with language mirroring that of the statutes of Richard II.[46] Their

---

44. Charles Merrill Hough, Reports of Cases in the Vice Admiralty of the Province of New York and in the Court of Admiralty of the State of New York, 1715–1788 (New Haven: Yale University Press, 1925) at 243–254.

45. *See* The Law Practice of Alexander Hamilton: Documents and Commentary (5 vols., Julius Goebel ed., New York: Columbia University Press, 1969). The papers relating to the prize case, *Owners of Sloop "Chester" v. Owners of Brig "Experiment"*, is reproduced in Volume II at 892. The papers for the salvage cases, *Thompson v. Ship "Masborough"* (1784–1787) and *March v. Sundry Goods Salvaged from a Deserted Vessel by the Brigantine "Port Roseway"* (1785–1787), are reproduced in Volume II beginning at 881. The bottomry cases, *Dall and Heathcote v. Ship "Betsy"* (1784) and *Bartholomew and Terason v. Moeity of the Ship "Diligent"* (1785), are reproduced in Volume II at 863 and 870 respectively. In addition to his trial-work, Hamilton also argued three prize cases in the Court of Prize Appeals created by the Continental Congress to hear appeals from state courts of admiralty. *Id.*, Vol. II, at 781–782.

46. "An Act to prevent encroachments of the Court of Admiralty" was enacted on February 14, 1787. It provided:

> "That the Court of Admiralty of this State shall not meddle or hold pleas of anything done within this State, but only of things done upon the sea, as it hath been formerly used; and further that of all manner of contracts, pleas and quarrels, and of all other things done arising within the body of any county of this State, as well by land as by water, and also of wreck, of the sea, the Court of Admiralty shall have no manner of cognizance, power, nor jurisdiction; but all such manner of contracts, pleas, and quarrels and all other things arising within the body of any county of this State, as well by land as by water, as aforesaid; and also all wreck of the sea shall be tried, determined, discussed and remedied by the laws of the land, and not before, nor in, or by, the Court of Admiralty."

Reproduced in Putnam, *supra* note 8, at 463 n. 9. For the texts of 13 Ric. II, c. 5 (1389) and 15 Ric. II, c. 3 (1391), *see* Chapter I, notes 132–133 and text accompanying. Despite the language of the statute limiting the court's jurisdiction, it should be noted that the legislature did not abolish instance jurisdiction altogether, but rather restricted it to those matters which Hale and Prynne acknowledged to remain within the cognizance of the English High Court of Admiralty at the close of the eighteenth century, namely salvage, express hypothecation, and—arguably—seamen's wage-claims and foreign contracts. To the extent that the court conducted surveys of ships, it would appear this power remained undiminished.

victory would be short-lived, as within two years the state court would be abolished and its former jurisdiction assumed by the new Federal District Court. While New York sought to limit instance jurisdiction late in the era of the Articles of Confederation, Rhode Island sought to expand the jurisdiction of its admiralty court. Originally conceived in 1776 as a prize court patterned after that of Massachusetts, the assembly granted it power to hear private maritime disputes in 1780.[47] This court operated with a jury, though if the defendant failed to appear to defend the case, the court was empowered to dispense with this requirement.[48] With regard to prize cases, the records reveal no conflict over appeals to Congress.[49]

The Continental Congress, beset by a myriad of other problems, had not devoted much deliberation to how appeals from the state prize courts would be handled. In the course of the war, only a small percentage of these matters were in fact appealed.[50] Nevertheless, the appellate process for prize cases would prove influential for the generation that subsequently drafted both the Constitution and the Judiciary Act of 1789. While Congress had been quick

---

47. For discussion, *see* Bourguignon, First Federal Court, *supra* note 15, at 61–62; *see also* Frederick Bernays Wiener, *Notes on the Rhode Island Admiralty, 1727–1790*, 46 Harv. L. Rev. 44, 59–62 (1933). Wiener notes that it was not generally the practice of the court to publish the *ratio decidendi* together with the outcome of a case, though one such opinion has survived. In it, the judge relied upon 15 Ric. II, c. 3 (1391), though it should be noted that the case was decided in 1779, a year before the assembly granted the court full-fledged instance jurisdiction. *Id.* at 61–62. In 1780, the court received the power to hear "Causes concerning Seamens Wages, Salvage, and all other Matters and Things of a maritime Nature, properly cognizable before, and to be heard and determined by a Court of Admiralty." Act of July 20, 1780, R. I. Acts & Resolves, July, 1780 (2d Sess.) at 9, *reproduced in* Wiener at 60. Although it was by no means the most active of the state courts of admiralty, surviving records reveal that it did utilize its newly-acquired power to adjudicate two claims for damage to cargo and another for damage to a vessel. *See* Gutoff, *supra* note 24, at 380 n. 85.

48. Bourguignon, *supra* note 15, at 63.

49. Davis, Appendix, *supra* note 19, at xxi, insists that the "right to appeal to Congress was curtailed" in 1780, though Bourguignon, *supra* note 15, at 62, asserts that there is no record of a conflict between Rhode Island's admiralty court and Congress over appeals in prize cases.

50. Davis, Appendix, *supra* note 19, at xxxv–xlix, provides a complete list of the 109 prize cases appealed to the *ad hoc* and standing committees selected by Congress to hear appeals, as well as those heard by their successor, the Court of Appeals in Cases of Capture. According to Bourguignon, First Federal Court, *supra* note 15, at 77, of the roughly 1,830 prize cases tried in the states of Maryland, Rhode Island, Pennsylvania, Connecticut, and Massachusetts, fewer than 4% (a total of 69 cases) were appealed to a national tribunal.

to recommend that the states establish their own prize courts, retaining for Congress itself the right to hear appeals from these courts, it was less than diligent in providing mechanisms for handling the appeals. When the first appeal came before it in August of 1776, Congress was obliged to create an *ad hoc* committee to hear the case. By January, 1777, the decisions in another seven cases had been appealed to Congress, which appointed *ad hoc* committees to hear each.[51] It soon became apparent that the procedure was unweildy, and on January 30, 1777, Congress created a standing committee to hear appeals.[52] A more satisfactory arrangement would have to await the states' adoption of the Articles of Confederation.

When Congress approved the Articles of Confederation on November 15, 1777, they included the following language:

> The United States, in Congress assembled, shall have the sole and exclusive right and power of... establishing rules for deciding, in all cases, what captures on land or water shall be legal, and in what manner prizes taken by land or naval forces in the service of the united states shall be divided or appropriated; of granting letters of marque

---

51. *See* Davis, Appendix, *supra* note 19, at xxiii; for a list of these eight cases, together with the outcomes, *see Id.* at xxxv–xxxvi. *See also* Bourguignon, First Federal Court, *supra* note 15, at 85–86. Lest one judge Congress harshly for creating such an unweildy system of appeals, it should be remembered that the High Court of Delegates, which heard appeals in private maritime disputes, was itself a series of *ad hoc* panels assembled pursuant to an appellant's petition to the Crown. At the conclusion of each of these appeals, the judges' appellate commissions would expire. *See* G.I.O. Duncan, The High Court of Delegates (Cambridge: Cambridge University Press, 1971) at 1–2, 178–179. Thus it was not the *ad hoc* nature of the panels that made them impractical, but rather that the panels were assembled of members of Congress, whose newly-assigned judicial duties often interfered with their legislative responsibilities.

52. Congress first provided for the creation of a permanent panel of five to hear appeals:

> "Resolved, That a standing committee, to consist of five members, be appointed to hear and determine upon appeals brought against sentences passed on libels in the courts of Admiralty in the respective States, agreeable to the resolutions of Congress; and that the several appeals, when lodged with the secretary, be by him delivered to them for their final determination."

Continental Congress, *supra* note 15, Vol. VII, at 75. Congress would make fourteen adjustments in the structure of this standing committee from May 8, 1777, through January 5, 1780, including provisions for the appointment of a "register", those regulating the number of judges on the standing committee as well as the quorum needed to form panel, and those appointing new members to replace those stepping down. Davis, Appendix, *supra* note 19, at xxiii–xxiv.

> and reprisal in times of peace; appointing courts for the trial of piracies and felonies committed on the high seas, and establishing courts for receiving and determining finally appeals in all cases of captures, provided that no member of Congress shall be appointed a judge of any of the said courts.[53]

Unfortunately, the process of ratification was an arduous one, with Maryland holding out for a provision aimed at preserving unsettled public lands for the collective benefit of all thirteen states.[54] With negotiations with Maryland still in progress, on January 15, 1780, Congress opted to act, creating a new appellate court to replace the standing committee:

> Resolved, That a court be established for the trial of all appeals from the courts of admiralty in these United States, in cases of capture, to consist of three judges, appointed and commissioned by Congress, either two of whom, in the absence of the other, to hold the said court for the dispatch of business: That the said court appoint their own register: That the trials therein be according to the usage of nations and not by jury…[55]

The resolution was drafted in part by Oliver Ellsworth,[56] who later would serve as a member of the Committee of Detail at the Constitutional Convention of 1787[57] and who, as a member of the first Congress, would draft the Judiciary Act of 1789.[58] On January 22, Congress appointed the court's first panel, consisting of William Paca of Maryland, Titus Hosmer of Connecticut, and

---

53. Continental Congress, *supra* note 15, Vol. IX, at 915–916, Articles of Confederation, art. IX, para. 1.

54. For discussion, *see e.g.* Davis, *supra* note 19, at xiii (listing the dates on which each state signed).

55. Continental Congress, *supra* note 15, Vol. XVI, at 61. For debates of the resolution, *see Id.* at 61–64. Apparently through oversight, Congress neglected to provide for the transfer of cases pending before the standing committee to the new tribunal. This was remedied by a resolution of May 9, 1780, which provided the court with its name: "the Court of Appeals in cases of capture". Davis, *supra* note 19, at xxvi.

56. On January 8, 1780, Congress appointed Ellsworth to a committee of four, including William Houstoun, Thomas McKean, and Robert Livingston, to draft the resolution, which was adopted by Congress a week later. *See* Continental Congress, *supra* note 15, Vol. XVI, at 29–32.

57. Farrand, Framing, *supra* note 6, at 122.

58. Maeva Marcus & Natalie Wexler, "The Judiciary Act of 1789: Political Compromise or Political Interpretation?", *in* The Origins of the Federal Judiciary: Essays on the Judiciary Act of 1789 (Maeva Marcus ed., Oxford: Oxford University Press, 1993) at 13.

George Wythe of Virginia.[59] In the course of its existence, this court would hear fifty-six appeals.[60]

While replacing the standing committee with an Appellate Prize Court removed a certain amount of administrative inconvenience, it left the most serious flaws of the former appellate structure untouched. Foremost among these was Congress' choice of a "resolution" as the means of creating the court. Lacking the binding force of law, a resolution was at best a hortatory document. Under the circumstances, Congress had no better option, as the Articles of Confederation had yet to be ratified by all thirteen states when the court was created,[61] leaving Congress with a tribunal the authority of which could be questioned when it found itself at odds with a state court.[62] In addition,

---

59. Davis, Appendix, *supra* note 19, at xxv. With regard to the apparent inconsistency with the plain language of the Articles of Confederation, Article IX of which forbids appointing members of Congress to an appellate prize court, Davis remarks: "...it may be noted that Mr. Read and Mr. Lowell [later appointees to the Court], the only judges elected after the ratification of the Articles by all the States, were members of Congress when elected. Congress thus construed that instrument as meaning only that no person could act in both capacities at the same time." *Id.* at xxvi–xxvii. The three first appointees were thus exempt from the requirements of Article IX because it was not yet in force. While Hosmer would die in office, Paca eventually would become a delegate to the Maryland Convention that ratified the Constitution as well as the first judge of the Federal District Court in Maryland in 1789. (For a biographical sketch, *see e.g.* Owen & Tolley, *supra* note 36, at 325.) Wythe (who ultimately declined to serve), was a renowned legal scholar and drafter of Virginia's revised admiralty-court statute (*see supra* note 25), and later became a delegate to the Constitutional Convention. (For a brief biography, *see* Farrand, Framing, *supra* note 6, at 17–18.)

60. *See* Julius Goebel, Jr., Antecedents and Beginnings to 1801, Vol. I *in* The Oliver Wendell Holmes Devise: History of the Supreme Court of the United States (New York: Macmillan Publishing Co., 1971), at 182 (hereinafter Goebel, Antecedents).

61. *Id.* at 146, 172, 175.

62. Several of these incidents occurred during the Revolution, among which the most notorious was that involving the sloop *Active*, of which Goebel gives the following terse synopsis:

> "[T]he sloop *Active*...had been condemned in the Court of Admiralty for Philadelphia. The Standing Committee in the course of hearing the appeal had re-examined the facts in disregard of the Pennsylvania statute which had declared jury findings to be conclusive. The decree was reversed December 15, 1778, but the state judge refused to obey the mandate issued pursuant to the reversal and ordered his own decree to be executed."

Id. at 165. (For Congress' handling of the incident, and the resolution of March 6, 1779, that it produced, *see* Continental Congress, *supra* note 15, Vol. XIII, at 281–286. For a full analysis of the case and its ramifications, *see* Bourguignon, First Federal Court,

when the states (both individually and collectively through Congress) repudiated British law, they had no ready substitute for the British substantive and procedural prize rules.[63] Americans' practical experience with prize cases in the late eighteenth century had been limited to that acquired before the colonial vice admiralty courts—which owing to the lack of trained civilians had employed hybrid procedures.[64] Reports of prize decisions were nonexistent,[65] and treatises on procedural and substantive prize law were in short supply in the states.[66] Lacking guidance from a common set of sources, differences

---

supra note 15, Chapter III, at 101–134.) Although this case arose under the court's predecessor, the Standing Committee, the new court—established by means of a non-binding resolution—would fare no better, suffering a similar experience with the admiralty court of New Hampshire in *Penhallow v. Doan's Administrators*, which ultimately reached the United States Supreme Court nearly two decades later: *see* 3 U.S. (3 Dall.) 54 (1794). For discussion, *see* Goebel, Antecedents, *supra* note 60, at 179.

63. As Bourguignon observes:

> "The procedures for prize adjudication became well defined by the late seventeenth century.... The Council in 1665 outlined procedures for a trial in the prize court. Without departing from this basic outline, Parliament, by the various acts of the eighteenth century, more fully spelled out the details of prize adjudication."

Bourguignon, First Federal Court, *supra* note 15, at 17. "Various acts" is a reference to four statutes—6 Anne, c. 37 (1708), 13 Geo. II, c. 4 (1740), 17 Geo. II, c. 34 (1744), and 29 Geo. II, c. 34 (1756)—which governed procedure in prize cases. Nonetheless, the Americans' practical knowledge of these procedures was derived from their experiences during the Seven Years' War in their own vice admiralty courts, the procedures of which differed from those employed the High Court of Admiralty and its appellate forum, the Lords Commissioners. For a detailed discussion of how British prize procedure in the late eighteenth century differed from the procedures of the colonial vice admiralty courts—*see* Bourguignon, First Federal Court, *supra* note 15, at 139–178; *see also* Goebel, Antecedents, *supra* note 60, at 153–154.

64. For discussion of prize cases in colonial vice admiralty courts, see *supra* Chapter II, notes 172–191 and text accompanying. Francis Hopkinson, the Pennsylvania admiralty judge who was later to publish the first American admiralty reports, commented in 1785 on the American bar's lamentable lack of knowledge about prize, observing it was not until the publication of Lord Mansfield's recent opinion in *Le Caux v. Eden* that "for the first time, did the distinction occur between the prize court and the instance court of admiralty." *Dean v. John Angus*, Bee, Reports, 369, 372 (1785), *quoted in* Bourguignon, First Federal Court, *supra* note 15, at 151.

65. Goebel, Antecedents, *supra* note 60, at 154.

66. Only two works on the substantive law of prize circulated in America during the Revolution—Richard Lee's *A Treatise on Capture in War* (1759) and *The Report of the Law Officers of the Crown* (1753)—though several general treatises on the law of nations were available that made references to the law of prize. Among these were Molloy's *De Jure Maritimo et Navali*, of which a revised tenth edition had appeared in 1778. In addition, the

arose—ranging from subtle to significant—as each of the states interpreted prize law in its own vacuum.[67] This lack of uniformity compounded the difficulties facing Congress—first in its *ad hoc* and standing committees and later in formulating rules for its Appellate Prize Court[68]—forcing it to arrive at standards for reviewing the decisions of thirteen different jurisdictions, each operating under its own substantive and curial rules.[69]

---

works of Hugo Grotius, Samuel von Pufendorf, and Emmerich de Vattel were available and mentioned in extant records, as were Wyndham Beawes' *Lex Mercatoria Rediviva* (1751), Giles Jacob's *Lex Mercatoria* (1718), and Connelius van Bynkershoek's *Quaestionum Juris Publici*. Each of these sources was used at least once by an American prize court. For a list of all known sources of substantive prize law confirmed to have been cited by American courts, *see* Bourguignon, First Federal Court, *supra* note 15, Chapter V at 179–190. By contrast, the only work on procedural law known to have been used was Francis Clerke's *Praxis Curiae Admiralitatis Angliae*, for which an English translation had become available by 1722. *See* Goebel, Antecedents, *supra* note 60, at 154. Nonetheless, in a court in which neither the judges nor the practitioners were formally trained in civil law, this work would have been at best of limited use.

67. Goebel summarizes the state of prize adjudication during the Revolution as follows:

> "Some of the vagaries which turn up in prize case papers during the Revolution may be attributed to continuing adherence to colonial usages, others were the result of colonial legislation and still others were probably due to lack-learned lawyers and judges."

Goebel, Antecedents, *supra* note 60, at 154.

68. As Bourguignon explains, the role of Congress underwent changes after it delegated the power to hear appeals to the Appellate Prize Court:

> "During the seven years that the Court of Appeals was established and functioning, Congress continued especially in three ways to remain involved with prize affairs. The delegates to Congress discussed and debated a plan to establish the Court of Appeals on the firmer basis of a fully integrated ordinance. They also revised from time to time the ordinances regulating capture of enemy vessels and tried to collate these into one ordinance. Congress also continued to receive petitions and reports concerning the domestic and foreign complications resulting from privateering activity."

Bourguignon, First Federal Court, *supra* note 15, at 125.

69. Goebel, Antecedents, *supra* note 60, at 164. A systematic analysis of variations in the procedures employed by the state courts is beyond the scope of the present work. Goebel provides this short synopsis:

> "Some jurisdictions, among which were numbered Maryland, North Carolina and South Carolina, employed a relatively formal admiralty procedure, tainted, of course, with the anomaly of jury trial. In others common law procedure and writs were used as well as admiralty instruments to produce an odd potpourri. Very occasionally replications and rejoinders appear. In only in one case was a demurrer interposed."

Id. at 154–155. For a more detailed example of the use of common-law procedures in a

On several occasions, Congress had sought to clarify the procedural and substantive rules to be used in appellate proceedings. While members reached consensus upon the need to adjudicate under the "law of nations", that body of law was not self-defining, and there remained some doubt as to its exact requirements.[70] To be sure, Congress had incorporated the "law of nations" into a resolution when conflict with the admiralty court of Pennsylvania had prompted the representatives to reassert in detail their appellate powers first set forth in the resolution of November 25, 1775. In March of 1779, when the standing committee clashed with the admiralty court of Pennsylvania over the national tribunal's right to review state courts' decisions in prize cases, Congress reaffirmed that the law of nations governed prize cases, adding furthermore that the power to interpret that body of law was vested in the national government.[71] Nonetheless, Congress did not set out substantive rules in detail until 1781, in the waning days of the Revolution following Cornwallis' defeat at Yorktown.[72] This ordinance established the rules that the Appellate Prize

---

prize case, see the description contained in BOURGUIGNON, FIRST FEDERAL COURT, *supra* note 15, at 231–234, of the case of the Spanish brigantine *"St. Antonio"*, libelled in Boston in 1782.

70. As early as 1777, James Wilson, concerned over Congress' lack of expertise in international law, had suggested that Congress appoint a person to advise Congress on questions arising under maritime law and the law of nations, though at the time no action was taken. BOURGUIGNON, FIRST FEDERAL COURT, *supra* note 15, at 93. As late as 1780, the problem had not been remedied; it was observed in debates on July 27 that few members had experience with the law of nations. *See* CONTINENTAL CONGRESS, *supra* note 15, Vol. XVII, at 672–674.

71. In reaffirming and extending the Resolution of November 25, 1775 (*see supra* notes 15–17 and text accompanying), Congress resolved that a committee constituted by Congress had the authority to review and, if necessary, to overturn findings of fact made by juries in state admiralty proceedings. Moreover, the resolution asserted that no state possessed the power to insulate its courts from review by a national tribunal, providing *inter alia*:

> "That Congress is by these United States invested with the supreme sovereign power of war and peace: That the power of executing the law of nations is essential to the sovereign supreme power of war and peace: That the legality of all captures on the high seas must be determined by the law of nations: That the authority ultimately and finally to decide on all matters and questions touching the law of nations, does reside and is vested in the sovereign supreme power of war and peace: That a controul by appeal is necessary, in order to compel a just and uniform execution of the law of nations..."

CONTINENTAL CONGRESS, *supra* note 15, March 6, 1779, Vol. XIII, at 283–284.

72. On December 4, 1781, Congress—at this time operating under the Articles of Confederation—passed an ordinance that sought to codify its understanding of the substan-

Court would apply on appeal, but as it was not directly binding on the states, it did not produce nation-wide uniformity of substantive standards. As late as 1782, Congress continued to grapple with the problem of uniformity, but its final efforts were in the form of an attempt to promulgate a model law for adoption by the states rather than a national law that would bind the states directly. The suggestion had come too late; many felt that the conflict was drawing to a close. Anticipating a peace treaty, further efforts to improve the method of prize litigation were abandoned.[73]

Throughout the Revolution, Congress had failed to produce an effective solution to the procedural problems that plagued the adjudication of captures. Its own procedures were at best skeletal, lacking the detail and precision of their British counterparts,[74] and the failure to standardize state practice with that of the national tribunals haunted Congress throughout the war. Of all the problems with procedure,[75] none was more troubling than Congress' inabil-

---

tive requirements of the law of nations in cases of capture. This ordinance pre-empted prior legislation, providing that: "all resolutions and ordinances of Congress relating to captures or re-captures on water, and coming within the purview of this ordinance, except as hereinafter excepted, shall be null and void..." For the text of the ordinance, *see* CONTINENTAL CONGRESS, *supra* note 15, Vol. XXI, at 1153–1159.

73. The last time that substantive prize law is mentioned in the *Journals* is on March 30, 1782, where it was noted that "The said committee also reported the form of a law to be recommended to the states for regulating the courts of admiralty". CONTINENTAL CONGRESS, *supra* note 15, Vol. XXII, at 154. For discussion, *see* GOEBEL, ANTECEDENTS, *supra* note 60, at 175.

74. BOURGUIGNON, FIRST FEDERAL COURT, *supra* note 15, at 48–49, 191–237.

75. The various appellate courts that Congress established—the *ad hoc* committees, the standing committee, and the Appellate Prize Court—attempted to reconcile their understanding of British appellate procedure with the states' use of common-law procedure at the trial level. The resulting problems were in part the product of the inherent incompatibility of the two systems, though inconsistency of the appellate courts' own approaches compounded the problems. This is most apparent in the courts' handling of the rules of evidence. In 1777, an *ad hoc* committee restricted evidence to be considered on appeal to that admissible under the rules of the common law, found credible by a jury, and transmitted by the trial court to the appellate tribunal in written form. At a later date, the Appellate Prize Court looked to the law of nations to determine what evidence was admissible: *see Miller v. Ingersoll*, 2 U.S. (2 Dall.) 19, 23 (1782). In general, the rules regarding what constituted the "record" of the trial court remained in flux throughout the Revolution. Moreover, the appellate judges often decided appeals in the absence of written briefs. As Bourguignon notes:

> "But... written arguments for an appeal and assignments of error were exceptions. Ordinarily the judges of appeals received only the records from the court below, depositions, interrogatories, and ship papers. Whatever legal argument

ity to find a way to reconcile the use of juries with the traditional practice—derived from the law of nations—of allowing appellate courts the power to review facts.[76] Within a few short years, this issue would resurface at the Constitutional Convention of 1787, where critics of the proposed judicial system would charge that to be functional, it would have to allow the federal courts to run roughshod over the fact-finding role of the jury, the most time-honored and jealously-guarded of common-law institutions.[77]

> was presented by counsel was oral, not written."

BOURGUIGNON, FIRST FEDERAL COURT, *supra* note 15, at 211; *see generally Id.* at 209–214.

76. The national prize courts, as Bourguignon observes, attempted to model their scope of review upon their knowledge of British standards of review:

> "[The] introduction of new testimony on appeal shows that the appellate judiciary of Congress, like the Lords Commissioners for Prize Appeals, considered its proceedings a trial *de novo*, and did not feel constrained by the record of the court below."

Id. at 212. Unfortunately, the domestic legislation of the various courts conflicted with this approach, as was the case with the law of Pennsylvania, which regarded its juries' findings of fact as conclusive and beyond the scope of review. These incompatible positions led to the conflict between Congress and Pennsylvania's court of admiralty over the disposition of the case of the *Active* in 1779. *Id.* at 105, *generally* at 101–134.

77. The debate over whether federal courts should be allowed full *de novo* review—resulting in some cases in a reversal of a trial-court jury's findings of fact—is amplified in the "pamphlet-wars" that followed the Constitutional Convention. For opponents of Article III, its apparent disregard for the traditional role of the common-law jury became a rallying point. *See e.g.* Henry J. Bourguignon, *The Federal Key to the Judiciary Act of 1789*, 46 S.C.L. Rev. 647, 662–663 (1995) (hereinafter Bourguignon, *Judiciary Act*). The antifederalist "Brutus XIV", first published on February 28, 1788, succinctly summarizes the antifederalist position:

> "...I do not know what the advocates of the system [of federal jurisdiction in Article III], would make it mean, for I have not been fortunate enough to see in any publication this clause taken up and considered. It is certain however, they do not admit the explanation which those who oppose the constitution give it, or otherwise they would not so frequently charge them with want of candor, for alledging that it takes away the trial by jury, appeals from an inferior to a superior court, as practiced in the civil law courts, are well understood. In these courts, the judges determine both on the law and the fact; and appeals are allowed from the inferior to the superior courts, on the whole merits: the superior tribunal will examine all the facts as well as the law, and frequently new facts will be introduced, so as many times to render the cause in the court of appeals very different from what is in the court below."

Reprinted in THE DEBATE ON THE CONSTITUTION: FEDERALIST AND ANTIFEDERALIST SPEECHES, ARTICLES, AND LETTERS DURING THE STRUGGLE OVER RATIFICATION (2 vols., Bernard Bailyn ed., New York: Library of America, 1993), Vol. II, at 258, 260 (hereinafter Bailyn, DEBATE).

In 1781, Mansfield wrote that:

> Mutual convenience, eternal principles of justice, the wisest regulations of policy, and the consent of nations, have established a system of procedure, a code of law, and a Court for the trial of prize. Every country sues in these Courts of the others, which are all governed by one and the same law, equally known to each.[78]

For an assortment of reasons, however, the fledgling United States found that Mansfield's simple formula was not so easy to implement. First, as one would expect, a newly independent nation cannot establish its infrastructure overnight, with the result that *ad hoc* solutions and trial-and-error adjustments generally mark the early stages of national development. Such was clearly the case with prize jurisdiction, which Congress altered—both subtly and drastically—at intervals of every several months throughout the war. Secondly, Mansfield referred to the nations of Europe, where allocations of power—and with it jurisdiction—were long established. The new American republic, by contrast, was just beginning to grapple with its identity as a "federal" nation; the place of the states *vis-à-vis* the national government was not yet resolved, nor would it be (if ever) until long after the ratification of the Constitution. In roughly one decade, however, Congress had learned all too well the practical problems associated with a national tribunal hearing appeals from state courts applying the law of nations. When many of its members met in Philadelphia in the spring of 1787 to revise the structure of the national government, memories of the tensions between the Appellate Prize Court and the state courts of admiralty were still fresh on their minds.

Congress also had learned through painful experience that entrusting jurisdiction over the rights of foreigners to state tribunals could lead to diplomatic crises, which the national government would be powerless to avert. In 1779 in Massachusetts, the seizure of several Spanish ships provoked a severe response from the ambassador of France, potentially threatening the United States' relations with a powerful neutral nation.[79] Similar incidents occurred

78. *Lindo v. Rodney*, 2 Douglas' Reports 613, 616; 99 Eng. Rep. 385, 388 (K. B., 1781).

79. As France had formal diplomatic relations with the United States, the Spanish "observer" in Philadelphia utilized the French as intermediaries to lodge his nation's complaint. At the time of the incident, Massachusetts had not yet revised its law to permit Congress to review the decisions of its court of admiralty (*see supra* note 41 and text accompanying), thus rendering the national government's ability to intervene a practical if not a legal nullity. Faced with diplomatic embarrassment, Congress wrote to the king of Spain:

"That Congress have every possible disposition to cultivate the most perfect har-

later that same year when a neutral Portuguese vessel and a ship belonging to French allies were also seized.[80] These crises were not restricted to prize cases. In Maryland, an ordinary case for seamen's wages raised issues of treaty-interpretation as the defendant-shipowner invoked a bilateral agreement between the United States and the Netherlands to challenge the state admiralty court's jurisdiction. A diplomatic protest was averted fortuitously when the court held for the defendant on the merits.[81]

By 1787, the shortcomings of Congress' attempts to create a national tribunal to address appeals of one class of maritime cases were all too apparent to the delegates, judges, attorneys, and litigants who had had experience with

---

> mony with his Catholic majesty, and to encourage the most liberal and friendly intercourse between his subjects and the citizens of these United States; but they cannot, consistently with the powers entrusted to them and the rights of the states and of individuals, in any case, suspend or interrupt the ordinary course of justice."
>
> "The Control by appeal, in the last resort, over decisions on captures made on the high seas, which is reserved to Congress, enables them to preserve the Law of Nations inviolate, without the necessity of *arbitrary* Interpositions in Judicial proceedings, which are no means tolerable under the free Government of the United States."

CONTINENTAL CONGRESS, *supra* note 15, May 22, 1779, Vol. XIV, at 635. Unfortunately, while Congress asserted its right to act as an appellate court, the domestic law of Massachusetts did not yet recognize it as such. Crisis was averted when Massachusetts agreed to change its law. *See also Id.*, April 24, 1779, Vol. XIV, at 508–510 (in response to the seizure of the Spanish ships, a resolution of Congress admonishing all states to allow for appeals to Congress in prize cases.) For further discussion, *see* GOEBEL, ANTECEDENTS, *supra* note 60, at 167–168.

80. The Portuguese vessel, the *Nostra Senhora de Carmo e Santo Antonio*, was seized by the Virginia privateer *Phenix*, in which Robert Morris had in interest. A French ship was similarly seized by a privateer based in Pennsylvania. For Congress' handling of these matters, *see* CONTINENTAL CONGRESS, *supra* note 15, July 16, 1779, Vol. XIV, at 838–842; Sept. 4, 1779, Vol. XV, at 1021 (relating to the *Nostra Senhora*); Aug. 12, 1779, Vol. XIV, at 950–951 (regarding the French vessel).

81. The papers relating to this case, discovered in manuscript in the Maryland State Archives by Judge Niles, date from 1785, as instance litigation began to supplant litigation of prize matters on the Maryland court's dockets. *De Jungste Elias* arose out of a claim for seamen's wages under articles signed in Amsterdam for a voyage to America. The shipowner challenged the jurisdiction of the court, arguing that jurisdiction rested with the Dutch Consul, under a bilateral "Treaty of Amity and Commerce" and the "Usage and Custom of Nations", both of which would bar the filing of the case in an American domestic court. Nonetheless, the court found that it had jurisdiction and addressed the case on the merits. A crisis was averted when the judge held for the defendant-vessel. *See* Niles, *supra* note 34, at 23–34.

the various solutions with which Congress had experimented for a dozen years.[82] For one commentator, the essential flaw of their efforts could be summarized succinctly in two sentences:

> The weak point of this whole judicial system was this: that it necessarily depended upon state officers to enforce the judgment of the appellate tribunal when it reversed the decree of a state court. State courts refused to enforce the rights of property acquired under Federal decrees.[83]

Nevertheless, despite its failings, the Continental Congress' experiment with maritime jurisdiction yielded two results that would have ramifications for the future organization of the federal judiciary. First, judicial review by a national tribunal alone would not provide a sufficient guarantee of uniformity in interpretation of law. So long as each state remained free to create its own procedural and substantive law, a national appellate court—in the absence of national legislation binding on all states—could not single-handedly reconcile the disparate rules generated by the several states. Ultimately, this practical experience would join together with theoretical and ideological objections to block the suggestion that the state courts could function as inferior federal courts.[84] Secondly, experience had shown that diplomatic crises are best

82. Bourguignon, *Judiciary Act*, *supra* note 77, at 653; *also see generally* BOURGUIGNON, FIRST FEDERAL COURT, *supra* note 15, at 238–318.

83. Davis, Appendix, *supra* note 19, at xxix.

84. Of course, today when a federal circuit court reviews the decision of a federal district court in a diversity case, it will look to the decisions of the state's supreme court for guidance in interpreting the applicable substantive and, where appropriate, the applicable procedural law. Nevertheless, it is not the goal of federal diversity jurisdiction to promote uniformity of law on the national level. At issue instead is whether entrusting state courts with interpretation of national law, with appeal to a national appellate court, would provide an efficient system for guaranteeing uniformity in law. The suggestion that the state courts could function as inferior federal courts is frequently associated with John Rutledge, who first raised the possibility in the debates at the Constitutional Convention on June 5. Together with Madison's response, this exchange outlines the essential features of the debate—both pro and con—which would resurface with greater embellishment periodically from 1787 until the passage of the Judiciary Act of 1789. *See* 1 FARRAND, RECORDS, *supra* note 3, at 119, 124, 128; *see also Id.*, Vol. II, at 45 (July 18, Pierce Butler endorsing Rutledge's position). Rutledge's suggestion remained a force to be reckoned with long after the debates had concluded; as late as August of 1789, Oliver Ellsworth felt obliged to challenge it in a letter. *See* Letter from Ellsworth to Richard Law (Aug. 4, 1789), *reprinted in* THE DOCUMENTARY HISTORY OF THE RATIFICATION OF THE CONSTITUTION (18 vols., John P. Kaminski & Gaspare J. Saladino eds., Madison: The State Historical Society of Wisconsin, 1976–1997), Vol. IV, at 495 (hereinafter RATIFICATION).

avoided by entrusting to national tribunals matters involving foreign interests—particularly those grounded in rights conferred by the law of nations. The end of the Revolution brought an end also to the Continental Congress' experiment with national jurisdiction. Dissatisfaction with the structure of the Articles of Confederation, however, soon would reopen the debate over the scope of jurisdiction of national courts, and many of the delegates who arrived in Philadelphia in the spring of 1787 would have their experiences with the state admiralty courts and the national appellate prize courts fresh on their minds.

The Constitutional Convention

On May 23, two days before deliberations began in Philadelphia, James Monroe wrote to Madison an encouraging—but foreboding—letter, wishing success to the delegates:

> We all look with great anxiety to the result of the Convention at Phila. Indeed it seems to be the sole point on which all future movements will turn. If it succeeds wisely & of course happily, the wishes of all good men will be gratified. The arrangements must be wise, and every way well concerted, for them to force their way thro the States. The experience of the federal govt. hath taught Congress, or rather those who have compos'd it, the sentiments of the several States upon the subject of the powers it shod. possess. Yet it may, by some be thought doubtful, whether it hath not taught them that it will be almost impossible to adopt any plan that will have the concurrence of all the states; or if it hath, that will be of any duration afterwards.[85]

Monroe's sense of urgency was lost on many of the delegates. Monday, May 14, originally had been scheduled as the first day of the Convention;[86] nonetheless, on the appointed day, only the delegations from Virginia and Pennsylvania were present.[87] Madison wrote to Jefferson on May 15 that:

85. Letter form James Monroe to James Madison (May 23, 1787), *in* The Papers of James Madison (17 vols., Robert A. Rutland & William E. Rachal eds., Chicago: University of Chicago Press, 1962–1991), Vol. IX, at 416–417 (hereinafter Madison, Papers).

86. 1 Farrand, Records, *supra* note 3, at 1.

87. The Diaries of George Washington (5 vols., Donald Jackson & Dorothy Twohig eds., Charlottesville: University of Virginia Press, 1976–1979), Vol. V, at 237 (hereinafter, Washington, Diaries).

"there is less punctuality in the outset than was to be wished. Of this the late bad weather has been the principle cause".[88] Poor attendance and bad weather—the inauspicious beginning tried even the patience of the normally stoic Washington, who remarked that the delays "serve to sour the temper of the punctual members who do not like to idle away their time".[89]

By May 25, the delegates of nine states had arrived, and the Convention formally opened.[90] Among those present was forty-two year-old Oliver Ellsworth, one-time judge of the Connecticut Supreme Court, delegate to the Continental Congress, and drafter of the ordinance that had created the Appellate Prize Court.[91] Also present was Nathaniel Gorham of Massachusetts, a former president of Congress and soon to be elected chairman of the Committee of the Whole.[92] Governor Edmund Randolph had served as attorney general of Virginia under the governorship of Thomas Jefferson, in which capacity in 1778 he had advised Jefferson on the jurisdiction of the state's admiralty court in the matter of the "*Phoenix*".[93] While in Congress, James Wilson of Pennsylvania had served on the committee that drafted the prize-court resolution of November 25, 1775, and later served on Congress' first *ad hoc* prize committee as well as on the standing committee that replaced it.[94] He subsequently represented private parties, appearing as counsel before the Appellate Prize Court in six cases.[95] Together with John Rutledge of South Carolina, these men would constitute the Convention's

---

88. Letter from James Madison to Thomas Jefferson (May 15, 1787), *in* MADISON, PAPERS, *supra* note 85, Vol. IX, at 415.

89. Letter from George Washington to Arthur Lee (May 20, 1787), *in* THE WRITINGS OF GEORGE WASHINGTON, FROM THE ORIGINAL MANUSCRIPT SOURCES 1745–1799 (39 vols., John C. Fitzpatrick ed., Washington, D.C.: United States Government Printing Office, 1931–1944), Vol. XXIX, at 213.

90. 1 FARRAND, RECORDS, *supra* note 3, at 1–2; WASHINGTON, DIARIES, *supra* note 87, Vol. V, at 237–239.

91. FARRAND, FRAMING, *supra* note 6, at 34–35; *see also supra* notes 56–57 and text accompanying.

92. *Id.* at 32, 72.

93. *Id.* at 16; *see also* BOURGUIGNON, FIRST FEDERAL COURT, *supra* note 15, at 97. Randolph also had experience as counsel in a number of prize appeals. *Id.* at 329. For discussion of the "*Phoenix*" (alternately spelled "*Phenix*" in the records), *see supra* note 80 and text accompanying.

94. All told, Wilson is confirmed to have served as judge in at least ten prize appeals while a member of Congress. For discussion of Wilson, *see* FARRAND, FRAMING, *supra* note 6, at 21; BOURGUIGNON, FIRST FEDERAL COURT, *supra* note 15, at 45, 81, 91–92, 329–337.

95. *Id.* at 221–226, 244–251, 329. The matters in which he served as counsel included two high-profile cases, the *Resolution* (1781) and the *Lusana* (1783).

Committee of Detail,[96] the body largely responsible for the language of Article III as it appears in the Constitution today.

In comparison with the debates over representation in the legislative branch and over the scope of power allotted to the president, the judiciary received scant attention from the delegates. It would be a mistake, however, to assume that the relative lack of debate indicates disinterest.[97] From the beginning there was a latent division of opinion regarding the proper role of the national judiciary. Unlike the struggles over representation in Congress, however, dissention over federal jurisdiction simmered in the background, often overshadowed in the discussions by other topics. The rift over the structure of the legislative branch was fought openly, producing the "Great Compromise", which satisfied the delegates from both large and small states by apportioning voting-power by state in the Senate and by population in the House of Representatives.[98] On the other hand, the compromise that gave structure to the judiciary[99] was less a product of an imaginative process of give-and-take than a tacit acknowledgement of the factions' inability to reach a consensus. In the end, the Convention did not complete its task of allocating jurisdiction to a national judi-

---

96. For biographical information on Rutledge, *see* Farrand, Framing, *supra* note 6, at 30, 122. On the composition of the Committee of Detail, *see* 2 Farrand, Records, *supra* note 3, at 97–98.

97. Bourguignon, *Judiciary Act*, *supra* note 77, at 651–652.

98. The "Great Compromise", by which the delegates settled the structure of the legislative branch, arguably has received more scholarly attention than any other event in American political and legal history. Farrand provides perhaps the best two-sentence synopsis:

> "The substance of these proposals was: 1. That in the first branch each state should have one representative for every 40,000 inhabitants, counting three-fifths of the slaves, and that money-bills should originate in the first branch and should not be amended by the second branch. 2. That in the second branch each state should have an equal vote."

Farrand, Framing, *supra* note 6, at 99; for more detailed discussion, *see Id.* at 92–112.

99. The compromise by which decision on creating inferior federal courts was to be left to Congress first surfaced in the Convention on June 5, when—as an alternative to Rutledge's suggestion that the state courts act as federal trial courts—Madison and Wilson offered amended language providing "that the National Legislature be empowered to institute inferior tribunals". 1 Farrand, Records, *supra* note 3, at 125. To that point in the debate, Rutledge's suggestion held a slim majority. The alternative offered by Wilson and Madison, however, provided a broader scope of consensus. For additional discussion, *see e.g.* William R. Casto, The Supreme Court in the Early Republic: The Chief Justiceships of John Jay and Oliver Ellsworth (Columbia: University of South Carolina Press, 1995), at 11–12.

ciary; it instead delegated it to the first Congress.[100] Gouverneur Morris, who served on the Committee of Style, years later wrote of the Constitution:

> Having rejected redundant and equivocal terms, I believed it to be as clear as our language would permit; excepting, nevertheless, a part of what relates to the judiciary. On that subject, conflicting opinions had been maintained with so much professional astuteness, that it became necessary to select phrases, which expressing my own notions would not alarm others, nor shock their selflove, and to the best of my recollection, this was the only part which passed without cavil.[101]

Absent from the Committee's draft were provisions for creating federal trial courts and courts of appeals. Even the number of federal courts remained in doubt. General federal-question jurisdiction was still a century away. Despite the vague language, obvious *lacunae*, and intentional omissions, there was at least one point on which the delegates had agreed. Among the enumerated classes of cases falling under its aegis, the federal judiciary would have jurisdiction over "all cases of admiralty and maritime jurisdiction."[102]

The deliberations had begun in earnest on May 29. Though the delegates had been slow in arriving, many came well prepared. Governor Edmund Ran-

---

100. Speaking before Pennsylvania's ratifying convention, James Wilson offered the following observations on why the Convention of 1787 had deferred to Congress the task of completing the structure of the federal judiciary:

> "Time, reflection, and experience, will be necessary to suggest and mature the proper regulations on this subject; time and experience were not possessed by the Convention; they left it therefore to be particularly organized by the legislature—the representatives of the United States—from time to time, as should be most eligible and proper. Could they have done better?"

JONATHAN ELLIOT, THE DEBATES IN THE SEVERAL STATE CONVENTIONS ON THE ADOPTION OF THE FEDERAL CONSTITUTION, AS RECOMMENDED BY THE GENERAL CONVENTION AT PHILADELPHIA IN 1787 (2d ed., 5 vols., Philadelphia: J.B. Lippencott & Co., 1861), Vol. II, at 488 (hereinafter ELLIOT, DEBATES). For a modern commentator's perspective on the delegates' decision to leave the structure of the federal courts to Congress, *see e.g.* Bourguignon, *Judiciary Act*, *supra* note 77, at 123.

101. Letter from Gouverneur Morris to Timothy Pickering, Dec. 22, 1814, *in* 3 FARRAND, RECORDS, *supra* note 3, at 419–420. Even allowing for substantial exaggeration in Morris' self-proclaimed role in the drafting, the text of Article III facially reveals an intent to defer to Congress resolution of most of the difficult choices on the courts' structure, scope of jurisdiction, and relationship with the states' courts.

102. With minor variations in punctuation, the text of the Committee of Style's draft of Article III, sec. 2 is ostensibly the same as that of the final draft of the Constitution. *See* 2 FARRAND, RECORDS, *supra* note 84, at 600–601.

dolph, acting on behalf of the Virginia delegation, presented the Convention with a collection of "sundry propositions" for the "establishment of a national government".[103] On the same day, Charles Pinckney of South Carolina, at twenty-nine one of the youngest delegates, also presented his own "draught of a federal government".[104] Scarcely more than two weeks later, William Paterson of New Jersey presented a competing plan in response to that of the Virginian delegation,[105] and that same week, Alexander Hamilton provided a set of written provisions to accompany his speech on the structure of the government.[106] All of these plans addressed the structure of the federal judiciary, and all envisioned the creation of both a supreme court and a number of inferior federal courts. In addition, all made some provision for maritime jurisdiction. Article IX of the Virginia Plan provided that:

> ...the jurisdiction of the inferior tribunals shall be to hear & determine in the first instance, and of the supreme tribunal to hear and determine in the dernier resort, all piracies, & felonies on the high seas, captures from an enemy; cases in which foreigners or citizens of other States applying to such jurisdictions may be interested, or which respect the collection of the National revenue; impeachments of National officers, and questions which may involve the National peace and harmony.[107]

The New Jersey Plan, less ambitious in its departures from the structure of the Articles of Confederation than Randolph's plan, also provided for federal jurisdiction over prize, national revenue, crimes committed on the high seas, and

---

103. *Id.*, Vol. I, at 21–22.

104. As Pinckney's plan was presented late in the day, the delegates did not discuss it, though it was referred to the Committee of the Whole and subsequently to the Committee of Detail. *See* FARRAND, FRAMING, *supra* note 6, at 30, 71–72; 1 FARRAND, RECORDS, *supra* note 84, at 16, 23.

105. FARRAND, FRAMING, *supra* note 6, at 84; 1 FARRAND, RECORDS, *supra* note 3, at 241.

106. Hamilton's speech and decision to deliver his own plan to the Convention appear from the records to have been motivated by his vehement opposition to the New Jersey Plan presented by Paterson three days earlier. *See* FARRAND, FRAMING, *supra* note 6, at 87–89; 1 FARRAND, RECORDS, *supra* note 3, at 281–291 (text of speech), 291–293 (text of plan).

107. 1 FARRAND, RECORDS, *supra* note 3, at 22. Farrand notes that Madison's surviving copy of the Virginia Plan contains slight variations in the language of Article IX, though it replicates the quoted language *verbatim*. For discussion, *see Id.*, Vol. III, Appendix C at 593–594.

matters involving foreigners, although the national courts were to exercise this jurisdiction only on appeal, thus preserving the state courts' power to hear such cases in the first instance.[108] Ironically, Hamilton, who had favored a central government with greater power than that contained in the Virginia Plan, likewise favored limiting national jurisdiction to appeals in matters involving national revenue and the claims of foreign nations or their citizens, though he did envision cognizance over prize cases in the first instance.[109]

Structurally, three of the plans—those of Virginia, New Jersey, and Hamilton—shared a common characteristic. Each granted enumerated spheres of jurisdiction over public-law matters, such as prize, piracy, and breach of the national revenue laws, while grouping national jurisdiction over private causes of action under the general heading of "claims of foreigners". There is a certain logic and intrinsic economy in this structure. The generation that had fought the Revolution perceived as essential the notion that the powers of government be carefully circumscribed. For federalists and antifederalists alike (though to differing degrees), this was best accomplished through a division of power among various branches of government, accompanied by expressly

---

108. Article 5 of the New Jersey Plan provided in relevant part:

> "...that the Judiciary so established shall have authority to hear & determine in the first instance on all impeachments of federal officers, & by way of appeal in the dernier resort in all cases touching the rights of Ambassadors, in all cases of capture from an enemy, in all cases of piracies & felonies on the high seas, in all cases in which foreigners may be interested, in the construction of any treaty or treaties, or which may arise on any of the Acts for regulation of trade, or the collection of the federal Revenue..."

Id., Vol. I, at 244. Farrand gives both a series of variant readings and the "Sherman amendments", though these have no bearing on the language relating to jurisdiction. *Id.*, Vol. III, Appendix E at 611–613.

109. Article 7 of Hamilton's plan addresses the judiciary:

> "The Supreme Judicial authority to be vested in Judges to hold their offices during good behaviour with adequate and permanent salaries. This Court to have original jurisdiction in all causes of capture, and appellative [*sic*] jurisdiction in all causes in which the revenues of the general Government or the citizens of foreign nations are concerned."

Id., Vol. I, at 292. This version of the plan is the one that Madison transcribed in his own notes of the proceedings. Farrand notes that other extant drafts simplify the language to read "for the determination of all matters of general concern". *Id.*, Vol. III, Appendix F at 618. In addition, a personal draft that Hamilton declined to present to the Convention provides (in Article V, Sec. 1) generally for jurisdiction over all matters relating to foreigners with no mention of either national revenue or maritime matters. *Id.*, Vol. III, Appendix F at 626.

defined limits on the powers of each.[110] The enumerated spheres of jurisdiction enhance the specificity of circumstances under which the national government may hail a citizen into court. On the other hand, listing classes of private claims (such as torts, breaches of contract, etc.) individually would not have added to the specificity of the provision. These private actions were all suitable subject-matter for federal jurisdiction because all implicated the interests of foreign nations. If left in the hands of the state courts, any one of these claims could have provoked a diplomatic crisis that the national government would have been powerless to avert. By coupling national jurisdiction over a generic category of claims with provisions designed to insulate the judges from local political pressure, the drafters sought to protect national interests from local prejudices.[111]

Of all the plans submitted to the Convention, only Pinckney's opted for a different structure. When Justice Wayne wrote in *Waring v. Clarke* that the phrase "all cases of admiralty and maritime jurisdiction" was in the "the first plan of government submitted to the Convention", he clearly was referring to the Pinckney Plan, as the other three plans make no specific reference to general maritime jurisdiction.[112] Unfortunately, Pinckney's precise language was lost to history for more than a century. In 1847, the source available to Wayne

---

110. Both federalists and antifederalists were deeply influenced by Montesquieu's writings, and in particular by his emphasis upon separation of powers. *See* Kenyon, *supra* note 9, Introduction at lxxvi, lxxx. In contrast, the unwritten English constitution lacked express limitations on the various branches, relying instead on an informal system of checks and balances that had evolved over time. Examining writings that preceded the Revolution, historian Bernard Bailyn traces a common thread of distrust for institutions that lacked transparent procedures and express limitations on their powers *vis-à-vis* the liberties of the citizen. Moreover, he maintains that the writers most frequently express this distrust through accusations of conspiracy. *See* BERNARD BAILYN, THE IDEOLOGICAL ORIGINS OF THE AMERICAN REVOLUTION (Cambridge, Massachusetts: The Belknap Press of Harvard University, 1967) at 144–159. With this environment in the formative years of their intellectual development, it would be natural for the delegates of the Convention to seek to establish clear lines of demarcation for separating the three branches of government from each other, for limiting their powers in relation to the states, and for defining the national government's relationship with the citizenry. This process was extended after ratification of the Constitution with the adoption of the Bill of Rights.

111. Hamilton's plan was quite specific in the need for independent judges, providing that they should hold tenure "during good behavior" and have "adequate and permanent salaries". 1 FARRAND, RECORDS, *supra* note 3, at 292. The independence of the judiciary was a recurring topic of debate at the Convention. *See e.g.* the debates of June 4, 1 FARRAND, RECORDS, *supra* note 3, at 106–110.

112. *Waring v. Clarke*, 46 U.S. at 457. For discussion, *see supra* notes 3–8 and text accompanying.

was the *Journal, Acts and Proceedings of the Convention.* This volume, edited in 1819 by then Secretary of State John Quincy Adams, had been published from extant manuscripts in compliance with a joint resolution by Congress. Adams made use of the papers salvaged by George Washington and deposited with the State Department in 1796, as well as an assortment of documents obtained from the collections of individual delegates.[113] In 1818, Pinckney had responded to Adams' request for a copy of his original plan by enclosing a draft which included a phrase that closely parallels the language quoted by Justice Wayne.[114] Nonetheless, contemporary witnesses—including the aging Madison and Rufus King—insisted that Pinckney had in fact sent a later draft, written as the Convention was coming to a close—after the work of the Committee of Detail and the Committee of the Whole had given the text much of its final structure.[115] For the next eighty years, scholars would debate the con-

---

113. 1 Farrand, Records, Introduction at xi–xiii; *see also* Jameson, *supra* note 8, at 112–115.

114. Article 9 of the plan that Pinckney sent to J. Q. Adams provides in relevant part:

> "The Legislature of the United States shall have the Power & it shall be their duty to establish such Courts of Law Equity & Admiralty as shall be necessary.... One of these Courts shall be termed the Supreme Court whose Jurisdiction shall extend...[t]o all cases of Admiralty & maritime jurisdiction..."

3 Farrand, Records, *supra* note 3, Appendix D at 600.

115. Jameson, *supra* note 8, at 114, notes that "the document had not been long published before its authenticity was privately disputed." Furthermore, the comments of King and Madison were brought to J. Q. Adams' attention shortly thereafter. In 1830, Adams recorded the following observations in his *Memoirs* regarding a conversation with Jared Sparks, who a short time earlier had spoken with Madison about the Pinckney Plan:

> "[Madison] said there was a paper presented by [Pinckney] to the Convention, but it was nothing like the paper now in the book. It was referred to the committee who drafted the plan of the Constitution, and was never afterwards in any manner referred to or noticed. In the book it has the appearance as if it was the original draft of the Constitution itself, and as if that which was finally adopted was Pinckney's plan, with a very few slight alterations. I told Mr. Sparks that Rufus King had spoken to me of C. Pinckney's paper precisely in the same manner as he says Mr. Madison now does; that it was a paper to which no sort of attention was paid by the Convention, except that of referring it to the committee, but when I compiled the Journal of the Convention, Charles Pinckney himself sent me the plan now in the book, as the paper which he had presented to the Convention; and with it he wrote me a letter, which obviously held the pretension that the whole plan of Constitution was his, and that the Convention had done nothing more than to deteriorate his work by altering some of his favorite provisions. Sparks said Mr. Madison added that this plan now in the book contained some things which could not possibly have been in Pinckney's paper, but which rose out of the debates upon the plan of Constitution reported by the com-

tent of missing document that Pinckney placed before the Convention on May 29.[116]

---

mittee. He conjectured that Mr. Pinckney's memory failed him, and that, instead of a copy of the paper which he did present, he had found a copy of the plan reported by the committee with interlined amendments, perhaps proposed by him, and, at a distance of more than thirty years, had imagined it was his own plan."

JOHN QUINCY ADAMS, MEMOIRS, Vol. VIII, at 224–225 (May 4, 1830), *reprinted in* 3 FARRAND, RECORDS, *supra* note 3, Appendix A, No. CCCLXVIII, at 481–482; *see also* letters of Madison: (from Jared Sparks, May 5, 1830) *Id.*, Appendix A, No. CCCLXIX, at 482, (to Jared Sparks, Nov. 25, 1831) *Id.*, Appendix A, No. CCCLXXXVII, at 514–515, (to Thomas S. Grimke, Jan. 6, 1835) *Id.*, Appendix A, No. CCCXCIII at 531–533, (to W. A. Duer, June 5, 1835) *Id.*, Appendix A, No. CCCXCVII, at 534–537. With nearly a century of hindsight, Jameson observes that: "the so-called Pinckney plan [submitted to J.Q. Adams in 1818] consists of the report of the Committee of Detail, as brought in on August 6, minus some of its lesser features, and plus some of those of the real plan." Jameson, *supra* note 8, at 124.

116. Some of this scholarly attention was focused upon attempts to reconstruct the original Pinckney Plan from a pamphlet that Pinckney published within weeks of the conclusion of the Convention. (For examples, *see* Jameson, *supra* note 8, at 120.) This pamphlet, released under the title *"Observations on the Plan of Government Submitted to the Federal Convention, in Philadelphia, on the 28th* [*sic: i.e.* 29th] *of May, 1787, by Mr. Charles Pinckney"*, was not placed in its final form until after the Convention had concluded, and speculation persists regarding how much of it was written before the proceedings convened. The pamphlet bore a striking resemblance to the final draft of the Constitution. When it appeared in print on October 14, Madison sent a copy to Washington. Their correspondence reveals that both men were of the opinion that Pinckney had written the pamphlet after the Constitution was in final form in order to claim credit for an undue level of influence over the proceedings. *Id.* at 115–116. Nonetheless, not all scholars are prepared to dismiss the pamphlet offhandedly. Both Jameson, the discoverer of the manuscript of the original Pinckney Plan (*see infra* note 117), and Andrew McLaughlin have argued that elements of the *"Observations"* are unique among the surviving papers of the Convention, lending credence to the notion that some of Pinckney's ideas were incorporated into the final draft. *See Id.* at 120–121; *see also* Andrew C. McLaughlin, *Sketch of Pinckney's Plan for a Constitution, 1787,* 9 Am. Hist. Rev. 735, 736, 741–747 (1903–04) (hereinafter McLaughlin). Farrand reprints the *"Observations"*, which states in relevant part:

> "The 10th article [of Pinckney's Plan] gives Congress a right...of appointing Courts of Admiralty for the trial of maritime causes in the States respectively.... At present there is no Tribunal in the Union capable of taking cognizance...of questions arising on the law of nations.... As the power of deciding finally in cases of Appeal and all Maritime Regulations, are to be vested in the United States, the Courts of Admiralty in the several States, which are to be governed altogether by their Regulations, and the Civil Law, ought also to be appointed by them; it will serve as well to secure the uprightness of the Judges, as to preserve an uniformity of proceeding in Maritime Cases, throughout the Union."

3 FARRAND, RECORDS, *supra* note 3, at 106, 117 (text), at 602–603 (commentary).

In 1901, the missing Pinckney Plan came to light. A summary of the original plan was found among the papers of James Wilson.[117] In relevant part, it provided that Congress "shall have the exclusive Right of instituting in each State a Court of Admiralty, and appointing the Judges &c. of the same, for hearing and determining all maritime Causes which may arise therein respectively".[118] Although contemporary scholarship confirms that Madison and King were right in identifying the Pinckney Plan published in the *Journal* as a later draft, it is clear that the original plan shared a common characteristic with the *Journal*'s version. Rather than grouping all private disputes within federal jurisdiction under the heading of "cases in which foreigners are interested", it instead identified them by subject-matter: *i.e.* maritime cases. For a Convention struggling to build a consensus, Pinckney's plan had several advantages. First, it retained for the federal courts at least one set of private claims in which both parties were citizens of the United States. In effect, it preserved the Virginia Plan's provision for diversity jurisdiction for the class of cases for which arguably it would be least controversial. Secondly, by limiting foreigners' access to federal courts to maritime cases, Pinckney's formulation dodged the controversial issue of pre-war claims, particularly those related to real property.

Nevertheless, the Committee of the Whole opted neither for Pinckney's approach nor for those of the other three plans. Instead, after two weeks of deliberations, it settled on more general language:

> Resd. that the jurisdiction of the Natl. Judiciary shall extend to all cases which respect the collection of the Natl. revenue, impeachments

---

117. Jameson, *supra* note 8, at 126–131.

118. The reconstruction is Farrand's, based upon two documents in Wilson's papers, which he also reprints. 3 FARRAND, RECORDS, *supra* note 3, at 608. The first of the two manuscripts, in Wilson's handwriting with emendations by John Rutledge, reads as follows:

> "[The Senate and the House of Delegates in Congress] shall have the exclusive Right of instituting in each State a Court of Admiralty, and appointing Judges &c. of the same for all maritime Causes which may arise therein respectively."

Id., Vol. II, Committee of Detail Doc. No. III, at 134, 136. The second manuscript (identified as a draft of the Pinckney Plan by McLaughlin—*see Id.*, Vol. III, at 606) contains variations in language, but the essential plan for admiralty jurisdiction is the same:

> "The Legislature of U.S. shall have the exclusive Right of instituting in each State a Court of Admiralty for hearing and determining maritime Causes."

Id., Vol. II, Committee of Detail Doc. No. VII, at 157, 159. For discussion, *see also* McLaughlin, *supra* note 116, at 735–736; Jameson, *supra* note 8, at 117–132.

> of any Natl. Officers, and questions which involve the national peace & harmony.[119]

By comparison with the language of the four plans, "national peace and harmony" is quite broad. Assuming that it stops short of granting full federal-question jurisdiction, at the very least it would appear to encompass all claims arising under the law of nations. A more expansive reading would include all claims by foreigners as well as disputes between citizens of different states—a full-fledged vesting of diversity jurisdiction. Unfortunately, the surviving records reveal little of the delegates' intended meaning. The only debate that sheds light on the language is found in the exchange between John Rutledge and James Wilson on June 5, in which Wilson remarks that "the admiralty jurisdiction ought to be given wholly to the national Government, as it relates to cases not within the jurisdiction of particular states, & to a scene in which controversies with foreigners would be most likely to happen."[120] Wilson is vague on precisely which controversies in admiralty he means, as both prize cases and private disputes had the potential to trigger diplomatic crises. In addition, the plain language clearly extends beyond cognizance over admiralty matters. Nonetheless, it is clear that the practical experience with admiralty jurisdiction under the Articles of Confederation provided a compelling example of how suits involving foreigners could prove problematic for the national government if entrusted to state courts.[121] Wilson soon would have an

---

119. 1 Farrand, Records, *supra* note 3, at 237. This language is found in Article 13 of the version of the Committee's Report as reproduced in Madison's journal. Two other versions of the Report have survived, both preserved among the materials that Washington donated to the State Department in 1796. Farrand labels them Drafts "A" and "B". Lacking numbers for the various articles, it appears that Draft "A" is an earlier version of Draft "B"; moreover Draft "A" lacks a provision establishing the jurisdiction of the federal judiciary. The language of Draft "B", however, is identical to that of Madison's version, except only for minor variations in spelling and punctuation. *See Id.* at 224–228 (Draft "A"), 231 (Draft "B"). All three versions reflect Wilson's and Madison's compromise on inferior courts, namely that Congress should have the power to create inferior federal courts. *Id.* at 226 (Draft "A"), 231 (Draft "B", Art. 12), 237 (Madison's journal, Art. 12).

120. *Id.*, Vol. I, at 124.

121. If Madison's notes are accurate, it is likely that Wilson's remark refers to private actions as well as prize cases, as prize cases always would involve the rights of foreigners, rendering the words "most likely" superfluous. Wilson's remark is the first reference to admiralty jurisdiction in the debates; the issue resurfaces periodically throughout the proceedings. The exchange between Wilson and Rutledge occurs during a debate over whether the federal judiciary should include inferior federal courts, and Wilson raises the scope of jurisdiction as an example of why federal trial courts are needed. In rebuttal, Rutledge's ally Pierce Butler could offer only the observation that inferior federal courts would be too

opportunity to debate the point with his interlocutor further. On July 24, both he and Rutledge would be appointed by their fellow delegates to the Committee of Detail.

While we have the recorded observations of Madison, Yates, King, and a handful of others from which to glean an understanding of the work of the Committee of the Whole, the Committee of Detail had no chronicler. Our knowledge is limited to what can be gleaned from the various scraps of paper—working drafts, personal notes, and marginalia—which escaped destruction. We know from Madison's notes that the delegates referred texts of the various plans to the five-man panel, as well as the draft generated by the Committee of the Whole.[122] We also have the personal papers of committee-member James Wilson, together with a few papers in the personal collections of other delegates. Taken together, these documents do not provide a chronological account of the debates, and thus is left to inference the process by which creative insight, debate, and compromise produced a draft of a judiciary article. The Committee, selected on July 24, began its work two days later, giving the other delegates a ten-day rest as it assembled a draft from the various plans and resolutions that had been given to

---

costly to maintain. *Id.*, Vol. I, at 124–126. For how private disputes could involve the whole nation in a conflict with a foreign government, *see* Judge Niles' discussion of the unpublished decision in *De Jungste Elias*, *supra* note 81 and text accompanying.

122. 2 Farrand, Records, *supra* note 3, at 97–98. The various drafts apparently did not include the Hamilton Plan. Among the papers before the Committee of Detail was a draft generated by the Committee of the Whole, dated June 6. With regard to the judiciary, it provides:

> "Resolved That the Jurisdiction of the national Judiciary shall extend to Cases arising under the Laws passed by the general Legislature, and to such other Questions as involve the national Peace and Harmony. Resolved That the national Legislature be empowered to appoint inferior Tribunals."

Id., Vol. II, Document I, at 129, 132–133. The language preserves both the Wilson/Madison compromise on creation of inferior federal courts and the broad, general formulation of national jurisdiction embodied in the words "national peace and harmony". It also incorporates a concept that underlies both the debates at the convention and those that soon would follow in the states' ratifying conventions, namely that the jurisdiction of the federal judiciary should be coextensive with Congress' law-making powers. Wilson summarized this view succinctly in his state-convention's debates several months later:

> "I believe [judicial powers and legislative powers] ought to be coextensive; otherwise, laws would be framed that could not be executed. Certainly, therefore, the executive and judicial departments ought to have power commensurate to the extent of the laws; for, as I have already asked, are we to give power to make laws, and no power to carry them into effect?"

2 Elliot, Debates, *supra* note 100, at 469.

it.[123] Considering the monumental task facing the Committee, and the many individual issues that confronted it, it seems unlikely that Wilson and his four colleagues spent much of their time debating the structure of the judiciary. A single sheet preserved among Mason's papers offers our only substantial clue as to their deliberations. An undated rough draft in Wilson's handwriting reveals that the Committee had given form to the general language "questions which involve the national peace and harmony" by appending a series of enumerated classes of cases. The draft made clear that the federal judiciary would have jurisdiction over claims arising under laws enacted by Congress, over disputes between citizens of different states (a clear reference to the Virginia Plan's grant of diversity jurisdiction), and over disputes involving foreign citizens. In addition, inserted between the lines of Wilson's text in the handwriting of John Rutledge are the words "& in Cases of Admiralty Jurisdn".[124] A document found among Wilson's papers—also undated but appearing to be a later draft—expands Rutledge's phrase to read: "The Jurisdiction of the Supreme (National) Court shall extend...to all Cases of Admiralty and Maritime Jurisdiction..."[125] From this point onward to the end of the Convention, the formulation of federal admiralty jurisdiction would not change.

Rutledge did not record his reason for inserting the reference to admiralty jurisdiction into Wilson's draft, nor is it clear that Wilson himself authored the variation "all Cases of Admiralty and Maritime Jurisdiction" which appears in the Committee's later draft. It is clear that the earlier draft represents a transitional step between the Committee of the Whole's phrase "national peace and harmony" and the later draft, which jettisons references to "national peace and harmony" entirely in favor of specifically enumerated classes of claims.[126] Nonetheless, we cannot dismiss Rutledge's phrase "Cases of Admiralty Jurisdn" solely as the product of a move from the general to the specific. If this had been the case, it is likely that the Committee would have reverted to the formulations of jurisdiction that the various plans had employed. The Virginia,

123. *Id.*, Vol. I, at xxii–xxiii.

124. Putnam, *supra* note 8, at 468, identifies the handwriting as belonging to Rutledge. For the text of the document from Mason's collection, *see* 2 FARRAND, RECORDS, *supra* note 3, Committee of Detail: Document IV, at 137, 147.

125. For discussion, *see* DAVID W. ROBERTSON, ADMIRALTY AND FEDERALISM (Mineola, New York: The Foundation Press, 1970) at 14, n. 31. The complete text of this draft is reproduced in 2 FARRAND, RECORDS, *supra* note 3, Committee of Detail: Document IX, at 163, 172–173.

126. 1 FARRAND, RECORDS, *supra* note 3, at 237 (Committee of the Whole: Draft of June 13); *Id.*, Vol. II, at 172–173 (Committee of Detail: Document IX).

New Jersey, and Hamilton Plans all had enumerated categories of cases over which the federal courts would have cognizance, but their categories (expressed in each plan in virtually identical language) nonetheless were very different from the one Wilson and his colleagues ultimately selected. The Virginia Plan had specified that the federal judiciary would have the power to hear cases involving the national revenue laws, foreign parties, "captures from an enemy", and "piracies & felonies on the high seas".[127] The New Jersey Plan also had specified that the federal judiciary was empowered to hear cases concerning the national revenue, foreign litigants, "captures from an enemy", and "piracies & felonies".[128] Hamilton chose similar language, granting the federal courts jurisdiction over breaches of the national revenue laws, captures, and matters involving foreigners.[129] In formulating its own draft, the Committee of the Whole had voted on June 12 to remove express references to piracy and prize,[130] replacing them with a general grant of jurisdiction over cases affecting "national peace and harmony".[131] In re-instituting enumerated categories of cases, the five-man panel somewhat surprisingly eschewed the language on which three of the plans concurred in favor of a new formula, one that preserved cases involving foreign citizens as a category[132] but made no mention of prize or piracy.[133]

When the Committee of the Whole abandoned specific references to piracy and prize, we reasonably might assume that they intended for such cases to fall within the class of cases affecting "national peace and harmony". In short, there is no reason to believe that the delegates rejected the notion that national

---

127. *Id.*, Vol. I, at 22.

128. *Id.*, Vol. I, at 244.

129. *Id.*, Vol. I, at 292.

130. Madison's notes for June 12 state that:

> "It was moved and seconded to strike out the words 'all piracies and felonies on the high seas' passed in the affirmative"
>
> "It was moved and seconded to strike out the words 'all captures from an enemy' passed in the affirmative"

Id., Vol. I, at 211; *see also Id.* at 220 for Yates' account of the vote.

131. *Id.*, Vol. I, at 237 (Art. 13). It is worth noting that the Committee of the Whole eliminated all language relating to Congress' power to define piracy and make rules for capture.

132. *Id.*, Vol. II, at 186–187 (Art. XI, sec. 3).

133. While Article XI, governing the judiciary, makes no express mention of either piracy or prize, Article VII grants to the Legislature the power "[t]o make rules concerning captures on land and water [and] to declare the law and punishment of piracies and felonies committed on the high seas", *Id.*, Vol. II, at 182; Article XII forbids states from issuing letters of marque. *Id.* at 187.

jurisdiction should extend over these matters.[134] Thus arises the question of why the Committee of Detail would substitute the words "all cases of admiralty and maritime jurisdiction" for the power to adjudicate prize and piracy cases as enumerated in three of the plans. It is clear that "admiralty and maritime" is not shorthand for prize, piracy, and private disputes involving foreigners, as the last is enumerated separately. This leaves two possible readings. Either the phrase simply replaces prize and piracy, or it reflects a conscious extension of the jurisdiction over private maritime disputes to those in which both parties are citizens of the United States. Largely through the efforts of one commentator, the former reading has become popular in recent years,[135]

---

134. When Wilson first argued for federal admiralty jurisdiction on June 5, Rutledge, Sherman, and Butler expressed their opposition only to the creation of inferior federal courts, not to federal appellate jurisdiction over maritime cases. The proposed trial courts, Butler contended, would be too expensive, and Rutledge maintained that the state courts could handle such cases in the first instance. *Id.*, Vol. I, at 124–125. If these three delegates were willing to allow appeals to a federal court in maritime cases, it is clear that they viewed these matters as different from disputes arising under state law.

135. This argument is most frequently associated with William Casto, *The Origins of Federal Admiralty Jurisdiction in an Age of Privateers, Smugglers, and Pirates*, 37 Am. J. Legal Hist. 117 (1993). Summarizing his thesis, Casto maintains:

> "There is no evidence, however, that the Founding Generation thought of maritime litigation primarily in terms of civil litigation. Eighteenth century Americans understood that admiralty courts adjudicated private claims, but this understanding was irrelevant to their decision to move maritime litigation from the existing state admiralty courts to national or federal admiralty courts. Surviving documentary evidence indicates quite clearly that the admiralty clause was placed in the Constitution and the federal admiralty courts were subsequently created to assure complete federal jurisdiction over three specific categories of litigation: prize cases, criminal prosecutions, and cases arising under the federal revenue laws. The evidence further indicates that the Founding Generation was unconcerned about the need for a national—as opposed to state—admiralty jurisdiction over private civil litigation."

Id. at 118. To interpret the work of the Committee of Detail, he utilizes—anachronistically—a report on the workings of the new federal judiciary drafted by Randolph in 1790, observing that "[t]he only direct evidence we have of the Committee's thoughts on this point is Randolph's Report in which he briefly noted that the Constitution embraced private maritime disputes but dismissed private disputes as of little national importance." *Id.* at 135. Randolph's report, a public document written three years after fact to serve the political ends of the moment, is unlikely to be the most objective of sources; furthermore, as Casto admits, even Randolph concedes that the Committee intended to grant instance jurisdiction to the federal courts, however much Randolph may minimize its importance to national interest. As for the contention that other evidence of the Committee's intent and rationale are lacking, these are supplied by various comments, correspondence, and pam-

though on closer examination it is not easily reconciled with either the debates at the Convention of 1787 or those of the states' ratifying conventions.[136] While

phlets produced during the debates on the Constitution, both in Philadelphia in the summer of 1787 and in the ensuing debates over ratification—in which the Convention's delegates (including the five Committee-members) had ample opportunity to clarify the language. For discussion, *see infra* notes 136, 142, 203; Chapter IV, notes 44–45 and text accompanying. Nonetheless, several recent articles and cases have adopted Casto's position, with some citing his article with approval. *See e.g. American Dredging Co. v. Miller*, 510 U.S. 443, 461 (Stevens, J., concurring); Bradford Clark, *Federal Common Law: A Structural Reinterpretation*, 144 U. Pa. L. Rev. 1245, 1353 n. 539, 1360 n. 568 (1996); LAURENCE H. TRIBE, AMERICAN CONSTITUTIONAL LAW (New York: Foundation Press, 2000), Vol. I, at 806 n.16.; Ernest A. Young, *Preemption at Sea*, 67 Geo. Wash. L. Rev. 273, 314–316 (1999). Martin Redish also argued against federal jurisdiction over private maritime disputes—on independent ideological grounds—though he has not gone so far as to maintain (as has Casto) that the original intent of the Framers was to exclude private maritime actions from the federal courts. *See* MARTIN H. REDISH, FEDERAL JURISDICTION: TENSIONS IN THE ALLOCATION OF JUDICIAL POWER (New York: Bobbs-Merrill Co., 1980) at 97–105. For a survey and analysis of recent case law and scholarly literature adopting Casto's position, *see e.g.* Joel K. Goldstein, *Federal Common Law in Admiralty: An Introduction to the Beginning of an Exchange*, 43 St. Louis L. J. 1337 (1999).

136. Farrand discovered a set of notes by Mason (dated August 27) that provide an example of the delegates' understanding of the term "admiralty". They contain a plan for the federal judiciary that would have vested federal jurisdiction in a supreme court and in "such Courts of Admiralty as Congress shall establish in any of the States." 2 FARRAND, RECORDS, *supra* note 3, at 432. Mason's proposal is significant for two reasons. First, it grants Congress the power to impose monetary limits on admiralty appeals to the supreme court, implying that private suits are envisioned. Secondly, by specifically incorporating the term "admiralty" to describe courts that were to hear private actions, it lends credence to the notion that the word was thought to encompass instance litigation. Notes of a similar proposal drafted on the same day—attributed to John Blair—incorporate the phrase "admiralty and maritime" in reference to courts with jurisdiction over private actions. *See* THE RECORDS OF THE FEDERAL CONVENTION OF 1787: SUPPLEMENT (James H. Hutson ed., New Haven: Yale University Press, 1987) at 244–245 (hereinafter FARRAND, RECORDS (Supplement)). For the debates on admiralty jurisdiction at the states' ratifying conventions, *see infra* note 203; Chapter IV, notes 44–45 and text accompanying. At this point one example will suffice. In the document by which New York ratified the Constitution on July 26, 1788, the delegates expressed their displeasure with the breadth of federal jurisdiction under Article III by including the following admonition to Congress:

> "...Congress shall not constitute, ordain, or establish any tribunals or inferior courts, with any other than appellate jurisdiction, except such as may be necessary for the trial of causes of admiralty, and maritime jurisdiction, and for the trial of piracies and felonies committed on the high seas..."

Bailyn, DEBATE, *supra* note 77, Vol. II, at 544. It is worth noting that the resolution makes a distinction between "admiralty and maritime" and "piracy". Moreover, New York's state admiralty courts exercised jurisdiction over instance matters as well as prize actions. *See*

piracy is inextricably connected with the sea and condemned by the law of nations, historically it was not an "admiralty" matter in the strictest sense. Parliament had removed it from the jurisdiction of the High Court of Admiralty during the Tudor period—at the zenith of the Court's power.[137] Moreover, the colonial vice admiralty courts—which had exercised a far broader sphere of jurisdiction than had the English Court—never exercised power over felonies committed on the high seas.[138] As for prize, it *was* within the jurisdiction of both the High Court of Admiralty and the colonial vice admiralty courts; in addition, the states' maritime courts clearly exercised jurisdiction over captures from the enemy. Nevertheless, as Mansfield once observed:

> The whole system of litigation and jurisprudence in the Prize Court, is peculiar to itself: it is no more like the Court of Admiralty, than it is to any Court in Westminster-Hall.[139]

In 1785, Judge Francis Hopkinson of Pennsylvania's admiralty court concurred, citing Mansfield as he explained that the procedural rules which a "prize court" applies are different from those of an "instance court of admi-

---

supra notes 44–46 and text accompanying. If the delegates drafted their resolution using the words "admiralty and maritime" in the same sense that these words would have been understood in their own state courts, it would appear that the limited role that they envisioned for the inferior federal courts nevertheless included instance cases.

137. The High Court of Admiralty lost jurisdiction over criminal cases under the reign of Henry VIII in 1537. *See* Thomas Lambert Mears, "The History of the Admiralty Jurisdiction ", *in* Select Essays in Anglo-American Legal History, Vol. II (Boston: Little, Brown, & Co., 1908) at 352. *See also* discussion, Chapter I, *supra* note 77 and text accompanying.

138. The Piracy Acts of 1700 and 1717—11 & 12 Will. III, c. 7 (1700) and 4 Geo. I, c. 11 (1717) respectively—granted the vice admiralty courts jurisdiction over piracy, though in the case of the former the courts were technically to sit in special sessions of Oyer and Terminer. The Act of 1717 provided further that the trials were to be by common-law procedures and by jury, thus removing the last vestiges of "admiralty" from the proceedings. Furthermore, there is no surviving record of an "admiralty" trial for piracy in the vice admiralty courts. With the exception of several cases of criminal assault, the colonial vice admiralty records are devoid of criminal cases. For discussion, *see* Chapter II, *supra*, notes 166–170 and text accompanying.

139. *Lindo v. Rodney*, 2 Douglas' Reports, 613, 614; 99 Eng. Rep. 385, 386 (K. B., 1781). For background of this case and *LeCaux v. Eden*, adjudicated the same year and raising the same jurisdictional issue, *see* The Mansfield Manuscripts and the Growth of English Law in the Eighteenth Century (2 vols., James Oldham ed., Chapel Hill: University of North Carolina Press, 1992), Vol. I, at 658–662.

ralty".[140] If the Committee of Detail had selected the phrase "all cases of admiralty and maritime jurisdiction" as a synonym for piracy and prize, it was a choice of words that strained the conventional usage and definitions of the day. Moreover, as we will see, such a reading is difficult to reconcile with the debates that followed in the states' ratifying conventions and on the floor of the first Congress.

As for the intended meaning of the phrase "admiralty and maritime", we would better understand it if we knew its origins. The debates provide few clues. Among all the delegates' proposed plans and records of their discussions, only one document employs similar language. Pinckney's plan, received and subsequently ignored by the Committee of the Whole, provided that the national legislature "shall have the exclusive Right of instituting in each State a Court of Admiralty, and appointing the Judges &c. of the same for hearing and determining all maritime Causes which may arise therein respectively".[141] Exactly how broadly Pinckney construed the phrase "all maritime Causes" remains a mystery. His only attempt at explanation, contained in his *"Observations on the Plan of Government"*, is likewise ambiguous. He defends the proposed grant of maritime jurisdiction as a means of ensuring uniformity in the interpretation of the law of nations, the civil law, and all "maritime regulations", language that could apply equally to instance, prize, or trade-act jurisdiction.[142] Nonetheless, it is significant that of the four plans presented to the Convention, Pinckney's alone fails to mention explicitly national jurisdiction

---

140. *See supra* note 64 and text accompanying; *see also* Bourguignon, First Federal Court, *supra* note 15, at 150–151.

141. 3 Farrand, Records, *supra* note 3, at 608 (Farrand's reconstruction); *see also Id.*, Vol. II, Committee of Detail: Document III, at 136 (summary of original Pinckney Plan in Wilson's handwriting, containing language identical to Farrand's reconstruction). The second summary of the Pinckney Plan (also in Wilson's handwriting) provides a variant reading for the section on federal jurisdiction: "The Legislature of the U.S. shall have the exclusive Right of instituting in each State a Court of Admiralty for hearing and determining maritime Causes." *Id.*, Vol. II, Committee of Detail: Document VII, at 159.

142. 3 Farrand, Records, *supra* note 3, Appendix A, No. CXIX, at 117. With regard to the admiralty courts' jurisdiction over "Maritime Regulations", it is worth noting that the original Pinckney Plan made reference both to admiralty courts and to another federal tribunal, which was to have exclusive cognizance over "Regulations of U.S. concerning Trade or Revenue". *Id.*, Vol. III, at 608. Assuming that Pinckney remained consistent in his views between the time of the drafting of the original plan and the writing of the *"Observations"* (admittedly a questionable assumption), it appears that the "Maritime Regulations" of the plan are not Trade Acts, leaving open the possibility (or reinforcing the notion) that Pinckney was referring to substantive maritime law—thus permitting private parties to file instance actions in the federal admiralty courts.

over matters in which foreign citizens are parties. On this point, the final draft of the Constitution reflects the position of the Virginia, New Jersey, and Hamilton Plans.[143] If "all maritime Causes" is read to mean instance actions involving foreigners as well as prize cases, the apparent gap between Pinckney's thinking and that of his fellow delegates narrows considerably.

The debt that Rutledge and his colleagues owe to Charles Pinckney is difficult to measure. Pinckney's draft was referred to the five-man committee without the benefit of debate.[144] Madison later denied that the draft was ever consulted.[145] Pinckney's own subsequent conduct did little to help his cause; his transparent effort to claim undue credit for the lion's share of the Constitution aroused contempt from his contemporaries and historians alike.[146] Nonetheless, at least two commentators have argued that Pinckney's influence has been underrated. Franklin Jameson, the scholar who first identified Pinckney's proposals among Wilson's papers, observes that "the articles of the so-called Pinckney plan, so far as they extend... run in exactly the same order as those of the committee's report."[147] He speculates that Wilson resorted to examination of the Pinckney and New Jersey Plans in drafting the section on the judiciary because the Convention's resolutions and the Virginia Plan on which they were based lacked sufficient detail on the organization and jurisdiction of the federal courts.[148] Andrew McLaughlin goes even further, contending

---

143. "The judicial Power shall extend to all Cases... between a State, or the Citizens thereof, and foreign States, Citizens or Subjects." U.S. Const. art. III, sec. 2.

144. 2 Farrand, Records, *supra* note 3, at 23; *Id.*, Vol. II, at 128.

145. *Id.*, Vol. III, Appendix A, No. CCCLXVIII, at 481–482; *see* discussion, *supra* note 115 and text accompanying.

146. Jameson, *supra* note 8, at 115–116. Jameson remarks further "that as a maker of the Constitution Charles Pinckney evidently deserves to stand higher than he has stood of late years, and that he would have a better chance of doing so if in his old age he had not claimed so much." *Id.* at 132. *See also* discussion, *supra* note 116 and text accompanying.

147. *Id.* at 127. After comparing the Pinckney Plan with the final draft of the Committee of Detail, Jameson adds:

> "Then let any person who has ever attended a committee meeting, and who remembers the process by which an important document was ground out, ask himself what the chance is that a document which was one of several put into the hopper on July 26 should, after such permutations as those above exhibited, emerge on August 6 as the final result of the committee's deliberations, with almost exactly the provisions with which it entered, and in almost exactly the same order."

Id. at 127–128.

148. Noting that Wilson's summary of the Pinckney Plan was found between pages of the resolutions of the Committee of the Whole, Jameson explains his inference:

that the Pinckney Plan contained roughly twenty original ideas that eventually were adopted into the final text of the Constitution.[149] Among these McLaughlin counts "cases of admiralty jurisdiction".[150]

Lacking personal correspondence or other direct indicia of how the committee members arrived at their decision to grant admiralty jurisdiction to the federal courts, we cannot know for certain whether Pinckney provided the inspiration. Circumstantial evidence, however, may provide clues as to why they opted for the particular formulation that they chose. When the Committee of Detail selected the phrase "all admiralty and maritime cases", they rejected as impractical the solution offered by the Committee of the Whole. To the extent that some members (particularly Rutledge) feared that federal trial courts would encroach upon the jurisdiction of the state courts, the phrase selected by the whole convention was certain to provoke alarm.[151] The language "questions which involve the national peace and harmony" was excessively vague, and an excessively zealous court could construe almost any matter as somehow affecting the national peace or harmony. Similarly, the five-man committee also rejected the somewhat more precise language of the Virginia and New Jersey Plans, which had called for federal jurisdiction over matters in which foreigners were parties. This bright-line rule no doubt would have limited the creativity of federal judges in determining whether the facts of a case

---

> "A possible reason for their being found at this point is that, in the main, they relate to what would naturally be the middle portion of Wilson's draft. They relate for the most part to the powers of Congress, of the Executive, and of the Judiciary. These three matters had received little elaboration in the Virginia plan or in the twenty-three resolutions of July 26. It was natural that Wilson, in essaying the task of amplifying this portion of the scheme, should draw off such passages as were germane to it from the other two documents [the Pinckney Plan and the New Jersey Plan] which, it will be remembered, had likewise been referred to his committee."

Id. at 128–129.

149. McLaughlin, *supra* note 116, at 735, 741–747, attempts to track Pinckney's contribution by comparing the text of the Pinckney Plan and Pinckney's *"Observations"* with the text of the Constitution. He concludes:

> "...we can say that Pinckney suggested some thirty-one or thirty-two provisions which were finally embodied in the Constitution; of these, about twelve were originally in the Articles of Confederation, and of course the fact that they were restated by Pinckney in his plan may not have had material influence in securing their adoption..."

Id. at 741. Those provisions not found in either the Articles of Confederation or in the other plans are listed at 739–740.

150. *Id.* at 740.

151. 1 FARRAND, RECORDS, *supra* note 3, at 124–128.

implicated national peace and harmony. In addition, both plans included jurisdiction over prize and crimes committed at sea. Nevertheless, when Rutledge (and perhaps several of his colleagues) opted to insert the phrase "cases of admiralty jurisdiction", they obviously believed that it added something which was absent from all of the other options suggested to that point. There are at least two possibilities—either one of which may have provided Rutledge with sufficient cause.

Both colonial experience and that of the Revolution had taught that "admiralty jurisdiction" involved procedures not employed in the courts of common law. The resolutions of the Continental Congress associate these procedures with the law of nations. Moreover, the vice admiralty courts, the work of which was familiar to many of the delegates, described these procedures as products of the *civil law*. Admittedly, neither the vice admiralty courts nor the state maritime courts that replaced them utilized procedures which would have passed muster at Doctors' Commons. Nevertheless, some practices—the *in rem* action, consolidation of claims, testimony by interrogatories, trials without juries, review of facts at the appellate level—were alien to the courts of common law. These features were, however, common to all American maritime courts, no matter how far they may have strayed from the details of the High Court of Admiralty's long-established practices. Unique procedures require specialized courts. The states had recognized the economy of having all maritime matters tried in the prize courts. These courts, already familiar with the procedures of the civil law (albeit in simplified or corrupted form), were better able to cope with the vagaries of maritime litigation—the civil arrest of ships, witnesses who were obliged to set sail before the trial date, etc.—than were their common-law counterparts. If such tribunals were to be created to hear prize cases, would it not be more efficient to open their doors also to other maritime matters, such as ships' surveys and instance cases? Had this not already occurred in the states, where local prize courts evolved in an *ad hoc* manner into full-fledged admiralty courts empowered to hear all manner of marine matters? The argument becomes even more compelling if one assumes that private maritime matters are governed by the law of nations. A specialized tribunal with expertise in the substantive law would be the logical forum for trying maritime cases. If these concerns were not enough, there is a second motive for opening the federal courts to private maritime suits. Dating back to the seventeenth century, there was some doubt as to whether the common law had cognizance over contracts signed on foreign soil. In the absence of federal jurisdiction, an American claimant might lack a remedy under the common law of his own state. In a fledgling nation dependent for its survival upon foreign trade, such shortcomings in the legal system would hardly be welcome. These concerns, seldom voiced in Philadelphia, would receive greater attention later at the states' ratifying conventions.

The Committee of Detail presented its draft on August 6; five days later the delegates submitted their own draft to the Committee of Style. It preserved the formulation of the Committee of Detail; the federal judiciary was to have jurisdiction over "all Cases of Admiralty and Maritime Jurisdiction."[152] There is no mention of the federal courts' cognizance over piracy or prize, although the draft expressly restored Congress' authority to regulate these matters.[153] The Committee of Style accepted the Convention's grant of maritime jurisdiction without amendment, save only for minor changes in punctuation.[154] On September 13, the Committee submitted its draft to the whole Convention; within four days, the document was presented for signatures. Ironically, Randolph, member of the Committee of Detail and drafter of the plan that the Convention had used as a basis for the draft which it sent to that committee, refused to sign.[155] In its final form, the judiciary article read as follows:

> The judicial Power shall extend to all Cases, in Law and Equity, arising under this Constitution, the Laws of the United States, and Treaties made, or which shall be made, under their Authority;—to all Cases affecting Ambassadors, other public ministers and Consuls;—to all Cases of admiralty and maritime Jurisdiction;—to Controversies to which the United States shall be a Party;—to Controversies between two or more States;—between a State and Citizens of another State;—between Citizens of different States;—between Citizens of the same State claiming Lands under Grants of different States, and between a State, or the Citizens thereof, and foreign States, Citizens or Subjects.[156]

---

152. *Id.*, Vol. II, at 576.

153. Article VII granted to Congress the power to "grant letters of marque and reprisal", to "make rules concerning captures on land and water", and to "define and punish piracies and felonies committed on the high seas". *Id.*, Vol. II, at 570. Rather than merely rubber-stamping the Committee of Detail's language, the Convention debated the provisions relating to piracy and the law of nations. *Id.*, Vol. II, at 312–316. Madison later would contend that the word "felony", "unknown to the law of nations", was an English common-law term that should not have been used as a replacement for "piracy". *Id.*, Vol. III, at 331–332. Nonetheless, the Convention opted to use "felonies" in its draft.

154. *Id.*, Vol. II, at 600–601.

155. *Id.*, Vol. II, at 646–647.

156. U.S. Const. art. III sec. 2. Section 2 provided further that:

"In all Cases affecting Ambassadors, other public Ministers and Consuls, and those in which a State shall be Party, the supreme Court shall have original Ju-

The Constitution settled several hotly debated issues while leaving others unresolved. Congress would have the power to enact legislation defining piracy and regulating captures during time of war. Individual states were prohibited from issuing letters of marque or reprisal.[157] Federal courts would employ juries in all criminal matters, but the requirement was disregarded for civil cases.[158] Revenue laws were to be uniform in all states, and states were forbidden to impose duties on ships of their fellow states.[159] On the other hand, the delegates ultimately accepted the compromise suggested by Madison and Wilson in the early days of the debates. Congress would determine whether to create inferior federal courts, how many were needed, and where they would be

---

> risdiction. In all the other Cases before mentioned, the supreme Court shall have appellate Jurisdiction, both as to Law and Fact, with such Exceptions, and under such Regulations as the Congress shall make."

It also provided that crimes would be tried by jury.

157. U.S. Const. art. I sec. 8, sec. 9.

158. The debate over whether to require juries in federal courts was in fact two-fold. Proponents—no doubt recollecting the handling of trade-act cases in the British vice admiralty courts—first wished to guarantee the right of trial by jury for all defendants. The second concern was for the treatment of juries' findings of fact on appeal. Traditionally, civil-law *fora* granted appellate courts the power to consider facts *de novo*. If the federal courts were to be constituted principally as tribunals for hearing prize and instance cases as well as those arising under the "law of nations", there was some concern that the courts' appellate procedures (designed primarily to review civil-law actions) would utilize the same *de novo* review for "common-law" actions, thereby rendering the jury's protection superfluous. Illustrative is the exchange between Gouverneur Morris and Wilson on August 27. Morris asked whether the proposed language would give the federal appellate courts the power to reconsider both law and facts in common-law as well as civil-law matters; Wilson remarked that it did. 2 Farrand, Records, *supra* note 3, at 431. In the end, the Convention reached a compromise. Criminal defendants would be entitled to a jury; juries would not be required for admiralty cases nor for any other matter arising under the law of nations. In addition, the appellate courts would have the power to review facts in all cases. *See* U.S. Const. art. III sec. 2.

159. U.S. Const. art. I sec. 9 contains the following provision:

> "No Preference shall be given by any Regulation of Commerce or Revenue to the Ports of one State over those of another: nor shall Vessels bound to, or from, one State, be obliged to enter, clear or pay Duties in another."

Also relevant to the issue of taxation is the second paragraph in Section 10:

> "No State shall, without the Consent of the Congress, lay any Imposts or Duties on Imports or Exports, except what may be absolutely necessary for executing it's inspection Laws: and the net Produce of all Duties and Imposts, laid by any State on Imports or Exports, shall be for the Use of the Treasury of the United States; and all such Laws shall be subject to the Revision and Controul of the Congress."

located.[160] Although desired by several delegates, the text made no express mention of a Marine Department to oversee private maritime business much as the Department of Commerce oversees the private sector today.[161] Similarly absent from Article I were explicit references to Congress' power to clear shipping channels of obstructions and to erect lighthouses and other aids to navigation.[162] The text also made no reference to the federal government's role in maintaining the navigability of inland waters, and it was silent even regarding the free navigation of the nation's rivers.[163] Admittedly, the Constitution did not forbid the national government from involvement in these activities, but any Congressional aid to navigation would have to be grounded in the Commerce Clause.

---

160. U.S. Const. art. III sec. 1 provides that:

> "The judicial Power of the United States, shall be vested in one supreme Court, and in such inferior Courts as the Congress may from time to time ordain and establish. The Judges, both of the supreme and inferior Courts, shall hold their Offices during good Behaviour, and shall, at stated Times, receive for their Services, a Compensation, which shall not be diminished during their Continuance in Office."

For a few members, even the Wilson/Madison compromise of allowing Congress to structure the federal courts was unacceptable. As late as September 15, George Mason scribbled the following on the back of his copy of the draft of September 12:

> "The Judiciary of the United States is so constructed and extended, as to absorb and destroy the judiciaries of the several States; thereby rendering law as tedious, intricate and expensive, and justice as unattainable, by a great part of the community, as in England, and enabling the rich to oppress and ruin the poor."

2 Farrand, Records, *supra* note 3, at 638. These themes—the inconvenience and expense of the federal courts and the opportunity that they offered for wealthier litigants to secure an advantage over their poorer adversaries—would resurface repeatedly at the states' ratifying conventions. *See infra* notes 188, 190–192, 212 and text accompanying.

161. As late as August 22, the Convention considered whether to provide for a Marine Department to advise the president on matters related to maritime affairs. 2 Farrand, Records, *supra* note 3, at 367.

162. The delegates debated this issue several times. *See e.g. Id.*, Vol. II, at 504.

163. One recent commentary has gone so far as to contend that Washington's own principal motive for attending the Convention had been to secure a national government that would "extend water transportation westward." *See* Stanley Elkins & Eric McKitrick, The Age of Federalism: The Early American Republic, 1788–1800 (Oxford: Oxford University Press, 1992) at 44. Even allowing for some exaggeration, the importance of inland waters as a political topic in 1788 is clearly established in the Convention's records. Hamilton raised the issue of navigation of the Mississippi River in his speech of June 18—*see* 1 Farrand, Records, *supra* note 3, at 308—and Randolph emphasized the importance of inland navigation in his opening remarks to the Convention on May 29. *Id.*, Vol. II, at 26. As late as September 14, both Franklin and Wilson favored inserting language granting the federal government the power of constructing canals. The suggestion was not incorporated into the text. *Id.*, Vol. II, at 615–616, 620.

Another crucial matter on which the Constitution remained silent was the source of substantive law to be applied in cases of admiralty and maritime jurisdiction—or in other cases not arising under the "Constitution, the Laws of the United States, and Treaties...made under their Authority".[164] Years later, Madison would deny emphatically that the Constitution incorporated the common law *sub silentio*.[165] The debates indicate that he believed Congress would supply a code of laws. While he defended the utility of allowing federal judges to interpret the code, it is unclear as to how far he was prepared to go in allowing them to create law interstitially by filling gaps in the enactments of Congress.[166] The opinions of others were more clearly expressed. Elbridge Gerry feared a strong federal judiciary and warned that allowing it the power to overturn Congressional statutes "was making States-

---

164. At issue here is the substantive law that the federal courts are to apply in diversity actions. During the debates in Virginia's ratifying convention, John Marshall turns to conflict-of-laws theory to answer the question. Federal courts will not create a separate body of substantive law, but rather will apply the law of the place where a contract is made to construe its terms. Debates of June 20, 1788, *reprinted in* Bailyn, DEBATE, *supra* note 77, Vol. II, at 730, 735. Admittedly, this does not guarantee that a federal court will always apply the rule of the state in which it is sitting, as it would in modern practice. (Moreover, it seems to imply universally accepted rules for conflict-of-laws.) Nevertheless, Marshall contends that federal courts will apply state law rather than rules of their own creation in diversity cases.

165. *See* Letter from Madison to Peter S. Duponceau (August, 1824), *in* FARRAND, RECORDS (Supplement), *supra* note 136, at 314. For discussion, *see also infra* Chapter IV, note 117 and text accompanying.

166. For discussion, *see e.g.* the debates of June 6, 1 FARRAND, RECORDS, *supra* note 3, at 138–139. There is much speculation regarding the degree to which jurists of the eighteenth century believed that judges "found" law rather than created it. One possible explanation for the more limited role eighteenth-century judges believed they enjoyed in creating law is grounded in the perceived nexus between positive law and natural law. One commentator provides a different explanation, tracing the more limited view of judicial law-making power to the seventeenth-century power-struggle between the Crown and Parliament:

> "[A]t this time the judges were fettered in their handling of legislation by the canons of statutory construction inherited from England. Under these rules, interpretation was less an art than an exercise in logic or grammar. If there had ever been much room for a court to indulge its own ideas of policy, it had shrunk to mere closet size once the hegemony of Parliament was settled. This was not without its effects in America, where legislatures were pretending to the same prerogative enjoyed by their prototype."

GOEBEL, ANTECEDENTS, *supra* note 60, at 228; *see also* discussion, *infra* note 169. Nonetheless, some delegates (such as Gerry: *see infra* note 166) recognized the potential power that judges have in making substantive rules.

men of the Judges."[167] His concern applied equally to granting federal judges the power of creating substantive rules independent of the will of Congress. The following year, Hamilton would respond in *Federalist No.* 78 that there is little danger of the judiciary usurping the role of the legislature, as judges "have neither Force nor Will, but merely judgment".[168] Startling as it may seem to modern sensibilities, his position was not out of step with the times. Scarcely two decades earlier, Blackstone had written that judges are "the depository of the laws; the living oracles" who "do not pretend to make new law", but instead infer latent, undiscovered rules through the intrinsic logic of the common law.[169] Nevertheless, even Hamilton concedes that judges may exceed their roles,[170] and

---

167. Gerry made his comment on July 21, as the Convention debated whether to allow the judiciary a power of veto over legislation parallel to that of the executive. *See* 2 FARRAND, RECORDS, *supra* note 3, at 73–75. Ultimately, the suggestion was rejected. This rejection, however, did not extend to judicial review, about which the Constitution remained silent. As one commentator explains:

> "The motion to associate the judicial in the veto was defeated 4–3, two states being divided. We cannot know what decided the issue—a rigorous view of separation [of powers], Ellsworth's intimation that the judges were free to employ standards other than the Constitution in the 'revisionary' process or the impact of Rutledge's final comment that judges ought never to give an opinion on law until it was before them. One thing remained: the judiciary was neither to meddle nor make with legislation except an issue of constitutionality should arise."

GOEBEL, ANTECEDENTS, *supra* note 60, at 228–229.

168. THE FEDERALIST, *supra* note 1, No. 78, at 523 (Alexander Hamilton).

169. WILLIAM BLACKSTONE, COMMENTARIES ON THE LAWS OF ENGLAND (4 vols., 1st ed., Oxford: Clarendon Press, 1765–1769; *reproduced in facsimile with commentary,* Chicago: University of Chicago Press, 1979), Vol. I, at 69–70 (hereinafter BLACKSTONE). The author elaborates on the notion that judges do not create law, but rather find it through an inferential process governed by reason:

> "And hence it is that our lawyers are with justice so copious in their encomiums on the reason of the common law; that they tell us, that the law is the perfection of reason, that it always intends to conform thereto, and that what is not reason is not law. Not that the particular reason of every rule in the law can at this distance of time be always precisely assigned; but it is sufficient that there be nothing in the rule flatly contradictory to reason, and then the law will presume it to be well founded. And it hath been an antient [*sic*] observation in the laws of England, that whenever a standing rule of law, of which the reason perhaps could not be remembered or discerned, hath been wantonly broke in upon by statutes or new resolutions, the wisdom of the rule hath in the end appeared from the inconveniences that have followed the innovation."

Id. at 70.

170. In anticipating a challenge to judicial review, Hamilton argues that the power is no more dangerous than those already granted to judges in the normal course of adjudication:

Blackstone admits that the judges' role is not always confined to a slavish adherence to *stare decisis*.[171] If judges in fact do create law, what constraints must they recognize? One constraint facing the eighteenth-century judge was the law of nations. Always present but ill-defined in the Continental Congress' resolutions on prize, the law of nations re-emerged intermittently in the Convention's deliberations. Wilson objected to language that would have given Congress the power to define the law of nations. Such power, he maintained, was beyond the unilateral competence of a sovereign nation.[172] As with other points of controversy raised at the Convention—the expense and (in)convenience of inferior federal courts, the use of juries in federal proceedings, and the need for uniformity in interpretation of law—the proper place of the law of nations in American jurisprudence would resurface in the states' ratifying conventions' debates.

On September 17, the Convention concluded its work. The mood was more cautious than enthusiastic as several delegates expressed last-minute

---

> "It can be of no weight to say that the courts, on the pretence of a repugnancy, may substitute their own pleasure to the constitutional intentions of the legislature. This might as well happen in the case of two contradictory statutes; or it might as well happen in every adjudication upon any single statute. The courts must declare the sense of the law; and if they should be disposed to exercise WILL instead of JUDGMENT, the consequence would equally be the substitution of their pleasure to that of the legislative body."

THE FEDERALIST, *supra* note 1, No. 78, at 525–526 (*emphasis in the original*). Thus in defending judicial review, Hamilton reveals a potential flaw in the Blackstonian view that judges merely find law. Courts *can* in fact make law; at issue to what extent they *should* exercise this power. As the thrust of Hamilton's exposition goes to checks and balances and separation of powers, one may infer that he believes that judges' law-making power will be held in check by the executive, who would refuse to enforce the judiciary's egregious overreaching. Where rules are made interstitially rather than in direct contravention of the will of Congress, however, inferring Hamilton's position is more difficult.

171. 1 BLACKSTONE, *supra* note 169, at 69–70.

172. Wilson's statement came late in the debates on September 14, in response to Gouverneur Morris' suggestion that Article I sec. 8 be amended to give Congress the power to "define" as well as "punish" offences against the law of nations. Madison summarizes Wilson's remarks as follows:

> "Mr. Wilson hoped the alteration would by no means be made. To pretend to *define* the law of nations which depended on the authority of all the Civilized Nations of the World, would have a look of arrogance, that would make us ridiculous."

2 FARRAND, RECORDS, *supra* note 3, at 615 (*emphasis in the original*). Morris defended his position, maintaining that the law of nations was "often too vague and deficient to be a rule." *Id.*

reservations before affixing their signatures to the new plan of government. Nevertheless, all but three—Rutledge, Mason, and Gerry—signed the document.[173] With its text complete and in final form, the Constitution emerged from the sheltered confines of Independence Hall into the open air—and public scrutiny. Despite the occasional heated debates, the Convention of 1787, with its small number of delegates working in secret sessions, was a comparatively tranquil prelude to the open deliberations, acerbic pamphlet-wars, and political maneuvering that characterized the process of ratification by the states.

General Debate over Article III in the States' Ratifying Conventions

On January 4, 1788, Connecticut convened its state convention in Hartford to deliberate on the proposed Constitution. Oliver Ellsworth arose before his fellow delegates to deliver the opening remarks. A strong national government, he insisted, was essential to defense.[174] He concluded his rather lengthy encomium on the virtues of the proposed system of government with a pithy summary: "The Constitution before us is a complete system of legislative, judicial, and executive power. It was designed to supply the defects of the former system; and I believe, upon full discussion, it will be found calculated to answer the purposes for which it was designed".[175] With minor variations, this scene played out in other states in much the same way throughout 1788. Not all delegates, however, were as optimistic as Ellsworth. In Massachusetts, Justus Dwight scribbled in his journal: "if any man advanced such a thing as this Constitution ten years ago, he would have been called a Tory."[176] As members of a generation immersed for nearly two decades in the rhetoric of the Revolution, it was natural that many participants in the process of ratification retained a strong suspicion of high concentrations of power. Government, if unchecked, posed the greatest threat to liberty. Defenders of the Constitution looked toward its intricate system of checks and balances for protection. Robert Lansing echoed the sentiments of many when he remarked:

173. *Id.*, Vol. II, at 641–650.

174. 2 Elliot, Debates, *supra* note 100, at 185–190.

175. *Id.* at 190.

176. Ratification, *supra* note 84, Vol. VII, Journal of Justus Dwight, at 1816.

> Scruples would be impertinent, arguments would be in vain, checks would be useless, if we were certain our rulers would be good men; but for the virtuous government is not instituted: its object is to restrain and punish vice; and all free constitutions are formed with two views—to deter the governed from crime, and the governors from tyranny.[177]

For many, however, checks and balances designed to prevent one branch of government from encroaching on the others provided insufficient safeguards to protect individual citizens from an overreaching central government.

As soon as the Convention concluded its work and released its final product, public opinion began to polarize. Newspapers published editorials—often written under pseudonyms—both for and against the new scheme of government. Longer pamphlets were printed privately and widely distributed. Surviving correspondence (at best a fraction of that actually exchanged) presents a lively picture of the debate among private citizens. Debates in the states' conventions, convened to ratify (or reject) the Constitution, became microcosms of the larger public dialogue. At the center of this dialogue was an issue often ignored in Philadelphia—the federal judiciary. The supporters of the Constitution, the self-styled "federalists",[178] defended the allocation of judicial power as a logical extension of Congress' law-making power. At the very least, it was necessary that the federal courts be granted jurisdiction over acts of Congress.[179] Hamilton outlined the federalists' vision of the place of the federal judiciary in the new national government:

---

177. 2 Elliot, Debates, *supra* note 100, at 295–296.

178. The term "federalist", first used by supporters of a more diffuse structure for the national government, later was co-opted by the advocates of strong central government during the pamphlet-wars that followed the Philadelphia Convention. *See* Merrill Jensen, The New Nation: A History of the United States During the Confederation 1781–1789 (New York: Alfred A. Knopf, 1950) at xiv. For how the self-styled "federalists" succeeded in expropriating the "democratic" rhetoric of their political opponents, *see e.g.* Gordon S. Wood, The Creation of the American Republic 1776–1787 (Chapel Hill: University of North Carolina Press, 1969) at 562.

179. The notion that the federal judiciary should have powers co-extensive with the law-making powers of Congress resurfaced throughout the debates in the states' conventions, as reflected in the comments of (among others) Wilson of Pennsylvania, 2 Elliot, Debates, *supra* note 100, at 469, and Davie of North Carolina, *Id.*, Vol. 4, at 156, 158. The notion retained an often-overlooked vitality even after the debates. Maeva Marcus has argued that John Marshall's opinions in cases raising issues of federalism were not a product of a dichotomy of nationalism and states' rights, but rather a reflection of the notion that the federal judicial power must be coterminous with Congress power to legislate. Origins of the Federal Judiciary, *supra* note 58, Introduction at 6.

> If there are such things as political axioms, the propriety of the judicial power of a government being co-extensive with its legislative, may be ranked among the number. The mere necessity of uniformity in the interpretation of the national laws, decides the question. Thirteen independent courts of final jurisdiction over the same causes, arising under the same laws, is a hydra in government, from which nothing but contradiction and confusion can proceed.[180]

Madison expounded on Hamilton's theme, concentrating on the two points that characterized the federalists' view of jurisdiction: the protection of national interests and the promotion of uniformity in legal interpretation in those cases in which national interests were implicated. Speaking before the Virginia convention, he encapsulated the federalists' position, providing in a few short sentences the essence of the arguments that would re-emerge repeatedly in longer form in all the debates, correspondence, and pamphlets throughout 1788:

> With respect to the laws of the Union, it is so necessary and expedient that the Judicial power should correspond with the Legislative, that it has not been objected to. With respect to treaties, there is a peculiar propriety in the Judiciary expounding them.—These may involve us in controversies with foreign nations. It is necessary therefore, that they should be determined in the Courts of the General Government. There are strong reasons why there should be a Supreme Court to decide such disputes. If in any case uniformity be necessary, it must be in the exposition of treaties. The establishment of one revisionary superintending power, can alone secure such uniformity.—The same principles hold with respect to cases affecting Ambassadors, and foreign Ministers.—To these same principles may also be referred their cognizance in Admiralty and maritime cases. As our intercourse with foreign nations will be affected by decisions of this kind, they ought to be uniform. This can only be done by giving the Federal Judiciary exclusive jurisdiction. Controversies affecting

180. The Federalist, *supra* note 1, No. 80, at 535. In structuring the ideal jurisdiction for the federal courts, Hamilton enumerates six categories of cases. These include jurisdiction over: 1) Congressional legislation, 2) constitutional questions, 3) cases in which the Unites States is a party, 4) cases involving the national peace, 5) admiralty and maritime cases, and 6) cases in which the state courts cannot be trusted to be unbiased. *Id.* at 534–536.

> the interest of the United States, ought to be determined by their own Judiciary, and not be left to partial local tribunals.[181]

Only one common federalist theme is missing from Madison's speech. In much of their rhetoric, the federalists were careful to stress that the federal courts would not interfere with the operation of the courts of the states because the sphere of federal jurisdiction was restricted to a handful of enumerated cases.[182]

As in Philadelphia the previous summer, some convention delegates and editorialists raised their concerns that the proposed federal courts would "swallow up" the jurisdiction of the state courts.[183] The federalists, however, generally met these attacks effectively by pointing to how carefully the Constitution

---

181. Ratification, *supra* note 84, Vol. X, at 1413–1414.

182. Typical is Hamilton's statement in the last of the *Federalist Papers* devoted to the judiciary:

> "[T]he judicial authority of the federal judicatures, is declared by the constitution to comprehend certain cases particularly specified. The expression of those cases marks the precise limits beyond which the federal courts cannot extend their jurisdiction; because the objects of their cognizance being enumerated, the specification would be nugatory if it did not exclude all ideas of more extensive authority."

The Federalist, *supra* note 1, No. 83, at 560. An anonymous editorial published by the *Connecticut Courant* on December 12, 1787, echoes Hamilton's sentiments, contending that the Article III's allocation of federal jurisdiction poses no threat to the state courts because the federal courts' jurisdiction is limited to enumerated classes of cases. *See* Ratification, *supra* note 84, Vol. III, at 487, 490.

183. Among the general objections to federal courts, those of delegates Maclaine, Spencer, and Locke at the North Carolina Convention provide good examples. All three expressed concern that the federal courts would absorb entirely the business of the state courts. *See* 4 Elliot, Debates, *supra* note 100, at 137, 160, 163–164, 169. In a letter to Adams (Jan. 5, 1788), an alarmed Samuel Osgood raises a novel point. In an argument harkening back to the times of Sir Edward Coke, he contends that legal fictions—reminiscent of the "Cheapside fiction"—will allow unscrupulous lawyers and federal judges to bring all cases within the ambit of the federal courts. *See* Bailyn, Debate, *supra* note 77, Vol. I, at 704, 706. Somewhat more convincingly, the author of "Agrippa V" (probably James Winthrop), expresses his fears that the federal courts will eschew state law entirely and adjudicate diversity cases under a body of federal common law of their own creation. *Id.*, Vol. I, at 474–476. Elsewhere, "Agrippa" defends the existing scheme of jurisdiction under the Articles of Confederation, contending: "It is now conceded on all sides that the laws relating to civil causes were never better executed than at present.... [C]an any reasonable man doubt whether he shall exchange a system, found by experience to be convenient, for one that is in many respects inconvenient, and dangerous?" "Agrippa I" (Nov. 32, 1787), *in* Ratification, *supra* note 84, Vol. IV, at 304–305.

had circumscribed federal jurisdiction.[184] More problematic were antifederalist criticisms of specific ambiguities in the text of Article III. Among these, four figure prominently in the debates. The Constitution made no specific provision for juries in civil cases. In addition, inferior federal courts (should Congress see fit to create them) would be costly to maintain. Furthermore, the new federal trial courts would not be geographically convenient for all litigants. Those financially able to absorb the costs of litigating in a more distant forum would have an unfair advantage over less affluent adversaries. The fourth objection was a variation on the third. Appellate *fora* would be even more distant, and the Constitution provided for appellate review of facts as well as law. Critics envisioned a system in which less pecunious litigants would be forced to incur the expense of a trial *de novo* far from home. While these four matters troubled the antifederalists alone, two others were troublesome to federalists and antifederalists alike. The Constitution had not specified the source of substantive law for those cases, such as maritime disputes and diversity cases, where federal statutory law might be lacking or inapplicable. In addition, the Constitution opened the door to *concurrent jurisdiction* without providing much guidance on how this would work in practice.

Of all the antifederalists' criticisms, those directed at the cost and convenience of the federal courts were both the most common and the most difficult for the federalists to answer. In December of 1787, an editorial in the New Hampshire Chronicle observed that: "From the great variety of cases to which this judicial power is to extend, it is apparent these courts must be numerous".[185] Numerous courts, as Pennsylvania delegate Whitehill admonished, would "be a great burthen".[186] At Virginia's convention, Patrick Henry echoed the same sentiment, saying: "I hope they will not have Federal Courts in every county."[187] Of course, the most effective way to reduce the costs of maintaining inferior federal courts was to limit their number. Nevertheless, it was impolitic for the federalists to suggest this solution. Fewer federal courts would reduce the costs to the federal government, but would increase the costs for

---

184. *See e.g.* Hamilton's remarks to the New York Convention, *in* 2 ELLIOT, DEBATES, *supra* note 100, at 353–356.

185. *See* "Cornelius" (*Hampshire Centinel*, Dec. 11, 1787), *in* RATIFICATION, *supra* note 84, Vol. IV, at 410, 415.

186. Pennsylvania Convention debates (Dec. 7, 1787), *in Id.*, Vol. II, at 515.

187. Virginia Convention debates (June 12, 1788), *in* Bailyn, DEBATE, *supra* note 77, Vol. II, at 687. Henry's concern was not only with the expense of the federal courts, but also with their impact on the state courts; he continued: "If they will, the State Courts will be debased and stripped of their cognizance, and utterly abolished."

litigants obliged to initiate or defend actions far from home. In a widely-circulated pamphlet, George Mason provided the model for the antifederalists' parade of horribles:

> The Judiciary of the United States is so constructed and extended, as to absorb and destroy the Judiciaries of the several States; thereby rendering law as tedious, intricate and expensive, and justice as unattainable by a great part of the community, as in England; and enabling the rich to oppress and ruin the poor.[188]

Similar statements soon followed in the states' conventions.[189] If federal trial courts would be inconvenient for many litigants, the same argument would apply *a fortiori* to federal appellate courts. In a letter to Randolph, Richard Henry Lee expressed his concern that if Congress fails to "regulate the right of appeal reasonably", that "the people will be exposed to endless oppression, and the necessity of submitting in multitudes of cases, to pay unjust demands, rather than follow suitors, through great expense, to far distant tribunals..."[190] Editorials echoed the same sentiment from Georgia[191] to Massachusetts, where one writer posed the question: "Would not such appeals serve to give every

---

188. George Mason, *"Objections to the New Constitution"* (*Massachusetts Centinel*, Nov. 21, 1787), *in* RATIFICATION, *supra* note 84, Vol. IV, at 288, 289.

189. *See e.g.* Pennsylvania Convention debates (Whitehill's remarks: Dec. 7, 1787), *in Id.*, Vol. II, at 514; North Carolina Convention debates (Spencer's remarks), *in* 4 ELLIOT, DEBATES, *supra* note 100, at 136.

190. Letter of Richard Henry Lee to Edmund Randolph (Oct. 16, 1787), *in* RATIFICATION, *supra* note 84, Vol. XIV, at 366, 369. Lee reprises his critique of the weaknesses of the proposed system for federal appeals four months later (Feb. 26, 1788) in a letter to James Gordon, Jr., in which he states that foreigners may carry appeals in cases of debt to "the supreme federal court, where distance and expense may ruin multitudes". *Id.*, Vol. XVI, at 210, 211–212.

191. The remarks of "Georgian" (*Gazette of the State of Georgia*: Nov. 15, 1787) are noteworthy not only for their inflammatory tone but also for recognizing that the expense of appeals might prove burdensome not only upon the poor, but upon the relatively well-to-do middle classes as well:

> "[T]he greatest injustice [would] be lawfully, nay constitutionally, committed by the rich against their brave fellow citizens whose only misfortune is to be, perhaps, not so rich as they, by dragging their lawsuits of any denomination and of any sum, however small, if they choose, before the GRAND TRIBUNAL OF APPEAL to which the poor will be unable to follow with their evidences and witnesses, and on account of the great expenses. Therefore, fellow citizens, pray restrain this encroachment so destructive to the inestimable rights the more numerous part of middle-circumstanced citizens now enjoy."

In Id. Vol. III, at 236, 241–242 (*emphasis in the original*).

advantage to the rich over the poor?"[192] The federalists were caught between Scylla and Charybdis. Nathaniel Gorham and Rufus King responded that the language of Article III mirrored that of the Massachusetts Constitution, and the legislature had not required litigants to travel across the state to defend appeals where small sums were at stake.[193] Madison, somewhat weakly, suggested that the problem might be solved by a nomadic Supreme Court, which would hold sessions in various locations throughout the country.[194] Hugh Williamson of North Carolina offered a stronger rebuttal:

> But we are told that justice will be delayed, and the poor will be drawn away by the rich to a distant Court. The authors of this remark have not fully considered the question, else they must have recollected that the poor of this country have little to do with foreigners, or with the citizens of distant States. They do not consider that there may be an Inferior Court in every State; nor have they recollected that the appeals being *with such exceptions*, and *under such regulations* as Congress shall make, will never be permitted for trifling sums.... Questions that are of a national concern, and those cases which are determinable by the general laws of the nation, are to be referred to the national Judiciary, but they have not any thing to do with a single case, either civil or criminal, which respects the private and particular concerns of a State or its citizens.[195]

Amid the usual litany of federalist arguments—protection of national interests, the availability of federal courts in each state, and the presumed foresight of Congress in setting monetary limits on appeals[196]—Williamson makes one novel observation. Ordinary citizens, for whom the costs of litigation in fed-

192. *See* "Candidus I" (*Independent Chronicle*: Dec. 6, 1787), *in Id.*, Vol. IV, at 392, 397.

193. This collaborative effort (*see Id.*, Vol. IV, at 186, 189), drafted in response to Gerry's speech in the Massachusetts Convention on October 31, 1787, was not published, although it does reflect the federalists' usual argument that Congress would not be either impractical or unfair in structuring the federal judiciary.

194. Virginia Convention debates (June 20, 1788), *in Id.*, Vol. X, at 1416–1417.

195. Speech of Hugh Williamson, delivered at Edenton, North Carolina (published by *New York Daily Advertiser*: Feb. 25–27, 1788), *in Id.*, Vol. XVI, at 201, 204 *(emphasis in the original)*.

196. William Paca, as delegate to the Maryland Convention, proposed an amendment to the Constitution that would have barred appeals to the Supreme Court where the amount in dispute did not exceed three hundred pounds sterling. In addition, echoing Samuel Osgood's fears (*see supra* note 183), he also sought to bar by constitutional amend-

eral courts might prove burdensome, generally are not involved in the classes of transactions over which the Constitution grants jurisdiction to the federal courts. Interstate and international sales contracts are the province of merchants and shipowners, for whom the comparatively higher costs of litigation were to be weighed against the federal judiciary's insulation from local prejudices. Moreover, where the contracts were with foreign parties, the additional costs of litigation were to be weighed also against the efficiency of specialized tribunals, staffed by judges conversant in the civil law and the law of nations.

The antifederalists' second line of attack on Article III centered on whether federal trial courts would employ juries.[197] In both the state-convention debates[198] and the press,[199] the opponents of Article III pursued the issue vigorously. The federalists had left themselves vulnerable on this point, as there was little agreement among them as to whether (or when) juries were necessary. Marshall maintained emphatically that juries would be used.[200] Hamilton was

---

ment legal fictions designed to "create" diversity jurisdiction. *See Maryland Journal* (April 29, 1788), *reprinted in* RATIFICATION, *supra* note 84, Vol. XVII, at 240, 241.

197. *See e.g.* Bourguignon, *Judiciary Act*, *supra* note 77, at 104.

198. *See e.g.* the comments of George Mason in the Virginia Convention debates (June 19, 1788), *in* Bailyn, DEBATE, *supra* note 77, at 727.

199. The examples are numerous; a few will suffice. *The Gazette of the State of Georgia* (Nov. 15, 1787) published a set of proposed constitutional amendments that included a provision for juries in all civil and criminal trials except impeachment. RATIFICATION, *supra* note 84, Vol. III, at 236, 242. Richard Henry Lee cited Blackstone in a letter to Randolph (Dec. 6, 1787), calling the privilege of trial by jury "most transcendent." *Id.*, Vol. XIV, at 366, 368. Shortly thereafter, he published a pamphlet entitled *"Observations on the System of Government"*, in which he reiterated his concern that federal courts would not utilize juries in civil cases. *See* PAMPHLETS ON THE CONSTITUTION OF THE UNITED STATES PUBLISHED DURING ITS DISCUSSION BY THE PEOPLE, 1787–1788 (Paul Leicester Ford ed., Brooklyn, New York, 1888) at 307 (hereinafter PAMPHLETS). A few antifederalist editorials even took the extreme view that juries should be employed in admiralty cases. This is the case with "A Democratic Federalist" (*Pennsylvania Herald*: Oct. 17, 1787). *in* RATIFICATION, *supra* note 84, Vol. XIII, at 386–392. This is also the case with "Cincinnatus III" (*New York Journal*: Nov. 11, 1787), the author of which quotes Blackstone and Mansfield in support of his position. *Id.*, Vol. XIV, at 124, 125–127.

200. In the Virginia Convention debates (June 20, 1788), Marshall asked: "Does the word Court mean only the Judges? Does not the determination of a jury, necessarily lead to the judgment of the Court? Is there anything here which gives the Judges exclusive jurisdiction of matters of fact? What is the object of a jury trial? To inform the Court of the facts. When a Court has cognizance of facts, does it not follow, that they can make inquiry by a jury? It is impossible to be otherwise." *See* Bailyn, DEBATE, Vol. II, *supra* note 77, at 736. Nonetheless, he acknowledged that some classes of cases (such as actions on replevin bonds) did not require a jury, noting that "[t]he Legislature of Virginia does not give a trial by jury where it is not necessary. But it gives it wherever it is thought expedient. The Fed-

less strident, frankly admitting his belief that juries should not be used in cases where the public peace was at stake.[201] James Iredell contended that the delegates in Philadelphia had not objected to use of juries in civil suits *per se*, but that they deferred to Congress only after they had failed to reach agreement on when juries were appropriate.[202] John Adams provided the most interest-

---

eral Legislature will do so too, as it is formed on the same principles." *Id.* at 739–740. Tench Coxe expressed similar sentiments in *"An Examination of the Constitution of the United States of America"*—his answer to R. H. Lee's pamphlet (*supra* note 199)—contending: "In trials about property in the foederal courts...there is nothing in the new constitution to prevent a trial by jury. No doubt it will be the mode in every case, wherein it is practicable." *in* PAMPHLETS, *supra* note 199, at 134, 149.

201. Constrained by the needs of propaganda, Hamilton's statements in *The Federalist* on the use of juries in federal courts are not entirely clear or consistent. In *Federalist No. 83*, he appears to equate cases concerning the "public peace" with some (though not all) cases in which the law of nations supplies the rule of decision. About this class of cases (in which he places all prize cases), he remarks:

> "Juries cannot be supposed competent to investigations, that require a thorough knowledge of the laws and usages of nations, and they will sometimes be under the influence of impressions which will not suffer them to pay sufficient regard to those considerations of public policy which ought to guide their enquiries. There would of course be always the danger that the rights of other nations might be infringed by their decisions, so as to afford occasions of reprisal and war. Though the proper province of juries be to determine matters of fact, yet in most cases legal consequences are complicated with fact in such a manner as to render a separation impracticable."

THE FEDERALIST, *supra* note 1, No. 83, at 568. Hamilton's most detailed statement on juries appears in *Federalist No. 83* (*Id.* at 558–562) and curiously makes no reference as to whether juries should be used in diversity cases. Elsewhere, however, he does note that it would be highly impractical to insist that federal trial courts sitting in admiralty apply the procedural rules (including the impaneling of a jury) that prevail in the various state courts of admiralty. *Id.* at 567. Obviously, the same rationale would apply equally to diversity cases. Nonetheless, in the opening paragraphs of *No. 83,* Hamilton goes to great pains to explain that the mere fact that the Constitution does not specifically require juries in civil cases does not imply it bars them. One might reconcile Hamilton's statements by assuming that he believes—as Adams and Iredell do (*see infra* notes 202–203)—that Congress should create uniform national rules for determining which classes of civil cases are eligible for employing a jury and which are not.

202. If Iredell is correct, the majority of delegates approved the use of juries in civil cases arising under acts of Congress or in diversity cases sounding in law. Controversy arose instead over whether to employ juries in admiralty or in diversity cases sounding in equity:

> "In some states, there are no juries in admiralty and equity cases. In other states, there are juries in such cases. In some states, there are no distinct courts of equity, though in most states there are. I believe that, if a uniform rule had been fixed by the Constitution, it would have displeased some states so far that they

ing analysis, explaining that the Constitution's silence on the use of juries in civil actions reflects the intention that they be used in some cases and not in others, such as admiralty, where (in Adams' opinion) the law of nations bars their use.[203] Adams was not alone in his belief that the law of nations required use of civil-law procedures in maritime cases.[204] While Iredell and Adams were confident that Congress would find a practical solution for when federal trial courts would employ juries and when they would not, many antifederalists were not. If Congress opted to create federal trial courts, they argued, such courts were needed primarily to handle maritime matters. Moreover, many agreed with Adams' view that the law of nations, and with it civil-law procedures, governed these matters. Furthermore, history provided them with no practical examples of courts that employed civil-law procedures in some cases

---

> would have rejected the Constitution altogether. Had [use of juries] been declared generally...it would have included equity and maritime cases, and created a necessity of deciding them in a manner different from that in which they have been decided heretofore in many of the states, which would very probably have met with the disapprobation of those states."

4 Elliot, Debates, *supra* note 100, at 170.

203. In a letter to Thomas Brand-Hollis (Jan. 4, 1788), Adams makes clear that the Constitution did not foreclose the use of juries in common-law diversity actions, but instead only in those cases in which the rules of procedure, supplied by the law of nations, would have rendered use of a jury awkward:

> "Our new constitution does not expressly say that juries shall not extend to civil causes.—Nor, I presume, is it intended, to take away the trial by jury in any case, in which you, sir, yourself would wish to preserve it.—Maritime causes, must be decided by the law of nations, and in conformity to the practice of the world. In these cases juries would not be willing to sit as judges, nor would the parties be contented with their judgment. Juries understand not the nature, nor the law of foreign transactions. We began, about twelve years ago, with juries in our courts of admiralty: but I assure you, the parties, witnesses, juries, judges, and all the world became so weary of the innovation upon trial, that it was laid aside by a new law with universal satisfaction. The examinations on interrogatories of witnesses and parties, in short the whole course of proceedings, as well as all the rules of evidence, must be changed, before juries could be introduced with propriety."

In Ratification, *supra* note 84, Vol. V, at 611. It is worth noting that Adams' reference to the "law of foreign transactions" indicates that he believes the constitutional language "admiralty and maritime cases" includes instance cases as well as prize.

204. *See e.g.* "Landholder VI" (*Connecticut Courant*: Dec. 6, 1787) stating: "In chancery courts juries are never used, nor are they proper in admiralty courts which proceed not by municipal laws, which they may be supposed to understand, but by the civil law and the law of nations." *in Id.*, Vol. III, at 487, 490.

and common-law procedures in others. Quite understandably, many antifederalists feared that Congress would structure inferior federal courts as civil-law tribunals for adjudicating disputes arising under the law of nations, only to have the courts apply the same procedures to other cases as well, such as common-law diversity actions and suits arising under acts of Congress.[205]

Closely connected to the debate over federal courts' use of juries was that over federal appellate review of facts as well as law. At the heart of antifederalist concern was the fear that federal appellate courts would be able to circumvent juries' findings by full review of facts *de novo*. The Declaration of Independence had specifically condemned the practice of transferring fact-finding from local juries to the judges of prerogative courts scarcely more than a decade earlier,[206] and for many already suspicious of centralized power, any suggestion that fact-finding be delegated to federal office-holders rather than one's neighbors naturally would provoke alarm. The dissention was exacerbated by the fact that the sphere of federal appellate jurisdiction was not yet established. The practice of reviewing facts at the appellate level, though limited in common-law systems, was commonplace in admiralty courts, where testimony was given through depositions and interrogatories rather than *viva voce*. In admiralty, there was no opportunity for the trier of fact to assess the demeanor of witnesses. Thus an appellate court, possessing a set of documents as complete as that examined by the court below, was at no disadvantage in reviewing the trial court's findings. Many antifederalists were willing to concede that appellate courts should have the power to review facts in admiralty, but balked at the notion that the courts should exercise the same power over common-law cases.[207]

---

205. *See e.g.* the "Democratic Federalist" (*Pennsylvania Herald*: Oct. 17, 1787), contending that admiralty procedure is derived from "foreign law", tainted with its ties to ecclesiastical law, and that if it were adopted, it would pave the way for the abolition of jury trials in federal court, even in common-law cases. *in Id.*, Vol. XIII, at 386, 388–389. While less vitriolic, the Minority Dissent of the Pennsylvania Convention (Dec. 18, 1787) expresses a similar fear that the use of civil-law procedures in admiralty proceedings would lead to their use in common-law matters as well. *Id.*, Vol. XIV, at 7.

206. The Declaration of Independence, para. 15, 20 (U.S. 1776).

207. From the extant records, it appears that the matter was most thoroughly debated in Virginia. On June 19, George Mason made explicit the distinction between appeals of admiralty and common-law cases:

> "A discrimination arises between common law trials and trials by Courts of Equity and Admiralty.—In these two last, depositions are committed to record, and therefore on an appeal the whole fact goes up; the equity of the whole case, comprehending fact and law, is considered, and no new evidence requisite. Is it so in Courts of common law? There evidence is only given *viva voce*. I know not a sin-

For many federalists, on the other hand, even the prospect of appellate judges reviewing facts *de novo* in common-law cases failed to arouse concern. Both Marshall and Hamilton defended the practice, with the former maintaining that appellate review of facts was necessary as a safeguard against local bias, particularly in matters relating to foreign diplomats.[208]

In the end, none of the antifederalists' overriding concerns about the structure of the judiciary in Article III were sufficient to prevent ratification. Nevertheless, the antifederalists' concerns arose out of the Framers' decision to vest in Congress the power to find solutions for the most controversial aspects of federal jurisdiction. Thus none of these issues could be resolved because the delegates did not yet know how Congress would opt to structure the federal courts. Instead, the arguments would be renewed in two years as the first Senate and House of Representatives met in Philadelphia. When they did, their views on admiralty jurisdiction would be instrumental in shaping the structure of the federal judiciary. Most of those views expressed in the first Congress were first heard in the debates of the states' ratifying conventions.

---

gle case, where there is an appeal of fact as to common law."

RATIFICATION, *supra* note 84, Vol. X, at 1404–1405. Continuing, Mason acknowledges that Congress may limit the appellate courts' fact-finding to the record, including transcripts of oral testimony, though he is quick to point out that there is no guarantee that Congress will do so. In the absence of such a requirement, he contends, parties may have to transport witnesses hundreds of miles to give testimony again. His proposed solution is to "confine the appellate jurisdiction to matters of law only, in common law controversies", leaving the courts free to review facts in maritime matters as was the usual practice. *Id.* at 1404. The following day, Patrick Henry takes up the same subject, noting that he would have no difficulty with appellate review of facts so long as it was limited to admiralty and chancery. When this power is extended to common-law matters, he warns: "The verdict of an impartial jury will be reversed by Judges unacquainted with the circumstances." *Id.*, Vol. X, at 1420.

208. Marshall's remarks were made at the Virginia Convention on June 20 in response to those of Mason (*see supra* note 207). *Id.*, Vol. X, at 1432–1433. Hamilton's views on the subject are found in *Federalist No. 81*. At the time of the writing of *The Federalist*, the structure of the federal judiciary had not yet been established, and Hamilton's arguments in favor of appellate review of facts include several possible solutions (*e.g.* the appellate court could impanel a second jury). He bases his rejection of amended language distinguishing appellate review of common-law matters from civil-law matters, oddly enough, upon an assumption that Congress would opt not to create federal trial courts. In the absence of federal trial courts, admiralty matters from the various states would receive disparate treatment on appeal, Hamilton contends, because some states chose to entrust fact-finding in admiralty to juries while others did not. *See* THE FEDERALIST, *supra* note 1, at 549–552.

Admiralty and the Concept of Concurrent Jurisdiction in the States' Ratifying Conventions

It is perhaps not surprising that the federalists generally supported the grant of admiralty and maritime jurisdiction to the federal courts. The grant was consistent with their overall desire for a stronger, more centralized government. Indeed, Hamilton selected it as the linchpin in his argument for the creation of inferior federal courts, observing that only "the most bigotted idolizers of state authority" would deny this jurisdiction to the federal courts.[209] The federalists' defense of the admiralty jurisdiction often was grounded in their desire for uniformity of law in matters affecting national interests.[210] Nonetheless, they were not alone in their support for vesting cognizance over maritime matters in the national judiciary—a political fact that was widely acknowledged in federalist circles.[211] Admittedly, a few antifederalists opposed the no-

---

209. The Federalist No. 80, *supra* note 1, at 538.

210. For Madison's views on the need for uniformity in interpretation of law where federal interests are at stake, *see supra* note 181 and text accompanying. Similar sentiments regarding national interests are expressed by the anonymous author of an editorial in the *Hampshire Gazette* (Jan. 9, 1788), who responds as follows to the contention of the antifederalist pamphleteer "Brutus" that federal jurisdiction will extend to "all civil causes except such as arise between citizens of the same state."

> "Very true! yet it ought to be attended to, that it extends to none but cases of national and general concerns: these cases are particularly stated and defined by the constitution, and [include] [a]ll cases of admiralty and maritime jurisdiction.... These are...cases to which the judicial power is extended. Let the impartial reader see and judge, whether there is great reason to apprehend that the business usually done in the state courts will be much affected or diminished; or, 'their power greatly abridged or their dignity eclipsed'."

Ratification, *supra* note 84, Vol. V, at 667, 668–669. The later work of "Brutus" (No. XIII: Feb. 21, 1788) reveals that the author of the editorial in the *Hampshire Gazette* misinterpreted his position; he has no objection to federal admiralty jurisdiction. *Id.*, Vol. XVI, at 172.

211. The federalists recognized that antifederalist opposition to Article III generally did not include its provisions for admiralty jurisdiction. As Timothy Pickering observes in a letter to Charles Tillinghast (Dec. 24, 1787): "The other cases [*i.e.* admiralty and maritime] enumerated in the constitution, seem to be admitted [by the antifederalists] as properly cognizable in the federal courts". Bailyn, Debate, *supra* note 77, Vol. I, at 289, 302. Instead, Pinckering contends, the real rift between the federalists and the antifederalists involves not maritime jurisdiction, but rather diversity jurisdiction and the question of whether juries should be employed in federal courts. *Id.* at 302. Other prominent federalists also took note of antifederalist support for admiralty jurisdiction. Both Wilson (*see* 2

tion,[212] while others wished to limit federal admiralty jurisdiction to appeals.[213] The remainder, however, favored some form of admiralty jurisdiction, which in turn would have required the creation of federal trial courts. At one end of the continuum were those, such as Spencer of North Carolina and the pamphleteer "Agrippa", who favored federal jurisdiction over prize and matters arising on the high seas.[214] At the other end of the spectrum, the *Gazette of the State of Georgia* published a suggested redrafting of Article III that preserved "admiralty and maritime" jurisdiction intact,[215] and the editorialist

---

ELLIOT, DEBATES, *supra* note 100, at 490) and Davie (*Id.*, Vol. 4, at 159) note the lack of antifederalist opposition to Article III's admiralty provisions in the conventions in Pennsylvania and North Carolina respectively.

212. *See e.g.* "A Democratic Federalist" (*Pennsylvania Herald*: Oct. 17, 1787), *in* RATIFICATION, *supra* note 84, Vol. XIII, at 386, 388–389. In an editorial in the *Baltimore Gazette* (Feb. 1, 1788), Luther Martin argued that granting maritime jurisdiction to the federal courts would increase the costs of litigation in actions for seamen's wages. *Id.*, Vol. XVI, at 8–10.

213. In the Virginia debates (June 19, 1788), Edmund Pendleton suggested that Congress would in all probability decide that the state courts could be used as inferior federal courts for admiralty trials, while federal courts would handle admiralty appeals. *See Id.*, Vol. X, at 1398.

214. In the debates in North Carolina (July 29, 1788), Spencer remarked that: "I wish them also [*i.e.* the federal courts] to have jurisdiction of maritime affairs, and to try offences committed on the high seas. But in the body of a state, the jurisdiction of the courts in that state might extend to carry into execution the laws of Congress. It must be unnecessary for the Federal Courts to do it, and would create trouble and expence [*sic*] which might be avoided." Bailyn, DEBATE, *supra* note 77, Vol. II, at 891. While Spencer's suggestion leaves open the possibility of instance jurisdiction over matters (*e.g.* collision) arising on the high seas, "Agrippa" suggests only public-law jurisdiction over prize and piracy. *See* "Agrippa" No. XII (Jan. 15, 1788), *in* RATIFICATION, *supra* note 84, at 720, 724–725; *see also* "Agrippa" No. XIV (Feb. 5, 1788), *in Id.*, Vol. V, at 863, 866. Though the identity of "Agrippa" is open to speculation, he is widely believed to be James Winthrop. *Id.*, Vol. V, at 303.

215. The author, who writes under the pseudonym "A Georgian", wishes to rewrite Article III to include guarantees for jury-trials in federal courts. *Id.*, Vol. III, at 236, 242. Given the tenor of the remainder of the editorial, it is significant that the author is willing to concede a full vesting of admiralty and maritime jurisdiction in the federal judiciary. On the whole, he is quite critical of the structure of the Constitution, although he concedes also that Congress should have the power to regulate maritime commerce:

> "[H]ad they added to the Articles of the Confederation a power to Congress, viz., to regulate foreign and internal trade, to lay and collect duties and imposts, uniform throughout the United States, to have the sole legislative power in maritime matters, to have coercive power to enforce the payment of the quota of each delinquent state, but to leave internal taxation and excise to the management of each individual state, the legislature thereof being certainly best acquainted with that important business, all would have been well and our federal government

"Cornelius" conceded that the nation needs national tribunals to adjudicate cases of "national importance".[216] As regards "cases affecting...admiralty and maritime jurisdiction", the moderate antifederalist pamphleteer "Brutus" remarked: "it is proper [that they] should be under the cognizance of courts of the union, because none but the general government, can, or ought to pass laws on their subjects."[217] Randolph, the drafter of the Virginia Plan who nonetheless declined to sign the final draft of the Constitution, echoed the same sentiments, remarking that: "national tranquility...and intercourse with foreign nations" requires a uniform maritime law, which can only be guaranteed by the federal judiciary.[218]

Particularly revealing of the widespread support for federal admiralty jurisdiction are the resolutions that accompanied the act of ratification in the various states' conventions. In some conventions, these resolutions took the form of recommendations for amendments to the Constitution, to be introduced into the first Congress pursuant to Article V. The structure of the federal judiciary had been argued at length in the Virginia Convention, with many speakers voicing strong objections to the language of Article III. In the end, the Constitution's supporters prevailed, but the "Resolutions" adopted by the delegates included the following suggested amendment to Article III:

> [T]he judicial power of the United States shall be vested in one Supreme Court, and in such Courts of Admiralty as Congress may from time to time ordain and establish in any of the different states: The judicial power shall extend to all cases in law and equity arising

---

> as good and fully adequate to its exigencies as could have been wished."

Id., Vol. III, at 237. This editorial is reprinted (with a one-paragraph introduction explaining its impact on the debate in Georgia) *in* THE COMPLETE ANTI-FEDERALIST (7 vols., Herbert J. Strong ed., Chicago: University of Chicago Press, 1981), Vol. III, at 129–136.

216. "Cornelius" (*Hampshire Chronicle*: Dec. 11, 18, 1787), *in* RATIFICATION, *supra* note 84, Vol. IV, at 410, 416–417.

217. "Brutus" No. XIII (*New York Journal*: Feb. 21, 1788), *in Id.*, Vol. XVI, at 172. It is worth noting that "Brutus" argues for only one fundamental change to Article III. That suggestion, the elimination of the right of citizens of one state to sue another state, later was incorporated into the Constitution as the Eleventh Amendment. It is widely believed that "Brutus" is the pseudonym of Robert Yates, the delegate to the Constitutional Convention today best remembered for his journal of the debates. *Id.*, Vol. XIII, at 411. Dissatisfied with the tenor of the proceedings, Yates left the Convention before it produced the final draft of the Constitution, and thus—unlike Mason, Gerry, and Randolph—he did not formally refuse to sign. *See* FARRAND, FRAMING, *supra* note 6, at 104–105.

218. Virginia Convention debates (June 21, 1788), *in* RATIFICATION, *supra* note 84, Vol. X, at 1451–1452.

> under treaties made, or which shall be made under the authority of the United States; to all cases affecting ambassadors, other foreign ministers or consuls; to all cases of admiralty and maritime jurisdiction; to controversies to which the United States shall be a party; to controversies between two or more states; and between parties claiming lands under the grants of different states.[219]

Thus in Virginia, a consensus on support for inferior federal courts extended no further than support for courts of admiralty. A short time later, North Carolina's convention passed resolutions of its own. It also proposed an amendment for limiting the jurisdiction of inferior federal courts to admiralty, incorporating *verbatim* the language of Virginia's convention.[220] The result was the same in New York, where the state's convention also recommended that Congress limit its creation of federal trial courts to courts of admiralty.[221] In Pennsylvania, the delegation as a whole did not publish proposed amendments to Article III. Nonetheless, opposition to the Constitution had been heated in some parts of the state, and the antifederalist faction in the state's House of Representatives had sought to block the convening of the state's convention. Having failed in their attempt, they published their objections to the Constitution in a Philadelphia newspaper. Somewhat surprisingly, even these most vehement opponents of the new form of government conceded that admiralty jurisdiction ought to be vested in national courts.[222]

---

219. *Form of Ratification, which was read and agreed to by the Convention of Virginia* (Amendments to the Constitution: Art. 14), *in* Bailyn, DEBATES, *supra* note 77, Vol. II, at 557, 563. In addition, the resolution waived the delegates' objections to the Supreme Court's power to review both law and fact in admiralty cases. *Id.* at 563.

220. State of North Carolina in Convention, August 2, 1788 (Amendments to the Constitution), *in Id.*, Vol. II, at 565, 570–571.

221. The Ratification of the Constitution by the State of New York, August 2, 1788, reads in relevant part:

> "That the Congress shall not constitute, ordain, or establish any tribunals or inferior courts, with any other than appellate jurisdiction, except such as may be necessary for the trial of causes of admiralty, and maritime jurisdiction, and for the trial of piracies and felonies committed on the high seas..."

in Id., Vol. II, at 536, 544.

222. The dissenters memorialized their objections in "An Address of the Subscribers Members of the late House of Representatives of the Commonwealth of Pennsylvania to their Constituents", which was published in the *Pennsylvania Packet* on October 4, 1787. In relevant part, it states:

> "The confederation no doubt is defective and requires amendment and revision, and had the convention extended their plan to the [*sic*] enabling the United States to regulate commerce, equalize the impost, collect it throughout the United States

While most federalists and antifederalists agreed that the federal judiciary should have cognizance over some classes of maritime disputes, the relationship between federal maritime jurisdiction and that of the states remained a source of controversy. In *Federalist No. 82,* Hamilton endorses concurrent jurisdiction of the state and federal courts.[223] Alexander Hanson, writing under the pseudonym "Aristides", also interprets Article III as creating a system of concurrent jurisdiction, of which he whole-heartedly approves.[224] At the other

---

> and have the entire jurisdiction over maritime affairs, leaving the exercise of internal taxation to the separate states, we apprehend there would have been no objection to the plan of government."

In The Complete Anti-Federalist, *supra* note 215, Vol. III, at 11, 15–16.

223. *Federalist No. 80,* while rhetorically brilliant, is (perhaps intentionally) not so clear as one would desire. Hamilton notes that: "the state courts will *retain* the jurisdiction they now have, unless it appears to be taken away in one of the enumerated modes". The Federalist, *supra* note 1, at 554. Thus on a cursory glance, it would appear that admiralty, as an enumerated jurisdiction under Article III, is removed from the cognizance of the state courts. Nevertheless, Hamilton emphasizes that state courts would have concurrent jurisdiction over "causes of which [they] have previous cognizance." *Id.* Moreover, he maintains that the state courts would be empowered to hear cases arising under statutes enacted by Congress. *Id.* at 555. Thus it would appear that the state courts would retain the power to hear diversity cases and cases involving foreigners, both listed together with admiralty among Article III's enumerated classes of cases entrusted to the federal courts. The dispositive point for Hamilton appears to be whether Congress has pre-empted state jurisdiction expressly: "[T]he inference seems to be conclusive that the state courts would have a concurrent jurisdiction in all cases arising under the laws of the union, where it was not expressly prohibited." *Id.* How these generalities relate to admiralty specifically remains a matter of speculation. It is clear that the states did in fact exercise admiralty jurisdiction. Presumably, in Hamilton's opinion, they could continue to do so:

> "I mean not therefore to contend that the United States in the course of legislation upon the objects entrusted to their direction may not commit the decision of causes arising upon a particular regulation to the federal courts solely, if such a measure should be deemed expedient; but I hold that the state courts will be divested of no part of their primitive jurisdiction, further than may relate to an appeal..."

Id. Clearly, Hamilton believes that Congress may bar the state courts from hearing certain cases arising under federal statutes, but what of the *lex maritima,* over which the states exercised "primitive jurisdiction"? Could Congress remove this from them by statute? It appears that the answer depends on whether the *lex maritima* is part of the law of nations and, if so, whether Congress has the power to change it. For discussion, *see infra* Chapter IV, notes 121–204 and text accompanying.

224. "Aristides", *"Remarks on the Proposed Plan of a Federal Government"* (Jan. 1, 1788), *in* Ratification, *supra* note 84, Vol. XV, at 517, 534, makes the following observations regarding the relationship between the state and federal courts:

> "The inferior federal courts, and the state courts, will, I conceive, have concur-

end of the political spectrum, Richard Henry Lee's "Federal Farmer" concedes that federal courts must have jurisdiction co-extensive with the law-making powers of Congress, but condemns concurrent jurisdiction as both inefficient and inordinately expensive for litigants.[225] The prospect of concurrent jurisdiction, held out as an olive branch by federalists to allay the antifederalists' fears that the new federal courts would absorb entirely the jurisdiction of the state courts, often produced the opposite effect. Many antifederalists, content to allow the federal courts to hear cases arising under congressional statutes, nonetheless feared overlapping jurisdiction even more than federal jurisdiction itself. As one anonymous editorialist remarked: "there never can be two several separate sovereign powers, holding a controul over the same persons, and the same property at the same time: one must be in subordination to the other."[226] Another alleged that "we shall be subject to all of the horrors of a divided sovereignty."[227]

> rent original jurisdiction in all the enumerated cases, wherein an appeal lies to the supreme court, *except only the cases created by or under the proposed constitution, in which, as they do not now exist, the inferior federal courts will have exclusive jurisdiction.*"

(*emphasis in the original*). As admiralty matters belong to those classes of cases that already existed at the time when the Constitution was drafted, they clearly fall within the ambit of concurrent jurisdiction. The author, Alexander Contee Hanson, was an ardent federalist and served both as a judge of the General Court of Maryland from 1778 through 1789 and as a delegate to the Maryland Convention in the summer of 1788. Despite his judicial credentials, several antifederalists, including "A Farmer" (*see infra* note 226) and fellow Marylander Luther Martin, found fault with his legal interpretations of the Constitution. *Id.*, Vol. XV, at 519. Nonetheless, the pamphlet was widely circulated, and serves as an excellent example of the federalists' optimism in assessing the viability of a system of overlapping jurisdiction.

225. First published October 10, 1787, the third in the series of Lee's "*Letters from the Federal Farmer*" makes the following observation regarding concurrent jurisdiction:

> "[The state courts] will have concurrent jurisdiction with the inferior federal courts in them [*i.e.* the private actions enumerated in Article III]; and, therefore, if the new constitution be adopted without any amendment in this respect, all those numerous actions, now brought in the state courts between our citizens and foreigners, between citizens of different states, by state governments against foreigners, and by state governments against citizens of other states, may also be brought in the federal courts.... I do not, in any point of view, see the need of opening a new jurisdiction in these causes—of opening a new scene of expensive law suits, of suffering foreigners, and citizens of different states, to drag each other many hundred miles into the federal courts."

in PAMPHLETS, *supra* note 199, at 275, 307.

226. "A Farmer" (*American Herald*: Jan., 14, 1788), *in* RATIFICATION, *supra* note 84, Vol. V, at 715–716.

227. "Agrippa V" (December 11, 1787), *in* RATIFICATION, *supra* note 84, Vol. IV, at 406, 408. For the identity of "Agrippa", *see Id.*, Vol. V, at 303; *see also* discussion, *supra* note 214.

The matter was debated in the states' conventions as well, with the federalists again offering concurrent jurisdiction as a means of alleviating geographic inconvenience and the antifederalists expressing concern that overlapping jurisdiction would create unnecessary expense and blur the lines of demarcation between the state and federal governments. In Pennsylvania, James Wilson assured his fellow delegates that citizens of other states or nations had the option of filing suit in the state courts as well in federal court.[228] In North Carolina, Governor Johnston told the delegates at the state convention:

> The opinion which I have always entertained is, that they will, in these cases...have concurrent jurisdiction with the state courts, and not exclusive jurisdiction. I see nothing in this Constitution which hinders a man from bringing suit wherever he thinks he can have justice done him.[229]

His colleague MacLaine concurred, maintaining that concurrent jurisdiction would not pose a threat to the states so long as claims that could be filed in federal court were such as could not affect the "internal policy and administration of the states."[230] Not all of the delegates, however, were convinced. Spencer summarized succinctly the sentiments of several of his fellow North Carolina antifederalists:

> I consider the concurrent jurisdiction of those courts with the state courts as extremely dangerous. It must be obvious to every one that, if they have such a concurrent jurisdiction, they must in time take away the business from the state courts entirely. I do not deny the propriety of having federal courts; but they should be confined to federal business, and ought not to interfere in those cases where the state courts are fully competent to decide.[231]

---

228. Pennsylvania Convention debates (Dec. 7, 1787), *in* 2 ELLIOT, DEBATES, *supra* note 100, at 491.

229. North Carolina Convention debates, *in Id.*, Vol. 4, at 141.

230. North Carolina debates, *in Id.*, Vol. 4, at 160, 163.

231. North Carolina debates, *in Id.*, Vol. 4, at 163–164. Spencer closes his argument with an observation that would prove prophetic for American admiralty jurisdiction: "Those courts will not take place immediately, and even when they do, it will be a long time before their concurrent jurisdiction will materially affect the state judiciaries." *Id.*, Vol. 4, at 164.

In Virginia's debates, Grayson added a further observation. Noting that the Constitution had not vested supreme power in one organ of government (as its unwritten English counterpart had vested in Parliament), he maintained that no branch of government was capable of resolving the conflict between the rival sets of courts which was sure to arise under a system of concurrent jurisdiction.[232] Nevertheless, not all antifederalists were adamantly opposed to concurrent jurisdiction. The *Minority Address* of the Maryland Convention expressly endorsed concurrent jurisdiction, stressing its potential benefits both for litigants and for the state-court systems themselves.[233]

In the end, opposition to the text of Article III was insufficient to block ratification. In general, the antifederalists had approved of federal admiralty jurisdiction *per se*, thus moving the focus of their opposition to other issues, such appellate review of facts and the absence of a provision mandating the use of juries in civil cases. These arguments, however, addressed only the courts' procedures; they did not question the wisdom of creating inferior federal courts. The strongest argument against creating federal trial courts voiced at the ratifying conventions was that they would be too expensive and impractical for litigants. The antifederalists' support for federal admiralty jurisdiction, however, had the effect of blunting their attack on the expense of cre-

---

232. Virginia Convention debates (June 21, 1788), *in* Ratification, *supra* note 84, Vol. X, at 1445. While Grayson does not mention it explicitly, his argument appears to be an oblique reference to the seventeenth-century struggle between the civilians and the common lawyers over equity and admiralty jurisdiction, which ultimately was resolved by Parliament in favor of the common lawyers.

233. The "*Address of the Minority of the Maryland Convention*" (*Annapolis Maryland Gazette*: May 1, 1788) presents an interesting case-study for antifederalist views on the federal judiciary. The report lists a series of proposed amendments to the Constitution, including a minimum value for disputes in federal court, mandatory impaneling of a jury where either party requests one, and an explicit ban on the use of legal fictions for the purpose of invoking federal jurisdiction. In general, the tone of the amendments reflects a distrust for much of Article III. Nevertheless, the authors applaud the prospective benefits of concurrent jurisdiction:

> "That in all cases of trespasses done within the body of a county, and within the inferior federal jurisdiction, the party injured shall be entitled to trial by jury in the state where the injury shall be committed; and that it be expressly declared, that the state courts, in such cases, shall have concurrent jurisdiction with the federal courts; and there shall be no appeal from either, except on matter of law; and that no person be exempt from such jurisdiction and trial but ambassadors and ministers privileged by the law of nations."

See Ratification, *supra* note 84, Vol. XVII, at 242. While the address approves appellate review of facts as well as law in revenue cases, it also provides for the state courts' concurrent jurisdiction over revenue cases if Congress opts to grant it to them. *Id.*

ating and maintaining inferior federal courts. If federal trial courts were necessary for hearing matters related to prize and piracy, the question of staffing them and paying their expenses would become moot. The expense, however onerous, was unavoidable. Thus the hurdle had been cleared; there would be inferior federal courts. At issue was only the extent of their jurisdiction. Ironically, the antifederalists' argument that federal trial courts would be too costly became the most compelling reason for extending their jurisdiction. The federal government, faced with the prospect of maintaining such courts, would have an incentive to make them as cost-effective as possible. Prize courts, staffed by judges with life-tenure whose salaries could not be diminished, would sit idly in peace-time, draining funds from the federal coffers while providing no useful service. The efficient solution was to establish them with jurisdiction that they could exercise in time of peace.

The debates in the states' ratifying conventions did little to resolve the other principal point of contention arising out of Article III. In their exuberance to defend the creation of inferior federal courts, the federalists put more effort into their rhetoric than into theory in expounding the virtues of concurrent jurisdiction. The antifederalists had raised a valid point. If both the federal courts and their counterparts in the states were to interpret the same body of law, how would uniformity of law—the ultimate goal of the federalists—be guaranteed? The states' ratifying conventions, convened only to vote "yes" or "no" on the Constitution, had not been forced to meet this issue head-on. That responsibility rested instead with the first Congress.

Chapter IV

"It is certainly to be wished that independent tribunals having concurrent jurisdiction over the same subject should concur in the principles on which they determine the causes coming before them. This concurrence can be obtained only by communicating to each the judgments of the other, and by that mutual respect which will probably be inspired by a knowledge of the grounds on which their judgments respectively stand. On great commercial questions, especially, it is desirable that the judicial opinions of all parts of the Union should be the same."

John Marshall[1]

Less than two years had elapsed between the closing of the Convention in Philadelphia and the opening of the first session of Congress in an adjacent room of the same building in 1789. Nonetheless, the political climate had changed greatly. William Maclay of Pennsylvania, a classically-educated country lawyer of modest means,[2] watched with dismay as his fellow senators' first debates centered on matters of titles and protocol. "Ceremonies, endless ceremonies, the whole business of the day", he remarked derisively in his journal.[3] Within a month, however, the Senate was hard at work debating a national tariff act,[4] and

---

1. Letter from John Marshall to Dudley Chase (Feb. 7, 1817), *reproduced in* Bradford R. Clark, *Federal Common Law: A Structural Reinterpretation*, 144 U. Pa. L. Rev. 1245, 1285 n. 181 (1996) (hereinafter Clark, *Federal Common Law*).

2. For biographical information, *see* The Journal of William Maclay: United States Senator from Pennsylvania 1789–1791 (1927 ed., Charles A. Beard ed.; *reprinted* New York: Frederick Ungar Publishing Co., 1965), Introduction at v–xiii (hereinafter Maclay, Journal). Maclay's Journal is also reproduced in its entirety in The Documentary History of the First Federal Congress of the United States of America: 4 March 1789—3 March 1791 (16 vols., Kenneth R. Bowling & Helen E. Veit eds., Baltimore: The Johns Hopkins University Press, 1988), Vol. IX: "The Diary of William Maclay and Other Notes on Senate Debates", at 3–402 (hereinafter First Federal Congress).

3. Maclay, Journal *supra* note 2, at 2 (April 25, 1789).

4. Maclay gives the most detailed surviving account of these debates on (May 25–June 17, 1789) in his *Journal. Id.* at 43–46, 49–78.

shortly thereafter it turned its attention to resolving the most controversial issue that the Convention of 1787 had delegated to it—the structure of the federal judiciary.[5] As one commentator has remarked, "The hot potato of whether to create lower federal courts had been consciously passed to the first Congress, and none of the heat had gone out of it in the intervening two years."[6] The intervening time, however, had changed the parameters of the heated debate. With the theoretical issues on the structure of government resolved by ratification of the Constitution, deliberations shifted to more practical concerns.[7] On the one hand, those opposed to a strong central government recognized that ratification had put to an end their preferred structure for the nation, and that survival of the United States depended upon making the Constitution work. On the other hand, the supporters of a strong national government recognized that their victory had been narrowly won, and approached with caution the task of creating a federal judiciary. Implicitly, each faction understood the importance of compromise, and the debates of the first Congress reflect not the strident tones of ideological opponents but rather a mood of reconciliation among politically savvy pragmatists.[8] The acrimonious

---

5. The debates commenced on June 22, 1789. *Id.* at 83.

6. Henry J. Bourguignon, *The Federal Key to the Judiciary Act of 1789*, 46 S.C.L. Rev. 647, 679 (1995) (hereinafter Bourguignon, *Judiciary Act*).

7. Noting the change in political climate since 1787, Marcus and Wexler contend that: "...those engaged in the drafting of the Judiciary Act paid less attention to the constitutional language, as ambiguous as it was, than to contemporary political necessities." Maeva Marcus & Natalie Wexler, "The Judiciary Act of 1789: Political Compromise or Constitutional Interpretation", *in* THE ORIGINS OF THE FEDERAL JUDICIARY: ESSAYS ON THE JUDICIARY ACT OF 1789 (Maeva Marcus ed., Oxford: Oxford University Press, 1993) at 13–14 (hereinafter ORIGINS OF THE FEDERAL JUDICIARY).

8. In assessing the tone of the proceedings in the first Congress, Julius Goebel characterizes their most noteworthy product, the Judiciary Act of 1789, as "an instrument of reconciliation deliberately framed to quiet still smoldering resentments." *See* JULIUS GOEBEL, JR., ANTECEDENTS AND BEGINNINGS TO 1801, VOLUME I *in* THE OLIVER WENDELL HOLMES DEVISE: HISTORY OF THE SUPREME COURT OF THE UNITED STATES (New York: Macmillan Publishing Co., 1971) at 458 (hereinafter GOEBEL, ANTECEDENTS). In his seminal article on the drafting of the Judiciary Act, Charles Warren characterizes it as a "compromise measure, so framed as to secure the votes of those who, while willing to see the experiment of a Federal Constitution tried, were insistent that the Federal Courts should be given the minimum powers and jurisdiction." *See* Charles Warren, *New Light on the Federal Judiciary Act of 1789*, 37 Harv. L. Rev. 49, 53 (1923) (hereinafter Warren, *Federal Judiciary Act*). Historians Stanley Elkins and Eric McKitrick note the caution with which the supporters of a strong centralized government approached the debates over the Judiciary Act:

"The fact was that a national judiciary as a branch of government was still

polemics of the pamphlet-wars had disappeared, replaced by the more subdued deliberations of a bicameral body whose members were—in the words of one commentator—"all federalists of varying shades and hues."[9] In this atmosphere of conciliation, it soon became clear that even the hard-line federalists would stop short of demanding that Congress vest in the federal courts the full extent of powers permissible under the Constitution.[10] In the end, the Judiciary Act of 1789 failed to please some of the more moderate federalists as well. Madison complained that it was "defective both in its general structure and, [in] many of its regulations."[11] Some modern scholars have agreed, with one characterizing the scope of Congress' grant of federal jurisdiction as "parsimonious".[12] Never-

---

> something of an abstraction.... Far more real to Federalist and Antifederalist alike were the already existing legal institutions of the states, going well back into colonial times and having been little altered by the Revolution.... Thus when it became a question of spelling out a federal system in detail, efforts to protect those interests and to resist encroachments upon state authority were only to be expected. Even the most thoroughgoing Federalists had little inclination to resist them, even assuming the alternatives to be self-evident, which apparently they were not. The natural drift, therefore, was toward conciliation."

See Stanley Elkins & Eric McKitrick, The Age of Federalism: The Early American Republic, 1778–1800 (Oxford: Oxford University Press, 1993), at 64 (hereinafter Elkins & McKitrick).

9. *See* Bourguignon, *Judiciary Act*, *supra* note 6, at 701.

10. For discussion, *see e.g.* Marcus and Wexler, observing:

> "[T]here is little indication...that those in Congress believed it necessary to legislate to the limits authorized by the language of Article III.... [M]ost of those in Congress acted on the assumption that the Constitution merely set the outer limits of their power. The Judiciary Act did grant federal courts jurisdiction over what are now called diversity cases, over cases in which the United States was a plaintiff, over admiralty cases, and over federal criminal offences. However, no provision was made for general 'federal question' jurisdiction in the lower federal courts, and the jurisdictional amount-in-controversy limitations restricted the federal courts to hearing only the most momentous cases within the universe defined by Article III."

"Judiciary Act", *in* Origins of the Federal Judiciary, *supra* note 7, at 16.

11. Letter from James Madison to Edmund Pendleton (Sept. 14, 1789), *quoted in* Goebel, Antecedents, *supra* note 8, at 507–508. It appears that Madison's remark was not aimed at admiralty jurisdiction or the Saving-to-Suitors Clause. For discussion of the context of his remark, *see* Warren, *Federal Judiciary Act*, *supra* note 8, at 130. Nevertheless, Madison had once expressed a belief that it would be constitutional for Congress to vest in state courts the powers to act as inferior federal courts. *Id.* at 66.

12. Eduardo C. Robreno, *Learning to Do Justice: An Essay on the Development of the Lower Federal Courts in the Early Years of the Republic*, 25 Rutgers L. J. 555, 560 (1998).

theless, the Judiciary Act was a reflection of the political realities of the time, and the fact that its basic structure has been altered little in the intervening two centuries stands as testimony to the practicality and foresight of its drafters.[13]

Congress faced two principal challenges in establishing a system of national courts. First, it had to define the scope of federal jurisdiction and the structure of the courts that would exercise it. In contrast to the states' ratifying conventions, where delegates debated whether inferior federal courts were necessary, the members of the first Congress tacitly conceded that these courts were needed and concentrated their efforts instead upon how to make them cost-effective.[14] As the debates progressed, the requirements of admiralty played a crucial role in shaping the structure of the federal courts. In the end, the Judiciary Act provided a well-defined structure, while the Process Act[15] established rules for the operation of these courts in meticulous detail. Congress was less successful, however, in meeting its second challenge. Madison had envisioned a

---

Observing that the federal courts did not receive "general federal question jurisdiction", he remarks that: "the grant of jurisdiction to the lower federal courts...did not reflect a policy judgment, but was, rather the result of political reality." *Id.* at 561.

13. Despite its inauspicious beginnings as the product of political compromise, Charles Warren gives testimony as to the remarkable longevity and utility of the Act:

> "[T]he Judiciary Act was a measure in the nature of a compromise between the extreme Federalist view that the full extent of judicial power granted by the Constitution should be vested by Congress in the Federal Courts, and the view of those who feared the new Government as a destroyer of the rights of the States, who wished all suits to be decided first in the State Courts, and only on appeal by the Federal Supreme Court. That the compromise was both wise and successful was seen from the fact that it was not until the lapse of forty-five years that jurisdiction of the Federal Courts was increased, to any substantial extent... [and] [i]t was eighty-six years before legislation was enacted, in 1875, vesting the Federal Circuit Courts with jurisdiction in all cases arising under the Federal Constitution and laws."

Warren, *Federal Judiciary Act*, *supra* note 8, at 131.

14. For discussion, *see e.g.* Marcus & Wexler, "Judiciary Act" *in* Origins of the Federal Judiciary, *supra* note 7, at 19–22. This is not to say that everyone in Congress believed that the Constitution required the creation of lower federal courts. In addition to hard-line opponents of a strong federal judiciary, others of more moderate political views, such as Madison and Francis Dana, also suggested that state courts could serve as federal trial courts. *See* Warren, *Federal Judiciary Act*, *supra* note 8, at 66. Nevertheless, the idea never received widespread support on the floor of either house.

15. An Act for the Regulation of Process in the Courts of the United States, 1 Stat. 93 (1789). This act was extended in force by a statute passed in the next session (*see* 1 Stat. 123 (1790)) and by another passed in 1791 (*see* 1 Stat. 191).

federal code of substantive laws.[16] To be sure, Congress did enact statutes covering topics as diverse as the collection of tonnage duties,[17] the registration of vessels,[18] the construction and maintenance of lighthouses,[19] and the regulation of merchant seamen.[20] Nevertheless, as useful as this legislation may have been, addressing the topic of substantive law in this piecemeal manner failed to provide a comprehensive solution to the source of substantive rules that federal courts were to apply in admiralty cases. In short, the Framers had declined to incorporate the common law into the Constitution, and—despite some vehement protests to the contrary—the first Congress followed their lead.

Had Congress merely neglected to enact a maritime code, federal judges would have been left to supply the necessary rules—as the common law had done for centuries—through incremental judicial innovation. That is not to say that the arrangement would have been free from friction. From Montesquieu to the present, the relations (and conflicts) between the legislative and judicial branches have been fodder for legal theorists, historians, and political scientists alike. The Constitution had structured the United States as a federal union. As such, resolving conflicts between the national government and those of the states was as crucial to the new nation's survival as maintaining checks and balances among the three branches of the federal government. While Congress created federal trial courts and empowered them to

---

16. *See* the debates of June 6, 1787, *in* The Records of the Federal Constitution of 1787 (3 vols., Max Farrand ed., New Haven: Yale University Press, 1966) Vol. I, at 138–139 (hereinafter Farrand, Records); *see also* discussion, Chapter III, notes 165–166 and text accompanying.

17. Congress' first efforts in this area consist of a series of statutes, beginning on July 20 with An Act Imposing Duties on Tonnage, 1 Stat. 27 (1789), and on July 31 with An Act to Regulate the Collection of Duties Imposed by Law on the Tonnage of Ships or Vessels, and on Goods, Wares, and Merchandise, 1 Stat. 29 (1789). These were followed by several others passed in rapid succession, which supplemented some of their provisions and repealed others. *See* 1 Stat. 69 (1789), 1 Stat. 112 (1790), 1 Stat. 135 (1790), 1 Stat. 145 (1790), and 1 Stat. 188 (1790). In addition, on April 2, 1790, Congress passed An Act to Prevent the Exportation of Goods Not Duly Inspected According to the Laws of the Several States, 1 Stat. 106.

18. On September 1, Congress passed An Act for Registering and Clearing Vessels [and] Regulating the Coastal Trade, 1 Stat. 55 (1789), and amended it a month later, 1 Stat. 94 (1789).

19. An Act for the Establishment and Support of Lighthouses, Beacons, Bouys, and Public Piers, 1 Stat. 53 (1789). Congress amended this act on July 22 of the following year; *see* 1 Stat. 137 (1790).

20. An Act for the Government and Regulation of Seamen in the Merchant Service, 1 Stat. 131 (1790).

hear maritime cases, its grant of jurisdiction was not exclusive. The Judiciary Act of 1789 provided that the federal district courts would have "original cognizance of all civil causes of admiralty and maritime jurisdiction... saving to suitors, in all cases, the right of a common law remedy, where the common law is competent to give it..."[21] The "common law" to which the Act refers is that of the individual states. Common law, as Matthew Hale had reminded his seventeenth-century readers,[22] was not a static body of abstract principles, but rather a process through which judges extrapolated new rules covering novel fact-patterns by analogy with the outcomes of past cases. This process is more art than science. A judge's discretion is not governed by a mechanistic system of logic, with a case's pre-ordained result merely awaiting discovery. When groups of judges disagree, it is, as Oliver Wendell Holmes observed, not because "one side or the other were not doing their sums right."[23] Thus where two separate sets of tribunals have cognizance over the same event or transaction, there is no guarantee that two separate courts will arrive at the same decision—either as regards the outcome or the rule to be applied. Indeed, the field of "conflict of laws" evolved as a response to this problem. To modern eyes, it appears only natural that Congress' grant of concurrent jurisdiction over maritime matters would pose a threat to national uniformity in substantive maritime law. Nevertheless, this result, so obvious to modern observers, was lost on the members of the first Congress.

It is unlikely that the first Congress' members were unaware of the potential for conflict where two sets of courts were empowered to hear the same set of cases.[24] In their own experiences, it was clear that the "common law", transplanted from England, had evolved somewhat differently in each of the

21. Judiciary Act, ch. 20, sec. 9, 1 Stat. 73, 77 (1789).

22. *See* "Sir Matthew Hale's Criticisms on Hobbes' Dialogue of the Common Laws", *reprinted in* William Holdsworth, A History of English Law (London: Methuen & Co., 1924), Vol. V, Appendix at 499–513. For discussion, *see also supra* Chapter I, note 177 and text accompanying.

23. Oliver Wendell Holmes, Jr., Collected Legal Papers, (New York: P. Smith, 1952), "The Path of the Law", at 167, 180.

24. Some antifederalists had opposed overlapping state/federal jurisdiction at earlier stages in the debates over the structure of the federal judiciary. For "Agrippa", this was only one facet of the larger problem of the same powers being exercised by both the federal and state governments, and he warned against the "horrors of a divided sovereignty". "Agrippa V" (Dec. 12, 1787), *reprinted in* The Documentary History of the Ratification of the Constitution (18 vols., John Kaminski & Gaspare Saladino eds., Madison: State Historical Society of Wisconsin, 1976), Vol. IV at 406, 408 (hereinafter Ratification). Even the moderate federalist Madison warned of the potential friction inherent in a system of concurrent jurisdiction. *See* Warren, *Federal Judiciary Act*, *supra* note 8, at 54.

colonies, thereby producing variations in substantive rules from one colony (and later from one state) to another. Moreover, it is also clear—from the records of their own proceedings—that Congress had no intention of enacting a comprehensive substantive maritime code, grounded in the Commerce Clause and binding on federal and state courts alike. Such a move both would have assured that all courts hearing maritime cases ground their decisions on the same substantive rules and would have limited the law-making discretion of state and federal judges. Instead, Congress opted to vest overlapping jurisdiction in the state and federal judiciaries, placing few constraints on the power of each set of courts to generate separate bodies of law for each class of maritime cases. As disconcerting as this may be to modern sensibilities, however, it was not perceived as problematic to the nation's newly-elected legislators in 1789. If we assume that the Judiciary Act's "Saving-to-Suitors Clause" was not a product of sloppy drafting, a sheer lack of foresight, or a failed attempt at political compromise by warring factions on the floors of the House and Senate, we must ask why members of the first Congress believed that concurrent state/federal jurisdiction over maritime matters—so potentially problematic in theory—would work well in the real world.

To understand why Congress approved the allocation of concurrent maritime jurisdiction, we must look past Montesquieu and abstract theories of federalism. The answer lies instead in how the generation of 1789 viewed substantive maritime law. The "common law" generally—those rules that govern contracts, torts, and real property—evolved through time. By a slow process of accretion, the cumulative efforts of succeeding generations of judges had constructed the body of the common law, an amalgam of the practical experience and collective wisdom of the English courts, distilled and refined through the ages. Thus it was in the minds and theories of Edward Coke and Matthew Hale.[25] How then, one might ask, does the *lex maritima* fit into this vision? The maritime law—at least to Coke, to Hale, and to those jurists falling under their influence—was indisputably part of the common law, and yet its history (such as it was understood in the eighteenth century) was markedly different from that larger portion of the common law that governed the affairs of "landlubbers". To the casual observer and the life-long practitioner at the admiralty bar alike, the substantive rules governing maritime affairs appeared to remain static, fixed in stone since time immemorial and rec-

25. For discussion, *see e.g.* J.G.A. Pocock, The Ancient Constitution and the Feudal Law: A Study of English Historical Thought in the Seventeenth Century (Cambridge: Cambridge University Press, 1957) at 163–181; *see also*, Chapter I, notes 174–191 and text accompanying.

ognized by all "civilized nations". Writing just six years after passage of the Judiciary Act, Richard Peters, the first judge of the federal district court of Pennsylvania and editor of the nineteenth century's first published American admiralty reports,[26] incorporated this notion into his opinion in a case involving seamen's wages, remarking:

> [T]he change in the form of our government has not abrogated all the laws, customs and principles of jurisprudence, we inherited from our ancestors, and possessed at the period of our becoming an independent nation.... It is, then, not to be disputed, on sound principles, that this court must be governed in its decisions, by the Maritime Code we possessed [in the colonial period].... These laws and the decisions under them, must be received as authorities, in this, and other courts...[27]

As late as the early twentieth century, this notion had not lost its vitality. In *Panama Railroad Co. v. Johnson*, the Supreme Court echoed Peters' sentiments in explaining the source of the substantive maritime law to be applied under Article III, sec. 2:

> As there could be no "cases of admiralty and maritime jurisdiction" in the absence of some maritime law under which they could arise, the provision presupposes the existence in the United States of a law of that character [predating the Constitution].... Such a law or system of law existed in Colonial times and during the Confederation and commonly was applied in the adjudication of admiralty and maritime cases.... The framers of the Constitution were familiar with that system and proceeded with it in mind.[28]

If this assessment of the Framers' state of mind is correct, it would go a long way toward explaining why two years later the first Congress would anticipate no complications arising from granting concurrent jurisdiction over maritime matters to the state and federal courts. In this view, the "general body of ad-

---

26. Admiralty Decisions in the District Court of the United States for the Pennsylvania District...to Which Are Added Cases Determined in Other Districts of the United States (2 vols., Richard Peters ed., Philadelphia; William P. Farrand, 1807) (hereinafter Admiralty Decisions). For discussion *see infra* Chapter V, note 55 and text accompanying.

27. *Thompson v. The Catharina* (Case No. 13,949), 23 F. Cas. 1028, 1030–1031 (D. Pa., 1795).

28. *Panama Railroad Co. v. Johnson*, 264 U.S. 375, 385 (1924).

miralty and maritime law" governs maritime transactions world-wide. It is not, in Holmes' phrase, "the articulate voice of some sovereign",[29] but rather a body of law separate from and antecedent to the laws established by the world's sovereign nations, which nevertheless is binding on all members of the international community. In such a world, presumably both state and federal courts would apply the same "general maritime law". The principal argument against concurrent admiralty jurisdiction is that, over time, state and federal courts would evolve different sets of substantive maritime rules, thereby threatening that uniformity of law so necessary for promoting maritime commerce. Shipowners and merchants would be unsure as to the rules governing their transactions, and litigants would seek the *fora* offering the most favorable rules. Such is the usual course of events where jurisdiction overlaps. If, however, the applicable body of law is both universally binding and unchanging, parties to maritime transactions know their rights and obligations *ex ante*, and the incentive for forum-shopping disappears.

Did the members of the first Congress believe—as Judge Peters did—that upon achieving independence, America incurred an obligation to enforce a body of substantive maritime law derived from the law of nations, and did that belief instill in them a sense of complacency regarding the potential conflict between state and federal courts in adjudicating maritime disputes? Is this belief at the core of Congress' decision to include the "Saving-to-Suitors Clause" in the Judiciary Act of 1789? Does this also explain why Congress opted not to enact a comprehensive maritime code? To answer these questions, we must examine the surviving evidence—the records of the debates in the first House and Senate, and the notes and correspondence of the participants.

Admiralty Jurisdiction and the Structure of the Federal Courts

Despite the diversity of regional and local interests represented in the first Congress, the qualifications of its individual members were remarkably similar. The overwhelming majority had served in the legislatures of their respective states. Roughly half had attended college, and nearly as many were

29. *Southern Pacific Co. v. Jensen*, 244 U.S. 202, 222, 37 S. Ct. 511, 531 (Holmes, J., dissenting, 1917).

practicing attorneys. Two out of every five had served in the military, while slightly more than half had served in the Continental Congress. Though by no means a majority, those who had been delegates to the Constitutional Convention two years earlier were well represented. Of the ninety-one members of both houses, twenty-one were Convention delegates who had returned to Philadelphia to represent their respective states in the national legislature.[30] While this provided a sizable contingent to inform their fellow congressmen of the drafters' original debates on the text of Article III, there was no guarantee that the new Congress would conform its decisions to the original intent of the delegates. The political climate had changed, and the task confronting the House and Senate was to accommodate those changes within the framework of the plain language of the Constitution.[31] Those favoring a strong federal judiciary were forced to concede that Article III provided the outer limits to which Congress could go in structuring the federal courts—not the minimal requirements.[32] On the other hand, as debates opened, it was already ob-

---

30. For statistics on the composition of the first Congress, *see* James Roger Sharp, American Politics in the Early Republic: The New Nation in Crisis (New Haven: Yale University Press, 1993) at 31–32. *See also* Warren, *Federal Judiciary Act, supra* note 8, at 64 (noting that while lawyers were a minority in the Senate, they constituted 75% of the membership of the House). While some authors (*e.g.* Marcus & Wexler, "Judiciary Act", *in* Origins of the Federal Judiciary, *supra* note 7, at 13–14) have opted to emphasize the comparatively small percentage of Philadelphia Convention delegates who were elected to the first Congress, it should be remembered that only fifty-five men had actually attended the Convention. *See* Max Farrand, The Framing of the Constitution of the United States (New Haven: Yale University Press, 1913) at 39. Moreover, some of the smaller states, such as Delaware, had sent delegations to the Conventions that were much larger than the number of seats allotted to them in Congress, and thus some Convention delegates were precluded from serving in the first Congress. Thus on the whole, the degree of overlap in membership between the Convention and the first Congress is astonishingly high.

31. Julius Goebel had described the Judiciary Act of 1789, embodying the structure of the federal courts, as "an instrument of reconciliation deliberately framed to quiet smoldering resentments". Goebel, Antecedents, *supra* note 8, at 458. More recently, Marcus and Wexler remarked that "those drafting the Judiciary Act paid less attention to the constitutional language, ambiguous as it was, than to contemporary political necessities." *See* "Judiciary Act", *in* Origins of the Federal Judiciary, *supra* note 7, at 13–14. For discussion the political compromise that produced the Act, *see also* Warren, *Federal Judiciary Act, supra* note 8, at 53, 67–68, 131.

32. As Bourguignon observes: "The basic skeletal outline of the final Act remained the same from the initial draft. An early sketch shows the committee from the beginning sought to create a stripped-down federal judicial system that was politically acceptable rather than one enjoying the full scope of power contained in Article III.... Article III provided a ceil-

vious to those seeking to restrict the powers of the federal judiciary that the creation of *some* inferior federal courts was inevitable. Their strategy shifted to limiting the scope of jurisdiction and minimizing the power that these new national courts would enjoy.

On April 7, 1789, the second day of its deliberation, the Senate appointed a committee to prepare a draft of a bill for organizing the federal judiciary. Among its members were Richard Bassett, William Few, William Paterson, Caleb Strong, and Oliver Ellsworth—all of whom had been delegates to the Constitutional Convention.[33] This committee in turn selected a subcommittee, consisting of Ellsworth, Strong, and Paterson, to pen the first draft. Chaired by Ellsworth, this subcommittee completed its draft of the bill in less than two months, and this draft was presented to the full Senate on June 12.[34] The bill, which provided for the creation of federal district and circuit courts, contained several especially noteworthy provisions, including the following:

> And [the district courts] shall also have exclusive original cognizance of all civil causes of admiralty & maritime jurisdiction, including all seizures under laws of impost, navigation or trade of the United

---

ing rather than a floor." Bourguignon, *Judiciary Act, supra* note 6, at 668. For further discussion see *e.g.* Marcus and Wexler, contending: "[T]here is little indication...that those in Congress believed it necessary to legislate to the limits authorized by the language of Article III.... [M]ost of those in Congress acted on the assumption that the Constitution merely set the outer limits of their power." "Judiciary Act", *in* ORIGINS OF THE FEDERAL JUDICIARY, *supra* note 7, at 16.

33. Bourguignon, *Judiciary Act, supra* note 6, at 667. *See also* Warren, *Federal Judiciary Act, supra* note 8, at 57–59. Among the members of the committee who had not been present in Philadelphia in the summer of 1787, Charles Carroll, Paine Wingate, Richard Henry Lee, and Ralph Izard had served in the Continental Congress; in addition, Izard had been a delegate to South Carolina's ratifying convention. Of all members of this committee, only William Maclay had not represented his state either in Congress or in the process of ratification. *See* THE DOCUMENTARY HISTORY OF THE SUPREME COURT OF THE UNITED STATES, 1789–1800—VOL. IV: ORGANIZING THE FEDERAL JUDICIARY: LEGISLATION AND COMMENTARIES (Maeva Marcus ed., New York: Columbia University Press, 1992), at 22–23 (hereinafter DOCUMENTARY HISTORY OF THE SUPREME COURT).

34. Bourguignon, *Judiciary Act, supra* note 6, at 667–668. Sections 1–23, including Section 9 and its "Saving-to-Suitors Clause", are in Ellsworth's handwriting, and eighteenth-century and modern writers are agreed that he is largely responsible for their substantive content as well. *See* Warren, *Federal Judiciary Act, supra* note 8, at 50, 59–61. For the texts of the various drafts of "S-1" (as the Judiciary Act had been known in committee) including those of June 12, July 17, and September 24, 1789, *see* FIRST FEDERAL CONGRESS, *supra* note 2, Vol. V, at 1150–1212; for history of the manuscripts of these drafts, *see* GOEBEL, ANTECEDENTS, *supra* note 8, at 463 n. 21, 465 n. 24, 466.

> States, where the seizures are made on waters which are navigable from the sea by vessels of (10) tons or more burthen, within their respective districts as well as upon the high seas. *Saving to Suitors in all cases the right of a common law remedy where the common law is competent to give it.*[35]

As soon as a printed copy became available, many senators sent copies to state officials and prominent members of the bars of their respective states, soliciting comments and advice.[36] In this correspondence, technical competence often weighed as heavily as political affiliation or doctrine. Maclay, the maverick populist, sought the advice of Richard Peters, a staunch federalist whose detailed knowledge of admiralty was well known both in Pennsylvania and throughout the nation.[37]

While the solicitation of advice accelerated with the publication of Ellsworth's first draft, the debate over the provisions of the Judiciary Act in fact had begun in private letters even before Congress had convened. From the outset, several themes emerged, and admiralty played a central role in each. Surviving letters reveal that the authors revisited the old issues of cost-effectiveness and geographical convenience of federal trial and appellate courts, the use of juries in federal trials, and *de novo* fact-finding at the appellate level. This time, however, the debate was not over a skeletal plan for the judiciary on "take-it-or-leave-it" terms; a simple "aye" or "no" would not suffice. The challenge facing the authors was to create a practical, functioning federal judiciary, complete from its underlying abstract concepts to the *minutiae* of its daily operations. The task demanded a close attention to detail, and as the authors re-examined the old issues, they made novel observations.

Owing to the nation's experience during the Revolution, federalists and antifederalists alike conceded that prize cases should be tried in federal

---

35. Judiciary Bill [S-1]: Sec. 10, June 12, 1789, *reprinted in* First Federal Congress, *supra* note 2, Vol. V, at 1177 (*emphasis added*). Other provisions of [S-1] relevant to admiralty are contained in Sections 20, 16, and 28. Section 20 allowed for appeals in admiralty cases where the damages totaled at least $300, indicating that even at this early stage Congress sought to shield the appellate courts from hearing trivial matters and/or to prevent affluent litigants from raising the costs for impecunious adversaries (as in cases of seamen's wages). *Id.*, Vol. V, at 1183–1184. Sections 16 and 28 mandated the use of oral testimony in federal courts sitting in admiralty and provided rules for implementing the requirement. *Id.*, Vol. V, at 1182, 1189–1191.

36. Documentary History of the Supreme Court, *supra* note 33, Vol. IV, at 23; for further discussion, *see* Goebel, Antecedents, *supra* note 8, at 458–461.

37. *See* Marcus & Wexler, "Judiciary Act", *in* Origins of the Federal Judiciary, *supra* note 7, at 15.

courts.[38] The antifederalists' concession on this point virtually guaranteed that Congress would establish some inferior federal courts under Article III; at stake, however, was the scope of jurisdiction granted to them. It soon became apparent that a court established to hear only prize cases would be impractical. The old vice admiralty courts had paid judges out of the proceeds of vessels sold at judicial auction. This practice, a source of controversy before the Revolution, had been virtually abandoned in the state admiralty courts in favor of fixed salaries.[39] Fixed salaries were efficient so long as the courts remained busy, and there was no shortage of prize litigation while the war was in progress. In peace-time, however, a prize court sits idle, and the judges' fixed salaries soon become a drain on the public coffers. The state admiralty courts solved this problem when they began to accept instance business, particularly in the late 1780s as the prize business waned and merchants and shipowners sought *fora* more knowledgeable and less overcrowded than the state common-law courts. As the debate on the federal judiciary progressed, it became apparent that the participants were cognizant of this problem; federal courts with jurisdiction over prize alone would not be cost-effective. Article III forbade the expedients of terminating federal judges' tenure or reducing their salaries until such time as the courts would be needed again. Nor was the financial burden of the courts during peace-time the only concern. Noting the lack of challenging work for prize courts in a nation at peace, one observer remarked that such courts would not attract judges of the highest caliber. Thus the courts, originally envisioned as specialized tribunals with expertise in the law of nations, might prove to be insufficiently prepared should the nation need their services during war-time.[40]

---

38. *See e.g.* "Brutus" No. XIII (New York Journal, Feb. 21, 1788), *reprinted in* RATIFICATION, *supra* note 24, Vol. V, at 495 (hereinafter RATIFICATION); for additional examples and further discussion, *see* Chapter III, notes 209–222 and text accompanying.

39. While it was generally the practice for state admiralty judges to be paid fixed salaries, the Revolutionary period was a time of *ad hoc* experiment, and there are recorded instances in some states (*e.g.* Maryland) in which judges' compensation came in part from the proceeds from the sales of condemned ships. *See* Judge Emory H. Niles, The Revolutionary Court of Admiralty of the State of Maryland: 1776–1789. Address before the Lawyers' Round Table, Maryland Club, Baltimore (Dec. 8, 1941) at 18 (hereinafter Niles).

40. This sentiment, later expressed in the Congressional debate, is summarized succinctly in William Bradford's assessment of Ellsworth's preliminary draft of [S-1]:

> "There is one thing observable in the jurisdiction of the district Judge, & that is, that it is very much limited, except in the case of seizures. Take away the jurisdiction over them, & in time of peace, he will have little to do, & a man of real talents will hardly be found to accept it: & with a jurisdiction so extensive over

One obvious solution to the idleness of the federal courts in peace-time was to vest in them the power to hear revenue cases. National taxes must be collected in peace as well as in war, thus guaranteeing a steady stream of business for the courts. The notion of revenue cases in "admiralty" courts, an anathema to the Sons of Liberty less than two decades earlier, provoked less cause for alarm in 1789.[41] Moreover, Ellsworth and his colleagues had sought to alleviate any lingering fears that federal courts would deprive defendants of their common-law rights by providing that all revenue cases would be tried before juries.[42] Nonetheless, even the addition of revenue cases to the federal courts' sphere of cognizance would not ensure that taxpayers would get their money's worth from their new courts. The next logical step was to grant instance jurisdiction as well. Despite subtle differences in procedure,[43] prize and

---

> seizures it seems to require a man of the first Abilities."

Letter of William Bradford, Jr. to Elias Boudinot (June 30, 1789), *reprinted in* DOCUMENTARY HISTORY OF THE SUPREME COURT, *supra* note 33, Vol. IV, at 430–431. For some contemporary critics, merely granting additional jurisdiction (*e.g.* over instance and revenue cases) alone would not solve the problem of the courts' inefficiency. Writing of Ellsworth's first draft of [S-1], federalist Paine Wingate maintained:

> "...that the administration of justice in the way proposed will cost more than it is worth. The judiciary is calculated by pretty good judges to cost between 50 & 60 thousand dollers pr. Annum & yet it will not extend to a tenth part of the causes which might by the constitution come into the federal court[s]."

Letter of Paine Wingate to Nathaniel Peaslea Sargeant (July 18, 1789), *reprinted in* DOCUMENTARY HISTORY OF THE SUPREME COURT, *supra* note 33, Vol. IV, at 474.

41. Upon hearing of a movement afoot in the House to amend [S-1], diplomat and judge Francis Dana, grandfather of the noted author and admiralty attorney Richard Henry Dana, Jr., cautioned against the dangers of depriving the federal courts of jurisdiction over "admiralty and revenue cases". *See* Letter of Francis Dana to John Adams (July 31, 1789), *reprinted in Id.*, Vol. IV, at 489–491. The lack of dissent on the Act's classification of trade-act cases as "admiralty" has not gone unnoticed. For discussion of the limited arguments on this provision, *see* Warren, *Federal Judiciary Act*, *supra* note 8, at 74–75.

42. Judiciary Bill [S-1], Sec. 10, June 12, 1789, *reprinted in* FIRST FEDERAL CONGRESS, *supra* note 2, Vol. V., at 1176–1177. It is worth noting that debate on the use of juries continued throughout the legislative history of the bill that would become the Judiciary Act, and that the Senate at first deleted the language "& the trial of facts shall be by jury" from Ellsworth's first draft. *See Id.*, Vol. V, at 1177, n. 35.

43. From the early eighteenth century onwards, both Anglo-American prize courts and instance courts had operated under procedures derived from the civil law. For discussion, *see* Chapter II, notes 251–260 and text accompanying. For procedural differences between instance and prize, *see e.g.* HENRY BOURGUIGNON, THE FIRST FEDERAL COURT: THE APPELLATE PRIZE COURT OF THE REVOLUTION 1775–1787 (Philadelphia: The American Philosophical Society, 1977) at 151 (hereinafter BOURGUIGNON, FIRST FEDERAL COURT); *see also* discussion, Chapter III, notes 139–140 and text accompanying.

instance litigation had much in common. In both, courts traditionally proceeded *in rem* against a vessel, and there is a certain intrinsic logic in Congress assigning all *in rem* claims to the same set of courts. To be sure, the textual grounds for granting instance jurisdiction to federal district courts is clear in the language of Article III—provided of course that one reads "admiralty and maritime" as encompassing private actions. Though James Kent's *Commentaries on American Law* later denied that the Framers had construed the language so broadly,[44] contemporary evidence indicates otherwise. At the close of the Constitutional Convention, the implacable antifederalist Luther Mar-

---

44. In his *Commentaries on American Law*, a seminal treatise in the nineteenth century that remains a classic work of legal literature today, Kent provides the following assessment of the Framers' intent:

> "But I apprehend it may fairly be doubted, whether the constitution of the United States meant, by admiralty and maritime jurisdiction, anything more than the jurisdiction which was settled and in active practice under the English jurisprudence, when the constitution was made; and whether it had any retrospective or historical reference to the usages and practices of the admiralty, as it once existed, in the middle ages, before its territories had been invaded and partly subdued by the bold and free spirit of the courts of common law, armed with the protecting genius and masculine vigor of trial by jury."

James Kent, Commentaries on American Law (3 vols., 2d ed., New York: O. Halsted, 1832), Vol. I, at 377–378 (hereinafter Kent, Commentaries). The "English jurisprudence" to which he refers more closely parallels that defined by Matthew Hale than that described by Leoline Jenkins. *Id.* at 371–377. He concedes, as Prynne had, that express hypothecation is within the exclusive cognizance of the admiralty, and maintains, as Hale had, that claims for seamen's wages are "an exception" to the rule that contracts signed on land do not sound in admiralty. As for the remainder of the instance jurisdiction of the English admiralty courts, Kent remarks:

> "[T]he English...instance court takes cognizance only of crimes committed, and things done, and contracts not under seal made *super altum mare*, and without the body of any county. This, of course, excludes all creeks, bays, and rivers, which are within the body of some county; and if the place be the sea coast, then the ebbing and flowing of the tide determines the admiralty. The cause must arise *wholly* upon the sea, and not within the precincts of any county, to give the admiralty jurisdiction. If the action be founded on a matter done partly on land and partly on water, as if a contract be made on land to be executed at sea, or be made at sea to be executed on land, the common law has the preference, and excludes the admiralty."

Id. at 378 *(emphasis in the original)*. It should be noted that Kent does not wholly endorse the "public law model" of admiralty jurisdiction espoused by modern critic William Casto. *Cf.* William R. Casto, *The Origins of Federal Admiralty Jurisdiction in an Age of Privateers, Smugglers, and Pirates*, 37 Am. J. Legal Hist. 117 (1993) (hereinafter Casto, *Origins*). Kent concedes that the Framers were not opposed to federal jurisdiction over instance cases *per*

tin had warned the Maryland legislature that Article III would place an undue burden upon mariners who wished to sue for their wages, raising their costs by forcing them to file their claims in inconvenient *fora*. Martin's criticism is premised on the notion that the Framers had intended for federal courts to hear private maritime actions. If Martin's assessment of the Framers' intent was accurate, the Constitution had empowered Congress to allocate instance jurisdiction to the federal judiciary.[45] Nonetheless, on the floor of the first Congress, it was not abstract debates over the Framers' intent but rather practical politics that would settle the matter of whether federal admiralty jurisdiction would extend to instance cases.

The subcommittee's draft of the judiciary bill came before the Senate on June 22, 1789. The antifederalists did have their objections, but, as in the states' ratifying conventions of the previous year, their counterattack was blunted by their own tacit concession that federal admiralty courts were essential. Richard Henry Lee suggested "[t]hat the jurisdiction of the Federal courts should be confined to cases of admiralty and maritime jurisdiction."[46]

---

se, but rather sought to limit its scope—with a few minor exceptions—to matters arising on the high seas.

45. In his letter to the Maryland legislature, Martin warns:

> "Should the mariners of an American or foreign vessel, while in any American port, have occasion to sue for their wages, or in any other instance a controversy belonging to the admiralty jurisdiction should take place between them and their masters or owners, it is in the courts of the general government the suit must be instituted; and either party may carry it by appeal to its Supreme Court. The injury to commerce, and the oppression to individuals, which may thence arise, need not be enlarged upon."

Letter of Luther Martin to the Maryland Legislature (Nov. 19, 1787), *reprinted in* 3 FARRAND, RECORDS, *supra* note 16, Appendix A, Doc. CLVIII, at 177, 220. As Martin was a delegate to the Convention, he was in a position as good as any to know what the delegates had intended when they adopted the language "admiralty and maritime" in Article III. Moreover, as he was highly critical of federal jurisdiction over instance cases, he had no incentive to exaggerate scope that his fellow Framers intended to ascribe to "admiralty and maritime". Given the context of the letter, it appears to reflect Martin's sincere belief regarding the Framers' intended meaning. In addition, his critique also provides insight into why the first Congress ultimately opted to include the "Saving-to-Suitors Clause" (*see supra* notes 21, 35; *infra* note 72) in the Judiciary Act: namely to guarantee geographically convenient *fora* for all private maritime actions. (For further discussion, see *infra* notes 73–84 and text accompanying.) For circumstantial evidence of the Framers' intention to include instance causes among "admiralty and maritime cases", *see* discussion, Chapter III, notes 124–143 and text accompanying.

46. MACLAY, JOURNAL, *supra* note 2, at 83. Maclay notes further that the language Lee selected to amend the bill was based upon the Resolutions that Virginia's ratifying conven-

Both Ellsworth and Maclay argued against the motion, and by the following day it became clear that Lee's motion was doomed to failure.[47] Ultimately, the bill passed the Senate with its provisions on the structure of the inferior federal courts largely intact.[48] In the House, however, the bill provoked more controversy. As in the Senate, it was clear from the outset that the debate in the House would focus on practical concerns, not on abstract theories of constitutional interpretation. James Jackson of Georgia set the tone for discussion, observing: "In fact the conveniency of the people is, or ought to be the first privilege of every government; and the people have a right to expect it. Our present constitution has set out with this declaration, 'We, the People', in its preamble; and therefore in the system before us, every attention of the Legis-

---

tion had wished to introduce for amending the language of Article III itself, namely: "the judicial power of the United States shall be vested in one Supreme Court, and in such courts of Admiralty as Congress may from time to time ordain and establish in any of the different states..." *Form of Ratification, which was read to and agreed to by the Convention of Virginia* (Amendments to the Constitution: Art. 14), *reprinted in* The Debate on the Constitution (2 vols., Bernard Bailyn ed., New York: Library of America, 1993), Vol. II , at 557, 563. It is worth noting that Charles Warren disputes Maclay's attribution of the motion to Richard Henry Lee. He reasons that:

> "It has always appeared to historians as somewhat remarkable that Lee should have thus attacked a fundamental principle of the bill which he himself had reported, and especially because of the fact that, while he had long been ardently advocating Amendments to the Constitution, he had never supported the Virginia proposition of limiting the Federal Courts to so narrow a scope as now proposed. It is possible that Maclay is mistaken in stating that Lee made this motion; for the original paper in the Senate Files is not in Lee's handwriting. Maclay reports, however, in detail Lee's speeches in favor of the motion, as well as those of William Grayson of Virginia; Ellsworth and Maclay, himself, opposed the motion, and it was finally rejected."

Warren, *Federal Judiciary Act*, *supra* note 8, at 67.

47. Unfortunately, the first Senate did not keep an official *verbatim* transcript of the proceedings, and Maclay's Journal lacks details on how Lee characterized "admiralty jurisdiction". He does, however, note that on June 23: "Mr. Lee endeavored to give the whole business a new turn, to elude the force of what I had said yesterday. According to his explanation on admiralty and maritime jurisdiction he would have taken in a vast field." Maclay, Journal, *supra* note 2, at 84. As most narrowly construed, admiralty would have encompassed public-law matters and/or cases arising on the high seas, it appears likely that this "vast field" included the full panoply of instance cases once litigated in the colonial vice admiralty courts and the state courts of admiralty.

48. The Bill passed the Senate on July 17, 1789, by a vote of fourteen to six. Ironically, despite supporting Ellsworth in opposing the motion to restrict the jurisdiction of federal trial courts to admiralty cases, Maclay joined five of his colleagues in voting against the Judiciary Bill as a whole. *See* Warren, *Federal Judiciary Act*, *supra* note 8, at 109.

lature ought to be drawn to this point."[49] Jackson's comment, with is emphasis on pragmatism over original intent, is equally applicable to the deliberations in both houses. Nevertheless, the old issues raised during the process of ratification—the convenience and cost of the federal courts, *de novo* review of facts at the appellate level, and the use of juries in federal trial courts—scarcely mentioned in the Senate debates, would receive detailed attention in the House. Moreover, as the debates unfolded, it became clear that each of these issues was inextricably interwoven with that of admiralty jurisdiction.[50]

Among the members of the first Congress, it was generally agreed that Article III set the outer boundaries of federal jurisdiction rather than a mandate that Congress grant the full measure of jurisdiction constitutionally permissible.[51] For those favoring "minimalist" approaches to federal jurisdiction, such as Richard Henry Lee, the threshold question was how to deal with admiralty and maritime jurisdiction. Cognizance over such cases was expressly granted to the federal judiciary in Article III, thus placing it on a sound constitutional footing. In addition, among all forms of jurisdiction that Congress contemplated granting to the federal courts, admiralty was the least politically controversial. Experiences of the Revolution had revealed the practical advantages

---

49. House Debates (Aug. 29, 1789), *reproduced in* First Federal Congress, *supra* note 2, Vol. XI, at 1353.

50. While the debate over *de novo* review of facts at the appellate level clearly implicated admiralty jurisdiction, it likewise was relevant to the debate over equity jurisdiction. As in admiralty, courts of equity determined facts without a jury, often on the basis of sworn statements rather than testimony *viva voce*. Where testimony is in the form of documents, an appellate court is at no disadvantage *vis-à-vis* a trial court in fact-finding. In common-law cases, however, appellate fact-finding threatened the role of the jury, and thus the appellate review of facts and the guarantee of a right to trial by jury are often linked in the debates. (*See infra* note 67 and text accompanying). Although most in each house agreed to appellate review of facts in admiralty cases, review of facts was hotly debated for federal equity jurisdiction. For discussion, *see* Warren, *Federal Judiciary Act, supra* note 8, at 96, 99, 102.

51. Marcus & Wexler, "Judiciary Act", *in* Origins of the Federal Judiciary, *supra* note 7, at 16. As the nineteenth-century admiralty scholar Erastus Benedict later would remark:

> "The [C]onstitution and the law must both concur in conferring jurisdiction. The judicial power of the government is derived from the Constitution. The disposal of it belongs to the Congress. Many subjects of jurisdiction which are clearly embraced in the [C]onstitution, lie actually dormant, because the Congress has never authorized their exercise by any of the courts."

Erastus C. Benedict, The American Admiralty: Its Jurisdiction and Practice (1st ed., New York: Banks, Gould, & Co. Law Booksellers, 1850), sec. 15, at 10 (hereinafter Benedict (1st ed.)).

of vesting some form of maritime jurisdiction in national *fora*. Moreover, as many maritime cases had been adjudicated outside of the common-law courts since the colonial period without significant conflict, the creation of a new set of specialized courts to hear maritime cases, in the minds of many, posed a less serious threat to the workings of the state courts. Federal admiralty jurisdiction did meet with more opposition in the House than in the Senate, where antifederalists such as Lee had conceded the point from the outset, but opposition was overcome in short order.

As debate opened in the House in August, opinion was divided as to whether state courts were competent to hear matters arising at sea. William Smith of Maryland believed they could not in the absence of authorization from Congress.[52] Fisher Ames of Massachusetts—which had established its own admiralty court during the Revolution months before the Continental Congress had authorized it—assumed that the Constitution had removed from the states power to hear cases arising on the high seas.[53] Others disagreed. Jackson observed that, as the state courts had "exercised the admiralty jurisdiction to the fullest extent",[54] there was no reason that they could not continue do so in the future. Michael Jenifer Stone of Maryland, an opponent of expansive jurisdiction for inferior federal courts, also contended that states' sovereignty—even after the ratification of the Constitution—encompassed the power to hear "all admiralty cases".[55] Agreement upon a "territorial" model for maritime jurisdiction would have made the House's task considerably eas-

52. Citing the practice under the state admiralty courts, Smith maintained that states' power to hear maritime causes was derived from Congress. While he does not elaborate, it appears his reasoning was based on the assumption that the power to hear such cases devolved to the national government—as an attribute of sovereignty—at the time of independence. Thus states could acquire jurisdiction over maritime causes only if that power were delegated to them by the sovereign that held it under the law of nations—in this case the national Congress. *See* House Debates (Aug. 29), *reproduced in* First Federal Congress, *supra* note 2, Vol. XI, at 1351.

53. Ames made his remark offhandedly in a speech regarding the limitations of state courts in enforcing federal statutes. With a touch of sarcasm, he quipped: "Can a State court sustain such an action? They may as properly assume admiralty jurisdiction, or sustain actions for forfeitures of the British revenue acts." Though not the principal point of the speech, the sarcasm would be out of place unless he believed that his colleagues understood the Constitution as removing maritime matters from the state courts as surely as independence had preempted American courts' powers to enforce the British Navigation Acts. *See* House Debates (Aug. 29), *reproduced in Id.*, Vol. XI, at 1358.

54. House Debates (Aug. 31), *reproduced in Id.*, Vol. XI, at 1389.

55. He did, however, admit that "admiralty courts [had not been] established in all the states", a practical observation which, as the debates progressed, would carry much weight

ier. If all had conceded that the jurisdiction of the states could extend no further than *terra firma* of their own respective boundaries, maritime jurisdiction would have belonged to the federal government by default. Some members did espouse this view, under which maritime jurisdiction was an attribute of sovereignty, conferred upon the United States by the law of nations.[56] Under such a theory, the debate over whether to create inferior federal courts would become moot; the creation of such courts would be necessary, as the states would lack the power to assume the jurisdiction. Egbert Benson of New York did not ascribe to the view that either the Constitution or the law of nations vested maritime jurisdiction solely within the national government. He saw no contradiction in the notion that both the state courts and those of the national government could exercise jurisdiction over the same territory simultaneously. The challenge, he maintained, was in finding a way for each to do so with the least friction possible.[57]

The members of the House did not reach agreement on the issue of whether state courts under the Constitution retained a residual power to hear causes arising at sea. If they had reached consensus on the notion that vesting maritime jurisdiction in state courts would have violated either the Constitution or the law of nations, Congress would have had no choice but to create inferior federal courts. The failure of those favoring the creation of inferior federal courts to convince their brethren that the Constitution and/or the law of nations rendered state-court jurisdiction over maritime matters *ultra vires* guaranteed that the debate over the structure of federal admiralty jurisdiction—and indeed over the structure of the entire federal judiciary—would focus on pragmatic rather than ideological grounds. As the discussion progressed, the representatives turned their attention to the issue that had preoccupied the pamphleteers and delegates to the states' ratifying conventions, namely the costs of establishing and operating federal courts. If the proponents of the bill were to succeed, they would have to convince a majority of their colleagues that inferior federal courts were cost-effective. As with Richard Henry Lee in the Senate, many in the House who were otherwise reluctant to

---

with his fellow representatives. House Debates (Aug. 31), *reproduced in Id.*, Vol. XI, at 1383–1385.

56. *See e.g.* House Debates (Aug. 29), *reproduced in Id.*, Vol. XI, at 1351, 1358.

57. House Debates (Aug. 29), *reproduced in Id.*, Vol. XI, at 1368. Benson's remark extends beyond admiralty to other classes of cases also (*e.g.* diversity cases) where both federal and state courts would have overlapping jurisdiction. If the Constitution (in his reading) mandated overlapping jurisdiction, it was not Congress' prerogative to question it, but rather to determine how best to make concurrent jurisdiction function smoothly.

grant an expansive jurisdiction to federal courts nevertheless believed that federal admiralty courts were necessary. Moreover, to be practical, federal admiralty courts had to be geographically convenient. At the very least, there had to be a court in each major port.[58] For smaller ports where permanent courts would not have been practical, some had suggested that federal judges take to the road, holding sessions at intervals in different cities, thus bringing federal trials to the litigants to save the litigants the expense of traveling to the courts.[59] Ultimately, however, this was rejected as impractical. For admiralty courts to be cost-effective, it was necessary that their jurisdiction extend beyond prize cases. Augmenting the scope of their cognizance by granting them power to hear revenue-act cases[60] was not alone sufficient to permit the nation to receive as much in service from the courts as the cost of their maintenance. Quite logically, the Senate's draft of the Judiciary Bill had opted to add jurisdiction over instance cases to the federal courts' powers; the House took up the debate at this point.

Once one accepts that instance cases must augment the federal courts' jurisdiction over prize and revenue cases in order to make efficient use of the courts, any notion of "ambulatory" federal courts becomes untenable. For disputes arising upon land between neighbors, merchants, or others whose respective places of business or domiciles generally remain unchanged for

---

58. *See e.g.* Letter of Richard Law to Oliver Ellsworth (July 14, 1789), *reproduced in* Documentary History of the Supreme Court, *supra* note 33, Vol. IV, at 467.

59. *See e.g.* Letter of David Sewall to George Thatcher (April 11, 1789), suggesting that: "Should these [Maritime or Admiralty Courts] be appointed over large districts they must be ambulatory, or at leat [*sic: i.e.* "least"] have Something like deputies that can attend to the Small matters of mariners [*sic*] Wages and Appraising & Bonding Vessels Where some of the owners differ about risking at Seas..." *Reproduced in Id.*, Vol. IV, at 374. Others, including Fisher Ames, Robert Treat Paine, and Nathaniel Peaslea Sargeant, suggested "ambulatory" federal courts in their correspondence as a means of reducing litigants' costs by bringing federal courts closer to their homes. *See* Marcus & Wexler, "Judiciary Act", *in* Origins of the Federal Judiciary, *supra* note 7, at 21, 36.

60. In his letter to John Adams of July 31, 1789, Francis Dana argues strongly for augmenting the jurisdiction of the federal courts by adding the power to adjudicate revenue-act cases. *Reproduced in* Documentary History of the Supreme Court, *supra* note 33, Vol. IV, at 489–491. Dana was not alone in his belief. Otho Williams, the newly appointed collector for the port of Baltimore, also urged the creation of admiralty courts to hear revenue-act cases in a letter of May 12, 1789 to David Humphries, secretary to President Washington. *Id.*, Vol. IV, at 377n. The notion that granting federal courts revenue-act jurisdiction would make them cost-effective in peace-time is often associated with Robert Treat Paine. *See e.g.* Marcus & Wexler, "Judiciary Act", *in* Origins of the Federal Judiciary, *supra* note 7, at 19; *see also* Goebel, Antecedents, *supra* note 8, at 460–461.

months or even years, waiting for the courts to be in session is at worst a minor inconvenience. In maritime matters, however, both ships and seamen frequently begin their next voyages soon after disputes arise. It is likely that witnesses—and even the parties themselves—would no longer be in port if the day of trial were delayed for months. Thus to be useful in resolving private maritime disputes in a timely fashion, courts must be open throughout the year.[61] Moreover, courts must be fairly numerous to be geographically convenient. For those in Congress who opposed the creation of inferior federal courts for political reasons, their best chance for defeating the Judiciary Bill lay in convincing their more moderate colleagues that the proposed system of courts was a luxury that the young nation could not afford. When consensus was reached on the need for admiralty courts, the argument that federal trial courts would be too expensive lost much of its force. If the United States were to incur the costs of establishing and maintaining a sufficient number of admiralty courts to serve the needs of maritime communities throughout the country, it was a small leap to the notion of allowing those courts to exercise jurisdiction over matters arising under acts of Congress or those in which one party was a domiciliary of a different state or nation. Some in Congress did contend that federal admiralty courts would be considerably less costly to operate than the system envisioned by Ellsworth and his colleagues on the Senate subcommittee,[62] but the argument appeared strained and was attacked by supporters of the bill as contrary to common sense.[63] William Smith of South

61. *See e.g.* Letter of James Sullivan to John Langdon (March 29, 1789), observing that "[t]he Admiralty ought always to be open in the Seaports on Account of Seizures mariners [*sic*] wages Botomrys &c.". *Reproduced in* Documentary History of the Supreme Court, *supra* note 33, Vol. IV, at 372–373. Sullivan makes the same point in a letter to Elbridge Gerry bearing the same date. *Reproduced in Id.*, Vol. IV, at 372.

62. Representative Samuel Livermore of New Hampshire, former chief justice of his state's Superior Court and delegate to the ratifying convention, sought to jettison the jurisdictional provisions of the Judiciary Bill in favor of creating "courts of admiralty", the expense of which, he remarked, would "not be by a fiftieth part so much" as the cost of the federal courts outlined in the Judiciary Bill. House Debates (Aug. 29, 1789) recorded in *The Gazette of the United States* (Sept. 2, 1789), *reproduced in* First Federal Congress, *supra* note 2, Vol. XI, at 1348. Livermore was not alone. Thomas Tucker also argued that federal jurisdiction should be restricted to admiralty and maritime cases. For discussion, *see* Warren, *Federal Judiciary Act*, *supra* note 8, at 123. Ultimately, only eleven of forty-two members of the House voted against the creation of federal district courts. Bourguignon, *Judiciary Act*, *supra* note 6, at 680–681; Warren, *Federal Judiciary Act*, *supra* note, at 125. For further discussion, *see e.g.* Goebel, Antecedents, *supra* note 8, at 504.

63. The response of the bill's supporters is best summarized in the remarks of William Smith of South Carolina:

Carolina laid to rest any lingering concerns about the costs of the federal courts, and moreover challenged the notion that the judicial system envisioned by the bill would cause friction between the state and federal courts. The need for admiralty courts formed the linchpin of his argument:

> All the difficulties and inconveniences which the gentlemen have started [*sic: i.e.* "stated"] as arising from the establishment of a district court arise from the government itself. All the objections made to this court apply equally against having any national judicature. Indeed if they had any weight they would as forcibly apply against the very institution which the gentlemen patronize, *viz.*, a court of admiralty and piracy. If there is to be this perpetual clashing of jurisdictions between the federal and State courts, this eternal jarring between their respective officers, will not these embarrassments exist under any judicial system which the ingenuity of man can devise? Will they not take place under the establishment proposed by the other side; and will the mere alteration of the court from a district to a court of admiralty and piracy remedy the evil?[64]

Thus for Smith, and ultimately for the majority of his colleagues, the additional "jarring" that would accompany the extension of the lower federal courts' jurisdiction from admiralty into diversity cases was not sufficient to block passage of the bill. Smith accepts a certain level of friction in the system as an unfortunate—but unavoidable—by-product of overlapping jurisdic-

---

> "But some gentlemen are of the opinion that the district court should be altogether confined to admiralty causes; while others deem it expedient that it should be intrusted with a more enlarged jurisdiction: and should in addition to admiralty causes, take cognizance of all causes of seizures of land, all breaches of impost laws, of offences committed on the high seas, and causes in which foreigners or citizens of other states are parties.... I am inclined to favor the latter.... The expence [*sic*: "expense"] is suggested as an objection to the system. It is admitted by [Livermore] that it is proper to have district courts of admiralty; these courts must of necessity have jurisdiction of offences committed on the high seas. Now the establishment of such a court will induce nearly all the expence that will be requisite; the extension of the system to the length I have stated will occasion a very trifling increase of expence, and if the latter plan should be found, after due consideration to be more conducive to the happiness and welfare of our constitutients than the other, a small increase of the expence ought to be no impediment to the attainment of so valuable an object."

House Debates (Aug. 29, 1789), recorded in *The Gazette of the United States* (Sept. 2, 1789), *reproduced in* First Federal Congress, *supra* note 2, Vol. XI, at 1349–1350.

64. House Debates (Aug. 29, 1789), recorded in *The Gazette of the United States* (Sept. 2, 1789), *reproduced in Id.*, Vol. XI, at 1362.

tion. The system is not ideal, but on balance the benefits outweigh the shortcomings. A contract-case arising under the laws of South Carolina will be heard in state court if both parties are domiciliaries of the state, but may be heard in either state or federal court if one of the parties is not. This system provides access to *fora* free from local bias, though it necessarily results in two separate sets of courts interpreting the same body of law. Smith recognizes the potential for conflict, though he opts to de-emphasize it. If one accepts diversity jurisdiction, this conflict is a natural consequence of it. More puzzling, however, is why he assumes that admiralty jurisdiction must carry the same potential for conflict. One can envision a scheme for federal jurisdiction in which diversity claims may be filed in either state or federal court, while all maritime claims must be filed in federal admiralty court. Diversity jurisdiction by its very nature implies concurrent jurisdiction; admiralty jurisdiction does not. Thus the friction and conflict that are inevitably present in the former are not in the latter. Nevertheless, Smith does not even consider the possibility of federal admiralty jurisdiction without concurrent jurisdiction vested in the state courts. Assuming that this is not a mere oversight, we must ask why he takes for granted that concurrent jurisdiction, embodied in the bill's "Saving-to-Suitors Clause", was a necessary component of federal admiralty jurisdiction.

Concurrent Admiralty and Maritime Jurisdiction

In its final form, the Judiciary Act of 1789 settled debate over many admiralty-related issues that plagued the deliberations over the judiciary since the Constitutional Convention. Those opposed to expansive federal jurisdiction long had feared the rules of procedure as the means by which citizens would be deprived of their common-law right to jury-trials.[65] The principal impetus

65. Typical of this common line of argument are the remarks of Richard Henry Lee in the third of his "Letters of a Federal Farmer" (Oct. 10, 1787), *reprinted in* Pamphlets on the Constitution of the United States, Published During Its Discussion by the People, 1787–1788 (Paul Leicester Ford ed., Brooklyn, 1888) at 294, 307–308. Federalist Tench Coxe, writing under the pseudonym of "An American Citizen" (1788), replies to such concerns, contending that the mere fact that federal trial courts will hear admiralty cases without juries does not imply that they will not employ juries in criminal cases and private actions arising on land. *Reprinted in Id.* at 147, 149–150. For further discussion of fears that civil-law fact-finding in admiralty cases would carry over to all cases heard in federal trial courts, *see e.g.* Bourguignon, *Judiciary Act*, *supra* note 6, at 662–663; Warren, *Federal*

behind the creation of federal trial courts had been the adjudication of prize and other matters arising under the law of nations. In the minds of many in the eighteenth century, the procedures of the civil law governed these matters.[66] Indeed, one of the chief justifications for extending the admiralty jurisdiction to instance cases was that courts already familiar with civil-law procedures would be more comfortable proceeding *in rem* or evaluating testimony in the form of depositions and interrogatories—both traditional elements of maritime litigation. Moreover, the availability of civil-law joinder of claims would make such *fora* better equipped to handle seamen's claims for wages. Some critics believed that if federal trial courts were structured as civil-law tribunals, they would extend civil-law procedure to all cases under their jurisdiction, including criminal and diversity cases, as well as any other matter arising under an act of Congress, thereby depriving defendants of trial by jury.[67] In the end, this did not happen. Federal district courts sitting in admiralty were to utilize a modified procedure derived from the civil law; when sitting in law, their procedures reflected those of the common law and preserved the common-law jury.[68] With regard to testimony, however, the Act changed traditional practice. From the colonial period through that of the Articles of Confederation, Amer-

---

Judiciary Act, *supra* note 8, at 75 (discussing the Senate's redrafting of Section 9 to assure jury-trials in all except "civil causes of admiralty and maritime jurisdiction").

66. *See e.g.* Letter of John Adams to Thomas Brand-Hollis (Jan. 4, 1788), contending that the law of nations bars the use of juries in admiralty cases. *Reprinted in* RATIFICATION, *supra* note 24, Vol. V, at 611. At roughly the same time, the anonymous author of an editorial in the *Connecticut Courant* (Dec. 10, 1787), also maintains that the law of nations requires the use of civil-law procedures in admiralty cases. *Id.*, Vol. III, at 487, 490.

67. The "slippery slope" argument—in essence that federal courts established as civil-law admiralty tribunals would for expediency's sake utilize civil-law procedures in common-law cases—was a popular feature of antifederalist pamphlets from the onset of the debate over ratification. Both Lee's "Federal Farmer" and Coxe's federalist rebuttal (*supra* note 65) address these concerns, as does "Brutus" No. XIV (Feb. 28, 1788–March 6, 1788), *reprinted in* DEBATE ON THE CONSTITUTION, *supra* note 46, Vol. II, at 260. It receives perhaps its most detailed elaboration, ironically, in John Adams' refutation. In a letter to Thomas Brand-Hollis (Jan. 4, 1788), Adams counters the antifederalists' argument, maintaining that the Constitution was silent regarding whether to employ juries in federal trial courts in order to permit their use in most cases while forbidding it in others, such as admiralty, where (in his opinion) the law of nations barred their use. *Reprinted in* RATIFICATION, *supra* note 24, Vol. V, at 611. For the debate over the use of juries, *see also* Bourguignon, *Judiciary Act*, *supra* note 6, at 662.

68. "(d) And the trial of issues of fact, in the district courts, in all causes except civil causes of admiralty and maritime jurisdiction, shall be by jury." Judiciary Act, ch. 20, sec. 9, 1 Stat 73, 77 (1789). The Act placed this same requirement on trials in the federal circuit courts. Judiciary Act, ch. 20, sec. 13, 1 Stat. 73, 80.

ican courts had bowed to tradition and accepted the notion that evidence should be received in the form of sworn statements. Nonetheless, American maritime attorneys were trained in the common law, and showed none of the attachment to the traditional forms so long defended by their counterparts across the Atlantic in Doctors' Commons. The result was a compromise. The Judiciary Act retained for the courts the power to proceed *in rem* and to consolidate seamen's wage-claims, both widely perceived as practical devices indispensable for maritime litigation. On the other hand, the Act empowered federal trial courts, even when sitting in admiralty, to receive testimony *viva voce*.[69] This decision would lay to rest another hotly contested point, namely whether federal courts would conduct complete *de novo* reviews. Such reviews were not practical where some of the testimony before the court below was oral. When the introduction of oral testimony was coupled with monetary limits on appeals,[70] the scenario outlined by George Mason, Patrick Henry, and others during the process of ratification failed to materialize.[71] Wealthy litigants would

---

69. "And be it further enacted, That the mode of proof by oral testimony and examination of witnesses in open court shall be the same in all the courts of the United States, as well as in the trial of causes in equity and of admiralty and maritime jurisdiction, as of actions at common law..." Judiciary Act of 1789, ch. 20, sec. 30, 1 Stat. 73, 88 (1789). Nevertheless, acknowledging the practical advantages of admitting testimony in the form of interrogatories, Congress allowed for the use of depositions and interrogatories in admiralty proceedings in the event that witnesses were "bound on a voyage at sea". For discussion, *see* Warren, *Federal Judiciary Act*, *supra* note 8, at 100, 106.

70. The notion of monetary limits on appeals was present in the Judiciary Bill since the first draft of Ellsworth's subcommittee in June. This amount, originally fifty dollars, was increased to three hundred dollars in the final draft of the Act. *See* Judiciary Bill [S-1], sec. 20, draft of June 12, 1789, *reprinted in* First Federal Congress, *supra* note 2, Vol. V, at 1184–1185. *See also* Judiciary Act of 1789, ch. 20, sec. 21, which provides: "And be it further enacted, That from final decrees in district court in causes of admiralty and maritime jurisdiction, where the matter in dispute exceeds the sum or value of three hundred dollars, exclusive of costs, an appeal shall be allowed to the next circuit court, to be held in such district". 1 Stat. 73, 83–84.

71. In traditional civil-law litigation, the trial court received testimony in the form of depositions and interrogatories. Thus an appellate court with a complete set of papers filed with the trial court would be in a position equal to that of the court below in evaluating the evidence. During the process of ratification, several antifederalists raised the concern that if federal courts were structured as civil-law tribunals, wealthy litigants would exploit appellate *de novo* review by forcing their opponents to travel to distant *fora*. Faced with the prospect of increased costs, many prospective litigants might forego litigation altogether. This notion, often recurring in antifederalist writings, is given detailed attention in the debates in Virginia's ratifying convention on June 19, 1788, principally in the comments of Mason and Henry. For a transcript of the proceedings, *see* Ratification, *supra* note 24,

not be able to manipulate the appellate process to force less affluent opponents to litigate whole cases *de novo* in inconvenient *fora.*

Of all provisions relating to maritime jurisdiction, however, the most interesting feature of the new statute was the "Saving-to-Suitors Clause". In its final form, the Act provided that:

> [The district courts shall] have exclusive original cognizance of all civil causes of admiralty and maritime jurisdiction, including all seizures under laws of impost, navigation or trade of the United States, where the seizures are made, on waters which are navigable from the sea by vessels of ten or more tons burthen, within their respective districts as well as upon the high seas... *saving to suitors, in all cases, the right of a common law remedy, where the common law is competent to give it.*[72]

Unfortunately, the extant records do not reveal details of debate over the Saving-to-Suitors Clause, as the provision has come to be known. Moreover, it is not clear that the clause, a product of the Senate subcommittee's original draft,[73] was ever debated on the floor of either house. Characterized in scholarly literature variously as "obscure" in aim and vague in content,[74] the clause

---

Vol. X, at 1404–1420. *See also* Chapter III, notes 206–208 and text accompanying. For a legislative history of the debates over appellate review of facts, *see* Warren, *Federal Judiciary Act, supra* note 8, at 102.

72. Judiciary Act of 1789, ch. 20, sec. 9, 1 Stat. 73, 77 (*emphasis added*). The opening lines of Section 9 also provide for the district courts' cognizance over crimes occurring at sea, on the following terms:

> "And be it further enacted, That the district courts shall have, exclusively of the courts of the several States, cognizance of all crimes and offences that shall be cognizable under the authority of the United States, committed within their respective districts, or upon the high seas; where no other punishment than whipping, not exceeding thirty stripes, a fine not exceeding one hundred dollars, or a term of imprisonment not exceeding six months, is to be inflicted..."

1 Stat. 73, 76–77.

73. Judiciary Bill [S-1]: sec. 10, June 12, 1789, *reprinted in* First Federal Congress, *supra* note 2, Vol. V, at 1177. *See* discussion, *supra* notes 33–35 and text accompanying.

74. Remarking "[a]t what the saving clause was aimed is obscure", Julius Goebel notes further that:

> "The Framers of the Constitution had established 'cases of admiralty and maritime jurisdiction' as a category to which the judicial power extended on the basis of the report of the Committee of Detail, but there had been no discussion of the implications of this combination. 'Maritime jurisdiction' had no fixed technical meaning in English law."

Goebel, Antecedents, *supra* note 8, at 474. Goebel speculates that the Saving-to-Suitors Clause was added to "restore jurisdictional balance between the common law and ad-

somewhat surprisingly also received little illumination in early case law. It would appear that both Congress and the courts accepted its meaning as self-explanatory and its purpose as self-evident. The fact that neither "admiralty" nor "maritime" were clearly defined terms of art in eighteenth-century America only deepens the mystery. Nevertheless, by adopting a scheme of concurrent maritime jurisdiction, Congress made a bold statement on how maritime litigation would evolve in the fledgling country. The choice of overlapping state/federal jurisdiction bears closer examination.

Once again, the underlying motive of Congress was convenience. The plain language of Article III leaves open the possibility that the Framers intended to exclude the state courts from admiralty jurisdiction entirely.[75] On the other hand, no less eminent authorities than Joseph Story[76] and the standard trea-

---

miralty courts as it had existed in the colonies." *Id.*, at 475. Casto goes further, maintaining that "Ellsworth drafted around the problem by opting for a vague and general definition". *See* Casto, *Origins*, *supra* note 44, at 147. It is Casto's contention that this approach was necessary to ensure that jurisdiction over private maritime cases remain exclusively with the state courts. Nonetheless, it would appear odd for Ellsworth to resort to such a strategy when—even by Casto's own admission—the issue of whether to vest the federal courts with jurisdiction over private maritime suits was not hotly debated. *Cf. Id.* at 146–147.

75. U.S. Const. art. III, sec. 2. The notion that the Framers' intent was to exclude state courts entirely from adjudicating admiralty matters has not received widespread support in the scholarly literature, though there are some notable exceptions. *See e.g.* George C. Sprague & Nicholas J. Healy, Cases on the Law of Admiralty (St. Paul: West Publishing Co., 1950), at 18; *see also* Frederick Bausman, *Admiralty and Maritime Jurisdiction*, 36 Am. L. Rev. 182, 185 (1902) (maintaining that the Saving-to-Suitors Clause passes constitutional muster only if Congress intended thereby to preserve common-law remedies *in federal court* in those cases that could sound in either admiralty or law) (hereinafter Bausman). One of the better discussions of this position (both pro and con) in the secondary literature is contained in David W. Robertson, Admiralty and Federalism (Mineola, New York: The Foundation Press, Inc., 1970) at 18–22.

76. Story explains Article III's grant of admiralty and maritime jurisdiction:

> "There is, then, a peculiar wisdom in giving to the national government a jurisdiction of this sort, which cannot be wielded, except for the general good; and which multiplies the securities for the public peace abroad, and gives to commerce and navigation the most encouraging support at home. It may be added, that, in many of the cases included in these latter classes, the same reasons do not exist, as in cases of prize, for an exclusive jurisdiction; and, therefore, whenever the common law is competent to give a remedy in the state courts, they may retain their accustomed concurrent jurisdiction in the administration of it."

He elaborates further in the accompanying footnote:

> "[The admiralty jurisdiction] is exclusive in all matters of prize, for the reason, that at the common law this jurisdiction is vested in the courts of admiralty, to

tise *Benedict on Admiralty*[77] have argued that the Constitution implicitly mandated concurrent jurisdiction. Although a few in Congress raised questions in

---

> the exclusion of the courts of common law. But in cases, where the jurisdiction of the courts of common law and the admiralty are concurrent, (as in cases of possessory suits, mariners' wages, and marine torts,) there is nothing in the constitution, necessarily leading to the conclusion, that the jurisdiction was intended to be exclusive; and there is as little ground, upon general reasoning, to contend for it. The reasonable interpretation of the constitution would seem to be, that it conferred on the national judiciary the admiralty and maritime jurisdiction, exactly according to the nature and extent and modifications, in which it existed in the jurisprudence of the common law. Where the jurisdiction was exclusive, it remained so; where it was concurrent, it remained so. Hence, the states could have no right to create courts of admiralty, as such, or to confer on their own courts, the cognizance of such cases, as were exclusively cognizable in admiralty courts. But the states might well retain and exercise the jurisdiction in cases, of which the cognizance was previously concurrent in the courts of common law. This latter class of cases can be no more deemed cases of admiralty and maritime jurisdiction, than cases of common law jurisdiction."

JOSEPH STORY, COMMENTARIES ON THE CONSTITUTION (1st ed., 3 vols., Boston: Hilliard, Gray, & Co., 1833), Vol. III, Bk. III, Ch. XXXVIII, sec. 1666, at 533–534 n. 3.

77. By the fifth edition of the treatise (1925), the editors had included the following assessment of concurrent jurisdiction:

> "The Judiciary Act, which in 1789 established the United States courts and defined their jurisdiction, is a contemporaneous construction of the Constitution and confirmed the existing right of the common law courts by providing that the United States District Courts should have 'exclusive original cognizance of all civil causes of admiralty and maritime jurisdiction,' etc., 'saving to suitors, in all cases, the right of a common law remedy, where the common law is competent to give it."

ERASTUS C. BENEDICT, THE AMERICAN ADMIRALTY: ITS JURISDICTION AND PRACTICE (5th ed., 3 vols., George V. A. McCloskey ed., Albany: Banks & Co., 1925), Vol. I, sec. 21, at 25. Nevertheless, the comment appears to be an interpolation by the editors, as the first edition of Erastus C. Benedict's original treatise states that:

> "[T]he constitutional grants of judicial power...are not grants to this or that court of the United States. The Constitution does nothing but draw the line between the cases which belong to the United States Government and those which belong to the State Governments. It transfers from the States and the people of the states to the General Government, the judicial sovereignty in great national classes of cases, to be exercised...by such courts, and in such manner as the congress of the newly created Government should provide."

BENEDICT (1st ed.), *supra* note 51, sec. 28, at 18. Thus for Erastus Benedict, it was theoretically possible for Congress to divest the states of all admiralty and maritime jurisdiction—a position clearly at odds with the later editors' contention that the power of state courts to hear admiralty cases was unimpaired by the Constitution—perhaps even to the point that Congress lacks the power divest them of the jurisdiction.

their private correspondence about the constitutionality of concurrent state/federal jurisdiction,[78] there is no record of such a debate in either house. Ultimately, the dispositive criterion was practicality. By granting concurrent jurisdiction over private maritime actions to the state courts, Ellsworth's subcommittee had sought to assuage the concerns expressed earlier by Luther Martin and others that federal maritime courts would be geographically impractical—forcing litigants to file or defend claims for small sums far from their homes.[79] The federal courts would be available for those litigants who felt the need for their particular maritime expertise or rules of procedure. Common-law courts were not accustomed to hear cases of salvage or to oversee ships' surveys. In addition, parties could opt for federal court where no common-law remedy was available, as when a contract was signed on foreign soil or on the high seas, in contemplation of performance at sea.[80] On the other hand, claimants who desired a jury[81] were free to file in state courts, pro-

---

78. *See* Marcus & Wexler, "Judiciary Act", *in* ORIGINS OF THE FEDERAL JUDICIARY, *supra* note 7, at 17.

79. Letter of Luther Martin to the Maryland Legislature (Nov. 19, 1787), *reprinted in* FARRAND, RECORDS, *supra* note 16, Vol. III, Appendix A, Doc. CLVIII, at 177, 220. (For text of the letter, *see supra* note 44.) For further discussion of the antifederalists' concern that federal courts would place less affluent litigants at a disadvantage, *see supra* Chapter III, notes 185–196.

80. For discussion, *see e.g.* Chapter I, notes 203, 227–228, 232–233 and text accompanying; *see also* Chapter II, notes 109–110, 129–138, 192–203 and text accompanying. Another practical concern often overlooked in the scholarly literature—eighteenth-century and modern alike—was the time-frame within which a seaman had to bring action. In *The Seaman's Friend*, a popular early nineteenth-century manual for merchant officers and seamen, Richard Henry Dana, Jr. admonishes his readers that one must commence his contract-action at common law within six years. In admiralty, however, the doctrine of *laches* prevailed, thus enabling a claimant to file an action *in rem* at his nearest convenience, even if the ship were not to return to port until after the six-year common-law limit had passed. RICHARD HENRY DANA, JR., THE SEAMAN'S FRIEND (6th ed., Boston: Thomas Groom & Co., 1851; New York: Scholars' Facsimiles & Reprints, 1979) Part I, Ch. XXI, at 223. For discussion of *laches*, *see also* THOMAS J. SCHOENBAUM, ADMIRALTY AND MARITIME LAW (Practitioner's Edition, St. Paul: West Publishing Co., 1987) sec. 4-17, at 156–157 (hereinafter SCHOENBAUM).

81. For the sailor, the preference between a local common-law court and an admiralty court varied according to personal circumstances. By opting for a common-law court, he would forego the advantages both of expedited proceedings and of joining his claim for wages with his shipmates in order to have his claim heard by a jury of his peers. It is an unfortunate fact that many judges took a patronizing view of sailors. Kent once described sailors as a "heedless, ignorant, audacious, but useful class of men" KENT, COMMENTARIES, *supra* note 44, Vol. I, at 136. Though less disparaging, Story regarded seamen as "wards of the admiralty", noting that they are "credulous and complying" and "thoughtless and require indul-

vided those courts could offer a remedy. Likewise, those who wished to reduce costs by litigating closer to home could do the same.[82] The system would work well for attorneys, many of whom had little experience with admiralty procedures. Reasoning that tort is still a tort, and a contract is still a contract, whether at sea or on dry land, most practitioners preferred not learning the intricacies of a new set of procedures simply in order to file claims in an admiralty court. So long as a claim could be characterized such that it would sound in common law, and so long as that law were to provide their clients with adequate remedies, most attorneys naturally would prefer the familiar surroundings and procedures of the local courts.[83] The proposed system like-

---

gence". *Harden v. Gordon* (Case No. 6,047), 11 F. Cas. 480, 485 (C.C., D. Maine, 1823). By the early nineteenth century, Richard Henry Dana, Jr., noted admiralty practitioner as well as author, concluded *Two Years Before the Mast* with a discussion the widespread perception of social-class prejudice in cases involving seamen: "The effect of a sailor's testimony in deciding a case must depend altogether upon the reputation of the class to which he belongs, and upon the impression he himself produces in court by his deportment, and by those infallible marks of character which always tell upon a jury." RICHARD HENRY DANA, TWO YEARS BEFORE THE MAST, AND TWENTY-FOUR YEARS AFTER (1st ed., 1842, *reprinted* New York: Collier & Son, Harvard Classics, 1937, 1968) at 360–361. Given the social and political climate, it is not surprising that some seamen would opt for a jury—particularly in their home ports—believing common citizens to be more sympathetic than the judiciary.

82. The principal impetus behind the Saving-to-Suitors Clause was convenience for litigants. *See e.g. State Gazette of North Carolina* (June 12, 1789), *reproduced in* DOCUMENTARY HISTORY OF THE SUPREME COURT, *supra* note 33, Vol. IV, at 403. For discussion, *see* Bourguignon, *Judiciary Act*, *supra* note 6, at 696.

83. While no comprehensive statistical study of practice under the states' admiralty courts has been published to date, those for the colonial period reveal an interesting trend. Of the 429 lawyers admitted to practice between 1666 and 1775 in Maryland, only eighteen are known to have represented clients in maritime cases. *See* DAVID R. OWEN & MICHAEL C. TOLLEY, COURTS OF ADMIRALTY IN COLONIAL AMERICA: THE MARYLAND EXPERIENCE, 1634–1776 (Durham: Carolina Academic Press, 1995) at 174–175 (hereinafter OWEN & TOLLEY). Similarly in New York, during a fifty-year period from 1739 through the Articles of Confederation, only twenty-five attorneys handled eighty percent of the admiralty business. *See* CHARLES MERRILL HOUGH, REPORTS OF CASES IN THE VICE ADMIRALTY OF THE PROVINCE OF NEW YORK AND IN THE COURT OF ADMIRALTY OF THE STATE OF NEW YORK, 1715–1788 (New Haven: Yale University Press, 1925), Introduction at xxiv. Even today, one scholar has noted that "some admiralty experts have a tendency 'to use the field's arcane vocabulary and conceptual apparatus as an instrument of power rather than of communication'". David W. Robertson, *Displacement of State Law by Federal Maritime*, 26 J. Mar. L. & Com. Law 325, 366 (1995); *see generally* David W. Robertson, *Admiralty and Maritime Litigation in State Court*, 55 La. L. Rev. 685 (1955). Forcing the plaintiffs' common-law bar to litigate in an unfamiliar court with unfamiliar procedures would only compound the problem. Indeed, the Federal Rules of Civil Procedure's 1966 amendments—

wise would benefit federal judges. By offering claimants a choice of forum, they would tend to gravitate to the courts with the shortest dockets.[84]

The Judiciary Act and the Constitution

By the second half of the nineteenth century, courts and commentators alike assumed that the Judiciary Act's system of concurrent state/federal admiralty jurisdiction squared with both the plain language of Article III and the Framers' original intent. A standard treatise of the era observes:

> [T]hough admiralty process and admiralty remedies are to be sought only in the District Court, the right is nevertheless preserved to suitors to avail themselves of any co-existing common law remedies, notwithstanding the subject matter in cases of contract or the locality in cases of tort be maritime. That which is saved is not a remedy in the common law courts but a common law remedy. That which is preserved is not for the benefit of courts, but for suitors. The election is in effect made by the plaintiff, and it is a choice which the defendant must abide.... To suitors there is preserved the right in all cases where a concurrent remedy exists, to elect between that afforded by the admiralty or by the common law, and in case the latter be deemed preferable to pursue it in the appropriate court wherein that jurisprudence prevails, either State or national, according to their residence.[85]

The author's first conclusion—that the purpose of the Saving-to-Suitors Clause was convenience for litigants, not protection of the state courts—is borne out by the extant records. Despite occasional vitriolic rhetoric about

---

which subsumed the old admiralty procedures under the streamlined Supplemental Rules for Certain Admiralty and Maritime Claims—serve to underscore the desire for admiralty procedures that are accessible to experienced litigators who are not specialists in maritime matters. FED. R. CIV. P, SUPP. R. A-F.

84. Convenience for the judiciary as a justification for concurrent jurisdiction appeared in correspondence on the judiciary which pre-dated the subcommittee's draft of [S-1]. *See e.g.* Letter of David Sewall to Caleb Strong (May 2, 1789), *reproduced in* DOCUMENTARY HISTORY OF THE SUPREME COURT, *supra* note 33, Vol. IV, at 384–385. It should be noted that Caleb Strong became a member of the subcommittee that drafted the Judiciary Act. *See supra* note 32 and text accompanying.

85. THEODORE M. ETTING, THE ADMIRALTY JURISDICTION IN AMERICA, (Philadelphia: Rees Welsh & Co., 1879; *facsimile reprint*, Littleton, Colorado: Fred B. Rothman & Co., 1986) at 85.

the federal courts "swallowing up" the jurisdiction of the state courts, the strongest argument of the opponents of expansive federal jurisdiction was that it would inconvenience litigants by forcing them to travel far from home to file or defend actions. This argument, not the rantings of the extreme antifederalists, had posed the greatest threat to the creation of inferior federal courts. The second conclusion—that a claimant may pursue admiralty remedies in federal court or common-law remedies in either state court or federal court (in the event of diversity)—comports with modern practice. The author, however, has the advantage of hindsight, and nearly a century of precedent can cloud one's perception.

At least one modern commentator has questioned the view that the first Congress intended the Judiciary Act to preserve concurrent jurisdiction for the state courts. Instead, the argument runs, Congress guaranteed to claimants a common law remedy in the federal courts. Although counterintuitive and contrary to two hundred years of case law, the argument is more profound than it looks on first glance. It deserves closer examination. "Admiralty", so the argument goes, refers to those matters that Coke and the common lawyers conceded to their civil-law rivals, while "maritime" refers to all cases the subject-matter of which is grounded in marine activities.[86] "Maritime" is thus more expansive than "admiralty". If one reads the Saving-to-Suitors Clause as allowing for common-law remedies in federal court, it guarantees a remedy in each maritime case. A federal court could not dismiss an action merely because the subject-matter lies outside the narrow definition of "admiralty" espoused by Coke, Prynne, or Hale. Over time, however, the courts developed a different view of "admiralty" and "maritime". The distinction became one of procedure and remedies. "Admiralty" cases were those adjudicated under modified procedures derived from the civil law. The substantive rules were those of the *lex maritima*, but admiralty's remedies—like its procedure—were unique unto itself. "Maritime" cases, on the other hand, were those that were marine in nature, arising out of events or transactions relating to navigation or the sea. "Maritime" implied no particular procedures or remedies. Hence it follows that Congress was free to delegate to the state courts the power to hear maritime cases, but not to delegate "admiralty jurisdiction".[87] The reason

86. *See* Bausman, *supra* note 75, at 183–184.

87. Bausman gives the following summary in his critique of the prevailing orthodox view, under which maritime jurisdiction is delegable and admiralty is not:

> "[T]he courts have held that the *Constitution means* exclusive. Exclusive as to what? Admiralty. As to maritime, too? Apparently not. Here they say that the Judiciary Act operates successfully to give jurisdiction to the courts of the States.

lay not in the grammar and syntax of Article III—for indeed the text treats the two words as parallel—but rather in the distinction between a class of cases defined by subject-matter and another defined by the procedures employed and the mode of relief granted. "Admiralty cases" were neither distinct from nor identical to "maritime cases". Moreover, to the extent that "admiralty cases" were a subset of the larger "maritime" category, they were not a subset defined by differences in the nature of the underlying disputes but rather differences in the available remedies.[88] In time, the notion that maritime jurisdiction was delegable while admiralty jurisdiction was not—in the hands of the federal judiciary—became penumbral to the plain language of the Constitution itself.[89] The notion spread to the states as well, as most abol-

---

> In other words, when it is admiralty that is to be defended it is not defended by the Judiciary Act's making the jurisdiction exclusive. It is defended out of the Constitution, which is interpreted to place admiralty above reduction by any Judiciary Act. The word maritime in the same clause is, however, left to the mercy of an act of Congress.

Id. at 185 *(emphasis in the original).*

88. An example of overlap between admiralty and maritime cases is that of seamen's wages. Such claims are obviously "maritime" as they relate to contracts to be performed at sea. Traditionally, seamen asserted claims for wages in admiralty court, where they were permitted to join their claims together in a proceeding against the ship. Claims thus filed were proceedings in admiralty. Nonetheless, some mariners sought redress for their grievances by hailing their employers into courts of common law. Indeed, Judge Holt had maintained that wage claims were by nature common-law claims, and that such claims in admiralty were spared from writs of prohibition only as "an indulgence to the poor sailors". Arthur Browne, A Compendious View of the Civil Law, and of the Law of Admiralty, Being the Substance of a Course of Lectures Read in the University of Dublin (2 vols., 3d ed. [1st American ed.], New York: Halsted & Voorhies, 1840), Vol. II, at 86–87 (hereinafter Browne). Thus two sailors could sue for unpaid wages for services rendered aboard the same ship on the same voyage—one against the ship in an admiralty court and the other against the owners in a court of common law. Both claims are "maritime". That one is "admiralty" and the other is not, however, is not a result of differences in the claims, but rather only in the procedures employed and the remedies sought.

89. State courts' power to hear "maritime" cases was never seriously challenged. On the other hand, it was widely believed that states could not create admiralty courts of their own to assume the full scope of admiralty and maritime jurisdiction described in Article III, even if Congress were to remove the jurisdiction from the federal courts. A generation after passage of the Judiciary Act, Justice Story raised this issue in *dicta*:

> "With regard to the admiralty and maritime jurisdiction, it would be difficult to prove that the states could resume it, if the United States should abolish the courts vested with that jurisdiction..."

Martin v. Hunter's Lessee, 1 U.S. 304, 373 (1816); *see also* discussion, *supra* note 87 and text accompanying.

ished their own admiralty tribunals in anticipation of the federal courts assuming all "admiralty" powers.[90]

One may ask whether either of these views—the time-honored interpretation of the courts or alternative supplied by the revisionist commentator—comport with Article III, and, in doing so, support the constitutionality of the Saving-to-Suitors Clause. The former requires that one accept the notion that Article III's "admiralty" refers to the structure and curial law of courts while "maritime" denotes the scope of substantive matters within the jurisdiction. The latter, by contrast, treats both "admiralty" and "maritime" as defining the substantive scope of jurisdiction; "admiralty" is a subset of "maritime", containing that restricted sphere of matters still within the purview of the English admiralty courts at the close of the eighteenth century. By rejecting the distinction between admiralty and maritime as one between court-structure/procedure and substance respectively, the revisionist's approach simultaneously rejects the grounds for maintaining that maritime jurisdiction is delegable while admiralty jurisdiction is not. This, at least to his mind, compels the conclusion that Congress could delegate *neither* admiralty *nor* maritime jurisdiction to the states. This approach displays real insight by showing that "admiralty" and "maritime" are of like kind, differing only in scope.[91] Gram-

---

90. Most states abolished their own courts of admiralty on the assumption that Congress would create replacements. Nevertheless, states were not unanimous in the view that federal law—either constitutional or statutory—barred states from creating or maintaining their own courts of admiralty. The state court of admiralty in Maryland was a true admiralty court in every sense of the term, utilizing modified civil-law procedures and empowered to proceed *in rem* against vessels. *See* Owen & Tolley, *supra* note 83, at 219–221. In 1792, an appellate court in Maryland awarded back-payments of salary to the estate of Benjamin Nicholson, the last judge of the state's admiralty court. Judge Nicholson received his salary for seven additional months following March 4, 1789—the date on which the Constitution came into force. (It should be noted that payment stopped at roughly the same time that Congress passed the Judiciary Act.) He resigned in December, 1790, not having been paid for the preceding thirteen months. Repeating an argument that Nicholson had made earlier in correspondence with the governor, the estate's attorneys argued that the state admiralty court was not abolished either by the Constitution or by the Judiciary Act, at the very least as regards its jurisdiction over maritime disputes in which all parties are Marylanders. The court decided in favor of the plaintiff, holding in effect that state admiralty jurisdiction was not pre-empted by federal admiralty jurisdiction. *See Nicholson v. Maryland*, 3 H. & McH. 109 (1792); for discussion, *see* Niles, *supra* note 39, at 1–11.

91. Citing the examples of shipbuilding contracts, trespass at sea, and ship's articles under seal, Bausman asserts that the Framers inserted "maritime" to expand the scope of marine jurisdiction beyond that of eighteenth-century admiralty:

matically, the text of Article III provides no support either to the notion that the Framers intended to equate "admiralty" with procedures and "maritime" with substantive issues or to the assertion that admiralty alone of the two is nondelegable. Moreover, the traditional interpretation is arguably anachronistic—at least to the extent that it equates admiralty with actions *in rem*.[92]

> "These things were maritime enough, but still the property, and the exclusive property, of the common law.... But the distinction between what is maritime and what belongs to the admiralty is perfectly clear. That this distinction was plain to the minds of the framers of the Constitution is not to be doubted. The words are not tautological."

Bausman, *supra* note 75, at 183–84. Although Bausman's assertion explains the need for "maritime" to increase the scope of "admiralty", it does not explain why the Framers retained the term "admiralty". While it is reasonable to assume that the words are not tautological, it is equally reasonable to expect that they not be redundant. One might salvage Bausman's reading by maintaining that the Framers included "admiralty" to reinforce the federal role in those matters outside of the common law that were related to marine activities, such as ships' surveys and disputes over salvage, express hypothecation, or contracts signed and performed on the high seas.

92. In modern practice, it is generally accepted that courts of common law can hear maritime cases, but that the power to entertain an action *in rem* belongs solely to the federal courts. The rationale underlying this rule is the protection of the maritime lien. Unlike a common-law mechanic's lien, the maritime lien confers not a *chose in action*, but rather a possessory interest in the vessel. Evolving out of the civil law's concept of *jus in re*, nineteenth-century courts held that claimants under maritime liens become part-owners. *See The Bold Buccleugh*, 13 Eng. Rep. 884 (1852); *The John G. Stevens*, 170 U.S. 113 (1898). (For how courts extended the concept of *jus in re* into a full proprietory interest in a vessel during the nineteenth century, *see* Paul Macarius Hebert, *The Origin and Nature of Maritime Liens*, 4 Tul. L. Rev. 381, 406–408 (1930); *see also* Edward F. Ryan, *Admiralty Jurisdiction and the Maritime Lien: An Historical Prespective*, 7 W. Ont. L. Rev. 173, 196–197 (1968).) The lien thus attaches to the *res* itself, and it follows the *res* even if its owners sell it to third parties. When a ship is party to an action *in rem* and subsequently sold at judicial auction to pay the claimants, however, all maritime liens are extinguished. *See e.g. Tucker v. Alexandroff*, 183 U.S. 424, 438 (Brown, J., 1902); *see also* Schoenbaum, *supra* note 80, Sec. 8-1, at 247–253. Nevertheless, the origins of the modern maritime lien cannot be traced back earlier than the 1790s. It evolved concurrently with—not before—the concept that common-law courts could not proceed *in rem*. The statements of some courts notwithstanding (*see e.g. The Rock Island Bridge*, 6 U.S. 215 (1867); *The Lottawanna*, 21 U.S. 582 (1875)), some modern commentators acknowledge the anachronism of grounding the presumed exclusivity of the federal action *in rem* in the protection of the maritime lien. Scholars supporting this position run the full gamut of the ideological spectrum, from Frederick Bausman, who believes that state maritime jurisdiction is unconstitutional, to William Casto, who contends that the Framers intended to vest instance jurisdiction exclusively in the states. For all of its other shortcomings, Casto's article debunks the notion that admiralty jurisdiction can be understood in terms of an *in rem/in personam* dichotomy:

Thus in revealing the weaknesses of the traditional interpretation, the alternate approach is quite useful. The theory goes awry, however, in assuming that the only course constitutionally available to Congress is to refrain from delegating *either* to the states. It overlooks the possibility that the Constitution permits Congress to delegate *both* admiralty and maritime jurisdiction.

Assuming that it was indeed possible to vest both admiralty and maritime jurisdiction in the state courts, it raises the question of why Congress opted for the formula embodied in the Saving-to-Suitors Clause. In the wake of our examination of the history of the marine jurisdiction under the Articles of Confederation, the reason is readily apparent. While the Judiciary Act establishes a scheme of concurrent jurisdiction, the scope of the state courts' maritime jurisdiction *vis-à-vis* that of the federal government is not identical, but rather overlapping. The Saving-to-Suitors Clause preserves state courts' power

---

> "The modern understanding of admiralty jurisdiction defines the national interest in particular maritime disputes by exclusive reference to the procedural nature of the remedy sought. In contrast, every piece of surviving evidence indicates that the Founding Generation's overriding concern was with the substance of the underlying dispute."

Casto, *Origins*, *supra* note 44, at 145. The notion that admiralty jurisdiction must be understood in terms of the *in rem* action, which must itself be understood in terms of the maritime lien, is a product of the "personification theory" of the maritime lien, expounded by Oliver Wendell Holmes and best exemplified by *Tucker v. Alexandroff*, which links the origin of the lien to the notion that ships are legal persons. (*See* Hebert, *Origin*, at 392–393.) Against this tradition stands both Clerke's *Praxis Curiae Admiralitatis Angliae* and the conclusions of most modern English legal historians, most notably Reginald Marsden, all of whom emphasize the procedural nature of the *in rem* action. (For discussion of the rift between advocates of the "personification theory" and the "procedural theory", *see* Hebert, *Origins*, at 382–392; *see also* William Tetley, Maritime Liens and Claims (2d ed., Montreal: Blais International Shipping Publications, 1998) at 53–55.) Originally, the action *in rem* was not the only procedural device by which admiralty courts could assume jurisdiction. Moreover, the procedural device of the action *in rem* pre-dated the substantive rights of the maritime lien. As Ryan observes:

> "Here then are the building blocks out of which were fashioned the maritime lien enforceable by an action *in rem*: the stipulation, the hypothec, the rights against the innocent purchaser, and the concept of the *actio in rem*."

Ryan, *Maritime Lien*, at 190. Courts did not use these building blocks to create the maritime lien until after the drafting of both Article III and the Judiciary Act. Thus the maritime lien, the action *in rem*, and admiralty jurisdiction were not inextricably connected, either in Britain or the United States, in 1789. One must take care not to assume that the rule of modern practice—namely that admiralty courts always proceed *in rem* and that common-law courts cannot—placed constraints upon either the Framers or the first Congress.

to hear maritime cases, but only to the extent that claimants seek "common law remedies". In essence, the Judiciary Act (*sub silentio*) prohibits states from operating their own prize courts. The experiences of the Revolution had taught the generation of 1789 the dangers of abandoning prize jurisdiction to the courts of the various states. Each state's prize court had operated under its own rules of procedure, making it nearly impossible for the national Appellate Prize Court to review the decisions effectively. In addition, the substantive law governing prize is derived from the law of nations. Unfortunately, however, in the eighteenth century no multilateral agreement embodied the law of prize; instead each court was obliged to infer the applicable rules from the "customs of civilized nations". The result was a deplorable lack of uniformity. When the Appellate Prize Court sought to remedy the problem by imposing its own interpretations of the law of nations on the cases before it, the Court found itself in conflict with the state tribunals. Lacking a mechanism for enforcing its decisions at the state level, the Court could neither resolve the conflict nor establish uniformity in procedural or substantive law. Such tensions would have been severe enough if they had implicated relations between the state and national governments alone, but with prize, the difficulties were not confined within the nation's borders. Prize cases by definition always implicate the rights of foreigners, frequently in ways that lead to diplomatic crises.[93] Thus the logical solution to the problems of prize litigation was national legislation—enforced by federal courts. As one would expect, the Judiciary Act granted prize jurisdiction to the federal courts.

National prize courts were necessary. Nevertheless, national prize courts were not practical. Article III provided for judges serving life tenures with undiminished salaries—hardly an efficient structure for courts that would hold sessions only during or immediately after a war. To render them cost-effective, Congress felt it necessary to augment their jurisdiction, allowing them to be useful during peace-time as well. For those in Congress most suspicious of a strong federal judiciary exercising a broad jurisdiction, conceding jurisdiction over revenue and instance cases was relatively painless. Courts of admiralty long had exercised cognizance over private maritime disputes without seriously threatening the independence and viability of common law courts. They had done so, in the form of the provincial vice admiralty courts, from their creation in the last decade of the seventeenth century through the 1760s.[94] Moreover, they had done so, in the form of the state prize courts,

93. For discussion, *see supra* Chapter III, notes 50–84 and text accompanying.

94. *See* discussion, *supra* Chapter II, notes 85–164, 192–203 and text accompanying.

which began hearing private maritime causes soon after their creation.[95] These courts were useful. They provided claimants with an understanding of maritime customs and business practices, as well as special expertise in construing the substantive rules that traditionally had governed them. Nevertheless, neither the vice admiralty courts nor their state-court successors ever wholly supplanted the common-law courts in adjudicating maritime disputes. Where claimants desired a jury or preferred the testimony of live witnesses to sworn interrogatories, the courts of common law stood ready and willing to hear their claims. Similarly, when claimants believed that the common law offered an adequate remedy, a common-law court close to home often was preferable to a court of admiralty located in a distant port. Many members of the bar no doubt also welcomed the availability of courts of common law, with their familiar rules of procedure. Merchants and shipowners engaged in complex commercial transactions, for whom an occasional legal dispute was part of the cost of doing business, desired a forum that understood the nature of those transactions—as well as the importance of structuring its proceedings so as to allow both ships and men to return to sea quickly. So too did some seamen, who appreciated the opportunity of joining their claims for wages with those of their shipmates. On the other hand, those for whom litigation was infrequent, particularly less affluent inland merchants or sailors in the coastal trades who returned to their homes between voyages, had recourse to their local courts, where remedy could be had at a reasonable cost.[96] *The Judiciary Act gave each group of claimants that which each most wanted. By doing so, however, it had not created a novel jurisdictional system, but rather merely had codified an old one. In essence, the Saving-to-Suitors Clause merely preserved the status quo.*

The foregoing explains the principal rationale underlying Congress' grant of concurrent jurisdiction under the Saving-to-Suitors Clause. Nonetheless, some questions remain unanswered.[97] Neither the Constitution nor the Judi-

95. *See supra* Chapter III, notes 15–49 and text accompanying for discussion.

96. *See supra* Chapter II, notes 204–270; Chapter III, 188–196 and text accompanying.

97. One issue not adequately debated in Congress is the rationale behind the provision empowering the Supreme Court to issue writs of prohibition to federal districts courts "when proceeding as courts of admiralty and maritime jurisdiction." *See* Judiciary Act of 1789, ch. 20, sec. 13 (b), 1 Stat. 72, 81. In order to determine whether an admiralty court's proceedings are *ultra vires*, and thus encroaching on the common law, one must have a clearly delineated concept of where admiralty ends and the common law begins. Unfortunately, neither the Constitution nor the Judiciary Act make this distinction. It was therefore left to the federal judiciary to set the line of demarcation in the next century. *See infra* notes 98–99 and text accompanying.

ciary Act provide a clear line of demarcation between "admiralty and maritime" and "common law".[98] Neither Article III nor the Judiciary Act expressly define either "admiralty" or "maritime" by reference to subject-matter. The statutes of Richard II, limiting the scope of admiralty jurisdiction to transactions and incidents occurring outside English counties, had been recognized by some American admiralty courts both before and after the Revolution.[99] This controversy would resurface in the nineteenth century, as federal courts grappled with the implications of the "tide-water doctrine".[100] In addition, the Judiciary Act left another crucial issue unresolved. Although the Act instructs federal courts to apply the "laws of the several states" in diversity

---

98. In the first edition of his treatise, Benedict provides a taxonomy of possible Constitutional definitions for "admiralty" that has not been improved upon in the last one and a half centuries:

"1. That this constitutional grant embraces only those few cases of which the English High Court of Admiralty, was permitted to take cognizance at the time of the American Revolution.
2. That it embraces all cases of which the English Admiralty anciently had jurisdiction, before the common law courts had by prohibition prevented exercise of most of its powers.
3. That it embraces only the cases which were within the acknowledged competency of the British colonial courts of Vice-Admiralty, as they existed at the time of the American Revolution.
4. That the actual jurisdiction of the States Courts of Admiralty, which were in existence at the adoption of the constitution of the United States, was alone embraced in the grant.
5. That the words admiralty and maritime, relate simply to subject matter, and were used in that general sense which embraces all those cases relating to ships and shipping, which arise under the municipal maritime regulations of each nation, and those which arise under the general maritime law."

Benedict (1st ed.), *supra* note 51, sec. 19, at 12–13.

99. *See* Owen & Tolley, *supra* note 82, at 28 n. 13 (Virginia), 138 (Maryland); Frederick Bernays Wiener, *Notes on the Rhode Island Admiralty*, 46 Harv. L. Rev. 44, 62 (1933). *See also supra* Chapter I, notes 132–136 and text accompanying (text of statutes of Richard II and discussion); Chapter II, notes 83 (Pennsylvania), 201–202 (Rhode Island, New York) and text accompanying; Chapter III, notes 25 (Virginia), 46 (New York) and text accompanying.

100. Courts spent much of the first half of the nineteenth century coping with the legacy of the jurisdictional statutes of Richard II. For the courts' adoption of the so-called "tidewater doctrine", *see The Thomas Jefferson*, 23 U.S. 428 (Story, J., 1825); *Peyroux v. Howard*, 32 U.S. 324 (Thompson, J., 1833); *Waring v. Clarke*, 46 U.S. 441 (Woodbury, J., 1847) (holding that "the admiralty jurisdiction of the courts of the United States extends to tide waters, though that may be *infra corpus comitatus*..."). Ultimately, the Court rejected the doctrine in *The Genesee Chief v. Fitzhugh*, 53 U.S. 443 (Taney, C. J., 1851).

cases,[101] it contains no parallel provision specifying which body of law shall apply in cases of admiralty and maritime jurisdiction.

Admiralty Jurisdiction and Substantive Law

The Judiciary Act's scheme of concurrent jurisdiction ensured convenient *fora* for adjudicating maritime disputes. Nonetheless, geographic convenience of courts merely facilitates the resolution of disputes in a cost-effective and timely manner; it does nothing to clarify the rights, duties, and obligations of ships' masters, owners, and mariners. The economic well-being of the United States depended upon maritime commerce; ships carried the exports necessary for improving the nation's balance of trade. Indeed, the carrying trades themselves—the largest sector of the American service industry—were the nation's chief means for offsetting massive deficits in the trade in goods.[102] It was thus essential that carriers and merchants know in advance the duties of care required of them in the stowage and transport of cargo. On whom would losses fall in the event of damage? What rules would apply to general average? Carriage of cargo involves a myriad of details, all of which must be regulated by legal rules. These rules must regulate interpretation of terms in charter-parties, including demurrage, delay, deviation, and *force majeure*. Masters and

---

101. Judiciary Act, ch. 20, sec. 34, 1 Stat. 72, 92.

102. By the late twentieth century, economic historians agreed both that international trade was crucial to the newly independent nation's survival and that earnings in the service sector—principally the carrying trades—were essential to offset American deficits in the trade in goods. The most complete statistical analysis of late eighteenth-century trade to date is that of Shepherd and Walton, covering the period just preceding independence. Of an annual trade deficit with Britain of 1.3 million pounds sterling, roughly 62% was offset by earnings from what the authors call "invisibles"—*i.e.* ocean-carriage and marine insurance. For tables of statistics and analysis, *see* James F. Shepherd & Gary M. Walton, Shipping, Maritime Trade, and the Economic Development of Colonial America (Cambridge: Cambridge University Press, 1972) at 113–130. Four years later, Shepherd and Walton followed up their study of late colonial trade with a comparison of trade in the late colonial period with that of the early republic. While trade fell slightly *per capita* by the early 1790s (owing largely to a large influx in population), there was nevertheless an increase of 37% in real value of total export of goods. At the same time, there had been an increase of 60% in American tonnage. Once again, it was earnings from the carrying trades that formed the backbone of American commerce with foreign nations. *See* James F. Shepherd & Gary M. Walton, *Change After the American Revolution: Pre- and Post-War Comparisons of Maritime Shipping and Trade*, 13 Explorations in Economic History 397, 412–420 (1976).

shipowners required knowledge of their legal duties in navigation of their vessels. Both shipowners and seamen needed to know in advance the rules that would regulate "ship's articles"—the seamen's employment-contracts. Salvors would not have exerted their efforts without assurance of salvage awards. Most importantly, marine insurers needed to know the risks to which their insureds were exposed. In essence, profitable maritime business required substantive legal rules that were available to and understood by all participants in the market. The Judiciary Act, however, provided no assistance in identifying the body of substantive law that federal courts were to apply in maritime cases.[103]

History provided American courts—both federal and state—with a series of possibilities. For Coke, Hale, and Molloy, the substantive maritime law was part of the common law of England.[104] Before the creation of the office of "Admiral", the common-law courts had tried maritime cases.[105] At the time, no

103. Congress did pass some statutes that regulated maritime business. The year following passage of the Judiciary Act, Congress enacted legislation that regulated the employer/employee relationship between shipowners and seamen. *See* An Act for the Government and Regulation of Seamen in the Merchant Service (June 20, 1790), 1 Stat. 131. Nevertheless, Congress did not embark upon a comprehensive solution to the need for substantive rules of maritime law.

104. In Hale's view, maritime customs gained force of law by incorporation into a nation's domestic law. In England, this meant absorption into the common law. In the absence of statutory law or common-law precedent, courts were permitted to look to the civil law, but only to fill gaps in the common law. Thus it would appear that for Hale the *lex maritima*, or "general maritime law", was not binding as part of the law of nations, but rather as part of the common law of the realm. *See* Matthew Hale, *A Disquisition Touching the Jurisdiction of the Common Law and Courts of Admiralty in Relation to Things Done Upon or Beyond the Sea, and Touching Maritime and Merchants' Contracts*, critical edition *reproduced from manuscript in* HALE AND FLEETWOOD ON ADMIRALTY JURISDICTION (M.J. Pritchard & D.E.C. Yale eds., London: Publications of the Selden Society, Vol. 108, 1992), Ch. IX, at 58–59 (hereinafter HALE AND FLEETWOOD). For discussion of Coke and Molloy, *see* DANIEL R. COQUILLETTE, THE CIVILIAN WRITERS OF DOCTORS' COMMONS, LONDON: THREE CENTURIES OF JURISTIC INNOVATION IN COMPARATIVE, COMMERCIAL AND INTERNATIONAL LAW (Berlin: Duncker & Humblot, 1988) at 115, 131, 145–146 (hereinafter COQUILLETTE, CIVILIAN WRITERS).

105. Before the creation of the office of Admiral in the fourteenth century, the courts of the boroughs had exercised jurisdiction over private maritime disputes, wrecks, and deodands. Among them were those of the Cinque Ports, as well as that of Ipswich, the "Domesday" of which contains the oldest surviving records of English maritime proceedings. Unfortunately, most of the borough-courts' records that pre-date the office of Admiral have been lost to posterity. *See* THE BLACK BOOK OF THE ADMIRALTY (*RERUM BRITANNICARUM MEDII AEVI SCRIPTORES* (ROLLS SERIES)): NO. 55 *MONUMENTA JURIDICA* (4 vols., Sir Travers Twiss ed., London: Her Majesty's Stationery Office, 1871; Krauss Reprints, 1965), Vol. II, at x–xxxvii (hereinafter TWISS); REGINALD G. MARSDEN, SELECT PLEAS IN

one would have thought to call the substantive law that these courts applied the "civil law". Centuries later, Blackstone would assert that substantive maritime law was part of the law of nations, which in turn had been "adopted by the [common law] of England".[106] Blackstone's assessment was not unique for his time. Lord Mansfield also treated the law merchant—and with it the *lex maritima*—as part of the law of nations. The law of nations was not foreign law, but instead the law of England.[107] It is Mansfield who generally is credited with incorporating the customs and practices of shipowners and merchants into the common law. To England's civilians, Mansfield's opinions were the culmination of the process begun by Coke and the common lawyers in the sixteenth century,[108] by which the common law co-opted the jurisdiction of

---

THE HIGH COURT OF ADMIRALTY: A.D. 1390–1404 AND A.D. 1527–1545, VOL. I (London: Publications of the Selden Society, Vol. 6, 1892), Introduction, at xv. Nonetheless, these courts continued to hear maritime cases even after the creation of the Admiral's courts. The records of some of these later port-courts have survived, providing us with a glimpse of maritime litigation beyond the activities of the Court of Admiralty and the vice admiralty courts. *See* THE ADMIRALTY COURT BOOK OF SOUTHAMPTON: 1566–1585 (Edwin Welch ed., Southampton: Southampton University Press, 1968). For further discussion, *see supra* Chapter I, notes 109–113 and text accompanying.

106. WILLIAM BLACKSTONE, COMMENTARIES ON THE LAWS OF ENGLAND (4 vols., 1st ed., Oxford: Clarendon Press, 1769; *reproduced in facsimile with commentary*, Chicago: University of Chicago Press, 1979), Vol. IV, at 67 (hereinafter BLACKSTONE).

107. Unlike Blackstone, Mansfield left behind no published writings except his opinions, and even these have come down to us filtered through the eyes of the reporter. Thus his theory of law must be reconstructed through examination of his opinions. In *Luke v. Lyde*, 97 Eng. Rep. 614, 617 (K.B. 1759), Mansfield identified the "maritime law" as "not the law of any particular nation, but the general law of nations." Citing Lord Talbot, he maintained further that: "The law of nations, in its full extent, [is] part of the law of England". *Triquet v. Bath*, 97 Eng. Rep. 936, 938 (K.B. 1764). Finally, in *Pilans v. Van Mierop*, 97 Eng. Rep. 1036, 1038 (K.B. 1765), he concluded that: "The law of merchants, and the law of the land, is the same." Taken together, the three cases form a perfect syllogism. The maritime law, as part of the *lex mercatoria*, is within the law of nations. The law of nations is part of the common law of England. Ergo, the *lex mercatoria* (and with it the *lex maritima*) is part of the common law of England.

108. It is perhaps ironic that the English civilians would group the staunch parliamentarian Coke together with the political conservatives Mansfield and Blackstone. Eighteenth-century Americans often saw Coke in contradistinction to the latter two. A letter by Jefferson, written in the last months of his life, reflects the view that had prevailed in the colonies on the eve of independence:

> "You will recollect that before the revolution, Coke Littleton was the Universal elementary book of Law students, and a sounder whig never wrote, nor of profounder learning in the orthodox doctrines of the British constitution, or in what were called English liberties.... But when his black-letter text, and uncouth but

the admiralty—even to the point of co-opting and applying admiralty's substantive rules as the common law's own.[109] Nonetheless, not all nineteenth-century readers would see in Mansfield the successor of Coke, Hale, and Molloy as the champion of notion of "*lex maritima* as common law". As Justice Bradley later would remark:

> [The law of the sea] reaches back to sources long anterior even to those of the civil law itself; which Lord Mansfield says is not the law of any particular country, but the general law of nations; and which is founded on the broadest principles of equity and justice, deriving, however, much of its completeness and symmetry, as well as its modes of proceeding, from the civil law, and embracing, altogether, a system of regulations embodied and matured by the combined efforts of the most enlightened commercial nations of the world.[110]

> cunning learning got out of fashion, and the honied Mansfieldism of Blackstone became the Students' Hornbook, from that moment, that profession (the nursery of our Congress) began to slide into toryism..."

Letter of Thomas Jefferson to James Madison (Feb. 17, 1826), *reproduced from manuscript in* The Republic of Letters: The Correspondence between Thomas Jefferson and James Madison, 1776–1826 (3 vols., James Morton Smith ed., New York: Norton, 1995), Vol. III, at 1964, 1965. For discussion, *see supra* Chapter I, note 167 and text accompanying.

109. Asserting that the *lex mercatoria* is part of the common law of England is not equivalent to stating that the *lex mercatoria* is, for example, part of the law of France. The *lex mercatoria* consists of the customs and practices of merchants; these change through time. In contrast, the common law is built upon precedent. That is not to say that the common law does not change, but rather that it changes through the interpretations of the courts, not those of the shipowners and merchants themselves. At least one school of thought contends that by incorporating the rules of the *lex mercatoria* into the common law, Mansfield essentially changed its character from flexible and responsive to the changing needs of merchants to static, with its rules frozen in the form in which they were first adopted. *See* Coquillette, Civilian Writers, *supra* note 104, at 132, 152, 157.

110. *Insurance Company v. Dunham*, 78 U.S. 1, 23 (Bradley, J., 1870). Bradley's thumbnail assessment of the *lex maritima* is more subtly sophisticated than often has been recognized. He avoids the pitfalls of those commentators who accept the civilians' contentions that the *lex maritima* derives directly from the law of the Rome, instead implicitly crediting the medieval customs and practices with its origins. Moreover, he recognizes (as few nineteenth-century commentators did) that modern Continental law—the "civil law"—later gave form and systematic organization to the maritime law. The result is a *lex maritima* born of medieval custom and reshaped by the civil law, deriving its modern content (and uniformity) from the mutual needs of trade among the community of nations.

Bradley acknowledges the international character of the *lex maritima*, as well as its debt to the civil law. Nevertheless, Bradley's assessment is not necessarily at odds with Mansfield's image as the heir to the tradition of Coke, Holt, and Hale. At issue is how Mansfield arrived at his conclusion that the maritime law, as part of the law of nations, became binding in England. Did the *lex maritima* have force of law in England because—and only because—it had been incorporated into the common law, or did it—as part of the law of nations—apply of its own force, thus compelling the common law to take notice of it?

To defend the former conclusion, namely that the *lex maritima* was binding only because the common law had incorporated it, one must view the relationship between the substantive maritime law and the common law as Holt, Hale, and Molloy viewed it. In all matters over which the High Court of Admiralty retained cognizance, the common law had concurrent jurisdiction. Even claims for seamen's wages were common-law claims, for which the common-law courts declined to issue writs of prohibition only as "an indulgence to the poor sailors".[111] Admittedly, there were a few areas, such as salvage and torts on the high seas, which were beyond the reach of the common law. There was also prize, the exclusive province of the Admiralty. Technically, however, the Court's procedures in prize differed from those employed in instance cases. Prize was thus *sui generis*, its jurisdiction vested in the High Court of Admiralty though by its nature not strictly speaking an "admiralty" matter.[112] Nonetheless, in general, Hale maintains that both the common-law courts and the admiralty courts are empowered to hear maritime cases, with both applying the same body of substantive law. This law is a subset of the common law of England.

As we have seen, Hale's theory squares well with the actual practice of maritime law in the American colonies. The varieties of maritime cases heard in the provincial vice admiralty courts differed little from those heard in the colonial courts of common law. The vice admiralty courts entertained actions for seamen's wages, breach of charterparties, and maritime torts—as did their common-law counterparts. Independence brought no significant changes. Despite some subtle differences in the scope of jurisdiction that the various states

111. For Chief Justice Holt's contention that the common-law courts refrained from issuing prohibitions only "as an indulgence to the poor seamen", *see* Browne, *supra* note 88, Vol. II, at 86–87. For Hale's views on the *lex maritima* as part of the common law, *see* Hale, *Disquisition*, *in* Hale and Fleetwood, *supra* note 103, Ch. IX, at 58–59.

112. *See* discussion, *supra* Chapter II, notes 175–179 and text accompanying; Chapter III, notes 64, 139–140 and text accompanying.

vested in their courts of admiralty, both the new state admiralty courts and the courts of common law continued to adjudicate maritime matters. Virtually any private claim that one could file in a state's admiralty court he could file also in a common-law court.[113] Thus had either the delegates to the Constitutional Convention or the members of the first Congress opted to incorporate the "common law", the course of maritime litigation arguably would have passed seamlessly from the Confederation to the Federal Republic.

Some, in fact, had argued for a general incorporation of the common law.[114] Edward Shippen, best remembered for serving as Chief Justice of the Supreme Court of Pennsylvania, gave his assessment of the Judiciary Bill to Robert Morris shortly before its passage:

> It is of the utmost Consequence that the Judiciary Law should establish in express terms by what Law we are to be governed—There are some loose Expressions in the Bill concerning the Common Law, but it is no where said the Judges should decide according to it—The American States have generally adopted it, either in their Constitutions or by Act of Assembly. The United States should likewise adopt it; and it should not be left to the Judges to make the Law, but only to declare it—Perhaps the Common Law alone would not be sufficient—there are many Statutes made in England before our Revolution which amend and improve the Common Law; some of these have been long practiced under in America, and are incorporated with the Common Law, which would be imperfect without them...[115]

---

113. *See e.g.* OWEN & TOLLEY, *supra* note 82, at 140 (noting that Maryland's Provincial Court had concurrent jurisdiction with the vice admiralty court and routinely heard all varieties of instance cases from 1642 through 1776. *See also* Table 5-A at 101, containing statistics relating to the types of maritime cases heard in both the vice admiralty court and in the courts of common law.) For a general discussion of the power of American common-law courts to hear maritime cases, *see supra* Chapter II, notes 97–270 and text accompanying; Chapter III, notes 15–49 and text accompanying.

114. *See e.g.* "Marcus" [James Iredell], "Answers to Mr. Mason's objections to the new Constitution, recommended by the late Convention", *reproduced in* PAMPHLETS ON THE CONSTITUTION, *supra* note 65, at 333, 336, maintaining that the common law had been incorporated *sub silentio* by the new nation, remaining in force until expressly repealed by acts of Congress.

115. Shippen's letter concedes that the latter suggestion, namely incorporating "useful" English statutes, would be frought with difficulty:

> "...I own it is a difficult and delicate Point to fix by any Rule the Extention of the Statutes; and perhaps here there may be a necessity to leave some latitude to the Judges—Such Statutes as do not suit our Circumstances, or which have never

From the states' ratifying conventions through the debate over the Judiciary Act, many expressed fears of wholesale incorporation of the common law.[116] Madison, though generally in favor of strengthening the national government, stopped short of endorsing incorporation of the common law. Not all of the common law, he maintained, was compatible with the republican underpinnings of the Constitution. Moreover, to the extent that the legislative power and judicial power were coterminous, and that the Constitution gave Congress the power to amend the law, incorporation would have placed Congress in the position to legislate over all matters within the common law's reach. Such a course of action would have serious ramifications for the powers of the state courts and legislatures.[117] Nonetheless, even Madison conceded the utility of adopting the common law provisionally at the state-level, if only to "obviate pretexts that the

---

> been at all admitted here, should certainly not be introduced— ..."

See Letter of Edward Shippen to Robert Morris (July 13, 1789), *reproduced from manuscript in* DOCUMENTARY HISTORY OF THE SUPREME COURT, *supra* note 33, Vol. IV, at 464, 466–467.

116. Antifederalists recognized the character of the common law. Even if it were adopted by Congress, it would be the federal courts, as well as Congress itself, that would shape the common law. Thus "Agrippa V" (Dec. 11, 1787) expresses fears that federal common law, over time, will diverge from that of the states. William Grayson expresses similar sentiments in Virginia's ratification debates (June 21, 1788), arguing:

> "The Court thus organized, are [*sic*] to execute laws made by thirteen nations, dissimilar in their customs, manners, laws and interests. If we advert to the customs of these different sovereignties, we shall find them repugnant and dissimilar. Yet they are all forced to unite and concur in making these laws. They are to form them on one principle, and on one idea; whether the civil law, common law, or law of nations.... It will involve consequences so absurd that, I presume, they will not attempt to make thirteen different codes. They will be obliged to make one code. How will they make one code without being contradictory to some of the laws of the different States?"

Reprinted in RATIFICATION, *supra* note 24, Vol. X, at 1446.

117. Shortly after the publication of the final text of the Constitution, Madison writes to Washington:

> "What could the Convention have done? If they had in general terms declared the Common law to be in force, they would have broken in upon the legal Code of every State in the most material points; they w[oul]d have done more, they would have brought over from G[reat] B[ritain] a thousand heterogeneous & antirepublican doctrines, and even the *ecclesiastical Hierarchy itself*, for that is a part of the Common law. If they had undertaken a discrimination, they must have formed a digest of laws, instead of a Constitution."

Letter of James Madison to George Washington (Oct. 18, 1787), *reproduced in* THE PAPERS OF GEORGE WASHINGTON (Dorothy Twohig, Philander D. Chase, Beverly H. Runge, et al. eds., Charlottesville: University Press of Virginia, 1998), Confederation Series, Vol. V, at 381, 382–383 (hereinafter WASHINGTON, PAPERS); THE WRITINGS OF JAMES MADISON (9

separation from G[reat] Britain threw us into a State of nature, and abolished all civil rights and Obligations".[118] By dodging the political maelstrom of incorporation, the first Congress opted to remain silent, thereby landing instead in a quagmire of uncertainty. Admittedly, Section 34 of the Judiciary Act gave a partial solution, providing that federal courts apply state law in diversity cases.[119] In addition, the district and circuit courts were to apply federal statutes to many matters—such as the collection of revenue. Congress' passage of a variety of acts relating to maritime activities confirmed the prevailing view that it had both the constitutional power and the inclination to legislate in the field of maritime commerce. Most of this legislation, however, would best be characterized as "regulatory".[120] Congress did not attempt to overhaul—or even to codify—those substantive rules that colonial and state admiralty courts had applied since the seventeenth century. The rules governing salvage, general average, breach of charterparties, maritime torts, and the rights and duties of ships' owners, masters, and mariners remained untouched by Congressional legislation.

If the United States did not inherit the *lex maritima* through a wholesale incorporation of the English common law, is there any other way in which it could have become binding in America? There remains one other possibility. At least one school of thought held that the English common law's adoption

---

vols., Gaillard Hunt ed., New York: G.P. Putnam's Sons, 1904), Vol. V, at 11, 14 (hereinafter MADISON, WRITINGS) *(emphasis in the original)*.

118. WASHINGTON, PAPERS, Vol. V, *supra* note 117, at 382; MADISON, WRITINGS, Vol. V, *supra* note 117, at 13. As Madison's objections to incorporation of the common law stemmed largely from his apprehension that the federal government might engulf the states, he expresses less concern at the notion of the states individually adopting the common law until such time as their respective legislatures should see fit to change it. He observes that: "Since the Revolution every State has made great inroads & with great propriety in many instances on this *monarchical* code."

119. Judiciary Act, ch. 20, sec. 34, 1 Stat. 73, 92.

120. However universal many substantive rules governing rights and obligations associated with maritime activities may have been among "civilized nations", it was clear that each nation determined for itself how to tax maritime commerce. Most of Congress' regulatory efforts were directed at collection of revenue—including acts for registering vessels (1 Stat. 94 (1789)), and for collection of duties on both tonnage and goods (1 Stat. 27 (1789); 1 Stat. 29 (1789); 1 Stat. 69 (1789)). Other measures that the first Congress enacted were of a similar "regulatory" nature, such as an act for construction and maintenance of aids to navigation (1 Stat. 53 (1789)) and another providing for inspection of goods before export (1 Stat. 106 (1789)). Admittedly, the Act for Regulation of Seamen in the Merchant Service (1 Stat. 131 (1790)) did make some minor incursions in a field long dominated by the customary maritime law, though most of the statute merely codified long-established rules. For a complete list of the first Congress' acts regulating maritime activities and commerce, *see supra* note 17 and text accompanying.

of the *law maritime* was not wholly voluntary. The *lex maritima* was part of the law of England not because the king, Parliament, and the common-law courts recognized it as such, but rather because it was binding in all "civilized nations". If the *lex maritima* were binding upon England, it would be equally binding upon all other nations, including its newly-independent former colony on the other side of the Atlantic. The notion of the *law maritime* as part of the law of nations was not new. When Judge Peters wrote in 1795 that the "change in the form of our government has not abrogated all the laws, customs and principles of jurisprudence, we inherited from our ancestors" and that a federal district court "must be governed in its decisions by the Maritime Code... possessed" and applied by its American predecessors in admiralty jurisdiction,[121] he was invoking a tradition older than American admiralty jurisdiction itself. Sir Richard Zouch, civilian, political polemicist, and antagonist of Edward Coke, maintained that both the *lex maritima* and the *lex mercatoria* were part of the law of nations,.[122] and he invoked no less eminent

---

121. *Thompson v. The Catharina* (Case no. 13,949), 23 F. Cas. 1028, 130–131 (D. Pa., 1795). For discussion, *see supra* notes 26–29 and text accompanying.

122. As Zouch intends his monograph as a defense of civil-law jurisdiction in England, his agenda is clear at the outset. He first must equate the *lex maritima*, or "*ley maritime*", with the law of nations, and then must connect the law of nations with the civil law. He observes:

> "... *England* is not destitute of special Laws for the regulating of Sea businesses, which are distinct from the Common Laws of the Realm; as namely, the *Civil Law*, and others, of which the Books of Common Law take notice by the names of *Ley Merchant, and Ley Mariner*."

RICHARD ZOUCH[E], THE JURISDICTION OF THE ADMIRALTY ASSERTED, AGAINST SIR EDWARD COKE'S *ARTICULI ADMIRALITATIS*, IN XXII CHAPTER OF HIS JURISDICTION OF COURTS (London: Francis Tyton & Thomas Dring, 1663) at 7 *(emphasis in the original)*. Continuing with a paraphrase of Sir John Davis, he remarks:

> "*[B]oth the Common Law and Statute Laws of* England *take notice of the Law Merchant, and do leave the cases of Merchants to be decided by the Rules of that Law, which Law Merchant... as it is part of the Law of Nature, and Nations, is universal, and one and the same in all Countries of the World; For as Cicero saith of that Law, Non erit alia lex Romae, alia Athenis, alia nunc, alia post haec, Sed et omnes gentes, et omni tempore una eademque Lex obtinebit*, whereby it is manefest, that the Causes concerning Merchants, are not now to be decided by the peculiar and Ordinary Lawes of every Country, but by the general Lawes of Nature and Nations.... [T]he Common Law of the Land did leave those cases [*i.e.* relating to "merchants and ships"] to be ruled by another Law, Namely, the Law Merchant, which is a branch of the Law of Nations."

Id. at 8–9 (*emphasis in the original*). It is ironic that Zouch, a defender of the civil law, would select the same quote from Cicero that Mansfield later offered in support of the proposition

an authority than Grotius to defend his position.[123] Charles Molloy, common lawyer and pragmatist, though careful to distinguish the customs and practices of modern European nations from the Civil Law of Rome, nonetheless treated the "law marine" as part of the law of nations.[124] Blackstone concurred.

---

that the law merchant was wholly incorporated into the common law. *See Luke v. Lyde*, 97 Eng. Rep. 614, 617 (K.B. 1759); discussion, *supra* Chapter IV, note 107 and accompanying text. *See also* discussion, *supra* Chapter I, notes 2, 103–104 and text accompanying. For Zouch, the reason for selection is clear. The law of nations trumps domestic law, thereby guaranteeing the independence of the civil-law courts from those courts that exist to construe national law. For Mansfield, the motive is more ambiguous. One could interpret Mansfield as saying that the common law incorporated the law merchant and law maritime because the law of nations compelled it to do so. On the other hand, one could argue that the common law took notice of the law merchant and law maritime because their universal appeal would have made it impractical to do otherwise. One must read both Zouch's statement and Mansfield's in the context in which they were written. Both sought to justify their respective courts' jurisdiction, and on this point one should expect more rhetoric than incisive reasoning from each. Nonetheless, both Zouch and Mansfield serve to reinforce the notion held by many Americans in the 1780s, namely that substantive maritime law was binding on all countries—including the United States—as part of the law of nations.

123. *Id.* at 6. Zouch's rather loose handling of the relationship between the law of nature, the law of nations, and nations' municipal law, while arguably rhetorically effective, blurs the careful distinctions that Grotius makes among the three. *Cf.* Hugo Grotius, *De Jure Belli ac Pacis* (1st ed. 1645; 2 vols., Latin critical edition with translation, Francis W. Kelsey trans., Oxford: Clarendon Press, 1925), Prolegomena: Vol. I (Latin edition) *(eighth through ninth pages: not paginated)*; Vol. II (English translation) sec. 39—sec. 41, at 23–24. Elsewhere in his work, Zouch displays greater clarity. While not abandoning entirely the nexus between the law of nature and the law of nations, Zouch is one of the first political theorists to ground the law of nations principally in voluntary and tacit agreement—*i.e.* treaties and the customs of nations. Thus Zouch's work may be seen as a transitional phase between the "naturalist" approach that characterized most early modern writings and the empirical or "positivist" approach that came to dominate the nineteenth century. For discussion *see e.g.* Edwin D. Dickinson, *Changing Concepts and the Doctrine of Incorporation*, 26 Am. J. Intn'l. L. 239, 251, 259–260 (1932) (hereinafter Dickinson, *Incorporation*).

124. Molloy's understanding of the "Law of Nations" is relatively modern by the standards of his contemporaries. He refers to it as the "Law of Will or of Common consent", observing further: "that which cannot by sure consequence be deduced out of sure Principles, and yet appears everywhere observed, must needs have its rise from free will and consent, which is that which is called the Law of Nations..." *See* Charles Molloy, *De Jure Maritimo et Navali*, or a Treatise of Affairs Maritime and of Commerce, in Three Books (3d ed., London: John Bellinger, 1682), Introduction *(not paginated)* (hereinafter Molloy (3d ed., Bellinger). This, he emphasizes—and not the continuing vitality of the ancient Roman Civil Law—is the source of the modern "law maritime". Nevertheless, portions of his text make a distinction between the "law maritime" and the "common law". *See e.g. Id.*, Bk. II,

His *Commentaries*, the standard reference work for American law students and practitioners alike, lends credence to the notion that the binding force of the *lex maritima* is supranational:

> Thus in mercantile questions, such as bills of exchange and the like; in all marine causes, relating to freight, average, demurrage, insurances, bottomry, and others of a similar nature; the law-merchant, which is a branch of the law of nations, is regularly and constantly adhered to. So too in all disputes relating to prizes, to shipwrecks, to hostages, and ransom bills, there is no other rule of decision but this great universal law, collected from history and usage, and such writers of all nations and languages as are generally approved and allowed of.[125]

When Peters,[126] Story,[127] and their brethren in the nineteenth century made reference to such sources, it was not mere window-dressing , hortatory exclamations and paeans to the distant past, inserted to lend credibility to their opinions.[128] By the early 1800s, it was commonplace for judges to treat the *lex maritima* as an intrinsic part of the United States' newly-acquired sovereignty—a body of rules that became binding upon the country's accession into the community of nations.[129] At issue is whether that view prevailed in the 1780s.

Ch. II (Masters of Ships), at 208–217. Molloy goes to some pains to explain that both bodies of law impose the same obligations. He does not, however, discuss the issue of whether in theory the courts of common law could derogate from the customs of civilized nations. He admits at least a small sphere of overlap between the jurisdiction of the courts of admiralty and the courts of common law *(divisum imperium)*, and implies that each will administer its own law. Whether the substantive maritime rules of the common law differ significantly from those of the "law maritime"/law of nations is largely unaddressed.

125. 4 Blackstone, *supra* note 106, Ch. V, at 67.

126. *Thompson v. The Catharina* (Case No. 13,949), 23 F. Cas. 1028 (D. Pa., 1795) (contending that the United States inherited a pre-existing "Maritime Code" via the law of nations at the time of its independence). In his published collection of American cases, Peters saw fit to include an Appendix containing the medieval Laws of Oleron, Wisbuy [*sic*], and the Hanse Towns, with the intention that they might prove useful for nineteenth-century judges and practitioners alike. *See* Admiralty Decisions, *supra* note 26, Vol. II, at i–cxi.

127. *Delovio v. Boit* (Case No. 3,776), 2 F. Cas. 418 (C.C., D. Mass., 1815).

128. *See* Edwin D. Dickinson, *The Law of Nations as Part of the National Law of the United States*, 101 U. Pa. L. Rev. 26, 34–35 (1952).

129. *Thompson v. The Catharina* (Case No. 13,949), 23 F. Cas. 1028 (D. Pa., 1795); *La Jeune Eugenie* (Case No. 15,551), 26 F. Cas. 832 (C.C., D. Mass., Story, J., 1822) (law of

The Law of Nations in Late Eighteenth-Century America

Three years after the passage of the Judiciary Act, Secretary of State Jefferson approached Attorney General Edmund Randolph for an opinion regarding the law of nations; he responded as follows:

> The law of nations, although not specially adopted by the constitution or any municipal act, is essentially a part of the law of the land. Its obligation commences and runs with the existence of a nation, subject to modifications on some points of indifference. Indeed a people may regulate it so as to be binding upon the departments of their own government, in any form whatever; but with regard to foreigners, every change is at the peril of the nation which makes it.[130]

For Randolph, the law of nations is binding on the United States as an attribute of sovereignty. Its application is unavoidable, at least as regards the rights of foreigners. For Americans of his generation, Randolph's words would provoke little dissent. The leading English jurists of the period—Mansfield and Blackstone in particular—treated the law of nations as part of domestic law. Scarcely a generation earlier, Jeremiah Gridley had admonished the young John Adams that "a Lawyer through his whole Life ought to have some Book on Ethics or the Law of Nations always on his Table."[131] He encouraged Adams to acquaint himself with the works of Grotius and Pufendorf as much as with Bracton and Glanville.[132] For Gridley, Adams, and their contemporaries, this field was known as the "law of nature and nations".[133] To some degree, this was a mark of the times. In the prevailing scholarly trends of mid-eighteenth-

---

nations incorporated into federal law, grounded in a theory of the law of nations derived from Vattel): for discussion, *see* Dickinson, *Changing Concepts*, *supra* note 123, at 259.

130. Letter of Edmund Randolph to The Secretary of State [Thomas Jefferson] (June 26, 1792) (examining the immunity of foreign diplomats from arrest), *in* OFFICIAL OPINIONS OF THE ATTORNEYS GENERAL OF THE UNITED STATES ADVISING THE PRESIDENT AND HEADS OF DEPARTMENTS (Washington, D.C.: Robert Farnham, 1852), Vol. I, at 26, 27.

131. THE DIARY AND AUTOBIOGRAPHY OF JOHN ADAMS (4 vols., L. H. Butterfield, Leonard C. Faber, & Wendell D. Garrett eds., Cambridge: Belknap Press of Harvard University, 1961), Vol. III, *Autobiography* at 272 (hereinafter DIARY AND AUTOBIOGRAPHY OF JOHN ADAMS).

132. *Id.*, Vol. III, *Autobiography* at 271, 274.

133. *Id.*, Vol. III, *Autobiography* at 271.

century discourse, the law of nature and the law of nations were often linked. As the colonies moved toward their break with the Crown, however, political considerations also weighed heavily in favor of adopting a view of the law of nations tied to notions of the law of nature.

By 1789, the notion of a "law of nations" as part of the "law of nature" had acquired a quite extensive pedigree. The earliest extant reference is found in the works of Cicero,[134] who admonished his readers that "nature is the wellspring of law".[135] To most modern legal scholars, Cicero's opinions on the law of nature (or its relation to the law of nations) are at best historical curiosities, the quaint passions of avocational antiquarians or the concern of professional philologists—not the foundations of contemporary jurisprudence. In the eighteenth century, however, a classical education was indispensable for advancement in the highest echelons of the legal profession. In his *Autobiography*, John Adams recounts his first meeting with Gridley. The meeting was not social, but rather an informal oral examination; at stake was whether Gridley would recommend that Adams be called to the bar. By his own admission, Adams' responses to questions about his reading of modern legal treatises left much to be desired. When Gridley asked about his proficiency in Latin, however, Adams remarked that he had read both the *Institutes of Justinian* and Cicero's *Orations* and *Epistles*. For Gridley, this was enough.[136] As one modern commentator remarked: "He had no formal legal education and only two years' apprenticeship in the countryside. But he could talk about Cicero.... So Cicero and Justinian helped Adams get sworn at the bar."[137] Within three years, Gridley had formed the Sodalitus Club, an association of the colony's elite legal practitioners, devoted to the improvement of the bar through study of Cicero, the *Corpus Juris Civilis*, and other classical sources.[138] Gridley, Adams, and their colleagues were not alone. Classical authors (and

---

134. *M. Tulli Ciceronis* [Cicero], *De Officiis* (Oxford Classical Texts: Michael Winterbottom ed., Oxford: The Clarendon Press, 1994), III. 17. 69 (hereinafter *De Officiis*). For discussion, *see e.g.* William W. Buckland, A Text-Book of Roman Law from Augustus to Justinian (3d ed., Peter Stein ed., Cambridge: Cambridge University Press, 1966) at 53 (hereinafter Buckland, Text-Book).

135. *Id.*, III. 17. 72 (*my translation*). "Law" in this context is "*ius*" rather than "*lex*".

136. Diary and Autobiography of John Adams, *supra* note 131, Vol. III, *Autobiography* at 270–272.

137. Daniel R. Coquillette, "Justinian in Braintree: John Adams, Civilian Learning, and Legal Elitism, 1758–1775", *in* Law in Colonial Massachusetts: 1630–1800 (Boston: The Colonial Society of Massachusetts, 1984), at 359, 366 (hereinafter Coquillette, "Justinian in Braintree").

138. *Id.* at 376–382.

by extension the classical languages) formed the basis of higher education in both the colonies and the early republic.[139] Indeed, despite a general shortage of books on law in America of the 1780s, volumes of Roman law and Continental treatises on the civil law and the law of nations were comparatively plentiful.[140]

Thus for the generation of the 1770s and 1780s, classical sources held weight. Their opinions on the law of nations could not be ignored, particularly when their conclusions leant support to notions of seminal importance to prevailing political agendas. It is not surprising that the political leaders and pamphleteers of the Revolution had turned to ancient sources—and in particular to their conceptions of natural law. When the American revolutionaries appealed to natural law, they did so for the same reasons that Coke had appealed to the common law. To Coke, the common law had pre-dated the king's prerogative, and thus "admeasured" it.[141] For James Otis, John Adams, and others, natural law held precedence over king and Parliament. Both Coke and the American revolutionaries needed an external yardstick by which to measure the legitimacy of the respective authorities that they opposed.[142] Coke

---

139. *See e.g.* ELKINS & MCKITRICK, *supra* note 8, at 48 (observing that: "[t]he chief propagandists of the Revolution had been classical scholars".) The importance of classical education did not end with independence; many of the Framers and members of the first Congress likewise had received classical educations. *See* Bourguignon, *Judiciary Act*, *supra* note 6, at 651. While one might expect such education from a Jefferson, an Adams, a Madison, or a professional scholar such as George Wythe, familiarity with classical authors and languages was common among the generation of the 1780s. Among the Framers, delegates as diverse in their backgrounds as Yates of New York, Rutledge of South Carolina, and Philadelphia merchant Mifflin all had classical educations. *See* CHARLES A. BEARD, AN ECONOMIC INTERPRETATION OF THE CONSTITUTION (1st ed. 1913; *reprinted* New York: The Free Press, 1986), at 132, 141, 149. Among members of the first Congress, even Maclay, remembered today chiefly for his implacable distrust of elitism, nevertheless had studied the ancient authors. *See* MACLAY, JOURNAL, *supra* note 2, Introduction at v.

140. *See e.g.* Coquillette, "Justinian in Braintree", *supra* note 137, at 367, observing: "The civil law and Roman law books were here, and in surprising numbers." For a quantitative examination of the works on civil law, Roman law, and the law of nations in American law libraries, *see generally* HERBERT A. JOHNSON, IMPORTED EIGHTEENTH-CENTURY LAW TREATISES IN AMERICAN LAW LIBRARIES: 1700–1799 (Knoxville: University of Tennessee Press, 1978) (hereinafter JOHNSON).

141. *See* CATHERINE DRINKER BOWEN, THE LION AND THE THRONE: THE LIFE AND TIMES OF SIR EDWARD COKE (1st ed., Boston: Little, Brown & Co., 1956) at 291; *see also* discussion, *supra* Chapter I, notes 164–192 and text accompanying.

142. *See* BERNARD BAILYN, THE IDEOLOGICAL ORIGINS OF THE AMERICAN REVOLUTION (Cambridge, Massachusetts: Belknap Press, 1967), at 26–28, 178, 188. Coquillette makes the following observation about Adams' use in the *Novanglus Letters* of the law of nations (*ius gentium*) grounded in notions of natural law:

found his in the process by which the cumulative wisdom of "most excellent men, in many successions of ages, by long and continual experience" refined the common law to the point where no man, limited to the wisdom gained through a single lifetime, should dare to replace it with a creation of his own ingenuity.[143] For the Americans, the yardstick was *ius naturale*, which neither the king nor acts of Parliament could supplant.[144]

The ancient Roman sources were nearly unanimous in tying the law of nations to the law of nature. For Cicero, all positive law [*i.e.* "*lex*"] must satisfy a threshold test of compliance with natural law.[145] While he concedes that a state may create positive law contrary to the dictates of nature, such law would

---

> "The core of the argument was the application of three legal principles of the *ius gentium*, namely: (1) that under the law of nature and nations resistance to arbitrary power is allegiance to the principles of law, i.e. '[r]esistence [*sic*] to lawful authority make rebellion'; and (2) that under the law of nations and the law of the English constitution itself there was no lawful parliamentary authority over the colonies...; and (3) therefore, resistance to attempts to subordinate colonial government to parliamentary edicts was, as a matter of universal legal principle, an affirmation of legal order."

Coquillette, "Justinian in Braintree", *supra* note 137, at 410–411.

143. [Edward Coke], The Reports of Sir Edvvard Coke, K[night], Late Lord Chief Justice of England...Faithfully Rendered into English (1st English ed., London: W. Lee, M. Walbanck, D. Pakeman, & G. Bedell, 1658), *Calvin's Case*, Part VII at 1, 3b; *see* discussion, *supra* Chapter I, notes 172–174.

144. Legal historian Stewart Jay offers the following assessment of the influence of treatise-writers in defining the natural law and the law of nations for Americans of the Revolutionary period:

> "Viewed from a modern vantage point, the reliance on treatise writers may be explained partially by the unavailability of other authority, such as published case-reports or diplomatic records. Nevertheless, in this prepositivist era the treatise writers were respected for their use of natural reasoning to discover the true principles of the law of nations. These were the same sources who had an established place in the intellectual foundation of the Revolution's ideology of natural rights. As revolutionaries, Americans quoted these authorities in the course of demanding respect for natural rights that were perceived as grounded in a body of law existing independently of positive enactment."

Stewart Jay, *The Status of the Law of Nations in Early American Law*, 42 Vand. L. Rev. 819, 824 (1989) (hereinafter Jay, *Law of Nations*).

145. "Indeed, true law [*lex*] is correct reason in harmony with nature—encompassing all people, unchanging, and eternal." *De Re Publica* III. 22. 33 (*my translation*), *in* Cicero, *De Republica*; *De Legibus* (Clinton Walker Keyes ed., Cambridge, Massachusetts: Harvard University Press, 1994) (hereinafter *De Re Publica*; *De Legibus*). (It is worth noting that this line opens the passage quoted by Mansfield, Story, and others, admonishing that there "will not be one law for Rome, and another for Athens...".)

lack legitimacy.[146] As for "*ius*" (translatable alternately as "law" or "custom"), this too has its origins in nature,[147] of which we gain acquaintance "by an innate power of perception".[148] When this *ius naturae*—the law of nature—underlies customary practices, these too may attain the force of law. In other words, when a custom that comports with the *ius naturae* is practiced universally among the citizens of a state, that custom, though unwritten, nonetheless becomes binding.[149] Where a custom is recognized among all nations, the result is the same. This universal, unwritten law is the "*ius gentium*"—the law of nations.[150] More than two centuries later, the *Institutes of Gaius* codified the view of the *ius gentium* that would most influence the thought of late antiquity, as well as that of early modern Europe:

> All societies that are governed by laws and customs observe in part those laws and customs unique to themselves, as well as that law which is common to all men. That law which a particular society adopts for itself is unique to it, and is called the *ius civile*—as it were the special law of that particular nation. On the other hand, that law

146. *See De Legibus* II. 4. 11., *supra* note 145; *De Officiis* III. 17. 69., *supra* note 134.

147. *De Inventione* II. 21. 65., *in* CICERO, *DE INVENTIONE, DE OPTIMO GENERE ORATORUM, TOPICA* (H.H. Hubbell ed., Cambridge, Massachusetts: Harvard University Press, 1993) (hereinafter *De Inventione*).

148. *De Inventione* II. 21. 65., *supra* note 147 (*my translation*). In the original language, Cicero's remark on human knowledge of natural law, the "*ius naturae*", is as follows: "... *ac naturae quidem ius esse, quod nobis non opinio, sed quaedam innata vis adferat...*".

149. Of the process by which custom becomes law Cicero remarks:

> "'Custom' [*i.e.* "*consuetudo*"] is thought to be that which long-standing practice has recognized through the common consent of mankind, despite it not having been reduced to writing. Nonetheless, through passage of time, fixed rules of law have crystallized around this custom."

De Inventione II. 22. 67., *supra* note 147 (*my translation*). (It is worth noting that the word that Cicero selects for "custom" in this context is "*consuetudo*"—the same that Malynes used as the title for his treatise on the law merchant. *See supra* Chapter I, notes 90–96 and text accompanying).

150. Cicero divides the unwritten Roman law into two categories, ancestral customs and the *ius gentium*, about which he writes:

> "Those rules that are not committed to writing apply either through customs, through the conventions of mankind in general, or through 'quasi-consensus', and most importantly, it is in this manner as prescribed by the law of nature [*ius naturale*] that our mores and laws are maintained."

De Partitione Oratoria 37. 130 (*my translation*), *in M. TULLI CICERONIS* [CICERO], *RHETORICA* (2 vols., Oxford Classical Texts, A.S. Wilkins ed., Oxford: The Clarendon Press, 1978), Vol. II.

> which the rational order of nature [*i.e.* "*ratio naturale*"] has established among all men—observed equally among all societies—is called the *ius gentium*, as all people observe it.[151]

Thus for Gaius, the law of nature and the *ius gentium* were inextricably connected. More that three centuries later his view would be incorporated into the *Digest of Justinian*.[152] Admittedly, the *Digest* contained a dissenting opinion; one passage from Ulpian distinguished between the law of nature and the *ius gentium*.[153] Moreover, modern scholarship questions the historical accu-

---

151. Gaius 1.1 (*my translation*). In the original language, the often-quoted passage reads as follows:

> "*Omnes populi qui legibus et moribus reguntur partim suo proprio, partim communi omnium hominum iure utuntur. nam quod quisque populus ipse sibi ius constituit, id ipsius proprium est vocaturque ius civile, quasi ius proprium civitatis; quod vero naturalis ratio inter omnes homines constituit, id apud omnes populos peraeque custoditur vocaturque ius gentium, quasi quo iure omnes gentes utuntur.*"

Latin text *in* The Institutes of Gaius (2 vols., Francis de Zulueta ed., Oxford: The Clarendon Press, 1948), Vol. I, at 2. Despite the reverence with which writers from the Renaissance onwards have referred to Gaius, his work is not of the highest order of scholarship. His *Institutes*, like the *Institutes of Justinian* that followed three centuries later, were originally designed as an introductory text, or a "students' hornbook" in modern parlance. Little is known of the author himself beyond his praenomen and his sympathy with the Sabinian school of legal thought. Nonetheless, even in late antiquity Gaius had achieved the status of authority, as the ill-conceived Law of Citations of 426 A.D. permitted his hornbook to be cited with a persuasiveness equal to the scholarly works of Ulpian, Paulus, and Modestinus, trumped only by the work of Papinian where fewer than two of these authors sided with his *Institutes*. Though the Law of Citations was repealed under Justinian, the *Institutes of Gaius* were nevertheless incorporated into the *Digest*. For discussion, *see* Buckland, Text-Book *supra* note 134, at 28, 33–34.

152. Dig. 1.1.9. (Gaius *Instit.*), *in Corpus Juris Civilis* (Latin ed., C. M. Galisset ed., Paris: Janet & Cotelle, 1830).

153. As the *Digest* structurally is a compilation of the works of various scholars, it is not surprising that the various authorities quoted often disagree on particular points of law. Nevertheless, Ulpian offers the lone dissenting opinion on the notion that the *ius gentium* is grounded in natural law. He remarks:

> "3. 'Natural law' [*i.e. ius naturale*]—that which nature has taught to all animals—is not unique to the human species, but instead is common among all animals, whether born on land or in the sea, and including also birds. From hence derives the union of man and woman which we call matrimony; from hence also derives the procreation and education of children. Indeed, we see also with clear certainty that animals—mere wild beasts—have an appreciation for this law. 4. The *ius gentium* is that which all societies of people observe. One can readily understand that this *ius gentium* falls short of the law of nature, since the law of nature is common to all living things, while the *ius gentium* is common

racy of the conclusions of both Cicero and Gaius. In the early days of the Republic, the *ius gentium* was not imbued with the aura of natural law that later writers ascribed to it.[154] There is also the matter of time. Chronologically, Ci-

---

to human beings alone."

DIG. 1.1. 3–4. (Ulpian, *Instit.* I.) (*my translation*), *supra* note 152.

154. Buckland maintains that originally in the early Republic, the *ius gentium* "...was merely the simpler part of the Roman Law, that part of it not bound up with typically Roman notions, and that it was in fact the simple rules observed in their intercourse by the trading peoples of central Italy." *See* W.W. BUCKLAND, A MANUAL OF ROMAN PRIVATE LAW (2d ed., Cambridge: Cambridge University Press, 1953) at 9 (hereinafter BUCKLAND, MANUAL). Elsewhere, he says of the *ius gentium*:

> "[I]t seems the better view that there is nothing imported about it: it is that part of the law which was applied also to aliens. It came to be thought of as universal, and therefore, by some at least, as implanted in man by nature, which brings it into touch with *ius naturale*."

W.W. BUCKLAND, THE MAIN INSTITUTIONS OF ROMAN PRIVATE LAW (Cambridge: Cambridge University Press, 1931) at 9. The notion of *ius gentium* imbued with the force of natural law, Buckland insists, is the creation of a later period, in which Roman legal thinkers, influenced more by Greek philosophy than Roman history, grafted a normative component onto Roman law's recognition of the customs of their trading-partners. Writing in the previous century, legal historian and anthropologist Sir Henry Maine was more blunt in his rejection of the notion that the early Romans believed *ius gentium* to be an outgrowth of the law of nature:

> "*Jus Gentium* was, in fact, the sum of the common ingredients in the customs of the old Italian tribes, for they were *all the nations* whom the Romans had the means of observing, and who sent successive swarms of immigrants to Roman soil. Whenever a particular usage was seen to be practiced by a large number of separate races in common it was set down as part of the Law common to all Nations, or *Jus Gentium*.... The circumstances of the origin of the *Jus Gentium* are probably a sufficient safeguard against the mistake of supposing that the Roman lawyers had any special respect for it. It was the fruit in part of their disdain for all foreign law, and in part of their disinclination to give the foreigner the advantage of their own indigenous *Jus Civile*.... The *Jus Gentium* was merely a system forced on [the Roman lawyer's] attention by a political necessity. He loved it as little as he loved the foreigners from whose institutions it was derived and for whose benefit it was intended. A complete revolution in his ideas was required before it could challenge his respect, but so complete was it when it did occur, that the true reason why our modern estimate of the *Jus Gentium* differs from that which has just been described, is that both modern jurisprudence and modern philosophy have inherited the matured views of the later jurisconsults on the subject.... This [revolution] arrived when a Greek theory of the Law of Nature was applied to the practical Roman administration of the Law common to all Nations."

HENRY SUMNER MAINE, ANCIENT LAW (1st ed., 1861; *reprinted* New York: Dorsett Press, 1986) at 40–43 *(emphasis in the original)* (hereinafter MAINE). Given Maine's underlying

cero was further removed from Gaius than the Framers are from us today, and he was more than a century more remote in time to Justinian than Sir Edward Coke is to the twenty-first century.[155] On close examination, the notion of a consensus among the ancients on the origins of the *ius gentium* is precarious at best. Nevertheless, there was no clear tradition among ancient writers that disputed the nexus between *ius naturale* and *ius gentium*, and the extant references supporting the nexus outnumbered those opposed to it. For the Generation of 1776, this was enough. Classical sources from the Roman Republic through Justinian's Byzantine Empire were pressed into service and cobbled together to form a coherent message—namely that no law is legitimate unless it complies with the dictates of "right reason" and "nature". Neither king nor Parliament could sanctify that which nature proscribes.[156]

For the Revolutionary generation, interest in the law of nations was not limited to classical texts. While Adams poured over the writings of Grotius, Pufendorf, Barbeyrac, and Burlamaqui,[157] Madison was reading the works of

---

premise—namely that law improves over time through a process of evolution—one might reasonably ask whether his analysis was driven by ideology. Nevertheless, his conclusions generally coincide with Buckland's.

155. The date of composition for the *Institutes of Gaius* is unknown, though the author himself is believed to have been born during the reign of Hadrian (*i.e.* between 117 and 138 A.D.) BUCKLAND, TEXT-BOOK, *supra* note 134, at 28. Cicero died in 43 B.C., and the *Digest of Justinian* was compiled between 530 and 533 A.D. *Id.* at 89.

156. It was common for American pamphleteers to cite classical sources to bolster the notion that supranational law could be used to curb the arbitrary exercise of power. One of the better examples is Adam's *Novanglus Letters*, of which Coquillette offers the following summary:

> "The core of the argument was the application of three legal principles of the *ius gentium*, namely: (1) that under the law of nature and nations resistance to arbitrary power is allegiance to the principles of law, i.e. '[r]esistence [*sic*] to lawful authority make rebellion'; and (2) that under the law of nations and the law of the English constitution itself there was no lawful parliamentary authority over the colonies...; and (3) therefore, resistance to attempts to subordinate colonial government to parliamentary edicts was, as a matter of universal legal principle, an affirmation of legal order."

Coquillette, "Justinian in Braintree", *supra* note 137, at 410–411.

157. Adams had been familiar with Burlamaqui prior to meeting with Gridley, and he began his study of Grotius and Pufendorf shortly thereafter. As a young lawyer, he also read Barbeyrac. *See* DIARY AND AUTOBIOGRAPHY OF JOHN ADAMS, *supra* note 131, Vol. III, *Autobiography* at 271–286. He continued to make use of these sources throughout his working life, citing both them and the classical sources on *ius gentium* periodically in litigation during the same time-frame in which Madison was at Princeton. *See generally* Coquillette, "Justinian in Braintree", *supra* note 137, at 376–400.

Montesquieu, Burlamaqui, and Vattel at Princeton.[158] The heavy emphasis upon authors of treatises, both ancient and modern, as a means of identifying and defining the law of nations is not surprising. In the late eighteenth century, empirical data on international custom and practice was not widely available. Not until the next century would case-law reports become common, and treaties, diplomatic correspondence, and similar records were rarely compiled into books.[159] To those whose intellectual leanings were of the "positivist" persuasion, this was no doubt somewhat of a disappointment. This school, which held that the law of nations was merely a human creation subject to change as custom and practice evolved, was foreshadowed by the works of Zouch, Alberico Gentili, and Cornelius van Bynkershoek.[160] At this early date, however, the positivists' rise to prominence was still several decades in the future. In the 1770s and 1780s, the field was dominated by the "naturalists"—Hobbes,[161] Pufendorf, Barbeyrac, and Burlamaqui—for whom the law of na-

158. In addition to these authors on the law of nations, the works of other major thinkers of the Enlightenment, including Locke, Voltaire, Rousseau, Hume, and Adam Smith, were standard fare in Princeton's curriculum while Madison was in attendance. *See* ELKINS & MCKITRICK, *supra* note 2, at 84–88. Princeton was not alone. King's College (later Columbia University) included literature on the law of nature in the fourth-year curriculum, in which the works of Grotius and Pufendorf were required reading. The curricular requirements of various American colleges account for numerous copies of treatises on the law of nature and/or nations appearing in the inventories of colonial libraries. *See* JOHNSON, *supra* note 140, Introduction at xxiv.

159. *See* Jay, *Law of Nations*, *supra* note 144, at 824.

160. *See* Dickinson, *Incorporation*, *supra* note 123, at 250–251.

161. If the law of nature were the basis of the law of nations, it is reasonable to assume that one could arrive at the content of the law of nature by tracing it "backwards" through the law of nations. Thus all that remains is to identify the "law of nations". For the early positivists, and indeed also for modern theorists in the field of international law, the law of nations consists of the custom and practice of nations. In *De Cive* (1641; revised, 1647), however, Hobbes emphatically rejects the notion that one can infer the content of *lex naturalis* empirically through examination of the customs and practices of the "wisest and most erudite nations". Admittedly, Hobbes' definition of the "natural law" may run askew of more traditional theories of the law of nature espoused by either Pufendorf or Vattel. One senses in these writers—to a greater or lesser degree—the view of natural law as somewhat akin to the Platonic forms, in that customs and practices that deviate from it are adjudged imperfect, even to the point of being morally inadequate. Hobbes does not imbue either *ius naturale* or *lex naturalis* with normative qualities such as "the good", opting instead to avoid the philosophical pitfalls of normative judgment. To those who dare to apply a normative yardstick to the customs of nations, he responds with skepticism. "It would scarcely be possible", he says, "to identify the person who shall judge the wisdom, erudition, and mores of all societies". Instead, he offers the following:

"Therefore, *lex naturalis* is, as I would define it, the dictate of right reason con-

tions was entirely subsumed under the law of nature,[162] and those who had staked out a middle ground between the positivist and naturalist positions—most notably Grotius, Wolff, and Vattel.[163]

Among writers of treatises on the law on nations, none was more influential in America than Emmerich de Vattel. Benjamin Franklin once wrote thanking Charles Dumas, the translator of Vattel's treatise, for receipt of a copy of the work, noting the timeliness of the gift and remarking that it had been "continually in the hands of members of our Congress", as they found it "necessary frequently to consult the law of nations".[164] James Otis had considered his work of sufficient importance that he struggled to reconcile it with that of Coke.[165] Indeed, so common were references to Vattel in late eighteenth-century America, that his name surfaced in places as diverse as attorneys' briefs, courts' opinions, discussions of foreign policy in Cabinet meet-

---

> cerning that which is to be done or omitted for the preservation of life and limb for as long as is possible.... As for 'right reason' in men's state of nature, I understand it not (as many do) to be an infallible faculty, but instead, it is an act of calculating—one's own rational appraisal both exact and true regarding whether his actions will redound to his own benefit—or to the detriment of the remainder of mankind."

See Thomas Hobbes, *De Cive*, Entitled in the First Edition "*Elementorum Philosophiae Sectio Tertia De Cive*" and in Later Editions "*Elementa Philosophica De Cive*" (Latin critical ed., Howard Warrener ed., Oxford: The Clarendon Press, 1983), Ch. II., sec. I., at 98–99 (*my translation*). Nevertheless, for Hobbes, no less than for undiluted naturalist Pufendorf or the eclectic Vattel, natural law provides the touchstone against which states' customs and practice must be measured. For the positivists—*e.g.* Zouch, Bynkershoek, and modern theorists—it is the other way around. Custom and practice *are* international law. One need not ask, as Hobbes does, whether these comport with "right reason".

162. Dickinson, *Incorporation*, *supra* note 123, at 244–247. Pufendorf completed *De Jure Naturae et Gentium*, his *magnum opus* on the relationship between the law of nature and the law of nations, in 1672. The following year, he published an abridgement entitled *De Officiis Hominis et Civis*. By 1691, this later work was available in English via a translation by Andrew Tooke; it was reissued in several editions, with some additions to the footnotes, on several occasions through 1735. *See* Samuel Pufendorf, [*De Officiis Hominis et Civis*] The Whole Duty of Man, According to the Law of Nature (1st English ed., 1691, Andrew Tooke trans., revised 1735; critical ed., Indianapolis: Liberty Fund, 2003), Introduction at xii–xv.

163. *Id.* at 242–244; 247–252.

164. Letter of Benjamin Franklin to Charles F.W. Dumas (Dec. 9, 1775), *reproduced from manuscript in* The Writings of Benjamin Franklin (10 vols., Albert Henry Smyth ed., New York: The Macmillan Company, 1906), Vol. VI, at 432.

165. *See* Gordon S. Wood, The Creation of the American Republic 1776–1787 (Chapel Hill: University of North Carolina Press, 1969) at 9.

ings, and even the popular press.[166] Eclectic in focus, Vattel found a place in his theories for both natural law and the custom and practice of nations, though the latter was required to pass muster under the former to ensure its legitimacy.[167] He did much to popularize Wolff's writings, but he parts company with Wolff in rejecting the latter's notion of *civitas maxima* as the source of the "voluntary law of nations".[168] As with Grotius, he accepts the idea that

---

166. For discussion, *see* Jay, *Law of Nations*, *supra* note 144, at 823.

167. *See* E[MMERICH] DE VATTEL, THE LAW OF NATIONS OR THE PRINCIPLES OF NATURAL LAW, APPLIED TO THE AFFAIRS OF NATIONS AND SOVEREIGNS (French ed. of 1758, trans. Charles G. Fenwick: Classics of International Law Series, Buffalo: William S. Hein & Co., 1994), Introduction, sec. 9, at 4–5; sec. 21, sec. 24–sec. 28, at 7–9 (hereinafter VATTEL). For Vattel, the law of nations is divided into the "necessary law of nations" and the "positive law of nations". This latter category consists of the "customary" (*i.e.* treaties), the "conventional" (*i.e.* customs and practices, binding only among participating nations), and the "voluntary". Arguably, this last category is an exception to the requirement that the law of nations be grounded in the law of nature. Vattel writes of this "voluntary" law:

> "It must happen, then, on many occasions that Nations put up with certain things although in themselves unjust and worthy of condemnation, because they cannot oppose them by force without transgressing the liberty of individual Nations and thus destroying the foundations of their natural society. And since they are bound to advance that society, we rightly presume that they have agreed to the principle just established. The rules resulting from it form what Wolff calls the *voluntary Law of Nations*..."

Id., Introduction, sec. 21, at 8 *(emphasis in the original). See also* discussion, *infra* note 169.

168. The relevant passages are found in VATTEL, *supra* note 167, Preface at 8a–11a; Introduction, sec. 13–sec. 21, at 6–8. Vattel notes:

> "...I differ entirely from Mr. Wolff in the foundation I lay for that division of the Law of Nations which we term *voluntary*. Mr. Wolff deduces it from the idea of a sort of great republic (*Civitas Maxima*) set up by nature herself, of which all the Nations of the world are members. To his mind, the *voluntary* Law of Nations acts as the civil law of this great republic. This does not satisfy me, and I find the fiction of such a republic neither reasonable nor well enough founded to deduce therefrom the rules of a Law of Nations at once universal in character, and necessarily accepted by sovereign States."

Id., Preface at 9a *(emphasis in the original)*. Dickinson gives one of the best short analyses of the differences between Vattel and Wolff, highlighting the fact that Vattel is not a mere "popularizer" of the latter's work:

> "[For Vattel], [t]he positive law of nations...consisted of the voluntary, the conventional, and the customary law. Vattel repudiated Wolff's derivation of the voluntary law from the conception of the *civitas maxima* and founded it instead upon the fiction of presumed consent, fortified by a curious process of reasoning which ran substantially as follows. Obligations, he said, are internal or external, the former binding the conscience only, the latter corresponding to rights in others. Rights corresponding to external obligations in others are perfect or

some portions of the law of nations are man-made, but he is more parsimonious in defining their scope.[169] He praises Hobbes' work for grounding the

---

> imperfect, the former including the right to compel performance, the latter including only the right to request performance. Now since nations are free, independent, and equal, as men are by nature, whatever is lawful or unlawful for one must be equally lawful or unlawful for another. Nations are free, therefore, to do whatever they please so long as they are under internal obligations only or affect only the imperfect rights of other nations. 'It must happen, then, on many occasions,' Vattel concluded, 'that nations put up with certain things although in themselves unjust and worthy of condemnation, because they cannot oppose them by force without transgressing the liberty of individual nations and thus destroying the foundations of their natural society. And since they are bound to advance that society, we rightly presume that they have agreed to the principles just established.' The rules arising from such unpreventable abuses of natural liberty constituted the voluntary law of nations."

Dickinson, *Incorporation*, *supra* note 123, at 249. For a more complete analysis, *see* Nicholas Greenwood Onuf, *Civitas Maxima: Wolff, Vattel and the Fate of Republicanism*, 88 Am. J. Intn'l L. 280, 300, *generally* 287–301 (1994) (hereinafter Onuf, *Civitas Maxima*); *see also* Peter Onuf & Nicholas Onuf, Federal Union, Modern World: The Law of Nations in an Age of Revolutions, 1776–1814 (Madison, Wisconsin: Madison House, 1993) at 15–16 (hereinafter Onuf & Onuf).

169. Vattel is quite emphatic in distinguishing his position from that of Grotius; he explains:

> "The celebrated Grotius understands by the 'Law of Nations' a law established by the common consent of Nations, and he thus distinguishes it from the natural law.... Grotius, by the very distinction which he draws, and by his application of the term 'Law of Nations' merely to those principles established by the consent of Nations, apparently gives us to understand that it is only these latter principles which sovereigns can insist upon being observed, the *internal* law remaining a guide for their consciences. If with his idea that political societies or Nations live together in a mutual interdependence in the state of nature, and that as political bodies they are subject to the Law of Nature, Grotius had considered, in addition, that the law ought to be applied to these new subjects according to their nature, this thoughtful writer would have easily perceived that the natural Law of Nations is a special science; that it gives rise among Nations even to an exterior obligation independent of their will, and that the consent of Nations is the foundation and the source only of that particular division of the Law of Nations which is called the 'arbitrary Law of Nations.'"

Vattel, *supra* note 167, Preface at 4a–5a. One might seriously question whether Vattel's characterization of Grotius' theories is correct. The gist of his criticism lies in his perception that for Grotius a portion of the "law of nations" (*i.e.* rules created by common consent) is not directly grounded in the law of nature—and that it is this portion alone with which nations can demand compliance of their fellow nations. Despite his condemnation of Grotius, Vattel himself has faced similar criticism on the same point. Political scientist Nicholas Onuf makes the following observation:

law of nations in natural law, though he criticizes its "paradoxes and detestable principles".[170] Like the naturalists before him, for Vattel "the Law of Nations, is in its origin, merely the Law of Nature applied to Nations", and the law of nature is by definition "not subject to change".[171] Admittedly, there is room for human innovation—in the form of acquiescence, tacit compliance with customs and practice, and overt consent expressed in treaties—but even these must comply with the unchanging "necessary" or "natural" law of nations.[172]

Vattel's influence, both explicitly and implicitly, underlies much of the debate on the law of nations in America in the last two decades of the eighteenth century. The Continental Congress' debates over the law of prize had been filled with references to Vattel; Franklin's gift of Dumas' translation clearly was

---

> "Had Vattel developed a coherent position on the several sources of a single law, that law would have had a foundation in the state practice it regulates. Instead, by rejecting the great republic [*i.e.* Wolff's *civitas maxima*] as a philosopher's conceit and a threat to the distinction between necessary and voluntary law, Vattel created a problem for himself. Natural society remains as a foundation for the necessary law. The voluntary law has nothing comparable. There is no evidence that Vattel recognized this problem as such."

Onuf, *Civitas Maxima*, *supra* note 168, at 301.

170. Vattel, *supra* note 167, Preface at 5a. While Vattel opts not to highlight the point, at the core of his differences with Hobbes are the conflicting views which the two men have regarding the notion of man in the state of nature. Vattel views man as a social creature; in his natural state he is part of a society. *Id.*, Introduction, sec. 10, at 5. Hobbes, in contrast, sees the state of nature as a condition from which man, desirous of self-preservation, seeks to escape through formation of social groups.

171. As Vattel explains:

> "We use the term *necessary Law of Nations* for that law which results from applying the natural law to Nations. It is *necessary*, because Nations are absolutely bound to observe it. It contains those precepts which the natural law dictates to States, and it is no less binding upon them than it is upon individuals. For States are composed of men, their policies are determined by men, and these men are subject to the natural law under whatever capacity they act. This same law is called by Grotius and his followers the *internal Law of Nations*, inasmuch as it is binding upon the conscience of Nations. Several writers call it the *natural Law of Nations*. Since, therefore, the necessary Law of Nations consists in applying the natural law to States, and since the natural law is not subject to change, being founded on the nature of things and particularly upon the nature of man, it follows that the necessary Law of Nations is not subject to change."

Id., Introduction, sec. 7–sec. 8, at 4 *(emphasis in the original)*.

172. *Id.*, Introduction, sec. 9, at 4–5. Arguably, this applies to the conventional and customary law of nations only. The "voluntary" law of nations (acquiescence in unjust practices—*see* sec. 21, at 8) appears to be exempt from compliance with the unchanging "natural" law of nations. *See* discussion, *supra* notes 167–168.

put to good use.[173] In many respects, Vattel's treatise found a niche in American thought that it never achieved in the author's native country, and that it arguably could not have attained in any other place or time. Sufficiently detailed to provide concrete information for answering practical questions on a myriad of topics—from the rules of war to those for interpreting treaties—it had the advantage of being well organized and provided with a very detailed table of contents, thus allowing for easy use in public debate. A strong argument can be made that Vattel's thoughts on treaty-formation lay at the heart of Jefferson's plan to ensure the United States' political security through economic interdependency facilitated by trade-agreements.[174] If the treatise lacked the theoretical complexity of Grotius or Wolff, for practical men grappling with daily problems of international relations it nevertheless served much the same function that Molloy's treatise had for the common lawyers as they struggled with the arcane rules of the *lex mercatoria* and the *lex maritima*. In addition, Vattel's emphasis on a nexus between the law of nature and the law of nations held a special appeal for the Revolutionary generation. That law grounded directly in the law of nature, the "necessary law of nations", was as immutable as the law of nature itself. Even the man-made portion of the law of nations—the voluntary, conventional, and customary law that constituted the "positive law of nations"—Vattel measured with the yardstick of natural law. For some of that generation, obeisance to a law of nations grounded in immutable nature ended with independence. Indeed, Thomas Paine, the quintessential revolutionary, was quick to renounce the law of nature as a basis for the law of nations once independence had been achieved.[175] For others,

---

173. *See* Bourguignon, First Federal Court, *supra* note 43, at 56–57; *see also supra* note 164 and text accompanying.

174. *See* Onuf & Onuf, *supra* note 168, at 105–111, 182–184); for discussion, *see also supra* Introduction, notes 117–122 and text accompanying.

175. In a pamphlet published in 1801, Paine foreshadows the ascendancy of the "positivist" view of the law of nations in a manner extreme even by today's standards. He repudiates the whole notion of a "law of nations", except that created by bilateral or multilateral treaties. Rejecting both Vattel and Grotius, as well as the naturalist Pufendorf, he maintains:

> "Nations in their original state are, with respect to each other, like individuals in a state of nature. From their original state they proceed to form treaties, and the treaty or treaties so formed between any two of them become a law to the parties forming them, and no more. They have no operation over other nations, neither do they make any part of a general law of nations, unless all treaties were formed on one and the same common principle: And it has been by confounding the law of treaties with the idea of a law of nations that has given rise to the error of a law of nations existing."

however, the nexus between the law of nature and the law of nations survived in their post-war thought.

James Wilson, co-drafter of the Constitution's Admiralty Clause, retained his belief that the law of nations was grounded in the law of nature—a belief that he would carry with him into his lectures on law and ultimately to the federal bench. In his lecture "Of the Law of Nations", Wilson begins emphatically, asserting: "The law of nature, when applied to states or political societies, receives a new name, that of the law of nations."[176] He criticizes Grotius for failing to base the "consensual" law of nations on the law of nature. Nevertheless, he likewise refuses to embrace wholeheartedly the position of Pufendorf and the naturalists, observing that: "Grotius and Pufendorff [*sic*] seem to have run into contrary extremes... [and] [t]he truth seems to lie between the two great philosophers."[177] While conceding that treaties and customs attain the force of law by consent, he simultaneously maintains that they are "under the control of" the law of nature.[178] Upon close reading, the influence of Vattel is unmistakable.[179] In his judicial career as well, his debt to the Swiss thinker is similarly apparent. In a charge to a grand jury in a maritime case, he remarks:

> The law of nations has its foundation in the principles of natural law, applied to states; and in voluntary institutions, arising from custom or convention. This law is universal in its authority over the civilized part of the world; and is supported by the consideration of its general utility, as well as that of its obligatory force.... True it is, that, so far as the law of nations is *voluntary* or *positive*, it may be altered by the municipal legislature of any state, in cases affecting *only* its own citizens. True it is also, that, by a treaty, the voluntary or positive law of nations may be altered so far as the alteration shall affect *only* the contracting parties. But equally true it is, that no state or states can,

---

THOMAS PAINE, COMPACT MARITIME (Washington, D.C.: Samuel Harrison Smith, 1801) at 3.

176. *See* "Lecture 'Of the Law of Nations'", *in* THE WORKS OF JAMES WILSON (2 vols., Robert Green McCloskey ed., Cambridge, Massachusetts: The Belknap Press of Harvard University, 1967), Vol. I, at 148 (hereinafter WORKS OF JAMES WILSON). The Lectures, delivered while Wilson served as a professor of law at the College of Philadelphia, were written over a two-year period immediately following Wilson's appointment to the Supreme Court in 1790, where he served until his death in 1798. *Id.*, Vol. I, Introduction at 28–31.

177. *Id.* at 151–152.

178. *Id.* at 150–151.

179. *Id.* at 149–152. *Cf.* VATTEL, *supra* note 167, Preface at 10a–11a, Introduction, sec. 7–sec. 9, sec. 24–sec. 28, at 4–5, 8–9.

> by treaties or municipal laws, alter or abrogate the law of nations any farther.[180]

In his treatment of the "voluntary or positive law", Wilson's language echoes Vattel, and yet he hints at something new. Vattel is quite clear that the positive law of nations comes in to being only at the instigation of two or more nations. Through acquiescence, unwritten custom, or express agreement, two or more nations may create positive law, so long as it does not offend the underlying natural law.[181] Wilson implies that this law already exists, subject to change by the agreement (either overt or tacit) of two or more nations. In practical terms, Vattel maintains that no nation is bound by either "voluntary" or "customary" law unless it acquiesces or consents.[182] Wilson, on the other hand, appears to assume that customs and practices of the community of nations apply as "default rules" unless two or more nations contract around them. Such a contract would be binding only among parties to the agreement; in their relations with other nations, the "default rules" would continue to apply. One of Wilson's contemporaries, George Nicholas, made the same point more explicitly in Virginia's debates on ratification:

> [T]here was no such thing as a particular law of nations; but that the law of nations was permanent and general—It was superior to any act or law of any nation. It implied the consent of all, and was mutually binding on all, being acquiesced in for the common benefit of all.[183]

Vattel is careful to distinguish between the permanent "necessary" or "natural" law of nations and the mutable "positive" law of nations, circumscribed but not dictated by the law of nature.[184] In Nicholas' thought, however, the "necessary" and "positive" law of nations have collapsed into one set of rules, both universally binding and immutable. For the fledgling United States,

180. WORKS OF JAMES WILSON, *supra* note 176, Vol. II, at 813–814 *(emphasis in the original)*.

181. *See* VATTEL, *supra* note 167, Introduction, sec. 9, sec. 21, sec. 24–sec. 26, at 4–5, 7–9.

182. *Id.*, Introduction, sec. 21–sec. 28, at 7–9.

183. Nicholas' remarks were made in response to Grayson's comments during the debates of June 18, 1788. *See* RATIFICATION, *supra* note 24, Vol. X, at 1383.

184. *See* VATTEL, *supra* note 167, Introduction, sec. 7–sec. 9 (necessary law of nations); sec. 21–sec. 27 (positive law of nations); sec. 27–sec. 28 (distinguishing the necessary from the positive law of nations), at 4–9.

Nicholas' view would have profound consequences. Under it, some portions of what Vattel termed the "positive law of nations" would bind the new republic irrespective of Constitutional recognition or Congressional consent.

The naturalist school (in both its undiluted form and the hybrid variety championed by Vattel) may have dominated American thought in the first decade following independence, but it did not go unchallenged. Positivism—the process of inferring the law of nations empirically from the custom and practice of nations—had begun to take root. Hamilton refers to this as the "modern law of nations", which he says "must necessarily be understood as that prevailing in Europe and acceded to by this Country".[185] Of this "modern" law, he writes:

> Does this customary law of Nations as established in Europe bind the U[nited] States? An affirmative answer to this is warranted by conclusive reasons. I The U[nited] States when a member of the British Empire were in this capacity a party to that law, and not having dissented from it when they became independent they are to be considered as having continued a party to it. II The common law of England which was & is in force in each of these states adopts the law of Nations, the positive equally with natural, as part of itself. III Ever since we have been an Independent nation we have appealed to and acted upon the modern law of Nations as understood in Europe. Various resolutions of Congress during our revolution—the correspondencies of Executive officers—the decisions of our Courts of Admiralty, all recognized this standard.... T'is indubitable that the

185. The statement was made in the context of the conflict between Britain and France in 1795. Hamilton (writing as "Camillus") begins, as Wilson does in his lectures, with a model of the law of nations apparently based on Vattel. In places, he goes so far as to cite Vattel by name. Nevertheless, as Wilson had done four years earlier, Hamilton modifies Vattel's model. While in Wilson's work, the positive law virtually collapses back into the necessary law of nations (reminiscent of Pufendorf, Burlamaqui, and their followers), in Hamilton's argument, the positive law (*i.e.* international custom and practice) takes on a life of its own. Customs recognized by most nations become binding on all others. The result is a theory that comports with twentieth-century models of international law. One reasonably might question whether Hamilton is being philosophically innovative, or merely acting as a good advocate, "hedging his bets" by paying homage to Vattel's eclectic brand of naturalism while simultaneously embracing the emerging empirical school of thought. *See* "To Defence No. XX" (Oct. 23–24, 1795), *in* The Papers of Alexander Hamilton (27 vols., Harold C. Syrett ed., New York: Columbia University Press, 1973), Vol. XIX, at 329–347 (hereinafter Papers of Alexander Hamilton).

> customary law of European Nations is as a part of the common law and by adoption that of the U[nited] States.[186]

Despite their obvious differences, the approaches of Hamilton and Wilson have one striking similarity. Both assume—*contra* Vattel—that the customs and practices of other sovereign states can bind a nation even without its express consent. Two or more nations may alter custom amongst themselves (albeit for the naturalist Wilson only within carefully circumscribed parameters), but one nation cannot unilaterally opt out of the positive law of nations.

Lex Maritima As Part of the Law of Nations

If the men of the Framers' generation indeed believed that the law of nations was universally binding on states individually, it remains to ascertain whether they also regarded the *lex maritima* as part of the law of nations. Vattel, characterizing the law of nations as that which regulates the relations between sovereign states, virtually ignores maritime law, mentioning it only briefly in the contexts of privateering and wreck.[187] Nonetheless, the notion of *ius gentium*, of which the *lex maritima* was a part, had enjoyed a long history in Europe. In Roman law, the *ius gentium* was originally law regulating private interaction—particularly among merchants.[188] This meaning was preserved from Cicero and Gaius onwards through the middle ages and down to the early modern era, despite some authors occasionally using the expression to refer to the *ius inter gentes*, or law among societies—the forerunner of that which today is generally called "public international law".[189] Some English civilians, wary of Coke's contention that all law common to all nations was

186. *Id.* at 341–342.

187. Vattel mentions the substantive law of wreck only in passing in a chapter devoted to that which we today would call the public international law of the sea. *See* VATTEL, *supra* note 167, Bk. I, Ch. XXIII, sec. 293, at 109–110. It is ironic that the Continental Congress looked to Vattel for assistance in adducing the law of prize. His treatise devotes only one section to privateering, and his description of the substantive rules are so rudimentary as to render them of little help to anyone seeking guidance on how to adjudicate cases of prize. *Id.*, Bk. III, Ch. XV, sec. 229, at 319.

188. *See e.g.* BUCKLAND, MANUAL, *supra* note 154, at 9; MAINE, *supra* note 154, at 41–43. *See generally* discussion, *supra* notes 134–155 and text accompanying.

189. For discussion, *see e.g.* COQUILLETTE, CIVILIAN WRITERS, *supra* note 103, at 35–36.

incorporated into the common law, sought to narrow the scope of the *ius gentium*. Nevertheless, even for these, the *ius gentium* retained a private-law component, namely the substantive law regulating transboundary transactions—*i.e.* the *lex mercatoria* and the *lex maritima*.[190] For the civilian Zouch it was self-evident that the "Law Merchant... is a branch of the Law of Nations" and that "Causes concerning Merchants, are not now to be decided by the peculiar and Ordinary Lawes of every Country, but by the general Lawes of Nature and Nations." Coupled in tandem with the "Law Merchant" was the "Law Mariner", which extended to those facets of mercantile activities that took place at sea.[191] The common lawyers concurred. Mansfield identified the substantive maritime law as "not the law of a particular country, but the general law of nations".[192] Blackstone added his opinion, expounding upon Mansfield's theme. The law merchant, "a branch of the law of nations", governed contracts of carriage, demurrage, general average, bottomry, marine insurance—in short the full panoply of instance cases. So also did it govern disputes involving both wreck and prize, for which "there is no other rule of decision but this great universal law, collected from history and usage, and such writers of all nations and languages are generally approved and allowed of".[193] The civilians and the common lawyers, so frequently at odds with each other in the course of English legal history, nonetheless managed to find common ground on one crucial point. The *lex maritima*—regulating both private maritime commerce and public-law matters such as prize—applied universally. Substantive maritime law was part of the law of nations.

---

190. English civilians felt obliged to respond to Coke's contention that if the *ius gentium* were binding on all nations, it should be characterized as part of the domestic law of England. In essence, the *ius gentium* would be a part of the common law. By thus cleverly turning the table on the civilians with a theory of their own creation, Coke forced some civilian writers to adopt a second line of defense. Borrowing from Gentili, they argued instead that the *ius gentium* was instead a form of universally applicable transboundary law, which governed both relations between states and business-relationships between citizens of different countries. For discussion, *see* Coquillette, Civilian Writers, *supra* note 103, at 91.

191. *See* Zouch, *supra* note 122, at 9–10, 66–67. (It is worth noting that Zouch cites as authority the same ubiquitous quote from Cicero's *De Officiis*, made famous by Mansfield and Story, which begins with the phrase: "There shall not be one law for Rome and another for Athens...". *Id.* at 9.)

192. *Luke v. Lyde*, 97 Eng. Rep. 614, 617 (K.B. 1759). For context and analysis, *see supra* note 107 and text accompanying.

193. 4 Blackstone, *supra* note 106, at 67; for the full text of Blackstone's comment, *see supra* note 125 and text accompanying.

Across the Atlantic, the men of the Framer's generation struggled with the same issue. Treatises on maritime law were in short supply in America, both before and after the Revolution. This was not the result of America being a legal backwater, but rather a reflection of a lack of treatises on the subject in England as well. Even in the Tudor period, the high-water mark of the High Court of Admiralty, there was no significant body of scholarly literature addressing the *lex maritima*.[194] Admittedly, there was the work of Francis Clerke, but this addressed only procedure, not the theoretical question of whether substantive maritime law was part of the law of nations. Hale's treatise was published posthumously—in the twentieth century. Both Malynes and Molloy[195] were more interested in practical questions about maritime law and the law merchant than in settling the academic question of whether the *lex maritima* was part of the law of nations. Those authors who did address the issue, from the civilian Zouch to the champions of the common law, Mansfield and Blackstone, were in agreement, as were the ancient authors from Cicero onward. In the history of Anglo-American maritime law, no quote was recycled more often than that taken from Cicero's *De Re Publica*: "There will not be one law for Rome, and another for Athens, nor one body of law now and another in the future, but in-

---

194. *See e.g.* Alain Wijffels, "*Ius Gentium* in the Practice of the Court of Admiralty Around 1600", *in* THE ROMAN LAW TRADITION (Cambridge: Cambridge University Press, 1994) at 121.

195. While Molloy avoids a detailed excursus on the theoretical underpinnings of the "law maritime", he does not dodge entirely the question of the relationship between the law of nations and maritime law. He observes that: "among all Nations there is a Common Law which governs the mighty thing of Navigation and Commerce". Nevertheless, he distinguishes those aspects of law that are grounded in the law of nature from those that are a product of custom. The former are immutable. The latter are susceptible to change and retain the force of law only so far as they reflect "justice" and "reason". Into this latter category, he places the Rhodian Laws and the Laws of Oleron. Although the substantive maritime law may not be immutable, Molloy leaves open the possibility that at any given time it may be binding on all nations, so long as it comports with "reason" and is generally recognized among nations. Thus Molloy never confronts head-on the question of whether a nation may opt out of "law maritime" recognized by custom among its trading partners. In essence, he dodges the question of whether the maritime law is supranational, applying automatically irrespective of the will of king and Parliament. The text—perhaps purposefully—is ambiguous on this point. As with the jurisdictional conflict between the common lawyers and the civilians, which Molloy deftly side-steps, the theoretical underpinnings of the maritime law provide ample opportunity for controversy. Molloy wished to market his book as a working-tool for litigators. Offending a portion of his prospective readership by taking sides in a theoretical/political debate would have served no useful purpose. *See* MOLLOY (3d ed., Bellinger), *supra* note 124, Introduction (*not paginated*).

stead among all people and for all times, the same imperishable and eternal law shall apply."[196] Zouch, Mansfield, Story, and James Wilson (among others) all expropriated it.[197] At the end of the eighteenth century, there were few published reports of courts' decisions and little Anglo-American scholarship dealing with the law of nations. It was to the ancient authors, the Continental treatise-writers, and Blackstone that American lawyers were obliged to turn for answers when confronted with questions concerning the relationship between domestic and international law. It was from these sources that the Framers' generation obtained information on the law of nations. The results were predictable. Charles Pinckney assumed that no nation could opt to utilize juries in maritime trials, since such a decision would violate the law of nations.[198] The choice was not one of purely domestic law, left to the discretion of a nation's sovereign judgment, but rather a duty imposed upon it externally. John Adams, whose career as a litigator included experience with maritime claims, remarked unequivocally in a letter in 1788 that: "Maritime causes must be decided by the law of nations".[199] James Wilson agreed. "Maritime law", he explained in 1791 in a charge to a grand jury "is not the law of any particular country: it is the general law of nations."[200] He reaffirmed this position the same year in one of his lectures at the College of Philadelphia, observing: "The law merchant as well as the law maritime forms a branch of the general law of nations."[201]

---

196. Cicero, *De Re Publica*, *supra* note 145, III. 22. 33 (*my translation*).

197. Zouch cited this line from Cicero's *De Re Publica* to support his contention that the maritime law transcends national boundaries. Zouch, *supra* note 122, at 9. Mansfield also included the line in the famous maritime/mercantile case *Luke v. Lyde*, 97 Eng. Rep. 614, 617 (K. B. 1759) (*See supra* notes 107, 192 and text accompanying). Story utilized the quote to support the notion of a universal maritime law in *DeLovio v. Boit* (Case No. 3776), 2 F. Cas. 418, 420 (C.C., D. Mass. 1815). Story subsequently quoted the same passage again in *Swift v. Tyson*, 41 U.S. 1, 19 (1842). (*See supra* Chapter I, note 2 and text accompanying.) Wilson found a place for the quote in his charge to a grand jury in a maritime case. Works of James Wilson, *supra* note 176, at 813. It is worth noting that all four cited Cicero in the original Latin—testimony to the importance of classical learning in Anglo-American law from the seventeenth through nineteenth centuries.

198. *See* Bourguignon, First Federal Court, *supra* note 43, at 335.

199. Letter of John Adams to Thomas Brand-Hollis (Jan. 4, 1788), *published in* Ratification, *supra* note 24, Vol. V, at 611. In context, Adams' remark (as had Pinckney's) clearly refers to curial law, although it may be read more broadly to encompass the substantive maritime law as well. Given Adams' use of the civil law and the *ius gentium* in arguing the case of *Doane v. Gage* (1766–1769) before the Revolution (*see supra* Chapter II, notes 158–164 and text accompanying), the broad reading is preferable. For discussion *see also* Coquillette, "Justinian", *supra* note 137, at 383–385.

200. Works of James Wilson, *supra* note 176, Vol. II, at 803, 813.

201. *Id.*, Vol. II, at 488.

Substantive Maritime Law and Concurrent Maritime Jurisdiction: Recapitulation

It is ironic that for Americans of the eighteenth century the concept of "*ius gentium*" was imbued with qualities of permanence and immutability. The hallmark of the *ius gentium* in the law of the Roman Republic had been its flexibility. The early jurists saw no need to regard the customs and practices of Rome's Italian trading partners as immutable. It was not until the twilight of the Republic that Cicero tied it to the law of nature in an unhappy marriage of Greek philosophy and Roman jurisprudence.[202] It is perhaps to be expected that that Cicero, clinging to the dying traditions of the old Republic on the eve of its eclipse by the new Empire, would seek to tie its law to something eternal and unchanging. Moreover, in the long history of western legal thought, he would not be the last to seek a substratum of coherency and order amid a collection of disparate rules that had evolved haphazardly over generations. Two millennia later, Arthur Browne and Joseph Story would do the same. This same impulse induced the jurists of the late Empire to codify the *ius gentium* in digests and institutes, thus fixing in stone the once flexible and mutable customs of the international community of merchants. In doing so, they deprived the Roman *ius gentium* of much of its character as a dynamic and practical tool of the mercantile community, much as the *lex mercatoria* of the middle ages lost those same qualities when it was co-opted by Holt, Mansfield, and the common lawyers in the seventeenth and eighteenth centuries.[203]

It was to these ancient sources, and to modern thinkers such as the naturalist Pufendorf and the eclectic Vattel, that the Americans of the Framers' generation turned for guidance in defining the law of nations. Cicero assured them that the law of nations was grounded in the law of nature; the naturalists—Pufendorf, Barbeyrac, and Burlamaqui—agreed. Vattel also gave his qualified assent, though he was careful to distinguish the "necessary" law of nations, intrinsically immutable, from the voluntary, consensual and customary law of nations—all susceptible to change, but only so long as those changes did not offend the law of nature. Not all Americans were as careful to make this distinction. For some, the distinction between the "necessary" and "positive" law of nations was blurred, with the latter collapsing back into the former. For these, the *ius gentium* became immutable and received bind-

---

202. Buckland, Text-Book, *supra* note 134, at 52–55.

203. *See* Coquillette, Civilian Writers, *supra* note 103, at 132, 145–146.

ing force in dealings with foreign nationals, irrespective of the wishes of the nation's law-makers. This is not to say that it was impossible for men of the Framers' generation to conceive of a law of nations grounded in the widespread consent of sovereign states rather than in the immutable dictates of nature. Indeed, one may find in Hamilton traces of the positivism that characterized Molloy's work, as well as that which came to dominate American thought in the early nineteenth century.[204] Nevertheless, even for those whose thought-processes were more empirically than teleologically inclined, obstacles remained. For those who sought to deduce the rules of customary international law from states' practices, there were few published compilations of diplomatic correspondence. In general, there were few law-books to be found in America that addressed the customary law of nations, and those that did—the writings of the Roman jurists, the naturalists, and Vattel—were of little use to those inclined to pursue empirical studies. There was little concrete information available for these neophyte positivists to use in challenging the prevailing assumptions that the *ius gentium* was grounded in the law of nature, and little reason to question the popularly held notion that the *lex maritima* was part of the *ius gentium*.

Even if the positivists had managed to convert the young nation to their principles, there is no guarantee that it would have changed popular opinion regarding the immutability of the *lex maritima*. The mere fact that substantive rules need not pass muster under the immutable principles of the law of nature does not necessarily prove that the rules of substantive maritime law prevailing among the community of nations remain in a state of evolution or flux. To determine whether, for example, the rules for general average recognized among the community of nations change over time, one would have to trace how nations have addressed general average in the past and compare the

---

204. Whether Molloy actually influenced Hamilton cannot be determined from extant evidence. Nonetheless, one can see a common theme in Molloy's definition of the law of nations as the "Law or Will of Common Consent" and Hamilton's "modern law of nations", under which a nation that participates or acquiesces in the customs or practices of its fellow nations becomes legally bound by them. In their treatment of the law of nations, both Molloy and Hamilton are positivists. Admittedly, Hamilton makes the expected passing remark on the "positive equally with the natural" law of nations—an oblique reference to Vattel. Nonetheless, the thrust of his comments rests upon two assumptions: first that one must infer the content of the law of nations from observing the customs of nations, and second, that a nation which participates in such customs implicitly accepts them as law. *See* Molloy (3d ed., Bellinger), *supra* note 124, Introduction (*not paginated*); Papers of Alexander Hamilton, *supra* note 185, Vol. XIX, at 341–342. *See also* discussion, *supra* notes 124, 186, 195 and text accompanying.

evidence to interpretations of the rules of general average recognized today. To do so, one would need resources, such as published reports of cases, which were largely unavailable to eighteenth-century Americans. Today, it is possible to trace the subtle changes in the rules of general average from antiquity through the middle ages and down to the eighteenth century. In doing so, one can readily recognize that the rules of antiquity bear little resemblance to those of early modern Europe. In the 1780s, however, there were no vast collections of ancient, medieval, or Elizabethan manuscripts readily available to the legal scholars and practitioners of Virginia, New York, Pennsylvania, or Massachusetts.[205] What they knew of substantive rules of law they had gleaned either from treatises or from their own personal experiences. This was the era of the common-place book, in which practitioners recorded the outcomes of cases and the substantive rules applied by the courts. These books were necessary, as digests of case law would not make their appearance until the next century. For the American lawyer attempting to master the substantive rules governing maritime commerce, their own clients were often their best resource—practical men who knew the rules through years of experience.[206]

---

205. At least since the late nineteenth century, scholars have recognized that the rules for general average are the best source of information regarding the origins of the various medieval maritime codes. As Sir Travers Twiss observed: "[T]he provisions on the subject of contribution in cases of jetison...may be regarded as a crucial test of the diversity of origin of any two systems of maritime law..." Twiss, *supra* note 104, Vol. III, at xxxiii. Writing in the 1870s, Twiss had access (as have all scholars who followed him) to extensive information on the history of the medieval and early modern manuscripts and early published versions of the various collections of sea-laws. This was clearly not the case for the men of the Framers' generation. Cleirac's seventeenth-century collection of Europe's maritime codes (although owned by Jefferson) was exceedingly rare, and Pardessus did not publish his collection of maritime codes until 1845. *See* Catalogue of the Library of Thomas Jefferson (5 vols., Millicent Sowerby ed., Washington, D.C.: Library of Congress, 1953), Vol. II, at 368; Twiss, *supra* note 104, Vol. III, at lxii. In the 1780s, even reports of case law were unavailable. Lord Stowell's published reports did not appear in print until 1799, and the earliest American reports were published until 1792 and 1807 respectively. Owen & Tolley, *supra* note 82, at 11; L. Kinvin Wroth, *The Massachusetts Vice Admiralty Court and the Federal Admiralty Jurisdiction*, 6 Am. J. Legal Hist. 251, 264, 365–366 (1962). Even Arthur Browne, the most eminent civilian of his day, was hampered by a lack of valuable information. This deficiency is reflected in his comments on general average. Writing in 1802, he observes: "The laws on average and contribution [of Roman law] do not materially differ from those of modern days, and have served as models for them". Browne, *supra* note 88, Vol. II, at 36. For further discussion, *see supra* Chapter I, notes 31–35 and text accompanying.

206. In his *Diary*, Adams remarks in passing that even the scholarly Jeremiah Gridley, owner of an extensive law-library, kept a common-place book. Diary and Autobiogra-

Had more resources been available to American attorneys in the 1780s, they would have seen that the *lex maritima* does in fact change. The changes, however, are rarely sudden. Throughout its long history, the *lex maritima* has been like a glacier, in perpetual but imperceptible motion. To the attorney assembling his common-place book or to the practical man of business, whose knowledge is limited to the experiences of one lifetime, the substantive rules of maritime law appear static, carved in stone in some distant age. Despite a rich history of gradual evolution in both England and on the Continent—buried in an assortment of public and private libraries awaiting discovery in the late nineteenth century—there was little in America's colonial experience to show that the law was in a state of flux. Even if most Americans had been convinced that *lex maritima* was not immutable through its connection to the law of nature, they had little reason to believe, as a practical matter, that it ever changed. Moreover, even most positivists would admit that one nation cannot unilaterally change the customary rules established by its fellow nations—nor in this instance was it clear that it would be desirable to do so. Colonial vice admiralty courts and state admiralty courts utilized substantive rules that differed little if at all from one jurisdiction to another.[207]

In 1789, jurisdiction over maritime matters, vested concurrently in the federal and state courts, posed no threat to the uniformity of substantive maritime law because it was virtually inconceivable that the two sets of courts would apply different sets of rules. In 1664, at the height of the struggle between the civilians and the common lawyers, John Exton had warned against the dangers of allowing two separate sets of courts to interpret one body of law; uniformity of substantive law was of paramount importance:

> I shall but once again put you in mind of what hath been already said concerning the necessity of upholding one and the same Law in all Na-

---

PHY OF JOHN ADAMS, *supra* note 131, Vol. I, at 155. Adams himself began compiling a common-place book, the text of which still survives. *Published from manuscript in* THE LEGAL PAPERS OF JOHN ADAMS (L. Kinvin Wroth & Hiller B. Zobel eds., Cambridge, Massachusetts: The Belknap Press of Harvard University, 1965), Vol. I, No. 2, at 3. For discussion, *see also supra* Chapter II, notes 230–254 and notes accompanying.

207. This is equally applicable to the early days after the passage of the Judiciary Act of 1789. Modern scholarship reveals that the substantive law that state courts applied was virtually identical to that applied by federal courts sitting in admiralty. For discussion, *see* Clark, *Federal Common Law*, *supra* note 1, at 1346; *see also* William Fletcher, *The General Common Law and Section 34 of the Judiciary Act of 1789: The Example of Marine Insurance*, 94 Harv. L. Rev. 1513, 1517 (1984) (contending that American courts of the early nineteenth century applied the "general maritime law". For discussion, *see infra* Chapter V, notes 52–71 and text accompanying.)

> tions in Maritime Causes, for one Nation's rendering of the same Justice to another that it doth from thence receive, which is the chiefest thing that maintaineth the Community of Traffique and Commerce, which cannot possibly be done, if the same should be rendered, by the various fancies of men, in no wise guided by any certain forme or rule, but by that thing (then [*sic*] which nothing can be more uncertain) which men call opinion, *tot capita, tot sententiae*.[208]

His warning comports well with those expressed in America in the 1780s. Nevertheless, despite the ominous tone, contemporary research reveals that by Exton's time, the common-law and civil-law courts utilized virtually the same substantive rules.[209] The same pattern would hold for the state courts and the federal courts in the early days of the United States. At this early date, it appeared that John Marshall's vision of uniformity might be achieved in maritime law.[210] On reflection, one should not be surprised that there was little if any variation in how various courts interpreted the substantive maritime law. The struggle for admiralty jurisdiction in England had been part of the overall struggle between the Crown and Parliament. At stake was political power and monetary reward for the victorious combatants, not vindication of one set of substantive rules at the expense of another. Similarly in America, the vice admiralty courts, the admiralty courts of the states, and the newly-created federal trial courts adjudicated maritime cases to the same end—the facilitation of maritime commerce essential to the preservation and growth of the American economy. The one constant through all these times and places was maritime commerce itself. Walter Ashburner once observed that the medieval *lex maritima* remained static for six hundred years; so too did the practices of mariners and merchants during that same time. "So long as the conditions which make the law remain unaltered, the law itself remains unaltered."[211] The same holds true for the United States in the eighteenth century. The world of wooden ships, driven by sail, was all that Americans of the 1780s had known. Merchants often owned their own ships. Individual entrepreneurs still dominated the mercantile centers of the new nation. The Industrial Revolution—and with it large concentrations of capital and corpo-

---

208. John Exton, The Maritime Dicaeologie, or Sea-Jurisdiction of England (1st ed., London: Richard Hodgkinson, 1664) at 145.

209. Coquillette, Civilian Writers, *supra* note 103, at 186.

210. Letter from John Marshall to Dudley Chase (Feb. 7, 1817), *quoted in* Clark, *supra* 1, at 1285 n. 1. *See supra* note 1.

211. Walter Ashburner, The Rhodian Sea-Laws: Edited from the Manuscripts (Oxford: Clarendon Press, 1909), Introduction at l, cxv.

rate ownership of vessels—had not yet entered the popular imagination.[212] Americans of the Framers' generation could not have predicted the demands that new technology would place on the existing legal rules. When vessels became self-propelled, the distinctions between sea-going and inland navigation became meaningless. In addition, self-propulsion gave rise to new activities—such as towage—which required new substantive rules. In the absence of Congressional legislation, it would be left to the courts to fashion such rules, and there was no guarantee that federal courts and state courts would arrive at the same conclusions when called upon to innovate.

Technology played a part in unsettling the carefully constructed scheme of concurrent jurisdiction, but it was not alone. In 1789, no one could have predicted that impetus for social change which would mark the close of the nineteenth century and the rise of the Progressive Era. Ironically, the maritime law—for centuries more compassionate in its treatment of seamen than the law of *terra firma*— appeared less so in the eyes of early twentieth-century reformers. The *lex maritima*, they insisted, had failed to keep pace with the times, and contemporary state statutes would provide better protection for impecunious sailors. Together, these factors served to undermine the assumptions upon which the Framers and members of the first Congress had structured admiralty jurisdiction. Concurrent jurisdiction would pose no threat of discord or friction between the state and federal courts so long as both applied the same substantive rules—dictated by international law—to the same forms of maritime and commercial activities. Nonetheless, navigation and commerce changed, as did society's expectations for justice and fairness for the nation's underprivileged classes. It would be left to the judges of

---

212. In the eighteenth and early nineteenth centuries, it was a frequent practice for individual entrepreneurs to vertically integrate their operations, carrying their cargo in their own ships. For discussion, *see* SAMUEL ELIOT MORISON, THE MARITIME HISTORY OF MASSACHUSETTS: 1783–1860 (1st ed. 1921; *reprinted* Boston: Northeastern University Press, 1979) at 24–25, 290. In the entrepreneurial era, it was also common for individuals to limit their exposure to risk by investing in shares of several vessels rather than investing the same amount in the acquisition of sole ownership of a single vessel. If a vessel were lost or failed to produce a significant profit for its owners, no single owner would face insolvency. *See* JOHN G.B. HUTCHINS, THE AMERICAN MARITIME INDUSTRIES AND MARITIME POLICY: 1789–1914 (Cambridge, Massachusetts: Harvard University Press, 1941) at 127. Corporate ownership—facilitating large concentrations of capital and offering limits on liability—changed the structure of the ocean-carrier industry. For discussion of the rise of corporate ownership of vessels, *see* HUTCHINS at 484–485 (corporate ownership of ocean-going vessels); LOUIS C. HUNTER, STEAMBOATS ON THE WESTERN RIVERS: AN ECONOMIC AND TECHNOLOGICAL HISTORY (1st ed. 1949; *reprinted* New York: Dover Publications, 1993) at 624 (corporate ownership of riverboats).

the mid-nineteenth century to deal with the pressures of the Industrial Revolution, and for those of the twentieth century to address the pressure for social change as manifested in substantive rules of maritime law. Both would have a profound impact upon how concurrent jurisdiction would function in practice.

Chapter V

"Don't undervalue Story—he did so much to make the law fluent."
Oliver Wendell Holmes, Jr.[1]

In January of 1842, in "the gathering fog of the early winter afternoon", eighty-three passengers boarded the steam packet *"Britannia"*, bound for Boston via Halifax. Traveling with his wife, Charles Dickens was among them, making his first transatlantic crossing. The accommodations were not as advertised, prompting the author to remark that he will never forget "the one-fourth serious and three-fourths comical astonishment" with which he beheld his cabin and the adjacent grand saloon. The former contained a bunk "than which nothing smaller for sleeping in was ever made except coffins"; the latter he characterized as "a long narrow apartment, not unlike a gigantic hearse with windows on the sides..." In the eyes of Victorian England's leading novelist, the century's latest marine technology was thus no more than a nautical coffin in a sea-going hearse, *and the ship was still at her moorings.*[2] Ten days out of port the *Britannia* encountered foul weather, and Dickens vented his frustration with steamships with an energy surpassing a North Atlantic gale:

> "But what the agitation of a steam-vessel is, on a bad winter's night in the wild Atlantic, it is impossible for the most vivid imagination to conceive. To say that she is flung down on her side in the waves, with her masts dipping into them, and that, springing up again, she rolls over on the other side, until a heavy sea strikes her with the noise of a hundred great guns, and hurls her back—that she stops,

1. Letter of Oliver Wendell Holmes, Jr., to Felix Frankfurter (Aug. 29, 1923), *in* Holmes and Frankfurter: Their Correspondence, 1912–1934 (Robert M. Mennel & Christine L. Compson eds., Hanover, New Hampshire: University Press of New England, 1996) at 158.

2. Charles Dickens, American Notes and Pictures From Italy (1st ed. 1842, 1846; *reprinted* London: Oxford University Press, 1957), *American Notes*, Chapter I at 1–7.

> and staggers, and shivers, as though stunned, and then, with a violent throbbing at her heart, darts onward like a monster goaded into madness, to be beaten down, and battered, and crushed, and leaped on by the angry sea—that thunder, lightening, hail, and rain, and wind, are all in fierce contention for the mastery—that every plank has its groan, every nail its shriek, and every drop of water in the great ocean its howling voice—is nothing. To say that all is grand, and all appalling and horrible in the last degree, is nothing. Words cannot express it."[3]

For Dickens, one transatlantic crossing under steam was enough; when he returned to England, he booked passage on a sailing ship.[4] Within a generation, however, steam had transformed ocean-travel forever. In closing the Victorian Era, Rudyard Kipling paints a picture far different than Dickens. A well-dressed traveler remarks to the ship's engineer: "Mister McAndrew, don't you think steam spoils romance at sea?" With more concern for speed and efficiency than ambiance, the practical Scot bites his tongue, but inwardly observes:

> Romance! Those first-class passengers they like it very well,
> Printed an' bound in little books; but why don't poets tell?
> I'm sick of all their quirks an' turns—the loves an' doves they dream—
> Lord, send us a man like Robbie Burns to sing the Song o' Steam![5]

Alas, McAndrew's prayer for a worthy successor to the bard of Ayrshire went unanswered; instead the nineteenth century had received John Ericsson. There was nothing (at least in the conventional sense) poetic about Ericsson. Brilliant, innovative, independent, and at times irascible, the Swedish-born inventor did more to alter ship-design and propulsion in one lifetime than had all of his predecessors for more than two millennia.[6] Despite his eccentricities

---

3. *Id.* at 15–16.

4. *Id.*, Chapter XVI, at 220.

5. Rudyard Kipling, *"McAndrew's Hymn", from* BALLADS AND BARRACK-ROOM BALLADS (New Edition with Additional Poems, 1893), *reprinted in* A CHOICE OF KIPLING'S VERSE (T. S. Eliot ed., London: Faber & Faber Ltd., 1942) at 57, 63–64.

6. Ericsson, designer in 1861–1862 of the Union ironclad *Monitor* and its innovative gun-turret, contributed to nineteenth-century naval architecture's advancements in iron ship construction and invented both the screw propeller (*infra* note 9) and the caloric engine, which sought to replace steam engines (with their dangerous boilers) with a mechanism driven by heating—and thus expanding—air. Of this latter invention, one biographer has remarked: "To the engineer of today, [the caloric engine] represent[s] the work of a pioneer progressing toward the gas turbine which, in half a generation, has come to dominate the sky." *See* RUTH WHITE, YANKEE FROM SWEEDEN: THE DREAM AND REALITY

and often tense relationship with the Department of the Navy,[7] he had become a hero to the Union for his engineering contributions during the Civil War, a service for which he was still fondly remembered nearly forty years after his death. As a crowd gathered in Washington in May of 1926, President Coolidge presided over the unveiling of a statue. It commemorated the life of the naval architect whose diminutive *Monitor* had repelled the behemoth *Virginia*, saving the Union Navy and bottling the Confederate ironclad up in port until its creators were forced to scuttle it. The various speakers recounted Ericsson's dedication to his adopted country, his opposition to slavery, and his refusal to accept money for his contribution to the war-effort.[8] Virtually ignored in the proceedings was the humble *screw propeller*.[9] Steam had freed ships from dependence upon the vagaries of the wind and weather, but the paddle-wheels employed by early steamers had been cumbersome, inefficient, and vulnerable to damage. Deriving inspiration from the ancient Greek mathematician Archimedes, Ericsson sought to simplify the unwieldy and often unreliable

---

IN THE DAYS OF JOHN ERICSSON (New York: Henry Holt & Co., 1960) at 39, 46, 63, 128–129, 149–153 (hereinafter WHITE, YANKEE). If Ericsson failed to produce poetry, his work nonetheless inspired it. Herman Melville's *"In the Turret"* (1862) describes Ericsson's innovative gun-turret, and his *"A Utilitarian View of the Monitor's Fight"* (1862) lists Ericsson's inventions as it describes graphically how technology has placed "War... Where War belongs, Among the trades and artisans", thus rendering it "Less grand than Peace":

"Yet this was battle, and intense—
Beyond the strife of fleets heroic;
Deadlier, closer, calm 'mid storm;
No passion, all went on by crank,
Pivot, and screw,
And calculations of caloric."

THE COLLECTED POEMS OF HERMAN MELVILLE (1st critical ed., Howard P. Vincent ed., Chicago: Packard & Co., Hendricks House, 1947) at 35–37, 39–40.

7. Ericsson's feud with the antebellum federal government stemmed from his contract to design the ill-fated *Princeton* for the Navy. Well designed but negligently manufactured, the *Princeton's* gun malfunctioned and exploded during publicly-held trials in 1844, wounding President Tyler and killing the Secretary of the Navy and other participants in the ceremony. Blaming Ericsson for the tragic mishap, the Navy refused to pay for his services and cancelled his contract. *See* WHITE, YANKEE, *supra* note 6, at 64–65, 96–126.

8. *See* PROCEEDINGS AT THE UNVEILING OF THE STATUE OF JOHN ERICSSON, IN POTOMAC PARK, WASHINGTON D. C., UNDER THE AUSPICES OF THE JOHN ERICSSON COMMISSION, MAY 29, 1926 (Washington, D. C.: U. S. Government Printing Office, 1929) at 42, 44. As further testimony to Ericsson's contribution to the Union's cause, a similar monument to him stands today in New York's Battery Park, near the north entrance to Castle Clinton.

9. Coolidge made only one passing reference to Ericsson's most significant invention, noting only that he "developed the screw propeller for marine use". *Id.* at 41.

steamship by tying its mechanism for propulsion directly to the engine.[10] He patented his invention in Britain in 1837 and in the United States two years later.[11] Ericsson's screw propeller completed the process that steam had begun. Equally adaptable to ocean-going and inland vessels, the propeller increased the efficiency and reliability of steam-driven craft.[12] Before steam, it was only with great difficulty that deep-water vessels could enter inland waters. Faced with a river's downstream currents and unable to tack with the wind within the confined spaces of the river-banks, square-rigged vessels rarely ventured beyond a river's mouth. When absolutely necessary, square-riggers could be towed upstream by a method known as "kedging", but this was not practical in the daily operations of commerce.[13] Steam-power and Ericsson's

---

10. Ericsson's American patent described his design as follows:

> "This invention...consists in two thin broad metallic hoops or short cylinders supported by spiral arms or spokes and made to revolve in contrary directions but at different velocities from each other around a common center, such hoops or cylinders being also placed entirely under the water at the stern of a boat and furnished each with a series of short spiral planes or plates; the plates of each series standing at an angle, the exact converse of the angle given to those of the other series and kept revolving by the power of a steam engine whereby a steam boat may be propelled effectually notwithstanding any variation in the draft of water."

United States Patent Office, Patent No. 588 (Feb. 1, 1838), Issued to John Ericsson, of London, England. One biographer later described how the propeller was intended to work in practice:

> "[To] keep the ship going in a straight line, Ericsson had employed two broad hoops devised to revolve in contrary directions around a spiral shaft running along the ship's bottom and into her hull; there, unlike anything previously conceived, *it connected directly with the motivating power of the steam engine*."

White, Yankee, *supra* note 6, at 46 (*emphasis added*).

11. Ericsson tested the first prototype of the screw propeller in 1829, and the design had proven commercially successful in England by 1831. *Id.* at 39, 63. He received his patent in Britain in 1836 and filed for a patent in the United States two years later. Unfortunately, as Ericsson was deeply absorbed in his work, he often displayed more interest in creative problem-solving than in worldly prosperity. Delinquency in filing opened the door for others to claim credit for his invention, thereby embroiling Ericsson in litigation for many years thereafter. *Id.* at 63, 138–141.

12. Ericsson originally designed his screw propeller for use on inland craft and canal boats, though it was through its use on ocean-going vessels, and particularly naval vessels, that the propeller had its most immediate impact on ship-design. Nevertheless, shortly after its invention, the propeller was in use on vessels as diverse as tow boats, canal barges, revenue cutters, and steamers engaged in trade on America's rivers and Great Lakes. *Id.* at 39, 129–130.

13. "Kedging" involved rowing a boat carrying an anchor upstream and dropping the anchor in the river. One end of a line was attached to the anchor, and the other to a ship's

invention removed this limitation. No longer would ocean-going vessels be obliged to anchor and transfer their cargoes to lighters, barges, and keelboats. Technological innovation blurred the distinction between "blue" and "brown" water.[14]

The marriage of steam and screw-propulsion had two immediate consequences for maritime law in the nineteenth century. First, it increased the frequency of some classes of claims (such as collision) already known to the *lex maritima*, and it added new classes of claims—in particular those relating to towage. Collisions in the age of sail were rarely major calamities; most often, damage was limited to rigging.[15] When steamships collided, however, it was likely that one, the other, or both would suffer serious structural damage, often resulting in sinking. Lacking statutory guidance, judges were forced to

---

capstan. Sailors aboard the ship then would haul the ship upstream by turning the capstan. *See* Samuel Eliot Morison, The Maritime History of Massachusetts, 1783–1860 (1st ed. 1921; *reprinted* Boston: Northeastern University Press, 1979) at 104 (hereinafter Morison). If one needed to get a ship a short distance upstream to a repair-yard, kedging was useful. Needless to say, this labor-intensive method was not used to carry overseas cargo up navigable rivers.

14. Admittedly, the custom of transferring ocean-going ships' cargoes to lighters and other craft for transport upstream remained the norm for the nineteenth century as it does for us today. Nevertheless, the jurisdictional statutes of Richard II were premised on the assumption that ocean-going ships *never* ventured inland. The mouths of navigable rivers below the bridges were thus natural bounds of jurisdiction in medieval England, as they constituted the furthest extremity of ocean-commerce in that era. (*See* discussion *infra* notes 142–143, 163–175 and text accompanying.) In the United States, where many rivers remained navigable hundreds of miles upstream, only the downstream current had prevented ocean-going vessels from venturing inland. Steam and self-propulsion removed that limitation. Early riverboats were patterned after their deep-sea counterparts, with keels and "v"-shaped hulls. *See* Louis C. Hunter, Steamboats on the Western Rivers: An Economic and Technological History (1st ed. 1941; *reprinted* New York: Dover Publications, 1993) at 65 (hereinafter Hunter); Erik F. Haites, James Mak, & Gary M. Walton, Western River Transportation: The Era of Early Internal Development, 1810–1860 (Baltimore: The Johns Hopkins University Press, 1976) at 18 (hereinafter Haites, Mak, & Walton). Some of these early craft moved regularly between salt and fresh water. Even after the flat-bottomed riverboats in the "wedding-cake" style had been perfected, some cargo continued to move hundreds of miles upstream in ocean-going vessels with hulls of moderate draft designed specifically for the hybrid blue-water/brown-water trade. *See* Robert Greenhalgh Albion, The Rise of New York Port, 1815–1860 (1st ed. 1939; *reprinted* Boston: Northeastern University Press, 1984) at 157, 308 (hereinafter Albion, New York Port).

15. *See supra* Chapter 1 n. 79, Chapter II, notes 153–155 and text accompanying.

innovate, creating new rules governing liability.[16] Towage was even more problematic. The activity was unknown in the age of sail, and the *lex maritima* lacked substantive rules governing duties of tug and tow boats. Once again, it was left to the judiciary to fashion rules.[17] Technology thus provided the first serious threat to the assumption underlying the Admiralty Clause and the Judiciary Act, namely that there was no danger of friction between state and federal courts since both sets of courts would apply a universal body of law unchanged since antiquity. A second and potentially more serious consequence remained. As ocean-going ships now could enter fresh water under their own power, the assumptions underlying the jurisdictional statutes of Richard II ceased to apply. While the vice admiralty courts had expanded their jurisdiction to include contracts signed on land "within the body of counties", they had not made serious incursions into the notion that "admiralty" was limited to ocean-going commerce. Steamships could cross an ocean, enter a river, and proceed miles inland beyond the ebb and flow of the tide. At issue was whether cases arising out of such voyages would be triable in federal court. Moreover, steamboats were developing a sizable interstate trade on the rivers of the Mississippi basin and on the Great Lakes. Was this trade to be governed by state or federal law? Both state and federal courts were forced to grapple with these questions, and the results were not always consistent. Often lacking guidance from Congress, the Supreme Court struggled to create a workable system for admiralty jurisdiction.

Blue Water: International and Coastal Maritime Commerce in the Antebellum Republic

Boston, the early center of the nation's carrying trades, virtually rebuilt itself in the two decades following ratification of the Constitution. Visitors returning from abroad scarcely recognized the city. New banks in the Federal Style, the offspring of an ever-growing foreign trade, lined the revamped State Street, and landfills had converted the jagged coastline of the city into usable space for additional wharves. New bridges allowed Bostonians easy access to

16. For a general discussion of how American courts sought guidance from foreign jurisdictions in formulating substantive rules for collision in the early age of steam, *see* Henry Flanders, A Treatise on Maritime Law (Boston: Little, Brown, & Co., 1852), Ch. IX, Sec. 349–Sec. 381, at 288–315 (Flanders provides the federal rule created by Judge Ashur Ware and Joseph Story's views on the subject in Sec. 357–Sec. 358, at 296–298.)

17. For the evolution of the federal rules for liability in towage, *see Id.*, Sec. 362–Sec. 363, at 300–301.

all parts of their city—a welcome addition, as the population had nearly doubled between 1790 and 1810.[18] By 1806, the revenues of New England's merchant fleet exceeded both the capital value of the fleet itself and the gross revenue of the federal government.[19] It was much the same in other coastal cities. By 1810, Baltimore had grown from a town of 6,000 to the nation's third largest city,[20] and New York would soon eclipse Boston as the center of the nation's shipping business,[21] becoming second only to London in quantity of tonnage passing through its port annually.[22] In 1828, revenue from the New York Customs House alone paid all of the federal government's expenses except for the interest due on the national debt.[23] This prosperity was not confined to foreign trade. Although trade with Europe, Asia, and South America continued to grow, coastal trade had surpassed it in volume by 1831.[24] The first decades of the new century were, in the words of one modern historian, "an era of unequalled affluence."[25]

Arriving in 1831 for his tour of America, Alexis de Tocqueville marveled at the success of the nation's maritime industries, praising its exports and observing that nine-tenths of its European imports were carried in American bottoms:

> It is difficult to say for what reason the Americans can navigate at a lower rate than other nations; one is at first led to attribute this su-

18. *See* Morison, *supra* note 13, at 124–125.

19. *Id.* at 189.

20. Baltimore had a population of roughly 6,000 at the outset of the Revolution and 13,000 in 1790. By the census of 1810, its population had reached nearly 36,000, surpassing Boston by roughly 2,000 inhabitants. *See* Jacob M. Price, *Economic Function and the Growth of American Port Towns in the Eighteenth Century*, 8 Perspectives in American History 123, Appendix B at 176 (1974); Douglass C. North, The Economic Growth of the United States: 1790–1860 (Englewood Cliffs, New Jersey: Prentice-Hall, 1966) at 49 (hereinafter North).

21. Albion, New York Port, *supra* note 14, at 266.

22. New York nearly tripled in population between the 1790 census and that of 1810, reaching 96,000 inhabitants. North, *supra* note 19, at 49. By 1821, more tonnage both cleared for and entered from foreign ports in New York than in Boston. Albion, New York Port, *supra* note 14, Appendices IV–V, at 392–393. New York had more than twice Boston's registered tonnage in 1815, and by 1817, it had passed the registered tonnage of the entire state of Massachusetts. *Id.*, Appendix XI, at 402–403. For the factors contributing to New York's success in luring the import/export business and the carrying trades away from New England's ports, *see Id.* at 374–386.

23. Albion, *supra* note 14, at 224.

24. Morison, *supra* note 13, at 297.

25. North, *supra* note 20, at 54.

> periority to the physical advantages that nature gives them; but it is not so. The American vessels cost almost as much to build as our own; they are not better built, and they generally last a shorter time. The pay of the American sailor is higher than the pay on board European ships, as is proved by the great number of Europeans who are to be found in the merchant vessels of the United States. How does it happen, then, that the Americans sail their vessels at a cheaper rate than we can ours? I am of the opinion that the true cause of their superiority must not be sought for in physical advantages, but that it is wholly attributable to moral and intellectual qualities.[26]

Tocqueville's efforts to tie the United States' success in ocean-carriage to national *ethos* were somewhat misplaced. The French critic's comments notwithstanding, America did in fact have a comparative advantage in shipbuilding

---

26. Alexis De Tocqueville, Democracy in America (1st ed. 1835, 1840; Francis Bowen trans. (1862), Phillips Bradley ed. (1945), *reprinted* New York: Alfred A. Knopf, 1994), Part I, Ch. XVIII, at 422–423 (hereinafter Tocqueville). Tocqueville's assessment is not merely a foreign traveler's penchant for excessive generalizations about another nation's "*ethos*". Instead, it appears to be a close paraphrase of a comment made to Tocqueville by Joel Roberts Poinsett, former ambassador to Mexico. Poinsett coined the phrase "from intellectual qualities, not physical" in answer to Tocqueville's question about the reasons for the success of America's carrying trades. Continuing, he conceded that American sailors earned higher wages than their European counterparts, but contended that American vessels sailed faster and spent less time in port than their competitors, thus allowing for more voyages and a reduction of costs. As for American ships' quality of construction, Poinsett maintained that ships were designed and built with an eye to cost/benefit analysis. In short, some vessels were indeed more cheaply built, with the understanding that they would pay for themselves in a few voyages, thus reducing the amount of capital invested. When a particular need arose, American builders could match or exceed the quality of any foreign shipyard. In an era in which any ship—well built or more economically constructed—stood a high chance of being lost at sea, the American cost/benefit strategy was quite effective, reducing the value of capital exposed to the risk of shipwreck and thus also reducing the cost of hull-insurance. *See* George Wilson Pierson, Tocqueville in America (1st ed., 1938; *reprinted* Baltimore: The Johns Hopkins University Press, 1996) at 644–645 (hereinafter Pierson). Tocqueville's estimate for the percentage of imports carried in American bottoms is not exaggerated. Official records of the time reveal that 922,952 of 1,204,900 of the registered tonnage (*i.e.* 76%) entering American ports in 1831 was American. Moreover, the same official records list the total value of imports into the Unites States as \$103,191,124, of which only \$9,229,014 (9%) entered in foreign bottoms. *See* United States Department of the Treasury, Statistics of the Foreign and Domestic Commerce of the United States (Washington, D. C.: U.S. Government Printing Office, 1864) at 10, 18 (hereinafter Treasury, Foreign and Domestic Commerce).

over the nations of Europe, as the cheaper costs of raw materials outweighed the higher costs of American skilled labor.[27] American shipyards were further aided by the invention of the "lift model", an American innovation that both improved efficiency in building ships and facilitated improvements in hull-design.[28] So long as the United States retained its comparative advantage in shipbuilding, American merchants and shipowners suffered no loss by Congress' requirement that all American-flagged vessels be of domestic construction.[29] As a result, American tonnage more than quadrupled between 1790 and 1810,[30] and by 1860 it had increased again ten-fold, nearly equaling that of the British Empire.[31] Tocqueville was correct in noting the higher costs of American labor,[32] but improvements in ship-design and efficiency in organization allowed Americans to spend less time in port and thus to make more voyages, more than offsetting the higher wages of American seamen.[33] American merchant-shipowners were especially aggressive in opening new markets in Asia[34] and in South America, the latter of which accounted for one-fifth of all the nation's trade from 1825 and 1860.[35]

---

27. JOHN G. B. HUTCHINS, THE AMERICAN MARITIME INDUSTRIES AND MARITIME POLICY, 1789–1914 (Cambridge, Massachusetts: Harvard University Press, 1941) at 72–102, 109–114, 172 (hereinafter HUTCHINS).

28. *Id.* at 113–114; MORISON, *supra* note 13, at 102.

29. For discussion of this policy, *see* HUTCHINS, *supra* note 27, at 73.

30. MORISON, *supra* note 13, at 96, 106, gives the figure of 450% for the increase in American tonnage during this period, estimating the size of the American merchant fleet at 500,000 tons.

31. HUTCHINS, *supra* note 27, at 259, provides the following estimates: "The tonnage of the United States engaged in all employments rose from 1,191,776 tons in 1830 to 5,353,868 tons in 1860, and that of the entire British Empire from 2,531,819 tons to 5,710,968 tons between the same years."

32. *Id.* at 73, 111.

33. For the most part, Americans' advantages in business-organization were refinements of those developed for saving time in port during the colonial period. For discussion, *see supra* Introduction, note 46 and text accompanying. *See also* Gary M. Walton, *Sources of Productivity Change in American Colonial Shipping*, 20 Econ. Hist. Rev. 67, 71–77 (2d ser., 1967); JAMES F. SHEPHERD & GARY M. WALTON, SHIPPING, MARITIME TRADE AND THE ECONOMIC DEVELOPMENT OF COLONIAL NORTH AMERICA (Cambridge: Cambridge University Press, 1972) at 6–9; PIERSON, *supra* note 26, at 644–645. For a description of the daily operations of foreign trade in the early nineteenth century, and the role of the merchant-shipowner's agent, the "supercargo", in facilitating efficient business operations, *see* MORISON, *supra* note 13, at 84–88, 112–113, 288–291.

34. For a description of the burgeoning trade with the Far East, and particularly with China, *see e.g.* MORISON, *supra* note 13, at 45, 64, 67.

35. ALBION, NEW YORK PORT, *supra* note 14, at 173.

Politics also played a significant part. During the Napoleonic Wars, the neutral United States had become carrier to the world. These gains were not without difficulties. Americans still faced discriminatory duties in the ports of many of their trading partners. Vessels flying the Stars and Stripes also were harassed at various times by both the British and the French navies as well as by ships of the Barbary States, and Jefferson's ill-fated Embargo of 1807 wreaked havoc upon American ocean-carriers while it lasted. Nonetheless, on balance the period from 1790 to 1812 was one of growth and profit for the nation's carriers.[36] Interruptions during the War of 1812 were more than offset by gains during the economic boom of the latter half of the decade, as well as those of the 1830s and 1850s.[37] Throughout the early nineteenth century, fisheries continued to provide the nation with an important product for both domestic consumption and export.[38] Although Massachusetts' whaling fleet had been decimated by the end of the Revolution, the industry made a swift recovery, becoming a mainstay of local economies until whale oil was replaced by petroleum after the Civil War.[39] In 1801, Salem native Nathaniel Bowditch first published his *Practical Navigator*, a series of tables that permitted mariners ascertain longitude without a chronometer. Printed in nearby Newburyport and reissued in countless editions, the book was of incalculable value to the expanding American merchant fleet.[40] Gradually, steam began to chal-

---

36. For discussion of both the obstacles faced by American ocean-carriers and their financial success during the Napoleonic Wars, *see e.g.* Hutchins, *supra* note 27, at 223–229. For the Federalists' reaction to Jefferson's ill-fated Embargo, including the Hartford Convention, *see e.g.* Morison, *supra* note 13, at 190–212. The letters exchanged between John Adams and Thomas Jefferson concerning the problem of the Barbary corsairs offer an interesting contemporary view of the problem. *See e.g.* Letter of Thomas Jefferson to John Adams (May 27, 1813) (on the need for a strong navy to protect against the Barbary States), *reprinted in* The Adams-Jefferson Letters (2 vols., Lester J. Cappon ed., Chapel Hill: The University of North Carolina Press, 1959), Vol. II, at 323, 324–325; Letter of John Adams to Thomas Jefferson (June 14, 1813) (agreeing with Jefferson's call for the strengthening of the navy to deter attacks from the Barbary States), *reprinted in Id.*, Vol. II, at 328, 329.

37. The United States' economy, and in particular its maritime sector, improved with the end of the War of 1812. While the nation experienced panics and depressions in 1819–1820, 1837, and 1857, most of the period from the mid-1820s through 1837 and the period from the late 1840s through the 1857 were times of prosperity. *See* Haites, Mak, & Walton, *supra* note 14, at 113; Albion, New York Port, *supra* note 14, at 285.

38. Morison, *supra* note 13, at 300–313, Appendix I at 395 (statistics).

39. For discussion, *see Id.* at 314–326; *also see generally* Granville Allen Mawer, Ahab's Trade: The Saga of South Seas Whaling (New York: St. Martin's Press, 1999).

40. Morison, *supra* note 13, at 114–115, 152.

lenge sail for supremacy at sea. Early ocean-going steam engines had operated at extremely low pressure and burned large volumes of coal; over time, however the engines had become more powerful and efficient.[41] While paddlewheels remained the norm for much of the first half of the century, screw propellers rapidly gained in popularity, owing to their simpler and more efficient design and their smaller size, which allowed more room in a ship's hold for cargo.[42] Despite its savings in size and weight, the screw propeller's vibrations placed additional strain on a ship's frame and timbers. For naval architects, the solution was obvious. First in ships' frames, and finally in their entire construction, iron replaced wood. More durable, stronger per cubic inch, and rendered less expensive than the dwindling supplies of timber by new technology, iron allowed for construction of ships the size of which could not have been imagined a few decades earlier.[43] The result was a dramatic increase in

---

41. While the lower pressures reduced the risk of explosion common on inland steamboats of the era, they both reduced the engines' power and increased their fuel-consumption through wasting energy. For discussion, *see* Edward W. Sloan, "The Machine at Sea: Early Transatlantic Steam Travel", *in* THE ATLANTIC WORLD OF ROBERT G. ALBION (Benjamin W. Labaree ed., Middletown, Connecticut: Wesleyan University Press, 1975) at 113–117 (hereinafter ATLANTIC WORLD).

42. As historian Edward Sloan observes:

> "A sidewheeler...was bound to be a clumsy sailer because of the paddle boxes. Buffeted by winds and waves, these large and vulnerable protuberances slowed the steamer and produced a jarring motion which left passengers wretched. When under both steam and sail, a sidewheeler often heeled over so far that one wheel was revolving uselessly in the air while the other was buried in the water. The consequent waste of power and difficulty in steering were obvious. To work the [auxilliary] sails on a sidewheeler was particularly frustrating, because the bulky machinery, the cumbersome paddle boxes, and the bridge extending between the two boxes thwarted the most adept sailor."

Sloan, "The Machine at Sea", *in* ATLANTIC WORLD, *supra* note 41, at 129. The fuel-consumption added even more problems. Not only did a sidewheeler's engines require more space for coal than for cargo (a characteristic that it shared with early screw-propeller ships), but weight of the coal in the hold affected its sailing-qualities. It sailed better mid-voyage, when a moderate amount of coal in the hold kept the water-line at the optimum level for the effective functioning of the paddle wheels. The screw-propelled ship had none of these disadvantages. The screw and shaft occupied less space than the paddle boxes and accompanying machinery, leaving more room for cargo, and the performance of the wholly-submerged propeller was not affected by the how low or high the ship rode in the water. *Id.* at 127–132.

43. *See* Sloan, "Machine at Sea", *in* ATLANTIC WORLD, *supra* note 41, at 114, 130–131 (observing that screw-propulsion shortened the lifespan of wooden hulls). HUTCHINS, *supra* note 27, at 422, maintains that "iron...hulls were in general probably nearly twice as durable, since they were subject neither to dry rot nor to serious loosening in the fasten-

both transatlantic cargo carriage and passenger service. Steam allowed shipowners to adhere to regular schedules. Where only 5,000 Americans had crossed the Atlantic by steamer in 1850, the number rose to 33,000 only four years later.[44] As the economy grew and diversified, trade and ocean-carriage would constitute an ever smaller percentage of the nation's output. Hamilton's prediction had been accurate. Manufacturing would dominate the American economy in years to come, but its development had rested upon the success of American maritime industry.[45] International trade and ocean-carriage reached their peak in the first half of the nineteenth century, and they served as the catalyst for the United States' entry into the Industrial Revolution.[46]

---

ings." Moreover, "[i]ron construction gave much more deadweight carrying capacity and internal volume than wooden construction." *Id.* at 443. The result was that iron hulls were no more than half the weight of wooden hulls of the same exterior dimensions, and were able to hold considerably more cargo. *Id.* at 443–444. Iron's impact on the size of ships was dramatic. Before 1840, any vessel measuring more than 130 feet in length and 500 tons was considered large. *See* MORISON, *supra* note 13, at 361. Nothing could have prepared shipbuilders of 1840 for Isambard Kingdom Brunel's *Great Eastern*. Powered by both sidewheels and screw propellers and constructed of iron, at her launching in the Thames in 1859 she measured nearly 700 feet in length and approached 20,000 tons—an astonishing forty times the size of the average large wooden sailing ship of a generation earlier.

44. Sloan, "Machine at Sea", *in* ATLANTIC WORLD, *supra* note 41, at 140 (giving the figures of 5,330 and 32,631 steamship passengers for 1850 and 1854 respectively). Historical data compiled by the Department of the Treasury testifies to the rapid expansion in registered steam tonnage for the same four-year period. In 1850, steamships measuring 89,642 tons arrived in American ports as part of the transatlantic trade, of which only 19,181 tons represented the American merchant fleet. By 1854, the total had risen to 259,059 tons, of which 107,713 tons were American vessels. *See* TREASURY, FOREIGN AND DOMESTIC COMMERCE, *supra* note 26, at 59.

45. *See* CATHY D. MATSON & PETER S. ONUF, A UNION OF INTERESTS: POLITICAL AND ECONOMIC THOUGHT IN REVOLUTIONARY AMERICA (Lawrence: University of Kansas Press, 1990) at 164; *see also* discussion, *supra* Introduction, notes 108–116 and text accompanying.

46. Foreign trade's impact on the American economy is a source of some controversy. In his 1966 study, economic historian Douglass North concludes: "Between 1793 and 1808, the economic development of the United States was tied to international trade and shipping." NORTH, *supra* note 19, at 46. According to North, this occurred not only directly through earnings in exports and the carrying trades, but also through the impact that these sectors had on other industries. He explains:

> "Shipbuilding was the major subsidiary industry. Its expansion followed closely the movements in ocean freight rates.... Ship-fitting industries, particularly ropeworks and sail-making, developed and flourished around the shipbuilding areas. More significant, particularly for later development, was the variety of complementary industries that arose to serve the re-export and carrying trades. Not only

Continental Influence on the Early Federal Courts

For modern federal courts, admiralty cases constitute a scarcely measurable portion of their dockets.[47] This was not the case in the courts' early years,

---

> did commission merchants, brokers and other business organizations evolve to implement these trades, but marine insurance companies and banks, and facilities for warehousing and docking also grew up as the carrying trade expanded.... Shipping and the re-export trade are the kinds of industries which, directly and indirectly, encourage increased urbanization. The income effect of these industries is to produce a multiplier effect through the growth of a variety of locally oriented manufactures and services to meet the needs of a growing urban population. The rapid growth of New York and other major ports reflected the development of a local consuming market. There was an increased demand for foodstuffs for this urban population, with a consequent widening of the market area around these urban centers and concerted efforts to reduce internal transport costs."

Id at 49–51. In essence, North contends that success of exports and the carrying trades contributed to the growth of the domestic economy in ways that a cursory perusing of export-earnings cannot wholly reveal. Later economists have disputed North's insistence on the crucial role of foreign trade in American economic development in the first three decades under the Constitution. *See e.g.* Paul A. David, *The Growth of Real Product in the United States Before 1840: New Evidence, Controlled Conjectures*, 27 J. Econ. Hist. 151, 188–194 (1967); Claudia D. Goldin & Frank D. Lewis, *The Role of Exports in American Economic Growth During the Napoleonic Wars*, 1793–1807, 17 Explorations in Economic History 6, 7–8 (1980). Goldin and Lewis conclude that: "Changes in the foreign sector from 1796 to 1807 probably did not lead to substantial growth in *per capita* income". *Id.* at 19. Nevertheless, they concede that the export sector was sufficiently large to account for 12% of total product. Even assuming significantly smaller annual *per capita* growth directly attributable to changes in the "foreign sector", this does not wholly refute North's claims regarding the "multiplier effect". With the foreign sector accounting for 12% of product, it is reasonable to assume that even small changes in earnings would have a significant indirect impact on the remainder of the economy. Ultimately, Goldin and Lewis concede this point:

> "Even though the increase in trade during the period from 1793 to 1807 did not dramatically increase incomes, we have not assessed its longer range effects. Impressive changes took place during these 14 years—the major port cities grew, towns developed in the hinterland, shipping tonnage expanded substantially, corporate chapters increased, and the banking and commercial sectors widened. The period of neutrality may not have greatly spurred income, but...it may have led to the emergence of a nascent national economy."

Id. at 23.

47. At present, admiralty accounts for roughly .045% of all cases filed in federal court. David W. Robertson, *Summertime Sailing in the U.S. Supreme Court*, 29 J. Mar. L. & Com. 275, 276 n. 3 (1998).

when maritime matters dominated the federal case-load.[48] Prize cases, controversy over which had fueled the demand for federal maritime courts in the first place, were unknown during peace-time and were never numerous in the nineteenth century—even when the nation was at war.[49] The bulk of the matters filed were instance cases.[50] Richard Peters—staunch Federalist, admiralty scholar, and the first judge of the Federal District Court of Pennsylvania—

---

48. *See* DONALD G. MORGAN, JUSTICE WILLIAM JOHNSON: THE FIRST DISSENTER (Columbia: The University of South Carolina Press, 1954) at 20 (hereinafter MORGAN); THE LAW PRACTICE OF ALEXANDER HAMILTON: DOCUMENTS AND COMMENTARY (5 vols., Julius Goebel ed., New York: Columbia University Press, 1969), Vol. II, at 788 (hereinafter LAW PRACTICE OF ALEXANDER HAMILTON).

49. Although difficulties with the states' handling of prize cases (*see supra* Chapter III, notes 50–84 and text accompanying) were among the principal reasons for vesting jurisdiction over prize in the federal courts, prize cases were never common. One commentator provides the following figures: "Between 1789 and 1918, the Supreme Court issued 192 opinions in prize and prize-related cases, for an average of just under 1.4 per year. The majority (114) of these, however, were handed down in the six years from 1814 through1819 and the four years from 1864 to 1867." Jonathan M. Gutoff, *Original Understandings and the Private Law Origins of the Federal Admiralty Jurisdiction: A Reply to Professor Casto*, 30 J. Mar. L. & Com. 361, 401 n. 166 (1999). It should be noted that some cases of "prize" appear in the records as cases of "salvage". In 1798, Congress provided that the crew of a private vessel should receive a "salvage" award for recapturing an American ship from the French during the "Quasi-War" (*see* 1 Stat. 572, sec. 2). The recapture entitled the privateer's crew to a portion of the proceeds of the sale, with the balance going to the original American owners. *See* LAW PRACTICE OF ALEXANDER HAMILTON, *supra* note 48, Vol. II, at 788. The "prize-related cases" to which Gutoff refers are presumably awards granted to naval personnel for capture of belligerents' merchant ships. Among most of the world's naval powers, a multilateral treaty signed 1856 in the wake of the Crimean War brought an end to letters of marque and privateering. While the United States was not a signatory, Congress has not issued a letter of marque or reprisal since the treaty came into force. *See* DONALD A. PETRIE, THE PRIZE GAME: LAWFUL LOOTING ON THE HIGH SEAS IN THE DAYS OF FIGHTING SAIL (Annapolis, Maryland: Naval Institute Press, 1999) at 140–142.

50. The claims filed in New York are representative of those filed in most of the major ports and provide a glimpse of federal maritime litigation in the 1790s; Goebel observes:

> "Most of the causes brought in the New York District Court were not of a nature to be pursued beyond the trial stage, if indeed so far. About 50 percent of the cases involved seamen's wages. If the minutes accurately reflect what went on, suits brought pursuant to the Collection Acts usually went by default. There were libels in restitution, bottomry, insurance, repairs, and salvage."

LAW PRACTICE OF ALEXANDER HAMILTON, *supra* note 48, Vol. II, at 788. Over the next two decades, the number of federal cases sounding in admiralty remained high, but the small claims for seamen's wages dwindled in importance in comparison with other matters. By the terms of 1817–1818, virtually all of the matters on the Supreme Court's dockets were

provided the best summary of the federal courts' first decade: "The Admiralty Part of the Business is here by far the heaviest. It requires much Knowledge on Subjects to which Common Lawyers seldom attend."[51] It is not surprising that the common lawyers were confused regarding the procedures and substantive law to be applied in federal maritime cases. Even federal judges with experience in maritime matters had reason to feel unsure about the law they were to apply, as Congress had provided them with little guidance.

The wishes of Madison and others notwithstanding, there would be no comprehensive Maritime Code. Federal judges would be expected to work within the framework of *stare decisis*. Moreover, theories of natural law were waning in acceptance. Once the implicit foundation of the law of nations and by extension also of the *lex maritima*, the law of nature gradually gave way to new concepts of international law grounded in the custom and practice of sovereign states. Stripped of the comforting notion of a *lex maritima* grounded in fixed, permanent principles and lacking resources for ascertaining international custom and practice, the challenge for federal judges would be to identify rules universal in character and to imbue their decisions with an aura of antiquity. The emerging result was the marriage between the positivist approach to the law of nations and the *lex maritima* as presented in the latest Continental treatises. Out of various and sundry medieval codes, the Roman Law, and the writings of contemporary civil-law scholars, federal judges created the "general maritime law".

Since the colonial period, there had been a deplorable shortage of readily available information on substantive rules governing maritime activities.[52] Independence, and with it the disappearance of the vice admiralty courts, brought with it an even more compelling need for sources of information on the *lex maritima*. For many of the Revolutionary generation, the notion of importing British substantive rules for adjudicating maritime cases was at best distasteful and at worst political apostasy.[53] They reasoned that the *lex mar-*

---

admiralty cases. *See* JEAN EDWARD SMITH, JOHN MARSHALL, DEFINER OF A NATION (New York: Henry Holt & Co. 1996) at 431 (hereinafter SMITH, JOHN MARSHALL).

51. Letter from Richard Peters to John Rutledge, Jr. (Jan. 4, 1801), *published in* THE DOCUMENTARY HISTORY OF THE SUPREME COURT OF THE UNITED STATES, 1789–1800, VOLUME IV—ORGANIZING THE FEDERAL JUDICIARY: LEGISLATION AND COMMENTARIES (Maeva Marcus ed., New York: Columbia University Press, 1992) at 680.

52. For discussion, *see supra* Chapter II, notes 231–254 and text accompanying.

53. The notion that British law was somehow antithetical to republican principles persisted long past the 1790s. The struggle intensified in the decades that followed, as the political battle-lines were drawn between Jeffersonian Republicans and conservative former Federalists, with some of the former maintaining that the transplanted British case-law system abrogated the power of the legislature undemocratically in favor of the judiciary. In

itima (either by nature or by custom and practice) belongs to the world as a whole. As such, the well-organized treatises of the Continental civilians should provide as much insight into the substantive maritime law as British case law, and with a considerable savings in time and convenience. Any British rule not recognized by the Continental civilians could be rejected as one nation's ill-considered innovation, not truly reflective of the law of nations and thus not binding on the United States. Thomas Jefferson was among the first Americans smitten with the impulse for collecting civilian maritime treatises. He began in the mid-1780s and continued through the first decade of the next century, amassing one of the largest such collections in the country.[54] In publishing his collection federal admiralty opinions in 1807, Richard Peters saw fit to include texts of the *Marine Ordinances of Louis XIV*, as well as translations of the laws of Oleron, Wisby, and the Hanse Towns, believing them to be well suited to the two-volume set, designed as a working tool for Ameri-

---

England, this view was championed by Jeremy Bentham, and Bentham's ideas, imported and adopted by some American Republicans, formed the basis of a movement away from a legal system grounded in *stare decisis*. This view reached its climax in the "codification movement" of the 1820s, as proponents sought to assure popular control over the law through enactment of comprehensive codes governing matters previously under the aegis of the common law. *See* James McClellan, Joseph Story and the American Constitution (Norman: University of Oklahoma Press, 1971) at 89–91 (hereinafter McClellan); William A. Fletcher, *The General Common Law and Section 34 of the Federal Judiciary Act of 1789: The Example of Marine Insurance*, 97 Harv. L. Rev. 1513, 1560, 1567 (1984) (hereinafter Fletcher). For further discussion, *see infra* notes 102–103 and text accompanying.

54. Noteworthy among Jefferson's Continental treatises are an English translation of Domenico Alberto Azuni's work on the maritime law of Europe, two books by Pierre Boucher—the treatise on substantive maritime law and the treatise on commercial law (both in the original French), Jean Francois Champagne's analysis of the Grotius/Selden debate on freedom of the seas (in French), and Estienne Cleirac's monumental collection of medieval sea-laws (French edition). Among the English books on civil and maritime law in Jefferson's collection were Clerke's *Praxis Curiae Admiralitatis Angliae*, Wynne's *Life of Sir Leoline Jenkins*, Marius' *Advice Concerning Bills of Lading*, Malynes' *Consuetudo*, Molloy's *De Jure Maritimo et Navali* (1722 ed.), and Browne's *Compendious View of the Civil Law and the Law of Admiralty*. Also in the collection were two of the six volumes of the opinions of the High Court of Admiralty in London, which first appeared in print in 1799. These opinions, commencing with the 1798 opinions of Lord Stowell, constituted the first published reports of the decisions of the High Court. Much of the remainder of Jefferson's collection dates from the period of his presidency and deals with the rules of prize and the rights of neutral vessels during war. *See* Catalogue of the Library of Thomas Jefferson (5 vols., E. Millicent Sowerby ed., Washington, D. C.: The Library of Congress, 1953), Vol. I, at 158–159; Vol. II, at 357–375. For additional titles acquired by Jefferson between the 1780s and 1808, *see supra* Chapter III, note 20.

can practicioners.[55] Federalist John Elihu Hall of Baltimore, attorney, legal scholar, linguist, and sometime literary critic,[56] in 1811 introduced the American bar to the influential French scholar, Balthazard Marie Emerigon, by translating his treatise on maritime loans into English, including such notes as were necessary for "explanation of technical terms in the Civil and French law, and such local usages as appeared to be necessary to the elucidation of the language of a foreign jurist."[57] As had Peters, Hall opted to include medieval materials in

---

55. RICHARD PETERS, ADMIRALTY DECISIONS IN THE DISTRICT COURT OF THE UNITED STATES FOR THE PENNSYLVANIA DISTRICT (2 vols., Philadelphia: William P. Farrand, 1807), Vol. I, Appendices at i–cxvii. Peters makes the following remarks in his Preface:

> "At the request of many of his friends, the Editor has added, as an appendix to each volume of the work, the maritime laws which are acknowledged as authority by most of the commercial nations of Europe, and some of which have been recognized as such by our own courts.... By the lawyer these will be received as a valuable and interesting addition to his stock of professional knowledge; and the American merchant will obtain much satisfaction, as well as advantage, from an acquaintance with the maritime codes of those countries with which he enjoys an extensive and frequent commercial intercourse. If to the legislator they should furnish any information which may be employed in the improvement of our maritime regulations, the editor will be amply compensated for having brought them into his notice."

Id., Preface at vi.

56. Born in 1783, John Hall attended Princeton and was admitted to the bar in Pennsylvania in 1805. Returning to his native Maryland three years later, at twenty-four he began publication of the *American Law Journal* (six volumes between 1809 and 1817), the first law journal in the nation. The *American Law Journal* was well-respected in its time and was cited by federal judges, including Justice Story. Hall subsequently became the first professor of modern history at an American university, accepting a chair at the University of Maryland at its founding. At thirty-three, he gave up both academia and the practice of law to become editor of *Port Folio*, a literary magazine published in Philadelphia. Over the remainder of his life, he published several more works on law, including a translation of Clerke's *Praxis* (*see infra* note 59), a treatise on constitutional law, and a work on the duties of the office of Justice of the Peace in Maryland. He died in 1829. *See* DICTIONARY OF AMERICAN BIOGRAPHY (1st ed. 1931; Allen Johnson & Dumas Malone eds., New York: Charles Scribner's Sons, 1960), Vol. IV, at 138–139; GEORGE C. CALCOTT, A HISTORY OF THE UNIVERSITY OF MARYLAND (Baltimore: Maryland Historical Society, 1966) at 32.

57. JOHN E. HALL, AN ESSAY ON MARITIME LOANS, FROM THE FRENCH OF M. BALTHAZARD MARIE EMERIGON: WITH NOTES (Baltimore: Philip H. Nicklin & Co., 1811), *quote in* Preface (*not paginated*). The Preface also makes reference to a forthcoming translation of Emerigon's work on marine insurance, though Hall did not fulfill this promise to his readers. It is worth noting that federal courts made use of Hall's translation of Emerigon. *See e.g. The Boston* (Case No. 1,669), 3 F. Cas. 918, 923 (S. D. N. Y., 1832) (citing Hall's translation in a case of bottomry).

appendices.[58] The translation of Emerigon followed publication two years earlier of his *Practice and Jurisdiction of the Court of Admiralty*, a three-part work designed to introduce American lawyers to the civil-law procedure for use in admiralty cases. Parts I and III were the author's own commentary; Part II was his translation of Clerke's *Praxis Curiae Admiralitatis Angliae*, the venerable sixteenth-century treatise dusted off and refurbished for American use.[59] Judge Samuel Betts of Federal District Court of New York followed Hall's example, publishing his treatise on admiralty practice in 1838. As was characteristic of the era, Betts tied the origins of admiralty law in the English-speaking world—both British and American—to Continental Europe, stating unequivocally in his introduction that "there is no controversy but that the court of the admiral had its proceedings in conformity to the civil law, from its earliest institution".[60] The notion of a cosmopolitan law of admiralty—both substantive and procedural, ancient and unchanging, time-honored and universal—had taken root in America. American legal scholars had begun to fill the vacuum left by Congress with the "general maritime law", complete with its mythical origins in the late Roman Empire and its descent in an unbroken legacy to the nations of the modern world.

The fascination with Continental materials was not confined to legal scholars and theorists. Courts actually consulted the medieval codes as well as modern civilians in deciding cases.[61] Federal judges examined medieval law in a di-

---

58. Hall's edition of Emerigon also contained excerpts of the Rhodian law of jettison taken from the *Digest* and *Codex of Justinian*, indicating that Hall felt that these ancient passages would be useful to nineteenth-century American practitioners. Moreover, though his Preface promised a forthcoming English edition of the *Consolato del Mare*, Hall abandoned the law for a career editing a literary magazine, and there is no record of him completing the project. *Id.* at 265–298.

59. John E. Hall, The Practice and Jurisdiction of the Court of Admiralty, (Baltimore: George Dobbin & Murphy, 1809).

60. Samuel R. Betts, A Summary of Practice in Instance, Revenue and Prize Causes, in the Admiralty Courts of the United States, for the Southern District of New-York; And Also on Appeal to the Supreme Court: Together with the Rules of the District Court (New York: Halstead & Voorhies, 1838), Introduction at vii.

61. Search of published opinions catalogued by Lexis for the years 1789 through 1859 reveals nearly sixty published opinions of federal courts that make express mention of the laws of Oleron, Wisby, the Hanse Towns, and the Consulate of the Sea. Others refer to the *Black Book of the Admiralty*, the Inquisition of Queenborow, the Table of Amalfi, and Roman sources. Continental civilians—particularly Boucher, Azuni, and Emerigon—also make frequent appearances in the case law. *See e.g. The William & Emmeline* (Case No. 17,687), 29 F. Cas.1288, 1289 (Betts, J., S. D. N. Y., 1828) (citing Azuni on ship's necessaries); *Certain Logs of Mahogany* (Case No. 2,559), 5 F. Cas. 374, 378 (C. C., D. Mass., 1837) (citing Boucher on freight); *Peters v. Warren Insurance Co.* (Case No. 11,035), 19 F. Cas. 373 (C. C., D. Mass., 1838) (Emerigon on liability of an insurer in case of collision);

verse set of disputes, encompassing salvage,[62] bottomry and materialmen's claims,[63] general average,[64] breach of charterparties,[65] collision,[66] ship's articles and seamen's wages,[67] seamen's right to maintenance and cure,[68] and disputes among ships' owners.[69] Joseph Story admonished against the profession, being as it was "split up into distinct provincial bars", becoming "devoted to mere state jurisprudence, and abandon[ing] those more enlightened and extensive researches which form the accomplished scholar, and elevate the refined jurist".[70] Use of the same body of sources produced a surprising level of

---

Pitman v. Hooper (Case No. 11,186), 19 F. Cas. 737, 742 (C. C., D. Mass., 1838) (Emerigon on freight); *The Fortitude* (Case No. 4,953), 9 F. Cas. 479, 483 (Story, J., C. C., D. Mass., 1838) (Emerigon on bottomry).

62. *See e.g. The Two Catherines* (Case No. 14,288), 24 F. Cas. 424 (Story, J., C. C., D. R. I., 1821); *Fisher v. The Sybil* (Case No. 4,441), 8 F. Cas. 141 (Johnson, J., C. C., D. S. C., 1816); *Lewis v. The Elizabeth Jane* (Case No. 8,321), 15 F. Cas. 478 (Ware, J., D. Maine, 1823); *Wilkie v. Two Hundred and Five Boxes of Sugar* (Case No. 17,662), 29 F. Cas. 1247 (Bee, J., D. S. C., 1796) (salvage of cargo); *Peabody v. Proceeds of Twenty-Eight Bags of Cotton* (Case No. 10,869), 19 F. Cas. 39 (D. Mass., 1829).

63. *See e.g. The William & Emmeline* (Case No. 17,687), 29 F. Cas. 1288 (Betts, J., S. D. N. Y., 1828) (bottomry); *The Fortitude* (Case No. 4,953), 9 F. Cas. 479 (C. C., D. Mass., 1838) (bottomry); *Zane v. The President* (Case No. 18,201), 30 F. Cas. 909 (E. D. Pa., 1824) (materialmen's claims).

64. *Mutual Safety Insurance Co. v. Cargo of the George* (Case No. 9,982), 17 F. Cas. 1088 (Betts, J., S. D. N. Y., 1846).

65. In addition to ordinary claims for breach of a contract of affreightment (negligence in handling of cargo, deviation, etc.), another context in which the ancient codes proved useful was for cases in which a ship's master had disposed of cargo to raise funds for repair of the vessel. *See e.g. The Gold Hunter* (Case No. 5,513), 10 F. Cas. 554 (Betts, J., S. D. N. Y., 1832); *Bulgin v. The Rainbow* (Case No. 2,116), 4 F. Cas. 612 (D. S. C., 1798).

66. *The Scioto* (Case No. 12,508), 21 F. Cas. 774 (Ware, J., D. Maine, 1847)

67. *See e.g. The Mentor* (Case No. 9, 427), 17 F. Cas. 15 (Story, J., C. C., D. Mass., 1825); *Emerson v. Howland* (Case No. 4,441), 8 F. Cas. 634 (Story, J., C. C., D. Mass., 1816); *Ex Parte Giddings* (Case No. 5,404), 10 F. Cas. 336 (C. C., D. Mass, 1814); *The Rovena* (Case No. 12,090), 20 F. Cas. 1272 (Ware, J., D. Maine, 1836); *The Martha* (Case No. 9,144), 16 F. Cas. 860 (Betts, J., S. D. N. Y., 1830); *The America* (Case No. 286), 1 F. Cas. 605 (Betts, J., S. D. N. Y., 1830); *Carey v. The Kitty* (Case No. 2,402) 5 F. Cas. 59 (D. S. C., 1808).

68. *See e.g. Harden v. Gordon* (Case No. 6,047), 11 F. Cas. 480 (C. C., D. Maine, 1823); *Natterstorm v. the Hazard* (Case No. 10,055), 17 F. Cas. 1243 (D. Mass., 1809); *Freeman v. Baker* (Case No. 5,084), 9 F. Cas. 754, (Betts, J., S. D. N. Y., 1833); *Reed v. Canfield* (Case No. 11,641), 20 F. Cas. 426 (Story, J., C. C., D. Mass., 1832).

69. *The Seneca* (Case No. 12,670), 21 F. Cas. 1081 (E. D. Pa., 1829).

70. Joseph Story, A Discourse on the Past History, Present State and Future Prospects of the Law (Edinburgh: T. Clark, 1835) at 35. For discussion, *see* McClellan, *supra* note 53, at 86.

uniformity among the various state and federal courts. Judges made a conscious attempt to consult both the practice of other nations and the decisions of their brethren, state and federal, in other jurisdictions in identifying and applying rules of substantive maritime law.[71]

Uniformity and the General Maritime Law

Support for an internationally uniform body of substantive maritime law transcended political affiliation; Federalists and Republicans alike accepted the notion that some substantive rules enforced by the maritime nations of Europe should be binding in the Unites States as well. St. George Tucker—Virginian, Republican, and editor in 1803 of the first American edition of Blackstone's *Commentaries*—vehemently rejected the notion that the common law of England was incorporated into federal law.[72] Moreover, he approached with skepticism the idea of uniform common law among the several states. His edition of Blackstone was designed to encourage similarity in the rules adopted in the various states, but only through persuasion.[73] Nevertheless, he accepted

---

71. Fletcher, *supra* note 53, at 1549, 1562.

72. Tucker first addressed the issue in print in a monograph published in 1800; he subsequently reworked the introductory portions of the monograph, adding new materials for insertion as an appendix to his edition of Blackstone's *Commentaries*. Only six copies of the monograph are known to be extant, two of which are held in Special Collections by the Swem Library of the College of William and Mary. The version included in Blackstone's *Commentaries* has been reissued (with new pagination) in a critical edition by Clyde N. Wilson. For convenience, the citations contained herein are given with reference (where applicable) to both of these editions. For rejection of the common law of England as a source of federal law, *see* St. George Tucker, Examination of the Question, "How Far the Common Law of England Is the Law for the Federal Government of the United States (Richmond: John Dixon, 1800) at 40–41 (hereinafter Tucker, Common Law); St. George Tucker, View of the Constitution of the United States, With Selected Writings (1st ed. 1803; critical edition, Clyde N. Wilson ed., Indianapolis: Liberty Fund, 1999) at 343–344 (hereinafter Tucker (Wilson ed.)).

73. Tucker's challenge to the notion of a uniform common law among the states is twofold. First, he notes that the common law was not identical in all of the colonies before independence:

> "[M]y readers will readily perceive that it would require the talents of an Alfred to harmonize and digest into one system such opposite, discordant, and conflicting municipal institutions, as composed the codes of the several colonies at the period of the revolution; united with the co-ercive arm of the Norman tyrant to enforce obedience to it, when digested. In vain then we should attempt, by

the notion of a uniform body of maritime law, binding on the community of nations,[74] though for him this body of law was carefully circumscribed such

---

> any GENERAL THEORY, to establish an uniform authority and obligation in the common law of England, over the American colonies, at any period between the first migrations to this country, and that epoch, which annihilated the sovereignty of the crown of England over them."

TUCKER, COMMON LAW, *supra* note 72, at 23 (*emphasis in the original*); TUCKER (Wilson ed.), *supra* note 72, at 338–339. Second, the Revolution put an end to any lingering hope that the common law might be uniform throughout the nation:

> "From that moment *there was no common law amongst them but the general law of nations, to which all civilized nations conform.* And no law could thereafter be imposed upon the people of any state, but by the legislature thereof, so no law could be obligatory in one state, merely because it was obligatory in another. And how much soever their municipal institutions might agree, one with another, yet as it was in the power of their legislatures, respectively, to alter the whole, or any part of them, whenever they should think proper, therefore, such coincidence by no means established a common rule amongst them; because, as was before observed, the establishment of a law within the jurisdiction of one state, gave it no authority within the jurisdiction of any other. From hence it follows, that the adoption of the common law, or statutes of England, in one state, or in several, or even in all, although it might produce a general conformity in their municipal codes, yet as such adoption was the separate act of each state, it could not operate so as to give to those laws a sanction superior to any other laws of the states, respectively; inasmuch as each state would still have retained the power of changing, or rejecting them, whenever it should think proper..."

TUCKER, COMMON LAW, *supra* note 72, at 24–25 (*emphasis added*); TUCKER (Wilson ed.), *supra* note 72, at 340.

74. In addition to acts of Congress (and the laws of the states in diversity cases), federal judges were to apply other bodies of law under certain circumstances. Among these bodies of law was the maritime law; he explains:

> "In short, as the matters cognizable in the federal courts, belong...partly to the law of nations; partly to the common law of England; partly to the civil law; partly to the maritime law, comprehending the laws of Oleron and Rhodes; and partly to the general law and custom of merchants; and partly to the municipal laws of any foreign nation, or of any state in the union, where the cause of action might happen to arise, or where the suit may be instituted; so, the law of nations, the common law of England, the civil law, the law maritime, the law merchant, or the LEX LOCI, or the law of the foreign nation, or state, in which the cause of action may arise, or shall be decided, must in their own turn be resorted to as the rule of decision, according to the nature and circumstances of each case, respectively. So that each of these laws may be regarded, so far as they apply to such cases, respectively, as the law of the land."

TUCKER, COMMON LAW, *supra* note 72, at 40 (*emphasis in the original*); TUCKER (Wilson ed.), *supra* note 72, at 361–362. Contentions of modern critics notwithstanding (*cf.* Fletcher, *supra* note 53, at 1523–1525), Tucker stops short of maintaining that there is a

that its parameters did not overlap those of the common law.[75] Belief in a cosmopolitan maritime law notwithstanding, American judges were well aware that uniformity would not be easy to achieve. Even when most legal scholars

---

body of "general common law" from which federal judges may draw to fill gaps in state law. Instead, each of these bodies of law—the law of nations, maritime law, the law merchant, foreign law—is to be applied where the rules for choice of law require it. In Tucker's time, choice of law was determined largely by geography. If a contract were drafted in a foreign country, that nation's law would apply. If the contract were between foreign merchants domiciled in two different countries, the law merchant would apply. Similarly, if a contract were to be signed at sea, the maritime law would supply the rule of decision. As he explains:

> "The judicial power extends likewise...8. To controversies between citizens of different states; and between citizens of any state and subjects or citizens of foreign states.—In these cases, the municipal law of the place where the cause of controversy arises, whether that be one of the United States, or Great Britain, or France, Spain, Holland, Hamburg, or any other country; or the general law of merchants; or the general law of nations, according to the nature and circumstances of the case, must be the rule of decision, in whatever court the suit may be brought. Thus if a bond be given in Philadelphia, the rate of interest must be settled according to the laws of Pennsylvania. If a bill of exchange be drawn in Virginia, the rate of damages must be settled by the laws of that state. If in England, Hamburg, or Cadiz, the custom of merchants in those places respectively must govern. *If a ransom bill be drawn at sea, the law of nations in that case must be consulted.*"

TUCKER, COMMON LAW, *supra* note 72, at 34 (*emphasis added*); TUCKER (Wilson ed.), *supra* note 72, at 353–354.

75. Conflict between the state's common law and the general maritime law appears to be impossible under Tucker's understanding of each. In his monograph of 1800, he remarks that "cases of admiralty and maritime jurisdiction...were never held to be within the jurisdiction of the common law." TUCKER, COMMON LAW, *supra* note 72, at 33; TUCKER (Wilson ed.), *supra* note 72, at 352. A notation in his manuscript of law lectures reinforces the point: "A Court of Admiralty impl[ies] a court that [has] no jurisdiction in common law cases...". *See* St. George Tucker, Ten Notebooks of Law Lectures (1790s) (unpublished manuscript, on file in Special Collections of the Swem Library, College of William and Mary), Vol. VII, at 57. Read together with his remarks on choice of law in his monograph of 1800 (*quoted supra* note 74), these statements outline the scope of matters that the general maritime law controls. Where a cause of action (tort or contract) arises at sea, the common law has no jurisdiction, and the general maritime law recognized by all "civilized nations" supplies the rule of decision. It appears that Tucker's understanding of the role of maritime law in relation to the common law matches Sir Edward Coke's. Unfortunately, Tucker's extant writings do not address the truly interesting question of which law a federal court should apply where a dispute arises over charterparty signed in Virginia. Should the court apply the general maritime law rather than the state's law in construing the contract if the two are in conflict?

and judges had believed that the substantive maritime law was tied to the law of nature, the content of the law was not necessarily self-evident. As belief in the law of nature waned, most recognized the law of nations as more fluid, and certainly less easily deduced from abstract principles. In the absence of a foundation firmly planted in natural law, one needs empirical data to ascertain the law of nations. By concentrating upon such data, judges became acutely aware of the subtle differences in the way the *lex maritima* was applied among the nations of Europe.

The general maritime law was neither self-executing nor entirely uniform from one nation to another. Compounding this problem was the fact that the United States had not inherited its admiralty traditions from a nation with a legal system grounded entirely in the civil law. The authors of the great Continental treatises understood how admiralty was to fit into the larger scope of their respective nations' legal systems. In a civil-law nation, admiralty formed an integral part of the legal system; this was not the case in the in the English system, where the common lawyers had viewed admiralty courts as unwanted branches grafted onto a system the underlying structure of which was ill-suited to them. In short, the precise parameters of American admiralty jurisdiction were not clear, and neither the English legal system nor the Continental legal systems provided models that federal judges could copy without making adjustments both for the requirements of federalism and for a judicial system grounded in *stare decisis*. As Judge Hopkinson once explained the nature of these *ad hoc* adjustments:

> When I am called upon to wield a power never before used, or directly claimed by any court of admiralty, in England or in our own country, the right should be made exceeding clear, from acknowledged principles and unquestionable deductions; and if any difference exists between the law of the United States and that of England, on the subject, arising from the nature of our political or judicial institutions, it should be brought home to the question, before the court can presume to add such a power to its jurisdiction. The courts of admiralty in England may have been, at one period, too much constrained by the watchful and rigorous jealousy of the common law, but, on the other hand the civilians have not been without ambition to extend their dominion; and, having the field very much to themselves on the continent, they must draw us over a wide range, if we follow them implicitly. By hastily disregarding the doctrines of the English courts, in favour of the apparent convenience of the civil law, we shall disturb the harmony of our system of jurisprudence, which has been essentially derived from that of England, and follows it in

> its leading arrangements. Let us be governed by a sincere desire to direct and regulate both jurisdictions by the great ends of public convenience, and individual justice, without rashly removing established limits and landmarks.[76]

Often called upon to adjudicate maritime matters, Judge Peters frequently found himself faced with a similar dilemma. In an action for seamen's wages in 1795, he remarks:

> If by our own municipal laws, there are rules established, our courts are bound exclusively to follow them. But in cases where no such rules are instituted, we must resort to the regulations of other maritime countries, which have stood the test of time and experience, to direct our judgments, as rules of decision.[77]

Peters then marshals an impressive collection of ancient and medieval authorities to support his holding.[78] After extrapolating a general rule from the sources he surveys, he awards wages to the libellants. Nevertheless, the facts of the case prevent Peters from confronting two problems that are usually present when a court adapts foreign rules for domestic use. First, as the rule derived from the medieval codes does not conflict with either federal law or public policy, he is free to adopt it without modification.[79] Second, the case is

---

76. *Davis v. The Seneca* (Case No. 3,650), 7 F. Cas. 166, 172 (Hopkinson, J., E. D. Pa., 1828). The dilemma facing Judge Hopkinson arose out of a suit by partners to compel a dissenting partner to sell his share in a vessel; the dissenter had refused to grant his permission for the ship to sail, thus forcing it to remain idle in port. This was a case of first impression in the United States. Relying on Continental theories, it was possible for the court to fashion such a remedy, but in England, the suit itself was beyond the jurisdiction of the High Court of Admiralty. Accepting Justice Story's argument in *DeLovio v. Boit* that federal admiralty jurisdiction was more extensive than its British counterpart, Hopkinson was first compelled to determine whether the claim lay within federal admiralty jurisdiction, and second, whether a substantive rule not recognized by Anglo-American case-law as an "admiralty" rule was in fact part of the general maritime law.

77. *Thompson v. The Catharina* (Case No. 1028), 23 F. Cas. 1028, 1029 (Peters, J., D. Pa., 1795).

78. The ancient and medieval materials include the Rhodian and Roman laws, the Table of Amalfi, the laws of Oleron, Wisby, and the Hanse Towns, the *Consolato del Mare*, and the *Ordinances of Louis XIV* of France. *Id.* at 1029–1031.

79. Peters acknowledges in *dicta* that his extrapolation of a rule from the collective provisions of the medieval maritime codes would have been for naught had the result offended the law or institutions of the Unites States: "The feudal parts of this law, and such as are inconsistent with the principles of our government are not, nor can they be, in force." *Id.* at 1031.

sufficiently simple that the sources Peters selects for the general maritime law are all in agreement. Thus Peters gives to the historically suspect Consulate of the Sea a weight equal to the Laws of Oleron, for which a pedigree is far better established both in England and on the Continent.[80] Another case reveals more clearly that augmenting federal maritime law with established foreign custom and practice is not simply a process of identifying the substantive rule recognized by all of the maritime nations of Europe. In adjudicating a case of salvage three years earlier, Peters found that the various medieval and modern Continental sources were in conflict regarding the method for calculating a salvage-award. Rather than choosing from among the established rules, he instead fashioned a new rule based in part upon the French Maritime Ordinances.[81] The case introduced a novel concept, namely that federal judges were not limited to selecting from among existing rules in settling a conflict in the customary rules recognized by the community of nations. At least for Peters, it appears that it was acceptable for federal judges to alter the general maritime law on an *ad hoc* basis if to do so would serve federal interests.[82]

Joseph Story and the Maritime Law

The grandson of the clerk of the Vice Admiralty Court of Massachusetts, in 1811 Joseph Story became at age thirty-two the youngest justice ever ap-

---

80. Peters goes to some length in defending his use of the "*Consolato del Mare*", asserting that despite its "origin...enveloped in obscurity", it is "a respectable part of the law of nations", which in Southern Europe "to this day, [is] the leading directrix, in their maritime affairs". *Id.* at 1030. Nevertheless, subsequent scholarship (based in part on analysis of manuscripts not available to Peters) has cast serious doubts on the age and authorship of the Consulate of the Sea. *See* discussion, *supra* Chapter I, notes 44–51 and text accompanying.

81. *See Warder v. La Belle Creole* (Case No. 17,165), 29 F. Cas. 215 (Peters, J., D. Pa., 1792).

82. Of his change in the rule established by the French Ordinance, he states: "Although I do not exactly follow, yet I have nearly as accommodated my determination to, this ordinance, as I think right." *Id.* at 217. Elsewhere he is more direct, stressing the importance of public policy in selecting or fashioning a rule. *See e.g. Willings v. Blight* (Case No. 17,765), 30 F. Cas. 50, 52 (Peters, J., D. Pa., 1800) (noting that rules should facilitate "the general interests and prosperity of commerce"); *Swift v. The Happy Return* (Case No. 13,697), 23 F. Cas. 560 (Peters, J., D. Pa., 1799) (selecting a rule for interpreting ship's articles that comports with local custom and business-practices). *See also* discussion *in* Stephen B. Presser, *A Tale of Two Judges: Richard Peters, Samuel Chase, and the Broken Promise of Federalist Jurisprudence*, 73 Nw. U. L. Rev. 26, 34–37 (1978).

pointed to the Supreme Court, a distinction that he holds to this day. He served simultaneously as an associate justice of the nation's highest court and a professor of law at his *alma mater*, Harvard, becoming one of the most prolific among American legal scholars in the nineteenth century.[83] His three-volume *Commentaries on the Constitution*[84] became a standard reference work immediately upon its publication in 1833, and it remains a legal classic today, indispensable reading for those who wish to understand constitutional interpretation in the early years of the republic. The abridged and simplified one-volume edition, *A Familiar Exposition of the Constitution,*[85] provided many students and laymen alike with their first exposure to constitutional theory. His American edition of Abbott's treatise became the nation's first standard reference book on substantive maritime law, pre-dating those of Erastus Benedict and Henry Flanders by more than a generation.[86] Scholarly, and with a gift for languages, Story managed to earn the respect of his colleagues in his first years on the bench largely through his expertise in admiralty, where his command of ancient and modern languages and detailed study of the civil law gave him a distinct advantage.[87] In an era when Chief Justice Marshall drafted most of the Court's opinions personally, Story alone among the associate justices amassed a significant total of majority opinions,[88] and many of these were

---

83. For Story's appointment to the Supreme Court, *see* GERALD T. DUNNE, JUSTICE JOSEPH STORY AND THE RISE OF THE SUPREME COURT (New York: Simon & Schuster, 1970) at 77, 81 (hereinafter DUNNE). For biographical information on Story's early years, tenure as a professor Harvard, appointment to the Supreme Court, and publications, *see* DUNNE at 15–44; R. KENT NEWMYER, SUPREME COURT JUSTICE JOSEPH STORY: STATESMAN OF THE OLD REPUBLIC (Chapel Hill: 1985) at 3–37, 237–270 (hereinafter NEWMYER); JOSEPH STORY, MISCELLANEOUS WRITINGS (Willian W. Story ed., Boston: Charles C. Little & James Brown, 1852), *Autobiography* at 1–42 (hereinafter STORY, MISCELLANEOUS WRITINGS).

84. JOSEPH STORY, COMMENTARIES ON THE CONSTITUTION (3 vols., 1st ed., Boston: Hilliard, Gray & Co., 1833).

85. JOSEPH STORY, A FAMILIAR EXPOSITION OF THE CONSTITUTION OF THE UNITED STATES (1st ed. 1840; *reprinted* Lake Bluff, Illinois: Regnery Gateway, Inc., 1986).

86. *See* CHARLES ABBOTT, A TREATISE ON THE LAW RELATIVE TO MERCHANT SHIPS AND SEAMEN: IN FOUR PARTS (3d American edition, Joseph Story ed., Exeter, New Hampshire: George Lamson, 1822).

87. For Story's record in drafting admiralty opinions, and the esteem in which his colleagues held them, *see* NEWMYER, *supra* note 83, at 93 (noting that Story drafted seventeen opinions in admiralty cases during that time). For Story's classical education and background in comparative law, *see* DUNNE, *supra* note 83, at 23, 92.

88. Between the years 1805 and 1833, Marshall drafted a total of 458 of 977 majority opinions; Story drafted 171 while serving on the court for seven fewer years than Marshall. Among the associate justices, only Story and William Johnson drafted more than seventy. *See* MORGAN, *supra* note 48, at 189; *see also* NEWMYER, *supra* note 83, at 81.

in admiralty. Moreover, there were the admiralty cases he heard while riding circuit.[89] In an age that saw the contributions of Ashur Ware, Samuel Betts, and Richard Peters, no one did more to shape American admiralty law than Joseph Story.

Immersed in the writings of Aristotle and Cicero, Story—against the trends of his time—believed firmly in natural law.[90] From this belief in natural law, it was a small step to the notion that law was governed by scientific principles.[91] Before Langdell and the legal scientists, Story pioneered the concept that law, properly understood, was governed by an intrinsic logic, and that it was the job of legal scholars and judges to sift through the amassed collections of case law to identify the abstract principles contained therein. There are at least two corollaries to this mode of thought. First, as law is an outgrowth of nature, it must be measured against a moral yardstick. To Story's New England Congregationalist mind, "nature" is "presumed coincede[nt] with the will of [the] Creator".[92] Second, as law is "scientific" and not random, it should be uniform.[93] That is not to say that the law of nature directly controls the outcome of cases. For Story as much as for Vattel or Pufendorf, the law of nature merely provides a touchstone against which positive law is to be measured; it does not provide the rule itself. Nonetheless, Story believed as Hale did that the process by which the common law developed substantive rules ensured their intrinsic logic. Through successive generations of judicial improvisation at the margins, slowly and incrementally optimal rules evolve.[94] While such

---

89. For discussion of Story's admiralty opinions while riding circuit, *see* DUNNE, *supra* note 83, at 93, 99. For a sampling of his circuit-court admiralty opinions, *see* cases, *supra* notes 61, 62, 67, 68.

90. In 1836, Story contributed an essay entitled "Natural Law" to the *Encyclopedia Americana.* It covered topics ranging from the origins of political society and decentralization of power, to society's need for a judiciary. The essay is reproduced in its entirety in MCCLELLAN, *supra* note 53, Appendix at 313–322. For the impact of Story's views on natural law on his judicial career, *see Id.* at 84, 108; *see also* NEWMYER, *supra* note 83, at 162.

91. Merging John Adams' distaste for "pettifogging" with his own brand of legal positivism, Story once wrote: "Law…I admire as a science; it becomes tedious and embarrassing only when it degenerates into a trade." Letter from Joseph Story to Thomas Welsh (Oct. 19, 1799), *quoted in* DUNNE, *supra* note 83, at 34. For discussion of Story's view of law as science, *see also* NEWMYER, *supra* note 83, at 211.

92. Joseph Story, "Natural Law", *reprinted in* MCCLELLAN, *supra* note 53, Appendix at 313.

93. For discussion of Story's belief in a need for uniformity in law, *see e.g.* NEWMYER, *supra* note 83, at 211; Fletcher, *supra* note 53, at 1554; MCCLELLAN, *supra* note 53, at 86.

94. For discussion of Hale's comment that the common law of England was "not the product or wisdom of some one man, or society of men, in one age; but of the wisdom,

an approach guards against radical innovation, it also guarantees that judges have some role in developing the law.

Story's confidence in the evolution of substantive rules over time was not limited to the common law; it applied equally to the law merchant and the general maritime law. While he greatly admired the Roman contribution to modern maritime law, he maintained that "[t]he glory of having reduced the principles of maritime law to a science belongs to later times."[95] As with the common law, *the lex maritima also was a product of the cumulative wisdom of many judges:*

> Let it not, therefore, be imagined, that the maritime law as acknowledged and practised upon by the most enlightened nations of the present day, was produced *per saltum*—by the sudden start of a single mind or nation, generalizing and analyzing the principles at a single effort. Far different is the case. It arrived at its present comparative perfection by slow and cautious steps; by the gradual accumulations of distant times, and the contributions of various nations. Industry and patience first collected the scattered rays, emitted from a thousand points through the dim vista of past ages; and philosophy reflected them back with tenfold brilliancy and symmetry. If, indeed, a professional mind might indulge in a momentary enthusiasm, it would perceive, that in this process had been realized the enchantment and wonders of the kaleidoscope, where broken and disjointed materials, however rude, are shaped into inexhaustible varieties of figures, all perfect in their order and harmonies, by the adjustment of reflected light under the guidance of philosophy.[96]

Here "philosophy" is the innate reason of the judge, acting in accordance with the law of nature. To the extent that reason can make sense of the "disjointed materials", it is appropriate to speak of the *science of law*. Nevertheless, for Story, law is not pure abstraction; it was to be made to serve the needs of society. As one of Story's biographers remarks: "American legal science, true to the spirit of the age, was applied science". One of the principal needs that law

---

counsel, experience, and observation of many ages of wise and observing men", *see* McClellan, *supra* note 53, at 85; *see also supra* Chapter I, note 177 and text accompanying. For Story's merging of the law of nature with Hale's view of the common law, *see* McClellan at 78–79, 84–85.

95. Joseph Story, "Literature of the Maritime Law", *in* Story, Miscellaneous Writings, *supra* note 83, at 98.

96. *Id.* at 99.

was to serve was the facilitation of commerce. Business functions most smoothly when rules are uniform in all markets and when all parties know the substance of the rules *ex ante*.[97] In his landmark opinion in *DeLovio v. Boit*,[98] Story cites numerous cases and provides a virtually exhaustive list of commentators on maritime law and jurisdiction. Against Coke's narrow construction of the scope of admiralty jurisdiction, he pits Zouch, Exton, Godolphin, Jenkins, Prynne, Clerke, Spelman, Hale, Selden, Hall, Valin, and even cases in Coke's own *Reports*. Nevertheless, in rendering his decision, he turns ultimately to concern for practicality:

> The advantages resulting to the commerce and navigation of the United States, from a uniformity of rules and decisions in all maritime questions, authorize us to believe that national policy, as well as juridical logic, require the clause of the constitution to be so construed, as to embrace all maritime contracts, torts and injuries, or, in other words, to embrace all those causes, which originally and inherently belonged to the admiralty, before any statutable restriction.[99]

Story's concept of uniformity does not stop at America's borders. Writing of the maritime law of America's trading partners, Story remarks:

> A great variety of curious and difficult questions are perpetually arising in our judicial tribunals, where the positive regulations or usages of other commercial nations would greatly assist us in forming decisions which should comport with general convenience, as well as with the general principles of law. Many are the cases, in which the reasoning is so nicely balanced on each side, that a settled foreign usage ought to incline the scale. We owe, indeed, a full moiety of our present commercial law to the positive ordinances or usages of France, Italy, and Spain, as they have been delivered to us by their eminent jurists. They seem now inclined to borrow from us in return; and thus, perhaps, national comity may gradually establish a nearly uniform system of commercial jurisprudence throughout the whole civilized world.[100]

"Uniform", however, does not mean "static". Story recognizes that the law must evolve to keep pace with changing commercial practices. The laws of the

---

97. For discussion, *see e.g.* NEWMYER, *supra* note 83, at 120–121.

98. *DeLovio v. Boit* (Case No. 3,776), 7 F. Cas. 418 (Story, J., C. C., D. Mass., 1815).

99. *Id.* at 443.

100. Joseph Story, "Literature of the Maritime Law", *in* STORY, MISCELLANEOUS WRITINGS, *supra* note 83, at 120.

ancient peoples of the Mediterranean, Story maintains, lacked the complexity of modern systems of maritime law because "the business of their commerce was extremely simple, their voyages were short, and their shipping was adapted to small cargoes and narrow reaches".[101] Complex commerce requires complex laws, and judges on occasion would be called upon to fashion new substantive rules. This fact lay at the heart of Story's ambivalence toward the "codification movement" of the 1820s. So long as codification was confined to distillation of general rules out of existing case law, Story initially supported it as a means of promoting uniformity.[102] Ultimately, however, he rejects the scheme as impractical, reasoning that a code would soon be out-of-date, "perpetually growing more and more defective, unless resort was had to new legislation."[103] Codification, Story concludes, hampers the ability of judges to adjust or fashion law incrementally as the needs of society and commerce demand.

---

101. *Id.* at 94.

102. As Story once wrote to Henry Wheaton:

> "I have long been an advocate for a 'codification' of the common law, at least of that part which is most reduced to principles & is of daily and extensive application. I do not suppose that such a code would render future legislation unnecessary, or would supercede the necessity of perpetual appeals to courts of justice. So long as human transactions are unlimited & are assuming new courses, & new forms, there must be an infinite diversity in the application of legal principles.... My opinion in favour of a code of the Common Law, therefore, rests on no visionary expectation of a perfect, infallible, or universal system. *But I am in favour of a Code, because I think it may reduce to certainty, method, & exactness much of the law, already passed upon by judicial tribunals, & thus give to the public the means, within a reasonable compass, of ascertaining their own rights & duties in many of the most interesting concerns of human life.*"

Unpublished letter of Joseph Story to Henry Wheaton (Oct. 1, 1825), *reproduced from manuscript in* McClellan, *supra* note 53, at 93 (*emphasis added*). For discussion, *see Id.* at 92–94.

103. Joseph Story, "Codification of the Common Law: A Report of the Commissioners Appointed to Consider and Report upon the Practicability and Expediency of Reducing to a Written and Systematic Code the Common Law of Massachusetts, or Any Part Thereof; Made to His Excellency the Governor, January, 1837", *in* Story, Miscellaneous Writings, *supra* note 83, at 698, 709. In a manner worthy of Matthew Hale, Story insists that law is too dynamic, too fluid to be frozen in codified form; it should be left instead to "its prospective operations in [the] future (as it has been in the past) to be improved, and expanded, and modified to meet the exigencies of society, by the gradual application of its principles in courts of justice to new cases, assisted from time to time, as the occasion may demand, by the enactments of the legislature." *Id.* at 713. For discussion, *see* McClellan, *supra* note 53, at 95–96.

With twenty-two years on the federal bench, Story had many opportunities to put his theories of jurisprudence into practice. Essentially conservative, Story's innovations are usually subtle, and frequently reflect a knowledge of business practices as well as a healthy respect for common sense. Although Story often favored the use of customs and practices of the trade in construing contracts between merchants, in *Brown v. Jones*, he declines to extend the same principle to ships' articles, reasoning in part that extending the rule of construction would serve no useful commercial purpose.[104] Merchants meet in the market-place as equals, and flexibility in their contracts aids both parties. Seamen signing ship's articles, however, are entering into an employee/employer relationship. A bright-line rule that construes ship's articles on the "four corners" of the contract better protects the interests of seamen—and thus encourages more men to go to sea. A native of Salem, Story understood all too well the advantage in both legal sophistication and economic bargaining power that shipowners had over sailors, and his opinion reveals an attempt to fashion a rule that discourages exploitation.[105] Story's opinions often reflect tension between the creative role of the judge and the adherence to *stare decisis*, which prevents one judge from, in Coke's words, "tak[ing] it on himself to be wiser than the law."[106] A two-page opinion that Story drafted while riding circuit reveals both his penchant for innovation and his respect for precedent. In *Ex parte Lewis*, he has no difficulty arriving at the conclusion that warfage creates a maritime lien of higher priority than a bottomry bond (a question of first impression), and yet he stops short of overruling a line cases holding that a personal contract for warfage between the warfinger and shipowner negates the maritime lien.[107] His respect for precedent shows most

---

104. *Brown v. Jones* (Case No. 2,107), 4 F. Cas. 404, 406 (Story, J., C. C., D. Mass., 1815). Story contends further that using custom and practice as understood in chartering to construe the term "voyage" in the context of ship's articles also would run afoul of the Act for the Regulation of Merchant Seamen (July 20, 1790), 1 Stat. 131.

105. The respondent in *Brown v. Jones* had wished to construe the term "voyage" as one would in a charterparty, permitting the ship's master to add another leg to the trip if to do would make sense commercially. Obviously, for sailors who were not to share in the additional profits, construing their contracts of employment in the same manner would be cause for alarm. Instead, Story requires that shipowners specify in the contract that extra voyages may be added. Story's attitude toward seamen was essentially paternalistic—if at times patronizing. In *Harden v. Gordon* (Case No. 6,047), 11 F. Cas. 480, 485 (C. C., D. Maine, 1823), he terms them "wards of the admiralty", characterizing them as "credulous and complying" individuals who are "thoughtless and require indulgence".

106. For discussion, *see supra* Chapter I, note 174 and text accompanying.

107. *Ex parte Lewis* (Case No. 8,310), 15 F. Cas. 451 (Story, J., C. C., D. Mass., 1815).

clearly in those opinions grounded in ancient and medieval texts.[108] Often more like a skillful advocate than a legal scholar, he deftly avoids the subtle conflicts among the venerable maritime codes, concentrating instead—as he did in *DeLovio*—upon the similarities among them. In the end, he creates the impression that the *lex maritima* is seamless, an amalgamation of disparate sources reconciled and synthesized into a coherent whole by centuries of time-tested judicial decisions. While his command of arcane texts often serves him well, he is nonetheless hampered by a lack of essential information on the provenance of some of the material he cites, and his command of languages cannot guard against corrupt or inaccurate texts. The quality of materials available to him, however, are beyond his control, and if his historical assumptions are not always flawless, the presentation is nonetheless rhetorically compelling and logically consistent.

Complex minds defy easy classification. A proponent of natural law, Story nonetheless displays great respect for the empiricist Bynkershoek, praising his works on commercial law and bottomry and remarking: "Every thing which

108. Story acknowledges that the "*Consolato del Mare* is a rare work in our country". Lacking access to modern scholarship on the Consulate of the Sea, he tends to overrate it, at one point chastising Hubner for his disparaging view of it. He is aware of extant texts and the leading scholarship of his own day, however, and he correctly notes that the earliest extant text is that of 1494. He errs, however, in ascribing this text to Francis Celelles, the editor who based his own edition of the early sixteenth century on the 1494 manuscript. Story does, however, correctly note that the first portion of the work is a later interpolation. *See* Joseph Story, "Literature of the Maritime Law", *in* STORY, MISCELLANEOUS WRITINGS, *supra* note 83, at 100–103. Even though Story accepts that the earliest text of the Consulate of the Sea was in Catalan, he had access only to an Italian translation, published in 1549. This version was not entirely accurate, and Story's correct rendering of a flawed Italian translation replicated the original translator's error in *DeLovio*. As Sir Travers Twiss observes:

> "As Mr. Justice Story's translation of this important chapter of the Valencian regulations has been made from the Italian version, which is not an accurate rendering of the original Catalan text, the Editor has subjoined the Catalan text in a note from which it will be seen that the words 'the partition of ships by public sale', used by Mr. Justice Story, do not accurately represent the meaning of the Catalan text, which should be rendered, 'of partnership in ship-building, of sales by public auction'..."

THE BLACK BOOK OF THE ADMIRALTY (*RERUM BRITANNICARUM MEDII AEVI SCRIPTORES* (ROLLS SERIES): No. 55 *MONUMENTA JURIDICA* (4 vols., Sir Travers Twiss ed., 1st ed. London: Her Majesty's Stationery Office, 1871; *reprinted* Kraus Reprints, 1979), Vol. III, Introduction at lxxv. For additional discussion of the texts of the Consulate of the Sea, *see Id.*, Vol. III, at xxvi–xxviii, xxxiii–xxiv, xli–xliv. *See also* discussion *supra* Chapter I, notes 44–51 and text accompanying.

came from this great man bears the marks of an original, vigorous, and independent mind."[109] Story shares Coke's respect for *stare decisis* and McReynolds' preference for order and tendency to view legal questions as grounded in morality, and yet he largely avoids the latter's propensity for mental inflexibility, once remarking in a letter to a friend: "He who lives a long life and never changes his opinions, may value himself upon his consistency, but rarely can be complimented for his wisdom. Experience cures us of many of our theories..."[110] Story's method for reconciling his views on natural law, uniformity, *stare decisis*, and judicial creativity defies simplistic summaries.[111] Propelled by his belief in the need for uniformity in the maritime law, he is will-

---

109. *See* Joseph Story, "The Literature of the Maritime Law", *in* STORY, MISCELLANEOUS WRITINGS, *supra* note 83, at 109–110. Story also cites Bynkershoek for authority in prize cases. *See* HERBERT A. JOHNSON, THE CHIEF JUSTICESHIP OF JOHN MARSHALL: 1801–1835 (Columbia: The University of South Carolina Press, 1997) at 41. For Bynkershoek's role as a founder of modern empirical theories of international law, *see* Edwin N. Dickinson, *Changing Concepts and the Doctrine of Incorporation*, 26 Am. Jur. Intn'l L. 239, 250–251 (1932); *see also supra* Chapter IV, note 160 and text accompanying.

110. Letter from Joseph Story to Harrison Gray Otis (Dec. 27, 1818), *reproduced in* DUNNE, *supra* note 83, at 35.

111. One biographer comes closer than most to providing a adequate brief account of Story's legal thought:

> "For Story, whose juristic system (following the systematic model of Blackstone) sought to integrate law and culture, the dilemma was especially intense. The problem was that he enthusiastically embraced all of the contradictory forces. The free market and economic individualism, in the style of Adam Smith, he accepted without question. He was a true believer in the transforming and civilizing forces of commerce and was willing to put the law at the service of the dynamic entrepreneurs who pioneered the commercial revolution. To this end he was a legal reformer and modernizer. But he also believed deeply in the sanctity of property and the moral values of traditional society as he experienced them in New England and Massachusetts. His plan for social-economic progress most assuredly carried with it a conservative, organic concept of community interest. There was no conflict, however: Story was convinced that American law might liberate and energize economic man and at the same time preserve property and keep the individual within the bounds of community well-being.
>
> To perform this feat, the law itself had to be moral and scientific. Thus did Story the jurist confront Story the instrumentalist: A symmetrical, principled, architectonic system of law was not just intellectually satisfying for him, though it was that; it was also, practically speaking, indispensable to moral economic progress. Law must serve the marketplace without being overwhelmed by it. By Story's reckoning only judges trained in the science of the common law could guarantee that this would happen."

See NEWMYER, *supra* note 83, at 137–138.

ing to challenge Coke on the basis of admiralty jurisdiction. Continental traditions, the dictates of commerce, and common sense compel the conclusion that admiralty jurisdiction should depend upon *subject-matter,* not geography. He is thus able to treat marine insurance as a matter for the admiralty, despite the fact that it was not within of the English High Court's cognizance, nor, generally speaking, within that of American admiralty courts before 1789.[112] Similarly, contracts of a purely maritime nature—charterparties, ship's articles etc.—are within the cognizance of the admiralty, irrespective of whether they were signed at sea, on foreign soil, or in a county of one of the United States. Nevertheless, he stops short of maintaining that *all* contracts with a maritime component also sound in admiralty.[113] More importantly, he stops short of asserting that all water-borne commerce is subject to federal admiralty and maritime jurisdiction. His motives clearly are not respect for the statutes of Richard II; he is all too ready to dispense with them when their application would make the court's cognizance over a charterparty depend on where it was signed. Nevertheless, neither the medieval maritime codes nor English practice had extended admiralty jurisdiction into fresh water above the ebb and flow of the tide. While ready to innovate in other contexts, Story

112. Contracts of marine insurance were triable in the High Court of Admiralty during the Tudor period under 32 Hen. VIII, c. 14. *See* Thomas Lambert Mears, "The History of the Admiralty Jurisdiction", *in* Select Essays in Anglo-American Legal History: Volume II (Boston: Little, Brown & Co., 1908) at 358. In 1601, cases involving marine insurance were assigned briefly to their own tribunal; subsequently the common law assumed this jurisdiction. *See* M. J. Pritchard & D. E. C. Yale, Hale and Fleetwood on Admiralty Jurisdiction (London: Publications of the Selden Society, Vol. 108, 1993) at lxxxi. It is worth noting that Story's interest in uniformity was not limited to the general maritime law. While some cases of marine insurance were tried in federal court as admiralty cases, most were heard as diversity cases. In either event, the substantive rules applied were the same. Rather than looking to state law, as Section 34 of the Judiciary Act required, Story and his brethren decided these cases under the "general common law"—*i.e.* the commercial law of the nation's trading partners adapted for use in the federal courts. For discussion *see* Fletcher, *supra* note 53, at 1553; *see also Peele v. Merchants' Insurance Company* (Case No. 10,905), 19 F. Cas. 98 (Story, J., C. C., D. Mass., 1822).

113. As Fletcher explains:

> "[Story] never suggested that cases arising out of commercial contracts between merchants engaged in interstate or international trade by water, or out of negotiable instruments used in such trade, were cognizable in admiralty."

Fletcher, *supra* note 53, at 1552 n. 195, *citing Plummer v. Webb* (Case No. 11,233), 19 F. Cas. 891, 894 (Story, J., C. C., D. Maine, 1827) (stating: "In cases of a mixed nature it is not sufficient foundation for admiralty jurisdiction, that there are involved some ingredients of a maritime nature. The substance of the whole contract must be maritime.")

hesitates to claim for the federal courts the power to hear cases arising out of the nation's burgeoning commerce on the western rivers and the Great Lakes.

Brown Water: Inland Navigation in the Antebellum Republic

For Alexis de Tocqueville, the United States' sheer size was almost incomprehensible. Of the Trans-Appalachian interior he wrote: "The valley of the Mississippi is, on the whole, the most magnificent dwelling-place prepared by God for man's abode; and yet it may be said that at present it is but a mighty desert."[114] America's early growth had been confined to the coast with good reason. Given the technology of the time, overland transportation of goods was generally impractical, and it was scarcely better for travelers. Only by water could people travel quickly and in comparative comfort. For goods, carriage by water was often the only cost-effective means of transporting them to distant markets. Fortunately, America's interior had been provided with one of the world's largest systems of navigable rivers and tributaries. As Tocqueville observed:

> Sometimes quietly gliding along the chalky bed that nature has assigned to it, sometimes swollen by freshets, the Mississippi waters over 1,032 leagues in its course. At a distance if 600 leagues from its mouth this river attains an average depth of 15 feet; and it is navigated by vessels of 300 tons for a course of nearly 200 leagues. One counts, among the tributaries of the Mississippi, one river of 1,300 leagues, one of 900, one of 600, one of 500, and four of 200, not to speak of a countless multitude of small streams that rush from all directions to mingle in its flow.[115]

In the early years, Americans made use of the rivers for transportation by floating flatboats laden with goods and agricultural products downstream. The trip upstream, however, was more arduous, accomplished by propelling keelboats against the current by human power, with or without the assistance of

---

114. Tocqueville, *supra* note 26, at 19.

115. *Id.* at 18–19. Tocqueville's estimate for the Mississippi's length in miles is approximately 2,500. The four larger tributaries to which he refers are the Missouri, the Arkansas, the Red River, and the Ohio. The four smaller tributaries are the Illinois, the St. Pierre, the St. Francis, and the Des Moines. According to modern estimates, the Mississippi River Basin contained more than 16,000 miles of navigable rivers. *See* Haites, Mak, & Walton, *supra* note 14, at 12.

draft animals.[116] By 1817, however, the first commercially successful steamboat began operations on the western rivers.[117] Within a generation, steam had entirely transformed river-transportation[118]—and in doing so transformed also the Trans-Appalachian West. As Tocqueville noted in his journal: "There isn't any one who does not recognize that the development of steam has added unbelievably to the strength and prosperity of the Union, and has done so by facilitating rapid communications between diverse parts of this vast body."[119] Success of western steamboats mirrored the success of the nation's economy. From the 1820s onwards, one can use the increases and decreases in active tonnage as a surrogate for measuring the West's economic booms and recessions.[120] Most revealing, however, is the correlation between the rise of the steamboat and the growth of population in the West. Before the advent of steam power, the Trans-Appalachian West had scarcely two million inhabitants; by 1860 that number had grown to thirteen million.[121] During that same period, from 1820–1860, the size of the steamboat fleet on the western rivers burgeoned from 14,208 tons to 195,022 tons,[122] thus forming a significant portion of total American commercial tonnage.[123]

---

116. For a detailed account of the economic importance of flatboats and keelboats on western rivers through the 1840s, *see* Haites, Mak, & Walton, *supra* note 14, at 14–15, 19–22.

117. *Id.* at 18.

118. Until the advent of steam, flatboats were unchallenged in carriage of goods downstream, and downstream freight had a ten-fold advantage over upstream freight. By 1840, estimates indicate that flatboats accounted for only 20% of all downstream freight. *Id.* at 20–21. Samuel Clemens, who as a young man working on the river was an eyewitness and a participant in the steamboat's replacement of the flatboat and keelboat, remarks that the steamboat "killed the old-fashioned keel-boating, by reducing the freight-trip to New Orleans to less than a week." Mark Twain, Life on the Mississippi (1st ed. 1883; *reprinted* New York: Library of America, 1982) at 367.

119. *See* Tocqueville's journals, *published in* Pierson, *supra* note 26, at 590.

120. Haites, Mak, & Walton, *supra* note 14, at 23–24. Citing "significant fluctuations in annual construction" of steamboats, the authors note: "Strikingly, this timing closely parallels the expansion and contraction of general economic activity in the West."

121. During the same period, growth of population in other parts of the nation was steady but not nearly of the scale experienced in the West. The nation as a whole had more than tripled its population from 1820 to 1860, increasing to nearly thirty-two million. *Id.* at 111–113.

122. *Id.*, Appendix A, at 130–131.

123. Albion gives the total registered, licensed, and enrolled blue-water tonnage of the United States as 1,280,000 tons in 1820 and 5,353,000 tons in 1860. Of these 867,000 tons were steamships in 1860. Figures for tonnage of steamships are not available for 1820. In 1828, the earliest year for which figures are available, 39,000 out of 1,741,000 total regis-

First secured by treaty in 1794,[124] and later permanently established through the Louisiana Purchase,[125] free navigation of the Mississippi was essential for putting western lands to profitable use. The Framers understood its importance; amid heated debates on the structure of government, the delegates occasionally turned their attention to free navigation of the Mississippi.[126] The advent of the steamboat intensified interest in the River and its navigable tributaries. No longer would the rivers merely provide a means of carrying agricultural products to market in New Orleans; self-propelled vessels could take goods upstream, thus opening new markets for Eastern manufactures. Steamboat-navigation was of sufficient importance in 1812 that the Virginia legislature selected John Marshall—then serving as Chief Justice of the Supreme Court—to lead a surveying expedition to the headwaters of the James River in order to ascertain whether it would be feasible to link the river by turnpike with a tributary of the Ohio.[127] Early on, the federal government assumed responsibility for improvements in navigation on the western rivers. Despite some controversy over the constitutionality of spending federal funds on repairing roads and building canals, even strict-constructionist Republicans conceded that such legislation was within the power of Congress, and President Monroe signed a bill authorizing surveys of the Ohio and Mississippi. Thereafter for the next twenty years, it was a rare appropriations bill that lacked a provision for improving the western rivers.[128] Considering the fairly small sums invested, the results were remarkable.[129] Active tonnage on the western

---

tered, licensed, or enrolled tons were steamships. *See* ALBION, NEW YORK PORT, *supra* note 14, Appendix at 402–405.

124. For discussion of the Pinckney Treaty of 1794, which opened the Mississippi to American navigation, *see* WILLIAM CASTO, THE SUPREME COURT IN THE EARLY REPUBLIC: THE CHIEF JUSTICESHIPS OF JOHN JAY AND OLIVER ELLSWORTH (Columbia: University of South Carolina Press, 1995) at 109.

125. For discussion, *see* SMITH, JOHN MARSHALL, *supra* note 50, at 318.

126. For discussion, *see Id.* at 119. *See also* THE RECORDS OF THE FEDERAL CONVENTION OF 1787 (Max Farrand ed., New Haven: Yale University Press, 1966), Vol. I, Debates of July 11, at 579 (Mason), at 585 (Madison), at 604 (G. Morris); Vol. II, Debates of Aug. 28, at 442 (G. Morris), Debates of Sept. 8, at 548 (G. Morris).

127. For discussion, *see* SMITH, JOHN MARSHALL, *supra* note 50, at 411–412.

128. Between 1824 and 1844, Congress appropriated $2,500,000, much of which was spent on removing "snags" (obstructions in the channels) and preventing the accumulation of bars. *See* HUNTER, *supra* note 14, at 190–205.

129. Opinion is divided on the extent to which federal expenditures actually aided the development of Western river transportation. In contrast to Hunter, HAITES, MAK, & WALTON, *supra* note 14, at 95–99, paint a less optimistic picture, noting that the level of appropriations dipped after 1839: "The river improvements had been yielding ever greater

rivers increased dramatically.[130] In a few short years, the steamboat had evolved from a blue-water craft adapted to inland use into a highly specialized vessel designed for maximum carrying capacity with a minimal draft. This was not radical innovation of the kind found on the drawing-boards of John Ericsson. The distinctive "wedding-cake" designs, ideally suited to the function that the boats were to serve, were instead largely the product of the practical experience and trial-and-error methods of Western entrepreneurs with little training in shipbuilding. Similarly, the engines were well-designed for their purpose. While ocean-going low-pressure steam engines were often unreliable and wasteful of fuel, the simply-designed high-pressure engines of the Western steamers were comparatively powerful and easy to maintain—even for an engineer with little formal training or experience.[131]

The impact of the rivers as avenues of commerce should not be underestimated. Inland navigation was largely responsible for integrating the nation's Eastern and Western economies.[132] Availability of inexpensive transportation made Western agricultural products competitive on Eastern markets, thereby enhancing farmers' profits, encouraging development of additional arable land, and giving Eastern consumers the benefit of lower prices for staple foods.[133] In the words of one modern commentary: "the river system...was the dominant medium until 1845 and was an integral part of the transportation network throughout the entire ante-bellum period".[134] As dominant as

---

economic dividends as western commerce grew; yet the efforts to maintain the rivers after 1838 were only sporadic." *Id.* at 97. The authors produce a table showing total appropriations for improvements by year. *Id.* at 96.

130. Haites, Mak, and Walton observe: "total annual tonnage in operation on all rivers had expanded a hefty forty-three fold from the first tentative decade of steamboat operations to the last decade of the ante-bellum period." *Id.* at 23.

131. Hunter, an engineer before becoming an economic historian, gives very detailed attention to the design of the high-pressure engines, noting both their power and ease of repair—as well as their unfortunate propensity to explode if not properly maintained. *See* Hunter, *supra* note 14, at 61–62, 108–113, 122–126, 142–153, 162, 175–180. For design of hulls, *see Id.* at 65–89.

132. Haites, Mak, & Walton, *supra* note 14, at 114, conclude:

> "As transportation developments more solidly linked its regions to the seaboard and abroad, the West evolved into an important segment of the national and international economy. Although economic unification on a national scale was far from complete in the early nineteenth century, considerable progress had been achieved fairly early in the commodity markets."

133. *Id.* at 117. For statistics on the increase in acres of Western farm-land by decade and the impact on wholesale prices of agricultural products, *see Id.* at 115–116.

134. *Id.* at 88.

they were, riverboats were only a portion of the West's growing system of transportation in the first decades of the nineteenth century. While railroads later provided competition and eventually would replace rivers as the conduit of Western commerce, in the early period the industries were complimentary, with the infant railroads actually expanding traffic on the rivers.[135] Moreover, inland transportation was not restricted to the Mississippi and its tributaries. Commercial navigation of the Great Lakes was expanding as rapidly as that on the rivers. By 1853, the tonnage of steam-powered vessels on inland waters, including the Great Lakes, exceeded the total steam-tonnage engaged in the interstate coastal trade, and inland vessels employed fifty percent more men than the coastal steamers.[136]

As important as the Supreme Court's opinion in *Gibbons v. Ogden*[137] was for establishing parameters for both Congress and the states in regulating commerce, often underestimated is its impact on inland navigation—and thus indirectly upon the century's next major struggle over the powers of the federal government *vis-à-vis* those of the states. Shortly after the Court declared New York's monopoly in interstate steamboat-service unconstitutional, entrepreneurs rushed in to take advantage of free competition, and soon the route between New Jersey and New York was saturated with new carriers. It was much the same on other routes as well.[138] With the level of traffic ever expanding on the nation's inland waters, it was only a matter of time before claimants would begin to characterize their claims as matters within the ambit of federal admiralty jurisdiction.

---

135. *Id.* at 120, Appendix at 131.

136. *See* Israel D. Andrews, Report on the Trade and Commerce of the British North American Colonies, and upon the Trade of the Great Lakes and Rivers (Sen. Exec. Doc. 112, 1853) at 49–52.

137. *Gibbons v. Ogden*, 9 U. S. 1 (Marshall, C. J., 1824). For discussion of the case *see e.g.* Smith, John Marshall, *supra* note 50, at 473–480; Morgan, *supra* note 48, at 190–192, 202–206 (concentrating on analysis of Justice Johnson's concurring opinion); Hutchins, *supra* note 27, at 329.

138. For discussion of the public's favorable response to the Court's decision and perception of it as a great benefit to commerce, *see* Smith, John Marshall, *supra* note 50, at 480–481. By 1825, the New York Court of Errors ended steamboat monopolies in intrastate commerce as well. *See* Albion, *supra* note 14, at 153. For a detailed examination of the facts behind the case, as well the decision's impact on navigation in New York's rivers, *see Id.* at 151–153.

Federal Jurisdiction over Inland Waters

The statutes of Richard II had grounded admiralty jurisdiction firmly in geography. Courts of admiralty were to exercise cognizance only over those matters arising aboard ships at sea or "hovering in the main stream of the great Rivers, only beneath the Bridges of the same rivers nigh to the Sea".[139] Some colonies, and later some states, conveniently had ignored the restriction as it related to contracts signed on land, reasoning that as the subject-matter was related to maritime commerce, so also the jurisdiction should properly be vested in a court of admiralty.[140] In the antebellum period, the federal judiciary concurred. Whether the statutes retained any vitality with regard to inland navigation was quite another matter. Some states under the Articles of Confederation had recognized the medieval limitations on admiralty courts—both as to contracts signed on land and as to inland waters. In 1811, the General Assembly of Maryland commissioned a report listing all English statutes that either remained in force in the state or should be considered by the legislature. The report's author, William Kilty, concluded that the statutes of Richard II were "found applicable and proper to be incorporated".[141]

---

139. For texts of the statutes and discussion, *see supra* Chapter I, notes 132–136 and text accompanying.

140. *See supra* Chapter II, notes 194–203 and text accompanying; *see also supra* Chapter III, notes 24–26, 46 and text accompanying.

141. William Kilty, A Report of All Such English Statutes as Existed at the Time of the First Emigration of the People of Maryland, and Which by Experience Have Been Found Applicable to Their Local and Other Circumstances; And of Such Others as Have Been Made in England or Great-Britain, and Have Been Introduced, Used and Practiced by the Courts of Law or Equity; And Also All Such Parts of the Same as May Be Proper to Be Introduced and Incorporated into the Statute Law of the State (Annapolis: Jehu Chandler, 1811) at 223–224. Despite Chancellor Kilty's recommendation, by 1811 the issue of incorporating the statutes of Richard II was moot in practice if not necessarily in theory. The last judge of the state's admiralty court, Benjamin Nicholson, received in 1777 an appointment to serve "during good behavior". After the ratification of the Constitution, the court received no further cases, and the governor and council treated the office—as well as the court itself—as abolished. At the same time, they discontinued payments of Nicholson's salary; Nicholson resigned in December of 1790. Two years later, the heirs of the recently deceased judge filed an action in the General Court to recover the salary unpaid from 1789 through 1790. Surprisingly, the court granted relief, lending credence to Nicholson's contention that the Constitution did not abolish state courts of admiralty, but instead merely relegated them to hearing maritime cases in which both parties were residents of the same state. *See Administratrix of Nicholson v. Maryland*, 3 H. & McH. 109 (1792). Nevertheless, as a practical matter, Maryland never appointed a judge to replace Nicholson, and the state's admiralty

In England, the statutes of Richard II merely reflected the local geography. Very few English rivers were navigable above the ebb and flow of the tide, and those that were, were not customarily navigated by vessels engaged in foreign or coastal commerce.[142] Early in America's history, observers had remarked on the geographic differences between it and the mother country. William Penn in particular expressed alarm over the prospect of vice admiralty courts trying revenue cases arising on colonial rivers, which in places reached a width of three miles more than one hundred miles upstream from the ocean. The rivers, he reasoned, were the principal avenues of communication and transportation in America. Most activities were in some manner connected to them, and Penn feared that the extension of vice admiralty jurisdiction over them would deprive colonists of juries in virtually all legal proceedings.[143] While his fears of admiralty courts absorbing the courts of common law proved unfounded, his observations on the importance of jurisdiction over inland waters was prophetic. Most of the population and its commercial activities remained near navigable water in the nineteenth century. Moreover, changes in technology made rivers "navigable" from their mouths both upstream and downstream and blurred the distinction between blue-water and brown-water commerce. To practical men of business, a legal distinction based upon where a vessel had committed a tort—on the ocean or upstream on a river—was meaningless so long as one were speaking of the same ship on the same voyage. At issue was whether the federal courts would agree with them.

Despite expansion of the general maritime law in the early decades of the nineteenth century, not all federal judges were proponents of an expanded ad-

---

court never again convened. Thus it appears inexplicable that Kilty would recommend that the state adopt two English statutes limiting the jurisdiction of a court that no longer existed. For discussion, *see* Judge Emory H. Niles, The Revolutionary Court of Admiralty of the State of Maryland 1776–1779, Address Before the Lawyers' Round Table, Maryland Club, Baltimore (Dec. 8, 1941) (transcript available in the Maryland Historical Society Library).

142. *See* David W. Robertson, Admiralty and Federalism (Mineola, New York: Foundation Press, 1970) at 106 (hereinafter Robertson, Admiralty and Federalism).

143. Petition of William Penn to Privy Council, *reprinted in* Winfred Trexler Root, The Relations of Pennsylvania with the British Government, 1696–1765 (New York: D. Appleton & Co. for University of Pennsylvania Press, 1912) at 97. As the proposed courts were to enforce the Navigation Act of 1694, a power not granted to the High Court of Admiralty, the statutes of Richard II did not apply—at least with regard to the courts' jurisdiction to hear revenue cases arising on colonial rivers. For the context of Penn's remarks, *see supra* Chapter II, notes 81–84 and text accompanying.

miralty jurisdiction. William Johnson, a Jefferson-appointee in 1804, nevertheless had shown himself amenable to defending broad federal powers to regulate commerce in a strong concurring opinion in *Gibbons v. Ogden*.[144] On the issue of expanded admiralty jurisdiction, however, he was more reticent, once warning in dissent against "this silent and stealing progress of the Admiralty in acquiring jurisdiction to which it has no pretensions."[145] Nevertheless, generally speaking Joseph Story shared little of Johnson's fears of an ever-growing admiralty jurisdiction depriving Americans of their right to a trial by jury. In *DeLovio*, Story had argued that the scope of admiralty jurisdiction recognized in America in colonial times was broader than that granted to the High Court of Admiralty.[146] The statutes of Richard II are thus inapplicable as regards maritime contracts, jurisdiction over which is properly grounded in

---

144. For discussion of Johnson's concurring opinion in *Gibbons v. Ogden*, 9 U. S. 1 (Marshall, C. J., 1824), *see* Morgan, *supra* note 48, at 190–192, 202–206; *see also* discussion *supra* note 137 and text accompanying).

145. *Ramsay v. Allegre*, 25 U. S. 611, 614 (1827). Johnson makes his statement in the context of an admiralty action *in personam* by a home-port materialman against a shipowner for the cost of repairs. The materialman had accepted a promisory note, which for the majority moves the matter out of admiralty and into the cognizance of the common law. While concurring in the outcome, namely that the materialman was unable to recover in admiralty, Johnson disagrees with the implicit assumption that in the absence of the promisory note the outcome would have been different. He concludes:

> "I am fortifying a weak point in the wall of the constitution. Every advance of the admiralty is a victory over the common law; a conquest gained upon the trial by jury.... Once establish the rights here claimed, and it may bring back with it all the Admiralty usurpations of the fifteenth [*sic*] century. In England there exists a controlling power, but here there is none. Congress has, indeed, given a power to issue prohibitions to a District Court, when transcending the limits of the Admiralty jurisdiction. But who is to issue a prohibition to us, if we should ever be affected with a partiality for that jurisdiction? I, therefore, hold, that we are under a peculiar obligation to restrain the Admiralty jurisdiction within its proper limits."

Id. at 640.

146. *See DeLovio v. Boit* (Case No. 3,776), 7 F. Cas. 418, 442 (C. C., D. Mass., 1815), contending that the statutes of Richard II, which bound the High Court of Admiralty, did not similarly bind the vice admiralty courts:

> "The commissions of the crown gave the courts, which were established, a most ample jurisdiction over all maritime contracts, and over torts and injuries, as well in ports as upon the high seas. And acts of parliament enlarged, or rather recognized, this jurisdiction by giving or confirming cognizance of all seizures for contraventions of the revenue laws.... Tested, therefore, by this exposition, the admiralty jurisdiction of the United States would be as large, as its most strenuous advocates ever contended for."

their subject-matter, not the fortuitous *loci* of their signing. Given Story's broad conception of admiralty jurisdiction, his opinion in *The Thomas Jefferson* continues to provoke surprise. The facts were uncomplicated. Members of the crew of a steamboat plying the Missouri libelled the vessel in federal court for unpaid wages; the respondent contended that the court lacked jurisdiction. Ultimately, the matter reached the Supreme Court, where Story, writing for the majority, held that a federal court could not entertain an action *in rem* against a vessel engaged in fresh-water commerce.[147] On first glance, it appears that Story has reversed his position on the archaic English acts, but on closer examination, his opinion pays no more regard to the statutes of Richard II than does *DeLovio*:

> In the great struggles between the Courts of common law and the Admiralty, the latter never attempted to assert any jurisdiction except over maritime contracts. In respect to contracts for the hire of seamen, the Admiralty never pretended to claim, nor could it rightfully exercise any jurisdiction, except in cases where the service was substantially performed, or to be performed, upon the sea, or upon waters within the ebb and flow of the tide. This was the prescribed limit which it was not at liberty to transcend. We say, the service was to be substantially performed upon the sea, or on tide water, because there is no doubt that the jurisdiction exists, although the commencement or termination of the voyage may happen to be at some place beyond the reach of the tide. The material consideration is, whether the service is essentially a maritime service. In the present case, the voyage, not only in its commencement and termination, but in all its intermediate progress, was several hundreds of miles above the ebb and flow of the tide; and in no just sense can the wages be considered as earned in maritime employment.[148]

For Story, there is no talismanic significance in place of performance. If a voyage begins or ends in fresh water above the ebb and flow of the tide, it may nevertheless be subject to admiralty jurisdiction. As with all other forms of maritime contracts, subject-matter controls jurisdiction. Nonetheless, "maritime" in Story's mind is limited to ocean-borne commerce. The ancient law, the medieval codes, the English High Court of Admiralty at the height of its powers, and the modern Continental commentators all defined it as such, and Story re-

147. *The Thomas Jefferson*, 23 U. S. 428, 429 (Story, J., 1825).
148. *Id.* at 430.

fuses to tamper with their definition.[149] He does, however, raise an interesting point in *dicta*. If "some act of Congress had extended the right to sue in courts having admiralty jurisdiction" to such cases under the Commerce Clause, the grant of jurisdiction would pass constitutional muster.[150] While Story followed his own opinion in *The Thomas Jefferson* in similar cases,[151] at the request of members of Congress he drafted an act extending federal admiralty jurisdiction to vessels engaged in interstate commerce on lakes "and the navigable waters connecting such lakes".[152] Congress approved his completed draft within six days, and it was signed into law by President Tyler on February 26, 1845.[153]

---

149. One modern commentator speculates that the composition of the Court and politics of the time may have influenced Story's opinion, forcing him to appease states-rights advocates by cloaking his opinion in a convenient definition of "maritime". *See* Robertson, Admiralty and Federalism, *supra* note 142, at 106–107.

150. *The Thomas Jefferson*, 23 U. S. 428, 430.

151. *See e.g. United States v. Coombs*, 37 U. S. 72, 76 (Story, J., 1838), noting: "Our opinion is, that in cases purely dependent upon the locality of the act done, it is limited to the sea, and to tide waters, as far as the tide flows; and that it does not reach beyond high water mark. It is the doctrine which has been repeatedly asserted by this Court and we see no reason to depart from it."

152. An Act Extending the Jurisdiction of the District Courts of the United States to Certain Cases Upon the Lakes and Navigable Water Connecting the Same, 5 Stat. 726 (1845). The act states:

> "[T]he district courts of the United States shall have, possess, and exercise, the same jurisdiction in matters of contract and tort, arising in, upon, or concerning, steamboats and other vessels of twenty tons burden and upwards, enrolled and licensed for the coasting trade, and at the time employed in business of commerce and navigation between ports and places in different States and Territories upon the lakes and navigable waters connecting said lakes, as is now possessed and exercised by the said courts in cases of the like steamboats and other vessels employed in navigation and commerce upon the high seas, or tide waters, within the admiralty and maritime jurisdiction of the United States; and in all suits brought in such courts in all such matters of contract or tort, the remedies, and the forms of process, and the modes of proceeding, shall be the same as are or may be used by such courts in cases of admiralty and maritime jurisdiction; and the maritime law of the United States, so far as the same is or may be applicable thereto, shall constitute the rule of decision in such suits, in the same manner, and to the same extent, and with the same equities, as it now does in cases of admiralty and maritime jurisdiction; saving, however, to the parties the right of trial by jury of all facts put in issue in such suits, where either party shall require it; and saving also to the parties the right of a concurrent remedy at the common law, where it is competent to give it, and any concurrent remedy which may be given by the State laws, where such steamer or other vessel is employed in such business of commerce and navigation."

153. *See* Robertson, Admiralty and Federalism, *supra* note 142, at 111–112.

In the interim, the Supreme Court continued to grapple with the implications of the "tide-water doctrine" announced in *The Thomas Jefferson*. In *Peyroux v. Howard* ("*The Planter*"), the Court addressed the issue of whether a materialman could maintain an action in admiralty for services rendered to a steamboat at the port of New Orleans. The port, though accessible to ocean-going and inland steamers alike, was located substantially above the ebb and flow of the tide in the conventional meaning of the words.[154] Nonetheless, the Court took judicial notice of the tide's subtle impact on the Mississippi and found it within the ambit of admiralty jurisdiction:

> We think that although the current in the Mississippi, at New Orleans, may be so strong as not to be turned backwards by the tide; yet if the effect of the tide upon the current is so great as to occasion a regular rise and fall of the water, it may properly be said to be within the ebb and flow of the tide.[155]

After even a casual perusing of the opinion, it is easy to understand why Justice Johnson would decry "the silent and stealing progress of the admiralty" in expanding its jurisdiction. It is difficult to believe that the Court itself took *The Planter's* sophistry seriously. The question of jurisdiction was made to turn upon whether published scientific reference works could identify any measurable effect of the tide upon a particular body of fresh water. As with the "Cheapside fiction" of Sir Edward Coke's time, it served the practical function of allowing a court to establish jurisdiction over a case by satisfying a legal prerequisite, even if the method for satisfying it was dubious at best. This solution obviously was not adequate in the long run, and eventually the Court would be forced to face the issue of jurisdiction over inland waters head-on.

By the time that *The Genesee Chief* came before the Court, its composition differed greatly from that which had decided *The Thomas Jefferson* more than twenty years earlier. William Johnson had died in 1834, and was replaced on the bench by James Wayne of Georgia.[156] Roger Taney, whose appointment to the court as associate justice had been thwarted by the Senate in 1835, received confirmation the following year to replace John Marshall as Chief Justice.[157]

---

154. *Peyroux v. Howard*, 32 U. S. 324, 340–342 (Thompson, J., 1833).

155. *Id.* at 343. The published source of which Justice Thompson took judicial notice was *Stoddard's Louisiana*.

156. *See* Smith, John Marshall, *supra* note 50, at 521.

157. President Jackson originally had submitted the name of the former Federalist to the Senate as a replacement for Justice Duvall, but the Senate narrowly declined to confirm Taney's appointment. Taney's service as Attorney General, in which capacity he worked with Jackson

Joseph Story's last significant act on behalf of American admiralty law had been the drafting of the 1845 statute; he had died in September of that same year.[158] Nonetheless, the Court's new membership[159] initially did little to change the scope of American admiralty jurisdiction. Justice Wayne's 1846 opinion in *Waring v. Clarke* largely mirrored *Peyroux v. Howard* on the issue of tide-waters, accepting the trial court's finding that a bayou ninety-five miles upstream from New Orleans and two hundred miles from the sea was in fact affected by the tide.[160] This would change with the *Genesee Chief v. Fitzhugh.*[161] In May of 1847, the steamer "*Genesee Chief*" struck the schooner "*Cuba*", sending her to the bottom of Lake Ontario together with her cargo of six thousand bushels of wheat. The owners of the *Cuba* filed their claim *in rem* in federal court, grounding the court's jurisdiction in Story's jurisdictional statute of 1845.[162] Chief Justice Taney delivered the opinion of the Court.

Recognizing the inherent impracticality of the rule established by *Peyroux v. Howard* and *Waring v. Clarke,*[163] Taney seeks to examine the origins of the

---

to dissolve the Bank of the United States, had made him politically unacceptable to many senators. When Marshall died a few months later, Jackson again submitted his name to the Senate, this time for confirmation as Chief Justice. Despite some political difficulties, Taney was confirmed to fill the vacant Chief Justiceship in March of 1836. *See* CARL B. SWISHER, THE TANEY PERIOD, 1836–1864, VOLUME V *in* THE OLIVER WENDELL HOLMES DEVISE: HISTORY OF THE SUPREME COURT OF THE UNITED STATES (New York: Macmillan Publishing Co., 1974) at 15–38 (hereinafter SWISHER); SMITH, JOHN MARSHALL, *supra* note 50, at 521–522.

158. *See* NEWMYER, *supra* note 83, at 381–382.

159. Justices of the Supreme Court at the time of Taney's appointment were Smith Thompson (the author of *Peyroux v. Howard*), James M. Wayne (who had replaced Duvall), John McClean, Henry Baldwin, Phillip Barbour, and Joseph Story. The following year, the membership of the court was increased to nine, and John Catron and John McKinley ascended to the bench. Peter Daniel replaced Barbour upon the latter's death in 1841, and Justices Grier, Nelson, and Woodbury had replaced Baldwin, Thompson, and Story by the time the court addressed the issue of maritime jurisdiction in *Waring v. Clarke*, 46 U. S. 441 (Wayne, J., 1846). *See* SWISHER, *supra* note 157, at 39, 437.

160. *Waring v. Clarke*, 46 U. S. 441 (Wayne, J., 1846). The tort that provided the basis for the case occurred in 1843, two years before passage of the jurisdictional statute, and there is some question as to whether the bayou upon which the collision had occurred would have been within the 1845 statute's ambit. For discussion of the case, *see supra* Chapter III, notes 2–8 and text accompanying.

161. *The Genesee Chief v. Fitzhugh*, 53 U. S. 443 (1851).

162. *Id.* at 460–463.

163. As Taney explains:

> "But [*Waring v. Clarke*] showed the unreasonableness of giving a construction to the Constitution which would measure the jurisdiction of the admiralty by the tide. For if such be the construction, then a line drawn across the Mississippi

assumption that admiralty jurisdiction ended with the ebb and flow of the tides. In England, he admits that the restriction was "a sound and reasonable one, because there was no navigable stream in the country beyond the ebb and flow of the tide; nor any place where a port could be established to carry on trade with a foreign nation, and where vessels could enter or depart with cargoes." Thus he concludes that in England "tide water and navigable water are *synonymous terms*, and tide-water, with a few small and unimportant exceptions, meant nothing more than *public rivers*..."[164] Such was not the case in the United States in the 1850s:

> At the time the Constitution of the United States was adopted..., in the States which were at that period in any degree commercial, and where courts of admiralty were called on to exercise their jurisdiction, every public river was tide-water to the head of navigation. And indeed, *until the discovery of steamboats, there could be nothing like foreign commerce upon waters with an unchanging current resisting the upward passage.* The courts of the United States therefore, naturally adopted the English mode of defining a public river, and consequently the boundary of admiralty jurisdiction. It measured it by tide-water.... *[T]he public character of the river was in process of time lost sight of, and the jurisdiction of the admiralty treated as if it was limited by the tide.* The description of a public navigable river was substituted in place of the thing intended to be described.[165]

Thus Taney rejects the notion that the language "admiralty and maritime" by definition incorporates the tide-water limitation, implicitly assuming the jurisdictional limits of "admiralty and maritime" to be a nation's *navigable public waters* and the high seas. Turning to the proper measure of admiralty jurisdiction, he reasons that if Congress were empowered to ground admiralty and maritime jurisdiction as established by the Judiciary Act of 1789 in "the navigable character of the water", so too should it be constitutional for Con-

---

> would limit the jurisdiction, although there were ports of entry above it, and the water as deep and navigable, and the commerce as rich, and exposed to the same hazards and incidents, as the commerce below. The distinction would be purely artificial and arbitrary as well as unjust, and would make the Constitution of the United States subject one part of a public river to the jurisdiction of a court of the United States, and deny it to another part equally public but a few yards distant."

Id. at 456–457.

164. *Id.* at 454–455 (*emphasis added*).

165. *Id.* at 455 (*emphasis added*).

gress to extend that jurisdiction inland through the act of 1845.[166] To deflect anticipated criticisms from advocates of states' rights, Taney adds that the act of 1845 provides both for concurrent state/federal jurisdiction and for the empanelling of a jury at the request of either party.[167]

Unfortunately the jurisdictional act of 1845 did not cover all inland waters. During the same term in which the Court decided *The Genesee Chief*, the justices also heard *Fretz v. Bull.* On a portion of the Mississippi well above the ebb and flow of the tide, a steamboat had collided with a flatboat, with the loss of the latter and its cargo.[168] As the river was neither a lake nor a river connected to a lake, the act of 1845 did not apply. Nonetheless, Justice Wayne reasoned that *The Genesee Chief* held that "the constitutional jurisdiction of the United States in admiralty was not limited by the tide-water, but was extended to the lakes and navigable rivers of the United States."[169] Implicitly, the decision rested upon the Judiciary Act of 1789, in which the jurisdiction is defined simply as "admiralty and maritime"—a phrase borrowed from the Constitu-

---

166. *Id.* at 457–458. As Taney concludes:

> "We have therefore the opinion of the legislative department of the government, twice deliberately expressed, upon the subject. These opinions of course are not binding on the judicial department, but they are always entitled to high respect. And in this instance we think they are founded in truth and reason; and that these laws are both constitutional, and ought therefore to be carried into execution. The jurisdiction under both laws is confined to vessels enrolled and licensed for the coasting trade; and the act of 1845 extends only to such vessels when they are engaged in commerce between different States or territories. It does not apply to vessels engaged in domestic commerce of a State; not to vessels or boats not enrolled and licensed for the coasting trade under the authority of Congress. And the State courts within the limits embraced by this [1845] law exercise a concurrent jurisdiction in all cases arising within their respective territories, as broadly and independently as it is exercised by the old thirteen States, (whose rivers are tide-waters,) and where the admiralty jurisdiction has been in full force ever since the adoption of the Constitution."

Id. at 458.

167. Taney adds:

> "But the act of Congress of which we are speaking...saves to the party a concurrent remedy at common law in any court of the United States or of a State which may be competent to give it. But it goes farther. It secures to the parties the trial by jury as a matter of right in the admiralty courts. Either party may demand it. And it thus effectively removes the great and leading objection, always heretofore made to the admiralty jurisdiction."

Id. at 459.

168. *Fretz v. Bull*, 53 U. S. 466 (Wayne, J., 1851).

169. *Id.* at 468.

tion itself. Thus for Justice Wayne, Taney's concept of "*navigable public waters*" became penumbral to the Constitution, and his holding in *Fretz v. Bull* opened the federal courts to a substantial class of potential litigants.[170] Six years later, the Court addressed the same issue again, but this time with a new twist. The steamboat "*Magnolia*" collided with the steamer "*Wetumpka*" on the Alabama River. The Alabama, unlike the Mississippi, did not form a boundary between states nor flow through more than one state. Instead it originated in the state from which it took its name and emptied into the Gulf of Mexico; moreover, it remained navigable well above the ebb and flow of the tide.[171]

While Justice Wayne had assumed federal jurisdiction with little discussion in *Fretz v. Bull*, Justice Grier examined the issue in greater detail in *The Magnolia*. The analysis is tripartite. First, he characterizes the Alabama as "a great public river, navigable from the sea many miles above the ebb and flow of the tide", noting further that "[v]essels licensed for the coasting trade, and those engaged in foreign commerce pass on its waters to ports of entry within the State".[172] Second, taking "navigability" as the touchstone for the Constitution's phrase "admiralty and maritime jurisdiction", he asserts that Congress had the power to vest either all or part of this jurisdiction in the lower federal courts.[173] Finally, Grier maintains that the Judiciary Act of 1789, by selecting language identical to that found in Article III, vested in the federal courts the full measure of admiralty jurisdiction permissible under the Constitution:

> But this act [*i.e.* the Judiciary Act of 1789] does not confine admiralty jurisdiction to tide-waters; and if the flux and reflux of the tide be

---

170. For discussion, *see* Richard Henry Dana, Jr., *History of Admiralty Jurisdiction in the Supreme Court of the United States*, 5 Am. L. Rev. 581, 591–592 (1871) (hereinafter Dana, *History of Admiralty Jurisdiction*); Robertson, Admiralty and Federalism, *supra* note 142, at 115–116.

171. *Jackson v. The Steamboat Magnolia*, 61 U.S. 296 (Grier, J., 1857).

172. *Id.* at 297–299.

173. Grier writes:

> "Congress might give any of these courts the whole or so much of the admiralty jurisdiction as it saw fit.... An act of Congress was therefore necessary to confer this jurisdiction on those [inland] waters, and was completely within the constitutional powers of Congress; unless, by some unbending law of nature, fresh-water lakes and rivers are necessarily within the category of those that are not 'navigable', and which, consequently, could not be subjected to 'admiralty jurisdiction', any more than canals or railroads."

Id. at 300–301.

> abandoned, as an arbitrary and false test of "navigable river", it required no further legislation of Congress to extend it to the Mississippi, Alabama, and other great rivers, "navigable from the sea". If the waters over which this jurisdiction is claimed be within this category, the act makes no distinction between them. It is not confined to rivers or waters which bound coterminous States, such as the Mississippi and Ohio, or to rivers passing through more than one State; nor does the act distinguish between them and rivers which rise and pass through one State only, and are consequently "*infra corpus comitatus*".[174]

Thus, Grier concludes, the Court is not extending federal admiralty jurisdiction, but merely recognizing a jurisdiction already constitutionally conferred by the first Congress. Unfortunately, while the conclusion resolves the jurisdictional question before the Court, it raises another in the process. Why had Congress passed the jurisdictional act of 1845, and had not the decision in *The Magnolia* rendered the act superfluous? Grier treats the statute as a reaffirmation of Congress' original intent in 1789, enacted both to overrule *The Thomas Jefferson* and to convince the Court to re-evaluate its recent decisions relating to admiralty jurisdiction over inland waters.[175]

---

174. *Id.* at 301.

175. *Id.* at 302. Subsequent case-law supports Grier's conclusion. With the Supreme Court recognizing the Judiciary Act of 1789 as the basis for admiralty jurisdiction over inland waters, counsel for some parties in the 1860s attempted to argue that the act of 1845 was intended to restrict rather than expand federal admiralty jurisdiction in the Great Lakes. The Supreme Court ultimately rejected this argument in *The Eagle*, 75 U. S. 15 (1868). Author, attorney, and legal scholar Richard Henry Dana provides a good analysis of the effect of the Court's holding:

> "The opinion therefore puts the jurisdiction on the broad ground that the act of 1845 is inoperative to restrict the admiralty jurisdiction allotted to the district courts by the act of 1789. The reasoning is this. Upon principles now settled, the only operation of the act of 1845 would be to restrict, so far as concerned the lakes and their connecting waters, the admiralty jurisdiction the district courts would otherwise have under the act of 1789. Now the act of 1845 was not only entitled 'An act *extending* the jurisdiction,' &c., but had in every part the aspect of an enabling act. It would be a violence to construe it as a restricting and disabling act. The reasons for passing it were well known to be the state of the decisions of the Supreme Court at the time; and, as those decisions were now overruled, and the act shown to be both needless and inoperative as an enabling act, the true course was to treat it as inoperative in all respects."

Dana, *History of Admiralty Jurisdiction*, *supra* note 170, at 600.

Thus in a space of four decades the Supreme Court had expanded the admiralty and maritime jurisdiction to include inland waters. Admittedly, there were still some details to be sorted out, such as how federal law defines "*navigable*"[176] and whether *intrastate* commerce on a river such as the Alabama falls within the jurisdiction of the federal courts.[177] The Court's decisions[178] met with a mixed reception. As early as 1838, steamboat owners and merchants in Louisville had petitioned Congress to extend federal admiralty jurisdiction to western rivers; similar petitions were circulated in the Ohio Valley in 1850. Steamboat owners saw in federal maritime law a means of strengthening the authority of their boats' masters and controlling strikes. A "strike" under state law was a "mutiny" under the general maritime law, subject to legal sanctions.[179] Moreover, the following year, Congress gave the owners an additional reason to lobby for admiralty jurisdiction. Congress passed the Limitation of Liability Act, under which owners could limit their liability in tort to freight pending and the value of the vessel after an accident.[180] Over time, however, the owners found the general maritime law more even-handed than they had expected. While it gave rights to owners unknown under state law, it simultaneously gave rights to labor. "Deck-hands" became "seamen" under federal law. They were, in Joseph Story's phrase, "wards of the admiralty" and were entitled to sign ship's articles. While the law forbade them to strike, they were nonetheless protected from discharge before the end of the voyage named in the articles, a rule that proved irksome to owners accustomed to discharging

---

176. *See Veazie v. Moor*, 55 U. S. 568 (1852) (holding that a state may grant a monopoly to shipowners who improve rivers upstream from waterfalls, as such waters are not "navigable" within the meaning of federal admiralty law); *The Daniel Ball*, 77 U. S. 557, 563 (1870) (stating the general rule that navigable waters are defined as those that "form in their ordinary condition by themselves, or by uniting with other waters, a continued highway over which commerce is or may be carried on with other states or foreign countries in the customary modes in which commerce is conducted by water."). For discussion, *see also* Dana, *History of Admiralty Jurisdiction, supra* note 170, at 593–594.

177. *See The Propeller Commerce* 66 U. S. 574 (1862); *The Belfast*, 74 U. S. 624 (1868). For discussion of the series of cases under which the Supreme Court established that federal admiralty jurisdiction embraces matters arising in intrastate commerce on a river wholly within the boundaries of one state, *see* Dana, *History of Admiralty Jurisdiction, supra* note 170, at 596–598.

178. For a synopsis in outline-form of the scope of federal admiralty and maritime jurisdiction in 1871, *see* Dana, *History of Admiralty Jurisdiction, supra* note 170, at 620–621.

179. *See* Hunter, *supra* note 14, at 474–475.

180. *See* 9 Stat. 635 (1851); for the history of the statute, *see* Joseph C. Sweeney, *Limitation of Shipowner Liability: Its American Roots and Some Problems Particular to Collision*, 32 J. Mar. L. & Com. 241, 246–262 (2001).

crew at any point on a voyage when their cost in wages outweighed their value to the enterprise.[181] Moreover, inland seamen were entitled to maintenance and cure if injured, and they could join together in one proceeding to sue for their wages. As the general maritime law benefited deck-hands in their contractual relationships with steamboat owners, so also it benefited merchants and others doing business with steamboats. Subject to admiralty jurisdiction, a river-boat could be sued *in rem*—a useful procedure where the owners were frequently not aboard nor even present in the state.

By the close of the antebellum period, federal admiralty jurisdiction had reached a scope roughly commensurate with that which it enjoys today. Despite his tireless, life-long efforts to bring order and uniformity to American maritime law, Joseph Story had been unwilling to extend federal admiralty jurisdiction into the nation's interior. On first glance, it is ironic that Story, Republican-turned-Federalist, would limit the federal courts' jurisdiction to the tide-waters, while Taney, Federalist-turned-Jacksonian Democrat, would expand federal admiralty jurisdiction to an unprecedented scope. The irony cannot be explained merely as a difference in political vision. No one believed more strongly in uniform, practical laws serving the interests of private enterprise and national economic growth than did Story. Had he been able to find a way to extend federal jurisdiction to inland waters without violating his understanding of the fundamental structure of maritime law, he would have done so. Similarly, despite serving as Jackson's Attorney General and playing a central role in toppling the Bank of the United States, Taney recognized the importance of brown-water commerce to the nation. His opinion in *The Genesee Chief* makes explicit reference to changes in levels of commerce and to foreign steamships entering America's inland waters. The difference between the two lay instead in their respective approaches to jurisprudence. Story proceeded *inductively*, and finding no precedent for inland jurisdiction either in the United States or abroad, he thus withheld federal admiralty jurisdiction from inland waters. On the other hand, Taney proceeded *deductively*, reasoning that the logical construction of the words "admiralty and maritime" in the act of 1845, the Judiciary Act of 1789, and the Constitution was as a reference to jurisdiction over commerce carried on upon the nation's public navigable waters. Taney's reading did not offend the plain language of Article III, responded to the economic pressures facing the nation, and provided a solution with popular support in its own day.

The pressures of the early nineteenth century were those of a rapidly growing economy, for which maritime commerce and the carrying trades served

---

181. *See* HUNTER, *supra* note 14, at 475–477.

as the principal catalysts for growth. Responding to these pressures was the principal challenge for the federal judiciary in its first seventy years. Predictably, the courts focused first on developing the "general maritime law" in order to fill the gap left by Congress' failure to promulgate a maritime code and second upon expanding the scope of federal admiralty jurisdiction in response to changes in technology and commercial activity. For their time, their solutions worked quite well. Nevertheless, expansion of federal admiralty jurisdiction inland created a larger sphere of concurrent jurisdiction and thus a greater chance of conflict between judge-made federal law and the law of the states. Ironically, so long as the Saving-to-Suitors Clause remained in effect, the expansion of admiralty jurisdiction to fresh water actually posed a threat to the desired goal of uniformity in the general maritime law. Nevertheless, it was not only those cases arising on rivers and lakes that would pit state law against the general maritime law in the coming decades. As Reconstruction gave way first to the Guilded Age and then to the Progressive Era, society became entangled in the struggles between the nation's corporations and the infant organized labor movement. Social reformers also challenged poverty and working conditions spawned by the practices of businesses that had come to maturity in the unregulated world of America's Industrial Revolution. The substantive maritime law, for generations more sympathetic than the common law to the plight of the common seaman, soon found itself less so than the state statutes enacted by Progressive legislatures. Accustomed to small innovations in federal maritime law, soon federal judges would have to decide whether to expand the federal substantive law rapidly to keep pace with state legislatures, and claimants would seek relief in state law—in both state and federal courts—when it afforded more favorable remedies.

Conclusion

"After seventy years of baffling winds and cross currents in the region of admiralty jurisdiction, the Supreme Court of the United States has sailed out into deep water. Before this was accomplished, principles were affirmed, disaffirmed, and re-affirmed, many decisions overruled, a good deal of reasoning corrected, and numerous dicta retracted."

Richard Henry Dana, Jr.[1]

In the decade following the end of the Civil War, a middle-aged Samuel Clemens returned to his boyhood home in Missouri. With *Tom Sawyer* recently completed and the author struggling with the first chapters of *Huckleberry Finn*, he needed time to rest and gather his thoughts. He had not traveled the Mississippi since he had earned a living on it, and he was unprepared for the changes confronting him. As he passed St. Louis aboard a riverboat, he found the city almost unrecognizable:

> [T]he change of changes was on the "levee".... Half a dozen sound-asleep steamboats where I used to see a solid mile of wide-awake ones! This was melancholy, this was woful [*sic*]. The absence of the pervading and jocund steamboatman from the billiard-saloon was explained. He was absent because he is no more. His occupation is gone, his power has passed away, he is absorbed into the common herd, he grinds at the mill, a shorn Samson and inconspicuous. Half a dozen lifeless steamboats, a mile of empty wharves...a wide and soundless vacancy, where the serried hosts of commerce used to contend. Here was desolation, indeed.[2]

---

1. Richard Henry Dana, Jr., *History of Admiralty Jurisdiction in the Supreme Court of the United States*, 5 Am. L. Rev. 581 (1871).

2. Mark Twain, Life on the Mississippi (1st ed. 1883; *reprinted* New York: Library of America, 1982) at 366.

The Civil War had accelerated a process that the railroads had begun; the river steamboat was slipping into history. Even with steam-powered towboats competing with traditional steamboats in the latter decades of the century, the tonnage on western rivers had dipped significantly below pre-war levels, and the fleet never again achieved the economic importance it had held before the war.[3] In the blue-water trades, the changes were even more drastic. American merchant-shipping had performed well in the world's markets in the first half of the century. True to John Adams' prediction[4], the British Navigation Acts had in fact injured Britain's merchant fleet, forcing the nation's own shipowners to forego buying technologically superior and less expensive American ships in a misguided effort to protect British shipbuilders. The result was a windfall for the Americans, whose ships dominated the carrying trades in the century's early years.[5] So long as the United States retained its comparative advantage in shipbuilding, it was able to hold its advantage in the carrying trades as well. Technological innovation coincided with increased demand for speed in the late 1840s, as the California Gold-rush spurred construction of the clipper ship, with its sleek hull-design, elaborate rigging, and relatively small cargo-space. Speed, reaching more than fifteen knots, offset the higher operating costs, thus allowing carriers to charge higher freights. With the clipper,

---

3. Basing his figures on records of inspections, Hunter lists the total tonnage of traditional steamboats on the western rivers as 128,249 tons in 1870. For the same year, Hunter lists the total tonnage of river-towboats at 35,722 tons. Over the next forty years, the tonnage for towboats remained roughly constant, while that of steamboats had dropped to 32,694 tons by 1910. *See* Louis C. Hunter, Steamboats on the Western Rivers: An Economic and Technological History (1st ed. 1949; *reprinted* New York: Dover Publications, 1993) at 638. Haites, Mak, and Walton contend that Hunter's methods of making estimates generally result in underestimating actual levels of tonnage. Moreover, they dispute his conclusion that riverboats were beginning to lose in their competition with the railroads in the late 1850s. Nevertheless, even if Hunter's estimates are too low, he, Haites, Mak, and Walton are all agreed that the curve representing tonnage on the western rivers in the post-war period slopes steadily downward. *See* Erik F. Haites, James Mak, & Gary M. Walton, Western River Transportation: The Era of Internal Development, 1810–1860 (Baltimore: The Johns Hopkins University Press, 1975), Appendix B at 129–133.

4. Letter from John Adams to Thomas Jefferson (Aug. 4, 1785), *published in* The Adams-Jefferson Letters: The Complete Correspondence between Thomas Jefferson and Abigail and John Adams (2 vols., Lester J. Cappon ed., Chapel Hill: The University of North Carolina Press, 1959), Vol. I, at 48, 49. For discussion, *see supra* Introduction, note 93 and text accompanying.

5. *See* Andrew Gibson & Arthur Donovan, The Abandoned Ocean: A History of United States Maritime Policy (Columbia: University of South Carolina Press, 2000) at 45–46 (hereinafter Gibson & Donovan). After two centuries of protection, the British repealed their Navigation Acts in 1849. *Id.* at 54–60.

the United States' merchant marine reached the apex of its technological and economic achievement. Its dominance, however, was short-lived. As the rush to California began to slow in 1854, demand for carrying services declined, and many of the clippers became too expensive to operate.[6] Moreover, iron had begun to surpass wood as the primary material in shipbuilding as early as 1846.[7] The United States' comparative advantage in shipbuilding had been largely a product of the cost of raw materials. Lacking a sufficient industrial base to compete with Britain in the latest technology, by 1856 American shipbuilders instead concentrated on constructing wooden sailing ships for use in those trades in which they remained cost-effective.[8]

Ultimately, the United States' maritime policy, both before and after the Civil War, failed for the same reasons that the British Navigation Acts had failed.[9] Each sought to tie protection of the carrying trades to protection of shipbuilding, a strategy that works only when one's nation has a comparative advantage in the construction of vessels. Faced with laws designed to ensure that American-flagged ships were built in America, many investors felt their capital would be better invested in other enterprises. As a result, the American merchant fleet began shrinking, and an ever-smaller percentage of goods entering and leaving American ports did so in American bottoms.[10] Outstripped by British technological advances and victimized by outmoded and ill-considered policy-choices, the American carrying trades were slipping into the backwater of the nation's commercial activity.[11] Having facilitated the nation's growth, provided capital for the development of manufacturing, and spurred the expansion of agriculture by cutting the costs of transporting

---

6. *See Id.* at 60–63.

7. *See* H. David Bess & Martin T. Farris, U.S. Maritime Policy: History and Perspectives (New York: Praeger Publishers, 1981) at 22 (hereinafter Bess & Farris).

8. Gibson & Donovan, *supra* note 5, at 54; *see also* John G. B. Hutchins, The American Maritime Industries and Public Policy, 1789–1914: An Economic History (Cambridge, Massachusetts: Harvard University Press, 1941) at 299–300, 356, 399–403, 455 (hereinafter Hutchins).

9. For the conflicting goals and ultimate failure of American maritime policy before the Civil War, *see* Hutchins, *supra* note 8, at 363–368; for similar failures after the war, *see* Gibson & Donovan, *supra* note 5, at 73–78.

10. Bess & Farris, *supra* note 7, at 27, estimate that the size of the nineteenth-century American merchant fleet reached its peak in 1860 at 2,379,396 tons; this figure had been reduced to 928,062 tons by 1890.

11. According to the estimates provided by Bess and Farris, between 1846 and 1858, an average of roughly 75% of all U. S. foreign trade was carried in American bottoms. By 1860, that figure had dropped to 66%, and by 1875 it had plummeted to 26.2%. *Id.* at 23, 26.

American farm-products to foreign markets, the carrying trades were by the end of the century of comparatively small economic importance.

The Framers had been very much products of their own times. They understood the importance of maritime commerce to the fledgling nation, and thus understood as well the importance of vesting admiralty and maritime jurisdiction in the federal courts. The experiences of the Revolution had shown them the dangers of entrusting maritime cases to state tribunals. Operating beyond the control of the national government, such courts posed a potential threat to the good will that Congress sought to cultivate and preserve among allies and neutral nations. Moreover, experience had shown that opportunities for friction were not limited to prize cases; on occasion even instance cases could involve the nation in conflict with other countries. While not often expressly mentioned at the Constitutional Convention, the national Appellate Prize Court—with which many of the delegates had first-hand experience—helped to shape the debate over the federal judiciary. Antifederalist opposition to the creation of inferior federal courts centered on the cost and convenience of such courts. If too numerous, the administrative expense of maintaining them would provide an unnecessary drain on the national coffers; if too few, wealthy litigants could hail their less affluent fellow-citizens into distant *fora*, thereby raising their costs and forcing them to settle on disadvantageous terms. The latter argument applied with even greater force to federal appellate courts. Nonetheless, federalists and antifederalists alike conceded the importance of national prize courts. The question remained, however, as to whether it would be practical to create national courts with jurisdiction only over prize. Common sense and the experiences of both the vice admiralty courts and the state prize courts of the Revolution held that the courts would be more cost-effective if permitted to hear private maritime disputes as well. So long as the text of the Constitution contemplated federal judges serving during good behavior with undiminished salaries, the argument for augmenting the federal courts' jurisdiction with a class of cases that they could hear during peace-time was even more compelling. Allowing federal trial judges to hear instance cases guaranteed both that the expensive system of federal courts would be utilized efficiently and that the occasional instance case with international overtones would be adjudicated in federal court. The antifederalists thus conceded that the establishment of a system of fairly numerous federal trial courts was necessary. From this point, it was a small step to the conclusion that it would be cost-effective and convenient to empower these courts to hear diversity cases and cases arising under federal statutes as well. In essence, by conceding the necessity of federal *maritime* tribunals, the antifederalists lost their strongest arguments against the creation inferior federal courts. To be sure, there was a backlash. Some antifederalists feared that federal trial courts structured as civil-law admiralty and prize tribunals would employ the curial rules of the civil law in common-law cases as well, thereby depriving defendants of the common-law right to a jury. At the appellate level, they feared that the courts would adopt admiralty's practice of reviewing facts *de novo*, forcing defendants to incur the expense of trying the same matter twice—the second time in an inconvenient forum. These fears were sufficient to prevent the Convention from agreeing on a full-fledged structure for the federal judiciary, but not to prevent agreement on a final text. Instead, the delegates reached a compromise whereby Article III deferred the decision on the structure of the federal courts to Congress.

The first Congress did in fact create inferior federal courts, vesting them with diversity as well as admiralty jurisdiction. Nevertheless, the same Judiciary Act that established these courts also preserved for maritime claimants "the right of a common law remedy where the common law is competent to give it", in effect granting concurrent jurisdiction to the state courts. Congress' choice of allowing claimants to file in state courts would not frustrate the underlying goal of keeping maritime cases with international overtones in a federal forum, so long as a foreign defendant could remove the action to federal court on the grounds of diversity. In addition, it allowed claimants to file their claims in the courts most convenient for them. When speed of adjudication was of paramount concern, or when witnesses would return to sea shortly, the federal courts sitting in admiralty were available. Similarly, where a party required special expertise, or desired from a court a service, such as a ship's survey, which the courts of common law were not able to provide, a federal admiralty court could hear the case. Seamen appreciated the procedural device that allowed all crew members to join their claims in a single action against the ship, and the action *in rem* provided merchants and materialmen with a means of enforcing their claims when a ship's owners were not within the court's jurisdiction. On the other hand, when the sums involved were too small to warrant traveling to a distant forum, or where a party desired a jury, there was the option of filing in the local courts of common law. It should be remembered, however, that Congress had not created a new jurisdictional regime, but instead merely had codified the *status quo*, established early in the colonial period and preserved by the states after independence. With regard to uniformity, which experience with the state prize courts had taught them was so essential, there was little concern. The substantive law applied in the state and federal courts would be identical, just as the substantive law applied in the vice admiralty courts and the colonial courts of common law had been. For the founding generation, the substantive maritime law, the "*lex maritima*", was a part of the law of nations and grounded in the law of nature, and as such was not susceptible to change at the unilateral whim of one nation. Under the Articles of Confederation, there had been no serious clash between the state admiralty courts and the courts of common law over the substantive rules that governed instance cases, and there was no reason to believe that such a clash would occur at the national level. As part of the law of nations, the *lex maritima* would apply with equal force in either a national or a state tribunal.

Uniformity in the substantive maritime law was long recognized as desirable, particularly in the eighteenth and early nineteenth centuries, when maritime commerce was the linchpin holding the American economy together. Shipowners are better able to conform their conduct to legal standards when the rules are clearly defined and when the same rules apply to the same conduct in all ports. There are advantages of efficiency in predictability *per se*, even apart from one's concern for selecting the best rule of law.[12] Moreover, there are distinct advantages in selecting substantive rules that comport with those of one's trading partners. Once Congress had vested admiralty and maritime jurisdiction in federal trial courts, the federal judiciary strove to ensure that the substantive law remained uniform. When their efforts were hampered in part by Congress' failure to enact a maritime code, federal judges turned to foreign sources, reasoning that the *lex maritima* was binding (if not entirely self-executing) in all civilized nations. The result was the development of the "general maritime law", the customs and practice of maritime nations formally incorporated into federal law through judicial decisions. In the early years, federal judges extended and embellished the myth of a universal *lex maritima*—Imperial Rome's legacy to the modern world, absorbed into the medieval maritime codes and transmitted from them into the civil law of modern Continental Europe. In part a relic of the era of the colonial vice admiralty courts, the myth was reinforced by the circumstances of the day. Admiralty case law was not published until the 1790s, and such reports as were published were not widely available until the nineteenth century. Initially, judges derived rules of law deductively from the few standard treatises at their disposal. More importantly, as there were no appreciable changes in marine technology in the early years of the republic, judges seldom encountered novel fact-patterns and thus were not often called upon to innovate. Nevertheless, federal judges' ap-

12. As legal scholar David L. Shapiro has phrased the argument: "[I]t would often be far better to have one bad (*i.e.*, unduly burdensome) federal rule on a particular topic than to have fifty less burdensome but significantly different state rules." David L. Shapiro, Federalism: A Dialogue (Evanston: Northwestern University Press, 1995) at 49 (hereinafter Shapiro). *See also* discussion, *supra* Chapter II, notes 194–196 and text accompanying.

proach to maritime issues began to change as the century progressed. Careful research into the history of the medieval codes—largely absent in the colonial period—revealed discrepancies in the manner in which they treated various issues, thereby challenging the notion that the law was unchanged since antiquity and uniform throughout Europe. In addition, new technology gave rise to new legal issues and blurred the traditional distinction between oceangoing and inland navigation. Moreover, as theories of the law of nations grounded in the law of nature gave way to empirical theories of international law, judges concentrated more heavily upon ascertaining the custom and practice of nations. No longer did they view these practices as unchanging. They were aided in their efforts by the availability of new sources for the substantive maritime law, and in particular published case law.

From the seventeenth century's "Battle of the Books" through the debates over the ratification of the Constitution, admiralty was held to be unique for its ties to the civil law. Nevertheless, as the nineteenth century progressed, the most salient feature of American admiralty law was its adoption of the case-law system of adjudication and its doctrine of *stare decisis*. The case-law system was a product of America's common-law tradition and the publication of courts' opinions, the latter wholly lacking in the colonial period. So long as published reports were unavailable, courts were not able to rely effectively upon precedent and thus could not develop the substantive law through the process of gradual accretion that characterizes the common law. Instead, judges handled each case as the civil law handles cases, namely by the judge's deductive reasoning grounded only in the texts available. Lacking both a maritime code and the plethora of Continental treatises available to European civilians, judges of the colonial and state courts of admiralty had muddled through as best they could, with *ad hoc* decisions more often grounded in common sense than in rules extrapolated from opinions in previous cases. To be sure, their decisions were neither arbitrary nor seriously at odds with those in similar cases heard by either the High Court of Admiralty or the maritime courts on the Continent. Nevertheless, while early American admiralty courts' decisions evinced a certain consistency, the system did not lend itself to the development of new law. A case might announce a new rule, but there was no effective mechanism for preserving the innovation for later cases. With the establishment of federal courts and the introduction of published reports, the complexion of maritime adjudication changed. The substantive law, long thought to be static, began to evolve. Thus also arose an issue largely overlooked by the founding generation. As long as a system of law is grounded in *stare decisis*, it is inevitable that judges will create rules of substantive law. Coke and Hale understood this, and indeed for them it was the strength of the common law.[13] For Americans concerned with separation of powers, however, judge-made federal law carried with it the potential for judicial encroachment

---

13. As Coke had cautioned in *Calvin's Case*:

> "[O]ur daies [*sic*] upon the earth are but as a shadow, in respect of the old and ancient dayes and times past, wherein the Laws have been by the wisdom of the most excellent men, in many successions of ages, by long and continual experience (the trial of right and truth) fined and refined, which no one man (being of so short a time) albeit he had in his head the wisdom of all the men in the world, in any one age could never have effected or attained unto."

[Edward Coke], The Reports of Sir Edvvard Coke, K[night], Late Lord Chief Justice of England... Faithfully Rendered into English (1st English ed., London: W. Lee, M. Walbanck, D. Pakeman, & G. Bedell, 1658), *Clavin's Case*, Part VII at 1, 3b. For Hale also, the cumulative wisdom of generations of common-law judges was to be preferred over the logical deductions of the most learned legal scholars of a single era:

> "Againe it is a reason for me to preferre a Law by w[hi]ch a Kingdome hath been happily governed four or five hundr[e]d yeares then [*sic: i.e.* "than"] to adventure the happiness and Peace of a Kingdome upon Some new Theory of my owne tho' I am better acquainted w[i]th the reasonableness of my owne theory then [*sic*: "than"] w[i]th that Law. Againe I have reason to assure myselfe that Long Experience makes more discoveries touching conveniences and Inconveniences of Laws then [*sic*: "than"] is possible for the wisest Councill of Men att first to foresee. And that those amendm[en]ts and Supplem[en]ts that through the various Experiences of wise and knowing men have been applyed to any Law must needs be better suited to the Convenience of Laws, then [*sic*: "than"] the best Invention of the most pregnant witts not ayded by Such a Series and tract of Experience.
>
> All these thinges are reasonable, the particular reason of the Laws & Supplem[en]ts themeselves perchance are not obvious to the most Subtill Witts or Reason.
>
> And this adds to ye difficultie of a present fathomeing of the reason of Laws, because they are the Production of long and Iterated Experience w[hi]ch tho' itt be commonly called the mistriss of Fooles, yett certainly itt is the wisest Expedient among mankind, and discovers those defects and Supplys w[hi]ch no witt of Man cou[l]d either at once foresee or aptly remedye."

[Sir Matthew Hale], *Reflections by the Lrd. Chiefe Justice Hale on Mr. Hobbes his Dialogue of the Lawe, published from manuscript as an appendix in* William S. Holdsworth, A History of English Law (7 vols., London: Methuen & Co., 1924), Vol. V, at 499, 504–505 (*page numbers from original manuscript omitted*). It is not by means of application of innate "reason", but only through mastering techniques of legal interpretation upon which the common law has been built that one can hope to contribute to the development of law. Hale concludes:

> "And upon all this that hath been said it appeares that men are not borne Comon Lawyers, neither can the bare Excerciss of the Faculty of Reason give a man a Sufficient Knowledge of it, but it must be gained by the habituateing and accustomeing and Excerciseing that Faculty by readeing, Study and observation to give a Man a compleate Knowledge thereof. And although a Man that hath long and

on the role of the legislature.[14] Moreover, judicially-created law had ramifications for the state/federal relationship as well. By establishing federal trial

---

> Industriously Excercised himselfe in that Study cannot p[re]tend either to Infallibilitie in his Judgm[en]t or to a full attainm[en]t of all that is attaineable toucheing the Laws of England, yett he will be much better fitted for right Judgm[en]t therein, then [*sic*: "than"] he that hath no other Stock to trade upon then [*sic*: "than"] the bare Excercise of his Faculty of reason, or that hath only taken the paines to read over the Titles of the Statutes or Indexes or Repertoryes of some Law bookes."

Id. at 505 (*page numbers from original manuscript omitted*).

14. At issue is the matter of degree. Holmes maintained that "[J]udges do and must legislate, but they can do so only interstitially; they are confined from molar to molecular motions." *Southern Pacific Co. v. Jensen*, 244 U. S. 205, 221 (Holmes, J., dissenting, 1917); *see also* Letter of Oliver Wendell Holmes, Jr. to Harlod J. Laski (Feb. 1, 1919), *published in* Holmes-Laski Letters: The Correspondence of Mr. Justice Holmes and Harold J. Laski 1916–1935 (2 vols., Cambridge, Massachusetts: Harvard University Press, 1953), Vol. I, at 183. At the very least, "interstitial" must include rules generated in interpreting statutes; as one modern scholar explains: "[J]udge-made law is unavoidable. That is, courts must make a certain amount of common law simply because there is no clear line between 'making' and 'applying' law, between commands that are clear on the face of a statute and those made through an exercise of judgment and creativity. Deciding individual cases thus generates some common law because the process of adjudication necessarily entails articulating rules to elaborate and clarify the meaning and operation of statutory texts." Larry Kramer, *The Lawmaking Power of the Federal Courts*, 12 Pace L. Rev. 263, 269 (1992) (hereinafter Kramer). Beyond this point, opinion is divided as to when judicial law-making is permissible. As to what justifies allowing judges to create law, Kramer offers the following:

> "The justification, in my view, is simply that common law and common lawmaking are exceedingly useful. Legislators have limited time and resources, and the legislature already has difficulty dealing with all the problems that make their way on to its agenda. Legislators cannot possibly minotor every aspect of daily life that could benefit from the enactment of positive law. Recognizing the authority of courts to make law thus improves governance by enlarging the state's lawmaking capacity and increasing citizen access to the lawmaking apparatus. This, by the way, is another benefit of separation of powers that tends to be missed: establishing independent departments with lawmaking responsibility multiplies the 'inlets' available to the citizenry and makes government more responsive to the needs of the people."

Id. at 270. For Kramer, federal judges' lawmaking powers should not be without limits, and he suggests that judicial lawmaking should preclude "federal common law that cannot be justified by reference to a federal statute." *Id.* at 288. His comments, however, are directed toward judicial law-making in those general fields in which the Constitution has granted law-making powers to Congress. Arguably admiralty stands on a somewhat different footing, as Article III grants admiralty and maritime jurisdiction exclusively to the federal courts, with no residual authority vested in the states. Presumably, the state-interests are less weighty in this context, and thus federal judges' law-making powers should be

courts operating under the case-law system and granting concurrent maritime jurisdiction to the state courts, the first Congress virtually had assured an eventual conflict between state law and federal judge-made law. While the members of the first Congress had anticipated some friction, assumptions regarding the nature of the substantive maritime law induced them to underestimate the degree of conflict.

So long as adjudication in federal admiralty courts offered advantages over that in the states' courts of common law, conflict rarely materialized. At the close of the nineteenth century, breach of maritime contracts sounded concurrently in admiralty and common law.[15] Moreover, state and federal courts exercised concurrent jurisdiction over cases of general average and salvage[16], as well as over torts committed at sea.[17] Nevertheless, claimants had little incentive to file cases of salvage or general average in the courts of common law[18], and even less for tort-cases, for which the common law's draconian doctrine of contributory negligence would have barred recovery in many cases in which admiralty would have allowed it.[19] There was one advantage to filing in federal court for all maritime claims, namely the maritime lien, which was held to be enforceable only in a court of admiralty. An innovation of federal judges, the maritime lien conferred a right in the *res* itself, and, under the American doctrine of personification of vessels, the lien would follow a vessel even if she were sold to another owner.[20] So long as admiralty's advantages

---

commensurately greater. In contemporary practice, however, the Supreme Court has not claimed an unlimited power to create federal maritime law. *See e.g. American Dredging Co. v. Miller*, 510 U. S. 443, 455 (Scalia, J., 1994): "While there is an established and continuing tradition of federal common lawmaking in admiralty, that law is to be developed, insofar as possible, to harmonize with the enactments of Congress in the field."

15. *See* George C. Holt, The Concurrent Jurisdiction of the Federal and State Courts (New York: Baker, Voorhis & Co., 1888) at 196 (hereinafter Holt).

16. *Id.* at 196–197.

17. *Id.* at 200.

18. *Id.* at 196–197. As Holt explains:

> "[C]ompensation for salvage services cannot exceed the value of the property saved, [and] it does not appear that any advantage can be gained by bringing an action to recover for salvage services in a State court. Claims for salvage constitute the first lien [in priority] in admiralty on the property saved, and such a claim can be more effectively prosecuted by the enforcement of such lien in admiralty than by an ordinary suit in common law."

Id.

19. *Id.* at 200, 207–208

20. *Id.* at 193–195. By the nineteenth century, the dispositive difference between the powers of federal district courts sitting in admiralty and those of state courts entertaining

in procedures and remedies outweighed the advantages of the substantive rules and remedies of the common law[21], the level of forum-shopping and state/federal friction remained minimal, and the substantive rules applied to maritime activities remained fairly uniform. The federal courts were free to generate rules for the "general maritime law" without serious risk of conflict with the laws of the states. In some cases, the innovations were minor modifications of rules already recognized in foreign courts[22]; in others, such as those involving towage, federal judges created new rules out of whole cloth in response to the demands of changing technology.[23]

Richard Henry Dana's assessment of the Supreme Court's success in resolving the problems of overlapping maritime jurisdiction was premature.[24]

---

maritime claims was that only the former could proceed against a vessel *in rem*. For discussion of the doctrine of personification of vessels and the development of the modern lien, *see* discussion *supra* Chapter IV, note 92 and text accompanying.

21. Admiralty's obvious procedural advantage was the action *in rem*. The other principal difference was the manner in which admiralty and the common law construed limitations on actions. By the nineteenth century, many common-law actions were governed by statutes of limitations, while admiralty continued to employ the doctrine of *laches*. Opinion was divided as to whether one had a longer period in which to file in admiralty. Holt, *supra* note 15, at 203–204 warned that in practice *laches* often produced a shorter period for filing one's claim than did states' statutes of limitations. Richard Henry Dana disagreed, cautioning seamen to heed states' statutory limits, as statutes of limitations often extinguished claims still deemed actionable in courts of admiralty. *See* Richard Henry Dana, Jr., The Seamen's Friend (6th ed., Boston: Thomas Groom & Co., 1851; *reprinted* New York: Scholars' Facsimiles and Reprints, 1979) at 223.

22. *See e.g. Talbot v. Seeman,* 5 U. S. 1, 43–45 (1801), in which Chief Justice Marshall reduced the award in a salvage case from a moiety to one-sixth of the vessel's value, based upon the unique fact-pattern. The American-flagged vessel in question had been captured by the French during the "quasi-war" and outfitted as a privateer without being formally condemned as a prize by a French court. While acknowledging that the recapture of a neutral ship not yet condemned would not give rise to salvage under either federal statutes in effect on the day of the recapture or under the law of nations, Marshall opted for a compromise. Although he found that the usual award of a moiety would have been too great, he also reasoned that denial of any award would have been inequitable. Instead, he settled on the reduced amount as fair compensation. Some modern commentators have speculated that the decision may have been designed in part as a compromise intended to placate both Federalists and Republicans, who were locked in a heated political struggle over the United States' relations with France. For discussion *see e.g.* Jean Edward Smith, John Marshall: Definer of a Nation (New York: Henry Holt & Co., 1996) at 291–295.

23. For nineteenth-century federal judges' innovations in the field of towage, *see e.g.* Henry M. Flanders, A Treatise on Maritime Law (Boston: Little, Brown & Co., 1852), Sec. 362–Sec. 363 at 300–301.

24. *See* quote, *supra* note 1.

Writing in 1871, he could not have predicted the changes in state law that would render the common law more sympathetic than the general maritime law to the plight of maritime tort-victims. Joseph Story had believed that judges should be responsive to the practical needs of the polities that they served. By this standard, the Supreme Court had met its principal challenge of the antebellum period with great success. Its extension of admiralty jurisdiction inland, its creation of the maritime lien, and its incremental development of the general maritime law served the needs of the nation's most valuable industry and thus facilitated growth of the national economy. In the years following, however, the economic and political climate had changed. After the Civil War, the Court was not under pressure to protect weighty national interests through its decisions in admiralty cases. The challenge was no longer one of responding to the needs of national commerce, but instead of responding to the needs of federalism itself. Admiralty opinions of subsequent years emphasized the interests of both the federal and state governments and the need to reduce friction between them. Irrespective of the merits of its legal reasoning, McReynolds' opinion in *Jensen* was politically an anachronism in 1917. It would have served the political contingencies of the antebellum period far better than those of the early twentieth century.

The first Congress incorporated concurrent jurisdiction over maritime matters into the Judiciary Act of 1789 for four reasons. First, there was geographic convenience; parties would have the option of filing their actions in the courts closest to their homes or places of business. Second, there was the convenience of the members of the bar; attorneys unfamiliar with admiralty's arcane procedures would be able to file their clients' claims in the familiar surroundings of the courts of common law. Third, allowing claimants the option of filing in either state or federal court would redistribute case-loads among courts. Self-interest would encourage claimants to seek relief where it could be granted most quickly, thus alleviating pressure on the courts with the longest dockets. Finally, concurrent jurisdiction allowed claimants to select the court with procedural rules most convenient for the fact-patterns of their cases. Today, the first (and most important) of these considerations is largely moot, as modern transportation has eliminated much of the inconvenience associated with traveling to a distant forum. With the elimination of the principal incentive for vesting concurrent jurisdiction in the state courts, one reasonably might ask whether the jurisdictional scheme embodied in the Judiciary Act is worth preserving. Added to these considerations is the unanticipated widening rift between state and federal substantive law as old assumptions regarding the immutability of the substantive maritime law have given way to the practical understanding that the general maritime law evolves in a *stare-decisis* system as does any other body of judge-made law.

The usual defense for overlapping jurisdiction in other contexts is that it allows states to serve individually as "laboratories" for the testing of new law, which in turn promotes competition between the states collectively and the federal government for enhancing public welfare.[25] Since *Jensen*, the Supreme Court's approach to resolving conflict between state law and the general maritime law has been one of accommodation rather than pre-emption, resting on the assumption that state law (which protects states' interests) has a part to play in maritime adjudication, even where its application may make inroads into the uniformity of the general maritime law.[26] Nonetheless, as a practical matter, the Court's decisions have not always been predictable or consistent.[27]

---

25. Justice Brandeis is often credited with the origins of this defense of overlapping state and federal law-making power. (*See New State Ice Co. v. Liebmann*, 285 U. S. 262 (Brandeis, J., dissenting, 1932).) For discussion of the merits of this defense of federalism—both pro and con—*see* SHAPIRO, *supra* note 12, at 38, 40–42, 76–79, 85–86, 123, 139.

26. McReynolds' decision in *Jensen*, resting on what the scholarly literature has termed "presumptive pre-emption", gives no thought to state interests. Moreover, *Jensen's* bright-line rule also gives no thought to the question of whether a judge-made federal rule should be allowed to trump a state's legislative enactment—the product of the democratic process. Nevertheless, even *Jensen* recognizes that state law may be applicable in certain limited circumstances: "[I]t would be difficult, if not impossible, to define with exactness just how far the general maritime law may be changed, modified, or affected by state legislation. That this may be done to some extent cannot be denied." 244 U. S. 205, 216 (1917). For discussion of "presumptive pre-emption" versus "accommodation" *see e.g.* David W. Robertson, *Displacement of State Law by Federal Maritime Law*, 26 J. Mar. L. & Com. 325, 337–338 (1995) (hereinafter Robertson, *Displacement*).

27. A survey of twentieth-century federal courts' opinions in matters requiring a choice between state and federal maritime law would be (and has been) the topic of a voluminous treatise (*see e.g.* DAVID W. ROBERTSON, ADMIRALTY AND FEDERALISM (Mineola, New York: The Foundation Press, 1970)), and it is beyond the scope of the present eighteenth/nineteenth-century historical study to review the topic in detail. Nevertheless, several trends have emerged. Conflicts between state law and the general maritime law arise most frequently in cases of death or personal injury in or adjacent to a state's navigable waters. *Pope & Talbot Inc. v. Hawn*, 346 U. S. 406 (1953), established the rule that the dispositive factors for determining whether a federal court must apply state law in preference to the general maritime law (or *vice versa*) apply with equal force when a state court must make the same choice between state law and federal judge-made law. Beginning with *Jensen*, federal courts traditionally have been reluctant to allow state workmen's compensation statutes to displace the general maritime law. Nevertheless, federal judge-made law does not always preclude the application of state workmen's compensation laws. *See e.g. Sun Ship, Inc. v. Pennsylvania*, 447 U. S. 715, 724 (1980) (applying a state workmen's compensation act where the court found it "more generous than federal law" and where Congress had not specified a need to limit recovery to the federal remedy). Owing in part to the Supreme Court's once-controlling decision in *The Harrisburg*, 119 U. S. 199 (1886) (denying a remedy for wrongful death under

Having flirted with a variety of theories over the years, including "gap theory" and the "maritime-but-local theory"[28], in 1961 the Court eventually opted for state/federal interest-balancing in *Kossick v. United States Fruit Co.*[29] Forty years

---

the general maritime law), federal courts of the early to mid-twentieth century were more open to application of state wrongful-death statutes, beginning with *The Hamilton*, 207 U.S. 398 (1907). A series of federal statutes enacted in the ensuing decades left gaps and ambiguities in the statutory scheme, thereby forcing federal courts to decide whether state statutes were applicable. *See* Death on the High Seas Act, 41 Stat. 537 (1920); Jones Act, 41 Stat. 1007 (incorporating remedies from the The Federal Employees Liability Act, 45 U. S. C. sec. 53). *See e.g. The Tungus v. Skovgaard*, 358 U. S. 588 (1959) (applying a state wrongful death statute *cum onere*); *see also Goett v. Union Carbide Corp.*, 361 U. S. 340, 346 (1960) (holding that "the substantive legal rights and liabilities are...to be measured by the standards of the general maritime law", while the state statute merely provides "a remedy for death resulting from an act made wrongful by other [*i.e.* general maritime] laws"). Similarly, the federal courts applied state survival statutes to death at sea. *See e.g. Just v. Chambers*, 312 U. S. 383 (1941); *Gillespie v. United States Steel Corp.*, 379 U. S. 148 (1964) (applying a state survival statute to the death of a seamen, whose drowning in state waters was caused by the unseaworthiness of the vessel on which he was employed). In the context of personal injury, however, federal courts generally have held that the general maritime law trumps state law. *See e.g. Kermarec v. Compagnie Generale Transatlantique*, 358 U. S. 625 (1959) (holding that a plaintiff's status as a "gratuitous licensee" did not bar his recovery for personal injuries sustained while visiting a crew-member aboard a ship docked in state waters). Nevertheless, despite this general trend, courts have not always been consistent in their treatment of personal injury. *See e.g. Caldarola v. Eckert*, 332 U. S. 155 (1947). In the final analysis, after *Jensen* and *Chelentis* federal courts failed for decades to provide a clear rationale for determining when judge-made general maritime law would take precedence over state law.

28. "Gap theory", often attributed to Oliver Wendell Holmes, holds that a court should look to state statutes to fill gaps in the statutory law and existing judge-made general maritime law rather than creating new substantive maritime rules. While yielding a bright-line rule, it provided no principled reason for adopting past judicial innovations while rejecting them as *ultra vires* in the instant case. Moreover, it failed to promote uniformity in the general maritime law while it simultaneously ignored both federal and state interests. *See* discussion, *supra* Introduction at 26; David P. Currie, *Federalism and Admiralty: The Devil's Own Mess*, 1960 Sup. Ct. Rev. 158, 167–173; Robertson, *Displacement, supra* note 26, at 339–341. The "maritime-but-local" test, derived from *dicta* in *Western Fuel Co. v. Garcia*, 257 U. S. 233, 242 (1921), sought to determine whether a "subject is maritime and local in character" and not addressed by the general maritime law. Other approaches suggested in the scholarly literature for explaining federal courts' decisions are the "pro-plaintiff rule", under which the court will base its choice of state or federal law the relative benefits of each to the plaintiff, and the preference for state statutes (in contradistinction to state common law) over federal judge-made law, on the grounds that they are products of the democratic legislative process. For discussion of the history of these suggested rules, *see* Robertson, *Displacement, supra* note 26, at 344–345.

29. *Kossick v. United Fruit Co.*, 365 U. S. 731, 738–740 (1961) (holding that the federal interest in the general maritime law's rule recognizing the validity of oral contracts out-

later, courts are still weighing the interests of the federal and state governments respectively in deciding whether to extend federal judge-made law or apply state law in maritime cases.[30] While the courts' method for weighing compet-

---

weighed New York's interest in the policy underlying its Statute of Frauds where a seaman had entered into an oral contract with his employer regarding health care).

30. The Supreme Court's two most recent decisions in this area reflect the process. In *Yahama Motor Corp. v. Calhoun*, 516 U. S. 199 (1996), the Court addressed the issue of whether a court should apply a state wrongful-death statute in preference to a federal judge-made remedy where the decedent was an operator of a pleasure-boat. In *Moragne v. United States Lines, Inc.*, 398 U. S. 375 (1970), the Court had created federal remedy for wrongful death on navigable water. (For discussion, *see infra* note 33 and text accompanying.) At issue in *Yamaha* was whether this remedy had pre-empted the application of state wrongful-death statutes. Distinguishing between "seafarers" (those covered by either the Jones Act or the Longshore and Harbor Workers' Compensation Act) and "nonseafarers", the court distinguished the facts in *Moragne* from those before it in *Yamaha*. The former had addressed an ambiguity in the law, under which a longshoreman performing the duties of a seaman within territorial waters could receive a remedy through state law for wrongful-death arising out of the unseaworthiness of the vessel, while a member of the ship's crew could not. Moreover, the various federal statutes applying to crew members also failed to provide a remedy. (*See* 398 U. S. at 395.) The court filled the gap by fashioning a parallel remedy for crew members under the general maritime law. Nevertheless, the Court in *Yamaha* declined to interpret *Moragne's* remedy as a pre-emption of state law. *Moragne* controlled only actions by seafarers, and furthermore, it "centered on the extension of relief, not on the contraction of remedies". 516 U. S. at 213. The state statute at issue in *Yamaha* provided a better remedy for the claimant than that fashioned by the Court in *Moragne*. Moreover, the decedent, a twelve-year old girl who had rented a pleasure-craft, had not been employed in the maritime industry. Finding the state's interest in protecting "nonseafaring" minors sufficiently strong to outweigh the federal interest in the uniformity of the general maritime law in this noncommercial context, the Court applied the state statute. 516 U. S. at 216. The Supreme Court revisited the issue of federal preemption of state law in admiralty five years later in *Norfolk Shipbuilding & Drydock Corp. v. Garris*, 532 U. S. 811 (2001). In *Norfolk Shipbuilding*, the Court addressed the issue of whether to extend *Moragne's* wrongful-death remedy where death is caused by unseaworthiness to cases in which death is caused by negligence. Rather than mechanically applying a state statute to supply a remedy, the court instead concentrated upon the rationale of its earlier decision in *Moragne* and the asymmetry that would result if the Court failed to extend the general maritime law. Justice Scalia observed: "The choice-of-law anomaly occasioned by providing a federal remedy for injury but not death is no less strange when the duty breached is negligence than when it is seaworthiness. Of two victims injured at the same instant in the same location by the same negligence, only one would be covered by federal law, provided only that the other died of his injuries." 532 U. S. at 816. Ultimately, the Court extended the holding in *Moragne* to cover wrongful death from negligence, and in doing so created a new remedy under the general maritime law. Thus the two most recent Supreme Court decisions on whether to apply federal maritime remedies in preference to state law came to opposite conclusions. Nevertheless, the cases

ing state and federal interests could use some additional clarification, with a few notable exceptions[31] judge-made federal law continues to apply where common sense dictates that the federal interest in uniformity is great, usually yielding to state law only in the context of tort-victims who do not earn a living in the maritime industry. Justice McReynolds' preference for clearly delineated jurisdictional lines notwithstanding, at least one school of thought holds that the benefits of overlapping state/federal power may outweigh the friction that it produces.[32] Empirically, this concept finds some support in the

---

have much in common. In both *Yamaha* and *Norfolk Shipbuilding*, the Court reaffirmed the notion that state law has a role to play in supplying remedies for injury and death occurring on navigable waters. In addition, the Court in both cases acknowledged that federal courts remain empowered to create new rules for the general maritime law despite the existence of parallel state statutes and despite the Constitution vesting the principal law-making power over such matters in Congress. The difference in the respective outcomes of the cases reflects only the differences in the Court's evaluation of the respective weights of the state and federal interests.

31. One of the most notable exceptions is the Supreme Court's highly controversial decision in *Wilburn Boat v. Firemen's Fund Insurance Co.*, 348 U. S. 310 (1955). In *Wilburn Boat*, the Court held that Texas state law rather than the general maritime law should govern the interpretation of a marine insurance policy covering a charter-fishing boat operating on navigable waters in a lake straddling the border of two states. While the boat was generally employed in a commercial activity, namely providing vacationing amateur fisherman with a means of fishing in the lake, at the time of the accident resulting in both its loss and the death of its operator, it had been borrowed for use as a pleasure-craft. It is worth noting that Texas law was more advantageous to the claimant than was the general maritime law. For a detailed analysis of the Court's decision in the case and its factual background, *see* Joel K. Goldstein, *The Life and Times of Wilburn Boat: A Critical Guide*, (Part I) 28 J. Mar. L. & Com. 395 (1997); (Part II) 28 J. Mar. L. & Com. 555 (1997). While today it is generally taken for granted that the federal interest in uniformity of law applied to marine insurance is great, it should be remembered that treating marine insurance as "maritime" is a comparatively modern concept. The first great treatise on the subject, James Allan Park's *A System of Marine Insurances*—the publication of which was roughly contemporaneous with the ratification of the Constitution—treated the subject as entirely within the common law. Moreover, in the antebellum period, most cases involving marine insurance reached federal court on diversity jurisdiction, though one commentator has observed that the courts treated these cases as governed by the "general commercial law" rather than by the common law of individual states. *See* William A. Fletcher, *The General Common Law and Section 34 of the Judiciary Act: The Example of Marine Insurance*, 97 Harv. L. Rev. 1513 (1984).

32. The notion that benefits accrue when allocation of power is "noncentralized" (*i.e.* diffused) and even redundant has received its most detailed defense in recent years in the works Daniel Elazar. *See* DANIEL ELAZAR, AMERICAN FEDERALISM: A VIEW FROM THE STATES (3d ed., New York: Harper & Row, 1984) at 3–9; for a critique, *see* discussion *in* SHAPIRO, *supra* note 14, at 75–91. While Elazar concentrates principally upon

recent history of overlapping maritime jurisdiction. In 1970, the Supreme Court in *Moragne v. United States Marine Lines*[33] overruled *The Harrisburg*, which for nearly a century had denied relief for wrongful death under the general maritime law. The wrongful-death remedy had originated in the states, an innovation of state legislatures concerned for the plight of deceased tort-victims' dependent families. For decades the Supreme Court had applied state-law remedies in similar maritime cases. By adopting the states' solution into the general maritime law, the Court standardized the remedy, thereby reaffirming the importance of uniformity, clarifying the standard to which courts would hold prospective tortfeasors, and rendering the results in such cases more predictable. Nevertheless, in the absence of pressure from competing state law, it is unlikely that the Court would have opted for such innovation without guidance from Congress. Even if the first Congress' reasons for es-

---

the legislative aspects of overlapping state/federal power, others have addressed overlapping judicial power as well. *See e.g.* discussion of "dual federalism" *in* Kramer, *supra* note 14, at 291–292; *see also* SHAPIRO, *supra* note 14, at 134–135 (discussing the role of the federal judiciary in requiring that Congress be clear in its intention to pre-empt state law).

33. *Moragne v. States Marine Lines, Inc.*, 398 U. S. 375 (1970). The Court concentrated on the need for logical consistency in the law, reasoning that Congress' intent to provide a remedy for breach of a duty to provide a seaworthy ship (recognized by federal statute as well as the general maritime law) had been thwarted through oversights in drafting of the controlling federal statutes, with the result that gaps appeared in which the Court either would have to fashion a remedy or apply state law. The incongruities noted were as follows:

> "[First,] within territorial waters, identical conduct violating federal law (here the furnishing of an unseaworthy vessel) produces liability if the victim is merely injured, but frequently not if he is killed. [Second,] identical breaches of the duty to provide a seaworthy ship, resulting in death, produce liability outside the three-mile limit...under the Death on the High Seas Act..., but not within the territorial waters of a State whose local statute excludes unseaworthiness claims.... The third, and assertedly the 'strangest' anomaly is that a true seaman—that is, a member of a ship's company, covered by the Jones Act—is provided no remedy for death caused by unseaworthiness within territorial waters, while a longshoreman, to whom the duty of seaworthiness was extended because he performs work traditionally done by seamen, does have such a remedy when allowed by a state statute."

Id. at 395–396. It should be noted that under the general maritime law, strict liability applies to unseaworthiness. For those states for which wrongful-death remedies were available only with a showing of negligence, the claimants' burden of proof was much higher, thus producing a lack of uniformity in liability to which potential tortfeasors were exposed. The Court's decision in *Moragne* placed all claimants on an equal footing where the general maritime law applied.

tablishing concurrent jurisdiction are not as compelling today as they were in 1789, *Moragne* nonetheless stands as an example of the potential benefits of retaining the overlapping jurisdictional scheme today.

Admittedly, maritime jurisdiction today does not occupy the place of central importance in the nation's economic life that it did in the antebellum years. Ocean carriage is of marginal significance to the United States' economy, and each year the size of the American merchant fleet continues to shrink. Nevertheless, the history of admiralty and maritime jurisdiction remains important. Even for those scholars of federalism with little interest in maritime law *per se*, the history of the nation's experiment with concurrent maritime jurisdiction provides a useful case-study of the theory of federalism in practice. We have been conditioned to think of state/federal conflict in terms of the federal government protecting individuals from the actions of the states. In the nineteenth century, admiralty reflected in part this stereotype, as the general maritime law afforded greater protection to seafarers than did the common law. In the twentieth century, however, this trend began to change as the states enacted statutes extending the rights of maritime workers beyond those recognized by the general maritime law. Conditioned in our responses to federalism by the history of the struggle for civil rights from the end of Reconstruction to the 1960s, we are apt to forget that the states are not by nature less disposed toward protection of individual citizens' rights than is the national government.[34] Admiralty stands as a reminder that the states too have a role to play in protecting citizens' rights and in encouraging both Congress and the federal judiciary to change, develop, and extend substantive law for the common benefit. That some friction results from this process is inevitable, but it is outweighed by the benefits to the nation as a whole.

For those with an interest in the law-making powers of the federal courts, admiralty of late has become a point of contention. It has been the goal of some critics to limit the law-making powers of federal courts. For most the goal is largely theoretical, a vindication of their views on separation of powers; for others, the goal is political, grounded in the belief that law-making by the federal judiciary poses a threat to the political decision-making of local majorities. Admiralty is especially problematic for adherents to these two schools of thought, as the federal courts' history of generating substantive law in this field is well-documented for the last two centuries and has remained untouched by the Supreme Court's decision in *Erie Railroad Co. v. Tomkins*.[35]

34. For discussion of the role of the states in protecting the rights of citizens in a federal system *see e.g.* Shapiro, *supra* note 14, at 52–56, 99–101.

35. *Erie Railroad Co. v. Tomkins*, 304 U. S. 64 (1938).

As both groups wish to restrict federal judges' power to generate substantive law, any Constitutional interpretation holding that these law-making powers in admiralty are *ultra vires* would go far in vindicating their respective theories. In recent years, it has become fashionable among some academics and courts alike to assume that federal courts of the early republic usurped jurisdiction over private maritime disputes in contravention of the Framers' original intent. If examination of the early history of admiralty jurisdiction serves no other purpose, at the very least it reveals that the Framers did not intend to limit admiralty jurisdiction to public-law matters. The delegates to the Convention of 1787 envisioned some role for the federal judiciary in the development of law; at issue is only the level and nature of their participation in the law-making process.

Finally, to study the history of maritime law and jurisdiction, one must place them in context. The history of both is tied inextricably to the law of nations, and concepts originally developed in the fields of maritime law and jurisdiction continue to have relevance in international law today. To those tempted to dismiss the history of maritime law as an arcane subject with little relevance to the world beyond its own limited sphere, the eighteenth-century French scholar Balthazard Emerigon once remarked:

> Researches into the antiquities of this legislation... will not appear useless to those persons, who may have remarked that these ancient doctrines, of which many are no longer in use, are nevertheless the foundations of others which are in vigour in the persent day, and which it is consequently difficult to comprehend throroughly without having reference to the ancient doctrines.[36]

Emerigon's observation remains true today. In most contexts, both domestic and international law have been grounded in the concept of territorial sovereignty. From the Middle Ages down to the present date, maritime commerce placed pressure on common-law and civil-law scholars alike to develop theories of jurisdiction not grounded in control over *terra firma*. The result was a mechanism for courts asserting cognizance both over events occurring on the high seas, a global commons, and over transboundary transactions. Analogies to maritime jurisdiction dominate our approach to jurisdiction over all global commons today, and it was to maritime law that we first turned for

36. *Quoted in* The Black Book of the Admiralty (*Rerum Britannicarum Medii Aevi Scriptores* (Rolls Series)): No. 55 *Monumenta Juridica* (4 vols., Sir Travers Twiss ed., London: Her Majesty's Stationery Office, 1871; *reprinted by* Krauss Reprints, 1965), Vol. III, at lxxxii.

conceptual guidance when technology made possible the exploration and commercial use of outer space. With the advent of the Internet, commerce itself is changing, and the old "territorial" models of jurisdiction must be modified if nations expect to exercise effective control over these new markets. In doing so, it is likely that they will draw upon international experience with maritime jurisdiction—the one jurisdictional sphere in which concepts of national territory are not of central importance. Viewed internationally, maritime jurisdiction has always been overlapping. Thus friction among competing sets of courts interpreting the same body of substantive law has not been limited to the domestic experience of the United States. Study of the United States' experiment with concurrent maritime jurisdiction may yet find a new use, serving as a microcosm of the tensions inherent in concurrent jurisdiction and as a springboard for addressing these tensions in the context of today's complex world economy.

Bibliography

I. English Legal History: Before 1789

Primary Sources

Acta Curiae Admirallatus Scotiae: 6th September 1557–11th March 1561–2 (Stair Society Publications, Vol. II, Thomas Callander Wade ed., Edinburgh: Robert MacLehose & Co., 1937)

The Admiralty Court Book of Southampton: 1566–1585 (The Southampton Records Series, Vol. XIII, Edwin Welch ed., Southampton: University of Southampton Press, 1968)

Walter Ashburner, The Rhodian Sea Laws: Edited from the Manuscripts (Greek critical edition, Oxford: Clarendon Press, 1909)

The Black Book of the Admiralty (*Rerum Britannicarum Medii Aevi Scriptores* (Rolls Series)): No. 55 *Monumenta Juridica*, (4 vols., Sir Travers Twiss ed., London: Her Majesty's Stationery Office, 1871; *reprinted by* Kraus Reprints, 1965)

William Blackstone, Commentaries on the Laws of England (4 vols., 1st ed., Oxford: Clarendon Press, 1765–1769; *reproduced in facsimile with commentary,* Chicago: University of Chicago Press, 1979)

Arthur Browne, A Compendious View of the Civil Law and of the Law of Admiralty, Being the Substance of a Course of Lectures Read in the University of Dublin (2 vols., 3d ed. [1st American ed.], New York: Halstead and Voorhies, 1840)

James Burrow, Reports of Cases Argued and Adjudged in the King's Bench, During the Time of Lord Mansfield's Presiding in that Court, From Michaelmas Term 30 Geo. II. 1756, To Michaelmas Term 12 Geo. III. 1772 (5 vols., New York: Hopkins and Bayard, 1808)

Cicero, *De Inventione; De Optimo Genere Oratorum; Topica* (H.M. Hubbell ed., Cambridge, Massachusetts: Harvard University Press, 1993)

M. Tulli Ciceronis [Cicero], *De Officiis* (Latin critical edition: Oxford Classical Text, Michael Winterbottom ed., Oxford: The Clarendon Press, 1994)

Cicero, *De Republica; De Legibus* (Clinton Walker Keyes ed., Cambridge, Massachusetts: Harvard University Press, 1994).

M. Tulli Ciceronis [Cicero], *Rhetorica* (2 vols., Latin critical edition, Oxford Classical Text, A.S. Wilkins ed., Oxford: The Clarendon Press, 1978)

Francisco [Francis] Clerke, *Praxis Curiae Admiralitatis Angliae* (London: William Crooke, 1667)

Francisco [Francis] Clerke, *Praxis Curiae Admiralitatis Angliae* (London: William Crooke, 1679)

[Francis Clerke], *Praxis Supremae Curiae Admiralitatis... Cui Adjiciuntur Articuli Magistri Rowghton* (Edward Simpson ed., London: C. Bathurst, 1743)

Edward Coke, The Institutes of the Laws of England (London: E. & R. Brooke, 1797)

[Edward Coke], The Reports of Sir Edvvard Coke, K[night], Late Lord Chief Justice of England... Faithfully Rendered into English (1st English ed., London: W. Lee, M. Walbanck, D. Pakeman, & G. Bedell, 1658)

A Collection of Sundry Statutes, Frequent in Use (Fardinando Palton ed., London: Flesher, Haviland & Young, 1636)

Corpus Juris Civilis (Latin edition, C.M. Galisset ed.: Paris: Janet & Cotelle, 1830)

Documents Relating to the Law and Custom of the Sea (2 vols., R.G. Marsden ed., London: The Navy Record Society, 1915–16)

John Exton, The Maritime Dicaeology, Or Sea-Jurisdiction of England (London: Richard Hodgkinson, 1664)

Extracts from Godolphin, Sea Laws, Jenkins, Malyne[s], Zouch and Exton, of All the Parts of those Treatises Which Relate to the Admiralty Jurisdiction in Cases of Contracts. Also the Commission of George III to the Vice Admiralty Court in New Hampshire in 1766 and an Abstract of the Records of the Vice Admiralty Court in Massachusetts Prior to the Revolution (Boston: Howe and Norton, 1826)

John Fortescue, *De Laudibus Legum Angliae* (London: Companie of Stationers, 1616)

Jonn Godolphin, *Synegoros Thallassios*: A View of the Admiral Jurisdiction, Wherein the Most Material Points Concerning That Jurisdiction Are Fairly and Submissively Discussed (1st ed. 1661; *reprinted* London: George Dawes, 1685)

Hugo Grotius, *De Jure Belli Ac Pacis, Libri Tres* (1st ed. 1645; 2 vols., Latin critical edition with translation, Francis W. Kelsey trans., Oxford: The Clarendon Press, 1925)

Hugo Grotius, *Mare Liberum Sive De Iure Quod Batavis Competit Ad Indicana Commercia, Dissertatio* (1st ed. 1608; Latin critical edition, Ralph van Deman Magoffin ed., New York: Oxford University Press, 1916)

High Court of Admiralty Examinations (Ms. Volume 53) 1637–1638 (Publications of the Anglo-American Records Foundation: Vol. II, Dorothy O. Shilton, Richard Holdsworthy & Eric G.M. Fletcher eds., London: Butler & Tanner, 1932)

Thomas Hobbes, *De Cive*: Entitled in the First Edition "*Elementorum Philosophiae Sectio Tertia De Cive*" and in Later Editions "*Elementa Philosophica De Cive*" (1st ed. 1641; 1647; Latin critical edition, Howard Warrender ed., Oxford: The Clarendon Press, 1983)

Thomas Hobbes, Leviathan, Or The Matter, Form, and Power of a Commonwealth, Ecclesiastical and Civil (1st ed. 1651; critical edition, Sir William Molesworth ed., London: John Bohn, 1839; *reprinted* London: Routledge/Thoemmes Press, 1994)

Institutes of Gaius (Latin critical edition, Francis de Zulueta ed.: Oxford: The Clarendon Press, 1946)

Stanley S. Jados, Consulate of the Sea and Related Documents (Tuscaloosa, Alabama: University of Alabama Press, 1975)

Gerard Malynes, *Consuetudo, Vel Lex Mercatoria*, Or The Ancient Law-Merchant (1st ed. 1622; critical edition, Katie F. Hamilton ed., Phoenix: Metheglin Press, 1996)

John Marius, Advice Concerning Bills of Exchange (1st ed. 1651; 2nd ed., London: W.H. for Nicholas Bourne, 1655)

Reginald G. Marsden, Select Pleas in the Court of Admiralty: A.D. 1390–1404 and A.D. 1527–1545, Vol. I (London: Publications of the Selden Society, Vol. 6, 1892)

Reginald G. Marsden, Select Pleas in the Court of Admiralty: A.D. 1547–1602, Vol. II (London: Publications of the Selden Society, Vol. 11, 1897)

Charles Molloy, *De Jure Maritimo Et Navali*: Or A Treatise of Affairs Maritime and of Commerce (3d ed., London: John Bellinger, 1682)

Charles Molloy, *De Jure Maritimo Et Navali*: Or A Treatise on Affairs Maritime and of Commerce (3d ed., London: Thomas Passenger, 1682)

James Oldham, The Mansfield Manuscripts and the Growth of English Law in the Eighteenth Century (2 vols., Chapel Hill: University of North Carolina Press, 1992)

James Allan Park, A System of Marine Insurances: With Three Chapters on Bottomry, on Insurances on Lives, and on Insurances Against Fire (1st ed., London: T. Whieldon, 1787; *reprinted* Philadelphia, Joseph Crukshank, 1789)

M.J. Prichard & D.E.C. Yale, Hale and Fleetwood on Admiralty Jurisdiction (London: Publications of the Selden Society, Vol. 108, 1992)

William Prynne, Brief Animadversions on, Amendments of, and Additional Explanatory Records to the Fourth Part of the Institutes of the Lawes of England, Concerning the Jurisdiction of the Courts, Compiled by the Late Famous Lawyer, Sir Edward Cooke, Knight (London: Thomas Ratcliffe and Thomas Daniel, 1669)

Samuel Pufendorf, [*De Officio Hominis Et Civis*] The Whole Duty of Man, According to the Law of Nature (1st Latin edition 1673, Andrew Tooke trans. 1691, rev. 1735; *reprinted* Indianapolis: Liberty Fund, 2003)

John Reeves, The Law of Shipping and Navigation from the Time of Edward III to the End of the Year 1805 (2d ed., London: W. Clarke & Sons, 1807)

Thomas Rowghton, *De Officio Admiralitatis Angliae Una Cum Articulis Concernentibus Idem Officium (Tr. Per Me T. Rowghton Ex Lingua Gallicana In Latinum.)* (London: R. Redman, 1530: xerographic facsimile available through University Microfilms International, No. 7681.8)

John Selden, *Mare Clausum seu, De Dominio Maris*: Of the Dominion or Ownership of the Sea (facsimile of Marchamont Nedham trans., 1652: New York: Arno Press, 1972)

James [Dalrymple], Viscount Stair, The Institutions of the Law of Scotland (1st ed. 1693; *reprinted*, David M. Walker ed., Edinburgh: University of Edinburgh Press, 1981)

The Statutes at Large, from the Fifteenth Year of King Edward III to the Thirteenth Year of King Henry IV Inclusive (Danby Pickering ed., Cambridge: Joseph Bentham, 1762)

The Statutes of the Realm: Printed by Command of His Majesty King George the Third, From Original Records and Authentic Manuscripts (facsimile of 1st ed.; *reprinted* Buffalo: William S. Hein & Co., 1993)

William Welvvod [Welwood], An Abridgement of All Sea-Lawes, Gathered Forth of All Writings and Monuments Which Are to Be Found among Any People or Nation, Upon the Coasts of the Great Ocean and Mediterranean Sea (facsimile of Humfrey Lownes ed., 1613: *reprinted as* No. 565, The English Experience—Its Record in Early Printed Books Published in Facsimile: New York: De Capo Press, 1972)

William Welvod [Welwood], The Sea-Law of Scotland (facsimile of Robert Wadlegrave ed., 1590: *reprinted as* No. 96, The English Experience—Its Record in Early Printed Books Published in Facsimile: New York: De Capo Press, 1969)

William Wynne, The Life of Sir Leoline Jenkins, Judge of the High Court of Admiralty, and Prerogative Court of Canterbury & C. Ambassador and Plenipotentiary for the General Peace at Cologn and Nimeguen, and Secretary of State to Charles II. (2 vols., London: Joseph Downing, 1724)

Richard Zouch[e], The Jurisdiction of the Admiralty Asserted, Against Sir Edward Coke's *Articuli Admiralitatis*, In XXII Chapter of His Jurisdiction of Courts (London: Francis Tyton & Thomas Dring, 1663)

Secondary Sources

J. H. Baker, The Legal Profession and the Common Law: Historical Essays (London: Hambledon Press, 1986)

Henry Bourguignon, Sir William Scott, Lord Stowell: Judge of the High Court of the Admiralty, 1789–1828 (Cambridge: Cambridge University Press, 1987)

Catherine Drinker Bowen, The Lion and the Throne: The Life and Times of Sir Edward Coke, 1552–1634 (1st ed., Boston: Little, Brown and Co., 1956)

W.W. Buckland, The Main Institutions of Roman Private Law (Cambridge: Cambridge University Press, 1931)

W.W. Buckland, A Manual of Roman Private Law (2d ed., Cambridge: Cambridge University Press, 1952)

W.W. Buckland & Arnold D. McNair, Roman Law and Common Law: A Comparative Outline (Cambridge: Cambridge University Press, 1936)

W.W. Buckland, A Text-Book of Roman Law from Augustus to Justinian (3d ed., Cambridge: Cambridge University Press, 1966)

Dorothy Burwash, English Merchant Shipping: 1460–1540 (1st ed. 1947; *reprinted* Toronto: University of Toronto Press, 1969)

Peter Wilson Coldham, English Adventurers and Emigrants, 1609–1660: Abstracts of Examinations in the High Court of Admiralty with Reference to Colonial America (1st ed. 1984; *reprinted* Baltimore: Geneological Publishing Co., 2002)

Peter Wilson Coldham, English Adventurers and Emigrants, 1661–1733: Abstracts of Examinations in the High Court of Admiralty with

REFERENCE TO COLONIAL AMERICA (Baltimore: Geneological Publishing Co., 1985)

PETER WILSON COLDHAM, MORE ENGLISH ADVENTURERS AND EMIGRANTS, 1625–1777: ABSTRACTS OF EXAMINATIONS IN THE HIGH COURT OF ADMIRALTY WITH REFERENCE TO COLONIAL AMERICA (Baltimore: Geneological Publishing Co., 2002)

DANIEL R. COQUILLETTE, THE CIVILIAN WRITERS OF DOCTORS' COMMONS: THREE CENTURIES OF JURISTIC INNOVATION IN COMPARATIVE, COMMERCIAL AND INTERNATIONAL LAW (Berlin: Duncker & Humblot, 1988)

DANIEL R. COQUILLETTE, FRANCIS BACON (Stanford: Stanford University Press, 1992)

Daniel R. Coquillette, "Justinian in Braintree: John Adams, Civilian Learning and Legal Elitism, 1758–1775", *in* LAW IN COLONIAL MASSACHUSETTS (Daniel R. Coquillette ed., University of Virginia Press, 1984)

J. Duncan M. Derrett, *The Works of Francis Clerke, Proctor (A Chapter in English Romano-Canonical Law)*, 40 *Studia et Documenta Historiae et Iuris* 52 (1974)

G.I.O. DUNCAN, THE HIGH COURT OF DELEGATES (Cambridge: Cambridge University Press, 1971)

Paul Macarius Hebert, *The Origin and Nature of Maritime Liens*, 4 Tul. L. Rev. 381 (1930)

WILLIAM S. HOLDSWORTH, CHARLES DICKENS AS A LEGAL HISTORIAN (New Haven: Yale University Press, 1928)

WILLIAM HOLDSWORTH, A HISTORY OF ENGLISH LAW (London: Methuen & Co. Ltd., 1924)

Lionel H. Liang, *Historic Origins of Admiralty Jurisdiction in England*, 45 Mich. L. Rev. 163 (1946)

HENRY SUMNER MAINE, ANCIENT LAW (1st ed. 1861; *reprinted* New York: Dorset Press, 1986)

F.W. MAITLAND, ENGLISH LAW AND THE RENAISSANCE (Cambridge: Cambridge University Press, 1901)

F.W. MAITLAND, EQUITY, ALSO THE FORMS OF ACTION AT COMMON LAW: TWO COURSES OF LECTURES (Cambridge: Cambridge University Press, 1929)

R.G. Marsden, "The High Court of Admiralty in Relation to National History, Commerce, and the Colonisation of America—A.D. 1550–1650", *in* TRANSACTIONS OF THE ROYAL HISTORICAL SOCIETY, VOL. 16 (New Series: London, 1902)

Joanne Mathiasen, *Some Problems of Admiralty Jurisdiction in the Seventeenth Century*, 2 Am. J. Legal Hist. 215 (1958)

Thomas Lambert Mears, "The History of the Admiralty Jurisdiction", *in* SELECT ESSAYS IN ANGLO-AMERICAN LEGAL HISTORY, VOL. II (Boston: Little, Brown, & Co., 1908)

G.L. PERUGI, *LEX RHODIORUM NAUTICA* (Greek critical edition, Rome: Ambrosian Library, 1929)

J.G.A. POCOCK, THE ANCIENT CONSTITUTION AND THE FEUDAL LAW: A STUDY OF ENGLISH HISTORICAL THOUGHT IN THE SEVENTEENTH CENTURY (Cambridge: Cambridge University Press, 1957)

FREDERICK POLLOCK & FREDERIC WILLIAM MAITLAND, THE HISTORY OF ENGLISH LAW BEFORE THE TIME OF EDWARD I (2 vols., 2d ed., Cambridge: Cambridge University Press 1899)

Timothy J. Runyan, *The Rolls of Oleron and the Admiralty Court in Fourteenth Century England*, 19 Am. J. Legal Hist. 95 (1975)

Edward F. Ryan, *Admiralty Jurisdiction and the Maritime Lien: An Historical Perspective*, 7 W. Ont. L. Rev. 173 (1968)

George F. Steckley, *Merchants and the Admiralty Court During the English Revolution*, 22 Am. J. Legal Hist. 137 (1978)

Joseph C. Sweeney, *The Admiralty Law of Arthur Browne*, 26 J. Mar. L. & Com. 59 (1995)

S.E. Thorne, *Courts of Record and Sir Edward Coke*, 2 Toronto L. J. 24 (1937)

STEVEN D. WHITE, SIR EDWARD COKE AND THE "GRIEVANCES OF THE COMMONWEALTH", 1621–1628 (Chapel Hill: University of North Carolina Press, 1979)

Alain Wijffels, "*Ius Gentium* in the Practice of the Court of Admiralty around 1600", *in* THE ROMAN LAW TRADITION (A.D.E. Lewis & D.J. Ibbertson eds., Cambridge: Cambridge University Press, 1994)

II. English, Colonial, and American Economic History before 1789

STUART BRUCHEY, THE ROOTS OF AMERICAN ECONOMIC GROWTH, 1607–1861: AN ESSAY IN SOCIAL CAUSATION (New York: Harper and Row, 1965)

Stuart Bruchey, *Success and Failure Factors: American Merchants in Foreign Trade in the Eighteenth and Early Nineteenth Centuries*, 33 Business History Review 272 (1958)

RICHARD BUEL, JR., IN IRONS: BRITAIN'S NAVAL SUPREMACY AND THE AMERICAN REVOLUTIONARY ECONOMY (New Haven: Yale University Press, 1998)

W.A. Cole, *The Arithmetic of Eighteenth-Century Smuggling*, 28 Economic History Review 44 (New Ser., 1975)

W.A. Cole, *Trends in Eighteenth-Century Smuggling*, 10 Economic History Review 395 (New Ser., 1958)

Rhoda M. Dorsey, *The Pattern of Baltimore Commerce During the Confederation Period*, 62 Maryland Historical Magazine 119 (1967)

Essays in the Economic History of the Atlantic World (John J. McCusker ed., London: Rutledge, 1997)

Christopher J. French, *Productivity in the Atlantic Shipping Industry: A Quantitative Study*, 17 Journal of Interdisciplinary History 613 (1987)

Herbert Alan Johnson, The Law Merchant and Negotiable Instruments in Colonial New York 1664–1730 (Chicago: Loyola University Press, 1963)

Cathy D. Matson & Peter S. Onuf, A Union of Interests: Political and Economic Thought in Revolutionary America (Lawrence: University of Kansas Press, 1990)

John J. McCusker & Russell R. Menard, The Economy of British America, 1607–1789 (Chapel Hill: University of North Carolina Press, 1985)

Merrill D. Peterson, *Thomas Jefferson and Commercial Policy, 1783–1793*, 22 William and Mary Quarterly 584 (3d ser., 1965)

Jacob B. Price, *Colonial Trade and British Economic Development*, 14 *Lex et Scientia* 101 (1978)

Jacob B. Price, *A Note on the Value of Colonial Exports of Shipping*, 37 Journal of Economic History 704 (1976)

Marcus Rediker, Between the Devil and the Deep Blue Sea: Merchant Seamen, Pirates, and the Anglo-American Maritime World, 1700–1750 (Cambridge: Cambridge University Press, 1987)

[John Holroyd, Lord Sheffield], Observations on the Commerce of the American States with Europe and the West Indies, Including Several Articles of Import and Export (*reprint of* 1st British ed., 1783, Philadelphia: Robert Bell, 1783; facsimile reprint, New York: Research Reprints Inc., 1970)

John [Holroyd], Lord Sheffield, Observations on the Commerce of the American States: A New Edition, Much Enlarged, with an Appendix (2d. ed, London: J. Debrett, 1784; facsimile reprint, New York: Augustus M. Kelley Publishers, 1970)

James F. Shepherd, *Commodity Exports from the British North American Colonies to Overseas Areas, 1768–1772: Magnitudes and Patterns of Trade,* 8 Explorations in Economic History 5 (1970)

James F. Shepherd & Gary M. Walton, *Economic Change after the American Revolution: Pre- and Post-War Comparisons of Maritime Shipping and Trade,* 13 Explorations in Economic History 397 (1976)

JAMES F. SHEPHERD & GARY M. WALTON, SHIPPING, MARITIME TRADE AND THE ECONOMIC DEVELOPMENT OF COLONIAL NORTH AMERICA (Cambridge: Cambridge University Press, 1972)

James F. Shepherd & Samuel H. Williamson, *The Coastal Trade of the British North American Colonies, 1768–1772*, 32 Journal of Economic History 783 (1972)

ADAM SMITH, AN INQUIRY INTO THE NATURE AND CAUSES OF THE WEALTH OF NATIONS (1st ed. 1776; Edwin Cannan ed., New York: Modern Library, 1937)

Gary M. Walton, *A Measure of Productivity Change in American Colonial Shipping*, 21 Economic History Review 268 (2d ser., 1968)

Gary M. Walton, *Sources of Productivity Change in American Colonial Shipping, 1675–1775*, 20 Economic History Review 67 (2d ser., 1967)

GARY M. WALTON & JAMES F. SHEPHERD, THE ECONOMIC RISE OF EARLY AMERICA (Cambridge: Cambridge University Press, 1979)

William Appleton Williams, *The Age of Mercantilism: An Interpretation of the American Political Economy, 1763–1828*, 15 William & Mary Quarterly 419 (3d ser., 1958)

III. English, Colonial, and American Social and Political History before 1789

BERNARD BAILYN, THE IDEOLOGICAL ORIGINS OF THE AMERICAN REVOLUTION (Cambridge, Massachusetts: Belknap Press, 1967)

JAMES BOSWELL, LIFE OF JOHNSON (1st ed. 1776; George Birkbeck Hill & L.F. Powell eds., 6 Vols. Oxford, Clarendon Press, 1934)

DANIEL DEFOE, A TOUR THROUGH ENGLAND AND WALES, DIVIDED INTO CIRCUITS OR JOURNIES (1st ed. 1724–1726; *reprinted*, Peter Davies ed., 2 vols., London: J.M. Dent & Sons, 1927)

DIARY AND AUTOBIOGRAPHY OF JOHN ADAMS (4 vols., L.H. Butterfield, Leonard C. Faber, & Wendell D. Garrett eds., Cambridge, Massachusetts: The Belknap Press of Harvard University, 1961)

RICHARD HOFSTADTER, AMERICA AT 1750: A SOCIAL PORTRAIT (New York: Alfred A. Knopf, 1971)

SAMUEL JOHNSON, TAXATION NO TYRANNY: AN ANSWER TO THE RESOLUTIONS AND ADDRESS OF THE AMERICAN CONGRESS (London: T. Cadell, 1775)

LAW AND AUTHORITY IN COLONIAL AMERICA (George Athan Billias ed., Barre, Massachusetts: Barre Publishers, 1965)

LEGAL PAPERS OF JOHN ADAMS (L. Kinvin Wroth & Hiller B. Zoebel eds., Cambridge, Massachusetts: The Belknap Press of Harvard University, 1965)

THOMAS PAINE, COLLECTED WRITINGS (New York: Library of America, 1995)

EDWARD ["NED"] WARD, THE LONDON SPY: THE VANITIES AND VICES OF THE TOWN EXPOSED TO VIEW (1st ed. published serially 1698–1703; Arthur L. Hayward ed., Cassell & Co., 1927)

IV. Colonial Maritime Law and Vice-Admiralty Jurisdiction

Primary Sources

James Barron, Richard Barron, et al. v. The Sloop "Adventure" and Cargo, Virginia State Court of Admiralty (decided Jan. 18, 1778) (unpublished opinion, on file with Special Collections of the Swem Library, College of William and Mary, The Tucker-Coleman Collection, 40 T79 Box 70)

CHARLES MERRILL HOUGH, REPORTS OF CASES IN THE VICE ADMIRALTY OF THE PROVINCE OF NEW YORK AND IN THE COURT OF ADMIRALTY OF THE STATE OF NEW YORK, 1715–1788 (New Haven: Yale University Press, 1925)

DAVID R. OWEN & MICHAEL C. TOLLEY, COURTS OF ADMIRALTY IN COLONIAL AMERICA: THE MARYLAND EXPERIENCE, 1634–1776 (Durham: Carolina Academic Press, 1995)

PROCEEDINGS IN THE COURT OF VICE-ADMIRALTY OF VIRGINIA, 1698–1775 (George Reese ed., Richmond: Virginia State Library, 1983)

RECORDS OF THE VICE-ADMIRALTY COURT OF RHODE ISLAND, 1716–1752 (Dorothy Towle ed., Washington D.C.: American Historical Association, 1936)

Several Laws and Orders, Made at the General Court at Boston in New England, October 14, 1668, Maritime Affairs, at 9–14 (*reprinted in* RECORDS OF THE STATES OF THE UNITED STATES OF AMERICA: A MICROFILM COMPILATION, Mass. B.2 Reel I 1661–1742, William Sumner Jenkins ed., Washington D.C.: Library of Congress Photoduplication Service, 1949)

THE STATUTES AT LARGE OF PENNSYLVANIA IN THE TIME OF WILLIAM PENN: COMPILED UNDER THE AUTHORITY OF THE ACT OF MAY 19, 1887 (1st ed. 1896; *reprinted with supplement by* Gail McKnight Beckman, New York: Vantage Press, 1976)

ANTHONY STOKES, A VIEW OF THE CONSTITUTION OF THE BRITISH COLONIES, IN NORTH-AMERICA AND THE WEST INDIES, AT THE TIME THE CIVIL WAR BROKE OUT ON THE CONTINENT OF AMERICA (London: B. White, 1783)

EMMERICH DE VATTEL, THE LAW OF NATIONS, OR THE PRINCIPLES OF NATURAL LAW APPLIED TO THE CONDUCT AND TO THE AFFAIRS OF NATIONS AND OF SOVEREIGNS (1st ed. 1758; Charles C. Fenwick trans., Washington D.C.: Carnegie Institution, 1916)

Secondary Sources

CHARLES M. ANDREWS, "THE VICE-ADMIRALTY COURTS" *in* THE COLONIAL PERIOD OF AMERICAN HISTORY, VOL. IV (New Haven: Yale University Press, 1938)

HELEN J. CURMP, COLONIAL ADMIRALTY JURISDICTION IN THE SEVENTEENTH CENTURY (London: Longmans, Green & Co., 1931)

DAVID DOBSON, AMERICAN DATA FROM THE RECORDS OF THE HIGH COURT OF ADMIRALTY OF SCOTLAND, 1675–1800 (Baltimore: Clearfield Co., 2000)

LAWRENCE A. HARPER, THE ENGLISH NAVIGATION LAWS: A SEVENTEENTH-CENTURY EXPERIMENT IN SOCIAL ENGINEERING (1st ed. 1939; *reprinted* New York: Octagon Books, 1973)

Matthew P. Harrington, *The Legacy of the Colonial Vice-Admiralty Courts*, (Part I) 26 J. Mar. L. & Com. 581 (1995); (Part II) 27 J. Mar. L. & Com. 323 (1996)

ELIZABETH EVELYNOLA HOON, THE ORGANIZATION OF THE ENGLISH CUSTOMS SYSTEM: 1696–1786 (New York: D. Appleton-Century Co., 1938)

WINFRED TREXLER ROOT, THE RELATIONS OF PENNSYLVANIA WITH THE BRITISH GOVERNMENT, 1696–1775 (New York: D. Appleton & Co. for University of Pennsylvania Press, 1912)

CARL UBBELOHDE, THE VICE ADMIRALTY COURTS AND THE AMERICAN REVOLUTION (Chapel Hill: University of North Carolina Press, 1960)

Frederick Bernays Wiener, *Notes on the Rhode Island Admiralty, 1727–1790*, 46 Harv. L. Rev. 44 (1933)

L. Kinvin Wroth, *The Massachusetts Vice Admiralty Court and the Federal Admiralty Jurisdiction*, 6 Am. J. Legal Hist. 250 (Part I), 347 (Part II) (1962)

V. The Constitutional Convention, the Admiralty Clause, and the Judiciary Act

Primary Sources

THE ADAMS-JEFFERSON LETTERS (2 vols. Lester J. Cappon ed., Chapel Hill: University of North Carolina Press, 1964).

The Antifederalists (Cecelia M. Kenyon ed., Boston: Northeastern University Press, 1966, *reprinted* 1985)

The Complete Anti-Federalist (7 vols., Herbert J. Storing ed., Chicago: University of Chicago Press, 1981)

The Debate on the Constitution: Federalist and Antifederalist Speeches, Articles and Letters during the Struggle over Ratification (2 vols., Bernard Bailyn ed., New York: Library of America, 1993)

The Diaries of George Washington (5 vols., Donald Johnson & Dorothy Towhig eds., Charlottesville: University of Virginia Press, 1976–1979)

Documentary History of the First Federal Congress of the United States of America: March 4, 1789–March 3, 1791 (14 vols., Linda Grant DePauw ed., Baltimore: Johns Hopkins University Press, 1972)

The Documentary History of the Ratification of the Constitution (John Kaminski & Gaspare Saladino eds., Madison: State Historical Society of Wisconsin, 1976)

The Documentary History of the Supreme Court of the United States, 1789–1800, Volume Four—Organizing the Federal Judiciary: Legislation and Commentaries (Maeva Marcus ed., New York: Columbia University Press, 1992)

Jonathan Elliot, The Debates in the Several State Conventions on the Adoption of the Federal Constitution, as Recommended by the General Convention at Philadelphia in 1787 (2d ed., 5 vols., Philadelphia: J.B. Lippencott & Co., 1861)

The Federalist (Jacob E. Cooke ed., Middletown, Connecticut: Wesleyean University Press, 1961))

Benjamin Franklin, Writings (J.A. Leo Lemay ed., New York: Library of America, 1987)

Industrial and Commercial Correspondence of Alexander Hamilton, Anticipating His Report on Manufactures (Arthur Harrison Cole ed., Chicago: A.W. Shaw Co., 1928)

Thomas Jefferson, Writings (Merrill D. Peterson ed., New York: Library of America, 1984)

The Journal of William Maclay: United States Senator from Pennsylvania 1789–1791 (1927 ed., Charles A. Beard ed., *reprinted* New York: Frederick Ungar Publishing Co., 1965)

The Journals of the Continental Congress: 1774–1789 (34 vols., Worthington Chauncey Ford ed., Washington D.C.: U.S. Government Printing Office, 1905)

William Kilty, A Report of All Such English Statutes as Existed at the Time of the First Emigration of the People of Maryland, and

Which by Experience Have Been Found Applicable to Their Local and Other Circumstances; And of Such Others as Have Been Made in England or Great-Britain, and Have Been Introduced, Used and Practiced by the Courts of Law or Equity; And Also All Such Parts of the Same as May Be Proper to Be Introduced and Incorporated into the Statute Law of the State (Annapolis: Jehu Chandler, 1811).

The Law Practice of Alexander Hamilton: Documents and Commentary (5 vols., Julius Goebel ed., New York: Columbia University Press, 1969)

Montesquieu, [Charles Louis] De Secondat, Baron De [Le Brède et De], The Siprit of Laws: Translated from the French, With Corrections and Additions Communicated by the Author (1st English ed., Thomas Nugent trans., London: J. Nourse & P. Vaillant, 1750)

Official Opinions of the Attorneys General of the United States Advising the President and Heads of Departments (Washington, D.C.: Robert Farnham, 1852)

Pamphlets on the Constitution of the United States, Published During Its Discussion by the People, 1787–1788 (Paul Leicester Ford ed., Brooklyn, New York, 1888)

The Papers of Alexander Hamilton, (27 vols., Harold C. Styrett ed., New York: Columbia University Press, 1973)

The Papers of James Madison (17 vols., Robert A. Rutland & William M.E. Rachal eds., Chicago: University of Chicago Press, 1962–1991)

The Records of the Federal Convention of 1787 (3 vols., Max Farrand ed., New Haven: Yale University Press, 1966)

The Records of the Federal Convention of 1787: Supplement (James H. Hutson ed., New Haven: Yale University Press, 1987)

The Republic of Letters: The Correspondence Between Thomas Jefferson and James Madison, 1776–1826 (James Morton Smith ed., New York: Norton, 1995)

The Works of James Wilson (2 vols., Robert Green McKloskey ed., Cambridge, Massachusetts: The Belknap Press of Harvard University, 1967)

The Writings of Benjamin Franklin (10 vols., Albert Henry Smyth ed., New York: Macmillan Co., 1906)

The Writings of George Washington: From the Original Manuscript Sources 1745–1799 (39 vols., John C. Fitzpatrick ed., Washington, D.C.: U.S. Government Printing Office, 1931–1944)

The Writings of James Madison (9 vols., Gaillard Hunt ed., New York: G.P. Putnam's Sons, 1904)

Secondary Sources

Frederick Bausman, *Admiralty and Maritime Jurisdiction*, 36 Am. L. Rev. 182 (1902)

Charles A. Beard, An Economic Interpretation of the Constitution of the United States (1st ed. 1913: *reprint*, New York: Free Press, 1986)

Henry J. Bourguignon, *The Federal Key to the Judiciary Act of 1789*, 46 S. C. L. Rev. 647 (1995)

Henry J. Bourguignon, The First Federal Court: The Federal Appellate Prize Court of the American Revolution 1775–1787 (Philadelphia: The American Philosophical Society, 1977)

Elizabeth Gaspar Brown, British Statutes in American Law, 1776–1836 (Ann Arbor: University of Michigan Law School, 1964)

William R. Casto, *The Origins of Federal Admiralty Jurisdiction in an Age of Privateers, Smugglers, and Pirates*, 37 Am. J. Legal Hist. 117 (1993)

Catalogue of the Library of Thomas Jefferson (5 vols., E. Millicent Sowerby ed., Washington, D.C.: U.S. Government Printing Office, 1953)

Bradford R. Clark, *Federal Common Law: A Structural Reinterpretation*, 144 U. Pa. L. Rev. 1245 (1996)

David P. Currie, *The Constitution in Congress: Substantive Issues in the First Congress*, 1789–1791, 61 U. Chi. L. Rev. 775 (1994)

J.C. Bancroft Davis, "Appendix to the Decisions of the Supreme Court of the United States: From September 24, 1789, to the End of October Term, 1888", *in* 131 U.S. ii (1889)

Edwin D. Dickinson, *Changing Concepts and the Doctrine of Incorporation*, 26 Am. J. Int'l L. 239 (1932)

Edwin D. Dickinson, *The Law of Nations as Part of the National Law of the United States*, 101 U. Pa. L. Rev. 26 (1952)

Stanley Elkins & Eric Mckitrick, The Age of Federalism: The Early American Republic, 1788–1800 (New York: Oxford University Press, 1993)

Max Farrand, The Framing of the Constitution of the United States (New Haven: Yale University Press, 1913)

Jonathan M. Gutoff, *Original Understandings and the Private Law Origins of the Federal Admiralty Jurisdiction: A Reply to Professor Casto*, 30 J. Mar. L. & Com. 361 (1999)

J. Franklin Jameson, "Studies in the History of the Federal Convention of 1787", *in* American Historical Association, Annual Report (H.R. Doc. No. 461) (2 vols., Washington, D.C., 1903) at 111–132.

Stewart Jay, *The Status of the Law of Nations in Early American Law*, 42 Vand. L. Rev. 819 (1989)

MERRILL JENSEN, THE NEW NATION: A HISTORY OF THE UNITED STATES DURING THE ARTICLES OF CONFEDERATION—1781–1789 (New York: Alfred A. Knopf, 1950)

HERBERT A. JOHNSON, IMPORTED EIGHTEENTH-CENTURY LAW TREATISES IN AMERICAN LIBRARIES 1700–1799 (Knoxville: University of Tennessee Press, 1978)

Andrew C. McLaughlin, *Sketch of Pinckney's Plan for a Constitution, 1787*, 9 Am. Hist. Rev. 735 (1903–1904)

JOHN C. MILLER, THE FEDERALIST ERA 1789–1801 (New York: Harper Torchbooks, 1963)

Judge Emory H. Niles, The Revolutionary Court of Admiralty of the State of Maryland 1776–1789. Address Before the Lawyers' Round Table, Maryland Club, Baltimore (Dec. 8, 1941) (transcript available in the Maryland Historical Society Library)

Nicholas G. Onuf, *Civitas Maxima: Wolff, Vattel and the Fate of Republicanism*, 88 Am. J. Intn'l L. 280 (1994)

PETER ONUF & NICHOLAS ONUF, FEDERAL UNION, MODERN WORLD: THE LAW OF NATIONS IN AN AGE OF REVOLUTIONS, 1776–1814 (Madison: Madison House, 1993)

ORIGINS OF THE FEDERAL JUDICIARY: ESSAYS ON THE JUDICIARY ACT OF 1789 (Maeva Marcus ed., New York: Oxford University Press, 1992)

Harrington Putnam, *How the Federal Courts Were Given Admiralty Jurisdiction*, 10 Corn. L. Q. 460 (1925)

Eduardo C. Robreno, *Learning to Do Justice: An Essay on the Development of the Lower Federal Courts in the Early Years of the Republic*, 29 Rutgers L. J. 555 (1998)

Franklyn C. Setaro, *The Formative Era of American Admiralty Law*, 5 N. Y. L. Forum 9 (1959)

JAMES ROGER SHARP, AMERICAN POLITICS IN THE EARLY REPUBLIC: THE NEW NATION IN CRISIS (New Haven: Yale University Press, 1993)

Charles Warren, *New Light on the History of the Federal Judiciary Act of 1789*, 37 Harv. L. Rev. 49 (1923)

GORDON S. WOOD, THE CREATION OF THE AMERICAN REPUBLIC 1776–1787 (Chapel Hill: University of North Carolina Press, 1969)

VI. American Economic, Social and Political History: 18th–19th Centuries

Primary Sources

ISRAEL D. ANDREWS, REPORT ON THE TRADE AND COMMERCE OF THE BRITISH NORTH AMERICAN COLONIES, AND UPON THE TRADE OF THE GREAT LAKES AND RIVERS (SEN. EXEC. DOC. 112, 1853)

U.S. DEPARTMENT OF COMMERCE, BUREAU OF THE CENSUS, HISTORICAL STATISTICS OF THE UNITED STATES, COLONIAL TIMES TO 1957 (Washington D.C.: U.S. Government Printing Office, 1960)

U.S. DEPARTMENT OF THE TREASURY, STATISTICS OF THE FOREIGN AND DOMESTIC COMMERCE OF THE UNITED STATES (Washington D.C.: U.S. Government Printing Office, 1864)

RICHARD HENRY DANA, JR., THE SEAMAN'S FRIEND (6th ed., Boston: Thomas Groom & Co., 1851; *reprinted* New York: Scholars' Facsimiles & Reprints, 1979)

RICHARD HENRY DANA, JR., TWO YEARS BEFORE THE MAST, AND TWENTY-FOUR YEARS AFTER (1st ed. 1842; *reprinted* New York: P. F. Collier & Son: Harvard Classics, 1937, 1968.)

CHARLES DICKENS, AMERICAN NOTES (1st ed. 1842; *reprinted* London: Oxford University Press, 1957)

CHARLES DICKENS, DAVID COPPERFIELD (1st ed. 1850; *reprinted,* Nina Burgis ed., Oxford: Clarendon Press, 1981)

[RUDYARD KIPLING], A CHOICE OF KIPLING'S VERSE (T.S. Eliot ed., London: Faber & Faber Ltd., 1942)

HERMAN MELVILLE, MOBY DICK, OR THE WHALE (1st ed. 1851; critical ed.: Harrison Hayford, Hershel Parker, & G. Thomas Tanselle eds., Evanston: Northwestern University Press, 2001)

[HERMAN MELVILLE], THE COLLECTED POEMS OF HERMAN MELVILLE (1st critical ed.: Howard P. Vincent ed., Chicago: Packard & Co., 1947)

TIMOTHY PITKIN, A STATISTICAL STUDY OF THE COMMERCE OF THE UNITED STATES (Hartford: Charles Hosmer, 1816)

ALEXIS DE TOCQUEVILLE, DEMOCRACY IN AMERICA (1st ed. 1835, 1840; *reprinted* New York: Alfred A. Knopf, 1994)

MARK TWAIN, LIFE ON THE MISSISSIPPI (1st ed. 1883; *reprinted* New York: Library of America, 1982)

United States Patent Office, Patent No. 588 (Feb. 1, 1838) Issued to John Ericsson, of London, England

Secondary Sources

Robert Greenhalgh Albion, Naval and Maritime History: An Annotated Bibliography (4th ed., Mystic, Connecticut: Munson Institute of American Maritime History, 1972)

A Supplement (1971–1986) To Robert G. Albion's Naval and Maritime History: An Annotated Bibliography, Fourth Edition (Benjamin W. Labaree ed., Mystic, Connecticut: Munson Institute of American Maritime History, 1988)

Robert Greenhalgh Albion, The Rise of New York Port, 1815–1860 (1st ed. 1939; *reprinted* Boston: Northeastern University Press, 1984)

The Atlantic World of Robert G. Albion (Benjamin W. Labaree ed., Middleton, Connecticut: Wesleyan University Press, 1975)

George C. Calcott, A History of the University of Maryland (Baltimore: Maryland Historical Society, 1966)

Paul A. David, *The Growth of Real Product in the United States Before 1840: New Evidence, Controlled Conjectures*, 27 Journal of Economic History 151 (1967)

Dictionary of American Biography (1st ed. 1931; Allen Johnson & Dumas Malone eds., New York: Charles Scribner's Sons, 1960)

Claudia D. Goldin & Frank D. Lewis, *The Role of Exports in American Economic Growth during the Napoleonic Wars, 1793–1807*, 17 Explorations in Economic History 6 (1980)

Erik F. Haites, James Mak, & Gary M. Walton, Western River Transportation: The Era of Early Internal Development, 1810–1860 (Baltimore: Johns Hopkins University Press, 1975)

Louis C. Hunter, Steamboats on the Western Rivers: An Economic and Technological History (1st ed. 1949; *reprinted* New York: Dover Publications, 1993)

John G. B. Hutchins, The American Maritime Industries and Maritime Policy, 1789–1914 (Cambridge, Massachusetts: Harvard University Press, 1941)

Granville Allen Mawer, Ahab's Trade: The Saga of South Seas Whaling (New York: St. Martin's Press, 1999)

Samuel Eliot Morison, The Maritime History of Massachusetts, 1783–1860 (1st ed. 1921; *reprinted* Boston: Northeastern University Press, 1979)

Douglass C. North, The Economic Growth of the United States, 1790–1860 (Englewood Cliffs, New Jersey: Prentice Hall, 1961)

George Wilson Pierson, Tocqueville in America (1st ed. 1938; *reprinted* Baltimore: The Johns Hopkins University Press, 1996)

Proceedings at the Unveiling of the Statue of John Ericsson (Washington, D.C.: U.S. Government Printing Office, 1926)

Shanties from the Seven Seas: Shipboard Work-Songs and Songs Used as Work-Songs from the Great Days of Sail (Stan Hugill ed., Mystic, Connecticut: Mystic Seaport Museum, rev. ed., 1994)

Ruth White, Yankee from Sweden: The Dream and the Reality in the Days of John Ericsson (New York: Henry Holt & Co., 1960)

VII. Law in the 18th–19th Centuries

Primary Sources

Charles Abbott, A Treatise on the Law Relative to Merchant Ships and Seamen: In Four Parts (3d American edition, Joseph Story ed., Exeter, New Hampshire: George Lamson: 1822)

Erastus C. Benedict, The American Admiralty: Its Jurisdiction and Practice (1st ed., New York: Banks, Gould & Co., 1850)

Erastus C. Benedict,The American Admiralty: Its Jurisdiction and Practice (5th ed., George V. A. McCloskey ed., Albany: Banks & Co., 1925)

Samuel Betts, A Summary of Practice in Instance, Revenue and Prize Causes in the Admiralty Courts of the United States, for the Southern District of New-York; and also on Appeal to the Supreme Court: Together with the Rules of the District Court (New York: Halstead and Voorhies, 1838)

Richard Henry Dana, Jr., *History of Admiralty Jurisdiction in the Supreme Court of the United States*, 5 Am. L. Rev. 581 (1871)

Theodore M. Etting, The Admiralty Jurisdiction in America (Philadelphia: Rees Welsh & Co., 1879)

Henry Flanders, A Treatise on Maritime Law (Boston: Little, Brown & Co., 1852)

John E. Hall, An Essay on Maritime Loans, from the French of M. Balthazard Marie Emerigon: With Notes (Baltimore: Philip H. Nicklin & Co., 1811)

John E. Hall, The Practice and Jurisdiction of the Court of Admiralty (Baltimore: George Dobbin & Murphy, 1809)

George C. Holt, The Concurrent Jurisdiction of the Federal and State Courts (New York: Baker, Voorhis & Co., 1888)

James Kent, Commentaries on American Law (1st ed., New York: O. Halstead, 1826–1830)

Reginald G. Marsden, Shipping and Marine Insurance Digest (1st ed. 1899; 2d ed., Reading: Eastern Press Ltd., 1926)

John B. Minor, Institutes of Common and Statute Law (4th ed., 4 vols., Richmond: Anderson Brothers, 1891)

Richard Peters, Admiralty Decisions in the District Court of the United States, For the Pennsylvania District (2 vols., Philadelphia: William P. Farrand, 1807)

Joseph Story, Commentaries on the Constitution (1st ed., Boston: Hilliard, Gray & Co., 1833)

Joseph Story: A Discourse on the Past History, Present State, and Future Prospects of the Law (Edinburgh: T. Clark, 1835)

Joseph Story, A Familiar Exposition of the Constitution of the United States (1st ed. 1840; *reprinted* Lake Bluff, Illinois: Regnery Gateway, Inc., 1986)

Joseph Story, Miscellaneous Writings (Boston: Little & Brown, 1852)

St. George Tucker, Examination of the Question, "How Far the Common Law of England is the Law of the Federal Government of the United States (Richmond: John Dixon, 1800)

St. George Tucker, Ten Notebooks of Law Lectures (1790s) (unpublished manuscript on file in Special Collections of the Swem Library, College of William and Mary)

St. George Tucker, View of the Constitution of the United States, With Selected Writings (1st ed. 1803; critical edition, Clyde M. Wilson ed., Indianapolis: Liberty Fund, 1999)

Secondary Sources

William R. Casto, The Supreme Court in the Early Republic: The Chief Justiceships of John Jay and Oliver Ellsworth (Columbia: University of South Carolina Press, 1995)

David P. Currie, The Constitution in Congress: The Federalist Period, 1789–1801 (Chicago: University of Chicago Press, 1997)

David P. Currie, The Constitution in the Supreme Court: The First Hundred Years, 1789–1888 (Chicago: University of Chicago Press, 1985)

Gerald T. Dunne, Justice Joseph Story and the Rise of the Supreme Court (New York: Simon and Schuster, 1970)

William A. Fletcher, *The General Common Law and Section 34 of the Judiciary Act of 1789: The Example of Marine Insurance*, 97 Harv. L. Rev. 1513 (1984)

JULIUS GOEBEL, JR., ANTECEDENTS AND BEGINNINGS TO 1801, VOLUME I *in* THE OLIVER WENDELL HOLMES DEVISE: HISTORY OF THE SUPREME COURT OF THE UNITED STATES (New York: Macmillan Publishing Co., 1971)

HERBERT A. JOHNSON, THE CHIEF JUSTICESHIP OF JOHN MARSHALL, 1801–1835 (Columbia: University of South Carolina Press, 1997)

JAMES MCCLELLAN, JOSEPH STORY AND THE AMERICAN CONSTITUTION (Norman: University of Oklahoma Press, 1971)

DONALD G. MORGAN, JUSTICE WILLIAM JOHNSON: THE FIRST DISSENTER (Columbia: University of South Carolina Press, 1954)

R. KENT NEWMYER, SUPREME COURT JUSTICE JOSEPH STORY: STATESMAN OF THE OLD REPUBLIC (Chapel Hill: University of North Carolina Press, 1985)

DONALD A. PETRIE, THE PRIZE GAME: LAWFUL LOOTING ON THE HIGH SEAS IN THE DAYS OF FIGHTING SAIL (Annapolis, Maryland: Naval Institute Press, 1999)

Stephen B. Presser, *A Tale of Two Judges: Richard Peters, Samuel Chase, and the Broken Promise of Federalist Jurisprudence*, 73 Nw. U. L. Rev 26 (1978)

JEAN EDWARD SMITH, JOHN MARSHALL, DEFINER OF A NATION (New York: Henry Holt & Co., 1996)

Joseph C. Sweeney, *Limitation of Shipowner Liability: Its American Roots and Some Problems Particular to Collision*, 32 J. Mar. L. & Com. 241 (2001)

CARL B. SWISHER, THE TANEY PERIOD, 1836–64, VOLUME V *in* THE OLIVER WENDELL HOLMES DEVISE: HISTORY OF THE SUPREME COURT OF THE UNITED STATES (New York: Macmillan Publishing Co., 1974)

F. L. WISWALL, JR., THE DEVELOPMENT OF ADMIRALTY JURISDICTION SINCE 1800: AN ENGLISH STUDY WITH AMERICAN COMPARISONS (Cambridge: Cambridge University Press, 1970)

VIII. Economic, Social, Political, and Legal History in the 20th Century

H. DAVID BESS & MARTIN T. FARRIS, U.S. MARITIME POLICY: HISTORY AND PROSPECTS (New York: Praeger Publishers, 1981)

JAMES E. BOND, I DISSENT: THE LEGACY OF CHIEF JUSTICE JAMES CLARK MCREYNOLDS (Fairfax, Virginia: George Mason University Press, 1992)

ANDREW GIBSON & ARTHUR DONOVAN, THE ABANDONED OCEAN: A HISTORY OF UNITED STATES MARITIME POLICY (Columbia: University of South Carolina Press, 2000)

HOLMES AND FRANKFURTER: THEIR CORRESPONDENCE, 1912–1934 (Robert M. Mennel & Christine L. Compston eds., Hanover, New Hampshire: University Press of New England, 1996)

THE HOLMES-LASKI LETTERS: THE CORRESPONDENCE OF MR. JUSTICE HOLMES AND HAROLD J. LASKI, 1916–1935 (2 vols., Mark DeWolf Howe ed., Cambridge, Massachusetts: Harvard University Press, 1953)

OLIVER WENDELL HOLMES, JR., COLLECTED LEGAL PAPERS (New York: P. Smith, 1952)

OLIVER WENDELL HOLMES, JR., THE COMMON LAW (1st ed. 1881; *reprinted* New York: Little, Brown & Co., 1923)

THE PAPERS OF WOODROW WILSON (69 vols., Arthur S. Link ed., Princeton: Princeton University Press, 1983)

G. EDWARD WHITE, JUSTICE OLIVER WENDELL HOLMES: LAW AND THE INNER SELF (New York: Oxford University Press, 1993)

IX. Admiralty in Contemporary American Law

BENEDICT ON ADMIRALTY (7th ed., revised [loose leaf], New York: Matthew Bender, 1959–1999)

GRANT GILMORE & CHARLES E. BLACK, JR., THE LAW OF ADMIRALTY (2d. ed., Mineola, New York: Foundation Press, 1970)

Joel K. Goldstein, *The Life and Times of Wilburn Boat: A Critical Guide*, (Part I) 28 J. Mar. L. & Com. 395 (1997); (Part II) 28 J. Mar. L. & Com. 555 (1997)

THOMAS J. SCHOENBAUM, ADMIRALTY AND MARITIME LAW (Practioner's Edition, St. Paul: West Publishing Co., 1987)

GEORGE C. SPRAGUE & NICHOLAS J. HEALY, CASES ON THE LAW OF ADMIRALTY (St. Paul: West Publishing Co., 1950)

WILLIAM TETLEY, MARITIME LIENS AND CLAIMS (2d ed., Montreal: International Shipping Publications, 1998)

X. Admiralty and Federalism

David J. Bederman, *Uniformity, Delegation and the Dormant Admiralty Clause*, 28 J. Mar. L. & Com. 325 (1997)

David P. Currie, *Federalism and Admiralty: The Devil's Own Mess*, 1960 Sup. Ct. Rev. 138 (1960)

DANIEL ELAZAR, AMERICAN FEDERALISM: A VIEW FROM THE STATES (3d ed., New York: Harper & Row, 1984)

Joel K. Goldstein, *Federal Common Law in Admiralty: An Introduction to the Beginning of an Exchange*, 43 St. Louis L. Rev. 1337 (1999)

Charles Merrill Hough, *Admiralty Jurisdiction—Of Late Years*, 37 Harv. L. Rev. 529 (1924)

Larry Kramer, *The Lawmaking Power of the Federal Courts*, 12 Pace L. Rev. 263 (1992)

MARTIN H. REDISH, FEDERAL JURISDICTION: TENSIONS IN THE ALLOCATION OF JUDICIAL POWER (New York: Bobbs-Merrill Co., 1980)

DAVID W. ROBERTSON, ADMIRALTY AND FEDERALISM (Mineola, New York: Foundation Press, 1970)

David W. Robertson, *Admiralty and Maritime Litigation in State Court*, 55 La. L. Rev. 685 (1995)

David W. Robertson, *Displacement of State Law by Federal Maritime Law*, 26 J. Mar. L. & Com. 325 (1995)

David W. Robertson, *Summertime Sailing in the U.S. Supreme Court*, 29 J. Mar. L. & Com. 275 (1998)

DAVID L. SHAPIRO, FEDERALISM: A DIALOGUE, (Evanston, Illinois: Northwestern University Press, 1992)

LAURENCE H. TRIBE, AMERICAN CONSTITUTIONAL LAW (Vol. I., 3d ed., New York: Foundation Press, 2000)

Ernest A. Young, *Preemption at Sea*, 67 Geo. Wash. L. Rev. 273 (1999)

Index